SUPERVISORY MANAGEMENT

The Art of Empowering and Developing People

Donald C. Mosley, Ph.D.
University of South Alabama

Leon C. Megginson, Ph.D.
University of Mobile

Paul H. Pietri, D.B.A.
University of South Alabama

Supervisory Management, 5e, by Donald C. Mosley, Leon C. Megginson, and Paul H. Pietri

Publisher: Dave Shaut
Acquisitions Editor: Pamela M. Person
Developmental Editor: Mardell Toomey
Marketing Manager: Rob Bloom
Production Editor: Anne Chimenti
Manufacturing Coordinator: Sandee Milewski
Internal Design: Jennifer Lambert
Cover Design: Jennifer Lambert
Cover Photographer or Illustrator: Brian Jensen, Stock Illustration Source
Photo Manager: Cary Benbow
Photo Researcher: Feldman & Associates, Inc.
Production House: Litten Editing and Production, Inc.
Compositor: GGS Information Services, Inc.
Printer: Quebecor World

Printed in the United States of America
3 4 5 03 02

For more information contact South-Western College Publishing, 5191 Natorp Blvd., Mason, OH 45040 or find us on the Internet at http://www .swcollege.com

For permission to use material from this text or product,contact us by

- **telephone: 1-800-730-2214**
- **fax: 1-800-730-2215**
- **web: http://www.thomsonrights.com**

Library of Congress Cataloging-in-Publication Data

Mosley, Donald C.
    Supervisory management : the art of empowering and developing people / Donald C. Mosley, Leon C. Megginson, Paul H. Pietri.—5th ed.
      p. cm.
    Includes bibliographical references and index.
    ISBN 0-324-02127-5 (alk. paper)
    1. Personnel management. 2. Supervision of employees. I. Megginson, Leon C. II. Pietri, Paul H. III. Title.
HF5549.M667 2001
658.3'02—dc21   00-033859

This book is printed on acid-free paper.

Preface

Supervisory Management, 5e, combines the study of traditional management principles and skill-building, "hands-on" techniques which prepare students to become supervisors. We emphasize that supervision is working *with* people to develop and empower them so they become better and more effective in their working roles.

We, as authors, strongly believe that the "laboratory" for management professors is in the real world of business organizations. Consequently, almost all of our research and consulting has involved thousands of team leaders and supervisors in many different types of organizations. We have found some of the most exemplary, creative, and exciting practices of supervision and leadership in this environment and have sought to pass this information along to you, always emphasizing good theory and techniques founded upon practical experience.

Our text closely follows the federal government's report of the Secretary's Commission on Achieving Necessary Skills (SCANS) requirements for workplace competencies and a three-part foundation of skills and personal qualities needed for job performance. Our text strives to maintain a workplace context and a practical emphasis throughout.

A number of changes have been made to keep the fifth edition fast-paced, relevant, and focused on building supervisory skills.

WHAT'S NEW IN THE FIFTH EDITION

- *Enhanced coverage of coaching and facilitation skills.* In the fourth edition, we became pioneers in introducing the coaching and facilitation skills that are so essential for team leaders. Because this information has been received so enthusiastically, we have enhanced the coverage of these topics in the fifth edition.

- *Significant revisions and coverage of new topics.* We have made significant revisions to Chapter 5, "Fundamentals of Organization," Chapter 8, "Motivating Employees," Chapter 9, "Leadership," and Chapter 10, "Managing Change, Group Development and Team Building." New coverage of current topics includes supervision of temporary workers, increased coverage of sexual harassment, impact of high employee turnover, diversity coverage, mentoring, information technology, and transformational leadership.

- *Another pioneering effort—Unique coverage.* In this edition we become the first in an introductory supervision book to introduce the concepts of developmental and servant leadership. These related concepts present innovative methods to building highly supportive work relationships between manager and employees. The emphasis is on reducing the dominance of the supervisor and developing the individual employee's innate potential. We believe this coverage is important based on current usage of these concepts in companies that are on the cutting edge.

- *Listings of Internet sites related to chapters topics.* Websites are included in all chapters and are readily identified by the "click" icon. These websites will help students become familiar with supervisory practices in real-world businesses while also improving their familiarity and ease with this important technological tool.

FEATURES OF THE BOOK

Designed to facilitate understanding and retention of the material presented, each chapter contains the following:

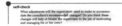

Understand the stages of organization growth.

- *Learning Objectives* Each chapter begins with a statement of Learning Objectives. Icons for identifying the learning objectives appear throughout the text material. The Chapter Review is also organized by the learning objectives.

The Conflict-Laden, Stressful Plant Environment

The Davis Chemical Company recently acquired the chemical division of a smaller company in a friendly divestiture. In the acquisition they acquired three profitable chemical plants and one unprofitable plant that we will call Plant D.

After the acquisition, Davis Chemical Company sent a home office human relations manager, Beverly Rogers, to gather information,

make a diagnosis, and provide recommendations to improve Plant D. In gathering data she utilized individual interviews and small-group discussion sessions. Beverly discovered considerable stress, insecurity, and low morale in the workforce of 500 people. In addition to a lack of teamwork, there was considerable conflict among departments, especially between production and maintenance.

- *Opening Preview Case* A Preview Case illustrates a major topic to be covered in the chapter and piques students' interest in the topic about to be discussed.

line organization
A line organization is concerned with the primary functions of the firm. In this case production, sales, and finance.

- *Key Terms and Phrases* New vocabulary is highlighted as it is introduced in each chapter. Definitions are also highlighted in notes that appear in the margin. Key terms are also listed at the end of the chapter, and appear in the glossary at the end of the text.

self-check
What adjustments will the supervisors need to make to accommodate the consultant's recommended changes? Do you think these changes will help or hinder the supervisor in the job of motivating and managing his or her crew?

- *Self-Check* Self-Check questions appear throughout each chapter, allowing students to test their understanding of concepts as they learn new material. This feature also helps improve their study routines by serving as a simplified self-study guide, covering all supervisory topics within the text.

- *Group Activities, Chapter Review, and Questions for Review and Discussion* Group Activities, Chapter Review, and Questions for Review and Discussion encourage students to reflect upon what they have read in a way that will help them better understand and learn the material.

skill builder 3-1
Proposed Change of Organization
group activity

Starting by himself in 1984, Jim Hardy built Hardy Pest Control until it operated in four states and employed over 1,000 persons.

In 1996 Hardy hired Derek Temple as vice-president of marketing. Temple, exceptionally bright and articulate, had previously owned an advertising agency. Before Temple was hired, all the employees in each local area reported to the local manager, and the service personnel went also the salespeople for the firm. The district managers were responsible for both operations and sales. Tem-

ple recommended that Hardy specialize by separating sales from service and placing all sales personnel under Temple. Under this new arrangement, even though sales personnel operated from the local manager's office, they reported organizationally to a district sales manager, usually located in another city (see Hardy organization chart). The sales manager positions, since they were new, had to be staffed with office help and supplied with office space. The proposed new organization is shown as follows:

- *Skill Builder Exercises* Skill-Builder Exercises appear at the end of each chapter; many of them relate to the SCANS requirements followed by many schools.
- *Cases* Cases located at the end of each chapter can be used to synthesize the chapter concepts and simulate the practice of supervision.

INSTRUCTOR'S MANUAL
Supervisory Management:
The Art of Empowering and Developing People
5E

INSTRUCTIONAL RESOURCES

Supervisory Management is accompanied by comprehensive instructional support materials.

Instructor's Manual. The instructor's manual (ISBN: 0-324-02128-3) provides resources to increase the value of the text for both students and instructors. The manual was prepared by Gayle Megginson Ross under the guidance of the authors. For each text chapter, the manual provides an outline and lecture notes

Supervisory
Management

The Art of Empowering
and Developing People

Mosley, Megginson, Pietri

that include specific suggestions for using transparency masters. There are answers to the end-of-chapter questions and Skill-Builders, responses to case questions, and notes for the video scenarios. Included within this supplement is a *test bank* that includes multiple-choice, true/false, and essay questions. A chart has also been created to accompany the test bank which shows how questions correspond with the chapter learning objectives.

ExamView Pro Testing Software. A new, user-friendly testing software program (ISBN: 0-324-02130-5) is new to this edition's product family. The test bank that is available in the instructor's manual has been recreated electronically in order to make test preparation easy for the instructor. This versatile software package allows the instructor to create new questions, edit and delete existing questions, and print out ready-to-use tests.

Video Scenarios. Two video collections accompany the new edition of the text. One video set (ISBN: 0-324-02131-3) contains ten skill-development scenarios. The second video set (ISBN: 0-324-07187-6) contains BusinessLink video case studies. These interactive videos, professionally developed by instructors, involve real companies and contain critical thinking questions that will provide an excellent forum for classroom analysis. These videos are the first of their kind offered for a supervision course.

Study Guide. The study guide (ISBN: 0-324-02129-1) that accompanies our text will be a real asset for your students. It has been carefully prepared by Gayle Megginson Ross under the guidance of the authors. For each text chapter, the study guide includes an overview, learning objectives, an expanded study outline, review questions, and activities, along with a feature new to this edition: Internet Web exercises, called "Exploring the Internet."

Web Site ISBN: 0-324-02797-5. We will offer support for both the instructor and the student. Instructors will be able to download the instructor's manual. Students will be able to view an online glossary of terms and more.

Acknowledgments

Rosemary Fittje was our unifying agent interfacing directly with the editors, putting our material into printed manuscript form, and keeping us on schedule. Her contributions were critical to completing this project. Additional keying support was provided by Jo Megginson, Susan Mosley, and Suzanne Barnhill. Special thanks go to Joy Harriman whose editing of Chapter 10 was most helpful. We also appreciate the efforts of our publishing team at South-Western College Publishing Company, which is one of the best if not *the* best in the industry. They are very customer-oriented and have provided us with trustworthy guidance. Their sales representatives are also very helpful to us, and we feel that all involved have a primary focus on you, the client. Individuals at South-Western we would like to thank include Acquisitions Editor Pamela Person, Developmental Editor Mardell Toomey, and Production Editor Anne Chimenti.

Others who have contributed to this edition include Gayle Megginson Ross, ancillary author who developed the Instructor's Manual with test bank and the study guide, Malvine Litten, Litten Editing and Production, Judy Hartman, GGS Information Services, Lorretta Palagi, Copy and Permissions Editor, Rachel Morris, Proofreader, and Cindy Kerr, Indexer.

We also acknowledge our colleagues and administrators, especially Carl Moore, Dean of the Mitchell College of Business, and Dr. Edward Harrison, Chair of the Management Department, both of the University of South Alabama.

We are very grateful to the many reviewers whose insights have served to improve this edition:

James H. Boyle
Glendale Community College

Craig Crick
Trukee Meadows Community College

Tom Deckelman
Owens Community College

Ken Hess
Anoka-Ramsey Community College

James T. McGrath
Community College of Baltimore County

Keith L. Mock
Bob Jones University

Fred Paricio
Gaston College

Michael G. Schaefer
Blinn College

Ron Weidenfeller
Grand Rapids Community College

The authors are firmly convinced that nothing is so practical as good theory. We are also convinced that the leading contributors to good management theory are professors whose laboratories are the real world of organizations and people. We were greatly influenced by role models, including Professor/Consultants Dr. Douglas McGregor and Dr. Rensis Likert.

While we cannot hope to make the contributions of these giants, we think our active involvement in the real world as consultants/facilitators/change agents has been a primary reason our book is one of the leaders in the supervisory field and is now entering its fourth edition.

Donald C. Mosley
Leon C. Megginson
Paul H. Pietri, Jr.

About the Authors

Donald C. Mosley. At the present time, Donald C. Mosley is professor emeritus of management at the University of South Alabama and also the founder and president of the Synergistic Consulting Group. Don and the Synergistic Group have been pioneers in the area of partnering, having designed and developed the original "quote partnering model" in the first formalized partnering workshop in the public sector. This model has been adopted throughout the United States and used internationally as well.

In the 1960s, as a young professor/consultant, Mosley developed his skills by being instrumental in helping a financially plagued chemical plant become the most profitable plant in the company's division within one year. During this period he was one of the first to utilize 360-degree evaluations by peers, work team members, and bosses as a basis for providing feedback and coaching for key managers.

Paul H. Pietri. Paul Pietri brings a wealth of knowledge of the supervisory field based on his over 25 years' experience as a trainer/consultant to private and public sector organizations. He has developed and conducted training designs in over 35 states for well over 5,000 supervisors from organizations such as International Paper Company, U.S. Department of Agriculture, Dupont, and others. Because of his extensive background in supervisory training, Pietri was chosen as one of seven U.S. team members to attend a Sao Paulo, Brazil, conference aimed at assisting Brazil's development of first- and mid-level managers. "Supervisors need and want answers to everyday, practical problems," Pietri feels. "A supervisory management textbook should employ, where possible, a strong hands-on approach that addresses real world issues and situations. I believe also that a good text emphasizes the practical, skills-oriented side of supervision throughout the entire text, not just in special applications tossed in at the end of a chapter."

Since 1986 Pietri has been actively involved in course design and training for Bowater Carolina, helping the company shift from a traditional, authority-based organizational culture towards one that emphasizes empowerment, teamwork, and quality. "Supervisors are especially strained and play a pivotal role in such change," he states. "The new culture entails a dramatic turnaround from the traditional way of managing that these supervisors practiced and were encouraged to practice in the past. These challenges—learning the new skills of empowering, facilitating, coaching, and managing conflict, to name a few—are being made to supervisors from all types of organizations throughout the country."

Leon Megginson. Leon Megginson has over ten years of managerial experience in the world of academics, practicing many of the skills found in our book. He served two years as associate dean of the business school at LSU and was chairman and dean of the school of business at the University of Mobile for eight years. He also served as operations officer of a squadron of over 100 pilots and airmen in the 25th Bomb Squad, U.S. Air Force, during WW II. He was a Fulbright Research Scholar in Spain during the 1960s and was a Ford Foundation Advisor in Pakistan, assisting the Pakistani in the area of management development.

Each year the Alumni Association at the University of South Alabama selects an Outstanding Professor. We are very proud that in 1993 the Association selected Paul H. Pietri, Jr., as the Outstanding Professor, and in 1999 Donald C. Mosley was selected.

Brief Contents

PART 1
OVERVIEW

1 Supervisory Management Roles and Challenges 2

2 Quest for Quality and Empowerment 34

PART 2
PLANNING

3 Fundamentals of Planning and Time Management 66

4 Decision Making and Problem Solving 98

PART 3
ORGANIZING

5 Fundamentals of Organizing 126

6 Delegating Authority 160

PART 4
LEADING

7 Communication 186

8 Motivation 218

9 Leadership 244

10 Managing Change, Group Development, and Team Building 272

PART 5
CONTROLLING

11 Exercising Control 304

12 Controlling Productivity, Quality, and Safety 326

PART 6
SKILL DEVELOPMENT

13 Coaching for Higher Performance 360

14 Meetings and Facilitation Skills 384

15 Managing Conflict and Stress 414

PART 7
MANAGING HUMAN RESOURCES AND DIVERSITY

16 Selecting, Training, and Compensating Employees 440

17 Appraising and Disciplining Employees 478

18 The Supervisor and Labor Relations 510

Endnotes 537
Glossary 543
URL Index 553
Subject Index 555
Photo Credits 569

Contents

PART 1 OVERVIEW

1 Supervisory Management Roles and Challenges 2

Preview: Sharon Olds, Supervisor 3

The Need for Management 6
What Is Management? 6   Levels of Management 8

What Do Managers Do? 9
Functions Performed by Managers 10   How the Functions Are Related 12
Roles Played by Managers 12

Skills Required for Effective Management 12
Conceptual Skills 13   Human Relations Skills 15   Administrative Skills 15
Technical Skills 16

The Transition: Where Supervisors Come From 17

The Improving Position of Supervisory Managers 18

Supervisory Relationships 20
Personal Relationships 20   Organizational Relationships 21   External
Relationships 22

Some Current Trends Challenging Supervisors 22
Dealing with a More Diverse Workforce 22   Emphasizing Team Performance 23
Coping with Exploding Technology 23   Adjusting to Occupational and Industry
Shifts 24   Meeting Global Challenges 25   Improving Quality and Productivity
26   Improving Ethical and Social Behavior 26

Skill Builder 1–1. The Personal Interest Inventory 28

Skill Builder 1–2. Effective and Ineffective Supervisors 31

Case 1–1. The Weak Supervisor 31

2 Quest for Quality and Empowerment 34

Preview: City Hospital 35

Empowerment 37
Levels of Empowerment 39

Quality 42
"Quality Is Job 1" 42   Reasons for the Recent Quality Revolution 42   Evolution
of the Quality Explosion in the United States 45   Approaches to Managing
Quality 49   Total Quality Management (TQM) 50

Role of the Supervisor in Empowerment and Total Quality 56

Major Impact at the Supervisory Management Level 56   The Emerging Supervisor:
Teacher, Leader, Coach 57

Skill Builder 2–1. Applying Empowerment 60

Skill Builder 2–2. The Quality Assignment 61

Case 2–1. Hillshire Farm/Kahn's 62

PART 2 PLANNING

3 Fundamentals of Planning and Time Management 66

Preview: Changes at Dixon 67

Some Important Points About Planning 68
Basic Steps in Planning 69   Planning is Most Closely Related to Controlling 70
Managers Tend to Neglect Planning 70   Contingency Planning Anticipates
Problems 72

Planning at Different Management Levels 72

Importance of Setting Objectives 74
What Are Objectives? 74   Objectives as a Stimulus for Motivation and Effort 75
Hierarchy of Objectives 75   Unified Planning Through Objectives 77
Guidelines for Setting Objectives 77

The Supervisor and MBO 78
Underlying Concepts 79   Key Aspects of the MBO Process 79   Some
Problems with MBO 80

Types of Plans 80
Standing Plans 80   Single-Use Plans 85

Managing Your Time 87
Time Management Matrix 88   The Time Log: Where Your Time Goes 89
Setting Priorities: A "Must" 90   Handling the Common Time Wasters 90

Skill Builder 3–1. Testing Your Planning Skills 94

Skill Builder 3–2. Determining Priorities 95

Case 3–1. Setting Performance Objectives 95

4 Decision Making and Problem Solving 98

Preview: The Advancing Landscape Architect 99

Role of Decision Making in Supervisory Management 100
Decision Making: The Heart of Supervisory Management 100   Why Supervisors
Need to Make So Many Decisions 100

What Is Decision Making? 102
Decision Making Defined 103   Elements Involved in Decision Making 103   Types
of Decisions to Be Made 104   How Decision Making and Problem Solving Relate
105

How to Make Decisions 106
Step 1: Define the Idea or Problem 106   Step 2: Develop Alternatives 107
Step 3: Collect, Interpret, and Evaluate Information About Each Alternative 107
Step 4: Select the Preferred Alternative 107   Step 5: Implement the Decision 109
Step 6: Follow Up, Evaluate, and Make Changes—If Needed 109

Factors to Keep in Mind When Making Decisions 109
The Right Person Should Make the Decision 109   Decisions Should Contribute to

Objectives   110   There's Seldom Only One Acceptable Choice   110   Both
Feeling and Thinking Should Be Used   110   Effective Decision Making Takes
Considerable Time and Effort   111   Decision Making Improves with Practice   111
A Decision May Not Please Everyone   112   A Decision Starts a Chain Reaction   112
Ethical Considerations Play a Part   112

Individual and Group Decision Making   114
Approaches to Decision Making   114   Advantages and Disadvantages of Each
Approach   114

Improving Decision Making   116
Bases of Decision Making   116   Some Guides to Less Stressful Decision Making
118

Skill Builder 4–1. Whom Do You Promote?   120

Skill Builder 4–2. Personal Problems   122

Case 4–1. Able or Baker?   122

PART 3   ORGANIZING

5   Fundamentals of Organizing   126

Preview: John Moody's Growing Organization   127

The Four Stages in Growth of an Organization   128
Stage 1: The One-Person Organization   128   Stage 2: The Organization with
Assistants Added   128   Stage 3: The Line Organization   130   Stage 4: The Line-
and-Staff Organization   131

Departmentalization   134
Functional Departmentalization   135   Product Departmentalization   136   Matrix
Departmentalization   136

Two Important Organizing Principles   138
Unity of Command   138   Span of Control   140

Relationships Between Line and Staff   143
Conflicts Between Line and Staff   143   How to Avoid Excessive Line-Staff Conflict:
Delineating Authority   143

Decentralization versus Centralization   146
Factors Affecting Decentralization   146   Effect of Decentralization on
Organizational Structure   147

Downsizing   148
Benefits of Downsizing   148   Costs of Downsizing   149   Impact on Remaining
Supervisors and Managers   149   Ways to Get Beyond Downsizing   149

Management Philosophy, Strategy, and Organization   150
The Horizontal Organization   151   The Inverted Pyramid   153   The Wagon Wheel
153

Skill Builder 5–1. Proposed Change of Organization   157

**Skill Builder 5–2. Reducing Costs in an Accounting
Firm   158**

Case 5–1. Conflicting Views   158

6   Delegating Authority   160

**Preview: Joe Allegro, An Effective Developer of
People   161**

Why Delegate? 162
Delegating Develops People 162   Delegating Allows a Supervisor to Do Other
Things 163   Delegating Allows More Work to Be Accomplished 163   Delegating
Improves Control 164

Process of Delegation 164
Granting Authority 165   Assigning Responsibility 165   Requiring Accountability
166

Effective Delegation 167
Knowing When to Delegate 168   How the Delegation Process Operates 168
The Principle of Parity of Authority and Responsibility 168   Time Required for
Effective Delegation 170

Parties Involved in Effective Delegation 171
The Role of Higher Management 171   The Role of the Supervisor 171   The Role
of Employees to Whom Authority Is Delegated 172

Why Supervisors Fail to Delegate 172

Dealing with Ineffective Employees 174

Relating Delegation to Success or Failure 175
Eight Ways to Fail 175   Turning a Weakness into a Strength 176

Ineffective Delegation: A Solution 176

Skill Builder 6–1. Test Your Delegation Habits 180

Case 6–1. The Promotion Decision 181

Case 6–2. Marion Dawson's Problem 182

Case 6–3. Preparing an Action Plan 183

PART 4   LEADING

7 Communication 186

Preview: Good News, Bad News? 187

What Is Communication? 188
Communication Process Model 188   Electronic Communication Technology 189
Importance of Nonverbal Messages 190

Flows of Communication 191
The Vertical Flows: Downward and Upward Communication 191   Lateral-Diagonal
Flows 196   Informal Communication 197

Barriers to Effective Supervisory Communication 198
Organizational Barriers 198   Interpersonal and Language Barriers 199

Improving Supervisory Communications 202
Set the Proper Climate 202   Plan for Effective Communication 204   Using
Repetition to Reinforce Key Ideas 205   Encourage the Use of Feedback 206
Become a Better Listener 207

**Skill Builder 7–1. Assessing Your Information-Disclosing and Information-
Receiving Style 212**

Skill Builder 7–2. Practicing Active Listening 214

Case 7–1. Developing a Communication Plan 216

8 Motivation 218

Preview: Sharon Olds: People Motivator 219

Motivation: Some Fundamentals of Understanding Human Behavior 221
Levels of Motivation 221 Intrinsic and Extrinsic Motivation 223 The Motivation–Performance Link 223

Maslow's Hierarchy of Needs Theory 224
Principles Underlying the Theory 225 Qualifying the Theory 227

Herzberg's Theory 228
Dissatisfiers and Motivators 228 Link to Intrinsic and Extrinsic Motivation 229 Qualifying Herzberg's Theory 230

Other Theories of Motivation 230
Expectancy Theory 230 Goal-Setting Theory 233 Reinforcement Theory 234

Lessons from the Theories: Five Steps to Motivating Employees 235
Help Make Employees' Job Interesting 236 Provide Clear Performance Objectives 237 Support Employees' Performance Efforts 237 Provide Timely Performance Feedback 237 Reward Employees' Performance 237

Skill Builder 8–1. Classifying Managerial Rewards 240

Skill Builder 8–2. Applying Motivational Theory 241

Case 8–1. The Motivational Challenge 241

9 Leadership 244

Preview: Kenny: An Effective Supervisor 245

Leadership: What Is It All About? 246
Factors Affecting Leadership Style 246 Two Leadership Models 250 Tannenbaum and Schmidt's Leadership Continuum 254 Is One Leadership Style Best? 256

Developmental Leadership 256
Heroic Managers 257 Developmental Managers 257

Transformational and Transactional Leadership 260
Transformational Leadership 260 Transactional Leadership 261

Servant Leadership 262
The Paradox of Servant Leadership 263 Characteristics of Servant Leadership 263

Core Leadership Functions 264

Skill Builder 9–1. The Debate Question 268

Skill Builder 9–2. Diagnosing and Selecting the Appropriate Leadership Style 268

Case 9–1. Kenny's Leadership—A Further Analysis 270

10 Managing Change, Group Development, and Team Building 272

Preview: The Ritz-Carlton Hotel Corporation 273

Managing Organizational Change 276
Forces Causing Change 276 Results of Ignoring Change 278 Ways of Dealing with Change 278 Planned Change 279

Importance of Work Groups 281
What Are Groups 281   Types of Groups 281   How Groups Develop 282
Evaluating Groups 283   Determining Group Effectiveness 285

Team Building 289
Partnering: Team Development Accelerated 290   What Is Involved in Partnering?
290   Partnering Successes 291   Partnering Failures and Their Causes 294

Self-Managing Work Teams 295

Skill Builder 10–1. Team Building 298

Skill Builder 10–2. Development of a Generic Project Partnering Approach 298

Skill Builder 10–3. Creating an Organizational Culture 300

Skill Builder 10–4. "Win as Much as You Can" Tally Sheet 300

Case 10–1. The Shift to Team Leadership 301

PART 5   CONTROLLING

11 Exercising Control 304

Preview: Ron Johnston: Controlling Operations 305

What Is Control? 306
Control's Close Links to Planning 306   Importance of Controls 307   Examples of
Controls 307

Characteristics of Effective Control Systems 307

Types of Control Systems 308

Steps in the Control Process 309
Step 1: Establishing Performance Standards 309   Step 2: Measuring Performance
312   Step 3: Comparing Performance with Standards and Analyzing Deviations 316
Step 4: Taking Corrective Action If Necessary 317

Management by Exception 318

The Impact of Technology on Controls 320

Skill Builder 11–1. The Overcontrolling Supervisor 323

Skill Builder 11–2. Setting Standards and Measuring Performance 323

Skill Builder 11–3. Setting Course Standards 324

Case 11–1. Controlling Absenteeism 324

12 Controlling Productivity, Quality, and Safety 326

Preview: Productivity Increase or Else 327

Improving Productivity and Cost Control 328
High U.S. Productivity Fuels the 1990s 328   Defining Productivity 328   Why
Productivity Is Important 331   Groups Influencing Productivity 333   The
Supervisor's Role in Improving Productivity 335   The Supervisor's Role in Cost
Control 335   Some Recent Productivity Improvement Methods 336

Controlling Quality 338
TQM and Quality Control 338   Understanding Variance in Controlling Quality 338
Some Tools for Controlling Quality 339   The Supervisor's Role in Achieving Quality
343

Promoting Employee Safety 347
What OSHA Does 347 Factors Influencing Safety 347 Causes of Accidents 350 The Supervisor's Role in Promoting Safety 350

Skill Builder 12–1. Quality Survey 354

Skill Builder 12–2. Increasing Safety Performance 355

Case 12–1. Using Quality Tools 356

PART 6 SKILL DEVELOPMENT

13 Coaching for Higher Performance 360

Preview: Coaching in Action 361

Introduction to Coaching 362
Coaching Is Performance Linked 362 Current Emphasis on Coaching 364 Why Supervisors Reject Coaching 364

The Coaching Functions 365
Tutoring 365 Mentoring 365 Confronting/Challenging 366 Counseling 367

Coaching and Understanding Diversity 367

The Skills of Coaching 368
Coaching: The Core Skills 369

Coaching for Improved Performance: Confronting and Challenging 370

Coaching: The Counseling Function 372
Areas of Employee Counseling 373 Role of EAPs in Counseling 375

Skill Builder 13–1. Practicing "I" Messages 378

Skill Builder 13–2. Practicing Coaching Responses 379

Case 13–1. The Coaching Meeting 380

14 Meetings and Facilitation Skills 384

Preview: Chuck Dansby, Facilitator "Extraordinaire" 385

Purposes of Meetings 386
Information Giving 387 Information Exchange 387 Fact Finding 387 Problem Solving 388 Achieving Consensus 388

Approaches Used at Meetings 389
Leader-Controlled Approach 389 Group-Centered Approach 390 Which Approach Should You Use? 392

Advantages and Disadvantages of Meetings 392
Advantages of Meetings 392 Disadvantages of Meetings 393

Making Meetings Effective 394
Factors to Consider Before the Meeting 394 Factors to Consider During the Meeting 395 Factors to Consider After the Meeting 399

What Is Group Facilitation? 399
Role of the Facilitator 400 Process Consultation 400 Facilitating Teleconferencing 403

Skill Builder 14–1. Achieving Group Consensus 406

Skill Builder 14–2. The Required Weekly Meeting 407

Skill Builder 14–3. Developing Skills as a Facilitator/Consultant 408

Skill Builder 14–4. Facilitator Training 409

Case 14–1. Meeting Facilitation Challenges 412

15 Managing Conflict and Stress 414

Preview: The Conflict-Laden, Stressful Plan Environment 415

Causes of Conflict 416

Conflict Management Styles 416

Using Principled Negotiation to Resolve Conflict 419

Overcoming Interpersonal Conflicts 419

What Is Stress? 421
Definition of Stress 422   The Costs of Stress 424   The Positive Aspects of Stress
424

Major Causes of Stress 424
Life Events 424   Personal Psychological Makeup 426   Organizational and Work-
Related Factors 427   Burnout 427

Ways to Cope with Personal Stress 430
Physical Exercise 430   Relaxation Techniques 430   A Sense of Control 430
Developing and Maintaining Good Interpersonal Relationships 432

Skill Builder 15–1. The Conflict-Laden, Stressful Plant Environment 434

Skill Builder 15–2. Up in Smoke-Are You Burned Out? 434

Skill Builder 15–3. A Planning Strategy to Cope with Success 436

Case 15–1. The Missed Promotion 436

PART 7   MANAGING HUMAN RESOURCES AND DIVERSITY

16 Selecting, Training, and Compensating Employees 440

**Preview: Bill Waldorf: Selecting and Supervising a Diverse High-Tech Work Team
441**

Responsibility for Selecting, Training, and Compensating Employees 443
A Shared Responsibility 443   The Supervisor's Role 443

Planning Human Resource Needs and Finding Employees to Fill the Jobs 444
Types and Number of Employees Needed 444   Filling Jobs from Within 446
Filling Jobs from the Outside 450

Complying with Equal Employment Opportunity Laws 451
Equal Employment Opportunity (EEO) Laws 451   Enforcement of EEO Laws 451

Selecting Employees for Specific Jobs 454
Requisition 454   Preliminary Screening 454   Application Form or Résumé 456
Preemployment Testing 457   Preemployment Interviewing 458   Checking
References and Records 459   Preliminary Selection by the Supervisor 459   Final
Selection 459   Physical Examination 460   Job Offer 460   Orientation 460

Training and Developing Employees 461

How to Determine Training Needs 461   How to Train Employees 461   Outside Assistance Available for Training 463

Compensating Employees 464
Importance of Compensation 464   Roles Played by Compensation 464   Types of Wages 465   Factors Affecting Wage Rates 466   The Comparable Worth Issue 468   Using Job Evaluation to Set Job Rates 469

Providing Employee Benefits 470
Legally Required Benefits 470   Voluntary Benefits 471   Flexible Benefits 472

Skill Builder 16–1. What Would You Do? 475

Skill Builder 16–2. What Do You Want from Your Job? 475

Case 16–1. John Wolf: The Bypassed Employee 476

17 Appraising and Disciplining Employees 478

Preview: When the Transfer Backfires (A) 479

The Role of Performance Appraisals in Supervisory Management 480
What Is a Performance Appraisal? 480   How a Performance Appraisal Operates 480   Purposes of the Performance Appraisal 481   Legal Aspects of the Performance Appraisal 482

Who Should Do Performance Appraisals? 482
Employees Rating Themselves 482   Employees Rating Supervisors 483   Peers Rating One Another 483   Immediate Supervisor Rating Employees 483

Some Selected Methods of Appraising Performance 483
Traditional Methods of Performance Appraisal 483   New Ways of Appraising Performance 486   Barriers to Effective Appraisals 487

The Role of the Appraisal Interview 489

The Need for Discipline 490
What Is Discipline? 491   Positive and Negative Discipline 493   Discipline as Due Process 494

Types of Disciplinary Problems 495
Number and Frequency of Occurrences 495   Severity of Consequences 495   Sexual Harassment 498

How Disciplinary Due Process Operates 498
Establishing Rules of Conduct 498   Determining Penalties 499   Imposing the Penalty Only After a Fair Hearing 499

The Supervisor and Discipline 500
The Supervisor's Disciplinary Role 500   Principles of Effective Discipline: The Hot-Stove Rule 500   Applying Discipline 503   Supervisors' Personal Liability for Disciplining Employees 504

Skill builder 17–1. Gloria Rogers Appraises Her Employees 506

Case 17–1. When the Transfer Backfires (B) 507

Case 17–2. Poor Interpersonal Relationships 507

18 The Supervisor and Labor Relations 510

Preview: The Union Organizer—Part 1 511

What Are Labor Relations? 512

How Unions Developed in the United States 513
  Early Union Activities 513   Period of Rapid Union Growth 513   Recent Limited
  Union Growth 515   Some Reasons for Declining Union Membership 516

Laws Governing Labor Relations 517
  Basic Labor Laws 517   Administration of Labor Laws 520

Union Principles, Objectives, and Methods of Attaining Objectives 520
  Organizing Employees 521   Becoming Recognized as the Employees' Exclusive
  Bargaining Agent 524   Engaging in Collective Bargaining 527   Conducting a
  Strike or Lockout 528   Reaching an Agreement 528

Living with the Agreement 529
  Supervisors' Rights Under the Agreement 530   The Supervisor and the Union
  Steward 530   The Role of Seniority 531   Handling Employee Complaints 531
  Caution Needed in Terminations 532

Skill Builder 18–1. The Union Organizer 535

Skill Builder 18–2. Would You Sign a Union Authorization Card? 535

Case 18–1. Major League Baseball Umpires Foul Out 535

Endnotes 537

Glossary 543

URL Index 553

Subject Index 555

Photo Credits 569

Overview

1   Supervisory Management Roles and Challenges

1 part

Supervisory Management Roles and Challenges

● outline

The Need for Management
What Is Management?
Levels of Management

What Do Managers Do?
Functions Performed by Managers
How the Functions Are Related
Roles Played by Managers

Skills Required for Effective Management
Conceptual Skills
Human Relations Skills
Administrative Skills
Technical Skills

The Transition: Where Supervisors Come From

The Improving Position of Supervisory Managers

Supervisory Relationships
Personal Relationships
Organizational Relationships
External Relationships

Some Current Trends Challenging Supervisors
Dealing with a More Diverse Workforce
Emphasizing Team Performance
Coping with Exploding Technology
Adjusting to Occupational and Industry Shifts
Meeting Global Challenges
Improving Quality and Productivity
Improving Ethical and Social Behavior

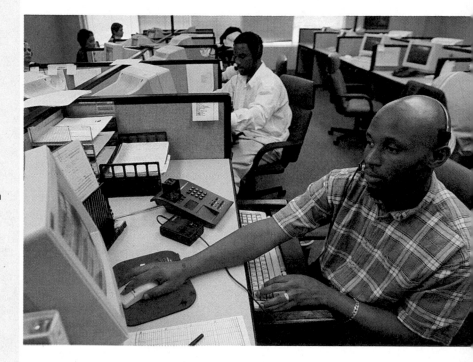

Supervisors are linking pins who are members of, and link or lock together, independent groups within an organization.

Rensis Likert

Sharon Olds, Supervisor

With over $3 billion of outstanding leases and 2,500 employees throughout the United States, AutoFin is a major player in the growing auto leasing business. Sharon Olds is one of six remarketing supervisors in the company's Southeast Division, which employs 300 plus employees (Exhibit 1–1).

As its primary function, the remarketing department contacts customers who have six months remaining on their auto lease agreements. The goal of Sharon's "remarketing associates" is to persuade a customer to (1) extend the lease, (2) buy the car and finance it through AutoFin, or (3) buy the car outright. A fourth customer option—that of allowing the lease to expire and returning the car—is the least favorable for AutoFin. In such cases, the company must take possession of the vehicle and sell it at auction. AutoFin will, at best, break even on the entire lease/sell transaction. Remarketing associates are goal-oriented, skilled communicators who must relate by telephone to people from all walks of life. Associate base pay is in the $20,000 range, but associates can earn as much as $35,000 to $50,000 through production incentives and overtime pay.

Presently age 31, Sharon joined the company six years ago as an associate trainee. She quickly became an excellent performer. Noting that most supervisors were either college graduates or had attended college, she took advantage of the company's tuition reimbursement plan and began working toward a

degree in business at a local university. She has since completed about two and a half years of her program, earning excellent grades. This initiative, coupled with her above-average job performance and excellent communication skills, caught management's attention. She was promoted to lead associate two years ago, a position in which she assumed a liason position between her supervisor and four associates. In this position, she mentored new associates and resolved for her associate team a range of customer-related problems referred to her. When one supervisor (not her own) left the company six months ago, Sharon was offered and accepted her present supervisory position, even though she initially took a pay cut.

I took it because I had confidence in being able to do it. This is an excellent company that is well managed and professional. You know where you stand. I think I can make a contribution and have more flexibility and freedom, even though there is more responsibility. But I really needed a different challenge—being on the phone most of the day with customers is not how I wanted to spend the rest of my life.

Sharon's supervisory effectiveness is gauged in terms of how successful her associates are in achieving their production goals. One production goal for each associate is to book 35 customers monthly to a new lease contract or to purchase and refinance their present vehicle. Another goal is that an associate must achieve a 40 percent success

*Partial Organization
Chart for AutoFin
Southeast Division*

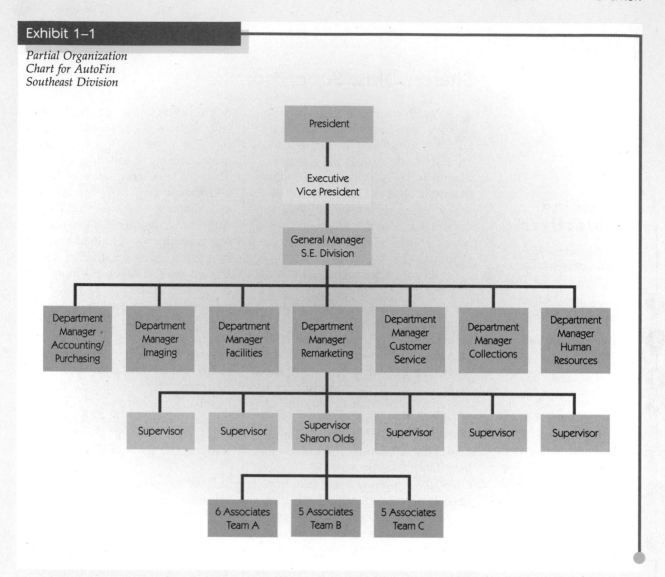

rate in having these customers purchase a warranty agreement on the vehicle. Regarding other departmental standards, associates must average (1) seven hours and 15 minutes each workday on line with customers, (2) fewer than 5 minutes with each customer contact, and (3) 30 or fewer seconds between calls.

Sharon's supervisory activities involve scheduling her associates' work, monitoring their calls (about 30 to 40 percent of her day), assess-

ing their daily performance reports, resolving customer situations referred to her by lead associates, conducting a 20- to 30-minute monthly performance review with each team member, conducting a weekly staff meeting with her associates, preparing performance reports for her department head, meeting weekly with her department head to review performance results, and attending supervisory meetings called by her department head. She also interfaces with department heads other than her own, for instance, when recruiting a new associate (human resources), ordering equipment and supplies (purchasing), or having equipment repaired (facilities).

Sharon's department typifies important changes in technology and employee diversity that are shaping organizations today. Each associate has a cubicle, complete with computer and phone. A customer call list, contract information, and a format for easily reporting the result of each associate's calls are computer generated; progress and results are networked to Sharon's computer for immediate performance tracking. Sharon's daily, weekly, and monthly performance reports are forwarded via computer format to her own department head. She and her associates are proficient in WordPerfect and Excel, and use e-mail routinely throughout the day. Sharon's 16 associates are comprised of 11 males and 5 females; there are ten Caucasians, four African-Americans, one Hispanic, and one Asian. They include a young 23-year-old single male, a 35-year-old single mother of four, and a grandmother of seven in her late fifties.

The issue that most challenged Sharon the past year came only one month after her promotion when her department manager, under pressure from corporate headquarters, increased associates' production quotas. Despite strong feelings of resistance by associates and supervisors, several supervisors said little at the meeting in which the departmental manager announced the change. Perhaps because she had only recently been promoted to supervisor, Sharon was among the most outspoken of her fellow supervisors in making her feelings known. She was concerned that this might not be the best thing politically for her to do, and this meant walking a narrow line with her boss and even fellow supervisors who may have resented her being so outspoken when they were not. But this seemed not to be the case; in fact, several supervisors told her they appreciated how Sharon had gone to bat in voicing associates' feelings about the new standards.

This case illustrates many aspects of a supervisor's job and some of the many challenges that supervisors must face. Sharon performs a broad set of duties, ranging from scheduling work, monitoring phone calls, having one-on-one performance reviews, and conducting meetings. She interfaces with people from multiple groups, including her own personnel, her department head, personnel from other departments, fellow supervisors, and, occasionally, customers. She uses a variety of skills ranging from computer know-how to the necessary diplomacy required when discussing poor performance with an associate.

She faces a common challenge of supervisors—obtaining results through others. She is totally dependent on her personnel to achieve the department's work goals. In a sense, Sharon's effectiveness is determined by how successful her personnel are. One way of looking at the supervisor's job then is to think of it in terms of "helping your people be as good as they can be."

This case indicates some of the many changes taking place that impact the work of supervisors and managers at all organizational levels, the increasing use of technology, and workforce diversity. At no time has the job of supervision been recognized as being so important. Likewise, at no time has it been

A common challenge of all supervisors is to help their employees learn, grow, and develop, so that objectives can be reached.

more challenging. This chapter is designed to introduce you in more depth to the roles and challenges of being a supervisor.

THE NEED FOR MANAGEMENT

① Explain why management is needed in all organizations.

Whenever a group of people works together in a structured situation to achieve a common objective, they form an **organization.** The organization may be a student group, a business firm, a religious group, a governmental institution, a military unit, a sports team, or a similar group. The main objective of such organizations is to produce a product or provide a service. Other organizational objectives may be to provide satisfaction to members, employment and benefits to workers, a product to the public, and/or a return to the owners of the business (usually in the form of a profit). To reach these objectives, management must perform three basic organizational activities: (1) **operations,** or producing the product or service, (2) **marketing,** or selling and distributing the product, and (3) **financing,** or providing and using funds. These activities must be performed in almost all organizations—both those operating for profit and those not seeking a profit.

organization
A group of people working together in a structured situation for a common objective.

operations
Producing an organization's product or service.

marketing
Selling and distributing an organization's product or service.

financing
Providing or using funds to produce and distribute an organization's product or service.

What Is Management?

Organizations are the means by which people get things done. People can accomplish more working together than they can achieve alone, but to combine and coordinate the efforts of the members of the organization, the process of management is required. Without management, people in the group would go off on their own and try to reach the organization's objectives independently of other group members. If small organizations lacked management, the members' efforts would be wasted. If management were absent in the larger, more complex organizations, objectives would not be reached and chaos would result. In summary, *managers are needed in all types of organizations.*

self-check

What managers have you come in contact with during the past week—either in person or on the phone, TV, or radio? What were their titles? At what level in their organization were they? What were some of their job responsibilities?

management
Working with people to achieve objectives by effective decision making and coordination of available resources.

human resources
The people an organization requires for operations.

physical resources
Items an organization requires for operations.

financial resources
The money, capital, and credit an organization requires for operations.

Management can be defined as the process of working with and through people to achieve objectives by means of effective decision making and coordination of available resources. The basic resources of any organization are **human resources,** which are the people involved; **physical resources,** which include buildings, furnishings, machinery, computers, equipment, materials, and supplies; and **financial resources,** such as money, capital, and credit. Exhibit 1–2 shows *the vital task of management: combining resources and activities into a productive system to attain organizational objectives.*

Consider the situation below:

Pete Bolton operates a one-person shoe repair shop. Pete performs all the necessary activities, including repairing shoes, serving customers,

Exhibit 1–2

How Management Combines the Organization's Resources into a Productive System

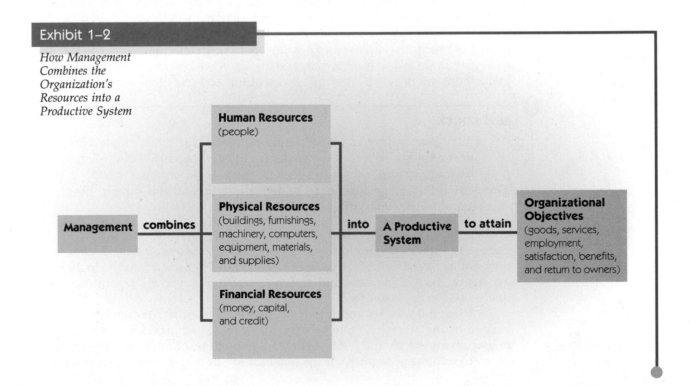

Management combines → Human Resources (people); Physical Resources (buildings, furnishings, machinery, computers, equipment, materials, and supplies); Financial Resources (money, capital, and credit) → into → A Productive System → to attain → Organizational Objectives (goods, services, employment, satisfaction, benefits, and return to owners)

ordering equipment and supplies, maintaining equipment, keeping records, paying bills, and borrowing money. He does it all.

Would you say that Pete is performing management? Our position is that he is not. On the one hand, he certainly employs *physical* and *financial resources.* While he does interact with customers, they are not an employed resource, because they do not perform work. The only *human resource* that Pete utilizes is himself. Now consider a new scenario for Pete:

> **Business is so good that Pete leases the adjacent office and removes the wall, creating five times more floor space for the shop. He hires four employees: Three perform shoe repairs and one is a counter clerk/ repairer. Pete must now perform management. Whereas in the first situation he was a doer, performing all activities himself, in the second situation he must manage, guide, and direct others who perform tasks. The skills required for Pete to perform successfully in this situation differ markedly from the first.**

This simple example explains why many individuals perform successfully in nonmanagement positions such as salespersons, technicians, operators, and professionals, but often fail when placed in positions of supervision. This book is about the skills needed to succeed in the second situation!

 2 Describe the different levels of management.

Levels of Management

Except in very small organizations, the different levels of management are usually based on the amount of responsibility and authority required to perform the job. Individuals at higher levels of the organization have more authority and responsibility than those at lower levels. **Authority** is the right to tell others to act or not act in order to reach objectives. **Responsibility** is the obligation that is created when an employee accepts a manager's delegated authority.

Large organizations usually have at least three levels of management, plus a level of operative employees. These levels are generally referred to as (1) *top management,* (2) *middle management,* and (3) *supervisory management.* In large organizations, there may be multiple levels of top and middle management.

authority
The right to tell others how to act to reach objectives.

responsibility
The obligation of an employee to accept a manager's delegated authority.

self-check

> In the chapter preview, for example, note that five levels of management exist at AutoFin: the president/CEO and executive vice-president comprise top management, the general manager and department managers comprise middle management, and supervisors comprise the supervising management level.

Exhibit 1–3 shows that authority and responsibility increase as one moves from the nonmanagerial level into the managerial ranks and then into the higher managerial levels. The titles and designations listed are only a few of those actually used in organizations.

Although the duties and responsibilites of the various management levels vary from one organization to another, they can be summarized as follows. **Top management** is responsible for the overall operations of the entire organization or oversees a major segment of the organization or a basic organizational activ-

top management
Responsible for the entire or a major segment of the organization.

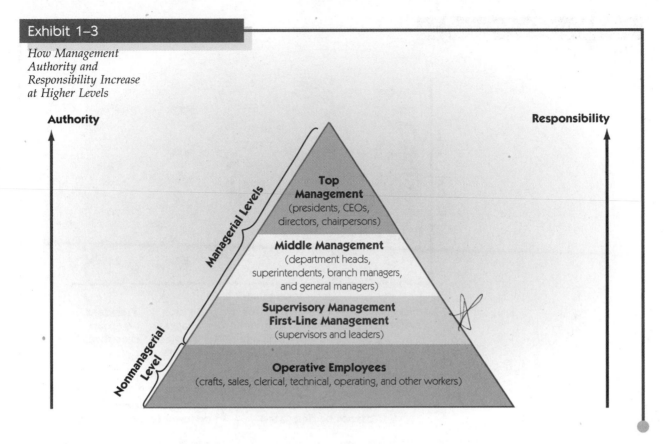

*How Management
Authority and
Responsibility Increase
at Higher Levels*

middle management
Responsible for a sub-
stantial part of the organization.

**supervisory
management**
Controls operations of
smaller organizational
units.

ity. **Middle management** is responsible for a substantial part of the organization (perhaps a program, project, division, plant, or department). Finally, **supervisory management** has control over the operations of a smaller organizational
unit (such as a production line, operating unit, office, or laboratory). Managers
in this last group, such as Sharon Olds' group, are in charge of nonmanagerial,
or rank-and-file, employees and are the managers with whom most employees
interact.

Another difference among managers at different levels is the amount of
time they spend carrying out various activities. Exhibit 1–4 shows how managers of one electrical appliance manufacturer spend their time. The terms and
titles are different from those used in this text, but the exhibit illustrates how
the importance of particular activities differs according to managerial level.

This book deals primarily with the first level of managers, who may be
called *supervisory managers* or simply *supervisors*.

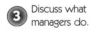 Discuss what
managers do.

WHAT DO MANAGERS DO?

It is now time to see what managers do that makes them so necessary to an organization's success. First we examine the functions managers perform. Then
we look at some roles managers play. Note at this point that not all managers
spend the same amount of time performing each management function or playing each role.

*How Managers Spend
Their Time*

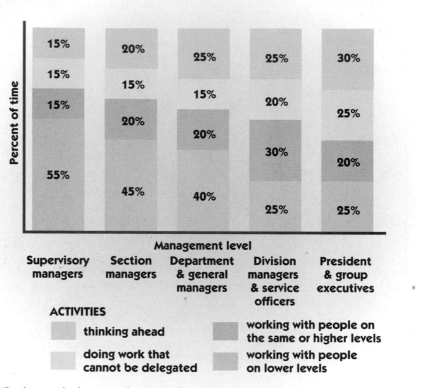

ACTIVITIES

	thinking ahead		working with people on the same or higher levels
	doing work that cannot be delegated		working with people on lower levels

SOURCE: *Based on a study of managers of a company that asked to remain anonymous.*

Functions Performed by Managers

managerial functions
Broad classification of activities that all managers perform.

Managerial functions are the broad classification of activities that all managers perform. There is no single generally accepted classification of these functions, but we believe that five separate, but interrelated, basic functions must be performed by any manager at any level in any organization. Successful managers perform these functions effectively; unsuccessful ones do not. The functions are:

1. Planning
2. Organizing
3. Staffing
4. Leading
5. Controlling

As shown in Exhibit 1–5, these functions reflect a broad range of activities.

planning
Selecting future courses of action and deciding how to achieve the desired results.

    Planning involves selecting goals and future courses of action and deciding how to achieve the desired results. It also encompasses gathering and analyzing information in order to make these decisions. Through planning the manager establishes goals and objectives and determines methods of attaining them. All other basic managerial functions depend on planning, because it is unlikely that they will be successfully carried out without sound and continuous planning.

The Management Functions in Action

Primary Function	Examples
Planning	Determining resources needed
	Setting daily, weekly, monthly performance objectives
	Developing work schedules
	Anticipating and preparing for problems before they occur
Organizing	Making sure members understand roles and responsibilities
	Deciding who is best suited to perform a given task
	Assigning tasks to team members
	Coordinating members' activities
Staffing	Interviewing and selecting potential employees
	Securing needed training to upgrade members' skills
	Helping employees grow and develop through coaching, job rotation, broadening of assignments
Leading	Communicating relevant information to members
	Coaching, encouraging, supporting members
	Praising, recognizing, rewarding for work well done
	Building employee acceptance of change
Controlling	Observing and monitoring employee performance
	Ensuring employee compliance with standards, procedures, rules
	Identifying and resolving crises, problems that occur
	Following up to ensure implementation of decisions

Chapters 3 and 4 are devoted to some of the more important aspects of planning.

Note that Sharon Olds' important activities involve planning and scheduling her employees' work.

self-check

What happens to managers' need to plan as they move up in an organization, as illustrated in Exhibit 1–4? Why does this happen?

organizing
Deciding what activities are needed to reach goals and dividing human resources into work groups to achieve them.

staffing
Recruiting, training, promoting, and rewarding people to do the organization's work.

leading
Conducting, guiding, influencing, and motivating employees in the performance of their duties and responsibilities.

Organizing. Deciding what activities are needed to reach goals and objectives, deciding who is to perform what task, dividing human resources into work groups, and assigning each group to a manager are tasks that make up the **organizing** function. Another aspect of organizing is bringing together the physical, financial, and human resources needed to achieve the organization's objectives. More will be said about the organizing function in Chapters 5 and 6.

Staffing. The process of recruiting, selecting, developing, promoting, and paying and rewarding people to do the organization's work is called **staffing**. This basic function is sometimes regarded as a part of the organizing function, but we think it is important enough to be considered separately. Chapters 16 and 17 will elaborate on this function.

Leading. The **leading** function involves guiding, influencing, and motivating employees in the performance of their duties and responsibilities. It consists of coaching and empowering employees, facilitating their activities, communicating ideas and instructions, and motivating employees to perform their work efficiently. As shown in Exhibit 1–4, middle managers and supervisory managers are more heavily involved in leading—that is, "working with people"—than are top managers. Because of this, more chapters in this book address "leading" than any other function.

controlling
Comparing actual performance with planned action and taking corrective action if needed.

Controlling. The **controlling** function involves comparing actual performance with planned standards and taking corrective action, if needed, to ensure that objectives are achieved. Control can be achieved only by setting up standards of performance, checking to see whether they have been achieved, and then doing what is necessary to bring actual performance in line with planned performance. This function must be executed successfully to ensure that the other management functions are effectively performed. Chapters 11 and 12 deal with various aspects of this function.

Note that Sharon Olds spends a large part of her workday monitoring other associates' phone calls and evaluating progress toward their work goals.

How the Functions Are Related

Although the five management functions must be performed by managers in all types of organizations and at all management levels, they may be performed in different ways and given different emphasis by various managers. One or more functions may be stressed over another at a particular level. For example, planning is done most often by top management, and leading and controlling are common among supervisory managers. Yet the functions are interrelated, interactive, and interdependent, as shown in Exhibit 1–6. Although they may be performed in any order, the functions tend to be performed in the sequence indicated by the numbers in the exhibit.

Roles Played by Managers

The preceding discussion of the management functions might lead you to believe that the manager's job is orderly, well organized, systematic, and harmonious. But this is just not so. In performing these functions, managers engage in a great many varied, disorganized, fragmented, and often unrelated activities. These activities may last for a very short time or may extend over a longer period.

roles
Parts played by managers in the performance of their functions.

In carrying out these activities, managers play **roles** as if they were actors, and these roles change rapidly and frequently. Ten managerial roles have been identified, grouped as follows: (1) interpersonal roles, (2) informational roles, and (3) decision-making roles. Exhibit 1–7 shows how each might be carried out by Sharon Olds (opening case).

Like managerial functions, these roles are given varying degrees of emphasis by managers in different organizations and at different levels in the same organization. Managers vary in how they interpret the roles, the time they devote to them, and the importance they assign to them. With training and experience, supervisors can learn to perform these duties effectively.

4 Explain the basic skills required for effective management.

SKILLS REQUIRED FOR EFFECTIVE MANAGEMENT

You may be wondering at this point what basic skills managers need in order to perform the managerial functions and play the managerial roles most

Exhibit 1–6

*How the Management
Functions Are Related*

1. Planning
Selecting and deciding how to
achieve future courses of action for
the organization as a whole and for
each of its subunits.

5. Controlling
Comparing actual performance with
planned performance, and taking
corrective action, if needed, to ensure
that objectives are achieved.

2. Organizing
Deciding the activities needed to reach
objectives, dividing human resources
into work groups, and assigning each
group to a manager with the authority
to carry out the activities.

4. Leading
Directing, guiding, and supervising
subordinates in the performance
of their duties and responsibilities.

3. Staffing
Recruiting, selecting, training and
developing, promoting, paying and
rewarding, and laying off and
terminating people to do the
organization's work.

Controlling   Planning   Organizing   Staffing   Leading

effectively. Although many skills are needed, a few of the most common ones
follow:

1. Conceptual skills
2. Human relations skills
3. Administrative skills
4. Technical skills

The relative importance of these skills varies according to the type of industry
in which the managers work, the organization to which they belong, their level
in the managerial ranks, the job being performed, and the employees being
managed. Exhibit 1–8 shows an estimate of the relative importance of these
skills at different management levels.

Conceptual Skills

Conceptual skills involve the ability to acquire, analyze, and interpret information in a logical manner. All managers need to understand the environ-

conceptual skills
Mental ability to be-
come aware of and
identifying relationships
among different pieces
of information.

Exhibit 1–7

Roles Played by Manager Sharon Olds

Role	What Is Involved	Examples
Interpersonal Roles		
Figurehead	Represents the unit as its symbolic head.	Greeting departmental visitors, attending meetings and ceremonies, representing company on community boards.
Leader	Helping personnel reach organizational and personal goals.	Motivating, encouraging, supporting associates; providing feedback about performance; building morale.
Liaison	Maintaining relationships between the unit and outsiders.	Meeting with departmental heads and other supervisors.
Informational Roles		
Monitor	Seeking out useful information that is especially relevant for the unit/organization.	Attending professional meetings, learning about forthcoming changes.
Disseminator	Providing relevant information to appropriate organization members.	Routing reports and information to associates and others; copying departmental head on memos to associates.
Spokesperson	Representing employees to supervisors and vice versa; representing the unit to others.	Representing the department at weekly meetings; speaking out against changes that adversely affect associates.
Decision-Making Roles		
Entrepreneur	Tackling problems; seeking changes to improve unit.	Introducing new equipment, encouraging improved methods, promoting innovation by associates, taking risks.
Disturbance handler	Responding to crises/ problems that arise.	Resolving associate conflicts, soothing associates' resistance to change.
Resource allocator	Allocating the unit's resources.	Preparing a budget, deciding which associates receive new equipment, which are offered overtime work.
Negotiator	Negotiating differences with employees, managers, and outsiders.	Negotiating with a difficult customer, bargaining for favorable terms with associates, other departments, own department head, and others.

SOURCE: *"Roles Played by Managers," adapted from* The Nature of Managerial Work, *by Henry Mintzberg. Copyright © 1973 by Henry Mintzberg. Reprinted by permission of HarperCollins Publishers.*

*The Relative
Importance of
Managerial Skills at
Different Managerial
Levels*

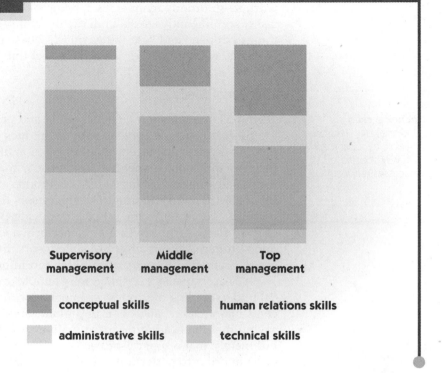

ments in which they operate, as well as the effects of changes in those environments in which they operate. In other words, managers should be able to "see the big picture." Top managers particularly need strong conceptual skills, because changes affecting the organization tend to be more important at their level than at other managerial levels. Around a third of their time is spent using conceptual skills.

Human Relations Skills

human relations skills
Understanding other
people and interacting
effectively.

Human relations skills consist of the ability to understand other people and to interact effectively with them. These skills are most needed in performing the leading function because they involve communicating with, motivating, leading, coaching, empowering, and facilitating employees, as well as relating to other people. These skills are important in dealing not only with individuals, but also with people in groups and even with relationships among groups. These skills are important to managers at all levels, but especially to supervisory managers, who spend almost one-half of their time using human relations skills.

Administrative Skills

administrative skills
Establishing and follow-
ing procedures to
process paperwork in an
orderly manner.

Administrative skills are the skills that permit managers to use their other skills effectively in performing the managerial functions. These skills include the ability to establish and follow policies and procedures and to process paper-work in an orderly manner. By lending *coordination*, *order*, and *movement* to tasks, administrative skills underlie the ability some people have to "make things happen" and "get things done." These skills are similar to those of good students, who are well organized and get things done efficiently.

Technical Skills

technical skills
Understanding and being able to supervise effectively specific processes required.

Technical skills include understanding and being able to supervise effectively the specific processes, practices, or techniques required to perform specific duties. While other managers should possess sufficient technical skills to keep their organization competitive, supervisory managers should have enough of these skills to see that day-to-day operations are performed effectively. Technical skills are more important for supervisors than for top managers, since supervisors are closer to the actual work being performed. They must often tell—or even show—employees how to perform a job, as well as know when it is done properly. About a third of supervisors' time is devoted to activities involving technical skills, such as computer and information management skills.

A head nurse in a hospital, for example, must have some degree of technical understanding of proper equipment use, nursing procedures, medication, chart maintenance, and other important aspects of a nurse's job. We are not saying that the head nurse, or any other supervisor, must be a technical expert, but merely that a supervisor needs a basic understanding of the work being done in order to perform the managerial functions and roles effectively.

The four skills we have just discussed form the basis for a wide variety of important management actions. For example, effective time management requires *conceptual* and *administrative* skills to prioritize activities and efficiently dispose of required paperwork; being an effective trainer requires the *technical*

Supervisors often use both their human relations and technical skills in their discussions with employees.

skills or an understanding of the subject matter and the *human relations* skills of being sensitive and able to communicate effectively with a trainee; political know-how requires *conceptual* and *human relations* skills to identify the potential implications of actions and to build strategic relationships.

In summary, effective supervisory management requires all of the skills—conceptual, human relations, administrative, and technical. The appropriate mix, however, depends on the level of management and the circumstances surrounding the managerial situation.

self-check

Which of the four skills are reflected when Sharon Olds performs these tasks?: (1) Prepares a to-do list for next week. (2) Monitors a newly hired associate's phone conversation with a customer. (3) Conducts a performance review meeting with the newly hired associate. (4) Completes her unit's daily performance report.

Explain where supervisors come from.

THE TRANSITION: WHERE SUPERVISORS COME FROM

Each year several hundred thousand nonmanagers trade in their toolboxes to become supervisors or managers. Teachers become principals, ministers become pastors, nurses become head nurses, salespersons become sales managers, and skilled operators or technicians become supervisors. Most of these supervisory positions are filled by promoting current employees.

Internal promotions make sense for at least three reasons. First, an inside candidate understands the organization and its culture. Also, if promoted within the same department, he will know the tasks required, the personnel, fellow supervisors, and likely his new boss. Second, management has firsthand knowledge of the employee's track record and can use this as a predictor of success. Third, to promote someone internally serves as a reward and as an incentive for those employees who have an interest in management and demonstrate management potential.

Unfortunately, organizations commonly make two crucial mistakes when selecting supervisors. One is to automatically select the best present performer to fill the position. Although the best performer may have excellent technical skills, as you saw earlier, technical skills are not the only skills needed to perform effectively as a supervisor. Other skills, especially human relations skills, are also important. Frequently, outstanding technical performers have unreasonably high expectations or little patience with nonproducers. Moreover, they may find it difficult to let go of their old positions, at which they were so good. Instead, they continue to perform their unit's operating work, neglecting the supervisory responsibilities of their position.

One of the authors was scheduled to interview a maintenance supervisor of a large paper manufacturer. His secretary informed the author that he was running late for the interview because of an equipment breakdown. An hour or so later he entered the office, sleeves rolled up, with grease covering his hands. "Sorry about missing the appointment; I'll be right with you after I wash up," he said. The author learned from this supervisor's crew that for this supervisor, almost every breakdown was a "major one." He micromanaged, insisted on being notified of

every development, and continually took over his technicians' jobs, especially the most challenging ones. His crew members had little opportunity for skill development and little initiative. As one stated, "our best work is done when he (the supervisor) is out of the plant, like on vacation."

Another crucial mistake made by organizations stems from inadequately preparing the employee to assume a supervisory position. Unfortunately, it is common to hear a supervisor say that the transition to supervisor went like this: "When I left work on Friday, I was a lab technician. With absolutely no training or warning, on Monday morning I learned I was a lab supervisor." Ideally, an organization takes great care when identifying potential successful candidates for supervisory positions and, once chosen, helps new supervisors make the transition. Before a permanent position is assigned, promising potential supervisors can be identified, assessed, and trained. Manufacturing companies frequently use the term "set up" to describe such a process. Thus, when someone is being "set up," it means that they are on track to ultimately be promoted to a permanent supervisory position. They may fill in as temporary supervisors when the supervisor is absent because of illness or vacation or may occupy a "lead" position that actually entails some supervisory responsibility.

Note in the chapter preview that Sharon Olds had occupied a lead associate position, which became her stepping stone for the advancement to supervisor.

Fortunately, organizations are doing a much better job nowadays of identifying people with supervisory potential and preparing them through appropriate training to help them make a successful transition. The topics in this book deal with skills that are important to supervisors-to-be, new supervisors, and experienced ones. For those of you who are not yet supervisors, mastering the skills of this book will surely assist your transition.

THE IMPROVING POSITION OF SUPERVISORY MANAGERS

(6) Discuss the improving position of supervisory managers.

Now let us concentrate on the supervisor's place in management. At one time, supervisors had autocratic power over employees. Employees either produced efficiently or were fired. The new concept today is one of leading or coaching a team or work group, rather than driving subservient workers. In essence, the supervisor must find a compromise between exercising too much authority and being a "rubber stamp" for higher managers.

Experts agree that the role of supervisory management is now in the process of changing drastically—but improving.

intermediaries
Go-betweens who act as mediators.

Supervisors are now viewed as **intermediaries,** or go-betweens, acting as mediators between their employees and higher levels of management. Supervisors stand between and among groups and have a sense of both belonging and not belonging to those groups. Thus, supervisors are caught between having to report to their managers and being representatives of management in relations with employees. Supervisors are transmitters of decisions made by their managers, but they also have authority to make recommendations to those managers. In other words, they are the "persons-in-the-middle" between the workers and higher level managers.

self-check

To what extent does this description of the supervisor as an intermediary fit Sharon Olds in relation to her employees?

No matter what type of role supervisors play, their goal is the same—getting out production, maintaining quality, holding down costs, maintaining high morale, and otherwise serving as management's representative while also acting as a spokesperson for employees. Although the knowledge and skills required today to perform most supervisory jobs have greatly increased from, say, twenty-five years ago, the central objective has remained the same—obtaining quality and quantity production while maintaining good human relationships.

A study of supervisors in two plants within the same company illustrates this point.[1] One plant followed traditional organizing practices: The supervisor had authority to supervise, to determine working conditions, to plan the work and schedule it, and to control it. In the other plant, "team advisors" were used instead of supervisors, with the focus being on facilitation rather than traditional direction of the work teams. As it turned out, "exceptional" and "average" supervisors at both plants, whether they were called supervisors or team advisors, exhibited characteristic behaviors.

"Exceptional" supervisors:

1. Were competent, caring, and committed both to getting the job done and to their employees.
2. Pushed for high quality, provided clear direction, and motivated employees with timely, accurate feedback.
3. Willingly shared information with personnel, even if the system didn't require it.
4. Were committed to teamwork and employee participation in the department's decisions.
5. Shared skills and knowledge willingly and saw their role as one of coach rather than driver.
6. Understood what was involved beyond their own units, from the broader perspectives of the plant.
7. Took the initiative in implementing changes and new approaches.

Supervisors considered only "average" in the two differently organized plants also exhibited similar behaviors. These supervisors:

1. Set narrowly defined goals and had more specific performance standards.
2. Were less attuned to the plant's overall goals and focused more narrowly on their own unit.
3. Provided less information or feedback about performance to their work groups.
4. Were less flexible, less innovative, and less willing to change.
5. Maintained tighter controls and were uncomfortable practicing participative management.

7 Clarify the different
relationships
supervisory managers have
with others.

SUPERVISORY RELATIONSHIPS

If we are to understand the role of supervisory managers in organizations, we must look at some of the relationships they have with different groups. For example, supervisors are legally a part of management and interact upward with other members of management. But they are often not accepted as peers by those managers, who usually have more education, come from outside the organization, and have higher social status and position. Before their promotion, supervisors typically worked as peers with those whom they now supervise.

The three major types of relationships that require supervisors to play different and demanding roles, as shown in Exhibit 1–9, are (1) personal, (2) organizational, and (3) external.

Personal Relationships

At one time it was believed that managers and employees left their personal problems at home when they entered the workplace. We now recognize that people bring their problems—as well as their pleasures—to their jobs. Supervisors' relationships with their families and their friends determine their attitudes and frame of mind as they perform managerial duties. Their attitudes, in turn, influence the relationships they have with other people, both inside and outside the organization.

Exhibit 1–9

*The Supervisor's
Relationships*

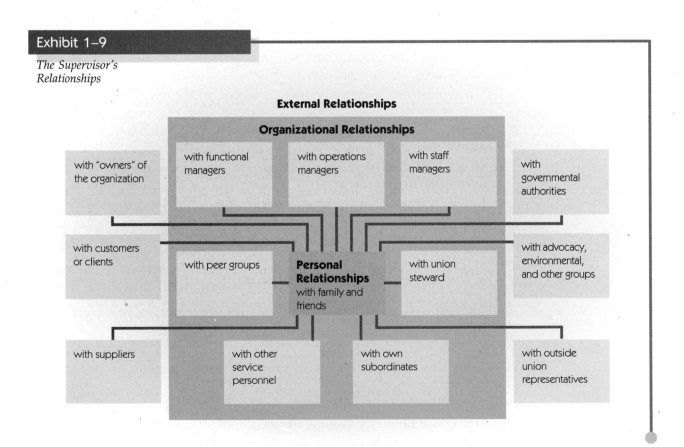

Organizational Relationships

Within the organization, supervisory managers have varied and often conflicting relationships. These relationships flow in three directions: from manager to employee, with peers or managers on same level, and from employee to manager, as shown in Exhibit 1–10.

Manager-to-Employee Relationships. Supervisory managers must relate to their own employees and to people from other units who perform some type of service for them. As Exhibit 1–10 illustrates, a manager-to-employee relationship exists where the supervisor facilitates and directs nonmanagerial personnel. It gives the supervisor a sense of importance.

Relationships with Peers or Other Managers. There are essentially two sets of horizontal relationships: those with other supervisory managers and those with the union steward or other representative(s) of the employees. Supervisors need the feeling of support and reinforcement that comes from associating with other supervisors who are considered their equals or peers. Yet the relationship can result in competition or even conflict if they seek to be promoted to the same job at the next higher level.

In a unionized organization, employees select a **union steward** to represent them in their dealings with management. Although the steward is a supervisor's peer—legally, if not organizationally—he or she does represent the supervisor's employees. Therefore, the association between the supervisor and the union steward may be competitive or even combative. This association provides supervisors with a challenge but can also be frustrating. For example, a supervisor will probably attempt to motivate employees to improve productivity, whereas a union steward may encourage them to maintain the status quo for fear that their jobs will be eliminated.

Supervisor-to-Manager Relationships. Supervisors have a *reverse* manager-to-employee relationship with managers at higher levels. As a result of downsizing, reengineering, empowering, and similar new managerial approaches, though, this relationship is being upgraded. Staff executives in other depart-

union steward
A union member elected by other members to represent their interests to management.

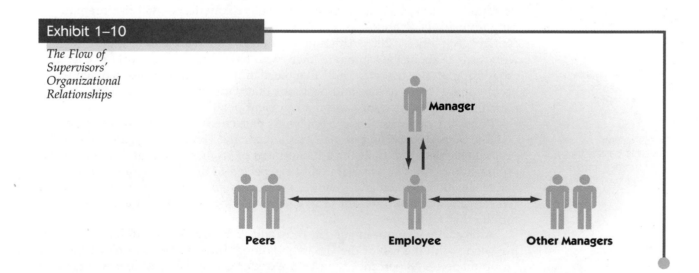

Exhibit 1–10

The Flow of Supervisors' Organizational Relationships

ments, such as legal and research, may also tell supervisors what to do. Functional executives, such as the controller and the human resource director, direct supervisors in handling certain activities. In this association, supervisors are the employees who must support and reinforce their managers.

External Relationships

Supervisory managers must also deal with people outside the organization. Some of the people who must be served or catered to are the owners of the business, customers or clients, suppliers, higher level union representatives, governmental authorities, and leaders of environmental and advocacy groups. These relationships can be quite difficult and frustrating for supervisors, who represent their organizations but usually do not have the authority to make decisions and enforce them.

8 Discuss some trends challenging supervisors.

SOME CURRENT TRENDS CHALLENGING SUPERVISORS

As shown earlier, today's supervisors must be prepared to adjust to the many current trends that will challenge their best performance. Among the more significant of these trends are (1) dealing with a more diverse workforce, (2) emphasizing team performance, (3) coping with exploding technology, (4) adjusting to occupational and industry shifts, (5) meeting global challenges, (6) improving quality and productivity, and (7) improving ethical and social behavior.

Dealing with a More Diverse Workforce

diversity
Refers to the wide range of distinguishing employee characteristics such as sex, age, race, ethnic origin, and other factors.

 http://www.dol.gov/

 http://www.ilr.cornell
.edu/library/e_archive/
glassceiling/

glass ceiling
Invisible barriers that limit women from advancing in an organization.

Diversity refers to the wide range of characteristics that distinguish employees, such as sex, age, race, ethnic origin, and other factors. At no time in our history has our workforce been so diverse, and this trend is expected to continue. Our comments here focus only on broad trends regarding gender, race, ethnicity, and age.

According to the Department of Labor,[2] the ethnicities of women workers— African-American, Hispanic, Asian, and Native American—will rise dramatically from 45, 11, 7, and 3 percent in 1986 to a projected 48, 12, 12, and 5 percent, respectively, by 2006. Although men and women are entering the workforce at about the same rate, men, who have been in the workforce longer, are retiring at a faster rate. Thus, like racial and ethnic minorities, women will occupy many types of jobs and positions that were previously the domain of men, including supervisory and management positions.

Providing opportunities for women is particularly challenging, as there appears to be a **glass ceiling** in many organizations. These ceilings are considered invisible barriers that limit the advancement of women into higher levels of the organization. Thus, supervisors will be expected to design programs to attract and to develop women and minority employees and to provide them with a full range of opportunities for growth and development, the same as they do for all other employees.

Along with changes in gender, race, and ethnicity, the workforce is also aging, along with the rest of the U.S. population. Those in the 45 or older age group made up 28 percent of the 1986 workforce, but their number will have

Younger, more diverse work groups are becoming the norm in today's organizations.

increased by more than 10 million employees and comprise 39 percent of the projected workforce by 2006.[3]

Being able to effectively manage such diverse individuals requires greater supervisory skills than was the case with the more homogeneous work groups of past decades.

Emphasizing Team Performance

As organizations seek to equip employees to function on their own, less direct supervision is required. This **empowerment** results in supervisors increasingly working with work groups or teams. These teams make suggestions for improvements in activities to make things run smoothly and accomplish goals effectively.[4]

When supervisors work with these teams, their roles are changed. No longer are they "bosses"; instead, they become leaders, facilitators, or **team advisors,** who share responsibility with the team for maintaining cost, quality, and prompt and effective delivery of products. Therefore, supervisors must provide further training to their teams in order to manage the production process more effectively.

Coping with Exploding Technology

Most working Americans now earn their living by creating, processing, utilizing, and distributing information, and the computer revolution shows no sign of slowing (Exhibit 1–11). As innovations in computer and other communications technology have displaced thousands of workers who used different skills, new opportunities are opening up for those who have the required education, training, and temperament. Conversely, employees with the older skills are being replaced in the workplace.

click! http://www
.generalmotors.com/
company/community_
involvement/diversity

empowerment
Granting employees authority to make key decisions within their area of responsibility.

team advisors
Share responsibility with team for cost, quality, and prompt delivery of products.

Technology Library

SOURCE: *"The Rotarian", May 1995, p. 10; by H. L. Schwadron. Used with the permission of the cartoonist.*

Computer-based information technologies continue to revolutionize how organizations function, impacting how tasks are performed, customers served, and people supervised.

Note that Sharon Olds was skilled in WordPerfect and Excel computer software, and used e-mail regularly to communicate to her department head, employees, and others in the organization.

The primary effect of exploding technology on supervisors will be the need to keep personally abreast of changes that can potentially improve effectiveness, improve training of employees, and overcome their resistance to change. Change brings with it uncertainty, and because most people resist that which is uncertain, overcoming employee resistance to technological change becomes an increasing part of the supervisor's job.

Adjusting to Occupational and Industry Shifts

The previously mentioned technological advancements, along with cultural and marketing changes, have resulted in shifts in occupation and industry mixes. First, there is a declining emphasis on the traditional industries, with a concurrent shift toward more people-related activities such as services and marketing.

reinvention
Organizations dramatically changing themselves in such elements as size, organizational structure, and markets.

reengineering
Rethinking and redesigning processes to dramatically improve cost, quality, service, and speed.

downsizing
Striving to become leaner and more efficient by reducing the workforce and consolidating departments and work groups.

 click! http://www
.reengineering.com/

Along with these shifts, there has been a **reinvention** of many organizations in which they have dramatically changed their size, organizational structure, and markets. Many of the large companies have also been **reengineering** their activities. A common reengineering approach is to ask "If we blew this place up and started over, what would we do differently to improve cost, quality, service, or speed? What should we eliminate entirely? What can we do that would make things easier for our customers?"[5] Not only are manufacturing companies reengineering, but so are many service companies.

These and other activities resulted in another trend, called **downsizing,** in which an organization strives to become leaner and more efficient by reducing the workforce and consolidating departments and work groups.

Some of the best known companies, such as American Express, Taco Bell, General Motors, IBM, and Sears, have been reinvented or reengineered. The results often included the elimination of 10 to 20 percent of a company's jobs, especially at the management level.[6] This means that frontline workers—and their supervisors—must handle more diverse tasks, think more creatively, and assume more responsibility. On the downside, though, those same people must work harder and therefore are under more pressure.[7]

In an effort by organizations to avoid costs associated with maintaining a larger workforce, temporary workers will increase from 2.8 million in 1998 to 4 million by 2006. Temporary services firms, such as Manpower and Kelly services, will be among the fastest growing U.S. industries.[8] Supervisors face numerous challenges when integrating temporaries into their teams of permanent employees, who often view temporaries as obstructing their own overtime, commissions, or higher pay. Temporaries themselves know little about the company and often show little inclination to be included as team members, knowing the assignment is only for a few days, weeks, or months.

Meeting Global Challenges

As business activities have become more global, those interested in supervisory management need to understand that they may have to operate in a one-world market. In fact, we estimate that up to one-half of all college graduates will work in some type of international activities in the future. And while we usually think of product exports as autos, movies, or computers, exports of financial information and other services are growing even faster.

An example of exporting services is AT&T, which aims to become the world's major provider of telecommunications services. In 1998, it formed a joint venture with British Telecom, and has since bought major stakes in Japan Telecom and Rogers Cantel Mobile, a leading Canadian telecommunications company.[9]

A result of the global challenge is the large number of U.S. businesses, such as Magnavox, Wilson Sporting Goods, Uniroyal, and B.F. Goodrich, that are foreign owned. This changing ownership may lead to differing cultures and management styles, especially at supervisory levels.

U.S. production facilities also are moving to Mexico, South America, Asia, and other countries where low wages and high productivity lead to a competitive advantage. When supervisors move to those areas to supervise local workers, or when a foreign company acquires a domestic company, supervisors must learn to adapt to cultural differences and find ways to adjust to nontraditional styles.

Improving Quality and Productivity

No organizational theme has run deeper in the past decade than has the search for improved quality and productivity. A reflection of this interest is shown by the fact that more than 200 books on quality have appeared in the last decade.[10] Global competition has been the primary force behind this interest.

The view of quality being embraced today—total quality management (TQM)—reflects a comprehensive organizational approach to customer satisfaction through continuous improvement in organizational processes.[11] As will be shown in more depth in Chapter 2, almost all major firms have adopted some form of total quality management focus that addresses not only such processes as product design and manufacturing, but also marketing, purchasing, human resource management, and others. The supervisor, as management's direct link with employees, plays an important role in an organization's quality initiatives. It is the supervisor who is challenged to find ways to gain employee commitment to high quality performance.

Equally as important as achieving better quality is achieving improved productivity, which is a measurement of the amount of input needed to generate a given amount of output. As productivity is the basic measurement of the efficiency of people and processes, it becomes a challenge for supervisors to improve through having people work better and smarter.

Improving Ethical and Social Behavior

ethical dilemmas
Situations in which the supervisor is not certain what the correct behavior is.

Today's supervisors face increased **ethical dilemmas,** that is, situations in which the supervisor is not certain what the correct behavior should be. Thus, they will have to define "right and wrong" conduct for themselves and their employees. As will be shown in Chapter 4, these ethical problems are becoming increasingly difficult in decision making and problem solving. Also, companies are under pressure from the government, media, and society to act in more socially acceptable ways.

---

chapter review

① **Explain why management is needed in all organizations.**

Management is needed whenever people form organizations. An organization is a group of people in a structured situation with a common purpose. People form organizations because they realize that they can achieve more by working together than they can alone.

Management is the process of working through people to achieve objectives by making effective decisions and by coordinating the development and use of scarce human, financial, and physical resources.

② **Describe the different levels of management.**

Large organizations usually have at least three levels of management. Top management oversees the overall operations—or a major segment of the organization or one of the basic organizational activities; middle management is responsible for a smaller part, such as a division or department; and supervisory management controls a smaller organizational unit.

(3) Discuss what managers do.

Managers at all levels do essentially the same things, but to different degrees. First, they perform the same functions—namely, planning, organizing, staffing, leading, and controlling. In performing these functions, managers engage in many varied and often unrelated activities that require them to play different roles. In playing interpersonal roles, a manager may act as a figurehead, a leader, or as a liaison between different groups. Informational roles include acting as a monitor, disseminator, and/or spokesperson. Finally, decision-making roles require the manager to be an entrepreneur, disturbance handler, resource allocator, and/or negotiator.

(4) Explain the basic skills required for effective management.

Effective managers need various skills in order to perform their functions and play their roles. Conceptual skills are needed in acquiring, interpreting, and analyzing information in a logical manner. Human relations skills involve understanding other people and interacting effectively with them. Administrative skills provide the ability to get things done by using other skills effectively. Technical skills consist of understanding and being able to supervise the processes, practices, or techniques required for specific jobs in the organization.

(5) Explain where supervisors come from.

By far most supervisory positions are filled through internal promotion. This has several advantages. Insiders understand the organization and its culture, and when promoted within their own department, the tasks, personnel, and other supervisors are familiar as well. Managers know something about the potential supervisor's capabilities through his or her track record. Also, internal promotion serves as a reward and incentive for present employees who desire to move up. Organizations can help to ensure a successful transition to supervision by identifying, assessing, and training potential supervisors and observing how they perform in temporary supervisory assignments.

(6) Discuss the improving position of supervisory managers.

The role of supervisory managers has drastically changed during the last century. No longer are they the foremen wielding autocratic power over subordinates; instead, they are supervisors leading people to be more productive. Until about 100 years ago, supervisors were essentially subcontractors, who tended to understand and relate to workers. Then, with growing organizational size and power, supervisors gained almost complete authority over their units. Now they are considered linking pins, or intermediaries, between their employees and higher levels of management.

(7) Clarify the different relationships supervisory managers have with others.

Supervisory managers are involved in at least three sets of relationships. First, they have personal relationships with their families and their friends. Second, they have sometimes conflicting organizational relationships with lower level employees, fellow supervisors, and higher levels of management. Third, they have external relationships with outsiders such as business owners, customers or clients, suppliers, union representatives, governmental authorities, and leaders of environmental and advocacy groups.

⑧ **Discuss some trends challenging supervisors.**

As the supervisory position grows in importance, it is becoming more complex because of many trends that are challenging supervisors' abilities to perform their jobs. The more important trends challenge supervisors to (1) deal with a more diverse workforce, (2) emphasize team performance, (3) cope with exploding technology, (4) adjust to occupational and industry shifts, (5) meet global challenges, (6) improve quality and productivity, and (7) improve ethical and social behavior.

important terms

administrative skills *15*
authority *8*
conceptual skills *13*
controlling *12*
diversity *22*
downsizing *25*
empowerment *23*
ethical dilemmas *26*
financial resources *7*
financing *6*
glass ceiling *22*
human relations skills *15*
human resources *7*
intermediaries *18*
leading *11*
management *7*
managerial functions *10*

marketing *6*
middle management *9*
operations *6*
organization *6*
organizing *11*
physical resources *7*
planning *10*
reengineering *25*
reinvention *25*
responsibility *8*
roles *12*
staffing *11*
supervisory management *9*
team advisors *23*
technical skills *16*
top management *8*
union steward *21*

questions for review and discussion

1. Why do people form organizations?
2. Identify the four functions every manager must perform and briefly explain each.
3. Why is management needed in organizations?
4. What are the three levels of management found in most large organizations? Describe each, giving its responsibilities.
5. Identify the four skills which managers need. Can someone be weak in one of these skill areas and still function effectively as a supervisor? Explain.
6. How are most supervisory positions filled? Explain why this is so.
7. What are the three types of supervisory relationships? Explain.
8. Identify each of the trends challenging today's supervisors and explain how each impacts supervisors.

skill builder 1–1

The Personal Interest Inventory

Directions: Each of the following questions is worth a total of 3 points. For each question, assign more points to the response you prefer and fewer points, in order of preference, to the others. For example, if one response receives 3 points, the other two must receive 0; if one receives 2, then the others must receive 1 and 0; or each may receive 1 point. Enter your scores in the Score Matrix.

1. Which activity interests you most?
   - _2_ a. Working with your hands
   - _1_ b. Working with people
   - _0_ c. Reading books

2. Which skills would you invest time in learning?
   - ___ a. Research and writing
   - ___ b. Organizing and leading
   - _1_ c. Crafts and art

3. Which job activities would you enjoy most?
   - ___ a. Counseling and coaching
   - ___ b. Building and doing
   - ___ c. Thinking and planning

4. Which trait is most characteristic of you?
   - _2_ a. Helper
   - _1_ b. Doer
   - ___ c. Scholar

5. Which would you most enjoy doing?
   - _3_ a. Talking with people
   - ___ b. Writing a book
   - ___ c. Building a house

6. How do you prefer to use your spare time?
   - _1_ a. Outdoor projects
   - _2_ b. Social activities
   - ___ c. Thinking

7. Which of these traits is most important to you?
   - ___ a. Physical coordination
   - _2_ b. Ability to deal with people
   - _1_ c. Mental ability

8. Which jobs most reflect your interests?
   - _1_ a. Teacher, social worker, counselor
   - _2_ b. Engineer, surveyor, craftsman
   - ___ c. Researcher, historian, author

9. Which ability is your strongest?
   - _2_ a. Communication skills
   - _1_ b. Creative thinking
   - ___ c. Physical skills

10. Which tasks do you perform best?
    - _1_ a. Operating and maintaining
    - _1_ b. Communicating and motivating
    - ___ c. Developing and planning

11. Which occupation interests you most?
    - _2_ a. Pilot
    - ___ b. Judge
    - _1_ c. Politician

12. Which of the following is most interesting to you?
    - _2_ a. Helping others
    - _1_ b. Thinking things through
    - ___ c. Using your hands

13. Which skills could you learn with the least effort?
    - _1_ a. Leading and negotiating
    - _2_ b. Artwork and handicrafts
    - ___ c. Language and theoretical reasoning

14. What tasks appeal to you most?
    - _1_ a. Developing new theories
    - _2_ b. Helping people with problems
    - ___ c. Developing a skill

15. What assignment appeals to you most?
    - ___ a. Working with ideas
    - _3_ b. Working with people
    - ___ c. Working with things

16. Which is your greatest attribute?
    - _1_ a. Creativity
    - _2_ b. Competence
    - ___ c. Sensitivity

17. For which occupation do you have a
natural talent?
    _2_ a. Counselor
    _1_ b. Builder
    ___ c. Scientist
18. Which subject interests you most?
    ___ a. Practical arts
    ___ b. Philosophy
    _3_ c. Human relations
19. To which group would you prefer to
belong?
    ___ a. Scientific society

_3_ b. Outdoor group
___ c. Social club
20. How do you like to work?
    _1_ a. In a group, discussing and
    recommending solutions
    _1_ b. Alone, using ideas and
    theories
    _1_ c. Alone, using tools and
    materials

Score Matrix

Question	Things		People		Ideas	
1.	a.	2	b.	1	c.	
2.	c.	1	b.	1	a.	1
3.	b.	1	a.	1	c.	1
4.	b.	1	a.	2	c.	
5.	b.		c.		a.	3
6.	a.	1	b.	2	c.	
7.	a.		b.	2	c.	1
8.	b.	2	a.	1	c.	
9.	b.	1	c.		a.	2
10.	a.	1	b.	1	c.	1
11.	a.	2	c.	1	b.	
12.	b.	1	c.		a.	2
13.	b.	2	a.	1	c.	
14.	c.		b.	2	a.	1
15.	c.		b.	3	a.	
16.	c.		a.	1	b.	2
17.	b.	1	a.	2	c.	
18.	a.		c.	3	b.	
19.	b.	3	c.		a.	
20.	c.	1	a.	1	b.	1
		20 TOTAL		25 TOTAL		15 TOTAL

Instructions: The Personal Interest Inventory should give you some insight into the
strengths you would bring to a management position. Basically, if you enjoy an activity,
it is likely to be something that you do well. The three areas shown in the Score Matrix—things, people, and ideas—correspond to the following skills, which managers
must use in doing their job:

Things: Technical skills
People: Human relations skills
Ideas: Conceptual skills

1. After scoring your inventory, break into groups of three to five and discuss your profiles. To what extent are they similar? Different? Are any of the areas dominant in the group? Underrepresented? Discuss.
2. Generalize about the kinds of supervisory jobs that might call for
   a. High technical skill
   b. High human relations skill
   c. High conceptual skill
3. Are your answers on this inventory consistent with the type of management job that you have in mind? If there are inconsistencies, what do they mean?

SOURCE: *Based on an exercise designed by Billie Stockton, Anita Bullock, and Anne Locke, Northern Kentucky University, 1981.*

skill builder 1–2

Effective and Ineffective Supervisors
group activity

Join with two or three of your classmates. Think of all the supervisors for whom you've worked—part-time or full-time. If any of you have not worked for a supervisor, try to observe a few in action in some organization or consider some of your teachers. Then, try to choose two supervisors: one who was most effective and one who was least effective. List the reasons each supervisor was effective or ineffective, and list the qualities that led to the effective or ineffective performance.

CASE 1–1

The Weak Supervisor

Henry Osmond was a participant in a supervisory training course conducted by one of the authors for a large clock manufacturing firm. He was in his mid-thirties, tall, quiet, and reserved—somewhat meek in appearance. He contributed little during the first two days of the course and during breaks didn't mingle with his 15 colleagues, all of whom, like himself, were first-line supervisors for the company. During one of the breaks, the instructor asked one of the participants about Henry.

"Well," said the participant, "don't blame yourself or the course for Henry's not getting involved. That's just Henry. He's a most interesting case. He's like that in the plant, too. It's a shame what's happened to him, really. Believe it or not, Henry is one of the top clockworks men in the country. His dad worked in this plant and had the same outstanding reputation—better, in fact, than Henry's. Henry Senior's retired now, but he makes more money running a clock repair operation than he ever did here. He's even had private planes land here, pick him up, and carry him to Europe to repair expensive collectors' or museum clocks. Well, Henry has the same skill. He picked up everything from his dad. The guy can look at a clock movement and immediately spot a problem that'd take someone else several hours to track down. I know—I've worked for three different firms in this industry—the guy has a special talent.

"Well, here's what happened. About nine months ago, the company moved Henry up to movement supervisor—this is the department that reworks, makes adjustments, or tries to correct any problems in the movements before we ship a clock to a retailer. The department also handles any defective movements that a retailer returns.

"Now our union contract doesn't allow supervisors to do actual 'hands-on' work, but ole Henry will generally bird-dog the best jobs—I mean, you'll see him looking over the shoulder of one of his people, giving step-by-step detailed instructions on what to do. He drives his technicians absolutely batty, interjecting himself into the most challenging jobs and oversupervising. Not only is he resented, but he's our weakest supervisor—very shy and timid, won't discipline, and doesn't get the paperwork done. He's a failure as a supervisor—and he

knows it. Never should have been offered the job and never should have taken it. It'd be a real loss of face now for him to be 'demoted' back to movement technician—at least in his eyes. I guess when they promoted him to supervisor, they didn't realize that they were taking away his toolbox. And Henry just doesn't have much else to offer. What a waste!"

Answer the following questions:

1. What did the supervisor mean when he said that the company "took away Henry's toolbox"?
2. What criteria besides technical skills could the company have used to determine whether Henry had supervisor potential?
3. Many companies automatically promote the top technical person in a department to fill a vacant supervisory position. What are the pros and cons of this practice?
4. Suppose that you are Henry's manager. What would you do about the situation, assuming the remarks about his performance are true?

Quest for Quality and Empowerment

• outline

Empowerment
Levels of Empowerment

Quality
"Quality Is Job 1"
Reasons for the Recent Quality Revolution
Evolution of the Quality Explosion in the United States
Approaches to Managing Quality
Total Quality Management (TQM)

Role of the Supervisor in Empowerment and Total Quality
Major Impact at the Supervisory Management Level
The Emerging Supervisor: Teacher, Leader, Coach

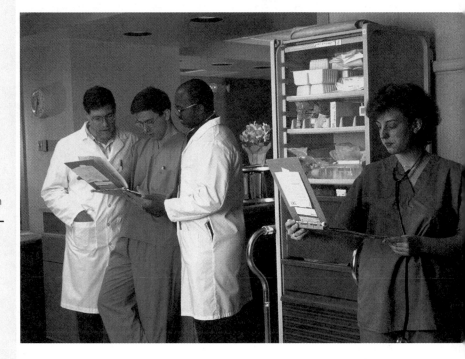

Quality begins with education and ends with education.

Kaoru Ishikowa

The quality movement . . . is in fact the first wave in building learning organizations—*organizations that continually expand their ability to shape their future.*

Peter Senge

City Hospital

learning
objectives

After reading and studying this chapter, you should be able to:

1. Define empowerment and give an example.

2. Identify and differentiate among the four levels of empowerment.

3. Describe how the recent U.S. quality resurgence began.

4. Identify the four approaches to managing quality.

5. Understand the three components of total quality management.

6. Explain how the supervisor's job is affected by empowerment and quality programs.

I n recent years City Hospital, a large 600-bed hospital in a major metropolitan area, faced many pressures. These included increased competition from other general hospitals, specialized orthopedic centers, women's and children's hospitals, and other health-care providers, such as outpatient surgery centers. Furthermore, all hospitals were coming under increasingly strong cost control pressure from private insurers as well as government. Two years ago a new administrator from outside the hospital was appointed, and within three months the hospital announced a "Total Quality Initiative (TQI)" that would "dramatically change the way the hospital was managed."

Under TQI, all areas of the hospital's operations, ranging from bedside care of patients to processing of patients' records to inventory control, would be targeted for continuous measurement and improvement. Employees at all levels, whether salaried or hourly, would be given greater responsibility for their own work. Numerous cross-functional, problem-solving teams would address major issues in the hospital in an attempt to unleash a wave of creativity and commitment.

A TQI task force was named, consisting of 20 persons representing all levels of the hospital. The task force's role was to chart the hospital's strategy in planning and implementing the new process. Task force members visited the country's outstanding hospitals to observe firsthand their programs.

They also visited Federal Express, Xerox, and other non-health-care firms that had won awards for quality excellence. A series of three-day training courses in problem solving, statistics, and group dynamics was initiated to help employees function in the new environment. Cross-functional TQI teams were formed to address high-priority hospital problems.

Several programs were initiated to spur greater involvement and commitment by employees. Monthly "peak performers" were selected for providing outstanding patient service. Communication between upper management and other levels opened considerably; the hospital administrator met regularly with employees from different departments, encouraging them to speak their minds. Supervisors were encouraged to delegate greater responsibility to their employees and to allow employees greater latitude in performing their work. A 360-degree feedback system was implemented in which managers were given performance feedback by peers and employees as well as managers.

Two years into the initiative the hospital's human resources director talked about the changes:

We've definitely made progress. Getting employees and supervisors to buy into the process has been difficult, though. Some of the more entrenched, longer term managers and professionals felt that nothing would really change. When they saw changes actually taking place in how we began operating, a number felt threatened by the potential loss of power or the feeling that they lacked the needed skills to effectively handle the new requirements. Under our new system, we're saying that the old ways of managing—intimidation and fear—are now out the window. That's been a hard pill for many old-line managers to swallow.

Most expected our TQI to be a lot of window dressing—all talk, no substance. However, our administrator means business. Recently a relatively young professional catapulted past two levels to be named one of our assistant administrators. That got everybody's attention, especially the more senior, old-line, management-style types who were vaulted over. Our nursing administrator, a 30-year vet, was as entrenched as they come and openly refused to change. She opted for early retirement, as did our rehab director. But people are buying in every week. We've had some terrific results already with some of our task force teams and we've empowered people. My own department is a good example. Each year the hospital has an annual management meeting where about 50 of our top managers assemble

for two days at a retreat site in a nearby resort. One day is for work, the other play. My training director and I usually put together the "whole show"—selecting a theme, developing the agenda, making the arrangements—the entire works. This year, given our team and involvement atmosphere, we selected a task force of managers to take on the assignment—the complete retreat planning and coordination—and we had the best retreat ever. We have run into some resistance at the salaried and hourly levels. Some employees, professionals included, would much rather have managers calling all the shots rather than having to stick their own necks out. "Why take on the added responsibility?" they ask. We hope they will realize that they must stick out their necks for this hospital to be its best. That may sound trite, but it's the only way we can be a quality, successful operation. They're beginning to realize that by learning a broader range of jobs, their value increases. And, if we downsize here, they will be more employable at a competitor or elsewhere in the industry.

 click! http://www.pfdf.org/

Peter Drucker, world-renowned management consultant, author, and academic, predicted in 1983 that tremendous organizational changes would impact the job of supervisory managers in organizations such as City Hospital.[1] One of the organizational changes would be brought about by the "quality" movement. In an effort to continuously search for improved quality of products, services, and processes, Drucker noted that top management would of necessity conclude that the rank-and-file employees, not supervisors, would be in the best position to lead the charge. The second change, Drucker said, would be to give greater authority to rank-and-file employees to do what was necessary to perform their jobs more effectively. This would include such things as planning, determining the resources to perform their jobs best, and interfacing directly with personnel who impact their job, such as customers, suppliers, service department personnel, and others. In combination, the quality goal and greater employee authority would directly affront the power and status of traditional supervisors and would require quite different supervisory roles. In the 13 years since Drucker wrote the article, much has changed in American organizations such as City Hospital. Drucker proved to be "on target." The two affronts to traditional supervisory status and power have become trends that are presently steam-rolling organizations of all types, large and small, profit and not-for-profit, manufacturing, service, and governmental. Today these changes are character-ized as "total quality" and "empowerment."

EMPOWERMENT

Define empowerment and give an example.

As indicated in Chapter 1, empowerment is part of the sweeping movement oc-curring in organizations today. One reason for the increasing use of empower-ment is the reduction in organizations' employee numbers in recent years. Downsizing eliminated more than 3.4 million jobs in America's largest firms (the *Fortune 500*) from 1982 to 1991. In 1998 almost 700,000 jobs in U.S. organiza-tions were chopped, making it the worst year of the decade.[2] The result—fewer corporate staff, fewer layers of management, and fewer operating-level employ-ees—has created leaner, trimmer organizations. The employees remaining share more power as they perform their daily tasks. Even in organizations that have grown rather than downsized, worker empowerment has become an increas-ingly important vehicle for improved organizational performance. It must be noted, however, that many so-called empowerment efforts motivated primarily by short-term labor reduction strategies have failed to produce the feeling of empowerment and instead create job stress, burnout, and helplessness.[3]

empowerment
Granting authority to employees to make key decisions within their areas of responsi-bility.

Empowerment means many things, but essentially it is the granting of au-thority to employees to make key decisions within their areas of responsibility. The driving idea behind empowerment is that the individuals closest to the work and to customers should make the decisions. Rather than being con-stricted by rigid rules and controls or by the need for approval from their su-pervisors, the best use of employees' skills and talents is to give them the re-sources—and the latitude—to make relevant decisions. Empowerment also may include authority to "bend the rules" as appropriate, given the employee's judgment of the circumstances. Note the consistent theme in the empowerment examples shown in Exhibit 2–1. In each case, employees are granted authority to impact their jobs in a meaningful way.

click! http://www
.americawest.com/

> **Ruth Thompson, customer service representative (CSR) for America West Airlines, tells a story that demonstrates well the empowered em-ployee. Ruth's home base was Phoenix and the flight to which she was assigned was Phoenix to San Jose, California. Shortly before takeoff, she saw a man jump up from his seat, visibly upset as he grabbed his belongings and ran from the plane. Ruth followed him and learned he was supposed to go to San Francisco. Apparently, he had been led to the wrong gate by another America West CSR. The San Francisco flight left from the adjoining gate, but as he and Ruth rushed there, they found it already closed and his plane backing away. The man was quite shaken, as he didn't fly much. But Ruth took over. "Our plane [to San Jose] was going to leave in five or ten minutes, but I took him over to one of our counters and calmed him down. Because I know reservations and the computer, we were able to look up his reservation. I made the deci-sion—America West encourages us to make decisions on our own, and they will back us up—to take him with us to San Jose. Once we got to San Jose, I knew that we could arrange ground transportation for him to San Francisco."**

*Empowerment
Through Job
Involvement*

The following examples of empowerment reflect power sharing in various organizations.

AT&T Universal Card Services

When a cardmember calls in for help, telephone associates at the second largest card service in the industry (behind the Discover Card) are empowered to do what it takes, even if it includes bending the rules. One desperate caller from Paris was stranded when an ATM "ate" his AT&T card on a Saturday afternoon. The cardholder had no cash and was scheduled to leave Paris the next day. With the cardmember on hold, an empowered associate contacted the American Embassy and arranged for a limo to take the traveler to the only bank open in Paris where an authorized emergency cash advance had been arranged.

Midas Muffler

At most Midas Muffler shops, a mechanic's job is narrowly defined . . . lift the car on the rack, determine what's needed, get a go-ahead from the service manager, and repair the vehicle as directed. But at some Midas shops, mechanics are empowered to do much, much more. A mechanic may handle phone customers, greet walk-in customers, inspect a vehicle, write up an estimate and discuss it with the customer, perform the repairs, test the car (as needed), explain and offer to sell an extended warranty, collect payment, and even adjust customers' bills when they are dissatisfied. "It's good business," said one Midas manager. "My mechanics have much more pride in their work and better understand our total operation. Also, we have customers who have identified with their service representative and only want to talk with that person."

The Ritz-Carlton

At the Ritz, top management has empowered its employees to assume ownership of customer problems. So when a customer comes to you with a problem, it's *your* problem. Employees can spend up to $2,000 to handle customer problems, ranging from mailing items left in a room by a checked-out guest to arranging for free accommodations or complimentary meals to remedy an error.

Motorola

Empowered employees work in teams and have authority to carry out a wide range of functions. They create their own production schedules, develop and manage budgets, schedule their training, select new team members, and choose their own leaders. As you will read later in the chapter, Motorola is considered a leading company in applying empowerment and quality principles.

L L Bean

Front-line employees have far-reaching authority to respond to the needs and problems of individual customers with speed and courtesy. One employee drove 500 miles from Maine to New York to deliver a canoe to a customer.

Disney World

Disney believes that front-line employees should be the first and last customer contact. Employees are highly trained and given the authority to do whatever is necessary to make customers happy. Even if a supervisor sees a front-line employee "giving away the store," the supervisor will not intervene, but will discuss it with the employee later.

The man was to meet an uncle in San Francisco. Ruth sent a computer message to San Jose to arrange the ground transportation to San Francisco and to notify the uncle of his nephew's change in plans. When the plane arrived in San Jose, Ruth accompanied him to the thoroughfare, making sure that ground transportation had been arranged and that the uncle had been notified.

Three days later when the man returned to Phoenix for his connecting flight home, Ruth was there to greet him and walk him to his connecting flight. "I brought him ten chocolate chip cookies for his trip back. And I went to a supervisor and got him to write up a travel voucher so that he could have another free round-trip on us. . . ."[4]

click! http://www.saturn.com

Perhaps the most publicized empowerment story is the GM Saturn Plant in Spring Hill, Tennessee. Built in response to U.S. automakers' loss of market share to Japanese imports in the 1980s, Saturn was planned with the premise that its workers would function far differently from a traditional U.S. auto plant. They were to be formed in about 150 teams of 15 or so each. Each worker was to be able to perform a wide range of jobs. Moreover, teams were to be empowered to make decisions traditionally reserved for their managers (recall Drucker's forecast), such as work scheduling, selection of team members, and greater control of their own work quality. In one 1995 television commercial, a Saturn production worker told of team members' pride in their work and points to the cord that runs over his work area. One pull of the cord, he states, is all it takes to shut down the line when he or his team members discover a quality problem. Then the race begins to track down its origin. In traditional auto plants, managers rather than workers make these decisions. Many aspects of the Saturn story have been a success, but because of its uniqueness—new physical plant, newly hired employees, a technology designed to encourage empowerment, and management/union cooperation—GM has not been able to fully generalize it to other plants.

Levels of Empowerment

② Identify and differentiate among the four levels of empowerment.

You can better understand the range of empowerment by thinking of it along a continuum as shown in Exhibit 2–2. In the lower left-hand corner, under traditional management, minimal empowerment exists. Major decision-making authority rests outside the control of employees, in the hands of managers or a system such as the traditional production line approach. The traditional production line breaks work down into a series of specialized, programmed activities of limited scope, dictates the speed of work, and so on. The worker's task is to complete the job as required; he or she can do little to influence the outcome. Even service work often employs traditional production line principles. The job of a McDonald's server, just like an assembly line worker, is carefully programmed. The server gives a standard greeting, secures the order and places it on the tray in prescribed format (cold drinks are put on the tray first, then hot, etc.), follows a set procedure in collecting payment, and gives a closing farewell to the customer. Thus, much work in production and service industries alike requires such consistent job behavior that little opportunity for employee empowerment exists.

suggestion involvement
Employees are actively encouraged to make suggestions to improve aspects of their work.

The second empowerment level is that of **suggestion involvement.** At this level, employees are actively encouraged to make suggestions to improve aspects of their work or to determine their opinion about tentative changes in the way work is conducted. This level of "involvement" doesn't change the fact that management or the "system," rather than employees, exercises true control over the primary work decisions that determine *what* is to be done and *how* to do it. The narrow job duties may remain, but *some* empowerment occurs through the suggestion process. McDonald's, for example, listens closely to its front-line employees. The Big Mac, Egg McMuffin, and McDLT were invented by McDonald's employees, as was the system of wrapping burgers that avoids leaving a thumbprint in the bun. The suggestion level of empowerment frequently utilizes employee teams designed specifically to address job or work environment problems and to make suggestions for resolving them. This is true of many "quality teams" or "problem-solving teams."

Exhibit 2–2

Levels of Empowerment

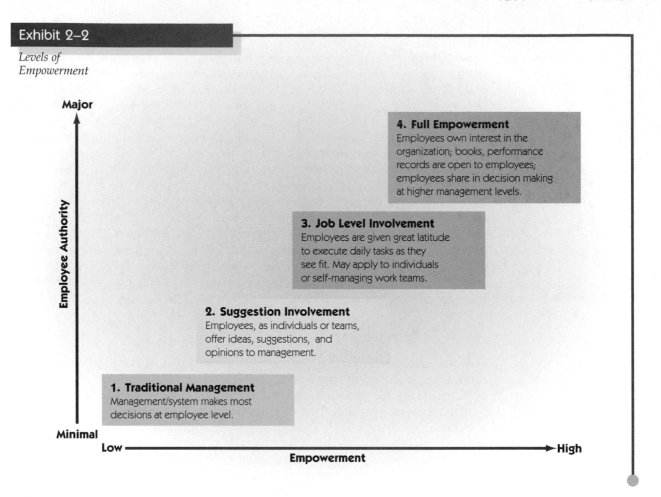

The third level is job involvement. In **job involvement,** jobs are defined so that employees use a broad variety of skills and control the work content of their jobs. Several conditions are necessary for individuals to become truly empowered at the job involvement level. These include the following:

job involvement
Employees use a broad variety of skills and control the work content of their jobs.

1. *Having self-confidence to perform the job well.* To be empowered, employees must feel that they have the skills and abilities to successfully perform their work.

2. *Being able to make work choices.* A condition of empowerment is that employees have significant latitude in determining how their work is performed. Often these choices include decisions about what, how, and when the work is done, as well as how work problems are handled.

3. *Believing the work is meaningful.* Empowered employees feel that their work has purpose and value—be it in the product or the service they produce. They feel that their extra effort and initiative contributes in an important rather than trivial way.

4. *Feeling that individual effort can "make a difference."* Truly empowered employees feel that they can personally impact job outcomes. The decisions that they make about their jobs largely determine whether the job results are a success or failure.

Empowerment at the job level allows workers to solve problems on the spot rather than having to first seek the permission of a supervisor. This saves time and money and also leads to improved worker morale.

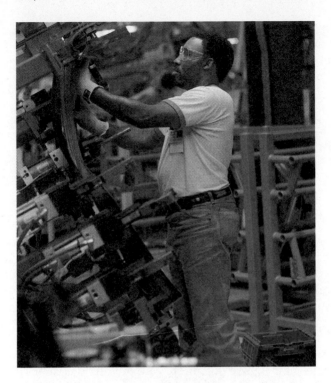

5. *Knowing there is management support.* Because empowered employees take risks in assuming responsibility, they must trust their own supervisors and higher managers to back them up.

self-check

How many of these conditions were reflected in the example given earlier about Ruth Thompson of America West Airlines?

Examples of job involvement given earlier from Saturn, AT&T Universal Card Services, Midas Muffler, and The Ritz-Carlton reflect empowerment at the job level. Employees are generally highly trained to be able to perform at this level. Saturn, for example, trained employees over 700 hours prior to startup of the company, despite the fact that most of its workforce consisted of veteran GM employees. Recall that the examples of Motorola and Saturn reflected empowered work "teams." Sometimes called **self-managed (autonomous) work teams,** these teams exercise a strong influence over the work content of their jobs. The employee teams, rather than supervisors or managers, control many aspects of their work, such as scheduling, assigning tasks, budgeting, selection of new team members, and evaluation of their own performance. This degree of empowerment is significantly broader than that given to the part-time, problem-solving teams found at the suggestion level of empowerment. At the job involvement level of empowerment, supervisors need to be reoriented toward supporting their people rather than closely directing them.

The fourth level is **full empowerment.** In a full empowerment organization the total organization is involved. The organization's performance information is openly shared and made available to all employees. Employees are highly

self-managed (autonomous) work teams
Teams that control many management aspects of their work, including scheduling, task assignments, and evaluation.

full empowerment
The total organization is involved.

skilled in teamwork and problem-solving techniques and actively participate in work unit and higher level management decisions. Some form of ownership is held by all employees through profit sharing and stock ownership. Because full empowerment represents such dramatic change from the traditional and even the suggestion and job involvement levels of empowerment, relatively few organizations incorporate *all* aspects of full empowerment.

self-check

What level of empowerment is found at City Hospital? Explain.

QUALITY

This section addresses the major impact that the search for ever-increasing achievement of high-quality products and services is having on organizations. As with the situation at City Hospital, employee empowerment plays an important role in the quest for high quality.

"Quality Is Job 1"

Maytag commercials show the lonely repairman who never gets called. British Airways claims, "We take more care of you." Pepsi and Coke wage huge advertising battles over which product tastes best. A small hometown diner advertises it has "the best burgers in town." Articles in *Business Week, Fortune, Industry Week, Forbes, The Wall Street Journal,* and others highlight quality as the hot current topic that it is. For the 1996–99 period, almost 2,000 articles on quality are listed by "INFOTRAC," a database of business periodicals. The governmental sector has also gotten into the act—a national survey showed that 40 states have adopted some form of "quality initiative" within state government; New York, Texas, Missouri, and Maryland have established annual quality awards. Training courses in "quality" management are regular offerings by consultants and training firms. Business schools at numerous universities have introduced courses in quality. Companies have allocated large budgets for quality training and created quality control departments, frequently headed by managers with high corporate visibility, such as vice-presidents. Despite the quality emphasis, however, we can all point to frequent experiences with poor-quality products and services (see Exhibit 2–3).

self-check

Think of a poor "quality" experience that you have had lately, either a product or service. What quality issue(s) shown in Exhibit 2–3 was involved? Do you believe that your poor experience with the product or service was an exception? Why?

Reasons for the Recent Quality Revolution

A number of reasons exist for the increased quality consciousness of organizations today. A primary reason for today's quality consciousness is the global economy. The ease of access of high-quality foreign makers and their products to world markets, including the United States, has raised the quality bar higher

Exhibit 2–3

Quality Issues in Manufacturing and Service

Manufacturing

1. Performance: a product's primary operating characteristics.
2. Features: the "bells and whistles" of a product.
3. Reliability: whether the product works consistently as specified.
4. Conformance: the extent to which physical and performance characteristics match preestablished standards.
5. Durability: how long the product lasts.
6. Serviceability: ease and costs of a product's repair.
7. Aesthetics: how a product looks, feels, sounds, tastes, and smells.
8. Perceived quality: subjective assessment resulting from image, advertising, brand names.

Service

1. Time: how long a customer must wait.
2. Timeliness: whether a service is performed when promised.
3. Completeness: the extent to which all items or services are performed.
4. Courtesy: the extent to which employees are polite, friendly, and accommodating.
5. Accessibility and convenience: the ease of obtaining service.
6. Accuracy: the extent to which the service is performed correctly the first time.
7. Responsiveness: whether service personnel react quickly and resolve unexpected problems.

SOURCE: *From "Total Quality" by James W. Dean, Jr. and James R. Evans. Reprinted with permission of South-Western College Publishing, a division of Thomson Learning. Fax 800-730-2215.*

http://www.iso.ch/
9000e/9k14ke.htm

ISO 9000
The global certification requirement of supplier firms that has been adopted by the United States and more than 90 other countries of the world.

for all competitors. Think of the highest quality auto tire, auto, or CD player that you can. Do names of foreign makers such as Michelin, Bridgestone, Toyota, Honda, Mercedes, Sony, and Panasonic come to mind? The openness of major global markets means that those firms with the best quality products/services will set the standard. No longer does a U.S. manufacturer have to beat out only its U.S. competitors; it must beat out foreign competitors as well.

A second reason, related to the global economy, is **ISO 9000,** the global certification requirement of supplier firms that has been adopted by the United States and more than 90 other countries of the world. ISO 9000 registration certifies that a supplier company meets certain quality standards in such areas as product design and development, manufacturing processes, testing, final inspection, and service (see Exhibit 2–4).

Companies whose systems are certified are listed in the ISO 9000 register and can publicize their registration as a marketing tool. ISO 9000 certification is critically important for U.S. companies doing business abroad, but also increasingly important within the United States because many U.S. companies require their suppliers to be certified. Started in 1987, ISO 9000 was originally viewed in this country as a European Common Market phenomenon, but by the end of 1995 almost 10,000 U.S. companies had registered. By the end of 1999 this figure had risen to over 22,000. One survey of U.S. manufacturing plants by *Industry Week* showed that more than 50 percent were ISO certified in 1999.[5] And the larger the firm, the higher the percentage. A study of U.S. distribution firms showed that 91 percent with revenues of $50 million or higher were certified, whereas only 37 percent in the $10 to $20 million range were certified.[6]

Exhibit 2–4

ISO 9000: The Standards for Certification

Companies that seek ISO certification must satisfy a team of outside auditors who evaluate the firm on the basis of 20 standards, related to these areas:

1. Management responsibility
2. Quality system
3. Contract review
4. Design control
5. Document control
6. Purchasing
7. Purchaser supplied product
8. Product identification and traceability
9. Process control
10. Inspection and testing
11. Equipment used to test, measure, and inspect
12. Inspection and test status
13. Control of nonconforming product
14. Corrective actions
15. Handling, storage, packaging, and delivery
16. Quality record keeping
17. Internal quality audits
18. Training
19. Servicing
20. Statistical techniques

To give you some idea of the rigor involved in satisfying ISO requirements, one well-known ISO consultant has developed a questionnaire for company audit teams to identify standards in which the company is weak. Questions for two such standards are given here:

Standard 1.0 Management Responsibility

1. With regard to quality, has your company defined its policy, objectives, and commitment?
2. Have you documented your policy, objectives, and quality commitment?
3. Is your quality policy understood, implemented, and maintained at all levels in the organization?
4. Have you defined the responsibilities and authority of persons involved in:
   a. final testing, control, and vertification requirements?
   b. identification and recording of any product quality problems?
   c. conducting internal audits?
   d. conducting design reviews?
   e. monitoring of the design process?
5. Are the design reviews, audits (quality system, procedures, product), and other inspection procedures carried on by persons other than those directly involved with the aforementioned tasks?
6. Has a management representative been assigned to ensure that ISO 9000 requirements are implemented and maintained?
7. Is the quality system periodically reviewed at appropriate intervals to ensure its continuing suitability and effectiveness?
8. Are records of the aforementioned reviews maintained?

Standard 2.0 Quality System

9. Do you have a quality manual?
10. Have you established written procedures in the areas of
    a. preparation of quality plans in accordance with specific customer requirements?
    b. updating, as necessary, of quality control, inspection, and testing techniques, including the development of new instrumentation?
    c. verification of design compatibility?
    d. identification and acquisition of any controls, processes, inspection equipment, fixtures, total production resources, and skills that may be needed to achieve the required quality?

SOURCE: *Adapted from James L. Lamprecht,* ISO 9000: Preparing for Registration *(New York: ASQC Quality Press, 1991).*

The questions given in Exhibit 2–4 relate to *only* 2 of the 20 standards, so you can see how rigorously a company must prepare for ISO certification. Preparation can take 18 months or longer for larger multiple-location firms to complete, but some can then complete implementation in a year or less, given considerable staff commitment. A small firm of 35 employees in a single location can achieve registration in 9 months. Registration fees alone can exceed $10,000 or more per site, not including the substantial amount of company resources involved. Once certified, registration must be maintained through successful revision at 6-month intervals.[7]

The third reason U.S. companies have become so quality conscious is the enormous cost associated with poor quality. Philip Crosby, a world quality expert, says that nonconformance—products and services that do *not* match up to requirements—costs the typical manufacturer about 20 percent of sales and the typical service firm 35 percent of sales. This includes the cost of scrapped materials, wasted time, costs of rework, and customers' exercise of warranties.

The fourth reason is the increase in policing of quality by external groups. The infrastructure for disseminating quality information has increased dramatically in recent years. Groups such as the Consumer Product Safety Commission and other consumer organizations have begun to police quality through public opinion, boycotts, adverse publicity, and legal action. Auto manufacturers eagerly (or perhaps dreadfully) await the annual results of auto quality ratings by J. D. Power and Associates, the independent rating agency, or automobile ratings assigned by other groups. Restaurants and hotels await ratings of their services by AAA, Mobil, and other travel-related rating services. All types of manufacturers await the ratings of groups such as *Consumer Reports*. The publication *Successful Meetings* annually lists the resorts with the best meeting facilities and services. Many other industry publications do the same for firms operating in their industry.

Evolution of the Quality Explosion in the United States

3 Describe how the recent U.S. quality resurgence began.

The background of today's surging quality movement in the United States can be traced to Japan. Following World War II, the words "Made in Japan" connoted cheap, inferior quality. As part of General MacArthur's program to help rebuild the country, 50-year-old W. Edwards Deming, a U.S. statistical quality control advocate, was brought to Japan to teach statistical quality control concepts. Deming addressed 21 top Japanese executives who were eager to learn and who represented the industrial leaders of the country. His theories formed the basis of **Deming's 85–15 rule.** This rule assumes that when things go wrong, 85 percent of the time the cause is attributed to elements controlled by management, such as machinery, materials, or processes, while only about 15 percent of the time are employees at fault. Thus, Deming believes that management rather than employees is to blame for most poor quality. The Japanese embraced Deming's message and transformed their industries by using his techniques. His "14 points for quality," as shown in Exhibit 2–5, are the actions he believed necessary for an organization to successfully make the quality "transformation."

Deming's 85–15 rule
Assumes that when things go wrong, 85 percent of the time the cause is from elements controlled by management.

Deming's contributions were recognized early by the Japanese. In 1951 the Deming Application Prize was instituted by the Union of Japanese Scientists and Engineers, and Deming was awarded the nation's highest honor, the Royal Order of the Sacred Treasure, from the Emperor of Japan. By the mid-1970s the

Exhibit 2–5

*Deming's Fourteen
Points for Quality*

1. Top management should establish and publish a statement of the organization's purpose and commitment to quality products and services and continuous improvement.

2. Everyone throughout the organization should learn the new philosophy.

3. Dependence on "inspecting" quality into products should be shifted to an attitude of "expecting" quality by having it built into the system.

4. There must be a systematic way to select quality suppliers, rather than simply on the basis of cost.

5. The organization must be devoted to continuous improvement.

6. All employees should be trained in the most modern quality and problem-solving techniques.

7. Leadership techniques consistent with getting the most commitment from employees should be practiced throughout the entire organization.

8. Fear should be eliminated from the work environment.

9. Teams and work groups must work smoothly together; barriers between functional departments must be eliminated.

10. Exhortations, posters, and slogans asking for new levels of workforce productivity must be backed by providing the methods to achieve these.

11. Numerical production quotas should be eliminated. Constant improvement should be sought instead.

12. Barriers that deprive employees from pride in their work must be removed.

13. A vigorous program of education, retraining, and self-improvement for all employees must be instituted.

14. A structure in top management that will push the thirteen points above to achieve the transformation must be created.

SOURCE: *From* Deming Management at Work *by Mary Walton. Copyright © 1990 by Mary Walton. Used by permission of G.P. Putman's Sons, a division of Penguin Putnam Inc.*

quality of Japan's products exceeded that of Western manufacturers, and Japanese companies made significant U.S. and global market penetration in areas such as autos, steel, computers, and electronics.

In the early 1980s, David Garvin of the Harvard Business School spent several years in Japan and the United States studying air conditioning manufacturers. He found that the failure rate in such key components as compressors, coils, and thermostats of the worst Japanese manufacturer was less than half that of the best U.S. manufacturer! He found that manufacturing techniques were basically the same, but the difference was in management. At Japanese plants, supervisors said quality was their major goal; at U.S. plants, supervisors said meeting production quotas was the major goal. At Japanese plants, meetings were held daily to discuss failure; at American plants, the range was anything from 10 meetings monthly in the best plants to just 4 a month in the worst plants. All Japanese companies had goals for quality, such as the percent of defects allowable, against which their managers and workers were measured; only one-half of U.S. plants had quality goals. In Japanese plants, the top quality manager reported to a higher level manager than in most American plants. New hires in Japanese plants received much broader training and for considerably longer time periods than their U.S. counterparts. Little wonder that "Made in the U.S.A." had become no match for Japan's higher quality products in many industries.[8]

Dr. W. Edwards Deming (1900–1993) was a visionary whose work is credited with creating the quality revolution. Deming continued lecturing into his 90s.

 click! http://www.quality
.nist.gov/

Malcolm Baldrige National Quality Award
A symbol of America's best in quality.

The United States' quality problem was first highlighted in a 1980 NBC program entitled "If Japan Can . . . Why Can't We?" The program introduced the then 80-year-old Deming who, although an American, was virtually unknown in this country. This program ignited a spark that awakened American executives and helped fuel a quality turnaround. Major companies, especially those that were threatened, embarked on extensive programs to improve quality. Ford Motors was among the first to invite Deming to help transform its operations. Within a few years, Ford's results improved dramatically; its profits became the highest for any company in automotive history, and by 1992 its Ford Taurus unseated the Honda Accord as the best-selling domestic model.

In 1987 Congress established the **Malcolm Baldrige National Quality Award** (see Exhibit 2–6), which generated a remarkable interest in quality by American business.

Dr. Joseph Juran, who, like Deming, was one of the premier leaders in the quality movement both in Japan and the United States, observed

I have become optimistic for the first time since the quality crisis descended upon the United States. I now believe that during the 1990s the number of U.S. companies that have achieved stunning results will increase by orders of great magnitude. I also believe that during the 1990s the United States will make great strides toward making "Made in the U.S.A." a symbol of world-class quality.[9]

In the 1990s the quality of U.S. goods and services has indeed achieved a stunning turnaround, leading the way to improved market competitiveness. U.S. automakers Ford, General Motors, and Chrysler have recaptured U.S. market share, and in 1998 Chrysler received its first J. D. Power quality award. Its Concorde received the highest rating in the premium mid-size car category and

Exhibit 2–6

*The Malcolm Baldrige
National Quality
Award*

The prize is only a gold-plated medal encased in a crystal column 14 inches tall. But since 1987, when the U.S. Congress created the Malcolm Baldrige National Quality Award at the urging of business leaders, it has symbolized America's best in quality. Named for the much-admired former U.S. Secretary of Commerce, Malcolm Baldrige, who died in 1987, the award is administered by the National Institute of Standards and Technology, with endowments covering costs of administration and judging of applicants.

Applications are scored by examination teams drawn from senior ranks of business, consultants, and academics. The highest scoring applicants move on to stage two—a site visit by four to six examiners who verify the facts in the application and probe more deeply into organizational processes. They report back to a nine-judge panel, which recommends winners to the Secretary of Commerce. The White House makes the formal announcements.

Winning a Baldrige has proved tough. In 1988, the first year of eligibility, only 3 of 66 applicants were winners; in 1989, only 2 of 40.

Organizations must observe eight essentials in order to win:

1. Establish a plan to seek improvement continuously in all phases of operations—not just manufacturing but purchasing, sales, human relations, and other areas.
2. Put in place a system that accurately tracks and measures performance in those areas.
3. Establish a long-term strategic plan based on performance targets that compare with the world's best in that particular industry.
4. Link closely in a partnership with suppliers and customers in a way that provides needed feedback for continuous improvement.
5. Demonstrate a deep understanding of customers in order to convert their wants into products.
6. Establish and maintain long-lasting customer relationships, going beyond product manufacture and delivery to include sales, service, and ease of maintenance.
7. Focus on preventing mistakes instead of developing efficient ways to correct them; that is, feedforward control is a must.
8. Perhaps most difficult, but imperative, is to make a commitment to quality improvement throughout all levels of the organization, including top, middle, and bottom.

Past winners since its inception in 1988 are given here:

1998	Manufacturing	Caterpillar Inc., Solar Turbines Division	1992	Manufacturing	AT&T Network Systems Group/Transmission Systems
		Boeing Airlift & Tanker Programs			Texas Instruments Defense Systems
		Texas Nameplate Co.			& Electronic Group, Dallas, TX
1997	Manufacturing	Solectron Corporation		Service	AT&T Universal Card Services
		3M Dental Products Division, St. Paul, MN			The Ritz-Carlton Hotel
				Small Business	Granite Rock Co.
	Service	Merrill Lynch Credit Corporation, Jacksonville, FL	1991	Manufacturing	Solectron Corporation
					Zytec Corp.
		Xerox Business Services, Rochester, NY		Small Business	Marlow Industries
1996	Manufacturing	ADAC Laboratories	1990	Manufacturing	Cadillac Motor Car Co.
		Trident Precision Manufacturing, Inc.			IBM Rochester
	Service	Dana Commercial Credit Corp.		Service	Federal Express Corp.
	Small Business	Custom Research, Inc.		Small Business	Wallace Co.
1995	Manufacturing	Corning Telecommunications Products	1989	Manufacturing	Miliken & Co.
					Xerox Business Products & Systems
		Armstrong World Industries	1988	Manufacturing	Motorola, Inc.
1994	Service	AT&T Consumer Communication			Westinghouse Commercial Nuclear Fuel Division
		GTE Directories		Small Business	Globe Metallurgical, Inc.
	Small Business	Wainwright Industries			
1993	Manufacturing	Eastern Chemical Co.			
	Small Business	American Rubber Co.			

Cirrus received best in the mid-size category. Xerox and Motorola have won the Deming prize for their high-quality operations in Japan. Harley-Davidson, which had seen its share of large motorcycles fall from 40 to 23 percent due to Japanese imports during a four-year period in the 1980s, had increased it to 48 percent by 1998. Today, "Made in the U.S.A." has again become a symbol of world-class quality.

Approaches to Managing Quality

4 Identify the four approaches to managing quality.

Organizations may seek to manage quality in one of several ways. These approaches are (1) traditional, (2) problem solving, (3) proactive, and (4) total quality.

Traditional Approach. The **traditional quality approach** to managing quality emphasizes quality assurance, quality control, or statistical quality control techniques based on random sampling. This approach focuses on inspection as the basis for ensuring that products or services meet the company's standards. The emphasis is not so much on error *prevention* as it is on error *detection*.

traditional quality approach
Emphasizes quality assurance, quality control, or statistical quality control techniques based on random sampling.

Problem-Solving Approach. The **problem-solving quality approach** emphasizes identification of defects through the traditional approach while rigorously seeking remedies to these problems through team problem-solving techniques such as quality teams. Training team members in problem solving and group dynamics is an important part of this approach.

problem-solving quality approach
Emphasizes identifying defects while seeking remedy to these problems through quality teams.

Proactive Approach. The **proactive quality approach** is a more aggressive quality approach, focusing on building quality into the process in advance rather than on "inspecting it into" the system. It emphasizes error *prevention* through training of employees, design of systems, selection of suppliers, and so on.

proactive quality approach
Building quality into the process in advance rather than "inspecting it into" the system.

Total Quality Approach. The **total quality approach**, also known as total quality management (**TQM**), reflects a major reorganization that strives to achieve customer satisfaction through continuous improvement of the organization's products and/or services and processes. It goes beyond the three approaches above; the term "total" reflects the fact that it is an overall organizational strategy initiated and committed to by top management and reflected at all organizational levels, including all employees, customers, and suppliers. The premise of the total quality approach is that a chain of events occurs when an organization's "quality" improves. Increased quality leads to increased market share, which increases profitability, as shown in Exhibit 2–7.

total quality approach (TQM)
Reflects a major reorganization to achieve customer satisfaction through continuous improvement of products or services.

Exhibit 2–7

The Total Quality Chain

Improved Products/Services → Increased Market Share → Increased Profitability

⑤ Understand the three components of total quality management.

Total Quality Management (TQM)

A major criticism of management is that it attempts to grab onto any perceived solution—any hot new buzzword of the decade—and quickly incorporate it. TQM, unfortunately, has been victimized in this same way. Many organizations adopted catchy TQM slogans, but, in fact, U.S. firms have not reached the commitment required to fully adopt a total quality management process. As one expert puts it, very few companies have considered adequately how they transform "the show"—the quality banners, slogans, and pep rallies—into a basic way of organizational life, that is, "the way we do things around here."[10] Approaches to total quality management vary greatly among organizations, not only because of different commitment levels, but also because each organization must fit the framework into its own unique environment.

There is growing evidence that companies which seriously embrace the total quality approach achieve good results. A study of 108 publicly traded companies that seriously embraced TQM over a five-year period experienced improved financial performance, including higher sales, greater income and increased stock value than peer group companies which did not undertake such a program.[11] Also, national housing quality award winners average more than twice the net income and one-third higher gross margins than builders who have not won awards.[12]

Whatever the abbreviation (such as City Hospital's TQI), the key to recognizing an organization's true commitment to quality is that it will enlist most of Deming's 14 points.

A true total quality process has three fundamental bases, as shown by the three-legged stool in Exhibit 2–8. These are (1) customer focus, (2) continuous improvement, and (3) employee involvement. Note how these are reflected in Motorola's overall statement of its fundamental objective, beliefs, goals, and initiatives (Exhibit 2–9).

Customer Focus. In the book *In Search of Excellence,* Peters and Waterman identified what they considered the excellent U.S. companies and what made them so.[13] One of the common characteristics of these companies was their excellent service to customers. They made a point of understanding and keeping up with their customers' problems and complaints and in maintaining a feedback system as to how they could be more effectively served. Under TQM the entire organization commits itself to the concept of customer satisfaction.

While external customers are the most obvious, each organization has many internal customer links. Maintenance personnel serve operating departments. The information provided by accounting departments serves operating managers who use the information to make decisions. Materials, products, and services contracted by purchasing specialists serve those internal customers for whom they are ordered. Even a manufacturing system can be viewed as a set of interrelated services: Manufacturing is a customer of product design; assembly is a customer of manufacturing; sales is a customer of packaging and distribution. Thus, the concept of "total quality" can be viewed as the umbrella under which everyone in the organization strives to create customer satisfaction.

At Bowater Carolina, for example, to increase employees' awareness and identification with the "entire company operations," external users of the company's products are frequently brought in to discuss what they require of good quality paper, special needs they may have, and the

Exhibit 2–8

Exhibit 2–8

*Three Bases of Total
Quality Management*

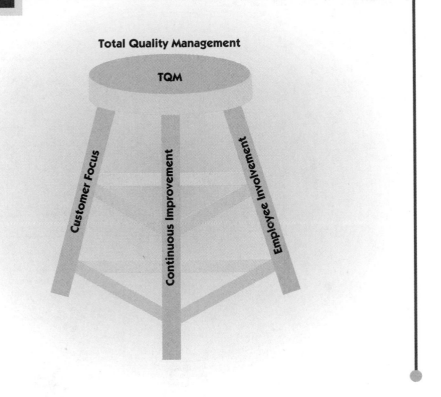

quality of Bowater's paper as compared to competitors. Bowater has also
arranged for employees to visit end-users of their products, such as the
Charlotte Observer, to observe the products they've created being put to
use. They also interface with *Observer* employees. The result is that
Bowater employees identify more with their own company, its products,
and their customers.

click! http://www.bmpcoe
.org/bestpractices

Continuous Improvement. A second important element of a total quality
process is continuous improvement, or *kaizen,* the Japanese term for it. Cum-
mins Engine provides a five-day employee training program that targets continuous improvement. The company's "Just Do It" principles give you a good idea
of what continuous improvement entails:

1. Discard conventional, fixed ideas about doing work.
2. Think about how to do it, rather than why it cannot be done.
3. Start by questioning current practices.
4. Begin to make improvements even if only 50 percent of them can be completed.
5. Correct mistakes immediately.[14]

Note that the approach not only emphasizes correction of errors, but complete
rethinking of current practices.

Often, improvements are stimulated by having employees work on special
problem-solving teams. Teams receive training in statistics, problem-solving

Exhibit 2–9

*Motorola's
Fundamental
Objective and Key
Beliefs, Goals, and
Initiatives Reflect
Commitment to
Quality*

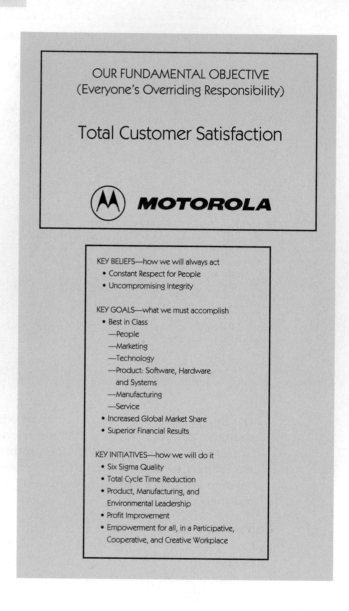

OUR FUNDAMENTAL OBJECTIVE
(Everyone's Overriding Responsibility)

Total Customer Satisfaction

Ⓜ MOTOROLA

KEY BELIEFS—how we will always act
- Constant Respect for People
- Uncompromising Integrity

KEY GOALS—what we must accomplish
- Best in Class
  —People
  —Marketing
  —Technology
  —Product: Software, Hardware
   and Systems
  —Manufacturing
  —Service
- Increased Global Market Share
- Superior Financial Results

KEY INITIATIVES—how we will do it
- Six Sigma Quality
- Total Cycle Time Reduction
- Product, Manufacturing, and
  Environmental Leadership
- Profit Improvement
- Empowerment for all, in a Participative,
  Cooperative, and Creative Workplace

skills, and team decision making to help them work effectively in solving problems and in generating improvement. As shown in Exhibit 2–10, all types of organizations employ such teams effectively.

Earlier you read about Deming's 14 points. Point 11 urges elimination of numerical production quotas. Deming felt that the emphasis on quantitative goals isn't conducive to the concept of continuous long-term improvement. Employees and managers obsessed with "making short-term quota" do it at the expense of quality. Managers may defer maintenance or allow lower quality work so as to meet production quotas. Additionally, Deming felt that quotas

Exhibit 2–10

Continuous
Improvement Teams
Work in All Sectors

Small Business

Fastener Supply Company has always been quality conscious. In 1993 Lucent Technologies had named it one of its 13 excellent suppliers for 11 years in a row. But because many of Fastener's customers, including Motorola and Polaroid, were demanding even higher quality, a team from purchasing, sales, and quality began meeting to seek improvements in all of the company's processes. As a result of the team's efforts, by 1996 the company had reduced its defective rate from 1,800 parts per million to 200. By 1996 all 250 of its own suppliers met or exceeded Fastener's own insistence on stringent internal quality standards. In 1994 Fastener received ISO 9000 certification; in 1995 it won the Level 1 Quality Award from the Massachusetts Council for Quality, and in 1997 it won the *USA Today*–Rochester Institute of Technology Quality Cup award for small business.

Manufacturing

The Eliminators, a nine-member team at Lears, a Virginia auto supplier, sought to improve performance of the No. 2 paint line, which suffered 35,000 rejected door pulls bound for General Motors, Ford, Chrysler, and Nissan vehicles. In an attempt to eliminate the paint "spots" that result from spraying the pulls, the team called vendors, visited other paint plants, and examined processes in an attempt to become more effective. The team's recommendation to switch from a waterfall to a vacuum air system to catch overspray lowered defects by 25 percent, improved productivity by 33 percent, and saved Lear $112,000 during the first year.

Manufacturing

A team at Motorola's Americas Parts Division in Schaumburg, Illinois, simplified the way its operation handled customer service calls. The changes slashed the percentage of customers who got a busy signal or hung up in frustration from 43 to 2 percent and saved the business at least $238,000 a year.

The regulatory streamlining team at circuit-board maker Solectron in Milpitas, California, worked with local government officials to cut red tape involved in getting a commercial building permit—a key problem in computer businesses where companies cannot afford delays. The suggestions made it possible for 95 percent of permits—including many complicated permits involving companies that produce hazardous waste—to be processed in one day, with most of the rest processed within a week. Previously, the process often would take weeks.

Health Care

In an effort to reduce patient time spent in hospitals and improve the quality of kidney transplants, Albany (New York) Medical Center's renal transplant quality improvement team of doctors, nurses, and technicians examined each step of the procedure and wrote a 26-page guideline list to help get patients home faster. The result cut hospital stays from 15 to 8 days by the end of 1998, increased the percentage of patients who survive one year after surgery from 87 to 97 percent, reduced readmission rates from complications by 50 percent and, importantly, cut costs by 25 percent or $10,000 per patient.

Not for Profit

To help the U.S. Postal Service reach its goal of next-day delivery for all letters mailed in its region, Charlean's Angels, a group of nine postal service workers at the Royal Oak, Michigan, Postal Distribution Center found ways to reroute mail that had been previously sorted by hand so that it could be processed by automatic sorting machines. The Angels' system will save the post office $700,000 yearly and will achieve the next-day delivery goal it sought.

SOURCE: *Marc L. Songini, "Setting Sights on Perfection,"* Industrial Distribution, *August 1997, pp. 34–38; Sara Nathan, "Hospital Speeds Recovery Time,"* USA Today, *May 7, 1999, p. 7B; Earle Eldridge, "After Spotting Paint Glitch, Lear Workers Eliminate It,"* USA Today, *May 7, 1999, p. 6B; Micheline Maynard, "More Machine-Sorted Mail Delivers Cost, Time Savings,"* USA Today, *May 7, 1999, p. 6B.*

imply a type of finality. For example, a cost-cutting program is thought of as a one-time event with a start and an end . . . the cost-cutting goal is reached, and therefore, additional cost cutting requires a new program. Under a total quality process, the continual, ongoing, cost-cutting effort would become built into the organization's continuous improvement culture.

Perhaps one reason that Western management tends to be complacent about methods, processes, and results is because at one time it did things the best way. Frederick W. Taylor and his associates in scientific management in the early 1900s asserted that the one best way to accomplish any job or work can be determined through systematic study. These best ways are carefully mapped out by industrial engineers, taught to workers, and monitored by supervisors to ensure that workers perform as taught. Taylor's philosophy is strongly pervasive today among U.S. managers. Times change, however, and today's "best way" is not likely to last. A total quality culture encourages continual change, a constant search for improvement. As shown below, there is no smugness at Motorola, the first Baldrige Award winner in 1988.

> **Perhaps the best known and most ambitious continuous improvement goal is that of Motorola. In 1987 Chairman Robert Galvin committed the company to a quality goal of 10 times improvement by 1989, 100 times improvement by 1991, and Six Sigma capability by 1992. Note that while it was quantitative, it was also continuous! To give you an idea of how much improvement this would be, "Six Sigma" reflects a defect rate of only 3.4 parts per million in each of the company's processes, whether manufacturing or administrative. Motorola has achieved Six Sigma quality in a number of its products, cutting defects from an average of 6,000 per million in 1987 to 26 per million in 1995.[15]**

Organizations have numerous tools/processes that can help them in their quest for continuous improvement. Two of these with which you should be familiar are benchmarking and reengineering.

benchmarking
Comparing company practices against those of world-class performers.

Benchmarking. **Benchmarking** is the process of comparing company practices and methods against the practices of firms who are world-class performers. Benchmarking gives you a lofty standard to reach for, but it helps you improve. A number of benchmarks, rather than only one, may be appropriate. For instance, IBM's Rochester, New York, division, in creating a new minicomputer, the AS 400, benchmarked top-notch internal IBM divisions as well as successful outside firms. Outside firms visited included (1) Xerox, the first U.S. firm to utilize benchmarking in the late 1970s and world-class in benchmarking processes; (2) Motorola, world-class for reducing quality defects; (3) 3M, which provided information for resource manufacturing planning capability; (4) Hewlett-Packard, which provided insights into the effective use of service representatives; and (5) Japanese firms, in the area of just-in-time inventory. IBM Rochester was able to produce from start to finish a minicomputer that exceeded all expectations.

self-check

> Assume that you are director of nursing at City Hospital, the hospital featured in the chapter preview. How would you apply the principle of benchmarking to continually improve "quality" in the nursing department?

reengineering
A redesign process for improving critical areas of performance.

Reengineering. As indicated in Chapter 1, **reengineering** is a fundamental rethinking and redesign process to achieve improvements in a critical area of performance, such as cost, quality, service, or speed. Rather than modifying current work procedures, reengineering begins with a clean slate and replans the job

Employee involvement is critical to bringing about improvements in the way a company does business.

from beginning to end. Thus, inefficiencies can be eliminated and productivity increased.

A good example of reengineering is the case of Wal-Mart and Procter & Gamble. The two worked together to reengineer the inventory system for Pampers Diapers, which were stored at Wal-Mart distribution centers. When distribution centers ran low, the order would be placed to Procter & Gamble, which shipped to the distribution centers, which then shipped to the stores. The reengineered system provides information on each store's inventory to Procter & Gamble, who now has authority to ship directly to Wal-Mart stores. This saves Wal-Mart the costs of ordering, storage, and distribution and allows Procter & Gamble to develop a closer link with its direct customers, the individual Wal-Mart stores. Both companies have benefited from this reengineering.[16]

Employee Involvement. The third major component of total quality management is the active involvement of employees in the process. You already learned about this topic in the section on employee empowerment, so our remarks here serve primarily as reinforcement. Because the spirit of a total quality philosophy is to unleash the creativity and capture the commitment of those workers most closely linked to the organization's services and products, it is essential that *all* employees, not just a select few managers or professionals, actively participate in the total quality process.

self-check

What were some of the methods used to promote employee involvement at City Hospital?

Employee involvement is the key vehicle used in achieving customer satisfaction and continuous improvement, the two other legs of the total quality stool. Employee involvement also helps achieve continuous improvement through participation in special problem-solving teams, natural work teams, or as individuals empowered to make their own job improvements.

In understanding total quality, organizations seem to underrate the commitment level needed to practice employee involvement. Major commitments to training in job skills, problem solving, and group dynamics require large commitments of money and time. Because management styles and attitudes are often inconsistent with the notion of "empowered" employees, some programs never fully leave the ground. Top management must not only lend support to the shift to employee involvement practices, they must visibly lead the way.

ROLE OF THE SUPERVISOR IN EMPOWERMENT AND TOTAL QUALITY

As you have seen throughout this chapter, the trends toward greater empowerment and the increasing emphasis on quality have their largest impacts on the way operating-level personnel perform their work. But the jobs of managers at all levels, and especially the first-line supervisory level, also require significantly changed roles.

Major Impact at the Supervisory Management Level

6 Explain how the supervisor's job is affected by empowerment and quality programs.

Since first-line supervisors work directly with operating-level employees, their own jobs are significantly modified under empowerment and total quality initiatives. Consider the major changes sought at the operation level: increased commitment, greater use of employee involvement, continuous improvement, increased pride in work, highly trained employees capable of solving their own job problems, design of jobs to allow employees greater responsibility, and the elimination of fear from the work environment. These factors, if they are actively sought by upper management, have a profound impact on the way supervisors perform their jobs.

Empowerment and total quality efforts require much top management commitment and even structural changes. But the fact remains: The employee level is where the "rubber meets the road." The first-line supervisor then becomes the agent of change in helping overcome numerous resistances. For example, employees may resist additional responsibility, may distrust management's commitment to the changes, or may feel threatened by having to learn new skills. They may resist empowerment because they fear taking risks. The supervisor's challenge becomes one of attempting to overcome these obstacles. As shown in the City Hospital chapter preview, managers and supervisors may also harbor many of the same, if not more, doubts as employees and also resist empowerment and total quality initiatives.

The Emerging Supervisor: Teacher, Leader, Coach

Some ways in which the supervisor's job in a traditional organization tends to differ from one in an empowered or total quality organization are discussed below and shown in Exhibit 2–11.

1. The traditional view focuses on the supervisor as the key to effectiveness. The supervisor plans, schedules, organizes, has the most responsibility for problem solving, and so on. In the empowered/quality view, work teams are the primary players. They often perform, plan, schedule, and provide much of their own work direction.

2. Traditionally the supervisor has the dominant work-unit role and is actively involved in all major elements of the work. Under an empowered/quality approach, employees assume more responsibility for their own work. Thus, the supervisor plays a supportive role.

3. In traditional systems supervisors are required to possess strong technical skills; often they are as technically competent, if not more so, than their work group members. This is less the case in empowered/total quality organizations. The supportive role played by supervisors requires primary skills in facilitation, such as helping, encouraging, and supporting.

4. The traditional supervisor's job may be seen as seeking stability, maintaining a consistent performance level, and managing the status quo. Supervisors of empowered/total quality groups seek constant improvement, encouraging change and departure from the status quo.

5. Because they were technically expert and the focal point of departmental decisions, traditional supervisors rely on their ability to inform, explain, and persuade. Supervisors of empowered and total quality organizations rely more on effective listening . . . to employees' needs, concerns, and ideas.

Exhibit 2–11

Changing Views of the Supervisor's Job

View of Supervisor's Job in Traditional Organization	View of Supervisor's Job in Empowered/Total Quality Organization
Supervisor-focused work unit	Team-focused work unit
Dominant role	Supportive role
Technical skills emphasis	Facilitation skills emphasis
Seeking stability	Encouraging change
Telling, selling skills	Listening skills
Personal responsibility for results	Shared responsibility for results
Personal problem solving	Team problem solving
Narrow, vertical communication	Broader, horizontal, external communication
Fear, pressure used to motivate employees	Pride, recognition, growth used to motivate employees
Autocratic decision style	Participative decision style

6. Under the traditional system supervisors bear primary responsibility for their work unit's results, whether good or bad. Supervisors of empowered groups share responsibility for results with employees, since employees strongly influence their own performance.

7. In the traditional system supervisors are expected to resolve most performance problems. In empowerment and total quality organizations supervisors are more likely to involve employees in problem solving. Or, as is the case in self-managed teams, teams themselves are expected to solve their own problems.

8. Traditional supervisors' primary interactions are vertical—with their own supervisor and their immediate work group. Supervisors or empowered employees interact with a broader constituency—peers, suppliers, service departments, and customers, as well as their immediate work group.

9. In the traditional system fear, pressure, and close supervision are common supervisory approaches. These are less appropriate in an empowered high-quality work culture, which values trust, recognition, pride, and employee involvement.

10. Because traditional supervisors are often the most knowledgeable about work processes in their department, they often use an autocratic approach; they make decisions and run the show. Today's empowerment/total quality culture invests heavily in trained, highly competent employees; supervisors are expected to use approaches that involve employees in decision making.

You might think of the supervisor's job in a high empowerment/total quality organization as being summarized by the two roles of leader and coach. As a *leader* the supervisor provides vision and ensures that members understand, accept, and are committed to the unit's goals. As a *coach* the supervisor trains, shows, explains, provides performance feedback, and helps members increase their levels of job performance.

As you recall, the title of this book is *Supervisory Management: The Art of Empowering and Developing People.* Also note that much of this text deals with topics that can be closely tied to the teacher–leader–coach roles: communication (Chapter 7); motivation (Chapter 8); leadership (Chapter 9); group development and team building (Chapter 10); coaching for higher performance (Chapter 13); meetings and facilitation skills (Chapter 14); managing conflict and stress (Chapter 15); selecting, training, and compensating employees (Chapter 16); and appraising and disciplining employees (Chapter 17).

We feel that empowerment and the three underlying components of the total quality movement—customer focus, continuous improvement, and employee involvement—will continue to become increasingly critical approaches to organizations in the future. And with it will come increasingly important challenges for employees, managers, and supervisors.

---

chapter review

 Define empowerment and give an example.

Two important trends currently impacting organizations of all types are empowerment and total quality. Empowerment is the granting of authority to employees to make key decisions within their area of responsibility. Empowerment exists along a continuum, ranging from traditional management to full empowerment.

(2) **Identify and differentiate among the four levels of empowerment.**

In traditional management most decisions are made above the employee level and little empowerment exists. At the suggestion level of involvement, employees are empowered to participate in suggestion system programs, or as part of problem-solving teams to make recommendations to resolve problems. Decision-making authority, though, rests with management. At the job involvement level of empowerment, employees are given much latitude to run their own jobs, making the major decisions involved. Finally, at full empowerment, (1) employees are involved to the highest extent on their own jobs, through profit sharing and ownership and/or stock awards; (2) company performance records are open to all employees; and (3) employees participate in making decisions beyond their own jobs and at the highest level of the organization.

A second recent trend is the quality movement. Quality of products and services has become increasingly important today because of (1) the major costs associated with poor quality, (2) the high-level quality of global conception, (3) activities of higher profile groups that police quality, such as governmental bodies, consumer groups, and industrial and service quality rating agencies, and (4) the increasing use of certification requirements for firms that export. An example of the latter is ISO 9000, a registration process that certifies that a supplier meets certain standards of quality.

(3) **Describe how the recent U.S. quality resurgence began.**

The history of the current emphasis on quality can be traced to Dr. W. Edwards Deming, who, following World War II, helped Japanese firms greatly increase their levels of quality and capture large market shares in key U.S. industries. It was not until the early 1980s that the U.S. quality movement gained momentum and Deming's work became popular. His "Fourteen Points for Quality" reflect his formula for improved quality. In 1987 Congress established the Malcolm Baldrige National Quality Award, given to U.S. firms who meet the highest standards of quality performance.

(4) **Identify the four approaches to managing quality.**

Organizations generally follow one of several approaches to managing quality. The traditional approach uses such processes as quality control and statistical sampling and essentially emphasizes error detection. The problem-solving approach emphasizes identification of defects while rigorously pursuing improvements through the use of quality teams. In a proactive approach, organizations use employee training and careful choice of suppliers and other processes to "do it right the first time." In the total quality (TQM) approach, the organization embraces a comprehensive systemwide effort that entails continuous improvement, customer focus, and employee involvement as its major parts.

(5) **Understand the three components of total quality management.**

The total quality approach is based on the "quality chain" where higher quality products and services lead to increased market share, which in turn leads to increased profitability. The customer focus of total quality includes internal as well as external customers.

Two important continuous improvement methods are benchmarking and reengineering. In benchmarking, a company compares its practices and methods to the practices of "world-class" performers as a basis for measuring its own progress. In reengineering, a company creates totally new approaches to how processes and activities can be performed effectively.

⑥ Explain how the supervisor's job is affected by empowerment and quality programs.

Since empowerment and total quality have their largest impact at the operating level, the first-line supervisor's job is greatly affected. The supervisor must overcome many program obstacles such as employee resistance to change, lack of trust in higher management, and lack of willingness to take on additional responsibility for effective performance. Whereas traditional supervisors may be directive and autocratic, the supervisor's role when total quality and empowerment programs are employed can be thought of more in terms of leader and coach.

important terms

benchmarking *54*
Deming's 85–15 rule *45*
empowerment *37*
full empowerment *41*
ISO 9000 *43*
job involvement *40*
Malcolm Baldrige National Quality Award *47*

proactive quality approach *49*
problem-solving quality approach *49*
reengineering *54*
self-managed (autonomous) work teams *41*
suggestion involvement *39*
total quality approach (TQM) *49*
traditional quality approach *49*

questions for review and discussion

1. What is empowerment? Identify the four levels of empowerment.
2. Explain how ISO 9000 has contributed to the recent quality revolution in American companies.
3. Who was W. Edwards Deming? Explain his role in helping make Japanese products so well known for their high quality.
4. Describe how the U.S. quality resurgence of the late 1980s began.
5. Isentify the four approaches to managing quality.
6. What are the three primary parts of TQM? Explain each.
7. Explain how benchmarking and reengineering can be used as continuous improvement tools.
8. Describe some of the changes in the supervisor's job because of empoerment and total quality.

●skill builder 2–1

Applying Empowerment

In Exhibit 2–1 you read about some actual examples of companies that practice "job involvement." These included specifics about employees at The Ritz-Carlton, Midas Muffler, AT&T, Motorola, LL Bean and Disney World.

You are likely to be familiar with some of the following positions. To test your understanding of empowerment, give examples of how *job involvement* might be applied to empower individuals who hold these positions.

a. Waiter/waitress position in a casual dining restaurant chain such as Chili's or Applebees.

b. Clothing department salesperson position for a national department store chain such as Sears, Penneys, or Dillards.

c. Administrative assistant to the department head of a college or junior college.

Your instructor may want you to discuss your answers as part of a small group.

● skill builder 2-2

The Quality Assignment
group activity

Assume the role of food service manager for City Hospital, referred to in the chapter preview. Your department's basic responsibility is the hospital kitchen and cafeteria. Each day your staff of 68 employees prepares all meals for patients, staff, and visitors, and serves staff and visitors in the hospital cafeteria. Included in your staff of 68 employees are an assistant director, three dieticians, seven supervisors, and kitchen and service personnel. Patient meals are planned for by the Department of Nutritional Services, which delivers meals to patient rooms. The major activities of your 68 personnel include the following:

a. Menu planning for the cafeteria's staff and visitor customers.
b. Preparing all patients' meals as specified by the Department of Nutritional Services.
c. Preparing and serving three cafeteria meals daily for hospital staff and visitors.
d. Ordering necessary food supplies.
e. Ensuring sanitary methods are used.

You and other department heads have attended a three-day course designed to teach the overall total quality approach. At the end of day one, the instructor concluded with, "You all have a good grasp now of what is involved in total quality. Accordingly, I have an assignment for you to bring to our next class. Be prepared to discuss your answers with your colleagues." The following tasks were on the assignment sheet given to you:

- Make a list of your department's key customers, both internal and external.
- List the important quality requirements that your department's customers have.
- Do they all have the same requirements or do some differ?
- Take one major activity of your department, and show how "continuous improvement" principles could be used.

Instructions:

1. Using the information presented in the five major activities of the Food Service Department, prepare the answers that respond to the instructor's assignment.
2. Meet in groups of three to five students and discuss.
3. Select a spokesperson who will present to the overall class a summary of your team's answers and discussion.

Hillshire Farm/Kahn's[17]

In 1988 Hillshire Farm merged with Kahn's to gain economies of scale and buying power in the smoked sausage market. Milton Schloss, president of Kahn's at the time of the merger, wanted to produce smoked sausage products that were equal to or superior to the market leader, Eckridge.

As president of Hillshire Farm and Kahn's, Schloss was a firm believer in "managing by walking around." He made a habit of making a daily tour of the plant and asking employees, "What's new?" One day an employee asked him if he really meant it. This surprised Schloss, and he arranged to meet privately with the employee early the next morning. The employee arrived with a balsa wood model of a new plant layout he had been working on at home. Recognizing the superiority of his ideas, Schloss asked him why he had not come forward sooner. The employee said that nobody had ever asked him. The design was implemented, and portions are still in place at Hillshire Farm in Cincinnati. This event was a catalyst for further quality efforts.

Drawing from a similar program at Procter & Gamble, Hillshire Farm developed a system called Deliberate Methods Change (DMC) to seek ways for continually improving processes. Using DMC, semivoluntary groups of salaried employees met to improve current processes. By emphasizing the positive aspects of improvement and refusing to place blame on workers for process design flaws, these groups built trust among the workforce.

Schloss was a firm believer in quality within the meat industry, and especially at Hillshire Farm. He used customer complaints—or more accurately, what customers found unacceptable—as the basis for defining quality. Schloss personally answered all customer complaints promptly, something that was unheard of at the time. Frequently customers were so surprised to hear from the company president that they apologized for their complaints. However, Schloss listened carefully to understand the nature of the complaint so that he could improve product quality. Also, he believed that a phone call from the company president would allow Hillshire Farm to keep the customer for life.

Schloss took a variety of steps to show his commitment and improve quality. He kept the plant grounds free of litter, freshly painted all the walls, and kept the grass and shrubbery neatly trimmed. In this way he communicated to employees the attitude they should adopt when they entered the building. Schloss also required that all telephone calls be answered after two rings and that the caller not be kept on hold for long.

The company defined four dimensions of quality—taste, particle definition, color, and packaging—and kept all employees continually informed of the company's quality standards. The accounting and finance departments judged quality according to how promptly and accurately they could make invoices and payments. Marketing and sales were responsible for identifying the features of the product that the customer perceived as most valuable and differentiable and for convincing the customer of Hillshire Farm's leadership in these features.

Schloss personally saw to it that these activities were performed throughout the company. He believed that management must act immediately on new ideas and suggestions. Getting commitment from supervisors was the most difficult task. Management had to explain the "hows and whys" behind the changes, motivate the workers, and recognize the top performers.

Instructions:

1. As described above, to what extent is Hillshire Farm/Kahn's incorporating each of the three components of total quality:
   a. customer focus
   b. continuous improvement
   c. employee involvement
2. What similarities/differences do you note between the quality/empowerment approaches taken by City Hospital (chapter preview) and Hillshire Farm/Kahn's?

Planning

3   Fundamentals of Planning and Time
     Management

4   Decision Making and Problem Solving

2 part

Fundamentals of Planning and Time Management

• outline

Some Important Points About Planning
Basic Steps in Planning
Planning Is Most Closely Related to Controlling
Managers Tend to Neglect Planning
Contingency Planning Anticipates Problems

Planning at Different Management Levels

Importance of Setting Objectives
What Are Objectives?
Objectives as a Stimulus for Motivation and Effort
Hierarchy of Objectives
Unified Planning Through Objectives
Guidelines for Setting Objectives

The Supervisor and MBO
Underlying Concepts
Key Aspects of the MBO Process
Some Problems with MBO

Types of Plans
Standing Plans
Single-Use Plans

Managing Your Time
Time Management Matrix
The Time Log: Where Your Time Goes
Setting Priorities: A "Must"
Handling the Common Time Wasters

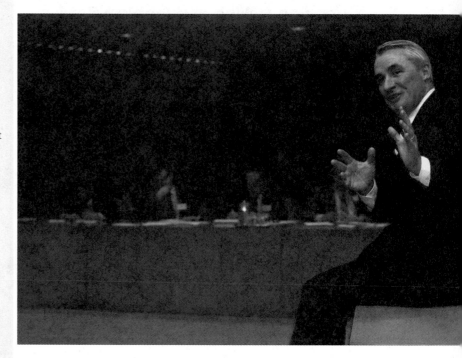

If you don't know where you're going, any road will get you there.
Author Unknown

After you have made up your mind just what you are going to do, it is a good time to do it.

Josh Billings

Changes at Dixon

Harold Marshall, newly promoted general manager of the Dixon Division of Computronix, Inc., was addressing a meeting of Dixon's 35 department heads, superintendents, and supervisors. The Dixon Division was one of the oldest in the Computronix system and one of the least cost effective. In fact, there were rumors that it would gradually be phased out of operation.

Most people at the meeting were seeing Marshall for the first time, although his reputation had preceded him. At age 32, he had gained widespread exposure as manager of the company's "experimental" plant in Fresno, California. That plant utilized totally new technology and many innovative management techniques.

Marshall began:

Ladies and gentlemen, it's good to meet many of you for the first time. We are faced with an important challenge—to increase the efficiency of this plant— and it's going to take dedication and commitment. I've promised Mr. Alexander [the vice-president] that I'll give it my best, and together we can show progress that will make top management commit itself to capital spending that will again make our division a top producer in the company.

If we're going to improve, our management system must change drastically. At Dixon, we have been practicing "defensive" management. That is, we react to problems when or after they occur. We've been good at doing that. But to be effective today, we must become far better at planning our future—setting goals and objectives, de-

veloping ways to reach them, and making sure we achieve them. Our industry cannot fly by the seat of its pants as we've done in the past. Each and every one of us is going to have to become adept at planning—for the division, for each department, and for each work unit. This is especially true of our supervisory level, for that is where the organization succeeds or fails. In the past, top management has done most of your planning for you, but now things will have to change.

Under the new unit planning system that we will establish, each of you will be required to commit to writing a plan for your operating unit, to be signed by you and your manager, with copies sent to the next higher level. The plan will contain five major objectives for your unit for the next six months. Each objective will be specific and include actual figures, such as "to reduce labor costs in my unit by 12 percent in the next six months." These objectives should cover the most critical areas of your operation and, of course, will require your own manager's approval.

Additionally, your unit plan must include the steps you'll need to take in order to achieve each objective, along with a timetable and names of employees responsible for each step. It should also identify the major potential impediments to reaching each objective, as well as your contingency plans for addressing these potential impediments. Finally, the plan should identify the process you'll use to monitor progress toward achieving the objectives.

Those of you who know me know that I am a firm believer in effective planning at all levels. I'm confident that implementing such a planning system—along with good follow-

learning objectives

After reading and studying this chapter, you should be able to:

1. Explain the steps involved in planning.

2. Explain how planning differs at top, middle, and supervisory management levels.

3. Explain how the hierarchy of objectives works.

4. Discuss important guidelines in setting objectives.

5. Identify the steps in management by objectives.

6. Differentiate the various kinds of standing and single-use plans.

7. Draw a simple PERT chart.

8. Discuss some ways to effectively manage time.

through—can help us make Dixon the most profitable division in the Computronix system.

Marshall continued to speak for about 15 minutes on such topics as the need to involve employees in the planning system, the importance of delegation, and the need for effective teamwork. He closed with an announcement that workshops would be held for all managers and supervisors to acquaint them with specific details of the new unit planning system.

We wish Marshall well in his attempt to turn Dixon around. Note the emphasis he places on effective planning. He is correct in his assessment of the role of supervisory management. Many managers see themselves as being strictly "fire fighters"—handling first this problem, next another, and then another. He is also correct in his view that supervisors at all levels must become more proficient at planning—perhaps the most neglected function of management.

As you have learned, *planning* involves selecting future courses of action for your organization and deciding how to achieve the desired results. This chapter builds on that definition and the ideas presented in Chapters 1 and 2. In Chapter 1 we discussed what management is, the managerial functions performed by managers, and the changing role of supervisory management. We now focus on the first of the management functions—planning. As you learned in Chapter 2, much planning must precede effective empowerment of employees and achievement of improved quality.

SOME IMPORTANT POINTS ABOUT PLANNING

Suppose you and a group of friends decide to take a weekend camping trip. Effective planning requires answers to the following kinds of questions: What constraints impact the group, such as the distance you can travel or the funds you have available? What activities most interest the group, such as hiking, boating, fishing, or mountain biking? What camping sites are available to choose from, and which activities are offered at each? What supplies and equipment will be needed, and does the group have the means to obtain them? Only after questions such as these are answered can the plan develop. Your group can then decide when and where to go, what time to leave, who will bring what, and perhaps even schedule your planned activities. Your plan should also anticipate future contingencies such as weather and occupancy of sites. Should rain be forecast, might you postpone the trip to a later date? If not, might you bring rain gear or have games available for indoor use? Might you reserve a site in advance or, if not, have a nearby backup site in mind?

Obviously, the trip's effectiveness greatly depends on the quality of planning that you and your group put into it. Supervisory planning works much the same way. Supervisors do planning—both routine and more detailed—as an ongoing part of their jobs. These may include plans for scheduling work, developing and living within budgets, making job assignments, and so on. They must also plan for major events that happen infrequently, such as when a department manager of a major department store plans for an annual inventory count or when a pizza store manager knows a week in advance that he must deliver 300 freshly baked pizzas to a convention of 600 people.

Cafeteria services must plan for supply and demand of food consumption—they want to make enough so that they don't run out, yet they don't want an oversupply, which would increase waste and therefore costs.

 Explain the steps involved in planning.

Basic Steps in Planning

As stated in Chapter 1, planning means deciding what will be done in the future; in other words, planning is forward looking. A manager must have a lot of discipline to set aside the time needed to solve present problems and to plan for the future. Moreover, much planning is intellectual; it is a "between the ears" activity that is hard work. Do you recall the discussion in Chapter 1 of the conceptual, human relations, administrative, and technical skills used by managers? Planning is normally an example of a conceptual skill. But it also requires other skills, especially to get the plans adopted and implemented.

Planning covers a wide variety of activities, from simple to complex, and from short to long term. But in all such cases, the three basic planning steps listed below exist. These are shown in Exhibit 3–1.

1. Setting an objective, or goal.
2. Identifying and assessing present and future conditions affecting the objective.
3. Developing a systematic approach by which to achieve the objective (the *plan*).

Exhibit 3–1

The Three Planning Steps

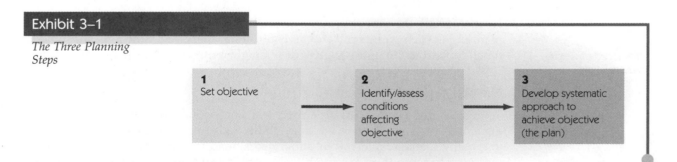

1 Set objective → **2** Identify/assess conditions affecting objective → **3** Develop systematic approach to achieve objective (the plan)

Three additional steps must also be taken in order to achieve the objective or goal established in step 1, though they are not exactly planning steps. These include the following:

4. Implementing the plan (organizing, leading, staffing).
5. Monitoring the plan's implementation (controlling).
6. Evaluating the plan's effectiveness (controlling).

These last three steps illustrate how closely related planning is to the other managerial functions, especially controlling.

The first step in planning—setting objectives or goals—addresses the issue of what one hopes to achieve. Notice in the chapter preview that Marshall's new planning system would require each manager to develop a plan that addresses five major objectives that their unit seeks to achieve.

The second planning step—identifying and assessing present and future conditions affecting objectives—recognizes important variables that can influence objectives. In our camping trip example given earlier, these would include factors such as equipment needed, weather, site availability, and so on. Since planning involves the future, certain assumptions about the future must be made.

The third step of planning is the developing of a systematic approach to achieve the objective. This third step becomes the *Plan*. It addresses such issues as the what, when, who, where, and how of the plan. The plan's complexity and importance are major factors in determining how formal and detailed this final step must be. The plan to build a new 200-bed wing expansion for City Hospital (Chapter 2 preview) will be much more formal and detailed than a plan to shut down a paper making machine for routine maintenance. Many daily plans are routine, however, and are carried about in supervisors' heads rather than being committed to paper.

Planning Is Most Closely Related to Controlling

Of the managerial functions, planning is probably most closely related to controlling. As you will see in more detail in Chapter 11, the steps in controlling are as follows:

1. Setting performance goals, or norms.
2. Measuring performance.
3. Comparing performance with goals.
4. Analyzing results.
5. Taking corrective action as needed.

Note carefully the first step in the above list. It involves planning! Because planning is such an integral part of controlling, these two functions are sometimes called the **"Siamese twins" of management.**

"Siamese twins" of management
Planning and controlling.

Managers Tend to Neglect Planning

Poor planning results in disorganized and uncoordinated activities, thus wasting time, labor, and money, but since thinking is often more difficult than doing, many managers, including supervisors, tend to slight planning. It is very tempting to forgo thinking about the future in order to get busy performing a

Exhibit 3–2

Lack of Planning

task or solving present work problems. The result is frequently unsatisfactory, as shown in Exhibit 3–2.

As Harold Marshall, the new Dixon general manager in this chapter's preview, pointed out, it's not unusual for a supervisor to spend his or her day fighting one "fire" after another—seemingly never catching up. Consider the following example:

> **Hank Green, a supervisor, had a hectic schedule and was about to be driven up a wall. He said: "Today I had three no-shows because of the weather, and my department is absolutely swamped. I'm pitching in myself, but I've also got to conduct a tour for some of our home office staff personnel after lunch. I'm supposed to meet with our industrial relations people on a case that goes to arbitration next week. To cap it off, Barbara Brown is asking for a transfer out of the department and wants to talk about it today. She and two of the other workers can't get along. This afternoon, I've got to have some important figures ready for the cost accounting department. On top of all this, I'm supposed to supervise my 19 people, three of whom are new hires who are just being broken in. What a day! But they all seem to be like this."**

Is it any wonder that this supervisor forgoes planning when his typical daily schedule is so demanding? But, ironically, many of the short-run crises that confront supervisors could be greatly eased by proper planning. As shown in Exhibit 3–3, when a supervisor devotes too little time to planning, short-run problems are likely to result, including impossible deadlines, unforeseen obstacles, crises, and crash programs. These problems preoccupy the supervisor, leaving little time to devote to planning—and the cycle goes on.

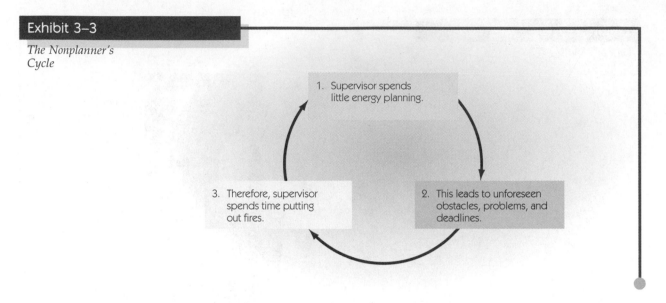

Exhibit 3–3

The Nonplanner's Cycle

1. Supervisor spends little energy planning.

2. This leads to unforeseen obstacles, problems, and deadlines.

3. Therefore, supervisor spends time putting out fires.

Contingency Planning Anticipates Problems

contingency planning
Thinking in advance about possible problems or changes that might arise and having anticipated solutions available.

It is important for supervisors to build flexibility into their plans by preparing contingency plans. **Contingency planning** means having anticipated solutions in advance for problems or changes that may arise and being prepared to deal with them smoothly when they do arise. Consider the following examples:

When the x-ray unit in the radiology department went down, Nurse Ratchett knew exactly whom to contact and how to divert patients to the x-ray machine in the hospital's emergency room.

Three weeks earlier, Charlie Fay had been relieved of his regular duties for a few days so that he could be trained as a backup forklift operator. Although not as expert as Willie Burns, Fay performed smoothly on the forklift when Burns was absent twice in one week.

You might think of contingency planning as the responses to the "what if . . . ?" questions that describe serious scenarios or events.

Contingency planning separates effective managers from ineffective ones. Proper anticipation of a crisis may prevent it from happening. If you are to be a good contingency planner, you will need to ask yourself the following questions and find answers to them:

1. What might happen that could cause problems within my area of responsibility?
2. What can I do to prevent these events from happening?
3. If these events do occur, what can I do to minimize their effect?
4. Have similar situations occurred in the past? If so, how were they handled?

PLANNING AT DIFFERENT MANAGEMENT LEVELS

2 Explain how planning differs at top, middle, and supervisory management levels.

Management planning differs according to the level of management at which it occurs, as shown in Exhibit 3–4. Top managers are more involved in **strategic planning,** which has longer time horizons, affects the entire organization, and

Companies in earthquake-prone areas such as Japan and California must have contingency plans for providing supplies, parts, and other necessities in case of disaster, such as the frequent earthquakes which plague the country.

click! http://www.dell.com/corporate/vision/index.htm

strategic planning
Has longer time horizons, affects the entire organization, and deals with its interface to its external environment.

click! http://www.whirlpoolcorp.com/whr/ics/story/value.html

deals with the organization's interaction with its external environment. Strategic plans include these:

1. The **mission,** which defines the fundamental purpose the organization attempts to serve and identifies its services, products, and customers
2. The overall **objectives** that drive the organization, such as profitability, customer satisfaction, employee relationships, environmental protection, or other critically important ends to be sought

Exhibit 3–4

Planning at Three Management Levels

Level	Planning Periods	What Is Planned
Top managers	Strategic long-term and intermediate-range plans of 1 to 5 or more years	Growth rate Competitive strategies New products Capital investments
Middle managers	Intermediate- and short-range plans of 1 month to 1 year	How to improve scheduling and coordination How to exercise better control at lower levels
Supervisors	Short-range plans of 1 day, 1 week, 1 to 6 months	How to accomplish performance objectives How to implement new policies, work methods, and work assignments How to increase efficiency (in costs, quality, etc.) Employee and supervisor vacations

mission
Defines the purpose the organization serves and identifies its services, products, and customers.

objectives
The purposes, goals, and desired results for the organization and its parts.

strategies
The activities by which the organization adapts to its environment in order to achieve its objectives.

operational planning
Consists of intermediate and short-term planning.

 http://www.amazon .com

 http://www.benjerry .com/mission.html

3. **Strategies,** the activities by which the organization adapts to the important factors that comprise its external environment, including consumers, customers, suppliers, competitors, and social, political, economic, and technological conditions

Middle and supervisory level managers are more concerned with operational planning. **Operational planning** consists of intermediate and short-term planning that facilitates achievement of the long-term strategic plans set at higher levels. As shown in Exhibit 3–4, these plans "operationalize" the plans made at higher levels and are much narrower in scope and much shorter term than those planned for at higher levels. As one first-line manager related:

> **Planning? Sure, I spend time planning. But most of my department's goals, objectives, and schedules are handed down to me from others. My planning is more along these lines: How can I get better performance from my work group members? How can I cut down turnover and absenteeism? Given my group's workload for the week, or for the day, what's the best way to attack it? Whom should I assign to various jobs? Take last week for example. Four of my people were out—two sick and two on vacation—and I had a lot of planning to do figuring who'd work where and when. Things seemed to go a lot more smoothly because I'd put in some time anticipating the problems. I've learned to plan on having a few people out "sick" on the opening day of hunting season!**

As you can see, all managers need to plan, regardless of their position in the hierarchy. Although planning at the supervisor level generally is less complex and involves less uncertainty than planning at higher levels, it is still crucial that such planning be done effectively.

self-check

What are other examples of events that supervisory managers must plan for?

IMPORTANCE OF SETTING OBJECTIVES

Objectives are crucial to effective planning. As the opening quotation in this chapter implied, only if you first know where you are heading can you effectively plan to get there.

What Are Objectives?

Objectives are the goals that provide the desired purposes and results for an organization and its parts. They answer the question "What do I want to accomplish?" Plans are aimed at achieving objectives.

Is there a difference between an *objective* and a *goal*? Management experts disagree on this matter. Some say that goals are broad and nonspecific, whereas objectives are narrow and specific. Others reverse the distinction just given. Still others do not distinguish between the two. Since the terms *goal* and *objective* are often used interchangeably, we will treat them as synonyms in this book.

Objectives as a Stimulus for Motivation and Effort

If you follow organized sports, you know that athletes frequently have objectives. Baseball players strive to hit .300; basketball players, to average 20 points; and football quarterbacks, to average 50 percent pass completions. A weekend golfer steps up to the first tee with an 85 in mind. A Friday-night league bowler shoots for an average of 150. Just as athletes are motivated by goals or objectives, so are people in the world of work.

> **Richard Ost owns three of the smallest drugstores you've ever seen. They are located in Philadelphia's "most bombed-out and burned-up neighborhoods." Yet he does more than $5 million worth of business a year—more than twice the rate of average drugstores. He succeeded by becoming "culturally competent." He labels prescriptions in Spanish for his Hispanic customers. He's also loaded some 1,000 common regimens in Spanish into his computer. With a single keystroke, any one of these can be printed in Spanish rather than English.**
>
> **He recently bought a second location with an Asian clientele. Soon he was filling more than 400 prescriptions a day—half in English, 30 percent in Spanish, and 20 percent in Vietnamese.[1]**

Objectives provide a stimulus for effort; they give people something to strive for. If Ost had no set goal—if he simply planned to go out and sell—he'd have no benchmark for telling whether he was doing well or poorly.

> **Lou Holtz, the now-famous coach from Notre Dame, is a firm believer in objective setting, as he tells in his video, *Do Right*. Fired from his first job as an assistant coach even before he reported to work (the coach who had hired him was fired, as were all his assistants), Holtz, with no contract, no job, and no money, became despondent and moped around the house.**
>
> **His wife bought him David Schwartz's *The Magic of Thinking Big*. Holtz stayed up all night reading it. One exercise required him to list 100 things he wanted to achieve in life. Enthusiastically, he showed the list to his wife. It included such aspirations as skydiving, meeting the Pope, and going into a submarine.**
>
> **Before reading the book, Holtz had been unsure he wanted to be a football coach. But there, included in his list of 100 things he wanted to do in life, were two important items: to be head coach at Notre Dame and to win a national football championship!**
>
> **Holtz credits Schwartz's book with turning his life around by making him focus on his objectives—what he wanted to achieve in life. He continues to stress the importance of objective setting among his coaches and players—not just in football but in academic performance and their personal lives as well.**

3 Explain how the hierarchy of objectives works.

Hierarchy of Objectives

In any organization, objectives are first needed at the top-management level. Once top management has determined broad objectives or goals, other levels of the organization, including supervisory management, reflect these in objectives or goals of their own, thus creating a **hierarchy of objectives.** Exhibit 3–5 pres-

Exhibit 3–5

Hierarchy of Objectives for Computronix

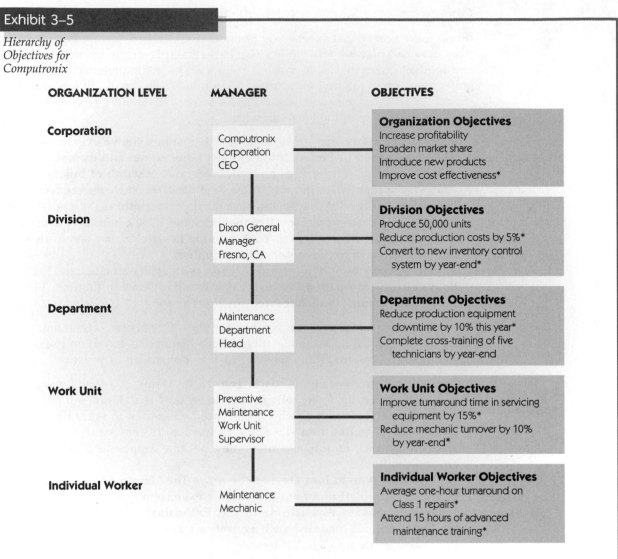

*Objectives directly linked to improved cost effectiveness.

---

hierarchy of objectives
A network with broad goals at the top level of the organization and narrower goals for individual divisions, departments, or employees.

ents a hypothetical hierarchy of objectives for Computronix, the firm described in the chapter preview.

Computronix's overall organizational objectives are increased profits, improved market share, new product introductions, and cost effectiveness, as well as others not mentioned. Note how one of these, the cost-effectiveness objective, is reflected at progressively lower organizational levels. At the division level, Dixon's objectives address cost effectiveness through objectives that seek a 5 percent reduction in production costs and the implementation of a new inventory control system. The Dixon maintenance department reflects the plant's 5 percent production cost reduction through the objectives of reduction of equipment downtime and upgrading the training of maintenance technicians. The preventive maintenance supervisor's objectives reflect the maintenance department head's objectives, and so on down the line. This diagram, though simplified, shows how the individual worker can be linked to top corporate levels through objective setting.

Unified Planning Through Objectives

unified planning
Coordinating departments to ensure harmony rather than conflict or competition.

A major advantage of organizational objectives is that they give managers at lower levels guidance in developing their own operational plans and coordinating their own activities. Ideally, top management's objectives should give tactical plans at lower levels unity of purpose. **Unified planning** means ensuring that plans at all organizational levels are in harmony, rather than at cross-purposes, with one another. Unified planning is especially important where coordination is required among departments or work units. Many supervisors are extremely dependent on other departments in accomplishing their own objectives. As shown in the example below, lack of unified planning at Computronix's Dixon Division has led to difficulties!

> **"This is ridiculous! They are trying to cut me down," stormed Juan Fernandez, supervisor of the processing department at the Dixon Division. The division was under the gun to reach its monthly production quota, and Fernandez's department absorbed a lot of the pressure. Fernandez continued: "If _we_ don't process quota, the division doesn't make quota. It's as simple as that. But those jerks in maintenance are killing me. Last week, they were supposed to shut me down for PM [preventive maintenance]. But what happened? Absolutely nothing! They couldn't get to me because they were caught shorthanded. You tell me why they had to send three of their technicians to a training school last week. I built my whole departmental schedule around last week's being slack. They knew I was scheduled for PM last week. There's no way they're shutting me down for even one minute during the next three weeks."**

Dixon has a problem here! Fernandez doesn't want to shut down for maintenance, but he risks some downtime later if his equipment doesn't receive the proper preventive maintenance. The lack of unified planning at lower levels may cost Dixon its objectives. It has already strained the relationships among personnel in the plant.

self-check

What action would you take now if you were Juan Fernandez? What should be done to prevent this type of situation in the future?

As you will see shortly, other types of plans may also be established to aid in unified planning at lower levels. These other types of plans—policies, procedures, and rules—are more specific than objectives and spell out the methods used at lower levels.

Guidelines for Setting Objectives

Discuss important guidelines in setting objectives.

Objectives set out for employees what they must do to make their performance acceptable. Since all supervisors should set objectives in their departments, the following guidelines should prove helpful to managers at all levels.

1. *Select key performance areas for objectives.* Since objectives focus attention and effort, the more important areas will suffer if there are too many objectives. Instead of having 15 objectives, select four or five key areas of performance, such as quality, quantity, customer relations, and cost controls, that really count!

2. *Be specific, if possible.* The objective "to have good quality" probably means different things to you and to your employees. "To produce parts with a 99 percent acceptance rate by the inspection department" is more specific, and it gives the worker a tangible measure of progress.

3. *Set challenging objectives.* Objectives should not be set so low that they can be met through "average" effort. Instead, they should require some stretching, but they should not be so difficult to achieve that an employee is discouraged from attempting to achieve them.

4. *Keep objective area in balance.* Effort expended in one performance area frequently affects another. The quality of work required influences the quantity of work, and the quantity of work may affect employee safety. Therefore, objectives may be needed in each of these areas so as to balance them properly.

5. *Objectives should be measurable.* If you want to determine whether employees are achieving objectives, there should be some way of measuring the extent to which they are being attained.

6. *Involve employees in setting objectives.* What do employees consider the key performance areas of their job? What do they think is a challenging but fair objective in a given area? When possible, ask these questions. There are times, however, especially during periods of financial difficulties and other crises, when it is not feasible or desirable to involve employees in objective setting.

7. *Follow up.* Once objectives have been set, supervisors tend to let up. Frequently only the supervisor knows the results of a worker's performance. Discuss progress with employees. Sharing results and discussing employees' progress will improve their commitment and demonstrate your own.

self-check

Note the quality objective in guideline 2: "to produce parts with a 99 percent acceptance rate by the inspection department." Do you see any problems with making this the only objective? Explain.

5 Identify the steps in management by objectives.

THE SUPERVISOR AND MBO

Although it was used by Du Pont in the early 1920s, management by objectives was first publicized by Peter Drucker in his book *The Practice of Management* in 1954.[2] This process has grown to be quite popular, especially in larger organizations. It has certainly called much attention to the role of planning and objective setting.

In general, **management by objectives (MBO)** is a process that involves the superior and subordinate managers of an organization in jointly setting common goals, defining each individual's major area of responsibility in terms of the results expected of him or her, and using those measures as guides for operating the unit and assessing the contribution of each of its members. The steps of the MBO process are shown in Exhibit 3–6.

Exhibit 3–6

*How the MBO
Process Operates*

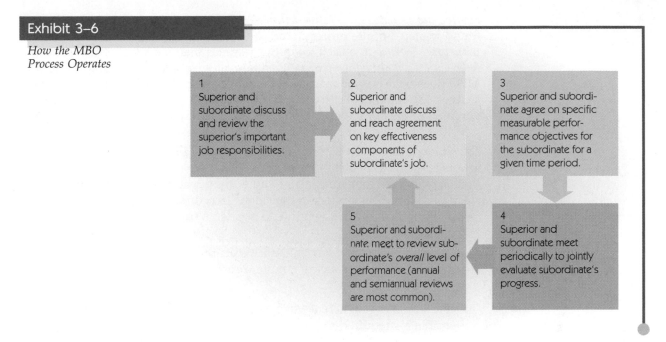

1
Superior and
subordinate discuss
and review the
superior's important
job responsibilities.

2
Superior and
subordinate discuss
and reach agreement
on key effectiveness
components of
subordinate's job.

3
Superior and subordi-
nate agree on specific
measurable perfor-
mance objectives for
the subordinate for a
given time period.

5
Superior and subordi-
nate meet to review sub-
ordinate's *overall* level of
performance (annual
and semiannual reviews
are most common).

4
Superior and
subordinate meet
periodically to jointly
evaluate subordinate's
progress.

**management by
objectives (MBO)**
Process whereby supe-
rior and subordinate
managers jointly set
overall organizational
goals, define each indi-
vidual's area(s) of re-
sponsibility in terms of
the results expected,
and use those measures
as guides for operating
the unit and assessing
the contributions of
each of its members.

Underlying Concepts

MBO's success is based on two underlying hypotheses. The first is: *If one is strongly attached to a goal, one is willing to expend more effort to reach it than if one were less committed to it.* The second concept is: *People prefer to be evaluated according to specific criteria that **they** perceive to be realistic and standards that **they** view as reasonably attainable.* Under this method, people participate in setting the goals and identifying the criteria that will be used to evaluate and reward their performance. Some of the goals may be measurable in quantitative terms (such as sales—or production—volume, expenses, or profits), whereas others may be assessed qualitatively (such as good employee relations, safety record, or employee development).

Key Aspects of the MBO Process

There are five key parts of MBO that are critical to its success. Some of these are directly tied to the five steps outlined in Exhibit 3–6.

1. *Link to organizational goals.* Note that the first step in the MBO process enables the subordinate to understand his or her supervisor's objectives. An effective MBO program can produce a clear understanding of how division, department, section, and individual objectives are related.

2. *Force managerial planning.* In steps 2 and 3 of the MBO process, employees are required to think their own jobs through. They are more likely to visualize the big, overall picture and to focus on the truly important performance areas. Instead of wasting their energies working on minor, less important activities, supervisors direct their efforts toward achieving the major performance targets they have established jointly with their superiors.

3. *Involve subordinates in objective setting.* Perhaps the unique feature of MBO is found in step 3 of the process. Here subordinates play an active role in establishing their own objectives. MBO assumes that *individuals are more likely to be highly committed to objectives that they have had a hand in setting.* Note that MBO does not give subordinates blanket privilege in setting their own objectives; the supervisor also provides his or her input. MBO emphasizes the jointness of the objectives and indicates that both parties can play an active role. The final decision for approval, of course, rests with the supervisor.

4. *Establish specific, measurable performance objectives.* Important to MBO programs is the need in step 3 for objectives that are specific and measurable—that is, objectives that are concrete rather than ambiguous. For example, instead of saying "Let's improve the safety record in the department," say "Let's reduce lost work hours due to accidents from 1,000 to 950, or by 5 percent."

5. *Increase communication and interaction.* When properly developed and executed, MBO establishes a closer, more direct communication between the supervisor and employees.

Exhibit 3–7 shows an actual MBO format used by one hospital. Notice that the subordinate is required to identify the basic objective and also must state the key action plans that will be taken toward completion of the objective. The supervisor's completed evaluation serves as the basis for determining the employee's annual performance rating and, ultimately, the merit increases or other rewards given by the organization.

Some Problems with MBO

Among the common problems encountered in MBO programs is the fact that, for many managers, allowing subordinates to participate in objective setting is contrary to their own styles and philosophy. They may therefore resist implementing MBO properly. MBO can also be time consuming, especially for supervisors with many subordinates. Paperwork may also increase as a result of supervisors' attempts to stay abreast of subordinates' progress. Finally, the need for specific, measurable objectives (that is, objectives that are readily quantifiable, such as production volume, costs, or profits) may result in less attention being paid to qualitative factors such as employee attitudes and satisfaction.

TYPES OF PLANS

6 Differentiate the various kinds of standing and single-use plans.

Once objectives have been set to determine *what* needs to be accomplished, plans can be developed to outline *how* the objectives can be attained. Basically, these plans fall into two categories: *standing plans* and *single-use plans.*

Standing Plans

standing plans or repeat-use plans
Plans that are used repeatedly over a period of time.

Standing plans, or **repeat-use plans,** are those that are used repeatedly over a period of time. The three most popular types of standing plans are *policies, rules,* and *procedures.*

Exhibit 3–7

MBO in Action

CHARITY HOSPITAL
MANAGEMENT OBJECTIVE STATEMENT (A)

Name: Larry C. Henderson	**Title:** Human Resource Manager

Objective Number: 1 of 7　**Initials: (Supervisor)** *A.R.H.*　**Initials: (Employee)** *L.C.H.*

Objective Statement (What)

To implement by Oct. 1, 1995 an In-House Physical Fitness Program that attracts 10% of hospital employees.

Action Plan (How) (give broad overview only)	Date Due	Responsibility Assigned To:
1. Create a PFP task force of persons from key departments to generate ideas, help plan PFP implementation.	March 1, 1995	Henderson
2. Interview a minimum of five responsible PFP directors in organizations that have established similar programs.	April 1, 1995	Henderson, Sanchez
3. Conduct written survey of all hospital employees to determine interest in various types of programs.	May 15, 1995	Henderson

---

CHARITY HOSPITAL
SEMIANNUAL PERFORMANCE EVALUATION (B)
Supervisor: Evaluate the employee´s attainment of the work objectives shown on Form A.
Your evaluation should be discussed with your employee.

Supervisor´s Evaluation of Employee´s Attainment of Work Objectives

Employee achieved objective well. Initial aerobics class, offered since September 1, has averaged 12% employee attendance during the week; the first lecture series was attended by 14%. Program has been well received, with many favorable comments encouraging expanded offerings.

Final Performance Rating (Check One)

☐ **Unsatisfactory**　☐ **Satisfactory**　☐ **Competent**　☐ **Commendable**　☒ **Superior**

Employee´s signature (I acknowledge having read and discussed the comments and performance rating noted above.)

Larry C. Henderson

Supervisor´s Signature *Anna R. Hightower*　**Date:** Jan. 18, 1996

Title: Assistant Administrator

NOTE: *Names of organizations and individuals are disguised.*
SOURCE: *Donald C. Mosley, Paul H. Pietri, and Leon C. Megginson,* Management: Leadership in Action. *Copyright © 1996 Addison Wesley Longman, Inc. Reprinted by permission of Addison Wesley Longman.*

policy
Provides consistency
among decision makers.

Policies. A **policy** is a guide to decision making—a sort of boundary on a supervisor's freedom of action. That is, it's a way to provide consistency among decision makers. For example, suppose that an *objective* of Computronix (recall the chapter preview) is "to operate our divisions so as to achieve high safety." Note that this objective tells the "what." A *policy* for achieving this objective at the various divisions could be that "All flammable substances will be stored and handled in a manner consistent with federal, state, and local regulations." Another policy might be "Each division shall emphasize safety performance of employees through a well-designed promotional campaign."

Within the Dixon Division of Computronix, an overall policy established by Marshall might be "Each operating department shall hold safety meetings at least once every three months to encourage adherence to rules and solicit employee safety suggestions." Other examples of policies are shown in Exhibit 3–8.

Supervisory managers fit into the policy picture in two key ways. First, they play an important part in implementing organizational policies that have been established by higher management. Second, they create policies within their departments as guides for their own work groups. Here are some examples:

1. *Absence notification.* "Employees who will be absent should notify me in advance, assuming this is feasible."
2. *Decision making.* "You are encouraged to make decisions on your own within your area of responsibility."

self-check

What are some other examples of supervisory policies? Can you think of any examples of policies established by the teacher of this course?

Policies established by upper level managers should be put into writing, since they must be enforced at operating levels by supervisors. Also, they often form the basis for legal proceedings against the organization and its manage-

---

Exhibit 3–8

Examples of Policies

Compensation policy: "This company shall establish and maintain wages on a level comparable to those paid for comparable positions in other firms in the community."

Overtime policy: "Supervisors shall offer overtime opportunities first to the most senior employees in the department."

Grievance policy: "Each employee shall have an opportunity for due process in all disciplinary matters."

Purchasing policy: "Where feasible, several sources of supply shall be utilized so as not to be solely dependent on one supplier."

Supervisory policy: "Managers shall periodically hold group meetings with employees for the purposes of discussing objectives, explaining new developments that may affect employees, responding to questions, and, in general, encouraging more effective and accurate communications within the organization."

ment. Supervisory policies like the ones mentioned above, however, may be communicated orally. Some policies may be unwritten, implied, or based on past practices because "that's the way things actually happen."

> **It was Mary Hicks's first week on the job. Her supervisor, Clara Sanchez, had been very helpful in showing her the ropes. Each day, Mary had shown up for work a few minutes before starting time—just to make sure she was on time. She noticed, however, that at least a third of the employees drifted in five to ten minutes late. This was true not only in her department, but also in others throughout the building. On asking one of her coworkers about this, she was told, "Yeah, they don't get really upset about five or ten minutes, just so it's not the same person all the time."**

The above example describes a practice that has become so widespread that supervisors may treat it as a policy. Supervisors must keep in mind that action or even inaction may come to be thought of as policy by employees and serve as a guide to their behavior.

Policies are relatively permanent but should not be "set in stone." Circumstances change, and management must from time to time reexamine the appropriateness of its policies.

rule
A policy that is invariably enforced.

Rules. Like policies, rules provide guidance. But a **rule** is stronger than a policy in that the guidance given by a rule is final and definite. Rules are inflexible and *must* be obeyed, under threat of punishment. If you work in a plant that has the rule "No smoking on the premises," you cannot smoke, and that is that. Note the difference between a policy and a rule as shown in the following examples:

1. *Policy:* "Employees who violate the no-smoking rule are *subject to discharge.*"
2. *Rule:* "Employees who violate the no-smoking rule are *automatically discharged.*"

Why distinguish between rules and policies, especially when the distinction is sometimes a fine one? First, as a supervisor, you must know when you do not have flexibility. Second, too many rules can result in overmanagement. Taking too much discretion away from the employees leads them to say "Well, let me look in the rule book and see what I'm supposed to do."

self-check

> What are some examples of rules that you can think of? Can a supervisor establish his or her own rules? Give an example.

Although rules have an important place in organizations, their overuse can lead to problems. When there are too many rules, supervisors lose their individualism and may use the rules as crutches. Or they may offer weak, apologetic reasons when they enforce the rules. For example, consider the following dialogue:

> *Supervisor:* **"Catherine, I'm sorry to have to write you up for punching in three minutes late."**

Catherine: "But you know I was actually here ten minutes early and just forgot to punch in. I was at my desk all the time. I can't afford to get laid off half a day for being written up."

Supervisor: "Sorry, Catherine. It doesn't seem fair to me, either, but I've got to stick by the rule book. A rule's a rule."

Procedures. The need for procedures arises when an organization or department requires a high degree of consistency in activities that occur frequently. Procedures are established to avoid "reinventing the wheel" and ensure that an effective sequence is followed. A **procedure** outlines the steps to be performed when a particular course of action is taken. Organizations have procedures for obtaining leaves of absence, ordering parts through central purchasing, taking weekly inventory, processing an employee's grievance, and so on.

procedure
Steps to be performed when a particular course of action is taken.

self-check

Can you think of a procedure for a regular activity that takes place in each of the following organizations: airline, hospital, retail store, college? Procedures used in driving a car? Preparing a payroll?

Not only do businesses need organized programs, but so do scientific undertakings such as the space program.

Single-Use Plans

single-use plans
Developed to accomplish a specific purpose and then discarded after use.

Single-use plans are developed to accomplish a specific purpose and are then discarded. Unlike policies, rules, and procedures, single-use plans detail courses of action that won't be performed on a repetitive basis. Examples of single-use plans are programs, projects, and budgets. These plans are more numerous and diversified than standing plans.

program
A large-scale plan composed of a mix of objectives, policies, rules, and projects.

Programs. We hear and read about programs daily—the U.S. *Gemini* and *Apollo* space programs, your city's pollution control program, a voter registration program, and so on. A **program** is a large-scale plan that involves a mix of objectives, policies, rules, and smaller projects. A program outlines the specific steps to be taken to achieve its objectives and the time, money, and human resources required to complete it. It is essentially a set of single-use plans carried out over a period of time. Other examples of programs are:

1. A tourism marketing program undertaken by your state.
2. A research program undertaken by drug producer Pfizer to develop vaccines for major diseases, such as AIDS and Parkinson's.
3. An upscaling program by Kmart to modernize the appearance of their stores.

project
A distinct part of a program.

Projects. A **project** is a distinct, smaller part of a program. For example, a state's tourism program involves many projects, such as selecting a tourism committee, benchmarking several states with outstanding tourism programs, promoting public attractions, and upgrading of the welcome centers that greet transit visitors on interstate highways. Each project has its own objectives and becomes the responsibility of personnel assigned to oversee it.

 click! http://www.gpo.gov/ usbudget/

budget
A forecast of expected financial performance over time.

Budgets. Every individual, family, or organization uses some form of budgeting. A well-planned budget serves as both a planning and a controlling tool. Simply stated, a **budget** is a forecast of expected financial performance over a period of time. A departmental budget covers such items as supplies, equipment, scrap, overtime, and personnel payroll.

schedule
A plan of activities to be performed and their timing.

Schedules. A **schedule** is a plan showing activities to be performed and their timing. Scheduling techniques range from a simple note or appointment book used to schedule your day to sophisticated schedules for such major challenges as building a new plant or launching a space shuttle. Two scheduling approaches with which you should be familiar are the Gantt chart and PERT network.

Gantt chart
Identifies work stages and scheduled completion dates.

The **Gantt chart** is a visual progress report that identifies work stages or activities on a vertical axis and scheduled completion dates horizontally. It is named after its developer, Henry Gantt, a management consultant who introduced the basic idea in the early 1900s. Since then, Gantt charts have been used extensively as a planning tool. Exhibit 3–9 illustrates a simplified Gantt chart. Note the specific activities that proceed from contract negotiation to job start-up and the scheduled times for each. Also note that one activity, long lead purchasing, can be carried on simultaneously with development of a manufacturing schedule. In actual practice, Gantt charts may include movable strips of plastic to represent bars, with different colors to indicate scheduled and actual progress. At a glance, a manager or supervisor can see whether a project is on time, ahead of schedule, or behind. While the Gantt chart is helpful as a planning tool, it does not show directly how the various activities involved in a job

Exhibit 3–9

Example of Gantt Chart Showing Activities Needed in Production Start-Up

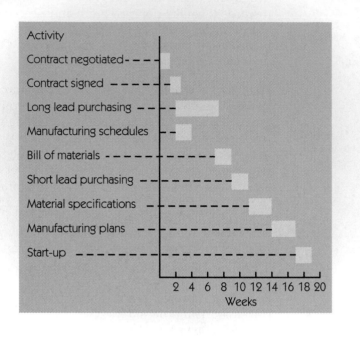

depend on one another. It is in showing such dependencies of activities that PERT network analysis can be helpful.

7 Draw a simple PERT chart.

PERT
Shows relationships among a network of activities to determine the completion time of a project.

Program Evaluation and Review Technique (PERT) is a management scheduling tool that shows relationships among a network of activities and events to determine the completion time of a project. Typically, PERT is used on highly complex, one-time projects, such as building a skyscraper or completing the prototype of a new jet aircraft, and requires the use of a computer. However, its principles are relevant for many supervisors, especially in planning and scheduling various aspects of their jobs.

Let's examine a PERT chart that can be applied at the supervisory level. Suppose that you are a maintenance supervisor and your department has to overhaul an important machine. You have determined that the following activities must be done to complete the job:

A. Remove the machine from its foundation.

B. Haul the machine to the repair shop.

C. Dismantle the machine.

D. Order and receive new replacement parts from the manufacturer.

E. Repair the machine.

F. Test-run the machine.

G. Build a new machine foundation.

H. Move the repaired machine to the factory floor.

I. Secure the machine to the new foundation.

Now, assume that you are asked to estimate when the machine can be ready for use again. The PERT network of events and activities involved in your analysis is shown in Exhibit 3–10. The numbered squares represent events at which the different activities to complete the job *begin* and are *completed*. For example, Event 2 marks the completion of Activity A and the beginning of Activities B and G. The lines represent the activities to be performed. The hours represent your estimate of how long each activity will take to complete based on your experience or on information supplied by others.

Exhibit 3–10

PERT Network for Completing Machine Overhaul

Note that the estimated completion time for the job is 62 hours. This total time is obtained by adding the hours necessary to complete the series of activities that comprise the *longest* route, in terms of time, to complete the job. This route is called the **critical path.** The series of activities on the critical path include A, B, C, D, E, F, H, and I. These are the activities that determine the completion time for the job. Activity G is not a critical step in the network because it can be begun and completed independently of activities B through I and is not included on the critical path.

A major advantage of PERT networks, even for simple problems, is that they graphically display the dependent parts of a total job. The supervisor thus has a better grasp of the total job to be completed.

critical path
The series of activities in a PERT network that comprise the longest route, in terms of time, to complete the job.

self-check

Suppose that it takes you four hours rather than the two hours estimated to repair the machine (activity E) as shown in Exhibit 3–10. Will this cause your project to be completed later than planned?

MANAGING YOUR TIME

In Chapter 1 we said that an organization's three types of resources are human, physical, and financial resources. Some management experts would include *time* as a fourth resource. *Make no mistake about it, time is one of the greatest resources a supervisor has.* Therefore, effective time management is essential for effective supervision. **Time management** is the ability to use one's time to get

time management
Ability to use one's time to get things done *when* they should be done.

things done *when* they should be done. Another definition, which reflects planning and prioritizing, is "arranging to accomplish the things you choose to get done within the time available." Without this ability, all of your other management skills are for naught. Even if you have excellent human relations skills, poor time management can leave you too easily distracted to effectively listen to an employee's problems. Or pressures can keep you from thinking clearly enough to use your conceptual skills fully. You may not even be able to take the time to display your technical skills by showing a new employee the ropes. To be effective as a supervisor, then, you must make effective use of your time.

Time Management Matrix

Stephen Covey has shown that we spend our time in one of four ways. These ways can be diagrammed as shown in Exhibit 3–11. As you can see, two variables govern our usage: (1) the *importance* of what we do—or the results expected, and (2) the *urgency*—or whether the action requires immediate attention or not.

Exhibit 3–11 shows how our activities can be classified on this matrix. Quadrant I shows activities that are both "important" and "urgent." Activities that are important but lack urgency are shown in quadrant II. Urgent but unimportant activities fall into quadrant III. Finally, quadrant IV contains activities that are neither important nor urgent.

While this matrix is helpful in managing our time, we need to see how the supervisor can use it in a practical manner. The following discussion should be useful to busy supervisors who want to improve their time management skills.

Exhibit 3–11

The Time Management Matrix

	Urgent	Not Urgent
Important	**I** ACTIVITIES: Crises Pressing problems Dealine-driven projects	**II** ACTIVITIES: Prevention, PC activities Relationship building Recognizing new opportunities Planning, recreation
Not Important	**III** ACTIVITIES: Interruptions, some calls Some mail, some reports Some meetings Proximate, pressing matters Popular activities	**IV** ACTIVITIES: Trivia, busy work Some mail Some phone calls Time wasters Pleasant activities

The Time Log: Where Your Time Goes

Time management experts say that the first step in making effective use of your time is to determine how your time is actually being spent. Conscientiously filling in a time log like the one shown in Exhibit 3–12 is an excellent way to get this information.

Exhibit 3–12

Daily Time Log

DAILY TIME LOG

Name _____ *Hoi Mon Sol* _____

Date _____ *March 1, 200–* _____

On this log record each activity that you performed during the workday. Make sure that you include every activity performed such as telephone calls, conversations, rest breaks, reading, and so on. Do this for a period of time long enough to reflect normal "workdays." A week should normally be sufficient.

From – To	Minutes	Type of Activity	People Involved	Priority A	B	C
8:00 – 8:05	5	Talked in hall	Dan, Patsy			
8:05 – 8:15	10	Read status report on work progress				
8:15 – 8:20	5	Checked progress on slow job	Ronald			
8:20 – 8:30	10	Prepared for supt. meeting				
8:30 – 9:30	60	Attended supt. meeting	Dept. heads & Supt.			
9:30 – 9:45	15	Coffee	Al, Peter, Karen			
9:45 – 9:50	5	Tried to return two phone calls -- no luck				
9:50 – 10:02	12	Completed questionnaire from Personnel Dept				
10:02 – 10:06	4	Went for mail				
10:06 – 10:20	14	Opened & read mail				
10:20 – 10:23	3	Called Purchasing Dept to check status of order	Kawahara			
10:23 – 10:50	27	Discussion with Supt. about objectives for Dept.	McWilliams			
10:50 – 11:00	10	Visited Personnel office to check status of applicants	Alice			
11:00 – 11:55	55	Met with United Way Committee	too many!			
11:55 – 12:10	15	Began work on dept. budget proposal				
12:10 – 12:50	40	Lunch	Dan, Patsy, Al			
—						
—						

Setting Priorities: A "Must"

Once you know where your time is going, you can analyze whether it is going in the proper direction. Not everyone can do all that he or she wants to do. The secret, then, is to spend time on those activities that are most important and urgent and that contribute most significantly to your doing a top-notch job.

click! http://www.fambiz
.com/

Hoi Mon Sol, whose time log is shown in Exhibit 3–12, said that he could not find enough time to do everything he wanted to do because he was so busy. Yet, when he got home, he looked back at his day and called his activities "wheel spinning." He didn't feel good about what he had accomplished. Sol, like many supervisors, typically spent his day handling many low-priority activities rather than the high-priority ones!

To use a time log most effectively, one must establish a rating system for classifying the priority of activities to be performed in a given day, such as the following:

1. A activities are the most important—they are critical to your job.
2. B activities are of medium priority—important, but less so than A's.
3. C activities are of low priority—routine and/or relatively unimportant.

The more efficient supervisor will spend a greater percentage of his or her time performing A activities.

Many of the "brush fires" to which supervisors devote a large percentage of their time are B or perhaps even C priority items. In the next section, we hope to help you learn to spend more of your time on your A's!

self-check

Examine the list of activities shown in Exhibit 3–12. Identify an A activity and a C activity. On what types of activities did Sol spend most of his time?

Handling the Common Time Wasters

Many activities that you carry out during a typical day are time wasters— inefficient uses of your time (see Exhibit 3–13). These may include doing rou-

---

Exhibit 3–13

Eight Common Supervisory Time Wasters

- Distractions and interruptions
- Failure to set priorities
- Procrastination
- Doing routine work that subordinates could handle
- Indecision
- Personal disorganization
- Failure to delegate
- Excessive or unnecessary paperwork

tine work that someone else could handle, excessive socializing, or fighting a losing battle against paperwork.

⑧ Discuss some ways to effectively manage time.

Supervisory jobs vary a great deal in terms of the demands on the supervisor's time. That's why maintaining a time log is an important first step in diagnosing your time management habits. Exhibit 3–14 is a broad list of "do's," which may help you to use your time more effectively.

Exhibit 3–14

How to Use Your Time More Effectively

1. *Set priorities.*
   a. Establish A, B, and C priorities.
   b. Determine daily priorities.
   c. Focus effort on high-priority items.

2. *Do not procrastinate.*
   a. Break big jobs into smaller parts.
   b. Get started, even if on a minor part of a job.
   c. Do the more unpleasant parts of a job first.
   d. Reward yourself for doing things on schedule.

3. *Manage the telephone effectively.*
   a. Have someone else take your calls and handle them if possible.
   b. Handle all return calls at set times of the day.

4. *Make your meetings effective.*
   a. Prepare and announce an agenda before the meeting.
   b. Begin meetings on time.
   c. Stick to the topics on the agenda.
   d. Make decisions or come to conclusions.

5. *Learn to delegate.*
   a. Delegate details that are time consuming.
   b. Delegate jobs that will help employees to develop.
   c. Delegate jobs that employees can perform better than you.

6. *Handle people who drop in.*
   a. Close your door for periods of time.
   b. Stand up and remain standing until the visitor leaves.
   c. Meet long-winded persons at their work area, so that you can leave when you are ready.
   d. Train your boss and work group to respect your time.

7. *Be decisive.*
   a. Set a personal deadline for making a decision.
   b. Once you have the facts, make the decision.

8. *Get organized.*
   a. Use a daily time planner.
   b. Implement a filing system.
   c. See 1b above.

9. *Stay on top of paperwork.*
   a. Handle papers only once!
   b. Handwrite short notes directly on original documents and forward them to the persons concerned.
   c. Have someone classify papers according to importance and route them for you.

10. *Avoid distractions and interruptions.*
    a. Keep a neat desk; work and papers piled on a desk are distracting.
    b. Try to set aside uninterrupted blocks of time.
    c. Face your desk away from the view of others.

chapter review

(1) Explain the steps involved in planning.

Planning is deciding what will be done in the future. The three planning steps are (1) setting an objective or goal, (2) identifying and assessing present and future conditions affecting the goal, and (3) developing a systematic approach to achieve the goal. Properly done, planning helps managers accomplish the four other management functions of organizing, leading, staffing, and controlling. Of these functions, planning is most closely linked to controlling. In fact, they are sometimes called the "Siamese twins" of management.

Because it is a difficult and time-consuming process, many supervisors tend to neglect planning. Instead of planning, they scurry about solving one problem, then another, seemingly too busy to plan anything. Effective planning anticipates many problems so that they are more easily handled when they occur. Contingency planning is thinking about anticipated problems in advance, and having potential solutions available.

(2) Explain how planning differs at top, middle, and supervisory management levels.

Planning differs for top-, middle-, and first-level management. Top managers spend a greater proportion of their time developing strategic long-term and intermediate-range plans of one to five or more years. Strategic plans include the organization's mission, objectives, and strategies and interfacing with its external environment. Middle-level and supervisory managers perform operational planning—intermediate-range and short-range plans of one year to one day—that operationalize strategic plans.

(3) Explain how the hierarchy of objectives works.

Objectives are crucial to effective planning. Once established, objectives provide a stimulus for individual effort. The objectives set at one management level reflect the objectives of the next higher operational level. This network of objectives is called a hierarchy of objectives. Objectives permit unified planning and coordination at lower management levels.

(4) Discuss important guidelines in setting objectives.

Among the guidelines for setting objectives are (1) setting them in only selected, key performance areas; (2) making them specific; (3) making them challenging rather than easy; (4) balancing them properly, as may be the case with volume and quality; (5) stating them in measurable terms; (6) involving employees in setting them; and (7) following up on results.

(5) Identify the steps in management by objectives.

Management by objectives (MBO), also commonly known as management by results and joint target setting, is a system whereby managers and employees jointly establish objectives and develop a systematic approach for achieving results. MBO typically involves five steps: (1) the supervisor and each employee discuss the supervisor's responsibilities and objectives; (2) the supervisor and the employee discuss the employee's job; (3) the supervisor and the employee jointly set specific, measurable objectives for a given performance period; (4) the supervisor and the employee meet periodically to review the employee's progress; and (5) the supervisor and the employee meet at the end of the period to review performance. The supervisor and the employee can then begin a new cycle.

(6) **Differentiate the various kinds of standing and single-use plans.**

After objectives have been established, plans can be developed throughout the organization. Standing, or repeat-use, plans direct action that deals with recurring situations. They include policies, rules, and procedures. A policy is a guide to individual decision making. Policies allow some flexibility, whereas rules are final and definite as to what action must be taken. A procedure outlines the steps that should be taken to complete a given action, such as applying for vacation leave or processing a grievance. Single-use plans are one-time plans that are discarded on completion. Examples of these are programs, projects, budgets, and schedules.

(7) **Draw a simple PERT chart.**

Two important types of schedules are Gantt charts and PERT charts, each of which provides a visual display of activities to be performed and the time frames involved.

(8) **Discuss some ways to effectively manage time.**

One of a supervisor's greatest resources is time. But activities performed by supervisors vary in importance and urgency. The effective supervisor will concentrate on the more important and most urgent activities. Maintaining a time log is a necessary first step toward becoming a more efficient time manager. Such a log enables a supervisor to see exactly where his or her time is being spent. More effective supervisors spend a greater proportion of their time on A priorities—activities that are ranked number one in terms of importance to the effective performance of their jobs. The following time-saving tips can help you to make better use of your time: (1) Set priorities, (2) do not procrastinate, (3) manage the telephone effectively, (4) make meetings effective, (5) delegate to others, (6) handle people who drop in, (7) be decisive, (8) get organized, (9) stay on top of paperwork, and (10) avoid distractions and interruptions.

---

important terms

budget *85*
contingency planning *72*
critical path *87*
Gantt chart *85*
hierarchy of objectives *75*
management by objectives (MBO) *78*
mission *73*
objectives *73*
operational planning *74*
policy *82*
procedure *84*
program *85*

Program Evaluation and Review
    Technique (PERT) *86*
project *85*
rule *83*
schedule *85*
"Siamese twins" of management *70*
single-use plans *85*
standing plans or repeat-use plans *80*
strategic planning *72*
strategies *74*
time management *87*
unified planning *77*

---

questions for review and discussion

1. What are the three steps in planning? Why do supervisors tend to slight the planning function?

2. How does planning differ among top, intermediate, and supervisory management levels?
3. What are some guidelines for setting objectives?
4. What is meant by a hierarchy of objectives? Explain.
5. What is MBO, and what are its steps?
6. What is the difference between a policy, a rule, and a procedure?
7. What is a Gantt chart? How does it differ from a PERT chart?
8. What actions can a manager take to effectively manage time?
9. What is contingency planning? Explain.
10. Distinguish between objectives and strategies.

● skill builder 3-1

Testing Your Planning Skills
group activity

Harold Marshall, general manager at Computronix's Dixon Division, has just named you as chairperson of the first annual blood drive, to be conducted at the plant site. A strong believer in the company's participation in community affairs and himself a member of the local Red Cross board of directors, Marshall has committed the division's 500 employees to the blood drive. Your committee will set the exact dates for the drive, which is to be held in three or four months.

As chairperson, you have been assigned a team of four other company employees to plan and implement the project. All members are highly respected, competent people, representing a true cross-section of the employees: One is a production worker who is president of the local union; another, an engineer, represents the professional segment; the human resources manager represents the management group; and a payroll clerk represents the administrative office group.

Marshall was given your name by your boss, who expressed confidence in your ability to lead a successful donor campaign at the plant. At 27, you are the youngest person on the committee and anxious to do a good job. You have called the first committee meeting, which you have advertised as a "preliminary planning meeting," to identify key factors that must be planned for in order

for the committee to meet its objective: having a successful blood drive at Computronix.

Instructions:

1. Make a list of what you consider the key planning issues to be identified by the committee at this initial planning meeting.
2. Of the items on your list, which two or three do you believe are the most crucial? Why?
3. Identify major problems that could prevent accomplishment of your objective. What contingency planning could be done to avert them or minimize their impact?
4. To help in your preparation for the planning meeting, identify 6 to 10 steps that you feel will be needed to achieve a successful blood drive. These steps might be such things as:
   a. Determine a date.
   b. Identify a location.
   c. Secure commitment from Red Cross, etc.
   Draw a PERT chart that shows the sequence and relationship of the activities identified. (You need not be concerned with the length of time needed for each activity.)
5. Compare your responses to questions 1, 2, 3, and 4 with those of other students. To what extent do they agree with you?

●skill builder 3–2

Determining Priorities
group activity

Assume that you are a high school principal. Organizationally, 12 teachers, 5 coaches, your assistant, and an assistant principal report to you. The assistant principal supervises another 8 teachers, 4 clerical workers, a custodian, a librarian, a counselor, and the cafeteria dietitian.

Listed below are a number of activities you performed during the past week.

a. Prepared a 15-minute speech to deliver to your school's PTA.
b. Met a sales representative from a local computer company to discuss possible purchase of computer equipment.
c. Filled in as a substitute teacher for an 11th-grade math teacher, who left school ill at lunchtime.
d. Met with the student homecoming committee to acquaint them with the guidelines for homecoming activities.
e. Prepared your list of yearly objectives and budget requests that must be submitted to the city superintendent's office.
f. Met with a group of four parents to discuss their complaints about unreasonably high demands by one of your teachers.

g. Listened to councilwoman Judith Johnson, who spoke to a civics class on "Your City Government."
h. Toured the school halls during changes in class periods.
i. Interviewed two final candidates for a woman's basketball and volleyball coaching position.
j. Discussed next week's homecoming game against a crosstown rival with the football coach.

Instructions:

1. Indicate how you would classify these in priority: MI (most important), RI (relatively important), or RU (relatively unimportant). Be prepared to defend your choices.
2. What additional information about the principal's activities may have helped you establish your priority listings? How would this information have helped?
3. Meet with groups of three to five other students to compare your choices of priorities. Discuss these and be prepared to report your results to the class.

Setting Performance Objectives

Jane Persons supervises the word processing center at Computronix, which consists of seven word processors. Work done by this section consists of word processing various reports and correspondence as required by other departments and handling all photocopying for the plant. Persons had just attended a meeting with the other section heads and heard Edna Strong, the administration department head, talk briefly about the new planning system in store for the Dixon Division. As Strong heard it from Marshall, the plant manager and all department heads and supervisors would be required to identify five key performance areas in their departments. These were supposed to be areas that

had a significant impact on performance.

It was the meeting with Strong
that puzzled Persons. Strong had
asked her to come up with the five
key performance objectives for her
word processing section. Persons
said: "I can understand how our sales
group or production groups can have
specific objectives. But I can't see
how our section can have anything
like that. What am I supposed to
come up with? Something like 'We
will process 9,500 pages in the next
year' or 'At least 99.5 percent of our
pages will be error-free'? This whole
unit planning system seems like a lot
of 'wheel spinning' to me. My people
know their objectives without this
planning stuff. Their objective is to
do a good job at getting the required

word processing done for these other
departments as quickly as possible."
Answer the following questions:

1. Do you agree with Jane Persons'
   view that the new planning system is "wheel spinning"? Why or
   why not?
2. Are there some key performance
   areas that Persons could identify
   for her action? What are they?
3. To what extent does Persons' last
   sentence meet the criteria discussed in the text under "Guidelines for Setting Performance Objectives"?
4. Can you develop one or more
   statements of objective for Persons' department that will be consistent with the "specific" criteria
   as required in MBO?

Decision Making and Problem Solving

- ● **outline**

Role of Decision Making in Supervisory Management
Decision Making: The Heart of Supervisory Management
Why Supervisors Need to Make So Many Decisions

What Is Decision Making?
Decision Making Defined
Elements Involved in Decision Making
Types of Decisions to Be Made
How Decision Making and Problem Solving Relate

How to Make Decisions
Step 1: Define the Idea or Problem
Step 2: Develop Alternatives
Step 3: Collect, Interpret, and Evaluate Information About Each Alternative
Step 4: Select the Preferred Alternative
Step 5: Implement the Decision
Step 6: Follow Up, Evaluate, and Make Changes—If Needed

Factors to Keep in Mind When Making Decisions
The Right Person Should Make the Decision
Decisions Should Contribute to Objectives
There's Seldom Only One Acceptable Choice
Both Feeling and Thinking Should Be Used
Effective Decision Making Takes Considerable Time and Effort
Decision Making Improves with Practice
A Decision May Not Please Everyone
A Decision Starts a Chain Reaction
Ethical Considerations Play a Part

Individual and Group Decision Making
Approaches to Decision Making
Advantages and Disadvantages of Each Approach

Improving Decision Making
Bases of Decision Making
Some Guides to Less Stressful Decision Making

There are few things as useless—if not as dangerous—as the right answer to the wrong question.

Peter F. Drucker

All the analyst really requires for the solution to a problem is: first, the painstaking assembly of all the phenomena; second, exhaustive patience; and third, the ability to comprehend the whole problem with a fresh and unbiased imagination.

Ellery Queen

The Advancing Landscape Architect

learning objectives

After reading and studying this chapter, you should be able to:

1. Explain the role of decision making in the supervisor's job.

2. Discuss why supervisors need to make so many decisions.

3. Define decision making and identify at least four elements involved.

4. Discuss how decisions are made.

5. Name some factors to keep in mind when making decisions.

6. Explain the role of ethics in the supervisor's decision making.

7. Decide whether to use the individual approach or the group approach when making decisions.

8. Discuss some ways of improving decision making.

Bobby Jones was hired as a landscape architect for Lane Corporation five years ago. His responsibilities include supervising a crew of 23 groundskeepers who are responsible for maintaining the corporate grounds. Because the work requires physical stamina and is performed mostly outdoors, the majority of the groundskeepers are men, although there are four women employed.

Brenda Lewis was hired by Jones six months ago. During her initial interview with Jones, she was told that she would be expected to perform the same duties as the male groundskeepers. However, once she was employed, she was assigned to work with a second female worker in the greenhouse. The two other female groundskeepers were assigned to caring for the indoor plants in the corporate offices. Brenda's duties consisted mainly of transplanting seedlings and watering plants. When she indicated to Jones that she would like to be given the opportunity to work outdoors with the rest of the crew, she was told that she was needed to work in the greenhouse because it was more suited for females and that she could not be expected to work like a man, mowing lawns and planting shrubs.

Jones frequently came by the greenhouse to see how the two female employees were doing. Although Lewis had been employed for six months and Maria Taylor had been there a year, Jones never called them by name. He always addressed them as "Babe" or "Honey." As he was giving them instructions, he had a habit of putting his arm around their shoulder or running his fingers through their hair. He always made a point to tell them his latest joke—usually one with sexual overtones.

On several occasions Jones insisted that Lewis help him deliver new plants to the grounds crew for planting. On these trips she rode with him in a golf cart. When the cart hit a bump or made a turn, Jones would put his hand on Lewis's leg to steady her. When she protested, he insisted he was just concerned for her safety.

In addition, Jones gave Lewis a book dealing with insecticides and told her that she would need to learn the information in order to work safely with the various chemicals stored near the greenhouse. He suggested that perhaps they should study the book together at her apartment after work.

At this point Lewis went to Jones's supervisor and filed a complaint of sexual harassment against Jones. She stated that she had never welcomed any of his "advances." When he put his arm around her shoulder, she pulled away. She did not laugh at his jokes, and she objected to his putting his hand on her leg. She also rejected his offer to study with him after work. She stated that she was afraid to tell him how she really felt because he was her supervisor, and she feared he would fire her.

SOURCE: Prepared by James D. Powell, Professor of Management, University of North Texas, Denton, Texas, and adapted from Leon C. Megginson, Geralyn M. Franklin, and M. Jane Byrd, *Human Resource Management* (Houston, TX: Dame Publications, Inc., 1995), p. 605.

Bobby Jones's supervisor is certainly in a difficult position! This chapter deals with his task—decision making and problem solving. As the chapter preview shows, supervisors must make effective, but often difficult, decisions if they are to be successful.

Chapter 3 covered the fundamentals of planning. Throughout this discussion, the need for decision making was implied. We now look at that subject in detail. Decisions must be made about people, about processes, and about priorities, to name just a few issues! Keep the supervisor's problem in mind, because we will return to his situation throughout the chapter.

1 Explain the role of decision making in the supervisor's job.

ROLE OF DECISION MAKING IN SUPERVISORY MANAGEMENT

Managers must make decisions whenever they perform any of the five management functions—planning, organizing, staffing, leading, and controlling—discussed in Chapter 1. Without decision making, the entire management system would cease to exist. For example, in planning, the supervisor must decide which objectives to seek, which policies to establish, and what rules and regulations to institute. In organizing, choices must be made as to who gets what authority and how duties and responsibilities are grouped. The function of leading entails deciding how best to communicate with and motivate employees. In staffing, decisions must be made concerning employee selection, placement, training and development, performance appraisal, compensation, and health and safety. In controlling, if actual performance does not conform to planned performance, decisions must be made about how best to bring them together.

The decisions that managers make often must be made quickly—and frequently with little information, or even conflicting information. Then, those decisions must be carried out in order to achieve the department's objectives!

Decision Making: The Heart of Supervisory Management

Decision making is central to the supervisor's job. Supervisors must continually decide what is to be done, who is to do it, and how, when, and where it is to be done (see Exhibit 4–1). As we will show throughout the chapter, although these decisions may be discussed separately, they are interrelated. One decision is affected by, and builds on, previous ones. For example, what your department produces determines what types of production facilities are needed. Decisions about production, in turn, influence the types of employees needed and the training and compensation they should receive. All of these decisions affect the amount of money budgeted for the department.

2 Discuss why supervisors need to make so many decisions.

Why Supervisors Need to Make So Many Decisions

Supervisory managers—even more than managers at other levels—are involved in directing employees' behavior toward achieving the organization's goals, as well as those of the employees themselves. Supervisors must make more decisions more frequently—and often more quickly—than other managers, since they're operating on a production-oriented, day-by-day, person-to-person basis. These decisions involve a variety of activities, as the following example illustrates.

Exhibit 4–1

Decision Making Is the Heart of Supervisory Management

Wilma Malone, nursing supervisor at Alquippa Medical Center, had been at work for only three hours, but she had already made seven major decisions.

1. She signed up to attend a one-day course on time management, to be offered the following week.
2. She assigned performance ratings to five of her new nurses on their performance appraisal forms.
3. She approved vacation requests for two nurses in her department.
4. She referred to the floor physician a patient's request to be taken off a prescribed medication.
5. She resolved a dispute between one of the nurses and a floor orderly.
6. She selected Jane Moore to serve as her replacement when she took her vacation in three weeks.
7. She requisitioned supplies needed by her department.

In many technical fields and in factories, just one layer of management separates the shop floor worker from the boss.

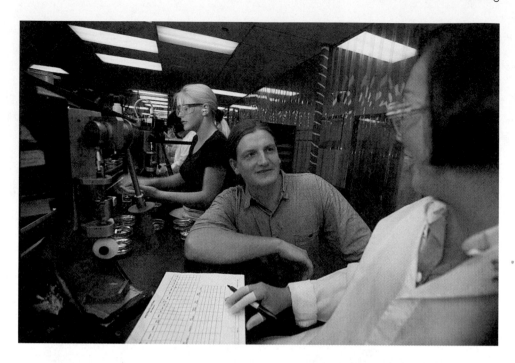

In addition, she made a handful of other minor decisions. The young trainee assigned to Malone said, "Are you always this busy, or is it just because it's Monday morning?" Malone replied, "It's all a normal part of a supervisor's job."

Employees look to their first-line supervisors for more direction, assistance, guidance, and protection than do subordinates of managers at higher levels. Also, in general, supervisors spend more time socializing with others in the organization since they have more employees than other managers. All of these activities require decision making.

As you saw in Exhibit 1–3, the lower the level of management, the greater the **span of management,** which is the number of immediate employees a manager can supervise effectively. Therefore, supervisors make decisions that affect not only their own behavior, but also that of many other people.

span of management
The number of immediate employees a manager can supervise effectively.

self-check

What was Jones's span of management in the chapter preview? Do you think that span was too great, just right, or too little for this type of business? Explain.

③ Define decision making and identify at least four elements involved.

WHAT IS DECISION MAKING?

Let us now define decision making, discuss its characteristics, look at some selected types of decisions, and consider some differences between decision making and problem solving.

Decision Making Defined

Have you known people who couldn't ever make up their minds? They might say, "I really don't know what to do. If I do this, such and such will happen. If I do that, then something else might happen." They just can't make decisions. The word *decide* comes from a Latin word meaning "to cut off." When you make a decision, you first consider a matter causing you some uncertainty, debate, or dispute and then make a choice or judgment that more or less results in a definite conclusion. You cut off further deliberation on the matter. Thus, **decision making** is the conscious consideration and selection of a course of action from among two or more available alternatives in order to produce a desired result.

decision making
Considering and selecting a course of action from among alternatives.

Elements Involved in Decision Making

There are several facts you should know about decision making. The most important ones are that (1) a decision may not be needed, (2) decisions involve the future, (3) the process is a conscious one, and (4) there must be more than one alternative solution.

A Decision May Not Be Needed. A wise decision maker begins by asking "Is a decision needed?" It may seem strange to include this question in a discussion of decision making, but it's important. In many supervisory situations, no decision is needed, and decision making would be in vain. If a given event is inevitable or if higher management is going to act in a certain way regardless of the supervisor's wishes, then making a decision is a waste of time. Some things cannot be changed regardless of the supervisor's wishes or actions.

> **"You really have guts, Will," said Carol Sheffield to Will Hauser, office supervisor for Gridtronics, Inc. "You didn't waste a lot of time with competing bids or even looking at what different word processors can do. Don't you feel uncomfortable getting the vice-president to approve the purchase of a $10,000 piece of equipment? What if he wants some evidence that you really shopped around?"**
>
> **"Well," said Hauser, "that's a good question, I suppose. But there's more to the story. Getting competing bids and spending a lot of time evaluating different systems would have been a waste of my time. A 'decision' really wasn't needed. The guy I bought that piece of equipment from is the vice-president's son!"**

Decisions Involve the Future. Surely you have heard others say "If only I had done this, then that wouldn't have happened." They assume that if they had made a different decision, it would have resulted in a happy marriage, a rapid promotion, or a killing in the stock market. It is said that hindsight is 20/20, but the supervisor's world is no place for Monday-morning quarterbacking. Rather, it's a place to prepare for today or tomorrow. Because a supervisor's decision making is oriented toward the future, it always contains an element of uncertainty.

Decision Making Is a Conscious Process. Decision making involves a conscious process of selection. No decisions are needed about breathing or digestion, because these are unconscious, reflexive actions. In making a decision, the individual consciously (1) becomes aware of a want that needs to be satisfied, (2) seeks relevant behavioral alternatives, and (3) evaluates them as a basis of choice, as shown in Exhibit 4–2.

Decision Making Involves More Than One Alternative. As indicated earlier, for a true decision to be made, there must be two or more available alternatives to choose from, including the possibility of doing nothing. Frequently, there are only two choices, as in a "yes or no" or "to do or not to do" situation. The decision to do nothing is sometimes the worst decision.

Most decision situations involve several alternatives with varying expected outcomes. You may not be aware of some of the alternatives and may not have decision authority over others. For other alternatives, you must estimate expected outcomes. You then evaluate each outcome in terms of its desirability. Sometimes there are no desirable alternatives. In such cases you have to decide between two undesirable ones.

self-check

What are the possible alternatives that Jones's supervisor can choose from in the situation described in the chapter preview?

Types of Decisions to Be Made

Although there are many ways of classifying decisions, we will discuss only one at this point—namely, categorizing decisions as either programmed or unprogrammed.

Exhibit 4–2

The Decision-Making Process

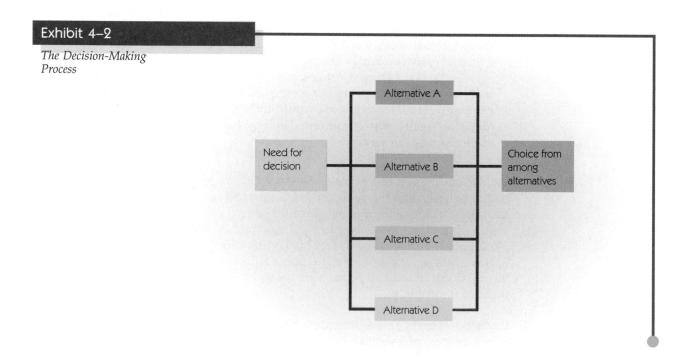

programmed decisions
Routine and repetitive decisions.

Programmed decisions are those that are routine and repetitive. Since such decisions tend to be similar and must be made frequently, supervisors usually establish a systematic way of handling them. Here are some examples of this type of decision:

1. How to handle an employee who reports to work late or is absent without permission
2. How to schedule work, shifts, vacations, and other time variations
3. How to determine which employees need training and what type of training should be given to them
4. How frequently to do maintenance servicing of machinery and equipment

The effective supervisor handles these decisions in a systematic way and may even set up a decision framework, including guidelines such as policies, procedures, or rules (see Chapter 3) to be followed.

unprogrammed decisions
Decisions that occur infrequently and require a separate response each time.

Unprogrammed decisions are those that occur infrequently. Because different variables are involved, requiring a separate and different response each time, it is difficult to establish a systematic way of dealing with such decisions. Some examples of unprogrammed supervisory decisions include the following:

1. Whether to buy an important piece of machinery or equipment, especially an expensive, complex piece
2. How to react to a union representative who says that a grievance will be filed if you give a written reprimand to a certain worker for a work-related violation of safety rules
3. How to handle a severe accident or explosion
4. Whom to promote to a supervisory position

How Decision Making and Problem Solving Relate

In one of his educational films, Joe Batten, a well-known management consultant, has a manager say "We have no problems here, just opportunities. Each problem should be considered an opportunity." Although we don't necessarily agree with that conclusion, it does give us a chance to show how decision making and problem solving are related. An **opportunity** is a set of circumstances that provides a chance to improve a situation or help reach a goal. A **problem** is an existing unsatisfactory situation causing anxiety or distress, which must be addressed.

opportunity
A chance for development or advancement.

problem
An existing unsatisfactory situation causing anxiety or distress.

Effective supervisors must be able to identify problems—and their cause(s)—to analyze complex and involved situations, and to solve problems by removing their cause(s). But placing too much emphasis on problems can prevent one from identifying opportunities. After all, solving a problem only eliminates or neutralizes a negative situation. Progress or advancement comes from seeking and identifying opportunities; recognizing the emotions, needs, and motivations of the people involved; and analyzing ways of satisfying them. Here are some examples of "opportunity" decision making at the supervisory level:

1. Replacing a piece of equipment that, while it is still functioning well, can be upgraded to increase efficiency.
2. Improving an already effective preventive maintenance system.

3. Cross-training employees to broaden their skills and raise morale.

4. Creating a new position for a highly skilled technician who has recently left the employ of a competitor.

5. Instituting the most innovative new processes and techniques.

self-check

> What other examples of "opportunity" decision making can you think of?

(4) Discuss how decisions are made.

HOW TO MAKE DECISIONS

Exhibit 4–3 shows that the decision-making process involves six basic steps. We have already mentioned most of them.

click! http://www.stanford.edu/group/decisions/

Step 1: Define the Idea or Problem

As Peter Drucker stated in the opening quotation, a decision is only as good as the correct definition of the problem. In other words, the right cure for the wrong problem is just as bad as the wrong cure for the right problem. But it is not always easy to know what the problem is or which opportunity is the best one to seek. When you have a fever, it is only a symptom of the true problem—an infection or other disorder. Likewise, as a supervisor, you should remember that low morale, high turnover, many complaints or grievances, waste, and declining sales are not the real problem. They are only symptoms of the real problem.

If the decision to be made involves solving a problem, its cause, or the factors that are creating it, must be determined. Without identifying the cause (or causes), it is difficult to solve the problem, for you may be treating its symptom rather than the root cause(s).

Exhibit 4–3

Steps in Decision Making

| **Step 1** Define idea or problem to be acted on. | **Step 2** Develop possible alternative solutions. | **Step 3** Collect, interpret, and evaluate relevant information about the alternatives. | **Step 4** Select the preferred alternative. | **Step 5** Implement the decision. | **Step 6** Follow up, evaluate, and make changes, if needed. |

Provide feedback.

self-check

What do you see as the real problem facing Jones's supervisor in the chapter preview? What was/were the cause(s) of the problem?

Step 2: Develop Alternatives

alternatives
Possible courses of action that can satisfy a need or solve a problem.

The second step is to develop alternative ways of solving the problem or taking advantage of the opportunity. **Alternatives** are possible courses of action that can satisfy a need or solve a problem. Several choices are usually available if you are able to identify and develop them. It is easier to choose from a few alternatives than from many, so reduce the number to as few as is feasible. Also, be aware that, if choices are limited, they may include only undesirable ones.

This is the stage where you decide whether you should make the choice or channel it to the person who has the authority or expertise to make it. If you decide that it is your "call," one choice is to do nothing, hoping that the problem will go away or solve itself in time. You must be careful, though, that this doesn't become an excuse for not making a difficult choice. If it does, you may get a reputation for being indecisive—the "kiss of death" to many promising supervisory careers.

Step 3: Collect, Interpret, and Evaluate Information About Each Alternative

Usually there are many sources from which to gather information affecting a decision. Sometimes standing orders, policies, procedures, rules, and regulations provide relevant information. In fact, these documents may have already made the decision for you—or at least may indicate how you should decide. Other sources of information include your own experience, company records and reports, discussion with the people directly and indirectly involved, and personal observations.

self-check

In the chapter preview, where do you think Jones's supervisor can get the information he needs to make his decision? What additional information beyond that given would be helpful to him in reaching the best decision?

Perhaps you've heard the saying "Tell me what you want to prove, and I'll get you the data to prove it." The effective evaluation of alternatives involves looking *objectively* at the pros and cons of each one. Choices can be evaluated in many ways. The information can be written down on a type of balance sheet, as shown in Exhibit 4–4, with the reasons for each alternative on one side and the reasons against it on the other. Or a process of elimination can be used in which the undesirable (or less desirable) choices are dropped.

Step 4: Select the Preferred Alternative

Finally, you reach the point where you must make a choice. You look at your conclusions from step 3 and then logically and rationally pick the alternative

The design stage is instrumental in selecting the prepared alternatives.

Exhibit 4–4

Evaluating Alternatives

you think is most desirable for all concerned from an objective, ethical, and practical point of view. Selecting the preferred alternative involves cost/benefit analysis and risk analysis.

cost/benefit analysis
Estimating and comparing the costs and benefits of alternatives.

Using the technique of **cost/benefit analysis,** you estimate what each alternative will cost in terms of human, physical, and financial resources. Then you estimate the expected benefits. Finally, you compare the two estimates. You choose the one with the greatest payoff, where the ratio of benefits to cost is most favorable.

risk
The possibility of defeat, disadvantage, injury, or loss.

Analysis of risk is inherent in decision making. **Risk** is the possibility of defeat, disadvantage, injury, or loss. Prudent decision makers try to minimize risk by effectively forecasting outcomes and considering all variables.

self-check

From the information you are given in the chapter preview, what decision should Jones's supervisor make? Why?

Step 5: Implement the Decision

Effective decision making doesn't stop when you choose from among alternatives. The decision must be put into operation. For example, you might need to obtain and allocate some equipment and supplies. Or you might need to develop methods and procedures. Or you might have to select, train, or even terminate some employees. This is a difficult part of decision making, because you must face and deal with people who may not like your choice. Many good supervisory decisions are ineffective because of the way they're implemented.

 click! http://www.kraftfoods.com

Step 6: Follow Up, Evaluate, and Make Changes—If Needed

This last step in the decision-making process involves exercising management's control function. It determines whether the implementation of the decision is proceeding smoothly and achieving the desired results. If not, and the decision can be changed or modified, it should be. If it can't be changed, then you "live with it" and try to make it succeed.

 click! http://www.pillsbury.com/

5 Name some factors to keep in mind when making decisions.

FACTORS TO KEEP IN MIND WHEN MAKING DECISIONS

It is relatively easy to describe the general steps in decision making, but actually making decisions is much more difficult because of several factors. The number and variety of such factors is extensive; we'll discuss only the more important ones.

The Right Person Should Make the Decision

Although there is no hard-and-fast rule as to who should make a given decision, in general, decisions are best made by the person in authority closest to the point of action. The key consideration is that the decision maker have adequate knowledge of the conditions and people involved as well as the authority needed to implement the decision.

Decisions Should Contribute to Objectives

Relating each decision to the organization's objectives facilitates decision making and helps the organization carry out its mission. It also helps in getting decisions accepted and carried out. If a given decision doesn't help achieve objectives, it should be questioned. For example, suppose the manager of an agricultural cooperative decides to buy fertilizer from a company owned by him, his wife, and his son. Although the manager and his family will make a nice profit on their operations, the farmers who buy the fertilizer will pay higher prices. You would expect the farmers to question this decision.

There's Seldom Only One Acceptable Choice

Most organizational problems can be solved, or resolved, in more than one way. The best choice depends on what factors you consider important, what weight you give to each, and what you do about them. Even when the outcome of a decision turns out to be not as expected, people tend to try to make it come out "right." For example, if a supervisor hires a computer programmer over the objections of the human resource manager, the supervisor will do everything possible to see that the new employee succeeds, regardless of any weaknesses the employee exhibits.

Both Feeling and Thinking Should Be Used

Supervisory decisions affect people. Such decisions may involve who is assigned which jobs, who receives overtime, how a new process will affect personnel, and so on. Supervisors must certainly be sensitive and understanding regarding the effects of their decisions on individuals. They must also, however, be willing to make decisions that affect people negatively.

Two basic ways in which people make decisions are through feeling and thinking processes. Supervisors who are primarily feeling oriented tend to use a **feeling decision process,** giving greater weight to the human issues—the "people" side of a decision. They essentially view many problems or inefficiencies as being explainable in human terms. They tend to focus on personal, human issues in decisions and give considerable weight to the effects their decisions will have on others.

Thinking-oriented supervisors, on the other hand, use a **thinking decision process,** focusing problem solving on analysis, logic, rationalization, and objectivity. Although the human factor may be relevant, it is not the dominant factor in the thinking decision process unless analysis and logic show it to be.

feeling decision process
Giving great weight to the "people" side of a decision.

thinking decision process
Focuses predominantly on analysis, logic, and objectivity to solve problems.

self-check

Which process should Jones's supervisor use in solving the chapter preview problem? Explain.

There is, of course, no one best approach; therefore, a balance of the two is needed. Supervisors who are overly feeling oriented may be considered too compassionate, too compromising, and wimpy. When carried to extremes, their sensitivity may cause them to fail to address issues or to make decisions that can have a negative effect on others (in disciplinary situations, for example). On the other hand, supervisors who are excessively thinking oriented may be considered too cold, too inflexible, too unsympathetic, and impersonal. Their failure to fully consider the human element may severely limit the effectiveness of their decisions. To be effective, supervisors must reflect a certain balance of dimensions in their decision making. The exercise in Exhibit 4–5 will give you some insight into your own style.

Effective Decision Making Takes Considerable Time and Effort

There is no such thing as a button-pushing, finger-snapping supervisor who spits out decisions with machine-gun rapidity. It takes quality time and effort—mental and often physical—to make effective decisions. Unfortunately, many choices are made simply on the basis of fatigue. After spending many hours evaluating various alternatives, the exhausted supervisor will subconsciously think "I'll choose the next one, regardless of what it is, just to get it over with." Or, to save time, a supervisor will say "That's not a bad choice. I can live with it if you can." Such decisions rarely turn out to be successful.

Decision Making Improves with Practice

People can't be taught to make effective decisions. They must learn by actually going through the process and living with the consequences. Like any learned skill, decision making improves the more you exercise it, assuming that you use it effectively.

Exhibit 4–5

Are You a Thinking-or Feeling-Oriented Decision Maker?

Instructions: Circle the response that seems to best describe you. Remember, there are no "correct" answers. If two answers are an absolute toss-up, leave that question unanswered and move on.

1. Are you more careful about (a) people's rights or (b) how people feel?
2. Are you more likely to be impressed by (a) principles and standards or (b) emotions and feelings?
3. In making decisions, which is more important to you: (a) objectivity or (b) how people will feel?
4. Do people who know you see you as basically (a) strong willed or (b) warm hearted?
5. If another person says something that is incorrect, would you normally (a) point out the error or (b) ignore it?
6. Are you best described as making decisions based on (a) logical, step-by-step analysis or (b) how your decisions make you and others feel?
7. Which do you feel is the greater mistake: (a) being too merciful or (b) being too firm?
8. Are you best described as (a) a rational person or (b) a caring person?
9. Assuming that you could perform equally well, would you feel more comfortable with the role of (a) judge or (b) counselor?
10. Which describes you better: (a) firm or (b) sympathetic?

Scoring: Count the number of "a" and "b" answers you gave. Your "a" answers tend to represent a thinking orientation; your "b" answers a feeling orientation. If there is a strong imbalance, you may need to be especially conscious of the overlooked dimension in your decision making.

A Decision May Not Please Everyone

Seldom does a decision please everyone concerned. The challenge facing the supervisor after the decision is made is to explain the decision and to win the individual's or group's cooperation.

> **An office manager was authorized to phase out 12 old computers over a period of a year, replacing three every four months. She assigned the first three new ones to the most efficient employees, only to hear complaints from those with the most seniority. She told them that, if their performance improved, they would get the next new ones.**

A Decision Starts a Chain Reaction

Since all parts of an organization are interrelated, don't be surprised when a decision made in another department affects yours, or vice versa. A decision maker should be prepared to defend, change, or drop a decision in view of the chain of events it starts.

> **Julie Acree was perplexed. She had recently made a decision to allow Maria Montano, one of her top technicians, to attend a two-day seminar on some of the new developments in her field. The superintendent had agreed and approved payment of the $150 tab for tuition. Now, Acree had just come from the superintendent's office, where she'd been told that supervisors in a number of other departments had also recommended their people for seminars. The decision to pay Montano's way was temporarily on hold until a policy could be worked out. "I can't afford to suddenly have 20 people attend seminars at the same time," the superintendent said.**

Ethical Considerations Play a Part

6 Explain the role of ethics in the supervisor's decision making.

Supervisors must be particularly concerned with ethical considerations when making decisions and solving problems. They should have a true concern for the well-being of others, both inside and outside the organization. Therefore, supervisors should not only obey all laws and conform to the ethical code(s) of practice established by their employer and society, but they should have a personal set of ethical principles that guides their actions. The difficult question, however, is: What is and what isn't ethical?

ethics
Standards used to judge "rightness" or "wrongness" of one person's behavior toward others.

Ethics are the standards used to judge the "rightness" or "wrongness" of one person's behavior toward others. As this concept of ethical behavior is the individual's personal *ethic*, it is the highest and most rigid level of behavior. The next highest level is adhering to professional and organizational *codes of ethics*, which are statements of what is and isn't acceptable behavior. The lowest level is the *legal level*, where we are all expected to adhere to the "law of the land."

In essence, ethical behavior requires considerations of *fairness*—that is, fair treatment of people with regard to hiring, job placement, grievances, benefits, terminations, and other employment activities. For an organization or supervisor to be fair, priorities must be balanced; that is, as much concern must be given to people and their problems as is given to economic and financial considerations. For example, there is often a conflict between job demands and personal considerations.

click! http://www.us.kpmg
.com/ethics/dilema
.html

Consider the dilemma of a supervisor in a software development company. An independent programmer has presented him with an exciting new software concept that would save his employer a considerable sum. It would also be an excellent new product for his wife's fledgling software development firm—if he doesn't refer the idea to his boss.[1]

In essence, to "be fair" means to balance your self-interest with the interests of others who are concerned with the problem. Thus, ethical supervisors know how and when to put aside selfish, personal needs and act favorably toward others.

self-check

> In the chapter preview, what ethical factors must Jones's supervisor consider?

While there are many guides to ethical behavior—most religions have them—there are two that we think deserve your attention. The first is Rotary International's "Four-Way Test." It requires that four simple questions be asked when considering an action.

1. Is it the truth?
2. Is it fair to all concerned?
3. Will it build goodwill and better friendships?
4. Will it be beneficial to all concerned?[2]

Kenneth Blanchard and Norman Vincent Peale have proposed a framework for managers to use as a guideline when facing an ethical dilemma in making a decision or solving a problem. Exhibit 4–6 summarizes their "ethics check."

Exhibit 4–6

*Blanchard and Peale's
"Ethics Check"*

To guide you in decision making when you face an ethical dilemma, ask yourself these three questions:

Ethics Check	Consider
1. Is it legal?	Will I be violating either civil law or company policy?
2. Is it balanced?	Is it fair to all concerned in the short term as well as in the long term?
	Does it promote win–win relationships?
3. How will it make me feel about myself?	Would I feel good if my decision were published in the newspaper?
	Would I feel good if my family knew about my decision?

SOURCE: *Kenneth Blanchard and Norman Vincent Peale,* The Power of Ethical Management. *Copyright © 1988 by Blanchard Family Partnership and Norman Vincent Peale.*

7 Decide whether to use the individual approach or the group approach when making decisions.

INDIVIDUAL AND GROUP DECISION MAKING

As a supervisor, should you make decisions by yourself, or should you involve your work group in decisions? In this section, we provide some ideas to help you answer this question.

Approaches to Decision Making

Exhibit 4–7 shows that there are three basic decision-making approaches. With Approach A, the individual supervisor runs the show. A supervisor using this approach would define the problem, determine and evaluate alternatives, and choose the most appropriate alternative. With the opposite approach (Approach C), the work group calls the shots. That is, the group defines the problem, develops and evaluates alternatives, and makes the decision as they think best. If you use Approach B, you get your group's help in defining the problem and in identifying and evaluating the alternatives. Perhaps you even ask them for a recommendation. But as supervisor you make the final decision.

Advantages and Disadvantages of Each Approach

Exhibit 4–8 shows the advantages and disadvantages of involving your work group in decisions. A major advantage is that, ideally, decisions will be improved. An old adage says that "two heads are better than one." The involvement of your employees in the decision-making process can also result in better

---

Exhibit 4–7

Role of Supervisor and Work Group in Decision Making

Influence of supervisor in decision-making process

Influence of group in decision-making process

Approach A
Supervisor defined problem, develops and evaluates alternatives, and makes decision.

Approach B
Supervisor solicits *group* input and advice about the problem, alternatives, and possibly even the recommended decision.
Supervisor makes the decision.

Approach C
Supervisor allows *group* to define the problem, develop and evaluate alternatives, and make the decision.

Exhibit 4–8 *Advantages and Disadvantages of Group Decision Making*	**Advantages** • Provides the supervisor with a broader range of information on the problem, alternatives, and recommended solution. • Lends a more creative approach to solving problems, since ideas may be "piggybacked." • Improves communication in the department because the work group becomes aware of issues facing the supervisor. • Creates higher morale in the work group. • Stresses a stronger commitment to the decision once it is made, since the work group helped to make it.	**Disadvantages** • Holds the supervisor accountable for the group's decisions. • Takes the work group's time away from other aspects of their jobs. • May force the supervisor to choose sides and thus cause morale problems. • Allows strong personalities to dominate the work group, in which case the decision may not reflect the entire group's opinion. • Requires more supervisory skill in communicating and clarifying the group's role in a given decision. • Is difficult to use if the decision must be made quickly.

communication, improved morale, and a stronger group commitment to the decision once it is made. Also, encouraging the free exchange of information by involving your staff in decision making is one way of overcoming employee apathy.

> **For example, Keith Dunn started his own restaurant because of the poor treatment he'd received from his former employers. After he had tried and failed at using such motivational gimmicks as benefits and contests, he started including his employees in decisions affecting the business. After they became a vital part of running the business, the annual turnover rate dropped from 250 percent, which was normal for the industry, to only 60 percent.[3]**

The major disadvantages, though, may outweigh the advantages in certain circumstances. The time the process takes, the personalities in the work unit, and the fact that as a supervisor you're still accountable for group decisions must all be considered. In some situations, group decision making may be a case of too many cooks spoiling the broth! You don't have to lock yourself into just one of the approaches mentioned earlier, however. As one supervisor at a large HMO put it:

> **My decision approach depends on the situation. Sometimes things are pretty routine, and I make the decision myself. At other times, I get input from just one or two people, or I might even hold a meeting to get the views of the entire group. Just recently, I pretty much let them make the decision about which of three new pieces of equipment we needed most. I said, "Whatever you guys decide on, I'll put it at the top of my list." I went with the majority vote, which was to rank a certain microcomputer Number One.**

self-check

Which of the three approaches mentioned in this section would you recommend to Jones's supervisor? Why?

Discuss some ways of improving decision making.

IMPROVING DECISION MAKING

To improve decision making, a supervisor should understand the basis on which decisions are made and the techniques used to make them. The *basis* of a decision is the frame of reference in which it is made. The *technique* is the method used in the decision process.

Bases of Decision Making

Some of the most frequent bases of decision making are authority of position, experience, facts, intuition, and a "follow-the-leader" attitude. From a practical point of view, there is no one best basis. Supervisors should use the bases that best suit the circumstances.

Authority of Position. The authority vested in the decision maker's position is probably the most frequently used basis. Decisions made on this basis tend to conform to the organization's strategies, policies, and procedures. For example, supervisory authority is the basis for decisions about job priorities, enforcement of company rules, and whom and when to discipline. Decisions made on the basis of authority of position also tend to provide continuity and permanence (since they are generally official), to be readily accepted, and to be considered authentic and legitimate. Yet these decisions may also reflect an unpopular company position, may be too routine, and may be made without due regard to the situation.

Experience. We see and understand things in terms of concepts and ideas with which we are familiar. Experience provides us with meaningful guides for selecting alternatives. It gives us practical knowledge of what has been done in the past and of the outcomes of those decisions. It also provides "tried and true" knowledge that tends to be accepted by those who have shared the experience. Yet a decision maker's experience may be limited or unique, and the choice made may be based on outmoded or obsolete experience.

Facts. Most discussions of decision making state that a decision should be based on "all the pertinent facts." If that ideal can be reached, well and good, for it gives the impression that the resulting choice is logical, sound, and proper. The pertinent facts may not be readily available, however, and if one waits to get them, no decision can be made. Also, getting the facts may be too costly or too time consuming. Furthermore, "facts" may be misleading—or even wrong—and may be merely someone's opinion or belief. Thus, although a supervisor must use the facts available, these facts must be carefully classified, diagnosed, and interpreted to reveal their inadequacies and flaws.

Recognizing that quick access to information is essential to decision making, many companies provide their supervisors and managers with

computer terminals. These people can now study cause-and-effect relationships among parts failure, process schedules, and reworking of production. As a result, they make consistently better decisions.

Intuition. Decisions may be unconsciously based on a person's cultural background, education, and training, as well as knowledge of the situation. This basis is called **intuition.** Conclusions reached on this basis may conflict with those resulting from other methods, as shown in Exhibit 4–9. According to Charles Sweet, president of A. T. Kearney Executive Search of Chicago, "Young execs in fast-changing high-tech companies, especially, rely on intuition, not planning, to make decisions.[4]

Choices based on intuition may be quite satisfactory, because they're based on the decision maker's total background. Also, these choices involve the person's emotions as well as mind, and a decision can be reached quickly. Finally, intuition often seems to work.

For example, Jack Chamberlin of General Electric decided to "go by gut" and select the cassette tape over eight-track cartridges in the early days of their development. His hunch proved correct. Charles Revlon, the founder of Revlon, has an uncanny knack for determining what customers want. And Albert Einstein attributed his theory of relativity to a "flash of insight."[5]

But intuition may not lead to optimal choices or solutions, and if your intuition is wrong, the decision will probably be wrong. Also, relying on intuition

intuition
Unconscious influence of a person's cultural background, education, and training, as well as knowledge of the situation.

Exhibit 4–9

Intuition or Facts

may lead you to minimize the use of other bases. Finally, it is practically impossible to defend an intuitive decision to your colleagues, higher management, or others. The primary concern is that you and others should know when the decision is based on intuition rather than factual analysis.

"Follow-the-Leader" Attitude. Some decisions are based on doing what others are doing. This approach is sometimes called the herd instinct and is based on the assumption that other people know more about the subject than you do. If you use this method, you'll be in the majority, but you may suffer if the "leader" is wrong.

Some Guides to Less Stressful Decision Making

In addition to the concepts discussed in this chapter, the following practical suggestions should help supervisors make better decisions with less stress:

1. *Try to avoid having to make crisis decisions.* With careful and adequate planning, fewer decisions will need to be made on a crisis basis. You usually have more time than you realize to make a sound decision. A few minutes of careful thinking can have a significant impact on the quality of a decision.

2. *Use established policies, procedures, rules, and regulations when applicable.* Most decisions on work situations are programmed decisions or are similar to those that have been made before, and guidelines exist for supervisors to follow. Use them and reserve your energy—and emotions—for the unusual problems.

3. *Give a decision the attention it warrants—and no more.* Small decisions don't require an elaborate decision-making process. Perhaps you can even delegate some of these. On the other hand, a major decision (such as the ones Jones's supervisor must make) can have a significant impact on the functioning of your unit—and on your career. In other words, don't get involved in counting the paper clips in the office or the toothpicks in the cafeteria.

4. *Seek help, if needed, from specialists and other managers.* Recognize (and accept) that some decisions are beyond your competence or knowledge. If you are faced with a complex problem, such as a question of environmental control, health and safety, or affirmative action, call in the experts.

5. *Don't dwell on your decisions, once made.* Few of us make the right decision all the time. Although you should follow up on the outcome of a decision, don't wallow in nonproductive worry about whether it was a good or bad one. Instead, follow the example of effective leaders: Do the best you can and then "leave it in the lap of the gods."

self-check

Which of these suggestions do you think apply to Jones's supervisor?

chapter review

1 **Explain the role of decision making in the supervisor's job.**

Decision making is the heart of management in that it is involved in performing all the managerial functions. To be successful, supervisors must make effective, but often difficult, decisions. And these decisions must be carried out in order to achieve the organization's objectives.

(2) Discuss why supervisors need to make so many decisions.

Supervisors must make more decisions, more frequently, and—often more quickly—than other managers, since they operate on a day-to-day and person-to-person basis and make decisions involving a great variety of activities.

(3) Define decision making and identify at least four elements involved.

Decision making is the conscious consideration and selection of a course of action from among available alternatives to produce a desired result. It involves at least four elements: (1) a decision may not be needed, (2) decision making involves the future, (3) it is a conscious process, and (4) more than one alternative is available. Decisions are termed *programmed* if they are routine and repetitive and hence can be made using an established, systematic process. They are *unprogrammed* if they occur infrequently and must be made without the benefit of an established system.

(4) Discuss how decisions are made.

Decision making allows one to take advantage of an opportunity for progress, development, or advancement. Problem solving focuses on removing a source of anxiety or distress. Decision making involves (1) defining the problem, (2) developing possible alternative solutions, (3) collecting, interpreting, and evaluating information about the alternative, (4) selecting the preferred alternative, (5) implementing the decision, and (6) following up, evaluating results, and making changes—if needed.

(5) Name some factors to keep in mind when making decisions.

Some of the factors to keep in mind when making decisions are that (1) the right person should make the decision, (2) decisions should contribute to objectives, (3) there's seldom only one acceptable choice, (4) both feeling and thinking should be used, (5) effective decision making takes considerable time and effort, (6) decision making improves with practice, (7) a decision may not please everyone, and (8) a decision starts a chain reaction.

(6) Explain the role of ethics in the supervisor's decision making.

The more effective supervisors use ethical value judgments in making decisions—especially those involving employees. Ethics are the standards used to judge the "rightness" or "wrongness" of one person's behavior toward another. Ethical supervisors know how and when to be ethical, by giving as much consideration to people and their problems as to economic and financial considerations.

(7) Decide whether to use the individual approach or the group approach when making decisions.

There are three basic decision-making approaches: (1) The individual supervisor runs the show, making all the decisions; (2) the work group calls the shots; and (3) the supervisor gets the group's help in defining the problem, evaluating the alternatives, and suggesting solutions, but the supervisor makes the actual decision. Group decision making improves communication and morale, broadens options, and increases commitment. However, the individual approach is quicker, provides for better accountability, and improves supervisory skills.

⑧ Discuss some ways of improving decision making.

Decisions are made on several bases. The most popular bases are (1) authority of position, (2) experience, (3) facts, (4) intuition, and (5) a "follow-the-leader" attitude. Effective decisions result from combining these bases so that both facts and feelings are considered. Some practical guides to less stressful decision making are (1) try to avoid having to make crisis decisions; (2) use established policies, procedures, rules, and regulations when applicable; (3) give the decision only the attention it warrants; (4) seek help, if needed, from specialists and other managers; and (5) don't dwell on decisions after they are made.

---

important terms

alternatives *107*
cost/benefit analysis *109*
decision making *103*
ethics *112*
feeling decision process *110*
intuition *117*
opportunity *105*

problem *105*
programmed decisions *105*
risk *109*
span of management *102*
thinking decision process *110*
unprogrammed decisions *105*

---

questions for review and discussion

1. What is meant by the statement "Decision making is central to the supervisor's job"?
2. How is decision making involved in performing the five management functions? Explain.
3. Define decision making, and explain the elements involved.
4. Define programmed and unprogrammed decisions, and give examples of each.
5. Is there really a distinction between decision making and problem solving? Explain.
6. Name and give a short explanation of each of the six steps in the decision-making process.
7. What is the role of ethical considerations in decision making? Explain.
8. What are the advantages and disadvantages of group decision making? With which approach do you personally feel more comfortable? Why and under what circumstances?
9. Evaluate the role of intuition in decision making.
10. Evaluate the "follow-the-leader" attitude toward decision making.

● skill builder 4–1

Whom Do You Promote?
group activity

Your company recently developed a plan to identify and train top hourly employees for promotion to first-line supervision. As a part of this program, your boss has requested a ranking of the six hourly workers who report to you with respect to their promotion potential. Given their biographical data, rank them in the order in which you would select them for promotion to first-line supervisor; that is, the person ranked Number One would be first in line for promotion.

Biographical Data

1. *Sam Nelson*—Caucasian male, age 45, married, with four children. Sam has been with the company for five years, and his performance evaluations have been average to above average. He is well liked by the other employees in the department. He devotes his spare time to farming and plans to farm after retirement.

2. *Ruth Hornsby*—Caucasian female, age 32, married, with no children; her husband has a management-level job with the power company. Ruth has been with the company for two years and has received above-average performance evaluations. She is very quiet and keeps to herself at work. She says she is working to save for a down payment on a new house.

3. *Joe Washington*—African-American male, age 26, single. Joe has been with the company for three years and has received high performance evaluations. He is always willing to take on new assignments and to work overtime. He is attending college in the evenings and someday wants to start his own business. He is well liked by the other employees in the department.

4. *Ronald Smith*—Caucasian male, age 35, recently divorced, with one child, age 4. Ronald has received excellent performance evaluations during his two years with the company. He seems to like his present job but has

removed himself from the line of progression. He seems to have personality conflicts with some of the employees.

5. *Betty Norris*—African-American female, age 44, married, with one grown child. Betty has been with the company for 10 years and is well liked by fellow employees. Her performance evaluations have been average to below average, and her advancement has been limited by a lack of formal education. She has participated in a number of technical training programs conducted by the company.

6. *Roy Davis*—Caucasian male, age 36, married, with two teenage children. Roy has been with the company for 10 years and received excellent performance evaluations until last year. His most recent evaluation was average. He is friendly and well liked by his fellow employees. One of his children has had a serious illness for over a year, resulting in a number of large medical expenses. Roy is working a second job on weekends to help with these expenses. He has expressed a serious interest in promotion to first-line supervisor.

Answer the following questions:

1. What factors did you consider in developing your rankings?
2. What was the most important factor you considered?
3. What information in the biographical data, if any, should not be considered in developing the rankings?

SOURCE: *This exercise was prepared for this book by Carl C. Moore, University of South Alabama.*

Personal Problems

An office manager was hired by a group of physicians in a small town in Kansas to head the employees at their private clinic. The office manager supervised a receptionist, two nurses, a lab technician, and a typist.

The receptionist was married and had three children. She was a long-term employee who was quite capable in her work and seemed to get along with everyone, including the patients. However, she began to receive many phone calls during work hours. Word got around that it was her husband who was calling her so often; everyone knew that he was an alcoholic. At times he kept her on the phone at great length, and she would ask the other employees to answer the other lines.

It eventually got to the point where the receptionist could not make appointments for patients or handle the incoming calls as she should. One day, when the receptionist had gone home early to handle a family problem, the office manager asked the other five employees to stay after work for a little while to discuss the problem.

Instructions:

Get together with four classmates and discuss what you would suggest to the office manager at the meeting.

CASE 4–1

Able or Baker?

Ken Parker was sent to Operating Department B of Petrochem Corporation to replace Dave Mann, who was retiring after 15 years as supervisor of the department.* Ken, 38 years old, with a B.S. in chemical engineering, had been with Petrochem 12 years and had been a supervisor for 4 years. On the basis of his excellent record, he was asked to see if he could improve the performance in Department B, which had about 15 operators.

Until about 3 years before, the company had been gradually reducing its workforce through attrition, as improvements in facilities decreased the number of workers needed. Consequently, no one had been involuntarily terminated in the past 20 years. Three years earlier, Petrochem had started hiring again and had hired people with much higher qualifications than those required of the older employees. Consequently, a third of Department B's employees were younger and better qualified than the rest.

Three months after Parker became supervisor, he received a call from the plant manager telling him that, because of a severe recession, all departments were being asked to terminate at least one person. The choice of who was to go was left up to each supervisor, but the terminations were to be permanent.

The two most likely candidates for discharge in Department B were Mr. Able and Mr. Baker. Able, 53 years old, with 25 years of service, was a high school graduate. His performance ratings for the past 11 years had varied from "poor" to "fair." His wife was an invalid; an only son was overseas with the U.S. Army; his divorced daughter and her young child, with no income of their own, lived with him. Baker, age 25 and unmarried, had 3 years of service and a B.S. in engineering. His performance ratings had consistently been "very good" to "excellent."

Parker knew that morale would suffer if he terminated Able. Yet, if he kept him and let Baker go, it would appear that good performance was considered of little value to the company. There was no union at Petrochem. The person whom Parker terminated would be released two weeks after notification and would receive only one week's severance pay for each year of service.

Answer the following questions:

1. If you were Ken Parker, which employee would you decide to terminate?
2. How would you go about telling the person you chose to terminate?
3. What would you tell the person you decided to retain?

---

*The name of the large energy company has been changed. These true events occurred before passage of the Age Discrimination in Employment Act, so Ken Parker was free to make whatever decision he chose.

Organizing

5   Fundamentals of Organizing

6   Delegating Authority

3 part

Fundamentals of Organizing

outline

The Four Stages in Growth of an Organization
Stage 1: The One-Person Organization
Stage 2: The Organization with Assistants Added
Stage 3: The Line Organization
Stage 4: The Line-and-Staff Organization

Departmentalization
Functional Departmentalization
Product Departmentalization
Matrix Departmentalization

Two Important Organizing Principles
Unity of Command
Span of Control

Relationships Between Line and Staff
Conflicts Between Line and Staff
How to Avoid Excessive Line-Staff Conflict:
Delineating Authority

Decentralization Versus Centralization
Factors Affecting Decentralization
Effect of Decentralization on Organizational
Structure

Downsizing
Benefits of Downsizing
Costs of Downsizing
Impact on Remaining Supervisors and Managers
Ways to Get Beyond Downsizing

**Management Philosophy, Strategy, and
Organization**
The Horizontal Organization
The Inverted Pyramid
The Wagon Wheel

*The only things that evolve by themselves in an organization are
disorder, friction, and malperformance.*

Peter Drucker

John Moody's Growing Organization

Our story begins in 1970 in a small Midwestern city of 75,000. Our main character is John Moody, 29, a high-school graduate and Vietnam veteran, who has been working in a large paper mill on the outskirts of the city since his discharge from the service in 1965. John still holds the same semiskilled job at the operative level that he started with. His wife's relatives believe he is a lazy person with a low IQ who will never amount to much. Actually, John is quite an intelligent person, but his basic satisfaction in life comes from the challenge of building and creating things in his garage workshop. Although he assumes that he will never get rich, he feels his take-home pay is sufficient to take care of the necessities of life and to support his hobbies. Even though his job at the mill is not very challenging, he gets all the challenge he needs from tinkering around in his workshop.

Unfortunately, in early 1980 the country begins to slide into an economic recession, which has an adverse effect on the paper industry. Several mill employees, including John, are laid off because of excessive inventory buildup. John signs up for unemployment compensation and decides to spend time building a new boat trailer in his garage. He puts a lot of thought and effort into the task. The result is an excellent trailer—such a fine one that several of his friends talk him into building trailers for them for 20 percent more than his expenses. Even at this price, his boat trailer sells for less than those sold in local stores. Before long, so many requests are coming in that John finds himself spending all his time in his garage.

At this point, John decides to work full time building boat trailers as long as he can make a living doing so.

In Chapter 1, we defined the term *organizing* and noted that it is one of the five functions of any manager or supervisor. In this chapter, we present concepts, principles, and a frame of reference for understanding this function. We do so by expanding on the John Moody preview case throughout the chapter to illustrate the stages of growth in most organizations and the principles of organizing.

Many first-level managers understand organization only from a narrow vantage point—their immediate department or perhaps one or two levels above them. We believe that it is equally important to be able to see and understand the organization from a much broader standpoint. The more completely supervisors understand the big picture, the better equipped they are to work effectively as key members of the management team. Consequently, organizing is presented from a broad, overall perspective in this chapter. In Chapter 6, we will focus on organizing concepts that are directly applicable to the supervisory management level.

Failure to understand the organizing function from a broader viewpoint can lead to the following problems:

1. Excessive violation of the unity of command principle

2. Failure to develop additional departments or work groups when needed

3. Unclear and improper assignment of duties and responsibilities to new employees

4. Ineffective use of organizational units and inadequate development of human resources because of improper decentralization of authority

5. Excessive and unhealthy conflicts between departments and between line supervisors and staff personnel

1 Understand the stages of organization growth.

THE FOUR STAGES IN GROWTH OF AN ORGANIZATION

To see the organizing function of management in operation, let us study the growth and development of John Moody's hypothetical manufacturing business. Usually a business organization grows in four stages. Stage 1 is the one-person organization; stage 2 is the organization with assistants added; stage 3 is the line organization; and stage 4 is the line-and-staff organization. Not all organizations go through all of these stages. Many skip the first stage and go directly to stage 2. For clarity's sake, however, we'll discuss each stage.

Stage 1: The One-Person Organization

From our reading of the preview case, we see that John Moody's business is in the first stage of organizational growth—that is, a one-person operation (Exhibit 5–1). This means that he alone performs the three basic activities common to all manufacturing operations: financing, producing, and selling.

Stage 2: The Organization with Assistants Added

After three months, so many orders are coming in that John Moody cannot fill them. In the past few years, the federal government has built a number of dams near John's town, creating four new lakes in the region. Fishing has been good, and there is a large demand for boats and

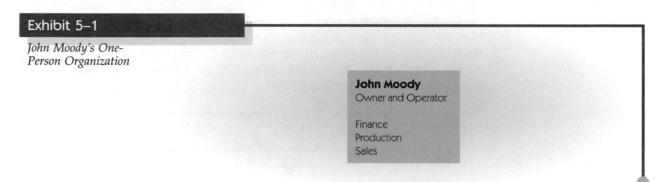

Exhibit 5–1

John Moody's One-Person Organization

John Moody
Owner and Operator

Finance
Production
Sales

boat trailers. John is now making more money per day than he did when he was with the mill. To keep pace with the orders, he hires Ray Martin, a former army buddy, to help build the trailers. For a small monthly salary, John also hires his wife, Nancy, to keep books and handle the financial details. Before the month is out, Ray has mastered his job so well that he and John are producing more boat trailers than they have orders for.

At this point, John and Ray start thinking about hiring someone as a salesperson. Ray's brother, Paul, has just graduated from college with a major in marketing. After hearing about John's business from John and Ray, Paul decides that it has possibilities. With the assurance of an opportunity to buy into the business in the future, Paul starts to work for John as a salesperson.

Exhibit 5–2 shows that John Moody has had to hire three assistants to help carry out the three primary activities of his business. This stage is a critical one; over 50 percent of new businesses fail in their first year of operation from lack of capital, ineffective management, or both.

Paul Martin proves to be an excellent salesperson, and the business continues to grow. To keep up with the increasing volume of orders, John hires additional people. Also, the business moves to a larger building.

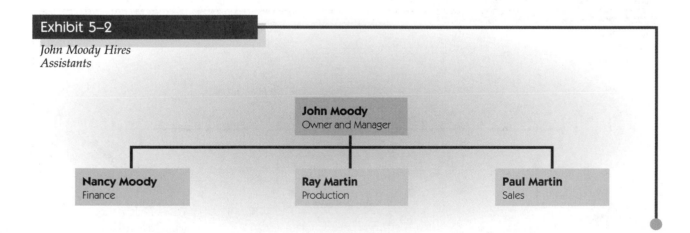

Exhibit 5–2

John Moody Hires Assistants

John Moody
Owner and Manager

Nancy Moody
Finance

Ray Martin
Production

Paul Martin
Sales

As Exhibit 5–3 shows, after two years John has 19 people working for him. His net income is such that Nancy has quit working, but John finds himself so busy that he cannot enjoy his higher income. More important, he feels that he is losing control of the business; the increased costs per trailer support this belief.

self-check

Before reading further, look at the organization chart in Exhibit 5–3. Can you explain why John Moody is losing control of his business?

In desperation, John Moody asks the Martin brothers for advice about his problem. Paul Martin recalls that in one of his college courses, the instructor talked about the management principle of *span of control*. This principle holds that there is a limit to the number of people a manager can supervise effectively. In Paul's opinion, the solution is to select managers for the areas of finance, production, and sales.

Paul's solution seems so simple that John Moody wonders why he didn't think of it himself. He places Beth Fields—his best accountant—in charge of finance, Ray Martin in charge of production, and Paul Martin in charge of sales.

Stage 3: The Line Organization

Exhibit 5–4 shows that John Moody has selected a manager for each of the three major departments, and his span of control has been reduced from 19 to 3 employees. Beth Fields is responsible for 3 employees, Ray Martin for 9 employees, and Paul Martin for 4 employees. In effect, John Moody's business is now structured as a **line organization.** This means that each person in the organization has clearly defined responsibilities and reports to an immediate supervisor.

There are two advantages to having a line organization at an early stage of a business organization's growth:

line organization
A line organization is concerned with the primary functions of the firm. In this case production, sales, and finance.

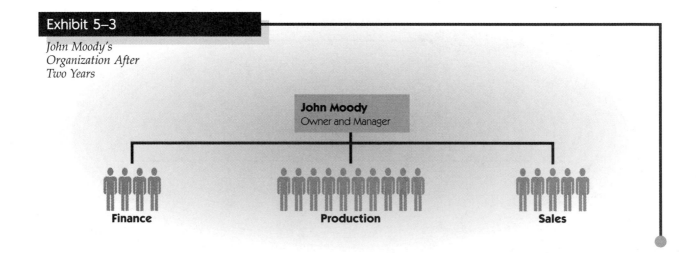

Exhibit 5–3

John Moody's Organization After Two Years

John Moody
Owner and Manager

Finance   Production   Sales

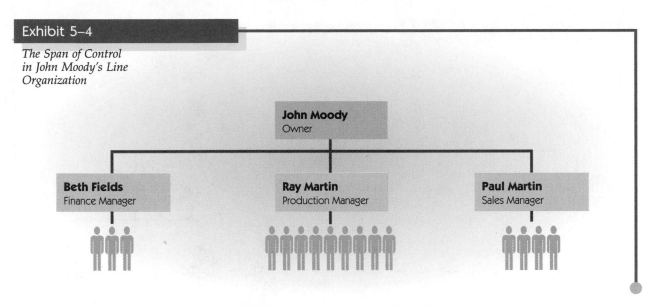

Exhibit 5–4

The Span of Control in John Moody's Line Organization

1. Quick, decisive action on problems is possible because authority is centralized—it is in the hands of John Moody and his three managers.
2. Lines of responsibility and authority are clearly defined. Everyone knows what his or her job and obligations are. Thus, evasion of responsibility is minimized and accountability is maximized.

As a result of the line organization and the capabilities of each manager, the unit cost of making each boat trailer is lowered. Under the leadership of sales manager Paul Martin, the business expands its sales territory to cover most of the states in the Midwest. As sales increase, production also increases. New people are added in both sales and production. The line organization develops to accommodate the increased growth. Keeping in mind the principle of span of control, John Moody adds new sections in production and sales whenever the volume of business justifies the new additions. He now also finds time to concentrate more on such tasks as developing plans for the future, coordinating the work of the three departments, and supervising his managers.

After 10 years, John Moody's business is employing over 700 people. During this period, John has promoted Ray Martin to be in charge of 5 production department heads. Exhibit 5–5 shows that this move has created an additional level of management in the production department. The department heads, in turn, are each responsible for 4 production supervisors. Each production supervisor is responsible for 10 production workers. Similarly, John has made Paul Martin sales manager in charge of 3 regional sales managers, each of whom is supervising 8 salespersons.

Stage 4: The Line-and-Staff Organization

Unfortunately, increasing sales require John Moody's business to add more people in order to meet production quotas. So the profit on each

*John Moody's Line
Organization After
Ten Years*

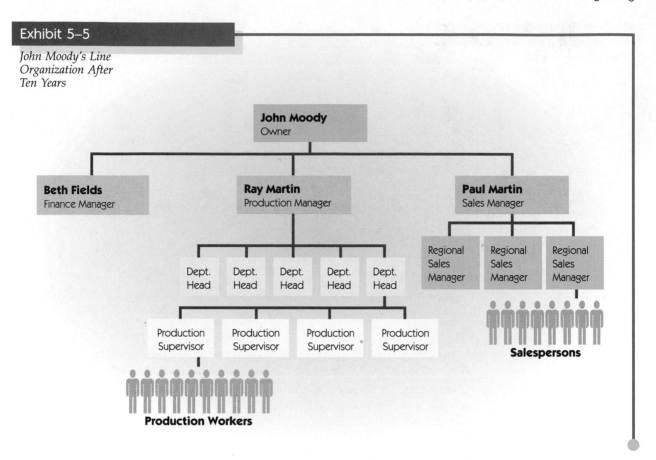

unit produced declines. Finally, Beth Fields, the head of finance, reports to John that each $1.00 in sales is costing $1.10. In other words, a boat trailer that the business sells for $300 is costing $330 to manufacture. Although the business is now financially sound, John is aware that, with the way things are going, it will not take long for the business to go bankrupt. He therefore decides to call in a reputable management consultant.

self-check

Before reading the consultant's recommendations, decide what you think is the primary problem or problems causing manufacturing costs to increase in John Moody's business.

line-and-staff organization
An organization structure in which staff positions are added to serve the basic line departments and help them accomplish the organization objectives more effectively.

The management consultant interviews managers from different levels in the company. After several days of investigation, the consultant makes the following report to John Moody:

My investigation reveals that you have made a mistake that many companies make: You are operating purely as a line organization, whereas at your stage of growth, you need to adopt a line-and-staff organization. This means that you need to hire several staff experts to perform some

of the activities your line managers presently do. As it now stands, your organizational structure tends to overload your managers. They are, in effect, wearing too many hats. More specifically, I have found evidence of the following three kinds of inefficiency:

1. Your supervisors are doing their own hiring, firing, and disciplining. Consequently, you have no uniform way of screening, selecting, promoting, and disciplining employees. Moreover, a number of the supervisors are hiring friends and relatives for their departments, and other employees believe that favoritism is rampant throughout the company.

2. The several department heads independently purchase materials and supplies for their departments. This duplication of effort has caused excessive space and dollars to be tied up in raw materials inventory. In addition, this practice has opened the door for waste and pilferage of supplies and materials.

3. Your department heads and supervisors are involved in method and layout studies, maintenance and repair work, scheduling and dispatching, and, to cap it off, quality control—all on top of their primary jobs of supervising the work and motivating their employees. The old proverb that "a jack of all trades is master of none" is certainly borne out by the situation I find in your plant.

My primary recommendation, therefore, is that you hire a human resources specialist to screen and select new employees, a production control manager to do all the purchasing and inventory control, and an industrial engineering manager to do method and layout studies and the like. [Their relationship to the organization is shown in Exhibit 5–6.] By adding these three staff specialists, you will give your department heads and supervisors a chance to concentrate on their primary job of overseeing production and motivating their employees. Equally important, you should receive immediate benefits and cost savings by eliminating inefficiencies and installing improved ways of operating.

self-check

What adjustments will the supervisors need to make to accommodate the consultant's recommended changes? Do you think these changes will help or hinder the supervisor in the job of motivating and managing his or her crew?

The consultant went on to report that, in the future, additional staff people would be needed if the company's rate of growth continued. He also stated that the company might want to consider diversifying by adding additional product lines that would require similar skills.

John Moody accepted the consultant's recommendations, and his line-and-staff organization went on to achieve not only record sales, but also record profits and growth. Ultimately, any growing business needs to pass into this fourth stage. Unfortunately, many do not, and some suffer the consequences of decline and bankruptcy.

Exhibit 5–6

John Moody's Line-and-Staff Organization

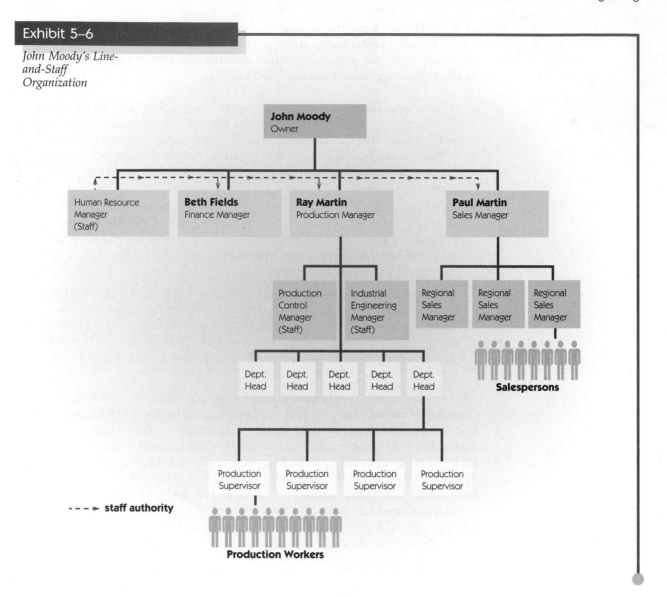

- - - ► **staff authority**

DEPARTMENTALIZATION

departmentalization
The organizational process of determining how activities are to be grouped.

The process of determining how activities are to be grouped is called **departmentalization.** There are many ways that these activities may be organized. For example, types of departmentalization include organizing by function, product, service, process, territory, customer, and matrix. Note that most organizations use a combination of these forms; that is, most organizations will use more than one of these approaches in their groupings. However, usually organizations use a functional approach at the top and other approaches at lower levels. Because three of these forms are more complex and are used extensively, we provide elaboration for functional, product, and matrix departmentalization.

2 Identify the advantages and disadvantages of the functional, product, and matrix departmentalization approaches.

Retail stores can run the gamut of departmentalization. One store may sell clothes of all kinds while another may specialize in sporting clothes.

Functional Departmentalization

functional departmentalization
A form of departmentalization that groups together common functions or similar activities to form an organizational unit.

Functional departmentalization groups common functions or similar activities to form an organizational unit. Thus, all individuals performing similar functions are grouped, such as all sales personnel, all accounting personnel, all nurses, all computer programmers, and so on. Exhibit 5–7 shows how functional departmentalization would be used at the top management level in dividing the three major business functions—production, sales, and finance.

Advantages of the Functional Approach. The primary advantages of the functional approach are that it maintains the power and prestige of the major functions, creates efficiency through the principles of specialization, centralizes the organization's expertise, and permits tighter top-management control of the functions. For example, having all library-related activities on a college campus reporting to a common "library director" permits unified library policy to be carried out.

This approach also minimizes costly duplications of personnel and equipment. Having all computers and computer personnel in one department is less expensive than allowing several departments to have and supervise their own computer equipment and personnel.

Disadvantages of the Functional Approach. There are also many disadvantages to a functional approach. Some of these are that responsibility for total performance rests only at the top, and since each manager oversees only a narrow function, the training of managers to take over the top position is limited. Organizations attempt to remedy this by transferring managers so that they become "rounded," with experience in several functions. Coordination between and among functions becomes complex and more difficult as the organization grows in size and scope. Finally, individuals identify with their narrow functional responsibilities, causing subgroup loyalties, identification, and tunnel vision.

Exhibit 5–7

*Functional
Departmentalization
at the Top-
Management Level*

Product Departmentalization

At some point, the problems of coordination under a functional approach become extremely complex and cumbersome, especially when rapid, timely decisions must be made. The functional approach is slow and cumbersome because there is no single manager accountable for all the given activities, with the result that considerable coordination and communication are required before decisions can be reached. Consequently, some products that top management feels have the most potential may not receive the attention they deserve. And no one person is accountable for the performance of a given product line. What can be done to resolve this dilemma? One solution for many organizations is to shift to smaller, more natural semiautonomous miniorganizations built around specific products, each with its own functional capabilities. This is known as **product departmentalization,** in which all the functions associated with a single product line are grouped.

Some of the advantages of product departmentalization are that attention can be directed toward specific product lines or services, coordination of functions at the product division level is improved, and profit responsibility can be better placed. Also, it is easier for the organization to obtain or develop several executives who have broad managerial experience in running a total entity.

Some of the disadvantages of product departmentalization are that it requires more personnel and material resources, it may cause unnecessary duplication of resources and equipment, and top management assumes a greater burden of establishing effective coordination and control. What a disaster it would be for GM's next economy-priced Chevrolet to have a body style almost identical to GM's top priced Cadillac Seville. Top management must use staff support to create and oversee policies that guide and limit the range of actions taken by its divisions.

Matrix Departmentalization

Matrix departmentalization is a hybrid type of departmentalization in which personnel from several specialties are brought together to complete limited-life tasks. It usually evolves from one or more of the other types of departmentalization and is used in response to demands for unique blends of skill from different specialties in the organization. The matrix structure is used not alone but in conjunction with other types of departmentalization. Say, for example, that a company had to complete a project requiring close, integrated work between and

product departmentalization
A form of departmentalization that groups together all the functions associated with a single product line.

matrix departmentalization
A hybrid type of departmentalization in which personnel from several specialties are brought together to complete limited-life tasks.

among numerous functional specialties. The project could be designing a weapons system or building a prototype for a supersonic aircraft. The traditional approaches to organization we have discussed do not easily provide for the flexibility to handle such complex assignments, which involve expertise from numerous functional areas of the organization. As shown in Exhibit 5–8, a project manager is given line authority over the team members during the life of the project.

The matrix organization provides a hierarchy that responds quickly to changes in technology. Hence, it is typically found in technically oriented organizations, such as Boeing, General Dynamics, NASA, and GE, in which scientists, engineers, or technical specialists work on sophisticated projects or programs. It is also used by companies with complex construction projects. Under this system, team members' functional departments maintain personnel files, supervise administrative details, and assemble performance reports while their members are on assignment.

Advantages of the Matrix Approach. One advantage of the matrix approach is that it permits open communication and coordination of activities among the relevant functional specialists. Another advantage is that its flexibility enables the organization to respond rapidly to change. This response to change is the result of a self-imposed and professional desire to respond—not a response to a hierarchically managed change effort. The use of this approach is essential in technologically oriented industries.

click! http://www.boeing.com/

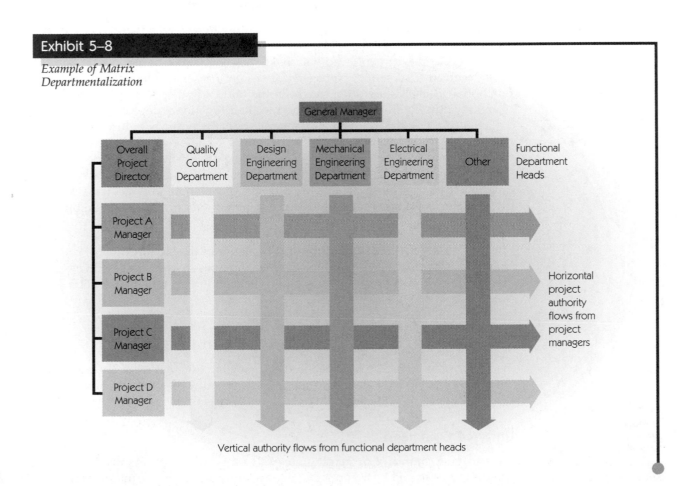

Exhibit 5–8

Example of Matrix Departmentalization

Disadvantages of the Matrix Approach. One disadvantage of matrix departmentalization relates to the lack of clarity and coordination in assigned roles. Conflict may occur when the requirements of the project team result in decisions contrary to the philosophy and viewpoint of the home office. For example, a project team might want the authority to make most decisions on site, while the home office wants tight control. Another possible source of conflict is the assignment of team members to more than one project; someone must determine how to allocate such team members' time on each project. Such situations require *facilitators*, who intervene to resolve clashes resulting from conflicting priorities.

> **Jean Johnson was a professor of management at Mid-Atlantic University. For the past year, she had been teaching in the management department and working half-time on an interdisciplinary project to improve the university computer system. For the life of the project, she had two bosses—the project director and the chairman of the management department. Until recently, this dual reporting had not caused any problem, but within the last month, the chairman of the management department had been putting increasing pressure on Jean to teach an additional course for the fall term. A professor had resigned suddenly, leaving the department shorthanded. The dilemma was that the computer study was nearing completion and required a major commitment of time and effort from all project members.**

In a matrix structure, who will decide on the members' advancement and promotion? Moreover, who will assign them to their next projects? Normally, the functional department head will make these decisions, based in part on reports received from project managers for whom the persons have worked. But functional specialists are often caught in the middle in disputes and torn between loyalties to project managers and to their functional department heads.

Finally, there are disadvantages relating to the temporary nature of assignments under this form of departmentalization. Psychologically, one may never feel that one has "roots" while drifting from one project to another—perhaps unrelated—project. Moreover, the close personal ties formed while working on a project team may be severed at the project's completion, in which case an individual's reassignment requires establishing a new set of working relationships with strangers.

Special Managerial Abilities Required. Because of the complexities of the matrix approach, managers should have special abilities in order to be successful. They should be adept at teamwork and coordination and also have facilitation skills.

TWO IMPORTANT ORGANIZING PRINCIPLES

③ Explain the principles of unity of command and span of control.

Two important principles involved in the organizing function were illustrated in the case of John Moody's organizations. These are unity of command and span of control (or span of management). Let us now discuss these principles in detail.

Unity of Command

unity of command principle
States that everyone should report to and be accountable to only one boss.

The **unity of command principle** states that everyone in an organization should report to and be accountable to only one boss for performance of a given activity. This supervisor should be responsible for evaluating performance, passing down orders and information, and developing employees to become better employees in the organization. It is to this person that employees should turn for help in carrying out their duties and should communicate any deviations, either positive or negative, in implementing their duties. In sum, the supervisor is only responsible for motivating his or her employees to achieve effective results and for taking action when employees deviate from planned performance.

Adherence to the unity of command principle is important for five reasons:

1. It prevents duplication and conflict when orders and instructions are passed down.

2. It decreases confusion and "passing the buck" because everyone—including managers—is accountable to only one person for a given assignment.

3. It provides a basis whereby a supervisor and his or her employees can develop a knowledge of each other's strengths and weaknesses.

4. It provides an opportunity for a supervisor and employees to develop supportive relationships and to realize their individual and group potential in achieving organizational objectives.

5. It promotes higher morale than is generally found in organizations that do not follow the unity of command principle.

Unfortunately, some managers only give lip service to this principle, although their organization chart seems to reflect it.

Recently, one of the authors of this book was working with a branch plant of a large company to tailor a management development program. Among other things, this author was examining the leadership styles practiced by key managers and their effect on employees. To determine those leadership styles, the author interviewed managers at all levels. The results showed that the plant manager, though unusually capable and generally effective, made one mistake with his employee managers: He violated the unity of command principle by periodically conducting inspections throughout the plant and making on-the-spot suggestions to operative employees. Oftentimes, he made these suggestions when the employees' supervisor was not present. As a result, operative employees were following instructions that their immediate supervisors were unaware of. Moreover, employees would stop working on their assigned duties in order to carry out the instructions of the plant manager. This practice caused a problem for supervisors, as illustrated by Exhibit 5–9.

As a result of this one error, a serious morale problem had developed. Many of the plant manager's otherwise effective managerial practices were being undermined. When this situation was called to his attention, he was quite surprised. It seems that he had slipped into this habit without being fully aware of its long-range consequences. When this manager thereupon began passing his suggestions and instructions through lower level managers, morale improved.

Although employees should have only one supervisor, they may, of course, have relationships with many people. For example, in a line-and-staff organization, line supervisors and department heads will have many contacts with staff personnel. These contacts are necessary so that both line and staff personnel can accomplish their duties. Later in this chapter, we will explain how these relationships can be developed without violating the unity of command principle. The important thing to remember is this: If a conflict results from a staff request

Exhibit 5–9

*Violating the Unity of
Command Principle*

and a line manager's command, the employee should have a single manager to
turn to for clarification or a final decision.

Span of Control

Before World War II, experts maintained that the span of control should be
three to eight people, depending on the level of management. In those days,
one of the first things an organizational consultant examined when a company
was having problems was the span of control at various levels. Today the three-
to-eight-people limit is no longer accepted as universally applicable. This is
why we state the **span of control principle** simply as follows: There is a limit
to the number of people a person can manage effectively. Just as you can span
only a limited number of feet and inches with your arms, your mental reach
can span only a limited number of the problems, situations, and relationships
that make up the activities of management.

**span of control
principle**
States that there is a limit
to the number of peo-
ple a person can super-
vise effectively.

Narrower Span of Control at the Top. One thing we can say without qualifi-
cation: The higher the managers are in an organization, the fewer people they
should have reporting directly to them. There are at least three reasons for relating span of control to management level:

1. Top-level managers must solve a variety of different, nonrecurring prob-
    lems. Much mental concentration is required to solve such problems.
2. Middle managers must spend much of their time in long-range planning,
    working with outside interest groups, and coordinating the various activi-
    ties of the organization. They cannot afford to be tied down by the excessive
    burden of supervision created when a large number of people report di-
    rectly to them.

3. First-level managers, by contrast, tend to be concerned with more clearly defined areas of operation. Although they are responsible for a certain amount of coordination with other departments, most of their contacts are directly with their immediate employees. Hence, they are able to supervise more people than are higher level managers.

Different Approaches to a Supervisor's Span of Control. Exhibit 5–10 depicts three different approaches to a supervisor's span of control, leading to quite different jobs for supervisors A, B, and C. Can we say that one of these approaches is best? No, because the correct size of a supervisor's span of control depends on a number of circumstances, as shown in Exhibit 5–11.

Companies that follow a policy of a narrow span of control are often hampered in achieving effective results. If an organization of, say, a thousand people rigidly adheres to a span of between three and seven, this tall, narrow organizational structure (with many, many management levels) will have some disadvantages. Numerous supervisory managers will be required, resulting in high payroll costs. Communication will have to pass up and down through

Exhibit 5–10

*Narrow, Wide, and
Very Wide Spans of
Control*

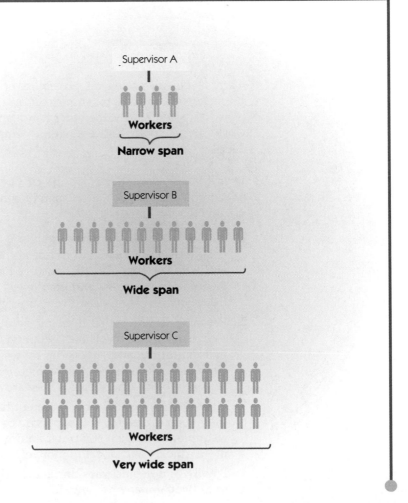

Factor	Narrow Span Indicated	Wide Span Indicated
How physically close are the people performing the work?	Dispersed, perhaps even in different geographical locations.	Very close, perhaps all in one physical work area in a building.
How complex is the work?	Very complex, such as development of a manned space station that will orbit the earth.	Rather routine and simple, such as an assembly-line operation.
How much supervision is required?	A great deal. So many problems arise that the supervisor needs to exercise close control.	Little. Workers are well trained and able to make normal job decisions easily.
How much non-supervisory work is required of the supervisor?	Much. The supervisor spends much time planning, coordinating, and performing nonsupervisory tasks.	Little. Not much planning and coordination is required of the supervisor. The supervisor spends most of his or her time supervising employees.
How much organizational assistance is furnished to the supervisor?	Little. The supervisor may do his or her own recruiting, training, and controlling.	Much. The supervisor may be aided by a training department, quality control department, etc.

many levels, increasing the possibility of distortion. Oversupervision may restrict decision making by employees and limit their opportunities to achieve their full potential. On the other hand, an advantage of tight control is that the work can be closely directed, so the company can hire relatively less skilled people.

Tendency Toward Wider Spans of Control. Over the years, many companies have tended to broaden their span of control at all levels. There are at least four reasons for this trend:

1. Higher educational attainment, management and supervisory development programs, vocational and technical training, and increased knowledge generally on the part of the labor force have improved the abilities and capacities of both managers and employees. The greater the supervisor's capacity, the more people he or she can supervise.

2. Research indicates that in many situations *general* supervision is more effective than *close* supervision. A supervisor practicing general supervision delegates authority and supervises by results; whereas a supervisor practicing close supervision provides detailed instructions and often does the same type of work as the workers they are supervising.

3. New developments in management have permitted businesses to broaden their span of control and supervise by results, without losing control. For example, by using a computer an organization can process information more quickly and develop more efficient information-reporting systems.

4. Finally—and sometimes this is the primary reason—wider spans of control save the company money.

RELATIONSHIPS BETWEEN LINE AND STAFF

4 Describe the difference between line and staff.

line personnel
Carry out the primary activities of a business.

staff personnel
Have the expertise to assist line people and aid top management.

Line personnel carry out the primary activities of a business, such as producing or selling products and/or services. **Staff personnel,** on the other hand, use their expertise to assist the line people and aid top management in various areas of business activities. Line departments, therefore, are like a main stream. Staff departments are like the tributaries serving and assisting the main stream, although they should not be thought of as being secondary to the line departments. Both line and staff people are important.

self-check

Of the various jobs you've held, which were "line" and which were "staff"?

Once a business has reached the fourth stage of growth and is no longer a small organization, it becomes more complex and difficult to coordinate. A line-and-staff structure that places competent specialists in certain positions, such as human resources management, legal and governmental departments, research and development, and public relations, will help eliminate confusion, duplication, and inefficiency. But it will not solve all problems for all time. A growing organization must be continually alert to pitfalls and potential trouble spots.

Conflicts Between Line and Staff

One common problem in most large organizations is excessive conflict between line and staff personnel and between different departments. Differences in viewpoint between people and departments are natural, inevitable, and healthy, but excessive conflict can disrupt an entire organization. As shown in Exhibit 5–12, many line and staff contacts are normal.

There are many reasons excessive conflict can develop between line and staff personnel within an organization. Exhibit 5–13 summarizes some reasons for conflict between line and staff personnel.

self-check

Before reading further, decide what you think might be done to decrease or eliminate the reasons for conflict between line and staff personnel.

5 Understand how to avoid excessive conflict between line and staff.

6 Explain the three types of authority found in organizations.

advisory authority
Authority of most staff departments to serve and advise line departments.

How to Avoid Excessive Line-Staff Conflict: Delineating Authority

Although conflict between line and staff people is not likely to be completely eliminated, a major way to avoid it is to ensure that people clearly understand the authority/responsibility relationships between individuals and departments. There are three types of authority: advisory, line, and functional.

Advisory Authority. The primary responsibility of most staff departments is to serve and advise the line departments. This type of authority is called **advisory authority** or the *authority of ideas.* However, some staff people may be so zealous in their efforts to sell their ideas to line personnel that they, in effect, hand

Exhibit 5–12

*Line and Staff
Contacts*

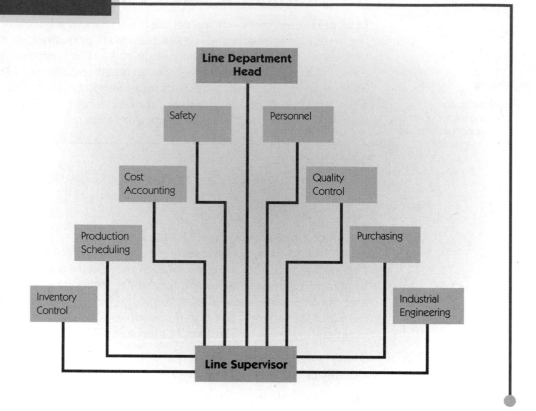

Exhibit 5–13

*Some Reasons for
Conflict Between Line
and Staff Personnel*

- Staff personnel give direct orders to line personnel.
- Good human relations are not practiced in dealings between line and staff personnel.
- Overlapping authority and responsibility confuse both line and staff personnel.
- Line people believe that staff people are not knowledgeable about conditions at the operating level.
- Staff people, because of their expertise, attempt to influence line decisions against line managers' wishes.
- Top management misuses staff personnel or fails to use them properly.
- Each department views the organization from a narrow viewpoint instead of looking at the organization as a whole.

out orders. If the line supervisor permits this to occur frequently, the unity of command begins to break down.

line authority
Power to directly command or exact performance from others.

Line Authority. The second type of authority, **line authority,** is the power to directly command or exact performance from others. Having this power to command does not mean that you will elicit effective performance simply by giving out orders. It does mean, however, that you are directly responsible for

Behind the scenes functions of research, accounting, quality control, and safety are found in many companies. What kind of authority would a staff person have working in this environment?

the results of a certain department or group of workers. Line authority is not restricted to line personnel. The head of a staff department has line authority over the employees in his or her department.

Functional Authority. The third type of authority, **functional authority,** is usually a restricted kind of line authority. It gives a staff person a type of limited line authority over a given *function,* such as safety or quality, regardless of where that function is found in the organization.

functional authority
A staff person's limited line authority over a given function.

For example, a staff safety specialist may have functional authority to insist that line managers follow standard safety procedures in their departments. The staff safety specialist may have top management's blessing to dictate to lower level line managers exactly what they must do and must not do concerning any matter that falls within the realm of safety. A quality control inspector may tell a line worker that certain parts need to be reworked. A human resources specialist may say to a line supervisor that the latter cannot fire a certain employee. A cost accountant may notify line departments that certain cost information must be furnished weekly, and so on.

self-check

Can you think of some other common examples of functional authority?

Are you thinking that functional authority seems to violate the unity of command principle? It does! For this reason, it is important that all individuals clearly understand what functional authority is. Top line managers have the major responsibility for defining the nature of functional authority. Moreover, it is important for line personnel to exercise their right to appeal to higher management levels when they have disagreements with staff personnel. Functional authority is necessary, but it can be dangerous if it is granted indiscriminately. Normally, it is given only to a staff area where there is a great deal of expertise and the staff expert's advice would be followed anyway.

Another way to avoid excessive conflict between line and staff people is to have effective communication between people and between departments. Key managers overseeing both line and staff people can improve the communication process by periodically bringing line and staff people together to discuss problems that cut across departmental lines. This example may inspire lower level managers to do the same thing with their key employees. Thus, the danger of seeing only part of the picture will be minimized.

⑦ Distinguish between centralization and decentralization.

DECENTRALIZATION VERSUS CENTRALIZATION

The concept of decentralization is closely related to the concept of delegation, which is examined in the next chapter. Briefly, delegation is the process by which managers allocate duties and authority downward to the people who report to them and assign responsibility for how authority is used.

> **An example of delegation occurred when John Moody called in assistants to help him do a better job than he could do alone. He assigned his assistants duties in finance, production, and sales.**

decentralization
The extent to which authority is delegated from one unit of the organization to another.

Both delegation and decentralization are concerned with the giving of authority to someone at a lower level. **Decentralization** is the broader concept, as it refers to the extent to which authority is delegated from one level or one unit of the organization to another. In a *decentralized* organization, middle and lower levels of management make broader, more important decisions about their units. In a *centralized* organization, upper management makes most of the important decisions that concern all levels or units within the organization.

Factors Affecting Decentralization

No organization is completely centralized or decentralized. Decentralization is a relative concept and depends on a number of factors, including the following:

1. *Top-management philosophy.* Some top managers have a need for tight control. They put together a strong central staff and want to make the most important decisions themselves. Others believe in strong delegation and push decisions to the lowest levels of their organization.

2. *History of the organization's growth.* Organizations that have grown by merging with other companies or acquiring them tend to be decentralized. Those that have grown on their own tend to be centralized.

3. *Geographic location(s).* Organizations that are spread out, with units in different cities or regions, tend to be decentralized so that lower level managers can make decisions that fit their territory or circumstances.

4. *Quality of managers.* If an organization has many well-qualified, well-trained managers, it will likely be decentralized. If it has few, top management will centralize and make the most important decisions.

5. *Availability of controls.* If top management has an effective control system—good, timely information about performance at lower levels—the organization will tend toward decentralization. Without a good flow of control information for monitoring end results, it will tend to be centralized.[1]

self-check

Select one of your past employers. Would you say that the organization was centralized or decentralized? Why?

Effect of Decentralization on Organizational Structure

 click! http://www.toyota
.com/

The degree to which an organization is decentralized will have a direct effect on the number of levels within the organization. As shown in Exhibit 5–14, Ford Motor Company, which is relatively centralized, has 12 layers of managers and supervisors between the operative employees and the chairperson. Toyota, which is relatively decentralized, has only 7 levels of management. The trend in the United States is toward reducing the number of levels of management and decentralizing. Both the Japanese success in the automobile industry and the re-

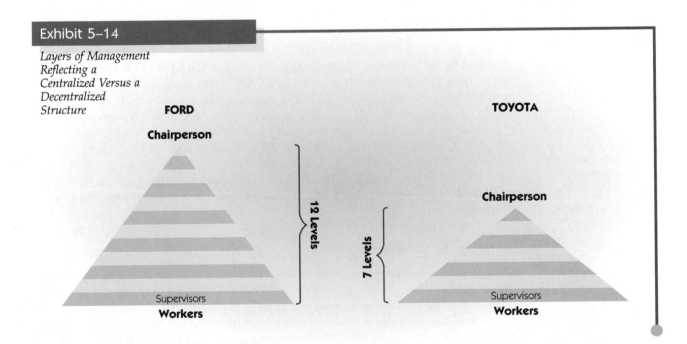

Exhibit 5–14

Layers of Management Reflecting a Centralized Versus a Decentralized Structure

FORD

Chairperson

12 Levels

7 Levels

Supervisors
Workers

TOYOTA

Chairperson

Supervisors
Workers

cession of the early 1990s, during which many U.S. companies trimmed organizational "fat," have had an impact on this trend. After Marvin Runyon retired as vice-president of Ford Motor Company, he accepted the position of chief executive officer with the Nissan Motor Manufacturing Corporation, U.S.A. When Runyon was asked how the Nissan plant in Tennessee would be operated, he replied that the plan would take the best of both American and Japanese management concepts and methods. He went on to state:

> **We are reducing the management levels that are customarily found in United States auto manufacturing companies. A lot of companies are very tiered. We're going to have five levels of management—president, vice-president, plant manager, operations manager, and supervisor. And then we have technicians. The reason we are doing that is to foster good communications, which I think is the key to running any business.**
>
> **We're going to have a very participative management style. What I mean is, everybody participates in what is done in this company. It will be more of a bottom-up management than top-down. Usually the top fellow decides everything that's going to happen, tells everybody, then expects everybody to march to that drummer. Japanese don't work that way. They work from a bottom-up technique. And that's what we plan to do.**
>
> **Now the reason for that is very simple. You go into a company and ask even a third-level person—say, the level of plant manager—"What are the problems in your operation?" He can give you about 4 percent of the real problems. Then you go to the operations-manager level, and they can give you, say, 40 percent. You go to the supervisor level, and maybe they can give you 70 percent. If you go to the technicians and ask them, they'll give you 100 percent of the problems. So, who better to participate in running the company than the people who actually know what's going on?**[2]

DOWNSIZING

8 Discuss the benefits and costs of downsizing.

In their book *In Search of Excellence,* Thomas Peters and Robert Waterman noted that one of the attributes of excellent companies is a simple organizational structure with a lean top-level staff.[3] In a 1988 article, management theorist Peter Drucker predicted that by 2008 a typical large business would have half the levels of management and one-third the managers of its counterpart today.[4]

Drucker's forecast is already coming true throughout the United States and Canada. **Downsizing** is the process of eliminating unnecessary levels of management and employees, thus reducing the number of staff personnel and supervisors. A survey of 1,200 human resource managers indicated that 35 percent of them had engaged in downsizing, and the average reduction was just over 10 percent.[5]

downsizing
Eliminating unnecessary levels of management.

Benefits of Downsizing

One of the major benefits of downsizing is the tremendous cost reductions that occur almost immediately. Perhaps even more important are the improvements that take place in the way the organization is managed. Turnaround time in decision making is speeded up, and usually communication improves in all directions. Moreover, the organization becomes more responsive to customers and provides faster product delivery. Downsizing also removes the tendency for each level to justify its existence by close supervision and by frequently asking for reports and data from lower levels. Without excessive interference and stifling of creativity at lower levels, line managers have more opportunity to develop and use their authority to make decisions affecting the bottom line. In the final analysis, all of these things translate into higher profits.

An illustration:

A. T. Kearney analyzed management layers among both highly successful companies and others whose performance was not above average in their industry. The 15 not-so-successful companies typically had at least four more organizational layers than the 26 successful ones. Interviews confirmed that more layers in the organization inhibit productivity because the decision-making process is slower and the chances are greater that opportunities will be lost.[6]

Costs of Downsizing

Downsizing has some costs that can wreck the prospect of higher profits if the process is not accomplished ethically and efficiently. Some companies downsize so rapidly and prune staff and middle management so much that they lose control. In addition, some companies are very insensitive in the way they go about downsizing, telling a number of loyal, effective managers that they are no longer needed. A heavy-handed approach can lead to morale problems with remaining employees for years to come. Some other potential disadvantages are increased workloads, diminished chances of promotion, and threatened job security for those remaining.

Perhaps the greatest costs are the least known—the social costs. Research shows that when employees lose their jobs because of downsizing, domestic problems increase. Fifteen percent lost their homes, despite an increase in the number of hours their spouses worked. Moreover, the suicide rate for laid-off workers is 30 times the national average.[7] Because of these costs, downsizing can never be painless, but thoughtful planning can minimize the pain.

Impact on Remaining Supervisors and Managers

Remaining managers and supervisors must adapt to fuzzier lines of authority and must develop skills in team building. In tall, narrow structures, middle managers and supervisors are accustomed to carrying out orders, and suddenly they must operate differently. As a first-line supervisor in an International Paper Company mill told one of the authors: "They used to tell us what to do; now they ask us." With the increasing emphasis on quality management, a supervisor has to function more as a coach, facilitator, expediter, and team developer.

Ways to Get Beyond Downsizing

Without question, downsizing has a negative impact on employee morale, and according to an American Management Association survey, just 45 percent of firms that have downsized have seen corporate profits increase.[8] Thus, it is important to look on downsizing not as an end in itself but as a means to an end. The way to get back to health is to focus on the remaining employees by developing a strategy of support for survivors and a strategic plan for growth and development for the organization.

click! http://www.xerox.com

Reengineering
"It means starting over.
. . . It means asking and
answering this question:
If I were creating this
company today, given
what I know and given
current technology, what
would it look like?"

However, it is important not to go back to a traditional management and organizational design based on principles of command, control, and compartmentalization.[9] Two ways to negate these dangers are (1) with the development of effective work teams discussed in a later chapter and (2) with a process called *reengineering.*

Reengineering is a reaction to the way many organizations do work today using the traditional methods of command, control, and compartmentalization. In a world of rapid change, firms that focus on division or specialization of labor with a resulting fragmentation of work end up with vertical structures built on narrow pieces of a process. Consequently, decisions are slow, and people look upward to their departments and bosses for answers, rather than getting information from internal and external customers to solve problems and get answers.[10]

When Michael Hammer and James Champy, two of the world's leading experts on reengineering, were asked for a quick definition, they gave this answer: "It means starting over. . . . It means asking and answering this question: If I were recreating this company today, given what I know and given current technology, what would it look like?"[11]

Their more formal definition of reengineering is "the fundamental rethinking and radical redesign of business processes to achieve dramatic improvements in critical, contemporary measures of performance such as cost, quality, service, and speed."[12]

Reengineering can be very expensive, and so firms should not use it for everything. If you have an unprofitable business, it may be better to close it, or if quality is a problem, focus on improving the quality rather than starting over. The general guideline is to save reengineering for big challenges that really matter, such as new product development or customer service. Although by one estimate, 50 percent of reengineering efforts fail to achieve the goals set for them, when it is done properly, reengineering has a big payoff. For example, Union Carbide used reengineering to save $400 million in three years.[13]

As Hammer and Champy have documented, the following types of changes occur when a company has successfully reengineered business processes:

- Work units change from functional departments to process teams.
- Jobs change from simple tasks to multidimensional work.
- People's roles change from controlled to empowered.
- Job preparation changes from preparation to education.
- Focus of compensation shifts from activity to results.
- Advancement criteria change from performance to ability.
- Values change from protective to productive.
- Managers change from supervisors to coaches.
- Organizational structure changes from hierarchical to flat.
- Executives change from scorekeepers to leaders.

MANAGEMENT PHILOSOPHY, STRATEGY, AND ORGANIZATION

9 Understand the relationship between management philosophy, strategy, and newer forms of organization.

Earlier in the chapter we discussed the impact management philosophy has on the organization. Management philosophy is particularly significant when we

http://www.wcom.com

http://www2.ford.com

discuss the newer forms of organizations, involving more decentralization, empowerment, team development, quality improvement, and networking. In a world of rapid change and global competition more and more firms are shifting to more decentralization, team development, and empowerment. Xerox, the company that invented the copier in 1959, is an example of a company that successfully changed its orientation and philosophy. For two decades Xerox dominated the copier market; unfortunately, "by 1981, however, the company's market share shrank to 35 percent as IBM and Kodak developed high-end machines and Canon, Ricoh and Iavin dominated the low-end segment of the market."[14] A wake-up call occurred when the company discovered that the Japanese were selling their machines for what it cost Xerox to make them.

Top management realized that the company had to make a cultural change and instituted a program of total quality management, including benchmarking. There was considerable resistance at first, but with perseverence the cultural change resulted in Xerox winning the Malcolm Baldrige National Quality Award in 1989. This was accomplished after reducing the levels of the hierarchical organization and the use of cross-functional teams. Here are some results:

- Suppliers were reduced from 5,000 to 300.
- Quality problems were cut by two-thirds.
- Manufacturing costs were cut in half.
- Development time was cut by two-thirds.
- Direct labor was cut by 50 percent and corporate staff was cut by 35 percent while increasing volume.[15]

We turn now to newer forms of organizations that enables companies to change cultures and will focus more on philosophy and strategy than organization charts per se.

The Horizontal Organization

Several experts believe that the organizations of the future will be more horizontal in nature and less hierarchical. The authors agree and believe the first- and middle-level supervisors will be the key players in this organization of the future. Although a number of companies such as Ford, Motorola, and General Electric have utilized **horizontal organization,** we will continue to use Xerox as our model.

horizontal organization
A flatter structure that uses a team in eliminating red tape and meeting the customer's needs.

One of Xerox's secrets in earning its first Malcolm Baldrige award was the realization that there are two aspects to TQM—a hard analytical side and a softer behavioral side involving teamwork. Pauline Brody of Xerox points out that it is the teamwork side that is more critical and more difficult to achieve. Thus, in their strategy they focus on developing teamwork and partnership relationships among the supervisor and the work group, the union and management, and different departments.

An organization structural change was undertaken in 1990 when Raul Allaire took over as CEO and chairman. As Allaire explains, "We were a $10 billion plus organization (now $18.2 billion), and we were functional in nature. So every function—sales, service, administrative, manufacturing, engineering, research and development—all came up the line and in the end reported to me."[16] Management consultant Frank Ostroff, one of the key developers of the horizontal organization, notes it was at this time that Xerox began its transformation from a vertical organization to a hybrid organization chart incorporating the horizontal philosophy (Exhibit 5–15).

Without going into detail, this philosophy and structure allowed Xerox to continue to use the vertical organization from the executive vice-president level upward, but everything below was organized horizontally. This move allowed the company to move decision making from the vertical structure into the Busi-

Exhibit 5–15

Xerox 2005: The Hybrid Organization Chart

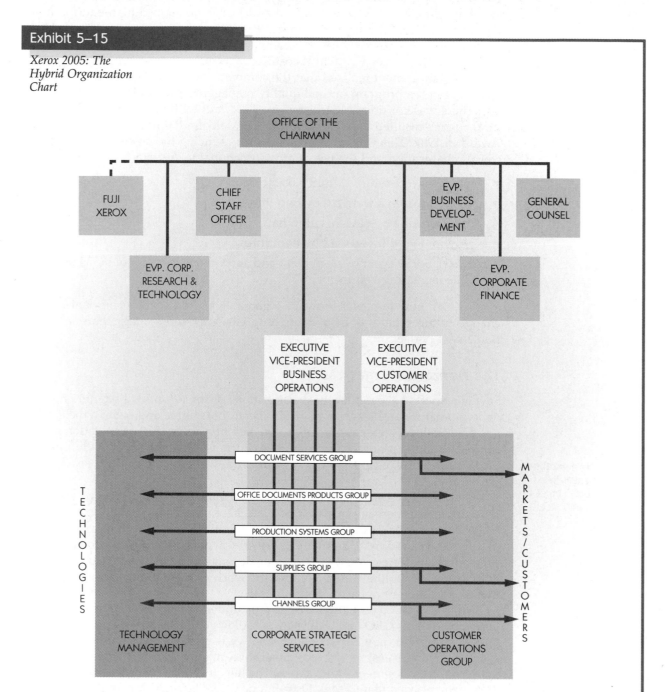

SOURCE: *Frank Ostroff,* The Horizontal Organization *(New York: Oxford University Press, 1999), p. 134.*

ness Division and the Customer Operations Division and made extensive use of teams in serving the needs of customers.

The outcomes continued to be outstanding in financial results and customer satisfaction. The company also received a second Baldrige award in the services category in 1998. Ostroff has identified a number of principles for designing and institutionalizing the horizontal organization. Several that have particular significance to supervisors are as follows:

Design

- Organize around cross-functional core processes, not tasks or functions.
- Make teams, not individuals, the foundation of organizational design and performance.
- Decrease hierarchy by eliminating non-value-added work and by giving team members, who are not senior managers, the authority to make decisions.
- Integrate with customers and suppliers.

Institutionalizing

- Empower people by giving them the tools, skills, motivation, and authority to make decisions.
- Teach people trained in specific functions or departments to work in partnerhips with others.
- Build a corporate culture of openness, cooperation, collaboration, and continuous performance improvement.[17]

Other organization forms that are influenced by philosophy and strategy are the inverted pyramid and wagon wheel.

The Inverted Pyramid

inverted pyramid
A strucutre widest at the top and narrowing as it funnels down.

The creation of the **inverted pyramid** has been attributed to Nordstrom, a very successful specialty retailer. Nordstrom's structure is very flat with few levels and employs a bottom-up management philosophy. The sales and sales support personnel, who are in direct contact with the customer, make the key decisions. The chart portrays "helping hands" symbolizing that all other levels are there to help and support the sales personnel to better serve and satisfy the customer. Exhibit 5–16 shows Nordstrom's inverted pyramid and the helping-hand concept.

The success of Nordstrom's management philosophy and empowered personnel is reflected in end results. During the past decade its sales have increased from $769 million (39 stores, 10,000 employees) to $3.4 billion (72 stores, 30,000 employees).[18]

The Wagon Wheel

wagon wheel
An organization form with a hub, a series of spokes radiating from the hub, and the outer rim.

Management consultant and author Nancy Austin points out that the **wagon wheel** is even more unorthodox than the inverted pyramid. In her words, "there are usually three main parts to these innovative formats: the hub of the wheel; a series of spokes, which radiate from the hub; and, finally, the outer rim. Customers are at the center. Whether you call the hub 'customers,' 'customer satisfaction,' or 'customer delight'—as AT&T Universal Card Services does—at last, customers show up inside the chart! Next come the spokes—busi-

*Nordstrom's Inverted
Pyramid*

SOURCE: *From* The Horizontal Organization *by Frank Ostroff, Copyright © 1999 by Frank Ostroff. Used by permission of Oxford University Press, Inc.*

ness functions (finance, marketing, engineering) or teams (new-product development, customer satisfaction, suppliers). Keeping it all together on the outer rim—where the rubber meets the road—are the chief executive and the board, who are placed there to make sure everybody has at his or her fingertips everything needed to serve customers. Here, too, managers are coaches and supporters, not naysayers and devil's advocates. The stubborn 'Us vs. Them' antagonism spawned by the old hierarchical mentality begins to even out a bit."[19]

---

chapter review

1 ## Understand the stages of organization growth.

This chapter focused on concepts that give supervisory managers a better understanding of their organization. A continuing case illustrated several phases of organization growth, from a one-person organization to a line-and-staff organization. It is important for a growing company to evolve from a line organization to a line-and-staff organization. This evolution allows the company to take advantage of specialization in such areas as human resources, quality control, purchasing, maintenance, scheduling, and safety. It also allows line managers and supervisors to concentrate on supervising and motivating their employees.

2 ## Identify the advantages and disadvantages of the functional, product, and matrix departmentalization approaches.

The span of control principle emphasizes that there is a limit to the number of people a person can effectively manage. As one moves down the organization chart from top management to supervisory management levels, the span of control should increase. The reasons for tying span of control to management level are that (1) top management requires the freedom to solve a variety of different, nonrecurring problems; (2) higher level managers must spend much of their time doing long-range planning, working with outside interest groups, and coordinating the various activities of the business; and (3) supervisory managers tend to be concerned with more clearly defined areas of operation.

(3) Explain the principles of unity of command and span of control.

Two important management principles for organizations are unity of command and span of control. Following the unity of command principle is important because it prevents duplication and conflict when orders and instructions are passed down. It also decreases confusion and "passing the buck" and provides a basis for managers and their employees to develop a better understanding of what they expect of each other. Finally, it promotes higher morale than is found in organizations that excessively violate the unity of command principle.

(4) Describe the difference between line and staff.

Though both line and staff personnel are important, their duties differ. Line personnel carry out the primary activities of a business, such as producing or selling products and/or services. Staff personnel use their expertise to assist the line people and to aid top management in various business activities.

(5) Understand how to avoid excessive conflict between line and staff.

A line-and-staff organization sometimes leads to excessive conflict between line and staff departments. Conflict can be minimized by ensuring that people understand the authority/responsibility relationships between individuals and departments.

(6) Explain the three types of authority found in organizations.

The three types of authority found in organizations are advisory authority (common in staff departments), line authority (direct command authority over employees), and functional authority (limited line authority in a narrow area of specialization). Another way to avoid excessive conflict is to have effective communication between people and between departments.

(7) Distinguish between centralization and decentralization.

The concept of centralization versus decentralization is important in understanding organizations. Some factors that influence the extent of centralization or decentralization are top management's philosophy, the history of the organization's growth, its geographic location(s), the quality of managers, and the availability of controls. Computer technology has increased the ability of higher management to shift in either direction. The trend, however, seems to be in the direction of decentralization.

(8) Discuss the benefits and costs of downsizing.

Many organizations are currently being streamlined by downsizing, or reducing the number of administrative levels. Although rapid downsizing can get out of control and there is unavoidable cost to the staff and supervisors who are laid off, the benefits to the organization in the form of cost reduction, faster decision making, and improved communication outweigh the costs. As a result of downsizing, supervisors often have more authority and responsibility, on the one hand, but they are called on to act more as leaders, coaches, facilitators, and team developers.

 Understand the relationship between management philosophy, strategy, and newer forms of organization.

Newer forms of organization are being developed that emphasize the role and importance of the customer and empowerment of employees who are close to the customer. These newer forms are the inverted pyramid, the wagon wheel, and horizontal forms. The horizontal form is particularly valuable in developing partnership relationships that emphasize interdependence, sharing of information, teamwork, and empowerment.

---

important terms

advisory authority *143*
decentralization *146*
departmentalization *134*
downsizing *148*
functional authority *145*
functional departmentalization *135*
horizontal organization *151*
inverted pyramid *153*
line-and-staff organization *132*
line authority *144*

line organization *130*
line personnel *143*
matrix departmentalization *136*
product departmentalization *136*
reengineering *150*
span of control principle *140*
staff personnel *143*
unity of command principle *138*
wagon wheel *153*

---

questions for review and discussion

1. Outline the four stages of organizational growth, and relate them to an organization with which you are familiar.
2. What two important management principles affect the successful operation of a growing organization? Do you think John Moody's difficulties could have been avoided if he had understood these principles? Discuss the advantages and disadvantages of functional, matrix, and product departmentalization.
3. What is the relationship between levels of management and span of control? Explain the advantages and disadvantages.
4. Distinguish between line and staff functions. Are they always easily identified in various types of business enterprises? Justify the existence of both line and staff departments.
5. What conflicts may arise between line and staff personnel? What reasons can you give for these problems? How does effective communication ease the conflict?
6. What are the three types of authority? Do they all exist in all four stages of functional growth?
7. What are some factors that favor centralization or decentralization?
8. How can a company minimize the negative effects of downsizing?
9. Why did Xerox shift to a hybrid organization form that emphasizes a horizontal philosophy?
10. What are the potential benefits and potential drawbacks of reengineering?

11. Discuss the relationship between management philosophy and organization. If you were the owner/manager of 10 convenience stores in the same city, what type of structure would you use? If you were the owner/manager of 10 CPA offices in various cities, what type of structure would you use?

●skill builder 5–1

Proposed Change of Organization
group activity

Starting by himself in 1984, Jim Hardy built Hardy Pest Control until it operated in four states and employed over 1,000 persons.

In 1996 Hardy hired Derek Temple as vice-president of marketing. Temple, exceptionally bright and articulate, had previously owned an advertising agency. Before Temple was hired, all the employees in each local area reported to the local manager, and the service personnel were also the salespeople for the firm. The district managers were responsible for both operations and sales. Tem-

ple recommended that Hardy specialize by separating sales from service and placing all sales personnel under Temple. Under this new arrangement, even though sales personnel operated from the local manager's office, they reported organizationally to a district sales manager, usually located in another city (see Hardy organization chart). The sales manager positions, since they were new, had to be staffed with office help and supplied with office space. The proposed new organization is shown as follows:

Prior to accepting the proposal, Jim Hardy decided to call in a management consulting firm to evaluate the proposal and suggest to him whether to accept or reject it.

Divide the class into teams of five to seven students who will play the role of a

consulting firm, and analyze the proposal.

Answer the following questions:

1. What do you see as the pros and cons of the new structure?

2. Based on your analysis, what is your recommendation to Jim Hardy?

●skill builder 5-2

Reducing Costs in an Accounting Firm
group activity

Divide the class into groups of five to seven students, each group representing the managing partners of an accounting firm. Have them discuss the following situation and report back to the class what their plan is, and how they would communicate it to employees.

There are 30 employees in your organization, and for the past year, sales and profits have been down. In fact, for the past six months, the firm has been operating at a loss.

Two months ago, a larger accounting firm acquired your firm in a friendly takeover. Its philosophy is to treat your smaller organization as a semiautonomous division of the accounting company, providing only general guidance and managing by results.

The accounting company CEO has asked your group, the managing partners, to develop a plan to reduce costs. It is important to note that 90 percent of your budget goes to salaries. Along with your plan, the accounting company CEO wants to know how you will communicate the plan to employees.

SOURCE: *Donald C. Mosley, Paul H. Pietri, and Leon C. Megginson,* "Management Leadership in Action." *Copyright 1996 Addison Wesley Longman, Inc. Reprinted by permission of Addison Wesley Longman.*

CASE 5–1

Conflicting Views

Conflicts between departments occur frequently. In production facilities, these conflicts often arise between production and maintenance departments, as illustrated by the following comments:

Production Supervisor: What a job! Top management is breathing down my neck to get the work out. My people do a real good job, considering our equipment problems and how crowded we are. But what a problem I have with that crew from maintenance! You'd think they owned the whole company, the way they carry on. They act as if they're doing you a big favor to do a repair job—letting you know how important they are and how they have to schedule their jobs. And they hate for you to tell them what's wrong with the equipment, as if they have to be the ones to do a "complete diagnosis." They always seem to drag their feet for me, and yet other production departments get things done right away. I've told the superintendent about their favoritism and cockiness, but it doesn't help.

Maintenance Supervisor: What a job! I've got production people running around here all day telling me what they've got to have done. I've got six mechanics, and sometimes we'll have 20 calls a day, not to mention our scheduled maintenance. So I try to assign priorities—that's the only way to survive. And then one of those @#$%&*! production supervisors takes his or her problem to the superintendent! What really burns me up is the abuse my people get from them. You try to do what's right, and some say you play favorites. I'd like to straighten that whole bunch of production yo-yos out!

Answer the following questions:

1. What concepts presented in the chapter are involved in this conflict?

2. What do you recommend be done to resolve the problem between the two supervisors?

3. Describe how a third party might work with the two supervisors to attempt to resolve the problem.

Delegating Authority

● outline

Why Delegate?
Delegating Develops People
Delegating Allows a Supervisor to Do Other Things
Delegating Allows More Work to Be Accomplished
Delegating Improves Control

Process of Delegation
Granting Authority
Assigning Responsibility
Requiring Accountability

Effective Delegation
Knowing When to Delegate
How the Delegation Process Operates
The Principle of Parity of Authority and Responsibility
Time Required for Effective Delegation

Parties Involved in Effective Delegation
The Role of Higher Management
The Role of the Supervisor
The Role of Employees to Whom Authority Is Delegated

Why Supervisors Fail to Delegate

Dealing with Ineffective Employees

Relating Delegation to Success or Failure
Eight Ways to Fail
Turning a Weakness into a Strength

Ineffective Delegation: A Solution

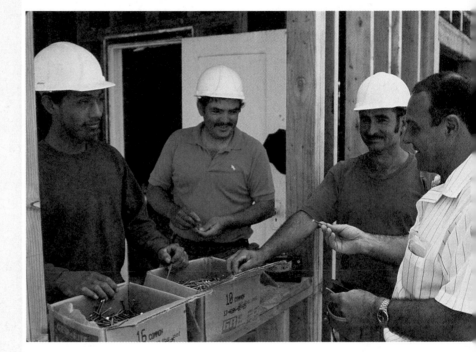

The greatest challenge in life is to be who you are and to become what you are capable of becoming.

Robert Louis Stevenson

The second greatest challenge is to assist and empower other people to become what they are capable of becoming.

The authors of this book

Joe Allegro, An Effective Developer of People

learning objectives

After reading and studying this chapter, you should be able to:

1. Recognize the importance of delegation.

2. Explain what is involved in the delegation process, including authority, responsibility, and accountability.

3. Discuss the roles of various parties in achieving effective delegation.

4. Understand why some supervisors are reluctant to delegate.

5. Gain insight into how to turn a delegation weakness into a strength.

6. Indicate ways to achieve effective delegation.

Joe Allegro is currently deputy director of construction for the Massachusetts Highway Department and is responsible for supervising construction at the largest publicly funded project in the United States, the Central Artery Tunnel (CAT) in Boston. Known as the "big dig," this series of tunnels will dramatically improve transportation in the city and has the potential to transform an interesting city into one of the world's most beautiful.

Growing up in Boston was a developmental experience in which sports played a key role. From sports Allegro learned the importance of relying on and supporting one another through teamwork, the value of preparation, and the good feeling that comes with success. Allegro states that from his teachers and coaches he learned that when a leader has high expectations and sets high standards, people generally will meet the challenge. In his own career he has found this to be the case nine out of ten times. Not only did his football coach, Paul Costello, have high expectations, he treated his players with respect and was very fair. Allegro states "he was a great motivator, and I learned from him that loyalty needs to go both ways. Some kids playing football at other schools felt that they were being used. But our coach worked very hard to get our players into colleges; he did not have to make this effort."

Allegro went to Cornell primarily because it had a good engineering school; there he played three years of college football. It was in college where Allegro really developed socially and became receptive to new ideas and concepts. He became interested in leadership and discovered he had some leadership ability.

Allegro graduated with a degree in civil engineering in 1982 and entered what many would consider a career down-period, but Allegro turned it into a leadership growth experience. During this time there was an economic downturn in engineering and he could not find a job in his field, so he took a job as a cook in a restaurant. Allegro gained a valuable lesson regarding authority and responsibility. Based on his job description, his real authority was limited, and he was rather low on the totem pole. In reality, Allegro did whatever needed to be done whether it went beyond his job description or not. Soon his *perceived* authority was much greater than his *real* authority. People turned to him for guidance and assistance, and he was running things whenever the boss was absent. The lesson learned was that if you assume authority and responsibility, people will give it to you as long as it is used to improve things.

In 1984 Allegro went to work for the Massachusetts Highway Department (MHD) as an engineer. The MHD had hired a large number of engineers after WWII to meet the expansion of the interstate highway program and had not hired many since that time. The average age of their engineers when Allegro went to work was 57, and he was one of 306 new engineering hirees. After going through an extensive job rotation

http://www.magnet.
state.ma.us/mhd/

program, Allegro advanced rapidly and joined the massive Central Artery project in February 1989. After spending time as an area engineer on the design side, he was made area manager for construction in April 1992.

Allegro had learned from sports and previous mentors that the essence of good performance and relationships is working *with* people rather than over or under people. While working on CAT, Allegro learned just how important good relationships are in getting a job done.

For example, one of the major tunnels of the Central Artery will connect downtown Boston with the Boston airport. Massport is the separate government agency that operates the airport and waterways surrounding the city. Completing the CAT project will take tremendous coordination and cooperation between Massport and Mass Highway. Allegro indicates that the only reason the project has not had excessive delays is because of the relationships that developed between people, enabling them to pick up the phone to call

someone for support or assistance in solving problems.

The people who work with Allegro have commented on how cool, calm, and collected he is in difficult situations. Margaret O'Meara is assistant area manager and reports directly to Allegro. She gives Allegro excellent marks as a boss, leader, and delegator. About the way he operates, she observes:

Allegro has the ability and confidence to motivate and empower people. He has helped me to grow and develop, and although I have had good managers in the past, he ranks number one. He challenges me and delegates to me major responsibilities and assignments. I, in turn, try to keep him informed on key issues, and I don't hesitate to seek his guidance on exceptional issues.

As we go through the chapter, we will return to Allegro and O'Meara to examine how they handle the delegation process.

SOURCE: *Discussions and correspondence with Joe Allegro and Margaret O'Meara and others associated with the Central Artery Tunnel Project.*

 Recognize the importance of delegation.

WHY DELEGATE?

The previous chapter covered the fundamentals of organizing—one of the management functions discussed in Chapter 1. Delegation is at the heart of organizing. Yet it is one of the concepts least understood and most underutilized by managers, especially middle managers. Research indicates that when people are elevated to middle-level management positions, they will either remain there for the rest of their careers or be demoted unless they learn to delegate authority effectively. The best time to learn to do this is at the first managerial level—the supervisor's level.

Delegating Develops People

People cannot grow and develop if they are oversupervised or not trusted to handle their normal duties and responsibilities. It is a well-known principle that we learn not only from books, but also from doing. In learning through doing, we will make mistakes. The wise supervisor realizes this truth and uses mistakes as an opportunity to discuss with employees what happened and

experiential learning
One learns by doing and uses mistakes as an opportunity to figure out how to avoid them in the future.

how it can be prevented in the future. The employees, in turn, learn from the experience. This procedure is called **experiential learning**. Exhibit 6–1 shows the steps the supervisor and employee follow in learning from successes and mistakes.

Delegating Allows a Supervisor to Do Other Things

A supervisor's job, as we have seen, involves more than just direct supervision. Effective delegation allows the supervisor to spend more time planning work and coordinating with other departments. It also allows more time for troubleshooting—dealing with problems before they get out of hand and taking advantage of opportunities in a timely manner.

Delegating Allows More Work to Be Accomplished

Instead of taking power away from supervisors, effective delegation expands the basis of their power. More people become knowledgeable about what the priorities are and assume responsibility for getting the job done. A climate of trust is established. In this environment, when the supervisor leaves the work

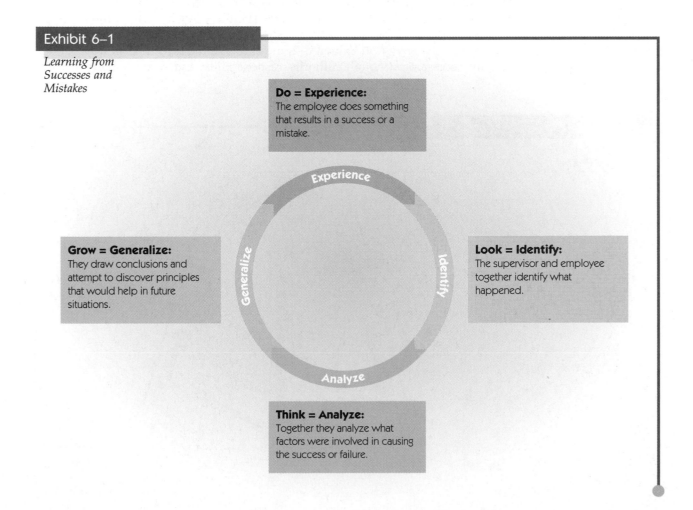

Exhibit 6–1

Learning from Successes and Mistakes

Do = Experience:
The employee does something that results in a success or a mistake.

Experience

Grow = Generalize:
They draw conclusions and attempt to discover principles that would help in future situations.

Generalize

Look = Identify:
The supervisor and employee together identify what happened.

Identify

Analyze

Think = Analyze:
Together they analyze what factors were involved in causing the success or failure.

area, employees continue to work effectively. They do so because of commitment and a sense of ownership in the work of the department.

Delegating Improves Control

In the effective delegation process, the emphasis is on results, not activities. Thus, the supervisor focuses on how well standards and objectives are met, not on the specific details of how they are met. In many cases, delegation also serves as a basis for evaluating people; they are compensated according to the results achieved. The key to improving control is to have an effective feedback system so that the supervisor can compare results with standards.

self-check

Can you identify other reasons effective delegation is so important? What are they?

Explain what is involved in the delegation process, including authority, responsibility, and accountability.

PROCESS OF DELEGATION

Delegation of authority refers to the process by which managers bestow authority on the people who report to them. The three key aspects of the process of delegation are granting authority, assigning responsibility, and requiring accountability. As shown in Exhibit 6–2, they are like the three legs of a stool, all equally necessary. Although authority, responsibility, and accountability are all

---

Exhibit 6–2

Three Aspects of the Delegation Process

delegation of authority
Managers grant authority to the people who report to them.

 click! http://www.ge.com

bound together, we will examine each aspect to sharpen our analysis and their interrelationship.

Granting Authority

In the previous chapter we defined line authority as the right and power to request others to carry out certain duties and responsibilities. When you delegate authority, you are granting an individual or team the power, freedom, or right to act within certain guidelines.

> **James Walker, supervisor of Department A, is concerned because four new workers have just been assigned to his department. Although normally he takes care of indoctrinating and training new workers, his schedule is so loaded for the next month that he cannot properly carry out the training assignments. He calls in his two most senior workers and, after expressing his confidence in their abilities, gives them the authority to indoctrinate and train the four new workers.**

In this example, Walker has just granted authority. The example illustrates that delegation to lower levels can occur above and beyond the normal assignment of duties and responsibilities. It also illustrates why it is important for supervisors to know both the weak and the strong points of their employees. James Walker knew his crew and chose the two people who could most effectively carry out the training function.

self-check

Can you think of other activities beyond the normal ones for which authority might be granted to workers at lower levels? What are they?

Assigning Responsibility

The second aspect of delegation is assigning duties and responsibilities. Most jobs, whether that of a nurse in a hospital, a teller in a bank, or an assembly worker in a manufacturing plant, have certain duties and responsibilities that usually go with them. For example, a bank teller not only is responsible for providing service to bank customers, but also is expected to be friendly, to identify prospective customers who do not have proper identification for cashing out-of-town checks, and to maintain the correct cash balances.

In addition, the unique nature of the banking industry or special priorities of the employing organization may result in the assignment of duties and responsibilities beyond the traditional requirements. An aggressive bank might add the extra responsibility of selling services. For example, a teller might be asked to present to each customer a form describing the bank's new money market account. If the customer shows interest, the teller can then engage in direct selling.

job descriptions
Written statements of the primary duties of specific jobs.

In medium-sized and large organizations, the key tasks associated with many jobs are listed in job descriptions, which are usually written by a human resources specialist after interviews with the jobholder and the jobholder's immediate supervisor(s). These **job descriptions**, which spell out the primary job duties and responsibilities, as well as other job-related activities, can assist in

Bank employees have a high degree of accountability since they are responsible for servicing customers and the bank's cash balances.

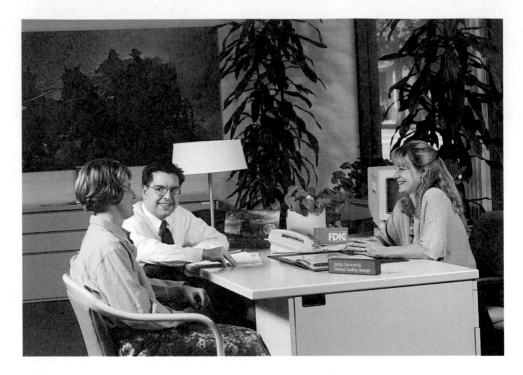

the process of delegation. Exhibit 6–3 provides an example of a job description for a production supervisor in a paper mill. It identifies 13 key duties and responsibilities, including crew leadership (1), crew work assignments (5), and safety and health management (11). For the purpose of illustration, we have spelled out the tasks for the coaching and counseling responsibility (8).

Requiring Accountability

accountability
The obligation created when a person accepts duties and responsibilities from higher management.

The third aspect of delegation is holding accountable those people to whom you have granted authority and assigned responsibility. **Accountability** refers to the obligation that is created when a person accepts duties and responsibilities from higher management; the delegatee is accountable to the next higher level to carry them out effectively. Accountability flows *upward* in an organization. It is in this aspect of the delegation process that the controlling function plays an important role.

self-check

Suppose that a department manager delegated a special assignment to a supervisor. The supervisor made a mistake in carrying out the assignment, and the mistake cost the firm $5,000. Who would you say should be held accountable for the mistake? Why?

If you answered that both the department manager and the supervisor should be held accountable, you are correct. The supervisor is, of course, accountable to the department manager, but the department manager is also accountable to her or his own supervisor.

Exhibit 6–3

Job Description for a Production Supervisor

Title: Production Supervisor, Finished Pruducts
Purpose of job: To plan, organize, control, and exercise leadership in the efficient and effective utilization of assigned crew personnel, equipment, and material resources for timely achievement of the crew's production performance objectives and standards.

1. Crew leadership responsibility
2. Crew performance standards
3. Crew performance improvement
4. Daily shift-change management
5. Crew work assignments
6. Crew performance supervision
7. Crew education, training, and development
8. Individual coaching and counseling
9. Production relationships management
10. Maintenance relationships management
11. Safety and health management
12. Labor contract administration
13. Work environment improvement

a. Observes and carries on conversation with individual crew members at their work stations daily to determine if there are any problems that require attention.
b. Provides on-the-job coaching in job skills at operator stations to reinforce classroom training and develop specific job skills.
c. Provides counseling to crew members on job relationship attitudes to improve their performance.
d. Refers crew members to company employee assistance resources for personnel problems that require special help.

An important fact to remember is that *accountability cannot be delegated!* Accountability is essential to maintain effective control over results. Therefore, a person who delegates an assignment should not be able to escape accountability for poor results. It is important to keep in mind, however, that this aspect of the delegation process is one of the primary reasons some supervisors are reluctant to delegate. Sometimes higher management mistakenly reinforces this reluctance of supervisors to delegate.

self-check

Could the $5,000 mistake mentioned earlier have been handled in such a way that it served as a learning experience and did not reinforce the manager's reluctance to delegate? How?

EFFECTIVE DELEGATION

In one of the classic books on the delegation process, Donald and Eleanor Laird point out that there is a big difference between making meaningful assignments to those below you and asking them to do the dirty jobs and meaningless activities you don't want to do yourself.[1] They emphasize that true delegation involves granting to the delegatee the authority needed to get the job done. Also, the decision making involved in the assignment is either shared or delegated entirely, and the delegatee is given freedom to handle details on his or her own initiative.

 click! http://www.saturn.com

To ensure accountability, controls are set up to check the effectiveness of the delegation. These controls can take many forms, such as personal observation by the delegator, periodic reports by the delegatee, or statistical reports concerning output, costs, grievances, and so forth. When mistakes occur, the supervisor can use these as a basis for coaching and developing employees.

Knowing When to Delegate

It's not always easy to know when to delegate authority—and what authority to delegate—to those working for you. Although there are no absolute guidelines to go by, there are at least a lot of red flags that signal a need to delegate. Consider the following:

1. Do you do work that an employee could do just as well?
2. Do you think that you are the only one who actually knows how the job should be done?
3. Do you leave the job each day loaded down with details to take care of at home?
4. Do you frequently stay after hours catching up on work even though your peers don't?
5. Do you seem never to get through with your work?
6. Are you a perfectionist?
7. Do you tell your employees how to solve problems?[2]

If you answered "yes" to many of these questions, you probably need to learn to delegate more effectively.

How the Delegation Process Operates

click! http://www.tvo.org/ pdonline/forprincipals/ delegate.html

Exhibit 6–4 illustrates how an effective delegation process operates. Notice that authority, such as for performing assigned duties, carrying out special assignments, achieving objectives, and meeting standards, is granted down the line from higher management to supervisory managers, then to workers. In turn, responsibility for using that authority is created, and accountability controls are established to ensure that the authority is properly used.

The practical steps in delegating authority effectively are listed in Exhibit 6–5. Notice that the process begins with creating an organizational climate in which delegation can occur effectively and ends only when other managers, as well as the employee, know about the delegation.

The Principle of Parity of Authority and Responsibility

When responsibilities and duties are assigned, adequate authority should be granted to meet the responsibilities and carry out the assignments. This is known as the **parity principle**. Some management experts go so far as to say that authority should be equal to responsibility. Quite candidly, first-line managers rarely have all the authority they would like to have to meet their responsibilities. This is also true of many other positions, including staff positions.

parity principle
When duties are assigned, adequate authority is delegated to those who must carry out the assignments.

Win Cagle, a supervisor with L. Hunter, a mail-order department store, was responsible for 25 employees who worked in the customer service

Exhibit 6–4

*Process of Effective
Delegation*

**Granting Authority and
Assigning Responsibility**
To perform duties, carry out
special assignments,
achieve objectives,
and meet standards.

Higher
Management

Supervisory
Management

Workers

**Establishing Accountability
Controls**
Reports on costs, production,
grievances, and turnover.
Special reports from lower
levels on delegated
assignments.

**When there are differences between actual
performance and planned performance, corrective
action takes place by coaching, counseling, or
correcting mistakes.**

department. He had just walked out of a meeting where the same old
line had been handed down—how supervisors were being given more
authority and should be accountable for results. "I've heard it all before—many times," he said. He continued: "Human Resources will send
me warm bodies. The training department will turn them loose before
they're ready, and the pay is so low we don't keep them very long. I
can't discipline the way I'd like to without running into opposition. The
maintenance department is stretched thin. Last week I had some computers locked up for four hours before they even got to it. We ran out of
office supplies last week because of the shippers' strike. And yet they
talk about how I'm responsible for results. That's a laugh! We have all
the responsibility, but no authority."

Exhibit 6–5

*Steps in Effective
Delegation*

- Management establishes an organizational climate in which delegation can occur effectively.
- Higher management makes sure that one manager's responsibility and authority do not overlap or duplicate those of other managers in the organization.
- Management establishes controls (feedback mechanisms) to measure the progress of an employee from start to finish of the assignment.
- The supervisor assigns specific duties and responsibilities to an employee, who accepts them.
- The supervisor grants enough authority to the employee to allow the latter to carry out the assignment.
- The supervisor and the employee agree on the specific results expected and how the results will be measured.
- The supervisor clearly communicates the delegated responsibility to all other managers so that the employee can carry out the assignment with a minimum of confusion and disagreement with other managers.

Proper delegation can help operations run more efficiently by enabling supervisors to focus on areas where their talents and knowledge are better utilized.

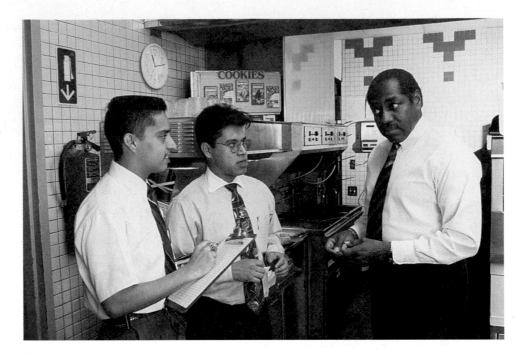

self-check

Is the situation described above true of most organizations? Do supervisors have authority to match their responsibility? Explain.

As we indicated in Chapter 1, many of the duties held by supervisors a number of years ago have now been shifted to staff departments such as the human resources department. Consequently, some of the authority that went with the supervisor's position years ago, such as the right to hire and fire, is no longer associated with the position or has been greatly modified. As a result, supervisors must be very wise in the use of what little authority is granted to them. This situation also places a premium on the supervisor's leadership abilities and skill in communicating with, motivating, counseling, coaching, and developing employees. We will explore these areas in depth in later chapters.

Note that in the chapter preview Allegro lacked the authority in the restaurant situation to do certain things. However, he used his leadership and influence to tackle problems outside his job description and got the job done with very little authority. Also, in the CAT project he used his influence with people outside the Massachusetts Highway organization to get problems resolved so that construction on the tunnel could continue. In these situations Allegro had tremendous influence but very little authority.

Time Required for Effective Delegation

Effective delegation does not occur quickly or easily. As we shall see in the chapter on leadership, how much a supervisor can delegate depends on the ability and willingness of employees to handle delegation. Sometimes a supervisor is faced with untrained and relatively new employees. In such situations, effective delegation is contingent on the training and development of the employees. Thus, the process requires planning and should proceed gradually. On the other hand, if a supervisor has a group of capable and well-trained employees, the process can occur more rapidly.

PARTIES INVOLVED IN EFFECTIVE DELEGATION

If a delegation system is to be effective, three important parties must have a role in it. These are higher management, the supervisor, and the employees to whom authority is delegated.

The Role of Higher Management

3 Discuss the roles of various parties in achieving effective delegation.

As we have already observed, higher management can have a major impact on whether effective delegation takes place. A fault-finding atmosphere—in which higher management is quick to criticize and fails to offer positive feedback for good results—will negate the process of effective delegation.

One reason delegation is so difficult is that either overcontrol or undercontrol by higher management can hinder the process. Other ways higher management can hinder the process include failing to provide objectives and policies, not sharing information with lower levels, and making decisions too slowly.

The Role of the Supervisor

In his practical book *No-Nonsense Delegation*, Dale McConkey has developed the role of both delegator and delegatee quite well.[3] The points that apply to the role of the supervisor are these:

1. Communicate clearly.
2. Specify authority.
3. Encourage employee participation.
4. Review results, not methods.
5. Show trust.
6. Seek recommendations.
7. Share credit, not blame.
8. Give support.
9. Be consistent.
10. Know your people.
11. Develop your people.

Points 3, 5, and 11 in the preceding list are especially important. No one has highlighted this idea better than Tom Peters, co-author of the bestselling book *In Search of Excellence.* After this book was published, Peters discussed what is involved in achieving supervisory excellence. He indicated that the biggest mistake managers make is forgetting that excellence comes not from a good reporting system or any other system of control but from people who care. He concluded that "managers have to be willing to give up enough control to allow the average person who works for them to honest-to-God own his or her job and feel responsible for it. A supervisor isn't going to win unless he or she does that."[4]

Most important for the supervisor is training employees so that they can do their jobs without the supervisor's intervention. Although it may be ego-satisfying to have employees frequently asking your advice and help regarding their duties, it does not develop them nor does it assist you in effectively carrying out your responsibilities.

> In the chapter preview, Allegro carried out the points listed by McConkey and worked with O'Meara as a true partner. He was especially interested in her growth and development, particularly in the technical aspects of the job. Since O'Meara has a degree in business management and not engineering, Allegro makes sure she is exposed to the technical issues. He also has arranged for her to manage complete programs, such as coordination with Massport and liaison with the laboratory. O'Meara has responded by exceeding Allegro's already high expectations and is doing great work.

The Role of Employees to Whom Authority Is Delegated

McConkey's tips for the employees to whom authority is delegated include the following:

1. Take the initiative.
2. Relate to the supervisor.
3. Be sure the delegation is realistic.
4. Determine and give feedback regarding results.
5. Report periodically to the supervisor.
6. Carry out the delegated assignments effectively.
7. Develop yourself to be able to handle more involved assignments.

It is important that employees not run to the supervisor each time a minor problem arises. Exhibit 6–6 illustrates how a wise supervisor might handle an employee who was reluctant to accept authority. Rather than take on a task (the monkey) that is the nurse's responsibility, the supervisor refuses to accept the responsibility and tosses the monkey back to the employee. Only when major problems arise should an employee solicit the supervisor's advice.

> Two things that Allegro really appreciates about O'Meara are that she demonstrates tremendous initiative and reports to him important developments—"Joe, I want you to know that I made this decision." She not only brings to his attention issues or problems, but also suggested solutions. If she has a question, she has the self-confidence to come to him for advice or assistance.

WHY SUPERVISORS FAIL TO DELEGATE

4 Understand why some supervisors are reluctant to delegate.

Industrialist Andrew Carnegie once said: "When a man realizes he can call others in to help him do a job better than he can do alone, he has taken a big step in his life." In the formative years of your life, most of your success in school work and in summer jobs depends primarily on your individual efforts. Achievement and success usually do not come from inspiring and working

Exhibit 6–6

The Supervisor "Placing the Monkey" Back on the Employee with the Primary Responsibility

with and developing people. Then, all of a sudden, you leave school. After working awhile, you are placed in a leadership position. Now, instead of being responsible for two or three assignments, you are responsible for working with and developing people to accomplish numerous assignments.

Perhaps, as a new supervisor, you can do several things better than anyone you supervise, but can you possibly do all things as well? Unfortunately, many supervisors apparently think they can, because they fail to delegate. Or, like Marion Dawson in Case 6–2 at the end of the chapter, they don't trust people and they destroy the effects of delegation by oversupervising.

Why do some supervisors have so much difficulty delegating authority? As we have already indicated, their previous experience in nonleadership positions sometimes gives them a mistaken notion of how a supervisor should function. In addition, since they are accountable for what their employees do or do not accomplish, it is natural for them to want to stay on top of everything that happens. However, this attitude usually causes resentment among the people supervised.

Supervisors who do not delegate must carry the entire burden of both their jobs and their employees' jobs. (See Exhibit 6–7.) The following are some of the reasons supervisors have difficulty delegating:

1. Since supervisors are held accountable for results, some of them hesitate to delegate out of fear that their employees will make mistakes.
2. Some supervisors believe that when they delegate, they surrender some of their power, thus decreasing their authority.

3. Some supervisors have a personality that makes them want to dominate things completely. We see this trait in the way some parents raise their children.

4. Some supervisors do not delegate because of a lack of trust in others.

5. Some supervisors do not delegate because they are insecure and are afraid that their employees will do so well that they will be recognized and promoted ahead of the supervisors.

6. Some supervisors correctly assess that some employees need more training, coaching, and experience before certain things can be delegated.

self-check

Can you identify other reasons some supervisors have difficulty delegating? What are they?

DEALING WITH INEFFECTIVE EMPLOYEES

Sometimes no matter how appropriate and effective a supervisor and his organization are in trying to assist, frame, coach, empower, and train an employee, things just don't work out. This type of situation is what the French management theorist Henri Fayol had in mind when he stated that a principle of leadership is to eliminate the incompetent. However, he went on to say that before doing so, one should do everything he or she can to help the employee to develop so that person can competently perform his or her duties and responsibilities.

Generally, Allegro has had very positive experiences with people meeting or exceeding his high standards and expectations. However, in one case an employee continually disappointed him in carrying out his duties and responsibilities. The following are steps Allegro followed in trying to turn an incompetent employee into a competent one.

1. He held a coaching session with the employee and, among other things, tried to share expectations in a more positive manner.

2. Together they discussed specifics of what could be done to improve the situation.

3. He spent more time with the employee and initiated routine end-of-the-day discussions. During these discussions, Allegro would provide feedback to the employee and explain how he, himself, would handle certain situations.

4. He started taking the employee to more meetings with him. Afterwards they would debrief by sharing how certain issues could be resolved.

5. After a period of time, Allegro backed away, delegated authority, and supervised by results. Unfortunately, the results were unsatisfactory and Allegro removed the employee from the position.

self-check

Do you think Allegro effectively carried out Fayol's leadership principle? Would you have handled it differently?

5 Gain insight into how to turn a delegation weakness into a strength.

RELATING DELEGATION TO SUCCESS OR FAILURE

Some of us are better delegators than others. In many cases, we use delegation only as a last resort. Perhaps we have no technical expertise in the area to which we have been assigned. Or perhaps we are stretched so thin that, against our better judgment, we are forced to call on others to help. Here's how one manager puts it:

> **Our company has an interesting approach to training high-potential supervisors in becoming delegators. We assign the supervisor who is disinclined toward delegation to head up a work unit of 30 or more people. Either the supervisor learns to delegate or he fails.**

Eight Ways to Fail

Undoubtedly, your ability to delegate becomes more crucial the greater your responsibility on the job. This ability becomes vital to your success or failure. Dr. Van Oliphant, a management consultant, has examined jobs from the standpoint of failure. His "eight ways to guarantee failure on the job" include several items related to delegation, as shown in Exhibit 6–8. These eight points are particularly applicable to the supervisor's job.

Exhibit 6–8

Eight Ways to Guarantee Failure on the Job

1. Develop a "know-it-all" attitude.
2. Do most things yourself, since you do them better.
3. Submerge yourself in details and trivia.
4. Disregard the need to cultivate peer relationships.
5. Procrastinate in making decisions.
6. Forget to balance the emphases on production and people.
7. Refuse to share the credit for success.
8. Place the blame for failure on subordinates.

self-check

Which of the items listed in Exhibit 6–8 seem most closely related to delegation? Explain. Are you guilty of practicing any of these? If so, which one(s)?

Turning a Weakness into a Strength

One of the premier banking schools in the United States is the Banking School of the South at Louisiana State University. Most of the bankers who are selected to attend commit to two weeks of training and education each summer for three years. They are also required to write answers to a series of home-study problems that are graded by the lead instructor in that particular subject. Several years ago one of the tasks in the supervisor/leadership area was "Write out and prioritize your life and five-year goals. Next, write out and prioritize your top five strengths and top five weaknesses or blind spots in achieving your top ranked goals. Finally, develop an action plan to turn your top ranked weakness into a strength."

A widespread goal of the bankers was to advance in the banking hierarchy based on their abilities. This goal was anticipated since most were already in supervisory/leadership positions and had been selected for the school in part because of their potential to advance within their respective banks. What may be surprising to our readers is that the number one weakness or blind spot identified by the majority of the junior class was in the area of delegation. Exhibit 6–9 illustrates an action plan of how one banker turned a potential weakness into a strength.

self-check

Do you think it would be a good idea to have all officers develop an action plan to improve their efficiency and effectiveness? Why or why not?

6 Indicate ways to achieve effective delegation.

INEFFECTIVE DELEGATION: A SOLUTION

Through her work with thousands of supervisors, management consultant Suzanne Savory has gained insight into the problem of ineffective delegation.[5] The supervisor's primary job is working with and developing people, she says, but unfortunately the people selected for that position throughout corporate America are often the best technicians, not the best managers of people. She goes on to say that these individuals get their "high" by developing their technical skills in order to become top achievers. Then, when they are promoted to the position of supervisor, they continue to try to get their high by being good technicians; consequently, they oversupervise or do the important technical work themselves.

reframing
Emphasizing management training and development programs.

The solution is what Savory calls **reframing**, or emphasizing management training and development programs. She states that this reframing is the goal of most management education today. "Generally," she concludes, "supervisory and management training is designed to teach the supervisor how to be a coach

Exhibit 6–9

Action Plan of James McKenney Vice President and Supervisor of Lending

I. Statement of my objective

To greatly improve my efficiency and effectiveness in carrying out the delegation process with the lending officers reporting to me.

II. Analysis of the problem or objective

A. At the banking school when we discussed the 16 problem styles (Myers-Briggs profiles and analysis), I discovered that the characteristics of my type can lead to being a very effective leader if a few potential blind spots can be overcome. It seems that those who are sensing/thinking types (as I am) are so conscientious that our attitude is "If you want it done right, do it yourself." This statement definitely applies to me.

B. When I was recently promoted to this position, the president of the bank gave me a number of positive reasons for my promotion. He also cautioned me that with my increased responsibilities, I could expect to get involved in activities as previously, but he wanted me to focus on developing the skills and knowledge of our loan officers and improve bottom line results.

C. I realize that most of my life I earned good grades in high school and college because of individual effort. This carried over to my work habits as a loan officer, but I now realize that to be a successful supervisor, I need to develop my team and make use of coaching and empowerment.

III. Development of alternative solutions

A. Start having biweekly meetings for one hour after banking hours.

1. At our first meeting we will jointly develop objectives that enhance and reinforce the bank's financial goal.

2. At our subsequent meetings we will review our progress and discuss any problem loans.

B. Set up a participative individual management-by-objectives program. This plan will allow individual bank officers to set performance objectives that support our lending division's objectives. During this process I will play the role of coach and mentor, and after the initial meeting, set up performance review sessions with each officer every six months or as needed.

C. Once every six months at our biweekly meeting we will conduct a brainstorming session to identify our strengths and any problems, issues, or missed opportunities we need to address.

D. I will explore educational opportunities available for our officers including scheduling several officers for our state banking school or the Banking School of the South.

IV. Final action plan

I have begun implementing all of the alternative ideas (A, B, C, and D in Section III). Prior to sending this to you, I met and discussed the ideas with our president and CEO. He was most enthusiastic and supportive and is presenting the concept to our executive committee for possible implementation in all divisions of our bank.

SOURCE: *This example is based on the experiences of Don Mosley when he served as coordinator and instructor for the management and leadership segment of the Banking School of the South at Louisiana State University. The name is fictional to ensure no embarrassment to the actual banker.*

rather than a player. If he is to be an effective supervisor, he must learn to get his high not from playing but from coaching."

If this reframing does not occur, the Peter principle may come into play. This principle was first espoused by Laurence Peter and Raymond Hull in a satirical—yet serious—analysis of incompetence in hierarchical organizations.[6] In examining hundreds of cases of occupational incompetence, Peter and Hull had seen the same phenomenon over and over: A competent person in a lower position in a hierarchy is promoted to a higher position and becomes incompetent. The competent student becomes incompetent as a teacher. The competent teacher becomes incompetent as a department head or principal. The competent technician becomes incompetent as a supervisor. Naturally, incompetent employees are not promoted further. From this analysis, Peter and Hull formulated the **Peter principle,** which states that "in a hierarchy, every employee rises to his [or her] level of incompetence."

Peter principle
States that in a hierarchy, every employee rises to his or her level of incompetence.

The authors of this text agree with Savory about the importance of reframing. In fact, this book is based on our observations in working with thousands of supervisors and managers, both experienced and inexperienced, in development programs. Almost without exception, those receiving management training for the first time rated the programs exceptional in helping them to do a better job of managing. They usually added, "I wish I had received this type of training earlier."

Organizations throughout the country are realizing that they have neglected the training of managers and are beginning to spend more energy and money on correcting the situation. For example, a large hospital designed a series of management development programs around the contents of this book, thereby making the Peter principle inoperative.

In 1995 Labor Secretary Robert Reich reported on studies conducted by researchers highlighting the considerable profits in employee empowerment. For example, Motorola estimates that it earns $30 for every $1 invested in employee training.[7]

chapter review

(1) Recognize the importance of delegation.

The delegation process is a partnering process between a supervisor and employees, bosses, and colleagues. Experiential learning is an important part of delegation, allowing employees to grow and develop by "learning through doing." If the employee's efforts result in a mistake, together the employee and supervisor can identify what happened, analyze factors involved, and discover principles to help in future situations.

Effective delegation is essential to performing the supervisory management job successfully. In addition to developing people, delegation (1) allows the supervisor to do other things, (2) accomplishes more work, and (3) improves control.

(2) Explain what is involved in the delegation process, including authority, responsibility, and accountability.

The process of delegation has three aspects: granting authority, assigning responsibility, and holding people accountable for results. Because accountability is essential to maintaining effective control over results, a person who delegates an assignment should not be able to escape accountability for poor results. Controls to ensure effective delegation can include personal observation by the delegator, periodic reports by the delegatee, and statistical reports concerning output, costs, and grievances.

③ **Discuss the roles of various parties in achieving effective delegation.**

Effective delegation also requires knowing when to delegate, understanding how the delegation process operates, attempting to follow the parity principle, and taking the time required to train employees. Although higher management should be supportive and the supervisor should delegate clearly and show trust, it is the responsibility of employees to function on their own and turn to the supervisor for help only when there is a major problem. Employees who frequently ask for advice may not be fully developing themselves or effectively carrying out responsibilities, though they may be stroking their supervisors' ego.

Employees to whom authority is delegated should (1) take the initiative, (2) relate to the supervisor, (3) make sure the delegation is realistic, (4) give feedback regarding results, (5) carry out assignments effectively, and (6) work toward handling increasingly involved assignments.

④ **Understand why some supervisors are reluctant to delegate.**

Despite the benefits of effective delegation, some supervisors fail to do so for a variety of reasons. A supervisor, for example, may closely monitor or even perform an employee's work because of his/her accountability to a manager. However, this attitude can cause resentment among employees and leave the supervisor little time to plan and coordinate with other departments.

⑤ **Gain insight into how to turn a delegation weakness into a strength.**

Many supervisors are so conscientious that they follow this guide: If you want it done right, do it yourself. However, in a supervisory position, it is important to develop an empowerment plan to share responsibilities and duties without losing control to offset this tendency. In Exhibit 6–9 James McKenney demonstrated one way this empowerment can be done.

⑥ **Indicate ways to achieve effective delegation.**

One of the solutions to ineffective delegation is to emphasize management training and development. This will reduce the probability that your organization will be subject to the Peter principle, which states that employees rise to their level of incompetence.

---

important terms

accountability *166*
delegation of authority *164*
experiential learning *163*
job descriptions *165*

parity principle *168*
Peter principle *178*
reframing *176*

---

questions for review and discussion

1. Discuss four reasons delegation is important.
2. Describe the process of delegation.
3. Explain the interrelationships among authority, responsibility, and accountability.

4. What is the principle of parity of authority and responsibility? How does it operate in practice?

5. Why do some supervisors fail to delegate effectively? If this situation were a common problem in an organization, what could be done to increase supervisors' skills in delegating effectively?

6. What are the roles played in effective delegation?

7. In what way or ways can higher management affect the delegation process?

8. In what way or ways can employees affect the delegation process?

9. Do you think Joe Allegro was correct in the way he dealt with the employee as detailed in the section dealing with ineffective employees? Why or why not?

10. Do you agree or disagree with Dr. Van Oliphant's eight ways to guarantee failure listed in Exhibit 6–8? Elaborate on your reasoning.

skill builder 6-1

Test Your Delegation Habits

Assume you are a supervisor. For each of the following statements, rate your agreement with a number between 1 and 5: 5 (strongly agree), 4 (agree), 3 (undecided), 2 (disagree), and 1 (strongly disagree).

_____ 1. I'd delegate more, but the jobs I delegate never seem to get done the way I want them to be done.

_____ 2. I don't feel I have the time to delegate properly.

_____ 3. I carefully check on employees' work without letting them know I'm doing it, so I can correct their mistakes if necessary before they cause too many problems.

_____ 4. I delegate the whole job, giving the employee the opportunity to complete it without any involvement on my part. Then I'll view the end result.

_____ 5. When I have given clear instructions and the job isn't done right, I get upset.

_____ 6. I believe that the staff lacks the commitment that I have, so any job I delegate won't get done as well as I would do it.

_____ 7. I'd delegate more, but I believe I can do the task better than the person I might delegate it to.

_____ 8. I'd delegate more, but if the individual to whom I delegate the task does an incompetent job, I'll be severely criticized.

_____ 9. If I were to delegate the task, my job wouldn't be nearly as much fun.

_____10. When I delegate a job, I often find that the outcome is such that I end up doing the job over again myself.

_____11. I have not found that delegation really saves much time.

_____12. I delegate a task clearly and concisely, explaining exactly how it should be accomplished.

_____13. I can't delegate as much as I'd like to, because my employees lack the necessary experience.

_____14. I feel that when I delegate I lose control.

_____15. I would delegate more, but I'm pretty much of a perfectionist.

_____16. I work longer hours than I should.

_____17. I can give employees the routine tasks, but I feel I must personally handle the nonroutine jobs.

_____18. My own boss expects me to keep very close to all details of the work.

_____TOTAL SCORE

Rate yourself:

Score

18–35   You are probably a superior delegator.

36–53   You have some room to grow.

54–71   Your delegation habits and attitudes could be substantially improved.

72–90   You are seriously failing to properly use your staff.

CASE 6–1

The Promotion Decision

Bert Ryborn is one of several candidates being considered for the position of division manager of one of the larger divisions of his insurance company. Ryborn's personnel file indicates that he joined the company as a trainee 16 years ago. His first assignment involved working in several departments on a rotation basis.

After the job rotation period, Ryborn was made a department supervisor. The work performed by his department was always in perfect order. One of the reasons for this high degree of accuracy was that Ryborn exercised close personal supervision over all aspects of the work. On more than one occasion, Ryborn became involved in the actual work to ensure that it was done correctly.

Later, Ryborn was promoted to area manager and given supervision of several departments. During his tenure in this position, there were signs that all was not well with Ryborn's supervision of his employees. In fact, one of his supervisors resigned during this period, stating that he had obtained a better position with another firm. However, during an exit interview with the human resources manager, he indicated that his real reason was Ryborn's management style. He added:

> **Bert demands personal approval of everything taking place within my department, even down to a pay change for the newest employee. He personally prepares most of the reports that provide data to the division manager. He also plans much of the work of the supervisors reporting to him.**

The vice-president, Ralph Johnson, is a staunch supporter of promoting Ryborn to division manager.

Answer the following questions:

1. Why do you think Ryborn has succeeded in his positions so far? Do you think that is the reason Johnson supports him for the promotion?
2. Do you think Ryborn will be a successful division manager?
3. Assume you are the human resources manager and Johnson has asked you for your advice on promoting Ryborn. Role play your meeting with Vice-President Johnson.

Marion Dawson's Problem
group activity

Marion Dawson was quite pleased when she graduated from Community College with an associate degree in business. While pursuing her degree, she had been employed as a worker with an international company specializing in fast foods similar to McDonald's, Wendy's, and Burger King. She was a very efficient worker and was soon elevated to handling the outside window sales where only the best employees were placed. She was also promised an opportunity to work for the organization upon completion of her associate degree program. After graduation, Dawson entered the company's management training program. From there she was placed in a busy store location as assistant manager. As an achievement-oriented person, Dawson saw this as the first step toward her long-range goal of becoming a regional manager or having her own franchise some day.

In her position as assistant manager, things went well. Dawson was familiar with all operations, and she practiced close supervision, stayed on top of things, and really stressed high production and fast service. Six months later she was promoted to manager at another busy store that was the most profitable within the region. In fact, the previous manager had just been promoted to regional manager and was now Dawson's boss.

At this stage of her career, Dawson was well ahead of schedule in her long-range program of becoming a regional manager. She had anticipated spending a minimum of two years as an assistant manager before having an opportunity to advance to manager. Her next career objective of becoming a regional manager seemed well within reach, since the industry

and company were growing at a rapid rate.

Dawson surmised that what had worked for her as an assistant manager would also work for her as a manager. She was not really concerned that the assistant manager and four supervisors who would be reporting to her were older and more experienced. After all, results were what counted. At her first meeting, she stressed her high expectations and set as an objective "to increase profits by 10 percent within three months." The yearly objective was to be a 20 percent increase. She indicated that she believed strongly in the management principle of follow-up. Not only would she be closely following up on their work, but she would expect them to do the same with store employees.

Two months later, overall profits in her store were down by 7 percent, and Dawson was beginning to worry. It seemed that the more she stressed profits and service and tried to follow delegated assignments closely, the more resistance she encountered. Although the resistance was not open, it was definitely present. In fact, she sensed hostility even from the part-time workers, a group with which she had always been close.

At the end of three months, profits had decreased by 10 percent.

Instructions:

Meet in groups of six or seven people. Make a diagnosis of what the problem is, and identify the critical issues involved. Select one member of your team to present what the team thinks Dawson's boss should do. After all teams have presented, the class should vote on which approach offers the best solution.

Preparing an Action Plan

Either consider your current job or one you will have in the future. In your current or future supervisory position prepare an action plan of how you will develop the personnel who report to you through the delegation process. Include in your plan how you can do so without losing control but still carry out the concept of empowerment and employee development.

Leading

7   Communication

8   Motivation

9   Leadership

10 Managing Change, Group
    Development, and Team Building

4 part

chapter 7

• outline

What Is Communication?
Communication Process Model
Electronic Communication Technology
Importance of Nonverbal Messages

Flows of Communication
The Vertical Flows: Downward and Upward
Communication
Lateral-Diagonal Flows
Informal Communication

**Barriers to Effective Supervisory
Communication**
Organizational Barriers
Interpersonal and Language Barriers

Improving Supervisory Communications
Set the Proper Climate
Plan for Effective Communication
Use Repetition to Reinforce Key Ideas
Encourage the Use of Feedback
Become a Better Listener

Communication

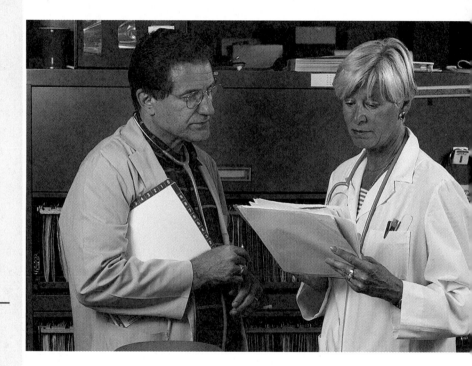

Communication is something so simple and difficult that we can never put it in simple words.

T. S. Matthews

I know you believe you understand what you think I said, but I am not sure you realize that what you heard is not what I meant.

Author Unknown

Too many people think they are wonderful with people because they have the ability to speak well. What they fail to realize is that being wonderful with people means being able to listen well.

Peter Drucker

Good News, Bad News?

learning objectives

After reading and studying this chapter, you should be able to:

1. Describe the five components of the communication process model.

2. Explain the forms of electronic communication technology.

3. Explain the different ways in which nonverbal communications influence supervisory communication.

4. Identify the three basic flows of formal communication in an organization.

5. Explain the managerial communication style matrix.

6. Identify and explain how organizational, interpersonal, and language barriers affect supervisory communication.

7. Identify five specific actions supervisors can take to improve their communications.

8. Show how a supervisor can use feedback to improve communication.

9. Define and illustrate active listening skills.

This chapter preview presents a dialogue between Ann Bishop, a medical records clerk with City Hospital, and Jean Curtis, the administrative section head. As you read this, think about the communication in this situation. Do you think it's effective? Why or why not? Would Bishop or Curtis answer this question differently?

Bishop: You wanted to see me?

Curtis: Yes, I did. I'll be right with you. Have a seat. (Curtis swivels her chair, facing away from Bishop, and continues talking on the phone for about four minutes. Her tone of voice and body movements show that she is upset about something. After hanging up, she swivels around, faces Bishop, and takes off her watch, placing it face up on the desk in front of her.) Ann, this will only take a few minutes.

Bishop: Okay.

Curtis: (Opens a personnel file folder, presumably Bishop's, looks at it and begins speaking.) As you know, I like to get right to the point, Ann. We've had two people leave us in the past three weeks, one involuntarily. The point is that you're ready to move on. You've been in archives for six months; we badly need some help in coding charts. Beginning next week I'd like to work you there.

Bishop: (Looks uncomfortable, shifts in her chair.) Into coding? But I've never done coding . . . .

Curtis: Don't worry about that. Of course you don't know coding yet. You'll have to learn. It's not really that complicated. You just have to be accurate. You'll do just fine.

Bishop: But I like working in archives. It's . . .

Curtis: When you were hired you were told you'd start off in archives, but people have to work where there's the greatest need. And you'll be making about $160 a month more in coding than where you are now. I know you'll like coding . . . in a few weeks you'll feel just as comfortable in coding as you do now in archives. I've alerted Stephanie Koval that you'll be working with her next week to learn the ropes . . . (Phone rings and Curtis tells the caller she'll be right up.) I've got to get some reports to the assistant administrator. I know you'll be really pleased in coding, Ann. It will be a wonderful opportunity for you. (Puts watch on and rises. Begins gathering papers as Bishop rises, turns, and walks away.)

The opening quotations certainly apply to this situation, don't they? Bishop will likely walk away from the meeting feeling pretty uncomfortable about the job change—perhaps not so much because of the change itself but because of the manner in which Curtis presented it. Each day, supervisors like Curtis and their organizations pay a high price for ineffective communication. These negative results include poor morale, reduced motivation, wasted money and time, lack of cooperation between people and departments, and even physical injury.

Communication plays a critical role in human relations, as well as in task-related areas of supervision. In a typical workday, supervisors assign jobs, discuss coordination efforts with people from other departments, have discussions with their own bosses, attend meetings, listen to and counsel employees—the list could go on and on. As you learned in Chapter 2, the emerging supervisor role of teacher, leader, and coach is strongly communication-linked. Studies of managers and supervisors have shown that they spend 60–80 percent of their time in some form of communication.[1]

WHAT IS COMMUNICATION?

Many supervisors think that communication is just a matter of "telling it like it is." They fail to recognize the difficulties involved in such a simple approach. When communication breakdowns occur, they are more interested in placing blame than in finding out what went wrong. To really understand a supervisor's role in communication, you must first learn about the basic communication process.

(1) Describe the five components of the communication process model.

Communication Process Model

Rather than define communication in words, we will use an illustration of the **communication process model** (see Exhibit 7–1). The components of the model are (1) the sender, (2) the message, (3) the channel, (4) the receiver, and (5) feedback. The barriers that interfere with the process are presented separately later in the chapter.

communication process model
Model of the five components of communication and their relationships.

sender
Originates and sends a message.

The Sender. The **sender** is the person who originates a message. Sometimes an inner need triggers the urge to communicate. When you say "Pass the salt, please," you are reacting to a physical need. When you say "I care about you," you may be reflecting a need for affection. When, as a supervisor, you say "You'll have to do this report over," you may be reflecting a need for esteem (you want to be proud of work done in your department) or a need for security (you fear that your own boss will reprimand you).

message
Words and/or nonverbal expressions that transmit meaning.

The Message. The **message** consists of words and/or nonverbal expressions that are capable of transmitting meaning. In the preceding examples, the messages are verbal. But as in the Curtis–Bishop interaction, nonverbal messages, such as placing a watch on the desk and smiling or frowning, are equally—if not more—important.

channel
The means used to pass a message.

The Channel. The **channel** is the means used to pass the message. Channels include face-to-face communication, the telephone, written forms (such as memos, reports, newsletters, or e-mail), and group meetings.

> One supervisor related how his crew was working on an important machine breakdown when the plant manager chewed him out for taking too long to complete the job. "I didn't mind getting chewed out as much as I minded the way he did it," said the supervisor. "It was via e-mail, and he copied the whole plant."

Exhibit 7–1

*Communication
Process Model*

Sender — **Message** — Channel — Receiver — Message — Feedback — Sender

receiver
The ultimate destination of the sender's message.

The Receiver. The **receiver** is the ultimate destination of the sender's message. The receiver is the one who assigns meaning to the message. On a daily basis, a supervisor frequently acts in the dual role of sender and receiver, as Exhibit 7–2 shows.

Feedback. Frequently we send a message in response to someone else's message. The response is called **feedback.** For example, your employee may ask "Why do I have to do the report over?" When you answer this question, you are then sending feedback in response to the employee's message.

feedback
The response that a communicator receives.

The communication process model makes communication appear very simple. In reality, though, the communication process is quite complicated and involves many variables.

 click! http://www.mars.com/

② Explain the forms of electronic communication technology.

Electronic Communication Technology

Communication practices at the supervisory level are being greatly impacted by advancements in electronic communication technology. Just as computer flu-

Exhibit 7–2

*The Supervisor as a
Sender and a Receiver*

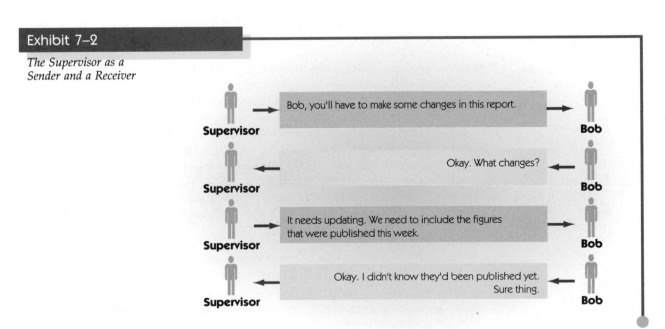

ency has become an essential employee requirement in many jobs, it has also become a prerequisite for increasingly more supervisory positions. More and more supervisors are making use of electronically linked computer networks within their organization (intranets) and external to their organization (the Internet) to access information, transfer information, and importantly, to communicate through electronic mail, simply known as e-mail. **E-mail** refers to documents created, transmitted, and read entirely on computer. Simply by entering into a computer a receiver's address and the desired message, a simple click of the Send command instantly conveys the message to the desired individual receiver or group.

e-mail
Documents created, transmitted, and read entirely on computer.

 http://www.hotmail .com

> **Sharon Olds, remarketing supervisor for AutoFin (see preview in Chapter 1), sends and receives daily in excess of 20 e-mail messages to people within her organization. These originate from and are sent to all levels. But even though she is physically housed near their cubicles in the immediate work area, Sharon frequently uses e-mail to communicate with her subordinates. E-mail allows her to be spontaneous, reduces the time involved in walking to see if someone is available, and enables easy record keeping—with a click of the Print button, she has a paper copy of the message. Sharon uses e-mail to pass on to her team members information about policy and procedure, but also uses it to recognize individual and group performance.**

Advances in voice communication technology have also considerably impacted supervisory communication. Regardless of the supervisor's location, cellular phones enable him or her to keep in touch with employees and others. Digital pagers accomplish the same. Voice mail enables supervisors to leave messages when a receiver is not present, and to hear recorded voice messages from callers. Teleconferences enable supervisors to communicate with people in different locations simultaneously; videoconferences provide the additional benefit of visual communication.

Importance of Nonverbal Messages

(3) Explain the different ways in which nonverbal communications influence supervisory communication.

Nonverbal messages play a big role in communication. One expert, Albert Mehrabian, found that only about 7 percent of emotional meaning is communicated verbally; the other 93 percent is communicated nonverbally.[2] In other words, your impression of someone's emotions, such as anger, happiness, or fear, is formed more strongly from that person's tone of voice, facial expression, or other nonverbal means than from the words the person uses.

Supervisors have to be careful that their verbal and nonverbal signals are consistent and do not give the wrong impression. Moreover, supervisors can obtain much information from the nonverbal signals of others.

Basically, nonverbal signals, which can send positive or negative information, fall into six categories:

voice signals
Signals sent by placing emphasis on certain words, pauses, or the tone of voice used.

body signals
Nonverbal signals communicated by body action.

1. **Voice signals**—emphasis on certain words, pauses, or tone of voice. For example, can you say "Nice job, Evans" in such a way that it's actually a put-down?

2. **Body signals**—slumped posture, clenched fist, raised eyebrows, or the act of kicking a piece of equipment.

Nonverbal messages such as the body signals shown here, play a pivotal role in communication.

object signals
Nonverbal messages sent by physical objects.

space signals
Nonverbal messages sent based on physical distance from one another.

time signals
Nonverbal messages sent by time actions.

touching signals
Nonverbal messages sent by body contact.

3. **Object signals**—office furniture, such as desks or chairs, plus carpet, plaques and awards on the wall, clothing or jewelry worn.
4. **Space signals**—huddling close, being distant, or sitting beside someone.
5. **Time signals**—being on time, being available, or saving time.
6. **Touching signals**—shaking hands, sympathetic pat on the back, or touching someone to gain attention.

self-check

What were the important nonverbal communications that occurred in the Curtis–Bishop meeting in the chapter preview?

FLOWS OF COMMUNICATION

4 Identify the three basic flows of formal communication in an organization.

To put the supervisor's communication role in perspective, we need to examine the flows of communication in an entire organization. Here we will look at communication *within* the organization, rather than with outside groups such as customers, suppliers, or government agencies. Exhibit 7–3 shows that there are several directions in which formal communication flows: (1) downward, (2) upward, and (3) laterally or diagonally. A fourth flow is the flow of informal communication, commonly known as the *grapevine.*

The Vertical Flows: Downward and Upward Communication

downward communication
Flows that originate with supervisors and are passed down to employees.

Downward communication originates with managers and supervisors and passes down to employees. Tremendous amounts of communication constantly flow in this direction. Examples of downward communication include announcements of goals and objectives, policies, decisions, procedures, job assignments, and general information.

Exhibit 7–3

Flow of Formal Communication in an Organization

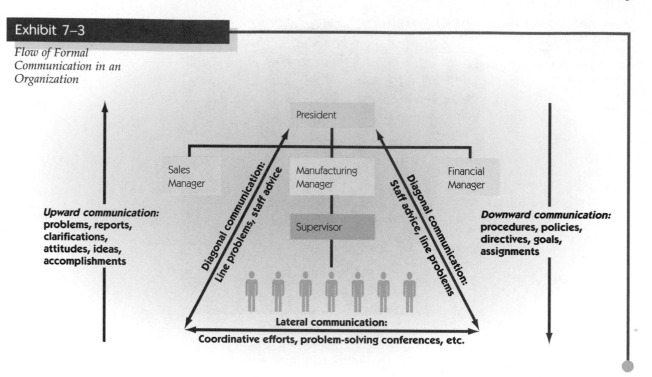

---

self-check

In the chapter preview, Jean Curtis's communication to Bishop was an example of downward communication. Note that Curtis passed the following specific verbal messages:

1. Three people have left the medical records section.
2. One was fired.
3. Bishop would begin working in coding next week.
4. Accuracy is an important part of coding.
5. Koval will help train Bishop.

Can you identify any other downward communications that Curtis sent?

Studies show that employees consistently rate their direct supervisor as their preferred choice of communication channel. Exhibit 7–4 lists communications that employees *like* to receive from their supervisor. Take a few seconds to examine the list before reading further. Do any items on this list strike you as being more crucial than others?

"Knowing where you stand" is listed by many employees as their single most important need. As one supervisor said to the authors in a workshop:

I think there's nothing worse than not knowing where you stand with your boss. I like knowing when I'm doing well, but I also need to know

Exhibit 7–4

Communications You Like to Receive from Your Supervisor

- *Role clarifications.* What's expected of you, how much authority and responsibility you have, and your job assignments.
- *Praise and recognition.* A supervisor's commendations on a job well done, compliments about you in the presence of third parties, and expressions of appreciation.
- *Constructive criticism and feedback.* Tactful criticism that demonstrates interest and implies a personal and professional concern on the part of the supervisor.
- *Demonstration of interest.* Communications reflecting interest in your professional growth and development, efforts to work with you to do a better job, and giving you undivided attention during conversation (as opposed to lack of eye contact or partial attention).
- *Requests for information or assistance.* Asking your opinion and advice, and consulting with you about relevant matters on the job.
- *Information that*
  a. Makes you feel important because you're "in the know"
  b. Pertains to department's progress, to other work team members, to plans for the department, and to contemplated changes
  c. Pertains to aspects of the overall organization, such as sales, forecasts, objectives, outlook for the future, and general internal changes of which the supervisor is aware
  d. Pertains to promotions, merit increases, desirable job assignments, and favors that can be granted by the supervisor

when I've goofed up. Having praise and compliments is nice; but when I screw up, I usually know it. So when my boss doesn't let me have some constructive criticism, he's really saying my work's not important enough to bother with or, even worse, that he expects no better from me. Performance feedback, good and bad, is my most important information need on the job.

upward communication
Flows from lower to upper organizational levels.

Upward communication flows from lower to upper organizational levels, as shown in Exhibit 7–5. It may consist of progress reports on a job; requests for help or clarification; communication about employees' concerns, attitudes, and feelings; or ideas and suggestions for improvements on the job.

Unfortunately, many supervisors do not seek these forms of upward communication, especially progress reports, from their employees. Neither do they obtain information about their employees' true attitudes, feelings, or suggestions for improvements. Japanese managers have a much better reputation than American managers for being receptive to their workers' needs and opinions, especially in the area of job improvements.

In Chapter 2 you learned that the cornerstone of a total quality management process is continuous improvement through employee involvement. Because of this, upward communication has become increasingly more important in today's organizational setting. In 1995, for instance, Toyota implemented over 60,000 new ideas that were received by workers at its five U.S. manufacturing plants.[3]

In addition to requesting oral or written progress reports, other means of encouraging upward communication from employees include suggestion systems, an open-door policy, attitude and morale surveys, group or individual meetings at which employees are encouraged to speak up, and hot lines where employees can anonymously solicit answers to questions or report unethical practices.

Exhibit 7–5

*Upward
Communication from
Workers to
Management*

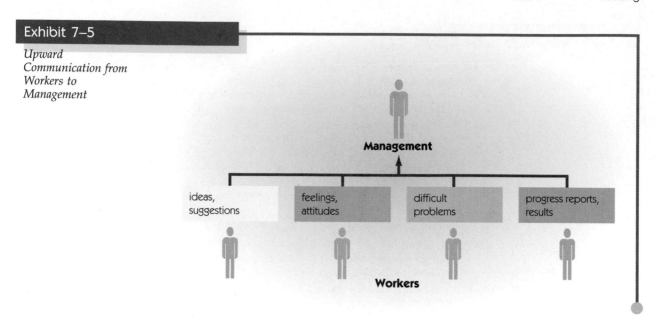

Superintendent Arch Patterson holds a weekly meeting of production supervisors to review work progress, discuss job changes, and resolve problems in the department. When issues are being discussed, he often makes sure that he gets others' opinions before giving his own. As he states, "I know personally that if this group knows how I feel about something, more of them will tell me what I want to hear. That's why I like to get their views first. Some of them will come right out and ask what I think, as if once I tell them, the discussion should end."

self-check

In Chapter 1 you learned of the dramatic changes taking place to make the workforce much more diverse. This included increasing percentages of women and of African-American, Hispanic, Asian, and Native American workers. In what ways do these changes impact the *downward communication flow* from manager/supervisor to work team members? The *upward communication flow* from team members to manager/supervisor?

5 Explain the managerial communication style matrix.

Managerial Communication Matrix. Now that you have a good understanding of the vertical communication flows, you can better understand each supervisor's communication relationship with his or her team members. As shown in Exhibit 7–6, the managerial communication matrix, a supervisor's basic communications with team members consist of disclosing information (downward communication) and receiving information from them (upward communication). A supervisor can be considered high as an information discloser and high as an information receiver (box 4), high in one but not the other (boxes 2 and 3), or low in both (box 1).

Supervisors who are high disclosers are very visible. When you work for a high discloser, you hear frequently about performance expectations, standards,

Exhibit 7–6

The Managerial Communication Matrix

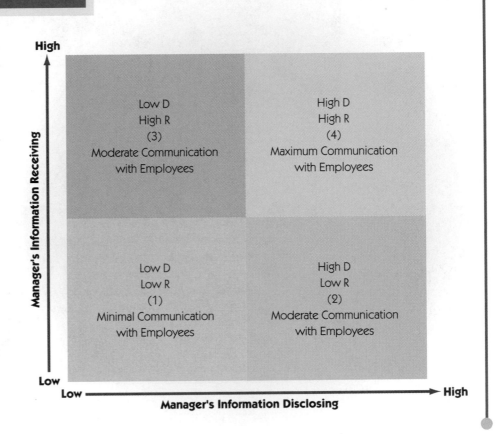

your boss's likes and dislikes, where you stand, and about the goings-on in the organization. Low disclosers tend to be less visible, communicating less frequently and openly about such matters.

High information-receiving supervisors are accessible and maintain an environment that encourages feedback from employees. They are apt to spend much of their time listening to employees' discussions about performance progress, problems being experienced, ideas and feelings about organizational and personal issues. In contrast, low information-receiving supervisors are less accessible and tend to create a less encouraging upward-communication environment than do high information receivers.

In this chapter's preview, how would you rate Curtis's communication style? Let us first qualify our answer. A supervisor's communication style is based on an ongoing, continual relationship with employees, rather than a single three- or four-minute interaction. But let's do some generalizing about Curtis. Let's take the easier choice first. Curtis seems definitely to be a *low information receiver.* She doesn't appear in the least interested in what Bishop has to say about the prospective new assignment in coding. Curtis *did* disclose some facts, as we mentioned earlier in this section. However, we heard nothing about Curtis's evaluation of Bishop's past work, which must be good, since she's being promoted. There was no discussion about why Bishop was chosen over other candidates for the position or how the new position is advantageous (other

It is important for supervisors to communicate with workers to build ongoing relationships.

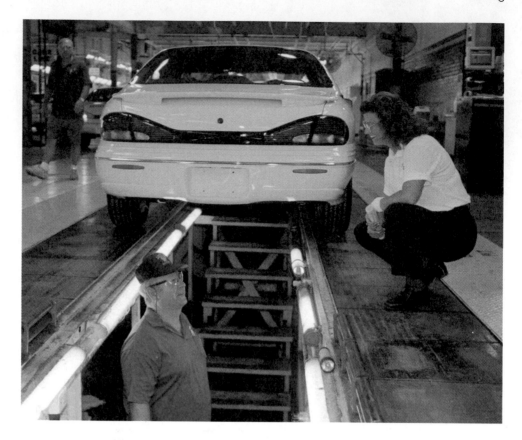

than higher pay). So if we had to generalize about Curtis's style, we'd bet that her normal, daily style is that of a *low discloser, low receiver.*

What would you like your own supervisor's style to be? In our workshops and seminars, about 90 percent of managers and supervisors state a strong preference in working for a high discloser, high receiver (box 4). When given a choice of their own boss's style being either a high discloser, low receiver (box 2) or a high receiver, low discloser (box 3), most opt for a supervisor whose style falls in box 2. This choice reflects the importance managers place on knowing clearly their boss's performance expectations and his or her feelings about their performance.

Lateral-Diagonal Flows

lateral-diagonal communication
Flows between individuals in the same department or different departments.

Lateral-diagonal communication takes place between individuals in the same department or different departments. This form of communication has become more important than ever in the past 25 years for several reasons. First, organizations have become greatly specialized. As indicated in the line-and-staff form of organization discussed in Chapter 5, members of staff departments such as purchasing, human resources, cost accounting, maintenance, and others interact regularly with line personnel. This may be to provide services, coordinate, advise, and sometimes actually give directives (recall the definition of functional authority in Chapter 5).

A second reason is the increased use of teams. Cross-functional, problem-solving teams comprising personnel from different departments have become an increasingly necessary approach to address problems that cut across organizational lines. As you learned in Chapter 2, one form of employee empowerment is the use of self-managed or autonomous work teams *within* departments. These teams often meet as a group on a daily basis and are highly dependent on communications among their members as they budget, schedule, assign jobs, and control quality of their *own* work.

Informal Communication

informal communication
Separate from a formal, established communication system.

The upward, downward, and lateral-diagonal communication flows that we have just presented are examples of formal communication. **Informal communication** is that which exists separately from the formal, established communication system. Some examples of informal communication are given below. Each example represents a communication channel that you will not find listed in the company's organization chart. Yet informal communications such as these are a way of life!

Lisa, Diane, Fred, and Roberto carpool, since they all work for the same company and live about 35 miles away. Their driving time is usually spent talking about their departments, people who work at the company, and other job-related matters. Because they all work in different departments, they are very much "in the know" about a number of company matters long before the formal company communication channels carry them.

Before seeing her boss about an important request, Mildred O'Neil dropped by to get Kathie Troy's opinion. Troy is a close friend of O'Neil's boss and would probably have some excellent advice for O'Neil as to how best to present her request.

grapevine
The "rumor mill."

The Grapevine. The best known informal communication method is the grapevine, also called the *rumor mill*. It is called a **grapevine** because, like the plant it is named after, it is tangled and twisted and seemingly grows without direction. Yet some surveys have found the grapevine to be employees' major source of information about their company, and it has been found to be surprisingly accurate. In fact, the research of Keith Davis, an authority on human relations, has shown that in normal work situations over 75 percent of grapevine information is correct.[4]

Purposes Served by Informal Communication. Informal communication accomplishes a number of purposes. Among these are (1) providing a source of information not ordinarily available, (2) reducing the effects of monotony, and (3) satisfying personal needs such as the need for relationships or status. Some people, in fact, take great pride in their unofficial knowledge of company matters.

Living with Informal Communication. Effective supervisors realize that informal communication serves important purposes. A supervisor must be aware that, unless employees are informed through formal channels, the informal channels will take up the slack. Keeping employees well informed is the best way to manage the grapevine, although it can never be eliminated. It will tend to be especially active when employees are concerned about job security or status.

BARRIERS TO EFFECTIVE SUPERVISORY COMMUNICATION

 Identify and explain how organizational, interpersonal, and language barriers affect supervisory communication.

Now that you understand the communication process, let's explore some typical communication barriers that a supervisor faces on the job. These barriers may be organizational, interpersonal, or language-related.

Organizational Barriers

Three types of organizational barriers to communication are (1) layers of hierarchy, (2) authority and status, and (3) specialization and its related jargon.

Layers of Hierarchy. Have you ever asked another person to give a message to a third person and found that the third person received a totally different message from the one you sent? The same thing occurs in organizations. When a message goes up or down the organization, it passes through a number of "substations" at each layer. Each layer can add to, take from, qualify, or completely change the original message!

At higher levels of management, messages are usually broad and general. At lower levels, these broad messages must be put into more specific terms. That's frequently the fly in the ointment, especially when lower and top levels have a gap of understanding between them.

Authority and Status. The very fact that one person is a boss over others creates a barrier to free and open communication.

self-check

Do you recall your feelings, as a student in elementary or high school, when you were told to report to the principal's office? Even if you had done nothing wrong, you were probably still very anxious and defensive about the visit.

The conference room patter before the superintendent walked in was loose and jovial. Some verbal horseplay occurred among the members, and there was kidding and joking. Some made very negative remarks about the major item on the agenda, which was a discussion of proposed changes in the company's system of performance evaluation. One person joked about another's being the one to tell the boss about the flaws in the new system, even though the boss strongly favored it. But when the boss walked in, the mood shifted dramatically. He did most of the talking; those in attendance listened attentively. Even when he asked for their opinions, he received only favorable comments about the proposal.

Since, as a supervisor, you must fill out employees' performance evaluations and determine rewards and penalties, employees will tend to give you the information that you are most likely to welcome. Information about frustrations, disagreements with your policies, job problems, below-standard work, and the like will tend to be withheld or changed to look more favorable.

Specialization and Its Related Jargon. The *principle of specialization* states that employees are more efficient when each performs just one task or only certain aspects of a task. For example, accountants do accounting work, salespersons sell, industrial engineers prepare efficiency studies, and safety specialists see to it that working conditions are safe.

Today's increased specialization, however, also creates problems. Specialists have their own technical language or jargon, interests, and narrow view of the organization. Many special terms used by maintenance technicians, electronic data processing specialists, and other groups are completely foreign to people in other departments. This can severely hamper communication.

self-check

What are some technical words that you're familiar with that your classmates probably wouldn't understand?

Interpersonal and Language Barriers

Even if the three organizational barriers just discussed do not exist, a supervisor's communication can still be distorted by interpersonal as well as language-related problems. Exhibit 7–7 lists a number of these barriers, some of which we will discuss.

perception
How one selects, organizes, and gives meaning to his or her world.

Differing Perceptions. The term **perception** may be defined as the process by which one selects, organizes, and gives meaning to his or her world. All of us have a special way of filtering things around us based on our culture, needs, moods, biases, expectations, experiences, and so on.

A major barrier to communication results from the increasingly diverse workforce, which reflects broad differences in age, race, sex, education, nationality, and other workforce factors. These differences result in quite different perceptions and interpretations of what is seen and heard, and they often result in different styles of communicating. This poses a much stronger communication challenge to supervisors than if all team members had similar backgrounds and shared similar characteristics with their supervisor.

One factor limiting our perception is that we can't grasp the whole situation at a given time. Some matters receive greater attention than others, while some matters receive none at all. Those matters we do focus on usually serve some immediate purpose. A person's needs, moods, cultural and social influences, and attitudes all come together to determine which things are important and what they mean.

> In a factory accident, for example, the following persons might "see" the accident differently: the supervisor, who may have lost a valuable worker; the safety engineer, whose safety record may have been blemished; the fellow worker, who is the injured worker's best friend; the company physician, who attends to the injured worker; and the human resources manager, who is concerned with workers' compensation and finding a replacement for the injured worker. If these persons were to communicate about the accident, each would have a different version.

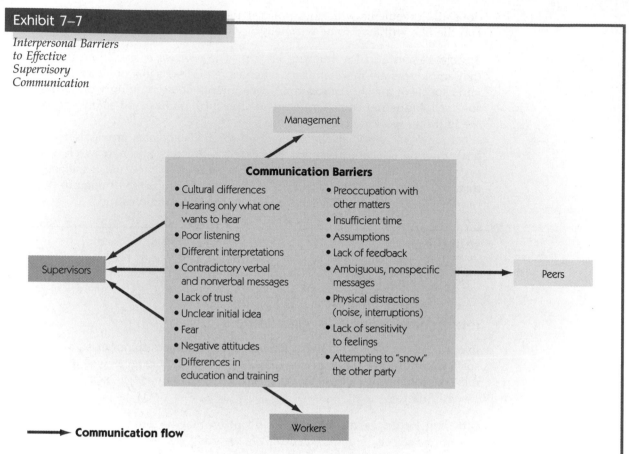

SOURCE: Business Communication Today, 4/e by Bovee/Thill, © 1998. Reprinted by permission of Prentice-Hall, Inc., Upper Saddle River, NJ.

When we go about interpreting things around us, we have a tendency to put similar things in the same category, to make them easier to handle. This tendency is called **stereotyping.** There are strong negative stereotypes for various nationalities, races, religions, sexes, occupations, and other groups in our society. For example, a male manager may label all women as "emotionally weak," all union officials as "agitators," and all staff employees as "meddlers." Obviously, such stereotyping will have a strong influence on this manager's communications to and from these individuals.

On the other hand, stereotypes may be favorable. As a supervisor, you must be aware that your attitudes, biases, and prejudices—both positive and negative—strongly influence your communications with others.

Language-Related Factors. We have already indicated how important language is in the process of communication. The fact that people interpret words differently can be traced to a lack of precision in the use of language. True, you can say that a drill press weighs 270 pounds, or that Sam Eggers is 5'11" tall, or that Judy Snead has completed 10 years of service with the hospital. Language is precise in that regard, and we can verify it.

Consider, however, a salesperson selling copiers who tells an office manager that the copier is "the finest on the market." Or one supervisor who tells

stereotyping
The tendency to put similar things in the same categories to make them easier to deal with.

click! http://www .daimlerchrysler.com/

another that "Sam is a loyal employee." Or a supervisor who says that "Judy Snead is a good nurse." What is "loyal" or "good"? What you consider to be "loyal" (for example, turning down several job offers from competing firms) may be "complacent" or "unambitious" to someone else. A "good" nurse to you may be one who is a sympathetic listener and spends a lot of time talking with patients and being cheerful and friendly; to someone else, a "good" nurse may be one who is knowledgeable and competent and goes about her or his work without trying to make conversation.

Sometimes a supervisor uses imprecise language when more precise language is necessary. Suppose a supervisor tells an employee, "You must improve on your absenteeism, as it has been excessive. Otherwise, you'll be disciplined." What does the supervisor mean by "improve on your absenteeism" and "excessive"? What "discipline" does the supervisor have in mind?

Another language barrier is the fact that words have multiple meanings and not all people have the same level of language skill, as exemplified in Exhibit 7–8. Many terms familiar to a veteran employee, for example, may be over the heads of a new crop of employees going through an orientation program. In some cases, people even try to "snow" others by using terms they know the others will not understand!

Linguistic Styles. Today, out of every seven people in the United States, one speaks a language other than English at home.[5] This greatly reflects the continuing diversity in the United States and the varying linguistic styles employees bring with them to work. Linguistic style refers to typical patterns in their speech, including factors such as volume, speed, and pauses; being direct or indirect; asking questions; and body language associated with their speech. Differences in linguistic styles are important communication barriers, especially among different cultures, where the styles vary greatly. For example, Japanese workers tend to communicate very formally and show much respect toward their bosses. They also use lengthy pauses to assess what is said. Americans, on the other hand, often forego formality and view pauses as signs of uncertainty or insecurity. Brazilians and Saudis favor closer physical speaking distances than do Americans. An American supervisor may find a Brazilian employee's

---

Exhibit 7–8

Multiple Interpretations of Words

FIX the machine to its foundation. (anchor)

FIX that nitpicking cost accountant. (give just due)

FIX the cash register. (repair)

FIXING to go to the storeroom. (getting ready to)

FIX our position regarding overtime policy. (establish)

FIX you up with that young engineer. (arrange a date)

A banquet with all the **FIXIN'S.** (special effects, side dishes)

FIX things up with the salespeople. (make amends, patch up a quarrel)

If we don't make quota, we're in a **FIX.** (a pickle, a bad position)

FIX the data outcome. (so that it's favorable, rig it)

FIX your hair before seeing the boss. (arrange, make orderly)

FIX the department meal on Friday. (cook, prepare)

FIX the company's mascot dog. (neuter)

manner aggressive, when in fact for the employee, it is a normal physical distance.

Another cultural linguistic style difference involves eye contact. Several years ago, Barbara Walters interviewed Libyan leader Colonel Moammar Gadaffi for a national U.S. television audience. She was reportedly taken aback because during the interview he refused to look directly at her as he spoke. Walters considered this insulting, as if the intent was to demean her. Her reaction was attributable to differences in linguistic style of the two cultures. In Gadaffi's culture not looking directly at her was a sign of respect.

Linguistic style may also vary among subcultures. Among some Native Americans, a child's continued eye contact with an adult is a sign of disrespect. Important differences exist between American males and females. American males may find swearing and racy joke telling acceptable among themselves, but females might find this offensive. Furthermore, women's linguistic styles tend to be more expressive and polite rather than direct and assertive, as is the case with males. Women view conversations as a means for establishing a "connection" and intimacy with others; males see conversations as a negotiation through which they seek to establish or maintain status and independence.[6]

self-check

After examining Exhibit 7–7, which barriers do you believe were involved in the Curtis–Bishop communication in the chapter preview?

7 Identify five specific actions supervisors can take to improve their communications.

IMPROVING SUPERVISORY COMMUNICATIONS

As we've indicated, communication is too critical to your success as a supervisor to be left to chance. Improving your skills in communication will help you accomplish your "task" and "people" goals. Some specific things you can do are (1) set the proper climate with your employees, (2) plan your communication, (3) use repetition to reinforce key ideas, (4) encourage the use of feedback, and (5) become a better listener.

Set the Proper Climate

A supervisor doesn't communicate in a vacuum. Communications take place within the entire supervisor–employee or supervisor–group relationship. A supervisor and his or her workers each bring a store of experiences, expectations, and attitudes to the communication event. These mental pictures strongly influence the meaning each person assigns to the messages sent and received. Thus, the setting is very important for good communication.

What type of setting best contributes to effective communication? We believe that two important factors are (1) mutual trust between the supervisor and employees and (2) a minimum of status barriers.

Establish Mutual Trust. Trust helps communication in two ways. First, if an employee trusts you, he or she is more willing to communicate frankly about job problems. Second, if employees trust you, they are less likely to distort your motives and make negative assumptions about your communications. If you fight for your employees' interests by bargaining with higher management, if you discipline fairly and consistently, and if you respect your employees' abili-

Explaining company procedures and policies to employees helps establish mutual trust.

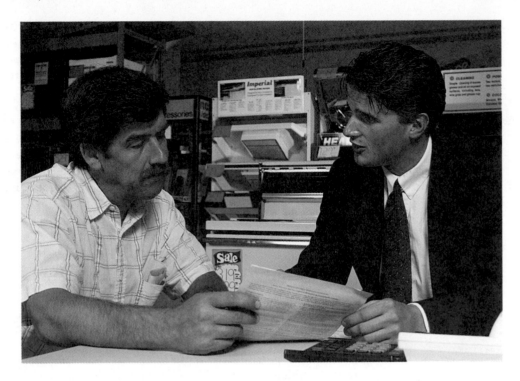

ties, you are more likely to be trusted by them. You'll be considered a source of help in reaching their goals.

Minimize Status Barriers. Status barriers consist of those factors that call attention to the fact that the supervisor ranks higher than his or her employees. Status barriers may be such things as dress, formality, office arrangement, and so forth. Generally, the best communication occurs in a setting where people are relaxed and comfortable and status differences are reduced. For example, the way a supervisor arranges his or her office furniture has much to do with establishing a relaxed setting, as shown in Exhibit 7–9.

Exhibit 7–9

Desk-Chair Arrangements that Affect Formality

Supervisor
Desk
Employee
Formal

Supervisor
Desk   Employee
Less Formal

Desk
Supervisor   Employee
Informal

One supervisor says he likes to discuss certain sensitive matters away from his own turf so as to make an employee feel more comfortable and less nervous. By design, supervisors may communicate in the employee's work area or in a neutral situation such as over a cup of coffee or lunch.

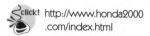
http://www.honda2000.com/index.html

At Honda of America, Honda President Shochiro Iramafiri wore no tie and ate in the company cafeteria. On the front of his white overalls, which were just like those everyone else in the plant wore, was his nickname, "IRI." He had no private office but worked at a desk in the same work area as the 100 others in his white-collar work group. This represented a distinct effort to diminish the status differences between himself and all other employees.[7]

Plan for Effective Communication

How many times have you completely blown a communication situation by not being prepared for it? After it's over, you think "Now why didn't I say this?" or "I never should have said such and such."

Anticipating Situations. If you are a supervisor, many of your contacts will occur without much warning and may not allow much planning. Yet there are a number of situations you can anticipate. For example, you can give thought to the following situations before they occur:

1. Giving employees their performance evaluations.
2. Disciplining employees and making work corrections.
3. Delegating authority for a job and communicating job assignments and instructions.
4. Persuading employees to accept changes in the job or work environment.
5. Trying to sell an idea to your boss or to other staff members.

If you understand how complex good communications are, you'll be more aware of the existing barriers and try to minimize their effects. To be understood by your team members, you must put yourself in their shoes and try to see things from their viewpoint. An old North American Indian prayer expresses the thought this way: "Lord, grant that I may not criticize my neighbor until I've walked a mile in his moccasins."

Examples of Planned Communications. Once you have established an objective for a communication, make a plan to achieve it. Let's look at two examples:

Suppose an excellent employee has asked in advance to speak to you about a transfer to another department. Assuming that you don't know all the facts, one objective of your meeting is to gain insight into the request for transfer, including the reasons for it and the timing. This will help you make a decision or make readjustments in your department. Your plan could be to take a listening role and use active listening techniques, which will be explained shortly. This strategy will prevent you from dominating the interaction, monopolizing the communication, and hindering the achievement of your objective.

Suppose you are going to ask a promising employee to participate in a voluntary training program. Your objective in this case is to gain the employee's acceptance of the program and to develop enthusiasm for it. Your plan, then, is to focus on how the employee will benefit from participating in the program. How will training aid the employee's development, future in the company, and so on? You would try to uncover any objections by using listening skills. And you would attempt to anticipate possible objections and determine how they can be overcome.

These two examples show the advantage of planning your communication. If you fail to plan when you can do so, you may depend too much on your spontaneous, off-the-cuff ability to communicate. Moreover, when you attempt to do your planning while the other person is talking, you can't listen effectively. The planning stage, therefore, spills over into the act of communication itself. The nature of your communication role, the message(s), and the strategy in message content and sequence can, to some extent, be predetermined. Thus, the three major concepts presented in the rest of this chapter relate clearly to planning.

Consider the Receiver's Frame of Reference. Earlier we discussed how each of us has unique filters that influence the way we interpret the world around us. Obviously, the better attuned you are to your subordinates' and others' patterns of evaluation, the more effective your communications to and from them will be. Effective communication, then, requires you to step into the shoes of others and visualize situations from their perspective.

self-check

Have you ever been in a class where the instructor was talking so far over the heads of the students that no one was even capable of asking an intelligent question? If so, what was your reaction? Why is it that some people overshoot their audience and don't even realize it?

A supervisor must frequently ask questions like these:

1. How is this person *like* me?
2. How is this person *different* from me?
3. How is this person *similar* to other employees?
4. How is this person *different* from other employees?
5. How will this person react if I say such and such?

These questions are especially important given the increased diversity of employees. A supervisor doesn't find out the answers to these questions by reading employees' biographical data from their personnel files. He or she must interact with them. The only way to discover employees' different motives, needs, attitudes, and ways of interpreting things is to be sensitive to these differences and to use effective feedback and listening techniques.

Use Repetition to Reinforce Key Ideas

Repeating a message plays an important part in communicating effectively. This is especially true when you have to communicate technical information or a direct order. Repetition, or redundancy, reduces the chance that incorrect assumptions will be made by the receiver. For example, you can state a complicated message in several ways, using examples, illustrations, or comparisons. You can also say the same thing several times, but in different words. Here, for instance, is how a supervisor might communicate an instruction to an employee.

> **Danny, we just got a telephone order for a 42-by-36-inch fireplace screen in our KL–17 series. I know you haven't done one up like it since last year, when that customer gave us so much trouble about the screen not fitting his fireplace opening. That's the same style this guy wants, with black and gold trim as shown in this catalog clipping. And you heard me right: He wants it 42 inches high by 36 inches wide—higher than it is wide.** (*Hands Danny the written specifications for the screen.*) **That's a new one for me, and I'm sure it's a new one for you too. Can you get it out in the next two weeks?**

Note how the supervisor used a past example and a catalog to clarify the style of the fireplace screen and how the supervisor repeated the required measurements, even though he also provided written specs!

8 Show how a supervisor can use feedback to improve communication.

Encourage the Use of Feedback

As mentioned earlier, feedback is the response that a communicator receives from the receiver of the message. Two ways in which a supervisor can encourage employees to provide feedback are (1) to create a relaxed environment and (2) to take the initiative.

Create a Relaxed Environment. Earlier in this section, we discussed the importance of establishing a favorable setting for communication. A relaxed setting is also required when the supervisor wants to obtain feedback from his or her employees. As a supervisor, you certainly should not look down on employees for asking questions or for openly stating their opinions, suggestions, or feelings on a subject. A defensive attitude on your part discourages feedback from employees. How you communicate also determines, to a large extent, the amount of feedback you will receive. For example, written instructions or memos don't allow for the immediate feedback that can be gained from face-to-face communication.

In ancient times, there was an Asian king who hated to hear bad news. Whenever a courier reported bad news or an unfortunate event to the king, the king became furious and had him beheaded. After three couriers bit the dust, the king began hearing only good news! The moral here for supervisors is that they must be receptive to all information, both good and bad, from their employees, or they too will be surrounded by a smokescreen.

Take the Initiative. Although the type of communication used and the setting for the communication are important in determining what feedback is obtained, the supervisor still must take the initiative in getting responses from the work group. For example, after giving a job assignment, you might ask "Do you have any questions?" or "Did I leave anything out?" An even better approach would be to say "To make sure I've gotten my message across, how about repeating it to me?" Frequently this approach produces a number of clarifications that someone might otherwise be unwilling to request for fear of looking stupid. You must be careful, however, not to use a patronizing tone of voice or to put too much of the burden of understanding on the employee. Remember—effective communication is a two-way street. Finally, you can set the stage for further feedback with comments such as "If anything comes up later or if you have some questions, just let me know."

The participative leadership style (discussed in Chapter 9) relies heavily on good two-way communication, which is a form of feedback. When a supervisor allows team members to make decisions or to express opinions, their responses are a form of feedback. This style helps the supervisor better understand the team members' thinking.

Feedback can also help you learn how to better send messages in the future. When you discover that your initial message wasn't clear or that your use of persuasion was not effective, you can refine future messages. A summary of tips about feedback appears in Exhibit 7–10.

Become a Better Listener

It has been said that Mother Nature blessed human beings with two ears and only one mouth as a not-so-subtle hint that, unfortunately, we often ignore. "How to Be a Good Listener" has become a popular subject and is being taught

---

Exhibit 7–10

Tips About Feedback

- Generally, feedback is better where there is a trusting relationship between people. If a person doesn't trust you, he or she is not likely to level with you or share feelings very readily. As a result, you are told only what you want to hear instead of what you *should* hear. For example, the person may say "Yes, sir, things are going okay on the Anders job," when in reality there is a lack of progress or some severe problem. Or the person may say "I certainly agree with you, boss," when in reality the person doesn't agree with you at all but doesn't want to upset you or risk being chewed out.

- Some people give feedback readily, but others need some encouragement. Examples of the latter type are people who are timid, quiet, or insecure or have learned that "it's best to keep your mouth shut around here." *Asking* such people for their ideas, suggestions, or feelings may elicit feedback. For example, you can say "Dale, how will this new policy affect your group?" or "What do you think about . . . ?"

- Complimenting people for providing feedback reinforces their willingness to *continue* providing feedback. When you say "I appreciate your honesty in discussing this" or "Thanks, Joan, for raising some issues that need to be clarified," you are encouraging the other party to give feedback in the future.

- When you are giving instructions, it is a good habit to ask the listener if he or she has any questions. For example, you can ask "Is this clear, Dick? Have you any questions?" Some supervisors end their instructions with "Now, Dick, let's see if we're together on this. In your own words, run by me what it seems I've just said." If the instructions are given over the telephone, you can say "Okay, Dick, read back to me those seven dates I just gave you so we can make sure we're together on this."

- When you have potentially negative feedback to give, it is helpful to begin by saying "Sarah, may I offer a suggestion about . . . ?" or "May I give you my impression of . . . ?" or "Can I share my feelings about . . . ?" This approach is less pushy, and the message will be received with less defensiveness than if you bluntly blurt out the negative information.

- Nonverbal signals and body language offer a wide variety of feedback. Frowns, nervous fidgeting, nods of the head, and other facial expressions and body movements give us a lot of information. Frequently, however, we overlook these signals completely because we are not looking at the other person or because we are absorbed in our own thoughts and messages.

today in many elementary and high schools throughout the country. Test your listening skills by completing the test in Exhibit 7–11. Studies of managers show that on average they spend a larger percentage of their work day (about 45%) in listening than in the other communication forms—speaking, writing, or reading.[8]

self-check

Our own research reveals that of the four communication skills (writing, speaking, reading, and listening) that managers and supervisors most frequently use, listening is the skill in which they have had the least training. Why do you think this is so?

Exhibit 7–11

Rate Your Listening Habits

As a listener, how frequently do you engage in the following listening behaviors? Place a check in the appropriate column, and determine your rating based on the scale at the bottom of the page.

Listening Habit	Very Seldom 10	8	6	4	Almost Always 2
1. Faking attention, pretending to be interested when you're really not.	___	___	___	___	___
2. Being passive—not asking questions or trying to obtain clarifications, even when you don't understand.	___	___	___	___	___
3. Listening mainly to what a speaker *says* rather than his or her feelings.	___	___	___	___	___
4. Allowing yourself to be distracted too easily.	___	___	___	___	___
5. Not being aware of the speaker's facial expressions and nonverbal behavior.	___	___	___	___	___
6. Tuning out material that is complex or contrary to your own opinion.	___	___	___	___	___
7. Drawing conclusions, having your mind made up before hearing the speaker's full line of reasoning.	___	___	___	___	___
8. Allowing yourself to daydream or wander mentally.	___	___	___	___	___
9. Feeling restless, impatient, eager to end the conversation.	___	___	___	___	___
10. Interrupting the speaker, taking over the conversation to get in your own side of things.	___	___	___	___	___

Your total score: _____

90–100	Superior
80–89	Very good
70–79	Good
60–69	Average
50–59	Below average
0–49	Far below average

9 Define and illustrate active listening skills.

active listening
The listener makes a response so as to encourage feedback.

Active Listening Techniques. A particular listening technique that places the supervisor in a receiver's role and encourages feedback from others is called **active listening** (also known as *feeling listening, reflective listening,* and *nondirective listening*). Basically, active listening requires the listener to make a response that tosses the ball back to the sender and says, "Yes, I understand; tell me more." It is used by psychologists, psychiatrists, counselors, and others when it is necessary to understand how someone feels and thinks. We think that active listening is of great value to supervisors as a method for encouraging more open feedback.

reflective statement
The listener repeats, in a summarizing way, what the speaker has just said.

The **reflective statement** is a form of active listening in which you repeat what you think the speaker has just told you.

> **Suppose the speaker is Jim Atkins, one of your employees. He tells you: "Say, I've got a little problem I'd like to discuss. It's about Klaric, the new guy in our department. He doesn't seem to fit in at all. Some of the guys have even kidded me about it, saying, 'Where did we dig this guy up? He's a real dork!' He won't even try to fit in, and the others seem to resent him for that. I've tried to help him work into the group, because you know the pride we have in our work and in getting along so well together. Klaric's a good worker, but he's causing us more trouble than he's worth."**

What is Atkins telling you? How would you respond? One way is to respond with a summary in your own words of what Atkins has just told you. For example, you could say "What you seem to be saying, Atkins, is that although Klaric is a good worker, you're concerned because he doesn't fit in well." This statement reflects back to Atkins what he has just said and allows him to continue talking about the subject.

Frequently, the speaker will elaborate on certain aspects of an earlier statement that seem to him or her to be critical. In the above example, Atkins might elaborate by saying "Well, the thing that gets me most, I guess, is that I really messed up in my evaluation of Klaric. When you asked my opinion, I honestly thought he would fit in. I just don't see how I could have been so wrong in evaluating him." By going into detail, you find that Atkins is mainly concerned about having made a poor evaluation of Klaric's ability to fit into the department.

probe
Directs attention to a particular aspect of the speaker's message.

The **probe** is more specific than the reflective statement. It directs attention to a particular aspect of the speaker's message. For example, in the Klaric case, your response to Atkins could be any of the following:

1. "He doesn't seem to fit in at all?"
2. "You say the other guys seem to resent him?"
3. "He's a real dork, eh?"

Note that these probes are more specific than the reflective statement, and they allow you to pursue what you feel may be important. The probe may provide additional insight into the problem by encouraging Atkins to discuss it more deeply. A probe is less likely to cause a speaker to become defensive than a direct question. If you asked "Who's been kidding you about it?" or "Why do you call him a dork?" Atkins might feel that you were putting him on the spot. You would do better to delay such questions until later stages of this communication situation.

Exhibit 7–12

*Tips for Better
Listening*

- Try to avoid doing most of the talking yourself. Give the other person an opportunity to speak.
- Avoid distractions. Close your office door or move to a quieter area.
- Act interested in what the other person says. Don't doodle, write, or work on something else. Give the employee your full attention.
- Ask questions. As long as the questions aren't considered nosy or brash, this will help keep you interested and encourage the employee to give more details.
- Summarize what you think someone has said. "What you're saying is. . . . " This will reinforce what you have heard and enable the other person to correct any misunderstanding on your part.
- Be empathetic. Try to put yourself in the speaker's shoes.
- Don't lose your temper or show signs of being upset by what the speaker is saying. Try to listen with an open mind.
- Don't interrupt. Let the person finish speaking before you respond.
- Use active listening techniques—reflective statements and probes—to ensure your understanding of key points, to help the speaker talk, or to steer the conversation in certain directions.
- After an important conversation or meeting, jot down notes to yourself about the main points discussed.

Other Listening Fundamentals. A number of other important techniques can help your listening effectiveness. These are presented in Exhibit 7–12.

As you can see, good listening is hard work. But it is an essential tool for the supervisor!

chapter review

1 Describe the five components of the communication process model.

Supervisors spend anywhere from 60 to 80 percent of their time in some form of communication. The communication process consists of five parts: a sender, a message, a channel, a receiver, and feedback.

2 Explain the forms of electronic communication technology.

Among the new forms of electronic communication that are impacting communication at the supervisory level are e-mail, mobile phones, digital pagers, voice mail, teleconferencing, and videoconferencing.

3 Explain the different ways in which nonverbal communications influence supervisory communication.

"Meaning" lies in people rather than in words, and nonverbal messages communicate our emotions more strongly than words. Six categories of nonverbal communication signals are voice, body, object, space, time, and touching.

4 Identify the three basic flows of formal communication in an organization.

In any organization there is a tremendous volume of formal communication that flows in three directions: downward, upward, and laterally or diagonally.

Downward communication includes announcements of goals, objectives, policies, decisions, procedures, job assignments, and general information. Upward communication consists of progress reports from employees; their requests for assistance; communication about their attitudes, feelings, and concerns; and ideas and suggestions for job improvement. Lateral-diagonal communication occurs between persons within a department or in different departments. It typically involves contacts between line and staff members and among team members in natural, cross-functional, and self-managed teams.

⑤ Explain the managerial communication style matrix.

The managerial communication style matrix reflects supervisors' behaviors toward disclosing information and receiving information. Supervisors who are high disclosers are active downward communicators to their employees. Supervisors who are high information receivers are open, accessible, and receptive to upward communication from their employees.

⑥ Identify and explain how organizational, interpersonal, and language barriers affect supervisory communication.

A number of organizational, interpersonal, and language barriers can hamper a supervisor's effectiveness in communication. Organizational barriers include the levels of hierarchy through which a message must pass, the authority and status of managers, and the jargon of specialized departments. Interpersonal and language barriers include people's differing perceptions, the general imprecision of language, and different linguistic styles.

⑦ Identify five specific actions supervisors can take to improve their communications.

There are several ways to improve supervisory communication. First, a supervisor should establish the proper setting when communicating with employees. The proper setting is a climate with a high trust level, where the supervisor is viewed as a source of help and where status barriers are minimized. Second, a supervisor should plan his or her communication. This involves determining in advance a communication strategy that will enable the supervisor to reach an objective. Third, a supervisor must consider the receiver's frame of reference. This requires looking at things from the receiver's view, which can be difficult. Fourth, a supervisor should use repetition to reinforce key ideas. Finally, a supervisor should encourage and induce feedback and become a better listener.

⑧ Show how a supervisor can use feedback to improve communication.

Two ways in which a supervisor can encourage employees to provide feedback are by (1) creating a relaxed communication environment and (2) taking the initiative to encourage feedback from others. A favorable feedback environment makes team members feel comfortable and relaxed and encourages open expression of their true feelings. Supervisors can take the feedback initiative by asking questions and creating situations which encourage or require their employees to communicate.

⑨ Define and illustrate active listening skills.

Active listening, known also as *feeling listening*, *reflective listening*, or *nondirective listening*, is a method of encouraging feedback from others. Two forms of active listening are reflective statements and probes. Reflective statements restate back to the speaker a summary of what the listener has heard the speaker express. Probes are more specific reflective statements that direct attention to a *particular* aspect of the sender's message.

important terms

active listening *209*	perception *199*
body signals *190*	probe *209*
channel *188*	receiver *189*
communication process model *188*	reflective statement *209*
downward communication *191*	sender *188*
e-mail *190*	space signals *191*
feedback *189*	stereotyping *200*
grapevine *197*	time signals *191*
informal communication *197*	touching signals *191*
lateral-diagonal communication *196*	upward communication *193*
message *188*	voice signals *190*
object signals *191*	

questions for review and discussion

1. What are the five components of the basic communication process model? Define each. Identify some of the important forms of electronic communication discussed in the text.
2. Explain the six different ways in which nonverbal signals influence supervisory communication.
3. Identify the three major flows of communication in an organization.
4. Explain the managerial communication style matrix. What are some purposes served by informal communication?
5. What are some examples of linguistic style communication differences that you have experienced? Explain.
6. How does planning aid communication effectiveness? Can you give a personal example?
7. Explain how a supervisor can use feedback to improve communication.
8. Define and give an example of active listening.

• skill builder 7–1

Assessing Your Information-Disclosing and Information-Receiving Style

Instructions: Please read the 16 items listed and circle the answer that best characterizes you.

To what extent do you:	Not much like you				Much like you
1. Make known your position on issues	1	2	3	4	5
2. Ask others for their advice about matters	1	2	3	4	5
3. Compliment/give recognition to others	1	2	3	4	5
4. Act friendly, approachable	1	2	3	4	5

To what extent do you:	Not much like you				Much like you
5. Offer constructive criticism to others	1	2	3	4	5
6. Indicate willingness to explore differences of opinion	1	2	3	4	5
7. Keep people informed about things you know are going on	1	2	3	4	5
8. Invite feedback about your own behavior or thinking	1	2	3	4	5
9. Make clearly known your expectations of others	1	2	3	4	5
10. Try to avoid distractions when listening to others	1	2	3	4	5
11. State your disagreement with opinions when they differ from your own	1	2	3	4	5
12. Hear out a position fully before making a judgment or decision	1	2	3	4	5
13. Provide adequate details when instructing or explaining	1	2	3	4	5
14. Ask questions of others to obtain information	1	2	3	4	5
15. Tell people when they've done something that irritates you	1	2	3	4	5
16. Keep an open mind to others' ideas and suggestions	1	2	3	4	5

Scoring: To calculate your information-disclosing score, add the results of items 1, 3, 5, 7, 9, 11, 13, 15 = _____ Information-Disclosing Score Total

To calculate your information-receiving score, add the results of items 2, 4, 6, 8, 10, 12, 14, 16 = _____ Information-Receiving Score Total

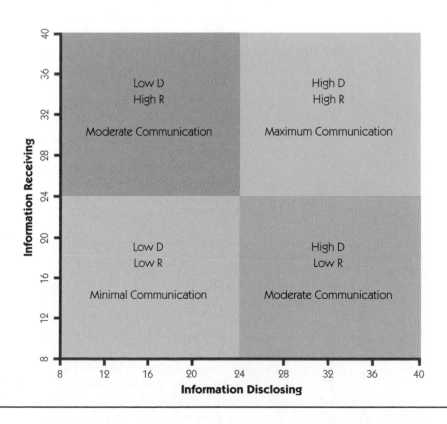

Practicing Active Listening
group activity

The interaction below is a replay of the chapter preview. Note that some of the super-visor's dialogue is missing; you will be asked to complete it. It is okay for you to read the entire case before beginning the assignment.

Bishop: (enters Jean Curtis's office) You wanted to see me?

Curtis: Yes, I did, Ann. Come in and have a seat. (Pauses) As you know, I've been very pleased with your performance in archives since you joined us six months ago. You seem to have an excellent handle on everything we do there. We have an opening in the coding department and it would be an excellent opportunity. I want to see how you feel about moving into coding. You are first choice, and that's what I want to discuss with you.

Bishop: Into coding? Gee, I don't know; I really don't know much about coding. I don't know what to say . . . .

Curtis: (Active listening response #1) _____

_____

_____

Bishop: I mean, yeah, this is a surprise. I've heard a little about what they do in cod-ing. Everyone's heard stories about some of the charts having the wrong codes on them and people getting into trouble because of that. It seems like a lot more pressure and responsibility . . . .

Curtis: (Active listening response #2) _____

_____

_____

Bishop: Yes, that's an important factor to me in any job. Not that I don't mind some responsibility. It's just that it seems there's a lot more in coding than in archives.

Curtis: Well, Ann, you're right about that; it is more responsibility because having up-dated, accurately coded charts is very important to both patients and insurers. That's why we're careful about who we ask to work in coding.

Bishop: But I like working in archives. I like the other clerks and we work together well. We work our lunch breaks out to cover for each other; we all pitch in and help when one of us gets overloaded. That's one thing I really like about working here—the cooperation.

Curtis: (Active listening response #3) _____

_____

_____

Bishop: Yeah, I really like that. At the last place I worked, nobody seemed to get along. I made more money than I make here, but getting along is more important to me than money. I know some people have left coding recently. Why is that?

Curtis: One left to work as a marketing assistant downstairs. Another married and moved out of the state. I've just finished writing her a letter of reference for a simi-lar coding position in a hospital in her new location. The third didn't work out be-cause of several reasons, including excessive absenteeism and marginal perform-ance when she was here. The first two had been with us for over five years each and seemed very happy in the department. (Pause) So money's not the most im-portant thing to you in a job?

Bishop: Oh, it's important, but there are other things—the people, the work, liking what I do. I guess money just isn't the only important thing.

Curtis: I think you're wise in looking at a job in ways other than just money. As a coder you would receive a $160 monthly increase, but it also would enable you to build a record of responsibility—this helped in landing the job in marketing for the person I just mentioned. It would also provide a stepping stone for you if you wanted to work in our legal records department.

Bishop: I don't know. It's just that I know the archives, I know what's expected of me there, and I know pretty much all there is to know about it. And I really was trained well before getting started . . . .

Curtis: (Active listening response #4) _____

_____

_____

Bishop: Yeah, I'm concerned about that. I just started really feeling comfortable in archives.

Curtis: We would want you to be comfortable before putting you on your own in coding. You'd work with Stephanie Koval, one of the senior coders for two or three days to get the hang of things. And we wouldn't turn you loose until you felt comfortable about your performance. In fact, since you seem to have some reservations that are understandable, we could let you try the job for two weeks and see how things go. Would that help any? I think you're ideally suited, but I don't want you to feel that I'm pressuring you.

Bishop: So you're saying you understand some of my concerns . . . .

Curtis: Yes, Ann, I think I do. And they're certainly normal. So why don't you give this some thought? I told Koval I'd be talking with you, so feel free to ask her any questions, or if you need to see me about anything further on this, please do. You've impressed us with your work in archives and that's what has led to today's meeting. Will you be able to let me know something by this Friday?

Bishop: I really like working here, Ms. Curtis, and I'm pleased by the confidence you have in me. The chance to switch jobs is a surprise to me . . . I just wasn't expecting it. You've given me some things to think about, so a few days will be fine. I'll let you know something by Friday.

Instructions:

1. Complete Curtis's four active listening responses as requested.
2. Identify any additional uses of active listening responses in the case.
3. Compare your active listening responses with those of other students and discuss.

Developing a Communication Plan

Brenda Watson is a cafeteria manager for a large cafeteria chain with over 250 cafeterias. The cafeteria has two assistant managers. One has responsibility for the kitchen and food preparation; the other has responsibility for other functions, including the service line personnel, cashiers, and the buspersons. Approximately 45 people work at the unit.

The following four situations occurred during the past week.

a. Tuesday was Watson's day off, but she'd forgotten a novel she'd left in her office. When she dropped by to pick it up at noon, she noted that several areas of the cafeteria line were not up to standard—there was spilled food on the floor in the customer line; the food line itself was not attractively displayed, and four leftover food trays cluttered the area. Watson didn't say anything at the time, because she was in a hurry. But she was shocked, to say the least. She planned to discuss this with the assistant manager the following day.

b. Reed Barton, one of Watson's most senior, trusted head cooks, asked her to intervene with John Casey, assistant manager of the kitchen. Kitchen employees have been turned off by Casey's hard-nosed, autocratic style, which of late seems to have turned up a notch. Casey, according to Barton, runs the kitchen like it's boot camp. And he gets angry when things aren't to his liking. Today he berated a senior employee loudly in front of several other employees; the employee, carving knife in hand, yelled back. Cooler

heads prevented the incident from escalating. Barton senses bad vibes between Casey and several employees, and most of it relates to Casey's aggressive style. Several employees asked Barton to tell Watson what's been going on. Watson is aware that Casey, who's been with her for four months, is very bright. However, she has noted his strong, aggressive style—a marked difference from his predecessor, one of the best kitchen managers Watson had. Watson pondered a plan for best discussing the situation with Casey.

c. At 1:30 p.m. Watson learned from her regional manager via a telephone call that the company was bought by Shoney's. The sale, totally unexpected, will be announced to the financial community within the hour and will likely make the morning paper. The regional manager knew little of the details, saying that Watson now knew as much as he did and should communicate this information to her employees.

d. Watson must communicate to her employees that a new overtime system will be installed companywide, effective in four weeks. In the past (ever since she could remember), managers would contact workers—by seniority—either in person or by phone to make sure that the most senior workers would have first opportunity for overtime. This was always slow and ineffective, since some senior workers declined overtime consistently. The new system should give each manager more flexibility in overtime assignments by getting monthly, advance overtime commitments from workers. While most employees will buy into the new system, Watson knew that several of the more senior people were likely to be upset.

Instructions:

1. In each situation, identify the major communication barriers that face Watson.

2. For each of the four situations, develop, in writing, a communication plan or strategy to help Watson in dealing with each. Include such factors as the objective, the appropriate setting, time, how she would organize her message, and other strategic factors you believe are relevant.

Motivation

● outline

Motivation: Some Fundamentals of Understanding Human Behavior
Levels of Motivation
Intrinsic and Extrinsic Motivation
The Motivation–Performance Link

Maslow's Hierarchy of Needs Theory
Principles Underlying the Theory
Qualifying the Theory

Herzberg's Theory
Dissatisfiers and Motivators
Link to Extrinsic and Intrinsic Motivation
Qualifying Herzberg's Theory

Other Theories of Motivation
Expectancy Theory
Goal-Setting Theory
Reinforcement Theory

Lessons from the Theories: Five Steps to Motivating Employees
Help Make Employees' Jobs Interesting
Provide Clear Performance Objectives
Support Employees' Performance Efforts
Provide Timely Performance Feedback
Reward Employees' Performance

Give me enough medals and I'll win you any war.

Napoleon Bonaparte

Journalist: "Your Eminence, the Vatican is such a huge place. About how many people work here?"

Pope: "About half, my son."

Anonymous

Sharon Olds: People Motivator

Sharon Olds (Chapter 1 preview) is rapidly becoming considered one of AutoFin's most effective supervisors. Since assuming a supervisory position only eight months ago, her department has consistently reached its production quotas and for the last two months ranked first among the six departments.

When she took over her present supervisory position, Sharon knew that she faced a strong challenge given the diverse ages, education, marital status, cultures, and needs of her personnel. Her department ranked in the middle of the pack from a performance standpoint. She felt that AutoFin was a solid organization to work for, with very good pay and benefits. Job security was excellent, assuming an employee met or came close to production quotas, which although difficult, could be attained with hard work. Working conditions were excellent once employees became accustomed to spending 95 percent of their work time on the phone with customers.

Sharon felt the biggest difference she could make was to soften the impersonal, bottom line attitude of upper management. "Although an excellent company to work for, AutoFin is very bottom line oriented. While our success comes from our people, top management is seen as impersonal and strictly numbers oriented," Sharon says. "They give an impression of being less concerned with their employees. I see my job as not only being concerned about my department's numbers, but also having my peo-

ple feel good about themselves. Motivating people to feel good about themselves and our department is an important key to my job."

A summary of some of Sharon's interactions reveals how she approaches the task of motivating her personnel:

1. Sharon uses weekly staff meetings as an opportunity for her associates to grow and learn from each other. For example, at each meeting, she has three or four members report to the larger group about a particular customer contact that began on a negative note and was turned into a positive outcome by the associate.
2. Sharon actively works at finding ways to encourage and support her newest associates. After listening in on one particularly difficult conversation in which her newest associate handled a sour, rude customer in a patient, highly professional manner, Sharon e-mailed the associate: "Jan, we should use the tape of your Miami phone call as the textbook example in effective communication. Great job!"
3. Sharon works hard at recognizing outstanding employee performance. When one associate set a weekly record for booked customer lease contracts, Sharon e-mailed her lauding the achievement and copied the department manager and other associates in the department. Sharon also congratulated the associate personally on her accomplishment, and at the

learning objectives

After reading and studying this chapter, you should be able to:

1. Identify the three levels of employee motivation.

2. Explain the relationship between performance and motivation.

3. Understand and explain Maslow's hierarchy of needs theory and the principle underlying his theory.

4. Differentiate between Herzberg's dissatisfiers and motivators.

5. Understand and explain expectancy theory.

6. Explain how supervisors can use goal-setting theory to motivate employees.

7. Define and explain reinforcement theory.

8. Identify five steps to motivating employees.

weekly associates' meeting Sharon led the team in giving her a round of applause.

4. Sharon finds a variety of ways to give recognition. When one associate shared at a team meeting suggestions for improving the customer database, Sharon e-mailed the suggestion to her own boss and recommended that all departments adopt the suggestion, crediting the employee for the suggestion. Sharon also championed the idea with her fellow supervisors. The recommendation was eventually implemented, and Sharon persuaded her boss to send a personal letter of appreciation to the employee.

5. Sharon particularly enjoys coaching and helping her lead associate learn the ropes. He is eager to learn and wants ultimately to become a supervisor. Sharon often seeks his advice and will delegate to him special assignments which give him an opportunity to learn more about the department. When Sharon was out with the flu, she missed for the first time her regularly scheduled meeting of supervisors with the department manager; she asked her lead associate to attend in her place. She could tell that he was quite pleased to do this.

6. While she is eager to praise for good performance, Sharon will not back off from addressing performance problems. But she does so tactfully and with concern for her associates' feelings. Several weeks ago her 57-year-old associate, one of the highest producers in the department, achieved only one-half of her daily quota on Monday and again on Tuesday. When Sharon approached her to

discuss it, instead of first bringing up the matter, Sharon began with some small talk. The employee herself brought up the issue with, "I guess you see where I've gotten off to a slow start this week. . . ."

7. Sharon is extremely sensitive about the best way to treat her associates. When one walked in twenty minutes late for the second time in a week, Sharon noted his hurried entrance, but withheld acknowledgment or eye contact. She talked with him within the hour about his tardiness, preferring not to address it immediately. During the eventual discussion, Sharon listened patiently to his explanations, which she considered plausible. She reinforced the reasons why punctuality was important and insisted that he be on time. The next day when the employee arrived on time, Sharon made sure she saw him, greeting him with a friendly "good morning," and asked if she could fix him a cup of coffee.

8. Sharon has worked hard to make her associates feel part of the team and to share team identity. At meetings, her language consists of "we" and "us." Two weeks ago, she ordered sandwiches and pizza and treated the associates to lunch in the conference room. Since her employees take lunch in two shifts, half went one day, the other half the next. Sharon intentionally avoided bringing up work-related issues at these outings, preferring that they be strictly social occasions. She and her lead associate felt the meetings were effective in establishing camaraderie, and Sharon plans do to this once every year or so.

MOTIVATION: SOME FUNDAMENTALS OF UNDERSTANDING HUMAN BEHAVIOR

motivation
Willingness to work to achieve the organization's objectives.

The opening case demonstrates that understanding and motivating employees is the core of effective supervision. Perhaps you've heard people say that no one can motivate someone else. They mean that **motivation** comes from within. It is the result of a person's individual perceptions, needs, and goals. We define motivation as the willingness of individuals and groups, as influenced by various needs and perceptions, to strive toward a goal. In organizations with enlightened management there is an attempt to integrate the needs and goals of individuals with the needs and goals of the organization. In the chapter preview, we saw that Sharon is trying to create compatibility between employees' needs and those of her company.

The quest for high quality and quantity of work, safety, cost effectiveness, compliance with company policies and procedures, and punctuality are important motivational issues that supervisors face each day. Getting employees to show up has proven a costly motivational challenge; in 1998 employee absenteeism rose 25 percent to a cost of nearly $700,000 annually for a 1,000-employee company.[1] In our management seminars we ask supervisors and managers to anonymously rate on a scale from 1 (lowest) to 10 (highest) the motivational level of employees whom they supervise. The ratings are turned in and written on a flipchart or board. Only rarely do scores higher than 8 appear; the average tends to be in the 5 to 6 range. When asked why ratings tend to be so mediocre, participants respond with comments such as "People today just don't seem to care as much," or "Some employees just want their paycheck and will do enough just to get by," or "There's no pride or commitment to their work."

Few social scientists would deny that people often act emotionally, but many would dispute that most people behave irrationally and unpredictably. They would argue that if more people understood the *why* of human behavior, other people's behavior would seem more rational and predictable. Why don't people have pride in their work? Why do they just do enough to get by? Why are others outstanding performers? The answer lies in their motivation.

Levels of Motivation

① Identify the three levels of employee motivation.

Broadly, when we say that someone is or is not motivated to engage in a certain behavior, we can refer to three distinct, but sometimes related, levels as shown in Exhibit 8–1. One level is the direction in which the individual behaves. Does an employee behave in desirable ways?

> **Does an AutoFin associate spend 95 percent of her time on the phone with customers? Does she key into her computer the result of each contact as it occurs, as desired by management? Does she attempt to sell a warranty agreement to each customer who extends a lease? Does she cooperate with other employees by providing information they may need about a customer she initially contacted?**

Note that the direction of an employee's behavior may be unfavorable from the supervisor's perspective. An AutoFin associate may spend 15 percent of her time making personal calls or reading the newspaper instead of contacting

Exhibit 8–1

The Three Levels of Motivation

customers. She may try to sell warranty agreements to only 50 percent of her contacts. She may choose *not* to share information that would be helpful to her colleagues. It is not enough for a supervisor merely to identify and communicate the desired practices; supervisors must meet the challenge of motivating employees to actually perform the desired behaviors.

A second motivation level relates to *how hard* the individual works to perform the behavior(s). While the employee may be aware of the need for the behavior, how much energy and effort does he exert to properly perform it?

> **John B. is keenly aware that safety is an important part of his job as a welder at Inland Marine's Yard 2. Yet, he often overlooks securing his safety harness when he works at heights over three feet above ground, despite the fact that this safety requirement is widely known and regularly discussed at weekly safety meetings held by his supervisor. Because he is experienced, John feels that this requirement is often a nuisance, so he usually "forgets." He'd rather put his energy into welding, which is what he is paid to do, he says. As John's supervisor states, John just isn't motivated to be conscientious in following established safety rules.**

For many supervisors, it is this second motivational level that provides the biggest challenge, getting employees to work hard, to put effort into what they do. A men's department manager complains that salespeople only go through the motions to keep their areas neat and orderly. "They know it, they just don't do it as well as they should." A branch bank manager laments her tellers who don't try very hard to make eye contact with customers, smile, call the customer by name, or attempt to cross-sell a CD or loan.

The third and final level responds to the motivational level of *persistence.* In the face of adversity, obstacles, or roadblocks, how hard does an employee keep trying to produce a behavior? The employee may be highly motivated when conditions for the behavior are favorable, but what happens in the face of adversity or roadblocks? When an employee isn't feeling well in the morning, will she call in absent? If she shows up, will she still persevere and perform the job well? If her equipment acts up, will she be motivated to find a makeshift way to get the work done?

> **Frito Lay is filled with tales of salespeople going to extraordinary efforts to meet their customers' needs. These include braving the fiercest**

http://www.frito-lay .com/

of weather to ensure their daily contacts, or going to great lengths to help a store clean up after a hurricane or fire. Letters about such acts pour into Dallas headquarters.[2]

Intrinsic and Extrinsic Motivation

intrinsic motivation
Behavior that an individual produces because of the pleasant experiences associated with the behavior itself.

Intrinsic motivation is that behavior which an individual produces because of the pleasant experiences associated with the behavior itself. Employees who are intrinsically motivated feel satisfaction in performing their work. This satisfaction may come from any of several factors, including enjoying the actual work done, the feeling of accomplishment, meeting the challenges, etc.

Anne Marie Bains has strong intrinsic motivation in her work as a pharmaceutical sales representative. She enjoys interacting with the professionals she calls on—nurses and physicians—and talking with them about her products. She enjoys traveling and the freedom of planning her calls. But the highlight is the actual time she spends communicating with the health care professionals—getting to know them on a professional basis, gaining their confidence, and knowing that they enjoy her visits.

extrinsic motivation
Behavior performed not for its own sake, but for the consequences associated with it. The consequences can include pay, benefits, job security, and working conditions.

By contrast, **extrinsic motivation** is performed not for its own sake, but rather for the consequences associated with it. The consequences can include such factors as the pay, the benefits, the job security, or working conditions.

Lonzo Gillis is a loan collector for a local bank. While he dislikes "putting the squeeze" on people, as he calls it, he can earn a nice bonus by exceeding his production goals. He also works in a nice air-conditioned office, and the bank's location is only 10 minutes from his home.

Lonzo is extrinsically motivated. It's not what he *does* in his job that he finds satisfying, but the indirect factors of pay, benefits, and working conditions.

② Explain the relationship between performance and motivation.

The Motivation–Performance Link

Many supervisors make a mistake in assuming that an employee's performance is directly related to an employee's level of motivation. Initially, one might conclude that the more highly motivated an employee is, the higher will be that employee's performance. This is not necessarily the case. Unquestionably, direction of behavior, level of effort, and persistence affect an employee's performance; however, the motivation–performance link is just not that simple.

For one thing, an individual's skill/ability level also influences performance. An employee with low motivation and exceptional skill may be able to outperform a more highly motivated, lesser skilled employee. And often, an employee's performance depends on such things as support of others. We all are familiar with sports examples of highly motivated players whose "performance" is below par, but the poor performance is not necessarily attributed to them: the NFL quarterback who last year was an all-star, but this year has three rookie offensive linemen and no pass protection; the outstanding pass receiver who this year is handicapped by a rookie quarterback; the pitcher whose infield leads the majors in errors. It works similarly in business organizations. The level of organizational support often influences performance.

Lucy Abruscato is a parts picker for a warehouse that provides auto parts to Chevrolet dealers in a large metropolitan area. A picker's job works like this: Lucy goes to a station, rings a bell, and is handed through a window an order sheet listing a customer's order. Each different part ordered is listed on one of the order sheet's 24 lines. Lucy's performance is measured by how many line items she picks each day, the normal range being 250 to 300 picks daily. She is paid at an hourly rate, so her performance is not directly tied to her pay. Each employee's weekly line total is shown on a large chart hung in the work area. Lucy noted that the line totals of new employees continually underperformed those of more senior employees, even after new employees became familiar with plant layout and part storage locations. She noted that the window attendant who hands each picker his line sheet rewards the more senior workers with the easier assignments—those involving smaller or more easily handled items such as nuts, bolts, gaskets, fan belts, and so forth. The more difficult assignments—tail pipes, trunk or hood assemblies, and engine blocks were assigned to the newer, typically younger, employees. As Lucy says, "I work harder than anyone, but my lines will not be up there with some of the old-timers. It upset me at first, but now I know—that's just the system."

To attribute an employee's low performance to low motivation or high performance to high motivation overlooks the fact that there are many other causes of performance besides just motivation level.

We conclude this discussion by stating that, *things being equal, employees who are more highly motivated will have higher performance.* But things are seldom truly equal, which challenges the supervisor's diagnostic skills when examining the true cause of a performance-related problem.

self-check

What variables other than motivation might impact the performance level of Sharon Olds' associates in the chapter preview?

Since the 1960s, much research has been done on the behavior of people at work. Some significant theories have been developed that are important to anyone in a position of leadership who wants to avoid unnecessary friction arising from human relationships in an organization. For a person of action, such as a supervisor who has to work with and through people, an understanding of motivation theory is essential. Kurt Lewin, famous for his work in the study of groups, once said that there is nothing so practical as good theory.[3] The remainder of this chapter will focus on the important theories of motivation, with emphasis on their application to effective supervision.

MASLOW'S HIERARCHY OF NEEDS THEORY

3 Understand and explain Maslow's hierarchy of needs theory and the principle underlying his theory.

One theory that is particularly significant and practical was developed by psychologist Abraham H. Maslow.[4] This theory is known as the hierarchy of needs. Of all motivation theories, it is probably the one best known by managers.

Principles Underlying the Theory

hierarchy of needs
Arrangement of people's needs in a hierarchy, or ranking, of importance.

The two principles underlying Maslow's **hierarchy of needs** theory are that (1) people's needs can be arranged in a hierarchy, or ranking, of importance, and (2) once a need has been satisfied, it no longer serves as a primary motivator of behavior. To understand the significance of these principles to Maslow's theory, let us examine the hierarchy of needs shown in Exhibit 8–2.

Physiological or Biological Needs. At the lowest level, but of primary importance when they are not met, are our **physiological** or **biological needs.** "Man does not live by bread alone," says the Bible, but anything else is less important when there is no bread. Unless the circumstances are unusual, the need we have for love, status, or recognition is inoperative when our stomach has been empty for a while. But when we eat regularly and adequately, we cease to regard hunger as an important motivator. The same is true of other physiological needs, such as those for air, water, rest, exercise, shelter, and protection from the elements.

physiological need
The need for food, water, air, and other physical necessities.

Safety or Security Needs. When the physiological needs have been reasonably well satisfied, **safety** or **security needs** become important. We want to be protected from danger, threat, or deprivation. When we feel threatened or dependent, our greatest need is for protection or security.

safety need
The need for protection from danger, threat, or deprivation.

Most employees are in a dependent relationship at work, so they may regard their safety needs as being very important. Arbitrary or autocratic management actions such as favoritism, discrimination, or the unpredictable application of policies can be a powerful threat to the safety of any employee at any level.

Social or Belonging Needs. **Social** or **belonging needs** include the need for belonging, for association, for acceptance by colleagues, and for friendship and

social need
The need for belonging, acceptance by colleagues, friendship, and love.

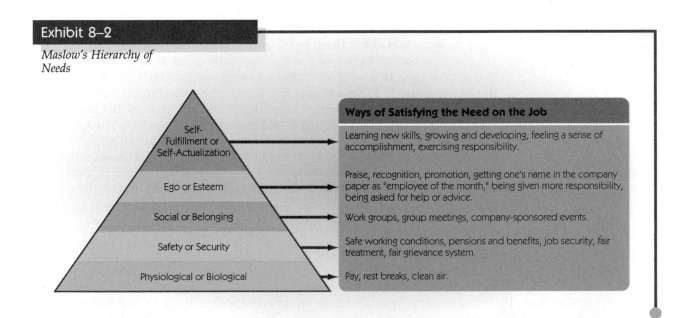

Exhibit 8–2

Maslow's Hierarchy of Needs

Ways of Satisfying the Need on the Job

Self-Fulfillment or Self-Actualization → Learning new skills, growing and developing, feeling a sense of accomplishment, exercising responsibility.

Ego or Esteem → Praise, recognition, promotion, getting one's name in the company paper as "employee of the month," being given more responsibility, being asked for help or advice.

Social or Belonging → Work groups, group meetings, company-sponsored events.

Safety or Security → Safe working conditions, pensions and benefits, job security, fair treatment, fair grievance system.

Physiological or Biological → Pay, rest breaks, clean air.

love. Although most supervisors know that these needs exist, many assume—wrongly—that they represent a threat to the organization. Fearing group hostility to its own objectives, management may go to considerable lengths to control and direct human efforts in ways that are detrimental to cohesive work groups. When the employees' social needs, as well as their safety needs, are not met, they may behave in ways that tend to defeat organizational objectives. They become resistant, antagonistic, and uncooperative. But this behavior is a *consequence* of their frustration, not the cause.

ego need
The need for self-confidence, independence, appreciation, and status.

Ego or Esteem Needs. Above the social needs are the **ego** or **esteem needs.** These needs are of two kinds: (1) those that relate to one's self-esteem, such as the need for self-confidence, independence, achievement, competence, and knowledge, and (2) those that relate to one's reputation, such as the need for status, recognition, appreciation, and respect from one's colleagues.

Unlike the lower level needs, ego needs are rarely fully satisfied, because people always seek more satisfaction of such needs once they have become important. A few years ago, the typical organization offered few opportunities for lower level employees to satisfy their ego needs. However, well-managed and innovative companies are doing a better job in this regard today.

 click! http://www.southwest.com/

Southwest Airlines was ranked number one of the top 100 best companies to work for in the U.S. by *Fortune* in 1998. A typical comment received from more than 100 enthusiastic Southwest employees was "Working here is truly an unbelievable experience. They treat you with respect . . . empower you . . . use your ideas to solve problems . . . they encourage you to be yourself."[5]

Still, the conventional method of organizing work, particularly in mass-production industries, gives little consideration to these aspects of motivation.

self-fulfillment needs
Needs concerned with realizing one's potential, self-development, and creativity.

Self-Fulfillment or Self-Actualization Needs. At the top of Maslow's hierarchy are the **self-fulfillment** or **self-actualization needs.** These needs lead one to seek realization of one's own potential, to develop oneself, and to be creative.

John B., age 64, is about three years from taking company retirement. He enjoys woodworking and has become quite good at it, his bowls and carved figures having won several awards at arts fairs. John is one of the most highly skilled mechanics in the company, but continually turns down overtime work on weekends. "The extra money just isn't worth it to me anymore," he says. "I'd much rather spend my time working in my shop or showing my work at an arts and craft show." John recently was asked on short notice to be flown over a weekend to another company location to help resolve a difficult maintenance problem which that site could not resolve. He accepted. As he stated, "It wasn't the money, it was the fact that nobody else could resolve it and I looked forward to the challenge."

It seems clear that the quality of work life in most organizations provides only limited opportunities to fulfill these needs, especially at lower organizational levels. When higher level needs are not satisfied, employees compensate by trying to further satisfy lower level needs. So the needs for self-fulfillment may remain dormant.

self-check

Reflect on the examples of motivation described in this chapter's preview case. Which need levels of employees are reflected in each of these?

Qualifying the Theory

Maslow's theory is a relative rather than absolute explanation of human behavior. You should be aware of the following four important qualifiers to his theory:

1. Needs on one level of the hierarchy do not have to be completely satisfied before needs on the next level become important.

2. The theory does not pretend to explain the behavior of the neurotic or the mentally disturbed.

3. Some people's priorities are different. For example, an artist may practically starve while trying to achieve self-actualization through the creation of a great work of art. Also, some people are much less security oriented or achievement oriented than others.

4. Unlike the lower levels, the two highest levels of needs can hardly ever be fully satisfied. There are always new challenges and opportunities for growth, recognition, and achievement. A person may remain in the same job position for years and still find a great deal of challenge and motivation in his or her work.

Raises and bonuses are not the only way to recognize employees' good work. Managers have a wide range of rewards that are motivations.

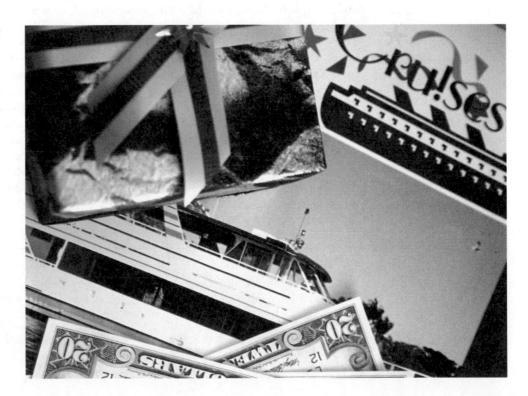

Bob Buschka, a computer programmer for a large bank in a midwestern state, has held his position for 20 years and would like to remain in that position. He enjoys programming and is looked on as one of the top programmers in banking in the area. The bank sends him to various schools to keep him growing and developing on the job.

"Bob's a remarkable person," says his boss. "He's passed up promotions into management to keep his present job, he's so into it. We know what a gem he is, and we do everything we can to give him lots of room to operate—special key projects, training and developing new programmers, and keeping up with the new applications to our industry."

HERZBERG'S THEORY

In the 1960s a researcher named Frederick Herzberg conducted in-depth interviews with 200 engineers and accountants from 11 different firms in the Pittsburgh, Pennsylvania, area.[6] Those interviewed were asked to recall an event or series of related events that made them feel unusually good and unusually bad about their work and how much the event(s) affected their performance and morale. Prior to Herzberg's study, a common assumption was that factors such as money, job security, and working conditions were all strong positive motivators, and pretty much worked the same way: If these things were not satisfied at work, people would be negatively motivated; if they were satisfied, they would be positively motivated. Herzberg's findings disproved this assumption and helped us better differentiate among various motivational factors.

④ Differentiate between Herzberg's dissatisfiers and motivators.

Dissatisfiers and Motivators

Herzberg found that two different lists emerged, one for factors that made the engineers and accountants feel unusually good, the other for those that made them feel unusually bad. Basically, he found that what people said most affected them negatively, or *dissatisfied* them (called **dissatisfier** or **hygiene factors**) about their jobs were things such as low pay, low benefits, unfavorable working conditions, poor job security, and poor company policy/administration. The things that *turned them on* (called **satisfier** or **motivator factors**) tended to be recognition, advancement, achievement, challenging work, being one's own boss, and the work itself. Interviewees indicated that satisfier/motivator factors had a stimulating effect on performance and morale, while the dissatisfier/hygiene factors had a negative effect. Note that the dissatisfier/hygiene factors are found at the lower level of Maslow's hierarchy, whereas the satisfier/motivator factors are at the higher levels. Exhibit 8–3 gives examples of Herzberg's factors.

dissatisfier factors
Factors that employees said most affected them negatively, or dissatisfied them about their job, including low pay, low benefits, and unfavorable working conditions.

satisfier factors
Factors that employees said turned them on, such as recognition, advancement, achievement, challenging work, and being one's own boss.

self-check

Try to answer Herzberg's survey questions yourself. Think about a particular job you have held in the past or presently hold. If you haven't had a job, think of your schoolwork.

1. What specific incident or event (singular or recurring) gave you the most satisfaction?

2. What caused the most dissatisfaction?

Exhibit 8–3

Herzberg's Satisfier/Motivator and Dissatisfier/Hygiene Factors

Satisfier/Motivator Factors

+ Recognition	"The boss says I've done a good job."
+ Advancement	"I was promoted to team leader."
+ Challenging work	"I solved a really tough job problem."
+ Being one's own boss	"I was given a free hand to do my job."
+ Work itself	"I got to design the new system."

Dissatisfier/Hygiene Factors

– Pay	"I'm not paid fairly for what I do."
– Benefits	"This company doesn't pay tuition or medical benefits."
– Working conditions	"It's so hot in the plant it's often unbearable."
– Job security	"With the seasonal work I never know for sure if I'll have a job."
– Company policy/administration	"We have so much red tape to go through."

Herzberg reasoned that the dissatisfier factors are what people take for granted about their jobs, so their presence is not particularly stimulating. For example, consider the employee who said that the most dissatisfying thing about his job was that the plant was too hot. Assume that the company addressed this issue and installed a crisp cooling system throughout the plant. Six months later would this employee be likely to say that one of the most satisfying things about the job was the cool plant? Not likely.

Conversely, factors that cause *strong dissatisfaction* do not tend to be such things as the lack of responsibility or challenge in a job or absence of recognition. If a company seeks to eliminate dissatisfaction it must address factors including wages, working conditions, and security.

Link to Intrinsic and Extrinsic Motivation

Earlier in the chapter we discussed the subject of intrinsic and extrinsic motivation. Note that the factors associated with positive motivation were intrinsic to the job, whereas those causing job dissatisfaction were extrinsic to it. When people felt good about their jobs, it was usually because something had happened that showed they were doing their work particularly well or were becoming more expert in their professions. In other words, good feelings were keyed to the specific tasks that they performed, rather than to extrinsic factors such as money, security, or working conditions. Conversely, when they felt bad, it was usually because something had happened to make them feel that they were being treated unfairly.

The crux of Herzberg's theory is that dissatisfiers and satisfiers are each important in their own way. Dissatisfier factors such as good pay, benefits, working conditions, and job security must first be addressed by management as a motivational base so as to prevent employee dissatisfaction. Once dissatisfaction is removed, management will get more "bang for its motivational effort" by focusing on employees' opportunities for responsibility, recognition, advancement, and challenge in their jobs.

More than 20 years ago, Walter Vaux was a young chemical engineer toiling in the lab when his boss walked in. "You're doing a wonderful job," he remembers the supervisor saying. "I'm so glad you're part of the department." It was just a few words, but the input was such a valuable motivator that Vaux, now 61 years old and retired, still talks of the lesson he learned: It takes more than cash. "Many other bosses have just taken my contributions for granted and felt that their reponse was more money. The real motivator was genuinely realizing my successes and telling me so."[7]

Qualifying Herzberg's Theory

Herzberg's results have been replicated in other studies involving nonprofessionals such as food service workers, assembly line workers, and others. However, there are some important qualifications to Herzberg's theory that you should bear in mind:

1. Money *can* be a motivating factor, especially when it is tied to recognition and achievement.

2. For some people, especially professionals, the absence of motivating factors such as recognition, advancement, and challenge can constitute dissatisfaction.

3. Critics contend that a built-in bias of Herzberg's findings is that when asked about something on the job that is positive, a person is biased toward mentioning something in which his or her behavior is the focal point, such as a feeling of achievement, meeting a job challenge, and so on. Conversely, when asked about dissatisfiers, one is likely to mention extrinsic factors over which he or she has no control, such as pay or working conditions.

Despite these qualifications, we feel that Herzberg's theory is valuable as a general guide to understanding behavior at work.

5 Understand and explain expectancy theory.

OTHER THEORIES OF MOTIVATION

This section explores some other theories of motivation with which you should be familiar. These include expectancy theory, goal-setting theory, and reinforcement theory.

Expectancy Theory

expectancy theory
Views an individual's motivation as a conscious effort involving the expectancy that a reward will be given for a good result.

The theories of Maslow and Herzberg focus primarily on the individual and his or her needs as dominant employee motivation factors. **Expectancy theory** is more dynamic. It views an individual's motivation as a more conscious effort involving the interplay of three variables: (1) expectancy that effort will lead to a given performance result; (2) probability of reward(s) associated with the performance result; and (3) the value of the reward to the individual.[8] Expectancy theory states that most work behavior can be explained by the fact that employees determine in advance what their behavior may accomplish and the value they place on alternative possible accomplishments or outcomes. Some writers have termed this a "payoff" or "What's in it for me?" view of behavior. Developed by Victor Vroom of the University of Michigan, expectancy theory is illustrated in Exhibit 8–4.

Let us take a look at how Vroom's theory operates. Suppose that Maria's boss says, "If you are able to complete the project ahead of schedule, Maria, I'll

Exhibit 8–4

Expectancy Theory

Motivation $=$ Expectancy that increased $\times$ Probability that a performance $\times$ Value attached to
effort will lead to a given   level will lead to a given   reward
performance level   reward

(Effort $\longrightarrow$ Performance link)   (Performance $\longrightarrow$ Reward link)

recommend you for a promotion to supervisor. I realize that it will mean your putting in some heavy work without pay, but think about it and let me know your answer." There are three important factors involved. As shown in Exhibit 8–4, one is the Effort → Performance relationship—Maria's expectancy that if she puts in the extra effort, she can realistically complete the project by Monday. The second factor is the Performance → Reward relationship, the likelihood that if she does complete the project by Monday, Maria will actually be promoted to supervisor. (In other words, does Maria's supervisor really have the influence to get her the promotion?) The final factor is the value Maria places on being promoted to supervisor. (Suppose the last thing in the world she wants is the responsibility and pressure of being a supervisor!) In expectancy theory, then, the three factors of the Effort → Performance link, the Performance → Reward link, and the value of the reward all interface to determine someone's motivation.

self-check

What example of expectancy theory explains your own motivational level in a given situation?

As shown in Exhibit 8–5, supervisors can do a number of things to apply the principles of expectancy theory. Here are three basic ways: (1) They can reward performance in ways that are meaningful to employees (the reward); (2) they can help employees reach desired performance levels through training and coaching (the Effort → Performance link); and (3) they can deliver on their commitments (the Performance → Reward link). Exhibit 8–6 illustrates a wide range of rewards that managers can provide. Note that many of these are absolutely free.

Each of Sharon Olds' sales remarketing associates has a sales goal to book 35 monthly customers to a new lease contract or to purchase and refinance their present vehicle. At that point, a financial incentive kicks in. Sharon works especially hard on the Effort → Performance aspect of expectancy theory by helping associates to be confident that if they work hard, they will actually achieve the 35 customer rate and higher.

Among the tools Sharon employs are continuous sales training of her associates, publicizing achievement levels and success stories, and performance feedback and coaching. "I do my best to make them feel that they have the right stuff and my support to succeed. It is especially important for new associates to know that if they work hard each day, they will achieve the necessary successes with customers. My full timers have done it before and know that they can get there, so my job is more one of encouraging them and rallying them."

Exhibit 8–5

Applying Expectancy Theory

1. Hire people who have adequate skill levels.
2. Set clear, recognizable performance goals.
3. Make sure employees know what is expected.
4. Continually stress employee training and skill development.
5. Use performance feedback and coaching to help employees gain skills.
6. Have employees share knowledge and expertise with others.
7. Give employees special jobs or assignments that stretch their abilities.
8. Celebrate performance successes.
9. Reward performance achievement.
10. Develop trust in your commitments by others; do not overpromise rewards.
11. Emphasize multiple rewards such as praise and recognition, being assigned desired work, receiving special training, attending a conference.
12. Determine what different individuals value as rewards (financial, social, being in the know, learning a new skill, etc.) and help make these happen.

Source: Copyright 1971. Reprinted with special permission of King Features Syndicate, Inc. World Rights reserved.

Sharon also works hard to reinforce the rewards received by top performers. She knows that the financial incentive is an important reward for most, but for others it is the fact that they have achieved a high level of success. "That's why I like to make it a big deal when someone gets there, like e-mailing everyone in sight about it," she says. "For many, that is as satisfying or more satisfying than the extra money."

Exhibit 8–6

Manager's List of Potential Rewards

Raises and bonuses
Social functions
Outings
A night on the town
A nice meal or lunch courtesy of the manager
Lunch as a group that the manager buys
Dinner
Day off or time off
Picnics for teams
Tickets to sports, special events
Direct oral praise to individual, one to one
Direct praise to individual in presence of others
Direct praise/recognition at group events
Peer recognition
Letters of recognition to file or place where customers can see them
Passing on customer compliments and commendations in voice mail or in writing
Written praise
Certificates and plaques
Shirts, phones, pins, hats, cups, jackets, and so on, all with the name of the company on them
Opportunity to attend conference, special training course
A parking space
Additional responsibilities
Personal call or visit from CEO or senior executive
New furnishings or equipment
Being assigned more favorable jobs
Allowing people to bid on projects/tasks they prefer

SOURCE: *Adapted from Peter Meyer, "Can You Give Good, Inexpensive Rewards? Some Real-Life Answers,"* Business Horizons, *November–December, 1994, pp. 84–85.*

---

(6) Explain how supervisors can use goal-setting theory to motivate employees.

goal-setting theory
The theory that task goals, properly set and managed, can be an important employee motivator.

Goal-Setting Theory

Task goals, in the form of clear and desirable performance targets, form the basis of Edwin Locke's **goal-setting theory** of motivation.[9] In Chapter 3 we emphasized the importance of objective setting as part of the planning process, but here we focus on the motivational aspects of goal setting. Locke's basic premise is that task goals can be highly motivating—if they are properly set and if they are well managed. Performance goals clarify the expectations between a supervisor and employee, between coworkers and subunits in an organization. They also establish a frame of reference for task feedback and provide a foundation for self-management. In these and related ways, Locke believes goal setting is of primary importance in enhancing individual motivation and job performance, and has spent much research since the 1970s substantiating that theory.

Listed here are the major ways in which a supervisor can use goal setting as a motivational tool:

1. Set specific goals. Specific, concrete goals consistently lead to better performance than general ones, such as "do your best," or no goals at all.

2. Set challenging but reasonably difficult goals. Be careful, though, not to set goals that an employee feels he or she has very little, if any, chance to reach. Several years ago, one professional football team's dressing room had posted the following offensive team goals:

    "Never allow our quarterback to be sacked; always score when inside the red zone (opponent's 20-yard line); never give up a fumble." Because they were unattainable, these goals were likely perceived as meaningless by the team's offensive players.

3. Ensure timely feedback to employees about goal achievement. This may be easier in certain situations, such as sales or production work, than in others.

4. Where practical, strengthen employee commitment by allowing them to participate in goal setting. Recall in Chapter 3 that an MBO cornerstone is employee involvement in helping establish their own key performance goals.

5. When multiple goals are established, make sure employees understand their priorities. For example, is meeting a quality goal more important than meeting a quantity goal or cost-effectiveness goal?

6. Reinforce goal accomplishment. When people exceed or reach goals, ensure timely rewards and recognition.

self check

In what way is goal-setting theory found in the chapter preview? Explain.

Define and explain reinforcement theory.

Reinforcement Theory

reinforcement theory
Based on the law of effect, holds that behaviors that meet with pleasant consequences tend to be repeated, whereas behaviors that meet with unpleasant consequences tend not to be repeated, and rewards and punishments are used as a way to shape the individual's behavior.

Reinforcement theory uses rewards and punishments that follow a person's behavior as a way to shape that individual's future behavior, as demonstrated in the following story.

> **A fisherman on a creek bank noted a small snake with something in its mouth swimming toward him with some difficulty. As it approached, he noted it was a small harmless water snake with a frog in its mouth that was too large. The poor little snake barely made it to the creek bank, so exhausted was it from trying to swallow the still alive, kicking frog. The fisherman reached down and pried open the little snake's jaws, allowing the frog to escape. But as he looked down at the poor little snake, he felt badly. Reaching into his bag, he opened his flask, picked up the little snake, and gave him a shot of fine distilled spirits. He then returned the little snake to the water and proudly watched him swim away, noting his two good deeds for the day, saving the frog and providing a lift to the little snake.**
>
> **About 20 minutes later, he again noted something rather smallish in the water, moving toward him, but with even greater difficulty than before. As it approached, he saw that it was the same little snake, this time with a much bigger frog. . . .**

Reinforcement theory is based on the law of effect, which holds that behaviors that meet with pleasant consequences tend to be repeated, whereas behaviors that meet with unpleasant consequences tend not to be repeated. To the extent that a supervisor has a degree of control of the reward and discipline system for employees, he or she has some control over the law of effect, just as did the fisherman with the frog. Suppose that a worker's attendance has been spotty recently. Reinforcement theory can work in two ways: (1) You can *positively reinforce* (praise, reward) the worker's favorable behavior (showing up on time), thereby encouraging him or her to repeat it, or (2) you can *discourage* (scolding, written disciplinary warning, assign nondesirable work duties) the worker's unfavorable behavior through punishment, thereby encouraging him or her not to repeat it.

Advocates of reinforcement theory argue strongly that positive reinforcement often is more effective than punishment in getting people to behave in desired ways.

> **Take, for example, an employee who gets punished for not treating a customer well. When the employee is called on the carpet, she might not necessarily know what specifically she must do to improve. Moreover, she might not be in a situation where she feels like listening, even if told. She might respond by associating "customer" and punishment, and try to avoid customers altogether.**
>
> **On the other hand, if, when the employee does something right and the supervisor says "I couldn't help but notice how patient and understanding you were in helping that customer work out her refund, I wanted to compliment you," then we are likely to get an employee out looking for customers to treat well. The specific behaviors (patience, understanding) lead to rewards that satisfy a person's need to enhance his or her self image.[10]**

Positive reinforcement, when properly applied, can be a very powerful motivator. Organizations and their supervisors have available a wide range of potential reinforcers, as listed earlier in Exhibit 8–6. Note that in addition to the more obvious raises and bonuses, a wide range of nonfinancial rewards was included. Recall how Sharon Olds used praise and recognition to reinforce associates when they performed their jobs well. Indeed, when praise is properly used, it is one of the most effective reinforcers a supervisor has; see Exhibit 8–7.

 click! http://www.hp.com

LESSONS FROM THE THEORIES: FIVE STEPS TO MOTIVATING EMPLOYEES

 8 Identify five steps to motivating employees.

Our intent in this chapter has been to explain a number of popular theories of motivation that can help you understand why people act as they do. You have noted the commonalities and close relationships among many of the theories. Based on these theories, we feel that there are a number of things that a supervisor can do to help create a motivating environment for employees. Moreover, these five actions apply broadly to supervisors in all types of organizations. These supervisory actions are:

1. Help make employees' jobs interesting.
2. Provide clear performance objectives.
3. Support employees' performance efforts.
4. Provide timely performance feedback.
5. Reward employees' performance.

Exhibit 8–7

How and When to Praise

1. **Praise should be genuine.** Often employees see through praise as simply a carrot used to motivate. Or some supervisors use it to compliment employees primarily when an upper manager is present to cast the supervisor in a good light. For praise to be meaningfully felt, the employee must feel it is intended as appreciation or recognition by the supervisor, with no additional conditions attached.

2. **Praise should be specific.** Assume that an employee has made a presentation at a safety meeting. After the meeting the supervisor says, "That was a terrific presentation, Anne. Thanks." While that *is* praise, there is no communication about the reason the behavior was praised. *More effective praise* would be "Ann, thanks for making the safety presentation. Your statistics and survey results were presented in a way that everyone could understand. And you are so good on your feet, in front of a group. I really appreciate your making us all aware of the need for continued safety awareness."

3. **Give praise for better than expected performance.** While recognition for expected results is important, especially in cases where you supervise below-average performers, some supervisors are too lavish in their praise of the expected and ordinary. When an employee who is always on time is greeted by his supervisor with "John, you're on time today, you're doing great," he may wonder what's really going on here and what the big deal is. In building a team of top performers, supervisory praise and recognition is especially important for better than expected results, such as putting out extra effort, exceeding performance goals, or going the extra mile.

4. **Praise should be timely.** To maximize its reinforcement potential, praise should be closely linked to the behavior. If you discussed yesterday with an employee his or her lack of punctuality, the time to recognize his or her punching in on time today is *today,* not the end of the week. You might make it a point to be near the clock and casually say "Thanks, Pete," which is sufficient to get the reinforcement across.

5. **Give praise for its own sake, not as a secondary motive.** When employees feel that praise is being used as a secondary motive, such as to soften their acceptance of another issue, it may be seen as superficial. Sometimes supervisors sandwich employee criticism with praise. They open with brief praise, then comes the "but" or "however" followed by criticism, which is the real purpose of the communication. Sometimes supervisors use praise to buffer bad news, such as when they disclose a turned-down promotion or reassignment. Positive conditional praise has its place, such as when coaching a new employee, but when viewed as an attempt to soften acceptance of another issue, praise is likely to be resented.

Help Make Employees' Jobs Interesting

Recall Herzberg's finding that employees said the most satisfying things about their jobs included feeling a sense of accomplishment, challenge, or responsibility. Granted, it is more difficult to make dull repetitive jobs more interesting, especially when you cannot alter an assembly line or change the nature of work being done. But you can do a number of things to make even dull, unchallenging jobs more interesting. Might you be able to rotate jobs/tasks? Might you assign team members to special projects that give them a break from the usual grind? Have them train a new employee? Learn skills to prepare them for a more advanced job? Make a safety presentation at a safety meeting? Might you elicit their help in resolving problems which you face, such as cost or deadline overruns, relationships with other departments, or ways to improve quality? As a supervisor, it is worth your effort to make employees' work provide opportunities for intrinsic satisfaction.

self check

If you are currently a supervisor, what actions could you take to help make your employees' jobs more interesting? If not currently a supervisor, select a job you have held that you considered dull and uninteresting. What actions could your supervisor have taken to make the job more interesting?

Provide Clear Performance Objectives

In line with expectancy and goal-setting theories, make sure employees clearly understand what is expected of them. If possible, set concrete, specific, challenging goals as discussed in goal-setting theory. Moreover, if these are not set by the system itself or by your own manager, try to obtain your employees' assistance in determining these. They are more likely to commit to goals they have had a hand in setting.

Support Employees' Performance Efforts

View yourself as a coach whose job is to support your team members. Help them through intangibles such as building confidence and encouraging them, but also support them in tangible ways through the resources you provide, your responsiveness to their needs, or by obtaining additional training for them, and so on. Be viewed not only as their best cheerleader, but as someone who delivers tangible support also.

Provide Timely Performance Feedback

Performance feedback is the fuel that employees need to sustain their effort. While the job itself may provide feedback to them, it is important that you acknowledge their progress. While reason would say that this is easier to do in favorable situations, our experiences with managers and employees indicate that it is not. Many employees state that they know things must be going well only because they *do not* hear from their supervisor. Managers must give favorable as well as unfavorable performance feedback. Note that we are not talking here about the feedback that accompanies an employee's 6- or 12-month formal review, but the feedback that occurs on a daily, regular basis.

Reward Employees' Performance

Be liberal with rewards, making sure that they are earned. Reinforce your high performers through the reward system available to you, such as merit increases, praise, and recognition, or opportunities to take on a more challenging job. Be creative with rewards, remembering that rewards are valued differently by different individuals (see Exhibit 8–7).

chapter review

① Identify the three levels of employee motivation.

The three levels of employee motivation are (1) the direction of an employee's behavior, (2) the level of effort, and (3) the level of persistence. Direction of behavior relates to those behaviors which the individual chooses to perform. Level of effort dictates how hard the individual is willing to work on the behavior. Level of persistence refers to the individual's willingness to pursue the behavior despite obstacles or roadblocks.

② Explain the relationship between performance and motivation.

While motivation is an important contributor to employee performance, it is not the only one. Also involved are an employee's skill and ability and organizational support in the form of physical resources and assistance. We conclude that other things being equal, employees who are more highly motivated will have higher performance records.

③ Understand and explain Maslow's hierarchy of needs theory and the principle underlying his theory.

The principle underlying Maslow's theory of a hierarchy of needs is that needs are arranged in a hierarchy of importance and that, once a need has been satisfied, it is no longer a primary motivator. The lower level needs include physiological, security, and social needs, and the higher level needs are esteem and self-fulfillment.

④ Differentiate between Herzberg's dissatisfiers and motivators.

Herzberg's research discovered that motivators are those factors that have an uplifting effect on attitudes or performance; whereas dissatisfier/hygiene factors are those that prevent dissatisfaction but do not motivate by themselves. Motivators are recognition, advancement, achievement, being one's own boss, and the challenge associated with the work itself. Dissatisfiers include pay, benefits, working conditions, job security, and company policy/administration. Motivators relate to the two highest levels of the Maslow hierarchy, self-fulfillment and esteem. Dissatisfiers are related to lower level physiological and security needs.

⑤ Understand and explain expectancy theory.

Expectancy theory views an individual's motivation as a conscious effort involving three variables: (1) expectancy that a given effort can achieve a given performance result; (2) probability that achieving the given performance result will lead to a reward; and (3) the value of the reward to the individual. Supervisors can apply expectancy theory by rewarding performance in ways that are meaningful to employees by helping employees reach desired performance levels through coaching and training, and by delivering rewards as promised to employees.

⑥ Explain how supervisors can use goal-setting theory to motivate employees.

The basic premise of goal-setting theory is that task goals can be highly motivating if properly set and well managed. To maximize their motivational impact, performance goals should be specific and difficult, but achievable. Ideally, employees should participate in the goal-setting process and, if multiple goals are involved, should understand their priorities. Performance feedback about progress toward goal attainment should be provided as well as timely rewards and recognition when goals are achieved.

(7) Define and explain reinforcement theory.

Reinforcement theory uses rewards and punishment that follow an individual's behavior as a way of shaping future behavior. It is based on the law of effect, which holds that behaviors that meet with pleasant consequences tend to be repeated, whereas behaviors that meet with unpleasant consequences tend not to be repeated.

(8) Identify five steps to motivating employees.

Supervisors, in general, can take five specific steps to motivate employees. They can (1) help make employees' jobs more interesting by enabling greater challenge, accomplishment, or responsibility; (2) provide clear performance objectives; (3) support employees' performance efforts through training, coaching, and assistance; (4) provide timely performance feedback to employees; and (5) reward employees generously for performance accomplishment.

---

important terms

dissatisfier (or hygiene) factors *228*
ego (or esteem) need *226*
expectancy theory *230*
extrinsic motivation *223*
goal-setting theory *233*
hierarchy of needs *225*
intrinsic motivation *223*
motivation *221*

physiological (or biological) need *225*
reinforcement theory *234*
safety (or security) need *225*
satisfier (or motivator) factors *228*
self-fulfillment (or self-actualization) needs *226*
social (or belonging) need *225*

---

questions for review and discussion

1. Identify and explain the three levels of employee motivation. Give an example of each for one of the situations below:
   - Customer associate at Home Depot
   - Bagboy at grocery chain
   - Carpenter for construction company
2. Explain the relationship between motivation and job performance. Can you identify a situation in which a factor other than your skill or motivation level impacted your performance?
3. Briefly outline Maslow's theory of the hierarchy of needs. What need levels are addressed by each of the following:
   - Being promoted from operator to supervisor
   - Setting a new record for individual performance
   - Being selected to attend a special training course
4. In what ways did Frederick Herzberg's research concerning employee motivation correlate with Maslow's hierarchy of needs?
5. In a recent management seminar taught by one of the authors to supervisors in a large shipyard, the supervisors commented: "We have very little opportunity to 'motivate' employees. All monetary factors—starting pay, yearly

merit increases, and bonuses based on the yard's profits—are controlled by upper management, with no input from supervisors. We don't have anything to motivate with." Do you agree or disagree with this supervisor? Why?

6. What are the elements of goal-setting theory? Explain.
7. What relationship, if any, do you see among expectancy theory, goal-setting theory, and reinforcement theory? Explain.

● skill builder 8–1

Classifying Managerial Rewards

Listed here are 15 actions that an organization's managers can take, each of which addresses one or more potential needs on the Maslow hierarchy. Some have been taken from Exhibit 8–6, "Manager's List of Potential Rewards," but others have been added.

Instructions:

1. For each item, identify the levels on the Maslow hierarchy of needs that the action addresses.
2. Select three items which you personally feel would be most important for you at the present time.
3. In small groups, discuss your results for items 1 and 2. To what extent did your team members agree on the three items? Why were there differences? Be prepared to report your results to the rest of the class.

Action	Maslow Need Level(s) Addressed
1. Day off or time off	_____
2. Personal call or visit from CEO or senior manager	_____
3. "Employee of the Month" parking space	_____
4. Direct oral praise from supervisor	_____
5. Opportunity to attend special training course	_____
6. Name in company newsletter	_____
7. Additional responsibilities	_____
8. Special task force assignment	_____
9. Company outing, picnic	_____
10. Being assigned favorable tasks	_____
11. Opportunity to attend special seminar	_____
12. New title, new office, new equipment	_____
13. Direct praise to individual in presence of others	_____
14. Receiving bonus for reaching production goal	_____
15. Being given more responsibility	_____

•skill builder 8-2

Applying Motivational Theory

Assume that you are a restaurant manager of a 30-employee restaurant chain. Your personnel consist of an assistant manager, cooks and food preparers, kitchen personnel, host/hostess, waiters, table bussers, and bartenders. Give an example of how you can use each of the following motivational theories to motivate your employees:

a. Expectancy theory
b. Goal-setting theory
c. Reinforcement theory

CASE 8-1

The Motivational Challenge

Assume you are 1 of 20 students attending a supervisory management course at a university. A paper assigned by the instructor asked each participant to write a one-page real-life case about an employee who posed a major motivational challenge for his or her supervisor. The paper was to describe the setting, giving some detail about the circumstances. At the beginning of class, the instructor collected all of the students' assignments and distributed them, one to each student. The case which you were given reads as follows:

My situation involves an employee in the technical department of my company. But first, I want to provide some background of the situation. This company is over 60 years old and was founded by a real buzz saw. He ran it like the military man he had been in WWII. He expected managers to have an answer for everything; that's what he was paying them for. If you punched a clock, you weren't being paid to think, just to do what you were told. We still joke around here about "leaving your brains at the gate" when you check in.

We seem to have two sets of people in the plant—the old-timers who were

brought up that way and the newer people who have been brought in since the company was bought from the family eight years ago by a national company. The company has brought in many new people. The new management now expects you to have more initiative and wants you to take the ball and run with it. Many of the older employees—at least some of them—have had difficulty doing that. We've gone to a mostly new generation of equipment in the plant, hired many new skilled technicians away from competition, and spent a lot on training.

The problem I want to address is a fellow technician I will call Barney Talbot. He's around 58 years old and is a holdover from the old days. While he has by far the most seniority at 24 years, he has not kept up with the rest of us. He is very insecure and hesitant to make decisions. Because we have now been given much more latitude with our work, Barney has posed a problem for all of us, especially our supervisor. Barney has been trained on maintaining the new equipment but is so insecure he takes up everyone's time (especially the supervisor) getting answers to even routine questions. He holds jobs up because of his indecision.

The supervisor gives him the most routine things to do, many of which don't involve the new equipment. This makes him fall even further behind everyone else. He takes a lot of his supervisor's and everyone else's energy, too. There's even resentment among the rest of us because he never gets any of the more difficult assignments and never gets called for weekend or holiday overtime like the rest of us. One reason I'm taking this course is *because I will probably be the next supervisor of the department when the current supervisor retires in two years, and I will inherit this problem.*

Instruction:

Assume the role of Barney Talbot's supervisor. Explain how you would try to motivate the employee, using the motivational theories/concepts found in your text.

chapter

9

Leadership

•─ **outline**

Leadership: What Is It All About?
Factors Affecting Leadership Style
Two Leadership Models
Tannenbaum and Schmidt's Leadership
Continuum
Is One Leadership Style Best?

Developmental Leadership
Heroic Managers
Developmental Managers

Transformational and Transactional Leadership
Transformational Leadership
Transactional Leadership

Servant Leadership
The Paradox of Servant Leadership
Characteristics of Servant Leadership

Core Leadership Functions

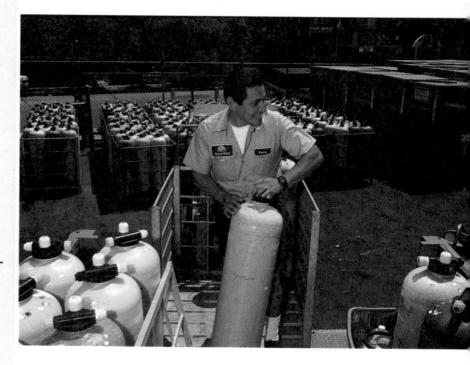

Leadership is of the spirit, compounded of personality and vision; its practice is an art.

Sir William Slim

Leadership is action, not position.

Donald H. McGannon

Kenny: An Effective Supervisor

learning objectives

After reading and studying this chapter, you should be able to:

1. Describe factors that affect the leadership style used.

2. Discuss and explain two frequently used leadership models.

3. Determine which leadership style is most appropriate in different situations.

4. Contrast heroic supervisors with developmental supervisors.

5. Contrast transformational leadership with transactional leadership.

6. Discuss how to inspire self-confidence, develop people, and increase productivity.

The most effective supervisor encountered by one of the authors of this textbook was named Kenny, and he was maintenance supervisor in a chemical plant of an international corporation.* The author was called in as a consultant because the plant was suffering from the results of the ineffective, autocratic leadership of a former plant manager. Such leadership at the top had adversely affected all levels, resulting in low morale and losses from plant operations.

In gathering data about the plant through interviews, questionnaires, and observations, the consultant discovered that one maintenance crew, unlike the rest of the departments in the plant, had very high morale and productivity. Kenny was its supervisor.

In the interview with Kenny, the consultant discovered that Kenny was a young man in his early thirties who had a two-year associate degree from a community college. The consultant was impressed with his positive attitude, especially in view of the overall low plant morale and productivity. Kenny said that the plant was one of the finest places he'd ever worked in and that the maintenance people had more know-how than any other group he had been associated with. Kenny's perception of his crew was that they did twice as much work as other crews, that everyone worked together, and that participative management did work with them.

One thing the consultant was curious about was why pressure and criticism from the old, autocratic manager seemed not to have had any effect on Kenny's crew. The crew gave the consultant the answer. They explained that Kenny had the ability to act as a buffer between upper management and the crew. He would get higher management's primary objectives and points across without upsetting his people. As one crew member described it:

The maintenance supervisors will come back from a "donkey barbecue" session with higher management where they are raising hell about shoddy work, taking too long at coffee breaks, etc. Other supervisors are shook up for a week and give their staff hell. But Kenny is cool, calm, and collected. He will call us together and report that nine items were discussed at the meeting, including shoddy work, but that doesn't apply to our crew. Then he will cover the two or three items that are relevant to our getting the job done.

Unfortunately, Kenny did have a real concern at the time of the consultant's interview. He was being transferred from the highest producing crew to the lowest producing one. In fact, the latter was known as the "Hell's Angels" crew. The crew members were a renegade group who were constantly fighting with production people as well as with one another. The previous supervisor had been terminated because he could not cope with them. In the course of this chapter, we will return to Kenny and what happened with the renegade crew.

---

*The company would not permit use of its name.

self-check

> Do you think Kenny can turn things around in a year with the renegade crew? Why or why not?

One thing we didn't say about motivation in the previous chapter is that it cannot take place in a vacuum. For things to happen, effective leadership must be exhibited. This chapter focuses on effective leadership.

We don't want the chapter preview to give you the idea that being an effective leader is easy. Today many supervisors and managers use a less effective leadership style than they could be using, often because they don't have the necessary skills or don't even realize the benefits of using other styles. They don't realize that the most effective style in one situation may not be the most effective in another. Hence, this chapter addresses such questions as the following:

1. Why do some leaders use one style and other leaders use another?
2. What effects do different styles have on employee productivity and morale?
3. What style is most appropriate in a particular situation?
4. Should a particular style be used consistently, or should the style be changed as circumstances change?

Such questions are vital for an organization, since supervisory leadership is one of the primary determinants of organizational performance and productivity.

LEADERSHIP: WHAT IS IT ALL ABOUT?

leadership
Influencing individual and group activities toward goal achievement.

Leadership is defined as a process of influencing the individual and group activities toward goal setting and goal achievement. In the chapter preview, Kenny successfully influenced his group toward the achievement of effective results, whereas the former supervisor of the "Hell's Angels" had not. This chapter provides insights and concepts that will assist supervisors in successfully leading their work groups.

Describe factors that affect the leadership style used.

Factors Affecting Leadership Style

Three factors, or variables, have a major impact on the choice of leadership style. These are (1) Theory X or Theory Y management philosophy, (2) the followers' readiness level, and (3) the situation faced by the supervisor. As Exhibit 9–1 shows, these factors are interrelated.

Theory X or Theory Y Management Philosophy. A supervisor's management philosophy is basically determined by his or her assumptions about the nature of people. Whether they are aware of it or not, most supervisors have a philosophy that influences their style in working with and through people. This philosophy is affected by several factors. Three critical factors interact to influence a supervisor's view of the nature of people and consequently shape his or her philosophy:

1. The supervisor's family and early school environment
2. The supervisor's experience and training in the area of leadership

Exhibit 9–1

*Factors Affecting
Choice of Leadership
Style*

3. The supervisor's present work environment, including the type of work and the general management system

Kenny had a very supportive and happy home environment. His father was a big influence and served as a role model. He always stressed to Kenny that he should treat people as he would want to be treated.

One of the most widely publicized approaches to the study of management philosophy is Douglas McGregor's concept of Theory X and Theory Y.[1] On the basis of his consulting and research work in industry, McGregor outlined two contrasting sets of assumptions about the nature of people. A manager's leadership style is influenced by the set of assumptions to which he or she subscribes. Following are the most significant assumptions of **Theory X:**

Theory X
The average person has an inherent dislike of work and wishes to avoid responsibility.

1. The average human being has an inherent dislike of work and will avoid it if possible.
2. Because of this human characteristic—dislike of work—most people must be coerced, controlled, directed, or threatened with punishment to get them to put forth adequate effort toward the achievement of organizational objectives.
3. The average human being prefers to be directed, wishes to avoid responsibility, has relatively little ambition, and, above all, seeks security.
4. The average human being cannot be trusted.

Supervisors who accept Theory X assumptions will be more inclined to prefer a structured, autocratic leadership style.

The basic assumptions of **Theory Y** are as follows:

Theory Y
Work is as natural as play or rest.

1. The expenditure of physical and mental effort in work is as natural as play or rest.

2. External control and the threat of punishment are not the only means of bringing about effort toward organizational objectives. People will exercise self-direction and self-control in the service of objectives to which they are committed.

3. Commitment to objectives is a function of the rewards associated with their achievement.

4. The average human being learns, under proper conditions, not only to accept but also to actively seek greater responsibility.

5. The capacity to exercise a relatively high degree of imagination, ingenuity, and creativity in the solution of organizational problems is widely, not narrowly, distributed in the population.

6. Under the conditions of modern industrial life, the intellectual potentialities of the average human being are only partially utilized.

7. The average human being believes that he is a winner so treat him like a winner.

Supervisors who hold Theory Y assumptions will be more inclined to prefer a supportive, participative leadership style when the situation calls for it. This last point is important because some people have misconstrued Theory Y by assuming that it always dictates a supportive participative approach. Although a leader holding Theory Y assumptions about people might prefer a participative approach, it does not preclude a tough-minded approach or decisions. For example, Henri Fayol, one of the pioneers of management thinking, used the term "commanding" for what today we call "leading." One of Fayol's principles of command (leadership) is to eliminate the incompetent. However, he indicates that before you take that step, you attempt to develop competence in the employee through training, coaching, counseling, etc. If these strategies do not work, you eliminate the individual through firing, and everyone knows the action was fair and warranted. This illustration reflects a Theory Y set of assumptions, and the outcome reflects a tough-minded decision.

Edgar Schein, an international expert on organization culture and process consultation, has stated "show me an organization that has a key leader with Theory X assumptions about people, and I predict they will eventually screw things up."[2] The authors agree with Schein. The former plant manager in the chapter preview was Theory X oriented and was a casualty of Henri Fayol's principle of command—eliminate the incompetent.

self-check

Which of these Theory X or Y assumptions did Kenny hold concerning his people? Also, what views did he hold regarding his boss and the new plant manager?

What if the renegade crew decides not to cooperate with Kenny and its members continue to be poor performers? Should Kenny continue to be supportive and use Theory Y strategies? Why or why not?

readiness level
The state of a person's drive or need for achievement.

The Followers' Readiness Level. **Readiness level** is the state of a person's drive and need for achievement. It results from his or her experience, educa-

A successful supervisor will adapt his or her management philosophy to individual and group activities.

 http://www.taci-hvac .com/frrbotto.htm

tion, attitudes, and willingness and ability to accept responsibility. These readiness variables should be considered only in relation to a specific task to be performed. The readiness concept is expressed by the following formula:

$$\text{Readiness} = \text{Ability} + \text{Willingness}$$

If followers are less ready, the leader should use a different style than if followers were more ready. Unfortunately, some supervisors fail to take into consideration the readiness level of their employees.

> After Kenny was assigned to the new crew, he had to make a decision on the leadership strategies he would use in dealing with them. His initial diagnosis was that the crew had the ability to do the work but lacked the willingness because of a poor attitude.
>
> Through discussion with members of the "Hell's Angels" crew, the consultant learned that the first day on the job Kenny called a meeting, shut the door, and conducted a "bull session" that lasted over two hours. Among other things, he told them about his philosophy and the way he liked to operate. He especially stressed that he was going to be fair and treat everyone equally. The crew members were allowed to gripe and complain as long as they talked about matters in the plant, while Kenny played a listening role without arguing with them. In the course of the session, Kenny expressed his expectations of the crew. They, in turn, told him they would do it his way for two weeks to see if he "practiced what he preached."
>
> As you may have surmised by now, Kenny's leadership made the difference. Before the year was out, his new crew was the most productive in the plant.

The Situation Faced by the Supervisor. Common sense dictates that the situation faced by a supervisor should have a major influence on his or her leadership style. A platoon leader directing troops in combat, an airline pilot who suddenly has engine trouble, or a supervisor faced with an immediate safety crisis would certainly not call for a group meeting and get people involved to deal with the emergency.

The nature of the work and the types of assignments must be considered in assessing a situation. Research scientists who perform creative and complex jobs, for example, require more freedom to operate than do workers who perform repetitive, assembly-line work. Finally, a leader's choice of style is influenced by how her or his unit is progressing. For example, a football team with outstanding potential that loses the first three games would get a different leadership response from its coach than a team that had won its first three games.

Two Leadership Models

② Discuss and explain two frequently used leadership models.

Of the many theories and theoretical models regarding leadership, we have selected two that are especially applicable for supervisors. These are (1) Robert Blake and Anne Adams McCanse's well-known Leadership Grid® and (2) Paul Hersey and Kenneth Blanchard's Situational Leadership® Model. Probably more supervisors have been trained using these models than any others. More than a million people have been trained in both the Situational Leadership and Grid models, including 40 countries worldwide.[3] Clearly businesses see these two models as more practical than the more theoretical models.

Leadership Grid®
Categorizes leadership styles according to concern for people and concern for production results.

Leadership Grid. The **Leadership Grid®** in Exhibit 9–2 (originally published as the Managerial Grid by Robert Blake and Jane S. Mouton) shows that a leader has two concerns: production and people.[4] "Concern for Results" is plotted on the horizontal axis of the grid, while "Concern for People" is plotted on the vertical axis. Although the exhibit identifies seven basic leadership styles, theoretically there are 81 combinations of "concerns" that could be plotted by using the nine-point system in the grid.

If a supervisor is primarily concerned with production and shows little concern for people, he or she is a *9,1* leader (9 in concern for production results and 1 in concern for people). The *9,1* leader is one who structures the work, delegates as little as possible, and usually is an autocrat in getting work accomplished. This style is called **authority compliance** or *task management*.

authority compliance
The leader's having a high concern for production results and using a directive approach.

Conversely, the supervisor who shows primary concern for people and little concern for production is a *1,9* leader. The *1,9* leader is supportive and somewhat permissive, emphasizing the need to keep employees happy and satisfied. Leaders of this type tend to avoid pressure in getting the work done. This style is called **country club management.**

country club management
High concern for people.

The *5,5* leader uses a **middle of the road management** style—this leader places some emphasis on production and some emphasis on people. Usually the unstated agreement in this style is "If you give me reasonable production, I will be reasonable in my demands on you."

middle of the road management
Places equal emphasis on people and production.

The *1,1* leader reflects the poorest of all styles on the grid, which is called **impoverished management.** Supervisors using this type of leadership have completely abdicated the leadership role. If any significant work gets done, it is due to the initiative of people working for this leader. In actuality, the leader has retired on the job!

impoverished management
Little concern for people or production.

Exhibit 9–2

*The Leadership Grid
Figure*

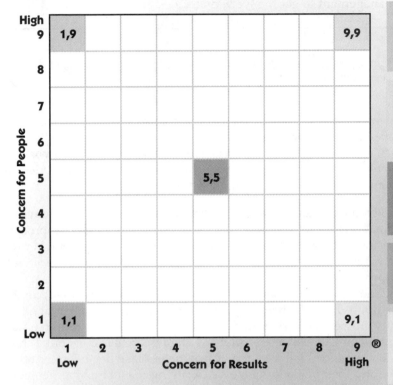

1,9 Country Club Management:
Thoughtful attention to the needs of the
people for satisfying relationships leads
to a comfortable, friendly organization
atmosphere and work tempo.

9,9 Team Management:
Work accomplishment is from committed
people; interdependence through a
"common stake" in organization purpose
leads to relationships of trust and respect.

5,5 Middle of the Road Management:
Adequate organization performance is
possible through balancing the necessity
to get work out while maintaining morale
of people at a satisfactory level.

1,1 Impoverished Management:
Exertion of minimum effort to get
required work done is appropriate to
sustain organization membership.

9,1 Authority-Compliance Management:
Efficiency in operations results from
arranging conditions of work in such a
way that human elements interfere to a
minimum degree.

**In Opportunisitic Management, people
adapt and shift to any grid style needed
to gain the maximum advantage.
Performance occurs according to a
system of selfish gain. Effort is given only
for an advantage for personal gain.**

**9+9: Paternalism/Maternalism
Management:**
Reward and approval are bestowed to
people in return for loyalty and obedience;
failure to comply leads to punishment.

SOURCE: *The Leadership Grid® figure, Paternalism Figure and Opportunism from* Leadership Dilemmas—Grid Solutions, *by Robert R. Blake and Anne
Adams McCanse (Formerly the Managerial Grid by Robert R. Blake and Jane S. Mouton). Houston: Gulf Publishing Company (Grid Figure: p. 29, Paternalism
Figure: p. 30, Opportunism Figure: p. 31). Copyright 1991 by Scientific Methods, Inc. Reproduced by permission of the owners.*

team management
High concern for both people and production.

The *9,9* leader believes that the heart of directing work lies in mutual understanding and agreement about what organizational and unit objectives are and about the proper means of attaining them. This type of leader has a high concern for both people and production and uses a participative approach called **team management** to get the work done.

self-check

Which style do you think Blake and associates advocate as the style that works best?

If your answer was the *9,9* style, then you are correct. Blake and associates strongly believe that the *9,9* style is the way to manage in leadership situations. They cite the many managers and supervisors with whom they have worked, regardless of political, religious, or business practices, who have concluded that a *9,9* (team management) leader is using the ideal style.

3 Determine which leadership style is most appropriate in different situations.

Hersey and Blanchard's Situational Leadership. It sounds as if we have leadership licked, doesn't it? You may have concluded that the best approach is a high concern for both production and people. But not so fast—a number of people disagree, saying that there is *no one best approach for every situation*, but only a best approach for a given situation.

life-cycle theory of leadership
Leadership behaviors should be based on the readiness level of employees.

One of the most popular situational approaches is called the **life-cycle theory of leadership.** It draws heavily on leadership research conducted at Ohio State University. In these studies, leadership behaviors and strategies in a number of different organizations were examined. The researchers concluded that many leadership behaviors fall into one of two areas—task behaviors or relationship behaviors. **Task behaviors** involve clarifying the job; telling people what to do, how to do it, and when to do it; providing follow-up; and taking corrective action. **Relationship behaviors** involve providing people with support, giving them positive feedback, and asking for their opinions and ideas.

task behaviors
Clarifying a job, telling people what to do and how and when to do it, providing follow-up, and taking corrective action.

relationship behaviors
Providing people with support and asking for their opinions.

These two concepts, along with the concept of the readiness level of followers, are central to understanding the Hersey-Blanchard model.[5] Recall that the readiness level of followers is assessed in relation to their ability to do a *specific* job or task. It encompasses their desire for achievement, experience, education, attitudes, and willingness to accept responsibility. Now that we have a few building blocks, let's examine Hersey and Blanchard's situational leadership model, as shown in Exhibit 9–3.[6]

Situational Leadership® Model
Shows the relationship between the readiness of followers and the leadership style.

The Hersey-Blanchard **Situational Leadership® Model** shows the relationship between the readiness of followers and the leadership style based on task and relationship behaviors of leaders. The model consists of four labeled blocks, or quadrants, with a curved line running through each quadrant. At the bottom of the model is a scale showing various ranges of readiness: high, moderate, and low. The direction of the arrow on the readiness scale and the direction of the arrow on the task behavior axis indicate that the higher the degree of readiness, the lower the degree of task behavior required.

To use this model, first identify the readiness level of the members of your work group (high, moderate, or low) on the readiness scale. Keep in mind that this point represents your assessment only in regard to their ability to carry out a *specific* task or assignment. Then draw a vertical line. The point where it intersects the curved line will fall within one of the four quadrants, and the la-

*The Hersey-Blanchard
Situational
Leadership® Model*

SOURCE: *Paul Hersey and Kenneth Blanchard,* Management of Organizational Behavior: Utilizing Human Resources, *7th ed. © 1996, p. 200. Reprinted by permission of the Center for Leadership Studies.*

bel on that quadrant gives the most effective leadership style for the particular situation.

Hersey and Blanchard use the model to explain not only leadership in dealing with adults, but also parents' leadership in raising children. Let's first illustrate the model using a family situation.

self-check

Assume that a four-year-old boy is to walk to a birthday party. Although the party is in the neighborhood, it is two blocks away and there are two busy streets to cross. Diagnose the leadership style the child's mother would use to get her son to the party.

If you responded that a high-task and low-relationship style is appropriate, then you are correct. The task involves some danger (crossing busy streets), and the follower is less ready. Hence, the mother should use a structured, high-task approach, accompanying the child and perhaps even holding his hand as they cross the streets.

The four quadrants in the top portion of Exhibit 9–3 can be translated into four basic leadership styles: (1) structuring and telling, (2) coaching and selling,

structuring and telling style
Used with individuals or groups relatively less ready for a given task.

coaching and selling style
Used with individuals or groups that have potential but haven't realized it fully.

participating and supporting style
Best used with ready individuals or groups.

delegating style
Used with exceptionally ready and capable individuals and groups.

(3) participating and supporting, and (4) delegating. The **structuring and telling style** (S1: high task and low relationship) usually works best with new or less ready employees and with individuals or groups whose performance is slipping. For example, if a department's costs have increased considerably beyond the standard, then a highly structured, close leadership style would be called for to correct the situation. Thus, the structuring and telling style would be used with an individual or group that is relatively low in readiness with respect to a given task.

The **coaching and selling style** (S2: high task and high relationship) is best used with individuals or groups that have potential but haven't completely mastered their assignments. For example, a high school football coach with young but talented players should probably use this approach. The coach would have a high concern for both task accomplishment (coaching) and convincing the players through positive reinforcement that they have the ability to win (selling).

An appropriate style to use as individuals or groups mature is the **participating and supporting style** (S3: high relationship and low task). The leader should use more participative management in getting ideas and should involve the followers in setting objectives and solving problems. Think of Maslow's hierarchy of needs theory (Chapter 8): As employees gain experience and competence, they have a need for more support for and involvement in their work.

The **delegating style** (S4: low relationship and low task) is one of the more difficult styles for a supervisor to use even when individuals or groups working under the supervisor are exceptionally ready and capable. A primary reason is that the supervisor is held accountable for results and therefore is reluctant to involve employees in her or his work. Perhaps you have heard the expression "If it ain't broke, don't fix it." This saying sums up why the wise supervisor will leave well enough alone as long as results are satisfactory. But what happens when conditions change?

self-check

Suppose you are a supervisor and have a skilled, capable worker who has never caused you any difficulties. For three years she has been a productive person in your department. Since she has proved to be a capable person, you would probably be using a delegating style in regard to her work. However, in the past two weeks her work has steadily deteriorated. Projects are late and the work, when completed, is of poor quality. As her supervisor, what leadership style would you use in this situation?

You certainly would not continue to delegate, would you? Most supervisors would shift all the way to a coaching and selling style or even to a structuring and telling style. Depending on what the problem is, either style could be appropriate. This situation shows how a leader might use a different style with an individual or group, depending on the situation.

Tannenbaum and Schmidt's Leadership Continuum

continuum of leadership behavior
The full range of leadership behaviors in terms of the relationship between a supervisor's use of authority and employees' freedom.

Robert Tannenbaum and Warren Schmidt are two writers who take a situational viewpoint toward leadership.[7] Their **continuum of leadership behavior,** shown in Exhibit 9–4, is especially useful when a supervisor is considering the degree to which employees should be involved in decision making. The figure is a rectangular block representing a continuum of power, which is divided by a diagonal line into two distinct parts: (1) use of authority by the supervisor and (2) the area of freedom for employees. The more authority the supervisor has, the less freedom there is for employees. Conversely, the more freedom employees are given, the less authority the supervisor uses. The continuum also indicates the range of available behaviors from which the supervisor can draw.

Tannenbaum and Schmidt maintain that each situation calling for a decision may require a different approach. The path the leader chooses to follow should be based on a consideration of the following three types of forces:

1. *Forces in the leader.* These include the leader's value system, confidence in employees, leadership inclinations, and feelings of security or insecurity.

2. *Forces in the employees.* These include the employees' need for independence, need for increased responsibility, knowledge of the problem, attitude toward and interest in tackling the problem, and expectations with respect to sharing in decision making.

3. *Forces in the situation.* These include the type of organization, the group's effectiveness, the pressure of time, and the nature of the problem itself.

These three types of forces can be compared to the three factors affecting leadership (discussed at the beginning of the chapter and shown in Exhibit 9–1). For example, a supervisor's management philosophy is greatly influenced by his or her value system.

Exhibit 9–4

Continuum of Leadership Behavior

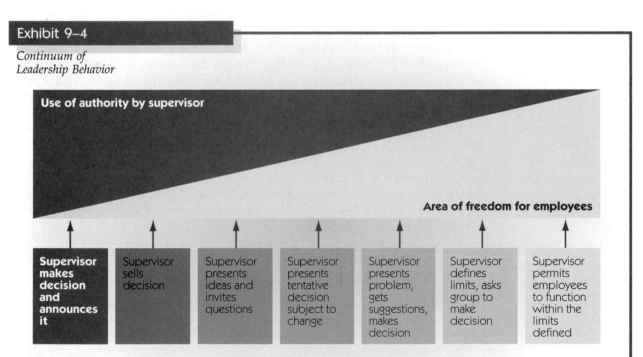

SOURCE: *Modified and reprinted by permission of* Harvard Business Review. *An exhibit from "How to Choose a Leadership Pattern" by Robert Tannenbaum and Warren H. Schmidt (May–June 1973). Copyright © 1973 by the President and Fellows of Harvard College. All rights reserved.*

The key point to remember is that the successful supervisor is skilled in assessing the appropriate behavior to use in a given situation.

Also, this approach preceeded the Vroom-Yelton decision-making model. Both approaches provide guidance for involving employees in the decision-making process. Utilizing this approach, how would you deal with the following self-check question?

self-check

As the result of a dramatic upward shift in sales, the XYZ firm has to rearrange vacation schedules. The previous supervisor consulted individually with employees and, when possible, gave them their first or second choice of vacation time. Because of time pressure, this approach would take too long now. Donna Douglas, the current supervisor, has a lot of confidence in her group of employees. They have a good work record. Drawing from the continuum of leadership behavior, what approach would you recommend that she use in rearranging vacation schedules?

Is One Leadership Style Best?

As we indicated, research supports the thesis that there is no one best style for all situations. However, Hersey and Blanchard and others recognize that, in most situations, the appropriate style is either coaching and selling or participating and supporting. So we can learn a lot from the Blake and associates thesis regarding the payoffs from utilizing a participative, team approach to managing.

The long-run trend in U.S. industry is for supervisory managers to use more participative styles, although they initially resist the move toward more participation.[8] An explanation for this trend is that employees are becoming better educated and their lower level needs have been relatively well satisfied. It is only through tapping the higher level needs, then, that significant motivation will occur.

We believe the next three leadership approaches to be discussed are the most affirming of supervisors who hold a Theroy Y set of assumptions regarding people. We also believe it is the most rewarding for the employees, the organization, and the supervisors in arriving at win–win outcomes. Although there is some overlap, there are enough differences that we present them individually. The approaches are developmental leadership, transformational leadership, and servant leadership.

4 Contrast heroic supervisors with developmental supervisors.

DEVELOPMENTAL LEADERSHIP

We noted earlier in the chapter that there is no one leadership approach that is effective in all situations, and that a contingency approach is called for to achieve effective results. In many environments, however, with educated personnel, a contingency diagnosis calls more and more for an approach known as *developmental leadership* that is especially effective in managing groups.

Developmental leadership is an approach that helps groups to evolve effectively and to achieve highly supportive, open, creative, committed, high-

developmental leadership
An approach that helps groups to evolve effectively and to achieve highly supportive, open, creative, committed, high-performing membership.

heroic managers
Those managers who have a great need for control or influence and want to run things.

performing membership. To understand developmental leadership better, let us first examine what David Bradford and Allen Cohen called "heroic management."

Heroic Managers

Heroic managers are those who have a great need for control or influence and want to run things. If they are dynamic and capable, they may do an effective job and produce good results, particularly in the short run. However, it is critical that they do not overcontrol and stymie the development of subordinates. They are depicted very heroically in films, especially those dealing with the Wild West. Some examples are the trail boss who gets the wagon train through to its destination and the sheriff who takes care of the bad guys.

From interviews with managers providing their views of what a good leader is like, Bradford and Cohen developed the following list of characteristics of heroic managers:

1. The manager should know at all times what is going on in the department. (In westerns, when asked for information, the trail boss always seems to know what is going on.)
2. The manager should have enough technical expertise to supervise subordinates. (The really good trail boss can not only outdraw and outshoot anyone around but also handle troublemakers quite effectively with his bare fists.)
3. The manager should be able to solve any problem that comes up or at least solve it before the subordinate does. (If the trail boss cannot handle any problem that arises, he loses face and his leadership position is undermined.)
4. The manager should be the primary (if not the only) person responsible for how the department is working. (The trail boss has total responsibility for the welfare of the group, so shared leadership is out of the question.)

Desirable though these characteristics are, if carried to extremes, they can lead to overcontrol and lack of development of subordinates, as shown in Exhibit 9–5. Therefore, what is needed is an orientation that focuses on *building heroes* rather than *being a hero*.

Developmental Managers

Building heroes is the goal of developmental leaders. Bradford and Cohen's model of the manager as a developer has three interrelated components: (1) building a shared-responsibility team, (2) continuously developing individual skills, and (3) determining and building a common department vision.[9]

Building a Shared-Responsibility Team. In talking about building a shared-responsibility team, we are really talking about shared leadership. Instead of using meetings primarily for reporting and providing information to the group, developmental leaders deal with real issues and actual problem solving.

self-check

Refer to the continuum of leadership behaviors shown in Exhibit 9–4. Which behaviors would support building a shared-responsibility team?

Exhibit 9–5

*The Self-Fulfilling
Consequences of
Using the Heroic
Management
Approach*

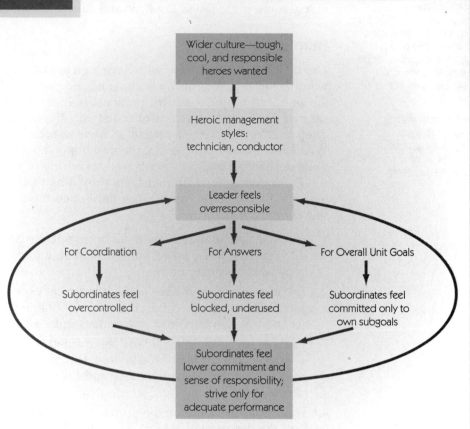

SOURCE: *Adapted from* Managing for Excellence. *David L. Bradford and Allen R. Cohen, Copyright © 1984, John
Wiley & Sons, reprinted by permission of John Wiley & Sons, Inc.*

Developing Individual Skills. The second component of developmental leadership, continuous development of individual skills, is closely interconnected
with the first. One of the best opportunities for individual development is offered by an effective team that deals with real issues. It is no secret that many
effective top executives derived considerable development from serving on
committees or task forces tackling tough issues. In addition, developmental
leaders encourage and seek out opportunities for their people to attend various
developmental courses of either a technical or a managerial nature and to increase both knowledge and skills continually.

Shaping a Common Vision. Many times, the final component, determining
and building a common group vision, is the first step in a manager's movement toward developmental leadership. Bradford and Cohen refer to this as developing the work group's *overarching goal,* which is supportive of the mission
and overall goals of the organization. They go on to say that creating a tangible
vision makes group members excited about where they are going. Exhibit 9–6
explains how one heroic manager evolved into a developmental leader.

Exhibit 9–6

International Paper's Turnaround Artist Bob Goins

In the fall of 1982, Bob Goins was considered to be one of International Paper Company's (IP) top-performing mill managers. Based on IP's criteria, the mill he managed in Bastrop, Louisiana, was consistently best in its peer group. But Goins was not satisfied. He felt that he had taken the mill about as far as it would go—from a productivity standpoint. In Goins's words, "I could try various things at getting production and performance pumped up, but shortly thereafter the air would go out."

As a heroic manager, Goins had a "can do" attitude and decided that next year was going to be a better year. This turned out to be a self-fulfilling prophecy, as the mill just had a great year. It was accomplished by Goins putting excruciating pressure on the work groups. In fact, when he sensed that they were at a breaking point, he pulled back and told them they were going to have fun again. Unfortunately, without the pressure and his intimidation style, the groups' performance declined.

Fortunately, around this same time, IP's top corporate management was initiating a number of strategies to change its culture. Among these was a series of two-day monthly meetings of a group of IP mill managers with representatives of an Atlanta consulting firm. The consultants played primarily a listening-facilitating role, allowing the groups unlimited brainstorming opportunities. Eventually the group developed a philosophy statement for the primary mill facility.

During this period, Goins started experimenting with various ways to allow people in the mill to do their own jobs. Among other things, Goins reduced the number of management levels in the mill. He used a shared-responsibility and joint problem-solving approach with what he calls the "lead team"—the group reporting directly to him.

One of the things he was most proud of at Bastrop was the initiation of team activity at the operative level. These area teams were organized into small groups for problem solving. Although each team had a trained facilitator, each selected its own leaders and own problems. The teams were made up of volunteers, and people rotated on and off the teams. Sometimes, after solving a particular problem, a team would disband, but sometimes it worked throughout the year.

The outcome of all this experimentation was a mill operating at historic performance levels and the transformation of Bob Goins from a heroic, benevolent autocrat to a developmental, participative manager.

Goins was next offered the challenge of managing IP's largest mill—one with a recent bitter strike and lockout. Not long after Goins took the job, an engineer commented, "I've heard a number of managers preach participative management, but Bob is the best I've seen at implementing it in a mill." After two years, Goins had IP's largest mill performing better than ever in its history.

Goins's next assignment was to the company's Texarkana mill—one that IP's higher management felt had never realized its potential. This turned out to be his greatest challenge. In the past, management had thrown people and extra supervision at production problems. Goins quickly found that empowering lower levels with decision-making and problem-solving authority did not motivate people to get the job done. They still deferred to foremen and higher levels for decision making and problem solving.

Goins's diagnosis was that the employees certainly had the ability but had been working a long time in a culture of top-down management, with an emphasis on telling people what to do rather than asking them and sharing leadership. Over a two-year period and without firing anyone, the following things happened:

1. There was a reduction of management levels in finished products and maintenance.
2. As a result of transfers and retirements, seven of the ten direct-reports are new.
3. High-performance, self-managing work teams are being used in several areas of the mill, and they operate the day shift without a foreman, reporting only to an area supervisor.
4. The mill is placing a high priority on training employees so they can operate effectively in a shared-leadership environment.

Oh, incidentally, Goins's developmental style and use of empowerment through shared leadership have been the catalyst behind the highest production level in the history of IP's Texarkana mill. Bob is now retired but his legacy is continuing to positively influence International Paper's culture.

SOURCE: *Conversations and correspondence with Bob Goins and other managers from his company.*

http://www
.internationalpaper.com

⑤ Contrast
transformational
leadership with
transactional leadership.

**transformational
leadership**
Converts followers into
leaders and may convert
leaders into moral
agents.

**transactional
leadership**
Leaders identify desired
performance standards
and recognize what
types of rewards em-
ployees want from their
work.

TRANSFORMATIONAL AND TRANSACTIONAL LEADERSHIP

Transformational leadership is one influential theory and way of looking at leadership that has emerged in more recent years. It is closely related to the team leadership discussed in Chapter 10.

John MacGregor Burns[10] and Bernard Bass[11] were the first to identify and explore the differences between transactional and transformational leadership. Both authors make the case that transformational leadership is a paradigm shift to a more visionary and empowering leadership style, particularly needed in a world of rapid and turbulent change. As Burns states, "the result of transforming leadership is a relationship of mutual stimulation and elevation that converts followers into leaders and may convert leaders into moral agents."

Transactional leadership is more of a traditional leadership approach and is similar to an exchange process. For example, a supervisor may implicitly or explicitly get the message across: "If you give me reasonable production, I will keep higher management off your back." Let us first examine transformational leadership and then transactional leadership.

Transformational Leadership

Bass and others have taken Burns' general framework and applied the concepts to the field of management. Their research has resulted in identifying a number of past and current transformational leaders. A recent study found three factors that were an integral part of being a transformational leader—charismatic leadership, individualized consideration, and intellectual stimulation.

The most important factor of transformational leadership is *charismatic leadership.* To receive a high score on this factor, a leader would need to

*Being familiar with
various leadership
styles will help to
inspire self-confidence
and increase
productivity of a work
group.*

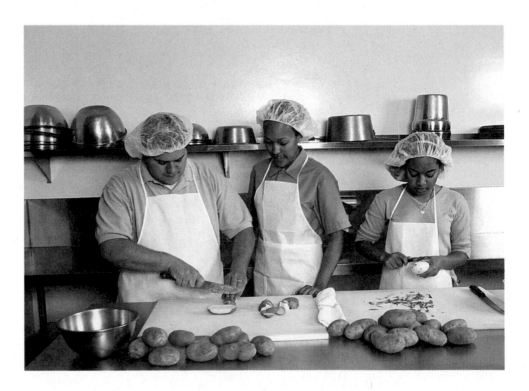

instill pride, respect, and esprit de corps and have a gift of focusing on what is really important, as well as a true sense of mission. The second factor, *individualized consideration*, indicates that the leader uses delegated assignments to provide learning and development and gives personal attention to individuals. The third factor, *intellectual stimulation*, indicates that the leader has vision and presents ideas that require rethinking of past methods of operation and allows for development of new ways of thinking.

click! http://www.wendys
.com

Some leaders who have scored exceptionally high on the charismatic leadership factor are Lee Iacocca, R. David Thomas (founder of Wendy's), George Patton, John F. Kennedy, Dr. Martin Luther King, Jr., Ronald Reagan, Sam Walton (founder of Wal-Mart), and Jack Welch, chief executive officer of General Electric. While charisma is important for effective leadership, it may be exercised to meet objectives that do not benefit society—Adolf Hitler and Saddam Hussein are cases in point.[12]

Research today reveals that transformational leaders are not limited to only world-class leaders. For example, Kenny in the chapter preview demonstrates many of the characteristics of this type of leader.

Transactional Leadership

Of course, not everyone can be a transformational leader, and there are many leaders who fall into the category of transactional leaders. These leaders identify desired performance standards and recognize what types of rewards employees want from their work. They then take actions that make receiving these rewards contingent on achieving performance standards. In essence, this exemplifies an exchange process, a quid pro quo or "I'll do this if you'll do that." The transactional leader operates within the existing culture and employs traditional management strategies to get the job done. Transactional leadership is based on the premise that the leader can positively reward or reinforce employees for their completion of the bargain. For example, if a leader utilized a management-by-objectives system and was able to reward employees who met or exceeded their objectives, this approach would work quite well.

A number of effective leaders demonstrate both transformational and transactional leadership behaviors. One example is Franklin D. Roosevelt, who "illustrated a balance with respect to transformational and transactional leadership. . . . Roosevelt played the consummate transformational leader with his inspiring addresses, encouragement of intellectual solutions, and fireside chats. He also played the consummate transactional politician in the give-and-take of the balance of powers among executive, legislative, and judicial functions."[13]

Comparison of Transactional and Transformational Leadership. One who believes that some people have the ability to grow and develop through levels of leadership and become transformational leaders is George McAleer, former air force pilot and now on the faculty of the National Defense University's Industrial College of the Armed Forces. McAleer agrees with Bass's thesis that transactional leadership can result in lower order improvements, but if one wants higher order improvements, transformational leadership is needed. This is the challenge that faces select military officers who were chosen to spend a year at a senior service college such as the Industrial College in Washington,

D.C. This year is critical in one's military career: Out of this select group, approximately one in five will become a general or admiral in the next 5 to 10 years.

In McAleer's words, "What made them successful up to this point in their career may not necessarily be the best avenue for them to proceed over the next several years. That's the formidable task my colleagues and I have at the Industrial College. Part of the challenge is encompassed in a course entitled "Strategic Decision Making."[14] The challenge is to convince these officers that the leadership style that will serve them best in the future as strategic decision makers is transformational. One way to convince them is to contrast the two leadership styles as shown in Exhibit 9–7.

6 Discuss how to inspire self-confidence, develop people, and increase productivity.

SERVANT LEADERSHIP

Although the concept of **servant leadership** has been around for centuries, only recently has it been seriously taught in management and leadership courses. In fact, there are very few supervisory books in which the concept is even mentioned, including the first four editions of this book. We are delighted to remedy that deficiency in this edition because it is a very powerful and useful concept and philosophy.

Exhibit 9–7

Contrasting Leadership Approaches

Transactional	**Transformational**
Characteristics	
Exchange Process	Relations Orientation
Evolutionary Ideas	Revolutionary Ideas
Within Existing Structure	Emerges in Crisis
Reactive	Proactive
Motivation	
Contingent Reward (Extrinsic)	Inspiration; Recognition (Intrinsic)
Power	
Traditional	Charismatic
Focus	
Outcomes	Vision
Leader	
Specifies Talk	Consultant, Coach, Teacher
Clarifies Roles	Emphasis on Empowering the Individual
Recognizes Needs	Gives Autonomy; Good Listener; Informal,
Manages by Exception	Accessible; Model of Integrity
Employees	
Seek Security; Needs Fulfilled	Transcend Self-Interests for the Organization
Separate Organization from Individual	Do More than They Are Expected to Do
Outcomes	
Expected Performance	Quantum Leaps in Performance

SOURCE: *George McAleer's presentation at APT Type and Leadership Symposium, Crystal City, VA, March 5–7, 1993.*

servant leadership
Defines success as giving and measures achievement by devotion to serving and leading. Winning becomes the creation of community through collaboration and team building.

The Paradox of Servant Leadership

Bennett J. Sims, Bishop Emeritus of the Episcopal Diocese of Atlanta and president of the Institute for Servant Leadership, provides a beautiful description of the nature of this paradox:

> The idea of paradox in the abstract is murky, but in a *person* it can shine like moonlight on tranquil water. Paradox will always need incarnation—embodiment—in order to be real. Logic falls short as a persuader.
>
> Consider the paradox of servant leadership. A servant is one who stands below and behind, while a leader's position is above and ahead. Logically then, it is impossible to make these two positions fit a single point in space or in the make-up of one person. But paradox, like servant leadership, is not bound by logic. When paradox is understood as a formula for great truth, then the opposite of a great truth becomes another great truth. Servant and leader combine to form an ideal blend of personal attributes in *toughness* and *tenderness*.[15]

When one of the authors first read this passage by Sims, he immediately thought of an officer he served under in the army. Captain Paul J. Padgent had won a battlefield commission in Korea and was the most highly decorated officer or enlisted man in the 82nd Airborne Division. He wore a pearl-handle revolver, and was tough and had exceptionally high expectations and standards for members of the infantry rifle company he commanded. His troops believed they were the best and would follow him anywhere. An example from a three-month peacetime simulated battle in south Louisiana swamps and forests gives us a clue to his troops' devotion and loyalty. Most of the company commanders had small tents where officers were served individually on plates. Their troops went through a long mess line being served on their mess kits. But in our company the officers were at the end of the line and followed the troops, and if any item was short, the officers missed it, not the troops. Incidentally, at the end of this three-month field exercise, Captain Padgent's company was singled out as the top performing company by the umpires.[16]

The United States Marine Corps has a history of training its troops, officers, and noncommissioned officers by placing the well-being of the group before the individual. This notion is an important part of servant leadership and is expounded on in an excerpt from a leadership autobiography by a former student. The excerpt is reprinted in Exhibit 9–8.

Characteristics of Servant Leadership

The person to whom we owe the greatest debt for providing us with insights into servant leadership is Robert K. Greenleaf, retired executive with AT&T. Prior to his retirement, he served seven years as director of management research and led an internal consulting group concerned with the values and growth of people. After his retirement, he worked as a consultant for businesses, foundations, professional societies, church organizations, and universities.[17] Greenleaf makes the important point that the servant leader wants to serve first and then lead. The servant leader focuses on meeting the needs of others and responding to problems first by listening. Greenleaf believes that

Exhibit 9–8

A Distant Drum

Joining the United States Marine Corps at age seventeen was the single most important choice I have made for my life. I graduated from boot camp, then from technical school with honors. I was meritoriously promoted and given my choice of duty stations. This was the first real accomplishment I had achieved on my own, and I knew that I didn't even really put forth much effort. It was then that I realized there was a whole world of opportunity available for me, and I was determined to go after a better way of life. I chose El Toro, California, as my duty station. I was proud to be a Marine, and I worked hard in my assigned unit.

I learned innumerable lessons throughout my military service, but the main ones were ingrained during boot camp, (the dreaded "Parris Island") and I live by them still:

1. Tell the truth.
2. Do your best, no matter how trivial the task.
3. Choose the difficult right over the easy wrong.
4. Look out for the group before you look out for yourself.
5. Don't whine or make excuses.
6. Judge others by their actions, not their race, culture, religion, or sexual orientation.

I cannot think of even one important situation in life which cannot be made better by applying these six creeds. I have tried to instill these lessons into my own child, and I am proud to say I believe he lives by them as well.

The exceptional men and women I met and worked with during my military service are still an inspiration to me. I feel a special kinship with each and every marine I meet.

SOURCE: *Cherl Templet,* My Leadership Autobiography, *March 1, 1999. A requirement in an MBA Leadership course taught by Donald C. Mosley, Spring Semester 1999, University of South Alabama, Mobile, Alabama.*

click! http://www.greenleaf .org

leaders who empathize with others provide a climate in which followers have the ability to grow and develop. In the chapter preview, this was one of Kenny's great strengths as a leader. Greenleaf also makes the point that leaders "who emphathize and who fully accept those who go with them on this basis are more likely to be trusted."[18] Again referring back to the chapter preview, the big challenge facing Kenny in his new assignment is gaining the trust and improving the performance of the "Hell's Angels" crew.

Larry Spears is a scholar who has studied Greenleaf's original writings for a number of years. He is also CEO of the Greenleaf Center for Servant Leadership. He has identified 10 characteristics of servant leadership that are shown in Exhibit 9–9.

self-check

Do you think training in servant leadership would be useful for business organizations? Why or why not?

CORE LEADERSHIP FUNCTIONS

The best of the contemporary leadership studies and books support the value of working toward developmental transformational and servant leadership. Also, as we saw in the opening case with Kenny, leadership of this nature is not restricted to the highest levels of management, but can occur at any level. Seven

Exhibit 9–9

*Ten Characteristics of
Servant Leadership*

1. **Listening.** Leaders have traditionally been valued for their communication and decision-making skills. Servant-leaders reinforce these important skills with a focus on listening intently and reflectively to others in order to identify and clarify the will of a group of people.

2. **Empathy.** Servant-leaders strive to understand and empathize with others. They accept and recognize others for their unique gifts and spirits. One assumes the good intentions of coworkers and does not reject them as people.

3. **Healing.** Learning how to help heal difficult situations is a powerful force for transforming organizations. Servant-leaders recognize that they have an opportunity to help make whole those people and institutions with whom they come in contact.

4. **Persuasion.** Another characteristic of servant-leaders is a reliance on persuasion, rather than using one's positional authority, to make organizational decisions. Servant-leaders seek to convince others, rather than coerce compliance. They are effective at building consensus with groups.

5. **Awareness.** General awareness, and especially self-awareness, strengthen the servant-leader. Awareness aids one in understanding issues involving ethics and values, and it enables one to approach situations from a more integrated, holistic position.

6. **Foresight.** The ability to foresee the likely outcome of a given situation is a characteristic that enables the servant-leader to understand the lessons from the past, the realities of the present, and likely consequences of a decision for the future. It is deeply rooted within the intuitive mind.

7. **Conceptualization.** Servant-leaders seek to nurture their abilities to dream great dreams. This means that one must be able to think beyond day-to-day management realities.

8. **Commitment to the growth of people.** Servant-leaders believe that people have an intrinsic value beyond their tangible contributions as workers. As such, servant-leaders are deeply committed to the personal, professional, and spiritual growth of everyone within an organization.

9. **Stewardship.** Greenleaf's view of organizations is one in which CEOs, staff members, and trustees all play significant roles in holding their institutions in trust for the greater good of society. In effect, everyone has a responsibility for being a good steward within an organization.

10. **Building community.** Servant-leaders seek to build a sense of community among those within an organization.

SOURCE: *Larry C. Spears, "Creating Caring Leadership for the 21st Century,"* The Not-For-Profit CEO *Monthly Letter 5, No. 9, July 1998 (The Robert K. Greenleaf Center for Servant Leadership, 921 East 86th Street, Suite 2000, Indianapolis, IN 46240).*

 click! http://academy.umd .edu

leadership functions reinforcing the transformational approach are valuing, visioning, coaching, empowering, team building, promoting quality, and listening with empathy. The effective leader is value driven and is able to implement these functions. A brief description of the core leadership functions are as follows:

Valuing. Having a good grasp of the organization's values and being able to translate these values into practice and elevate them to higher levels.

Visioning. Having a clear mental picture of a desired future for the organization or organizational unit.

Coaching. Helping others develop the knowledge and skills needed for achieving the vision.

Empowering. Enabling others to move toward the vision.

Team building. Developing a coalition of people who will commit themselves to achieving the vision.

Promoting quality. Achieving a reputation for always meeting or exceeding customer expectations.

Listening with empathy. Clarifying where others are coming from and acceptance of others even with imperfections. Anyone can lead perfect people if perfect people are to be found.[19]

Throughout the book we emphasize the importance of values, visioning, empowering, promoting quality, and listening with empathy. In the next chapter we focus on team building, and in Chapter 13, coaching employees. One thing we are certain of is that the supervisor who masters these core leadership functions will be an outstanding leader.

---

chapter review

(1) Describe factors that affect the leadership style used.

Leading is a process of influencing individual and group activities toward goal setting and goal achievement. How well this process is carried out has a major impact on both performance and morale.

Three interrelated variables have an impact on the choice of leadership style. These are (1) the supervisor's management philosophy, (2) the followers' readiness level, and (3) the situation faced by the supervisor. The followers' readiness level must be evaluated only with regard to carrying out a specific task or assignment.

(2) Discuss and explain two frequently used leadership models.

Two leadership models that are widely used in leadership training programs are Blake and associates' Leadership Grid® and Hersey and Blanchard's Situational Leadership Model. The Leadership Grid® plots five basic leadership styles. The one Blake and associates recommend as the ideal leadership style is the team management style.

(3) Determine which leadership style is most appropriate in different situations.

Hersey and Blanchard highlight four basic leadership styles: structuring and telling, coaching and selling, participating and supporting, and delegating. They make a strong case that the ideal style to use depends on the maturity level of employees and the situation faced by the supervisor. Research tends to support the Hersey and Blanchard position that there is no one best style for all situations. However, with the increasing readiness and education of employees today, there is a trend in U.S. industry toward using both the coaching and selling style and the participating and supporting style in influencing individual employees and groups. Tannenbaum and Schmidt maintain that each situation calling for a decision may require choosing a solution that balances the three forces found in the leader, employees, and the situation.

(4) Contrast heroic supervisors with developmental supervisors.

Heroic supervision often leads to overcontrol and lack of group development. By contrast, developmental supervision involves the group by using the three interrelated components of (1) building a shared-responsibility team, (2) continuously developing individual skills, and (3) determining a department vision in the form of an overarching goal.

⑤ **Contrast transformational leadership with transactional leadership.**

While research supports the thesis that no one leadership style is best for all situations, transformational and transactional leadership styles have emerged as two influential theories. Three important factors of transformational leadership are charismatic leadership (instilling pride, respect, and esprit de corps), individualized consideration (delegating assignments and giving personal attention), and intellectual stimulation (requiring rethinking of past methods and developing new solutions).

Transactional leadership is a more traditional approach. The transactional leader operates within the existing culture, positively rewarding and reinforcing employees for jobs well done.

⑥ **Discuss how to inspire self-confidence, develop people, and increase productivity.**

No one single leadership style or model provides a magic formula for inspiring self-confidence, developing people, and increasing productivity. However, by being familiar with all styles, using good common sense, and a contingency/situational leadership approach, one can become an effective leader who does realize the above objectives. Servant leadership is particularly valuable in inspiring self-confidence, tapping higher level needs, and developing people.

---

important terms

authority compliance *250*
coaching and selling style *254*
continuum of leadership behavior *254*
country club management *250*
delegating style *254*
developmental leadership *256*
heroic managers *257*
impoverished management *250*
leadership *246*
Leadership Grid® *250*
life-cycle theory of leadership *252*
middle of the road management *250*

participating and supporting style *254*
readiness level *248*
relationship behaviors *252*
servant leadership *262*
Situational Leadership® Model *252*
structuring and telling style *254*
task behaviors *252*
team management *252*
Theory X *247*
Theory Y *247*
transactional leadership *260*
transformational leadership *260*

---

questions for review and discussion

1. What is meant by *leadership?*
2. Briefly discuss the major factors that may influence the choice of an individual's leadership style. Correlate these factors with different leadership styles.
3. Discuss how a supervisor would determine the readiness level of an employee.
4. What leadership actions fall under the category of task behaviors, and what actions fall under the category of relationship behaviors?
5. Do you agree or disagree with Blake and associates that there is one best leadership style? Support your position.
6. In his early fifties, Bob Goins modified his leadership style from heroic to developmental. If you were trying to motivate managers to change as Goins did, how would you go about it? Do you think the majority of supervisors have the ability to modify their style? Why or why not?

7. Can you identify any transformational leaders from your own experience or reading? Please list the reasons why you placed them in the category of transformational leader. If you cannot identify someone, do you agree with the leaders identified in this chapter—John F. Kennedy, Martin Luther King, Jr., and George Patton? Why or why not?

8. What traits or characteristics appeal to you the most regarding servant leadership?

9. Of the various leadership approaches discussed in the chapter, which one would you most prefer your boss to use in working with you and your group? Explain your reasons.

10. How does transactional leadership differ from the telling and structuring style of Hersey and Blanchard?

● skill builder 9–1

The Debate Question
group activity

In general, are women or men more transformational in leadership approach? Judy Rosener, in her "Ways Women Lead," makes a case that, in general, women tend to be more transformational in leadership approach than men, who tend to be more transactional in approach. The comparison of the transactional and transformational leadership approaches found in Exhibit 9–6 should be referred to in completing the following instructions.

Instructions:

1. Have your class ask for five volunteers to form a team to debate on the side that, in general, women are more transformational in approach than men. Conversely, ask for five volunteers to take the opposite side. Allow a week for the two teams to prepare their respective cases. Two suggested starting reference sources are: Judy Rosener, "Ways Women Lead," *Harvard Business Review,* Jan.–Feb. 1990, pp. 119–125; and "Ways Men and Women Lead," *Harvard Business Review,* Jan.–Feb. 1991, p. 150.

2. After the week, the teams should present their cases in the form of a debate. A suggested format for the debate is to allow the affirmative team 15 minutes to present their case, and the opposing team also gets 15 minutes. Then, allow the affirmative team up to 5 minutes for rebuttal and the opposing team up to 5 minutes for rebuttal.

3. Who do you believe won the debate? Explain your reasoning.

● skill builder 9–2

Diagnosing and Selecting the Appropriate Leadership Style

In each of the following situations, choose the appropriate leadership style. Afterward, your instructor will give you the best and worst answer for each situation.

1. The interdepartment task force that you manage has been working hard to complete its division-wide report. One of your task force members has been late for the last five meetings.

He has offered no excuses or apologies. Furthermore, he is way behind in completing the cost figures for his department. It is imperative that he present these figures to the task force within the next three days.

a. Tell him exactly what you expect, and closely supervise his work on this report.
b. Discuss with him why he has been late, and support his efforts to complete the task.
c. Emphasize when the cost figures are due, and support his efforts.
d. Assume he will be prepared to present the cost figures to the task force.

2. In the past, you have had a great deal of trouble with one of the people you supervise. She has been lackadaisical, and only your constant prodding has brought about task completion. However, you have recently noticed a change. Her performance has improved, and you have had to remind her of meeting deadlines less and less. She has even initiated several suggestions for improving her performance.

a. Continue to direct and closely supervise her efforts.
b. Continue to supervise her work, but listen to her suggestions and implement those that seem reasonable.
c. Implement her suggestions and support her ideas.
d. Let her take responsibility for her own work.

3. Because of budget restrictions imposed on your department, it is necessary to consolidate. You have asked a highly experienced member of your department to take charge of the consolidation. This person has worked in all areas of your department. In the past, she has usually been eager to help. Although you believe that she has the ability to perform this assignment, she seems indifferent to the importance of the task.

a. Take charge of the consolidation yourself, but make sure you hear her suggestions.
b. Assign the project to her, and let her determine how to accomplish it.
c. Discuss the situation with her. Encourage her to accept the assignment in view of her skills and experience.
d. Take charge of the consolidation and indicate to her precisely what to do. Supervise her work closely.

4. Your staff members have asked you to consider a change in the work schedule. In the past, you have encouraged and supported their suggestions. In this case, your staff members are well aware of the need for change and are ready to suggest and try an alternative schedule. Members are very competent and work well together as a group.

a. Allow staff involvement in developing the new schedule, and support the suggestions of group members.
b. Design and implement the new schedule yourself, but incorporate staff recommendations.
c. Allow the staff to formulate and implement the new schedule on their own.
d. Design the new schedule yourself, and closely direct its implementation.

SOURCE: *W. Alan Randolph,* Understanding and Managing Organizational Behavior *(Homewood, Ill.: Richard D. Irwin, 1985), pp. 255–257. A complete 20-item Leader Behavior Analysis II questionaire is available from the Ken Blanchard Companies at 1-800-728-6000.*

Kenny's Leadership—A Further Analysis

In the chapter preview, we presented Kenny, an effective leader. Clues to his success may be found in the following comments made about him by his old crew, his new crew (the former "Hell's Angels" group), the plant's production manager, and Kenny's boss, the plant's maintenance manager.* It should be noted that both the production manager and the maintenance manager are relatively new to their positions and are not part of the former "autocratic management system." As you read these comments, review what you have learned in the preceding chapters and summarize the principles, points, and concepts from the text that Kenny puts into practice as a leader.

Maintenance Manager, Kenny's Boss:

- He's very knowledgeable in the maintenance area.
- He has considerable self-confidence.
- He interacts with people in the plant more than other supervisors do and works well with people from other departments.
- He has the ability to motivate his crew and gets along well with them.
- He functions well as a leader in one-on-one situations and in conducting crew meetings. For example, in both cases he lets people know how they stand and provides them with feedback, and together they discuss ways of improving performance.
- He's better organized than most supervisors, and there's less confusion in his department than elsewhere in the company.

Production Manager:

- He doesn't give the production people any hassle. He doesn't ask a lot of questions about why production wants it done. Instead, he tells the production people what needs to be done—and why.
- He's a team player—and he wants to get the job done.
- He's good with people—a great leader—and his crew work well together.
- He's conscientious—he does his job, does it right, and wants others to do the same.
- He goes out into the plant with his people, and he's there with them when they need help and advice.
- His crew doesn't give planners and coordinators a lot of static about what they put into a memo.

Kenny's Old Crew:

- He's fair.
- He has a good attitude and a positive outlook.
- He's concerned about and looks out for the welfare of his people.
- He keeps crew problems within the crew and doesn't run to upper management with every little detail.
- He has a broad-based knowledge of our work; people feel confident about his decisions.
- He's a good intermediary between upper management and the crew. He gets points across without getting the crew upset.
- When things are tight, he doesn't mind helping his men with the actual work.
- He has a level personality—he doesn't show much emotion.
- He's very supportive of his crew.

---

*Except for minor editing, the comments are presented as they were made to Donald Mosley.

Kenny's New Crew (the former "Hell's Angels"):

- He treats us fairly and equally.
- He takes up for the crew and his men.
- He doesn't threaten you and doesn't come back after a bad job and nit-pick and tell you what you did wrong. He takes a positive approach to solving problems.
- He can be trusted.
- He helps you with your personal problems.
- He's competent at what he does and relates the competency to us.
- He places his employees really well. We're not all like oranges—some are like apples—but he places us where we can do our best.
- He lets us work at our own pace—actually makes us want to work harder.
- He never appears to get angry; he's always the same—cool, calm, and collected.
- He's helpful on the job. He's there, but he's not there—doesn't hang over you, telling you what to do and how to do it. Instead, he wants results but lets us get them our own way.
- He seems to enjoy work and being around us.
- He listens to anything we have to say.

Answer the following questions:

1. How do you explain Kenny's acceptance by so many other people and the respect they have for him?
2. Can all supervisors operate the way Kenny does—and be effective? Explain your answer.
3. Given Kenny's effectiveness in his present job, would you recommend promoting him into high levels of management? Explain.
4. Review the characteristics of servant leadership in Exhibit 9–9 and transformation leadership in Exhibit 9–7. Which characteristics apply to Kenny?

10

Managing Change, Group Development, and Team Building

● outline

Managing Organizational Change
Forces Causing Change
Results of Ignoring Change
Ways of Dealing with Change
Planned Change

Importance of Work Groups
What Are Groups?
Types of Groups
How Groups Develop
Evaluating Groups
Determining Group Effectiveness

Team Building
Partnering: Team Development Accelerated
What Is Involved in Partnering?
Partnering Successes
Partnering Failures and Their Causes

Self-Managing Work Teams

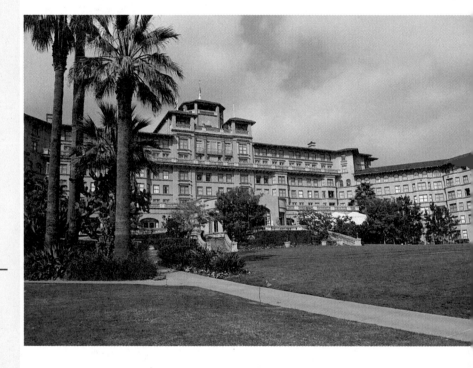

The essence of [collaboration] is working with people rather than over people or under people.

Mary Parker Follet

There is nothing permanent except change.

Heraclitus

learning objectives

After reading and studying this chapter, you should be able to:

1 Appreciate the impact of change on individuals and organizations.

2 Compare and contrast the reactive approach to change to the proactive approach.

3 Understand planned change.

4 Identify the stages of group development.

5 Compare the advantages and limitations of groups.

6 Describe the variables that determine a group's effectiveness.

7 Explain what is involved in partnering and why it is successful.

8 Describe how to work with self-managing work groups.

click! http://www.ritzcarlton.com/

The Ritz-Carlton Hotel Corporation

This chapter preview could easily have been placed in our leadership chapter because it involves transformational leadership. We have chosen to place it in this chapter because the case is a classic "textbook" example of the effective management of change and organizational development.

In 1850, Cesar Ritz was born in Neiderwald, Switzerland. "Blessed with virtues of ambition, courage and taste, Ritz strived for excellence in everything he did, and when he entered the hotel industry, his ideals were not to be compromised."

After working as a waiter at Voisin, then the most fashionable restaurant in Paris, Ritz teamed with the renowned French chef Auguste Escoffier, with whom he had worked in several of Europe's famous hotels. While both were employed at the Carlton Hotel in London, Cesar Ritz went to Paris to find a place for a hotel of his own. After selecting the perfect location for his hotel, he contacted Marnier La Postolle, an old friend and the originator of the liqueur Grand Marnier, who gladly loaned him the money to open his hotel.

June 1898 marked the opening of the Ritz of Paris of the Place Vendome, with, of course, Escoffier as *chef de cuisine.* The hotel, conceived by Cesar Ritz according to his own standards of perfection, initiated the European deluxe hotel industry. Ritz's idea was to create not a "grand hotel" but a new and original one, a home that would equal the comforts, security, and service that discriminating patrons would provide for themselves—a nonhotel.

Cesar Ritz insisted on certain criteria that would be the foundation for the Paris Ritz and all future hotels bearing the Ritz name: a central location, preferably overlooking a public park or square; comfortable and attractive rooms; food and beverage services second to none; and a wine cellar that would appeal to the finest connoisseurs. Combining all of these elements, Ritz still considered the most crucial aspect of his "perfect" hotel to be service. In order to provide the finest service and quality, the number of employees was to exceed the number of guests.

Both Ritz and Escoffier had an interest in the Carlton Hotel in London. They combined their efforts and established the Ritz-Carlton Company to give rights to the Ritz-Carlton name internationally. Under the supervision of Cesar Ritz, hotels developed all over the world, including New York City, bearing the Ritz-Carlton name, but few were able to survive the rigid standards established by Cesar Ritz.

The last sentence highlights the problem. Despite the Ritz-Carlton tradition, a number of the properties bearing the name failed to maintain the consistency and standards of excellence of the original founders.

This changed in 1983, when the current Ritz-Carlton Hotel Company acquired the rights to the name and bought the Ritz-Carlton in Boston. The hotel chain today owns outright only a few of the properties, but the company's 11,500 employees manage all 30 of the Ritz-Carlton properties located around the world. Under the transformational leadership of Horst A. Schulze, president and chief operating officer, the company's 30 properties have met or exceeded the standards of excellence of the original founders. Evidence of this achievement is reflected in the following:

1. In 1992, the Ritz-Carlton was selected best hotel chain in the United States by the Zagat U.S. Travel Service.

2. In 1992, Horst Schulze was chosen Corporate Hotelier of the World by *Hotels Magazine.*

3. In 1992, Ritz-Carlton became the first hotel company to win a Malcolm Baldrige National Quality Award (established by Congress in 1987 to promote quality management).

4. In 1994, the company was rated by *Consumer Reports* as the number one luxury hotel chain in the world.

At present, most Ritz-Carlton hotels are located within the United States; however, 10 or 12 new developments will be located outside the United States.

After a consulting trip to Honolulu in June 1994, one of the authors took a week's vacation and stayed at the Ritz-Carlton Kapalua, on the island of Maui. We had never stayed in a Ritz-Carlton and were curious to see if it lived up to its reputation. Afterwards we rated our stay a 10+ on a 10-point scale. Here are just a few reasons why:

- A basket of fruit was in our room upon arrival.

- A minor problem was presented to a staff member who solved it without fanfare. Later we found out that any staff member to whom a guest presents a problem is empowered to solve that problem.

- On two occasions when we asked for directions regarding a location on the hotel's 32 acres, we were not simply given directions; we were escorted there.

- The food was consistently excellent in all three of the hotel's restaurants.

Horst Schulze is given the credit for catalyzing the chain's reputation for quality and service. In regard to the awards received, Schulze has stated, "We are not resting on the momentary glory or satisfaction of these awards. We have embarked, and have worked diligently the last three years, on total quality management (TQM). We know that through TQM we will continuously improve our product and services. It is our intention to not only serve you with genuine care and comfort, but to fulfill all your needs in our hotels and give you complete service excellence all of the time.

"Today every employee, from housekeeper to server to manager, is committed to the ultimate dream and vision through TQM: 100% guest satisfaction."

Although the hotel's corporate managers have used consultants such as Joseph M. Juran and Steven Covey in their search for excellence, they have created their own version of total quality management. According to Sue Musselman, assistant to the vice-president of quality, it was pursuit of the Malcolm Baldrige Award that gave the organization the quantum leap in improving processes and services. Just a few of the tailored features of the Ritz-Carlton's focus on quality, service, and guest satisfaction are as follows:

1. President Schulze participates in employee orientation programs at each new hotel.

2. In the two-day orientation program for new employees, Rebecca

Powell, the training manager, emphasizes that "you serve but you are not servants"; rather, "you are ladies and gentlemen serving ladies and gentlemen."

3. In addition to the orientation program, 100 more hours of training are provided to employees.

4. When processes are improved or reengineered in one hotel, the information and concepts are shared with all hotels.

5. Every worker is empowered to spend up to $2,000 to fix any problem a guest encounters. Patrick Mene, director of quality, has reported that employees do not abuse this privilege. "When you treat people responsibly, they act responsibly."

Are employees achieving President Schulze's goal of 100 percent guest satisfaction? In the eyes of one customer, they are. "They not only treat us like a king when we hold our top-level meetings in their hotels, but we just never get any complaints," said Wayne Stetson, the staff vice-president of the convention and meetings division of the National Association of Home Builders in Washington, D.C.

The Ritz-Carlton credo—found in Exhibit 10–1 and carried by each employee—explains in more depth the chain's success. This is a hotel that has created a culture where the employees practice their credo.[1] They practice this credo so well that in 1999 they again won the Malcolm Baldrige National Quality Award and were announced as the first service company to be a repeat winner of this award. As they say in the business world, "they walk their talk."

Exhibit 10–1

The Ritz-Carlton Credo

The Ritz-Carlton Credo

THREE STEPS OF SERVICE		THE EMPLOYEE PROMISE	THE RITZ-CARLTON CREDO
1 A warm and sincere greeting. Use the guest name, if and when possible. 2 Anticipation and compliance with guest needs. 3 Fond farewell. Give them a warm good-bye and use their names, if and when possible.	*"We Are Ladies and Gentlemen Serving Ladies and Gentlemen"*	*At The Ritz-Carlton, our Ladies and Gentlemen are the most important resource in our service commitment to our guests.* *By applying the principles of trust, honesty, respect, integrity and commitment, we nurture and maximize talent to the benefit of each individual and the company.* *The Ritz-Carlton fosters a work environment where diversity is valued, quality of life is enhanced, individual aspirations are fulfilled, and The Ritz-Carlton mystique is strengthened.*	THE RITZ-CARLTON CREDO The Ritz-Carlton Hotel is a place where the genuine care and comfort of our guests is our highest mission. We pledge to provide the finest personal service and facilities for our guests who will always enjoy a warm, relaxed yet refined ambience. The Ritz-Carlton experience enlivens the senses, instills well-being, and fulfills even the unexpressed wishes and needs of our guests.

Continued

Exhibit 10–1

Continued

The Ritz-Carlton Basics

1. The Credo is the principal belief of our Company. It must be known, owned and energized by all.

2. Our Motto is: "We are Ladies and Gentlemen serving Ladies and Gentlemen." As service professionals, we treat our guests and each other with respect and dignity.

3. The Three Steps of Service are the foundation of Ritz-Carlton hospitality. These steps must be used in every interaction to ensure satisfaction, retention and loyalty.

4. The Employee Promise is the basis for our Ritz-Carlton work environment. It will be honored by all employees.

5. All employees will successfully complete annual Training Certification for their position.

6. Company objectives are communicated to all employees. It is everyone's responsibility to support them.

7. To create pride and joy in the workplace, all employees have the right to be involved in the planning of the work that affects them.

8. Each employee will continuously identify defects (M.R. B.I.V.) throughout the Hotel.

9. It is the responsibility of each employee to create a work environment of teamwork and lateral service so that the needs of our guests and each other are met.

10. Each employee is empowered. For example, when a guest has a problem or needs something special, you should break away from your regular duties to address and resolve the issue.

11. Uncompromising levels of cleanliness are the responsibility of every employee.

12. To provide the finest personal service for our guests, each employee is responsible for identifying and recording individual guest preferences.

13. Never lose a guest. Instant guest pacification is the responsibility of each employee. Whoever receives a complaint will own it, resolve it to the guest's satisfaction and record it.

14. "Smile – We are on stage." Always maintain positive eye contact. Use the proper vocabulary with our guests and each other. (Use words like – "Good Morning," "Certainly," "I'll be happy to" and "My pleasure.")

15. Be an ambassador of your Hotel in and outside of the workplace. Always speak positively. Communicate any concerns to the appropriate person.

16. Escort guests rather than pointing out directions to another area of the Hotel.

17. Use Ritz-Carlton telephone etiquette. Answer within three rings with a "smile." Use the guest's name when possible. When necessary, ask the caller "May I place you on hold?" Do not screen calls. Eliminate call transfers whenever possible. Adhere to voice mail standards.

18. Take pride in and care of your personal appearance. Everyone is responsible for conveying a professional image by adhering to Ritz-Carlton clothing and grooming standards.

19. Think safety first. Each employee is responsible for creating a safe, secure and accident free environment for all guests and each other. Be aware of all fire and safety emergency procedures and report any security risks immediately.

20. Protecting the assets of a Ritz-Carlton Hotel is the responsibility of every employee. Conserve energy, properly maintain our Hotels and protect the environment.

SOURCE: *© 1992 The Ritz-Carlton Hotel Company. All rights reserved. Reprinted with the permission of The Ritz-Carlton Hotel Company, L.L.C.*

MANAGING ORGANIZATIONAL CHANGE

1 Appreciate the impact of change on individuals and organizations.

In management, change is understood to be a part of everyday life. Change takes many forms. Internal change may include new technology, new work methods, different employee attitudes, new products or services, or new organizational structures. External change includes challenges imposed by increased global or local competition, regulations resulting from legislation, the swings of the economy, or the different work ethics of a younger generation entering the work force.

Forces Causing Change

Numerous factors affect an organization. Continuously changing forces leading to or causing change orginate both outside and within the organization, as shown in Exhibit 10–2. You might compare this situation to yourself. External stimuli require responses such as the condition of the weather, the requirements of the daily work schedule, and the different needs arising each day. Also requiring responses are the internal stimuli, such as your hunger level, the state of your health, or your attitude. A similar situation exists when we substitute an organization for yourself.

external change forces
Forces outside the organization that have a great impact on organizational change. Management has little control over these numerous external forces.

External Change Forces. Management has little control over the strong impact of numerous **external change forces.** Yet an organization depends on and must interact with its external environment if it is to survive. Specifically, resources, profits, and customers for products and services are all from the outside. Therefore, any force that impacts or changes the environment affects the organization's operations and brings about pressures requiring a change response. External forces—from technological advancements to changing consumers' requirements—cause an organization to alter its goals, structure, and methods of conducting business.

self-check

Suppose you were the director and owner of a 30-bed nursing home. What are some kinds of external change factors that might have an impact on your organization?

Experts have theorized that basic changes are needed in today's organizations. These changes are a move away from (1) a short-term rather than a long-term perspective, (2) a focus on ends rather than the means, and (3) an emphasis on the individual over the community.[2]

internal change forces
Pressures for change within the organization such as cultures and objectives.

Internal Change Forces. Change forces also come from within. **Internal change forces** may result from different organization goals or cultures, as we saw in the case of the Ritz-Carlton Hotel Company. Or they may be caused by new quality initiatives, changing technologies, or employee attitudes. For example, shifting the goal from short-run profit to long-term growth directly impacts the daily work of most departments and may lead to a reorganization that will

Exhibit 10–2

External and Internal Change Forces

SOURCE: *Donald C. Mosley, Paul Pietri, Leon Megginson,* Management—Leadership in Action, *5th ed, 1996, Harper Collins, p. 425.*

streamline overall operations. Changing to automated equipment and robots to perform work previously done by people will cause changes in work routine and just-in-time supplies. Altering incentive programs and personnel policies and procedures may result in different hiring and selection procedures. Employee attitudes about child and/or parent care, insurance needs, or flexible working hours may change daily business practices.

External and internal forces for change are often interrelated, not isolated from one another. At times, this linkage results from the changes in values and attitudes affecting people within the system. Some of these changes from within are from people who have entered the organization. For example, many of the changes now occurring in organizations are the result of the increasing availability of a highly trained workforce, including the need for increased flexibility and responsiveness of the organization to employee needs and a flattened hierarchy allowing greater responsibility to be placed with front-line workers.

Results of Ignoring Change

In serving to preserve many values and social, cultural, and technological innovations, businesses and other institutions help maintain our heritage. This is important in connecting the past, present, and future as well as establishing the foundation to allow the continuation of a high standard of living. However, in protecting themselves from further change, institutions strengthen their resistance by creating cultures of formalizing rituals, customs, and traditions much the same as any community. This resistance may lead to an inability to cope with new forces and paves the way for stagnation, decline, and failure. Coping effectively with change and embracing the need to plan to incorporate change for growth is necessary for an organization's future. This same reasoning is no less important on a personal level for managers and employees, who face change at an even more accelerated pace.

Ways of Dealing with Change

② Compare and contrast the reactive approach to change to the proactive approach.

There are two major ways to deal with organizational change: reactive and proactive. In the reactive process, management deals with problems or issues one-step-at-a-time or as they arise. The proactive process involves deliberate actions to modify the status quo.

reactive process of change
Management tries to keep the organization on a steady course by solving problems as they come up.

The Reactive Process of Change. When employing the **reactive process of change,** management solves problems as they come up, keeping the organization on a steady course. Change is initiated in reaction to something that has happened. For example, if you are a department store manager and complaints about customer service suddenly increase, one option would be to design a short training course for salespeople to correct the problem. If the quality of one of your major products becomes poor, you might search for another similar product from another producer. If new government regulations require you to have increased access for the handicapped, you will investigate adaptation of the facility.

Reactive approaches involve little planning and are aimed at solving an immediate, visible problem. Not usually viewed "threatening," the results of a series of small, incremental reactions can add up over time to a significant change in an organization. These "quick fixes" may not be compatible with one another—sometimes the overall end result is not desirable.

proactive (planned) process of change
Management tries to change things by setting a new course rather than by correcting the current one.

The Proactive (Planned) Process of Change. With the **proactive or planned process of change,** management tries to anticipate forces in both the external and internal environments, finding compatible, integrated ways to cope with the predicted new environments. Management's goal is to set a new course rather than correct the current one. Because of the rapidity and complexity of changes in today's world, we feel that managers must understand and practice planned organizational change.

self-check

Take a moment to review the chapter preview case. What type of action—reactive or proactive—is the Ritz-Carlton management taking? Explain your answer.

 Understand planned change.

organizational effectiveness
The result of activities that improve the organization's structure, technology, and people.

Planned Change

For management to plan for change, it must decide what needs to be changed in the organization. In general, management seeks to change things that prevent greater organizational effectiveness. **Organizational effectiveness** results from activities that improve the organization's structure, technology, and people so it can achieve its objectives.

The nature of the problem causing the organization to be less than ideally effective determines the choice of the particular technique used to achieve change. From a choice of alternatives, management must determine which one is most likely to produce the desired outcome. Diagnosing the problem includes defining the outcome that is desired from the change. In general, the desired outcome is either improved employee behavior or activities that will result in improved performance. This can be achieved by changing the organization's structure, technology, and/or people (Exhibit 10–3).

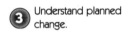 Exhibit 10–3

Organizational Effectiveness Results from Changing Structure, Technology, and/or People

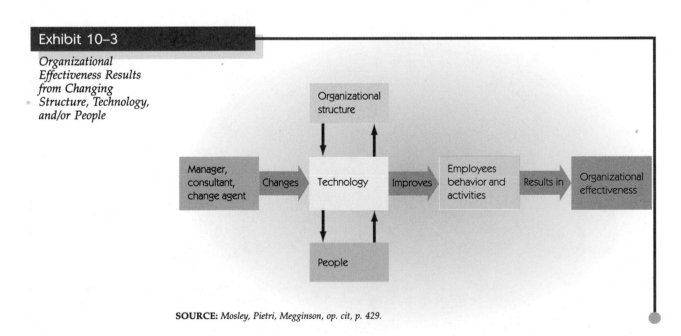

SOURCE: *Mosley, Pietri, Megginson, op. cit, p. 429.*

This classficiation of organizational elements in no way implies a distinct division among elements. According to the systems concept, a change in one element is likely to affect other elements. In general, the more change that is required, the more likely it is that management will change all three elements.

Management must decide the desired outcomes and the type of change programs to use to change the specific organizational element—including those activities needed to get the work done effectively (Exhibit 10–3).

Changing the organization's *structure* involves modifying and rearranging the internal relationships. This includes such variables as authority—responsibility relationships, communications systems, work flows, and size and composition of work groups.

Changing the organization's *technology* may require modifying such factors as its tools, equipment, and machinery; research direction and techniques; engineering processes; and production system, including layout, methods, and procedures. Changing technology may result from or contribute to changing tasks to be performed. Products and other inputs may be altered. For example, mechanization changes the nature of work performed.

Changing the organization's people may include changing recruiting and selection policies and procedures, training and development activities, reward systems, and/or managerial leadership and communication.

Supervisors and employees are likely to support change if they perceive the change as being directed at the real cause of the problem, as being an effective solution, and as not affecting them adversely. Most importantly, those who participate in a change process respond entirely differently from those merely affected by it. Exhibit 10–4 shows these different responses to change.

Next we turn to the study group dynamics that will provide greater insight into creating a climate of positive change.

Exhibit 10–4

Different Responses to Change

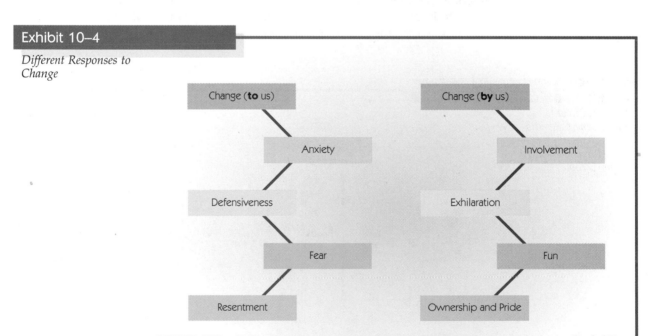

SOURCE: *William Walker, management consultant, presentation to the North Mississippi Health Services Board of Directors and staff, May 1, 1999. The Wynfrey Hotel, Birmingham, Alabama.*

IMPORTANCE OF WORK GROUPS

synergy
The concept that two or more people working together in a cooperative, coordinated way can accomplish more than the sum of their independent efforts.

To achieve synergy and, we hope, to gain the most of the employees, organizations require groups. **Synergy** means that the whole is greater than the sum of the parts. This is especially applicable when using teams and ad hoc task forces. Assume that a five person ad hoc task force is given the opportunity to solve a problem that has an impact on the entire organization. If the team reaches a synergistic solution to the problem, then synergy can be mathematically defined as $1+1+1+1+1 = $ more than 5.

It is important for supervisors to understand the basic concepts of group or team development because work groups or teams produce the synergistic effect needed for management to reach its goals.

What Are Groups?

group
Two or more people who communicate and work together regularly in pursuit of one or more common objectives.

Groups have been defined in various ways. The definition we prefer is that a **group** is two or more people who communicate and work together regularly in pursuit of one or more common objectives. This highlights the point that at least two individuals must work together to constitute a group. If a group becomes too large, it is difficult to interact with all members. This leads to the evolution of smaller groups. Remember, one finding of the Hawthorne studies was that groups can be either supportive of organizational goals or opposed to them overall.

Types of Groups

Groups in organizations are either formal and informal. Formal groups are those created by the organization. The most common example is the group formed by a manager and his/her immediate team members. Informal groups evolve out of the formal organization but are not formed by management. Neither are they shown in the organization's structure. An example would be a friendship group that enjoys discussing sports during lunch.

formal group
A group prescribed and/or established by the organization.

Formal groups. **Formal groups** are deliberately formed by management and are often shown on the organizational chart. For example, command groups are formal groups composed of staff who report to a designated manager, such as a group of vice-presidents for worldwide marketing. Committees and task forces are additional examples of formal groups. Later in this chapter, we examine the increasing use of self-managing work teams, another example of formal groups created by management. Exhibit 10–5 illustrates how one manager can be a member of several different groups while employed by one organization.

informal group
A group that evolves out of the formal organization but is not formed by management or shown in the organization's structure.

Informal Groups. **Informal groups** evolve out of employees' need for social interaction, friendship, communication, and status. While not a part of the formal organization, an informal group can sometimes be the same as a formal work team. The group members might give more allegiance to the informal leader than to the formal manager.

Other types of informal groups cross formal work team boundaries and are based on common interests. An informal interest group may come together to seek increased fringe benefits or attempt to solve a particularly broad-based software problem. Another type of informal group is a friendship group. Its

Exhibit 10–5

*A Manager's
Membership in
Different Groups*

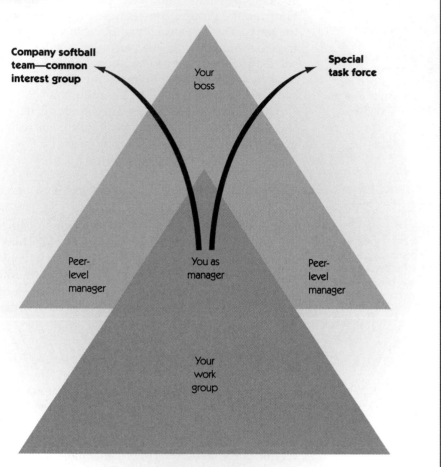

SOURCE: *Adapted from W. Alan Randolph,* Understanding and Managing Organizational Behavior *(Homewood,
Ill.: Richard D. Irwin, 1985), p. 385.*

members also have common interests, but they are more social in nature. Such
groups could include a running team, a band, or the people who gather to chat
during a break.

In general, informal groups provide a valuable service by helping members
meet affiliation and social needs. Ideally, management tries to create an environment in which the needs and objectives of informal groups are similar to the
needs and objectives of the formal organization.

 Identify the stages of
group development.

How Groups Develop

B. W. Tuckman developed a model of small-group development that encompasses four stages of growth.[3] A desirable feature of this classical model—
which basically has been followed by later researchers[4]—is that it examines the
stages in terms of task functions and interpersonal relations, both essential concerns of any group.

Stages of Group Development. The stages of group development defined by Tuckman are (1) forming, (2) storming, (3) norming, and (4) performing. There is some overlap between the stages, and the length of time spent in each stage can vary; however, the central concept is that a group will usually remain in a stage until key issues are resolved before moving to the next stage. Sometimes a group appears to have resolved key issues but really has not. In this case, after moving to the next stage, the group will have to shift back to the earlier stage to resolve the unsettled issue. The characteristics of each stage follow.

Stage 1: Forming. Forming is the stage in which members first come together and form initial impressions. Among other things, they are trying to determine the task of the group and their role expectations of one another. In this stage, members depend on a leader to provide considerable structure in establishing an agenda and guidelines, since they tend to be unsure of what is expected of them.

Stage 2: Storming. The storming stage is typically a period of conflict and—ideally—organization. Conflicts arise over goals, task behaviors (that is, who is responsible for what), and leadership roles. Relationship behaviors emerge, in that people have strong feelings and express them, sometimes in a hostile manner. It is a mistake to suppress conflict; the key is to manage it. If a group gets through Stage 2 successfully, it becomes organized and begins developing norms, rules, and standards.

 http://www.tvo.org/
pdonline/forprincipals/
norms.html

Stage 3: Norming. Norming is a stage of developing teamwork and group cohesion and creating openness of communications with information sharing. Members feel good about one another and give each other positive feedback, and the level of trust and cooperation is usually quite high. These desirable characteristics of team development result from establishing agreed-on goals and finalizing the processes, standards, and rules by which the group will operate. If the issues of the earlier stages have not been resolved, the group can regress. Later in this chapter, we will discuss norms in more detail.

Stage 4: Performing. Performing is the stage in which the group shows how efficiently and effectively it can operate to achieve its goals. Information exchange has developed to the point of joint problem solving, and there is shared leadership. As one organizational behavior text points out, "Some groups continue to learn and develop from their experiences and new inputs. . . . Other groups—especially those that have developed norms not fully supportive of efficiency and effectiveness—may perform only at the level needed for their survival."[5] Thus, group development, like individual development, is a continuing process.

Evaluating Groups

⑤ Compare the advantages and limitations of groups.

Groups, whether formal or informal, are a fact of organizational life. We have addressed many group-related issues in previous chapters. In this section, we discuss some important advantages and limitations of groups.

Advantages of Groups. Among the major advantages of groups are that they (1) provide members with opportunities for need satisfaction and (2) may function more effectively than individuals.

Provide Opportunities for Need Satisfaction.   Group membership provides an opportunity for members to satisfy security and relationship needs as well as higher level esteem and self-actualization needs. Group membership can be

Employees who work in groups often find they are able to accomplish more together than working as individuals. In addition, working in a group can be a satisfying social experience.

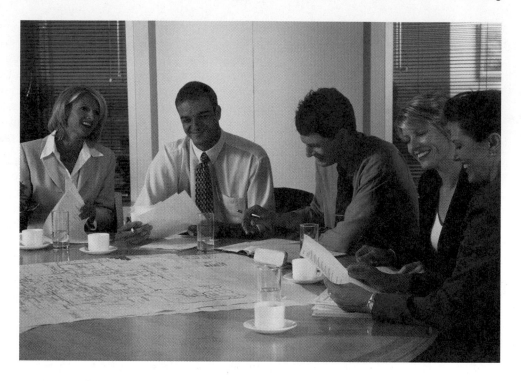

highly satisfying. For example, being viewed as a member of a high-performing problem-solving task force brings out feelings of pride. At times, a task you perceive as drudgery may actually turn out to be less distasteful when you are working together in a group.

May Function More Effectively Than Individuals. Synergy is the concept that two plus two can equal five. This is one of the major potential advantages of groups. The combination of members possessing different perspectives, experiences, and job skills can often work in a team's favor. Moreover, individuals operating as a group may feel a collective responsibility that often leads to higher motivation and commitment.

> **Ford's Taurus/Sable project is a good example. Whereas the typical new car project calls for planning, design, engineering, and manufacturing groups to complete their tasks in a sequential, step-by-step process, Ford's Taurus/Sable project used a group "team" focus by combining these groups from the start: Designers solicited input from manufacturing early in the process; numerous changes recommended by assembly-line workers were incorporated, enabling them to work more productively, with high-quality results. Even suppliers were part of the early, up-front planning process.**
>
> **Because of the huge success of "Team Taurus," as it was called, Ford will probably not return to the old Detroit system of insulated, independent, sequential new car planning.[6]**

Limitations of Groups. Among the general limitations of groups are that they may (1) encourage social loafing, (2) diffuse responsibility, and (3) be less effective than individuals.

Encourage Social Loafing.   *Social loafing* is the term used to describe "taking a free ride" when working with others as a team. We have all known team members who did not pull their weight as part of a team writing a group term paper or putting together a classroom presentation. Generally, social loafing occurs because some members genuinely believe that their contributions to the group are not that significant or they hope for a free ride. Free riders are reinforced when they receive rewards or recognition on an equal basis with those who have carried the greater load.

Diffuse Responsibility.   The diffusion of responsibility among members of a group is somewhat related to social loafing and is also one of its major causes. Because each person may be expected to do only a part of a project, no one person may feel totally responsible. Diffused responsibility may result in groups' assuming positions that individual members would not take if held individually accountable. The "Oh, what the heck" attitude, as well as the idea that "they" will handle it, leads to more liberal risk taking. This also means that the more mundane, routine, and undesirable group tasks may be neglected by individual members in the hope that someone else will complete them.

May Be Less Effective Than Individuals.   While the concept of synergy is an attractive argument in favor of group effort, the sad fact of the matter is that sometimes two plus two equals three. One classic study showed this effect dramatically. One would expect a group of three pulling on a rope to exert three times the pulling power that each could attain separately. Such was not the case: groups exerted a force only two and a half times the average of individual performance.[7]

Thus, as a result of social loafing, diffusion of responsibility, and other factors, groups may not necessarily be more productive and effective than individuals.

6 Describe the variables that determine a group's effectiveness.

Determining Group Effectiveness

What are the key factors determining the effectiveness of groups? Exhibit 10–6 highlights the essential variables affecting group satisfaction, goal accomplishment, and productivity. As the model demonstrates, there is a cause-and-effect

Exhibit 10–6

Model of Group Effectiveness

Causal Variable	Intervening Variables	End Result Variables
Leadership	Group size Member composition and roles Group norms Group cohesiveness	Satisfaction Goal accomplishment Productivity

relationship between leadership (the causal variable), group characteristics (the intervening variables), and the end result variables.

Variables affecting group effectiveness are (1) group size, (2) member composition and roles, (3) norms, and (4) group cohesiveness.

Group Size. Without question, the size of the work group has an impact on a group's effectiveness. The size of a group depends to a large extent on its purpose. Organizations can take a contingency approach to determining a manager's span of control (Chapter 5), which influences the size of the natural group. With the increasing use of committees, task forces, quality circles, and self-managing work teams, we need additional guidelines for determining the size of these types of groups. Exhibit 10–7 provides some guidelines on the effects of size on group leadership, members, and group processes.

It has been our experience that the ideal size for a problem-solving group is 5 to 7 members. As Exhibit 10–7 highlights, with this size, there is less chance for differences to arise between the leader and members, less chance of domination by a few members, and less time required for reaching decisions. In partnering workshops, we usually use ad hoc task forces of 5 to 7 to study an issue

Exhibit 10–7

*Possible Effects of Size
on Groups*

Category/Dimensions	Group Size		
	2–7 Members	**8–12 Members**	**13–16 Members**
Leadership			
1. Demands on leader	Low	Moderate	High
2. Differences between leaders and members	Low	Low to moderate	Moderate to high
3. Direction by leader	Low	Low to moderate	Moderate to high
Members			
4. Tolerance of direction from leader	Low to high	Moderate to high	High
5. Domination of group interaction by a few members	Low	Moderate to high	High
6. Inhibition in participation by ordinary members	Low	Moderate	High
Group Process			
7. Formalization of rules and procedures	Low	Low to moderate	Moderate to high
8. Time required for reaching judgment decisions	Low to moderate	Moderate	Moderate to high
9. Tendency for subgroups to form within group	Low	Moderate to high	High

SOURCE: *From "Organizational Behavior," 5th ed., by Don Hellriegel, John W. Slocum, Jr., and Richard W. Woodman. Reprinted with permission of South-Western College Publishing, a division of Thomson Learning. Fax 800-730-2215.*

and report back to the larger group with a recommended plan of action. Almost invariably, the action plan is accepted with only minor modifications.

The one time we ran into difficulty was when we used a larger group—14 people—to develop a partnering agreement. In that instance, the reported agreement was later sabotaged by a subgroup of the original group of 14. Their complaint was that the agreement had been rushed through by 2 of the more dominating members. On the other hand, one study has found that 14 members are the ideal size for a fact-finding group.[8] This shows once again that the ideal size depends on the group's purpose.

Member Composition and Roles. The composition of a group has considerable impact on productivity. At the minimum, the ability of members to carry out the mission is a major factor. The more alike members are in age, background, value systems, education, personality type, and so forth, the more similarly they will see things. The literature suggests that for tasks that are relatively simple and require maximum cooperation, homogeneous groups are superior.[9] Conversely, for complex tasks, groups composed of members with widely differing backgrounds are superior because more different ideas would be generated, increasing the probability of creativity.

Whatever the group's composition, key task and maintenance roles must be carried out if the group is to be effective (Exhibit 10–8). In carrying out the group's activities, members tend to shift back and forth between these roles naturally. This is especially true in problem-solving groups and in regular work teams where the formal leader is skillful in getting everyone to participate. Many members in a problem-solving group will play several task or maintenance roles. Unfortunately, there are ineffective roles or behaviors, such as dominating, that can have a negative impact on group effectiveness (see Exhibit 10–8). The skill is for the leader to operate so that members share the leadership role and ineffective behaviors are minimized. Exhibit 10–9 is a questionnaire allowing individual members of a group to assess how well they function in helping the group achieve its goals and in minimizing ineffective behaviors.

norms
Rules of behavior developed by group members to provide guidance for group activities.

Norms. **Norms** are generally thought of as rules of behavior developed by group members to provide guidance for group activities. Norms, standards, and action plans in an effective team are highly interrelated and are supportive of the organization's goals. However, if a group is not well led, negative norms will result, working against the organization's goals. An example of a negative norm is an informal leader in a construction team sending the message "Don't rush the work—they'll just give you more to do."

The critical role of leadership is especially important in influencing positive norms. An example of a positive norm is the informal leader in the marketing group sending the message "Make sure it looks nice—we want to be proud of our work." Business ethics are similar to norms in that they provide guides to behavior. The top leadership of an organization has significant influence on ethical normative values of groups as well as individuals.

group cohesiveness
The mutual liking and team feeling in a group.

Group Cohesiveness. The mutual liking and team feeling in a group are called **group cohesiveness**. As we have already seen, size plays a major part in the cohesiveness of a group. Another major factor is the frequency of communication. In the partnering workshops we have conducted, communications were frequently issue-oriented. This led to the development of group cohesiveness.

Exhibit 10–8

*Task and Maintenance
Roles in Groups*

	Effective Roles	**Ineffective Roles**
Work or Task* Functions	**Group Maintenance* Functions**	

Initiating. Proposing tasks or goals; defining need for action; suggesting a procedure or an idea for a course of action.

Information giving. Offering facts; providing relevant information; giving an opinion.

Information seeking. Requesting facts; seeking relevant information; checking on meaning; asking for suggestions or ideas.

Clarifying. Interpreting ideas or suggestions; defining terms; clarifying issues before group; clearing up confusions.

Summarizing. Pulling together related ideas; restating suggestions after group has discussed them; offering a decision or conclusion for group to consider.

Reality testing. Making a critical analysis of an idea; testing an idea; testing an idea against some data trying to see if the idea would work.

Consensus testing. Checking with the group to see how much agreement has been reached, or how near it is to a united conclusion.

Harmonizing. Attempting to reconcile disagreements; reducing tensions; getting people to explore differences.

Gate keeping. Helping to keep communication channels open; facilitating the participation of others; suggesting procedures that permit sharing remarks.

Encouraging. Being friendly, warm, and responsive to others; indicating by facial expression or remark the acceptance of others' contributions; giving others opportunity for recognition.

Compromising. When one's own idea or status is involved in a conflict, yielding status; admitting error; disciplining oneself to maintain group cohesion.

Sharing feelings. Sensing feelings, moods, relationships within the group; sharing feelings with other members; sharing observations on group processes.

Displays of aggression. Deflating others' status; attacking the group or its values; joking in a barbed or semiconcealed way.

Blocking. Disagreeing/opposing beyond "reason"; stubbornly resisting group wishes for personal reasons; using hidden agenda to thwart the movement of a group.

Dominating. Asserting authority or superiority to manipulate group or some of its members; hindering others' contributions; controlling through flattery or other forms of patronization.

Playboy behavior. Making a display, "playboy" fashion, of one's lack of involvement; "abandoning" the group while still physically in it; seeking recognition in ways not relevant to group task.

Avoidance behavior. Pursuing special interests not related to task; staying off subject to avoid commitment; preventing group from facing up to controversy; filibustering.

Sniping. Ridiculing opinions and ideas of others by word or action; personal criticism.

*The distinction between "task" and "maintenance" roles is somewhat arbitrary. Some of these terms could be classified in either column.

The agreement on overall goals, with the processes and plans to achieve those goals, also enhances group cohesiveness.

Conversely, the major factors preventing group cohesiveness are dysfunctional conflicts, internal power struggles, and failure to achieve goals. However, sometimes a group will be very congenial, agree on goals, and feel like a team, yet fail in its mission.

Three other concepts that play a key role in healthy group development are listening, supporting, and differing. How many times have you been in a group discussion and been cut off in midsentence? How many times have you been thinking about the point you want to make next rather than listening to the other person? The listening ideas presented in Chapter 7 are most applicable in groups. Sometimes we find ourselves responding to another person's idea or suggestion with the thought, "That's a great idea—I would never have come up with that." At those moments, it is important to give positive feedback in support of the suggestion if we want to create a supportive group environment for

Exhibit 10–9

Evaluating Your Behavior as a Group Member

Task-oriented behaviors: In a group, I ...	Never	Seldom	Often	Always
1. initiate ideas or actions.	1	2	3	4
2. facilitate the introduction of facts and information.	1	2	3	4
3. clarify issues.	1	2	3	4
4. evaluate.	1	2	3	4
5. summarize and pull together various ideas.	1	2	3	4
6. keep the group working on the task.	1	2	3	4
7. ask to see if the group is near a decision (take consensus).	1	2	3	4
8. request further information.	1	2	3	4
Relations-oriented behaviors: In a group, I ...				
9. support and encourage others.	1	2	3	4
10. reduce tensions.	1	2	3	4
11. harmonize (keep the peace).	1	2	3	4
12. compromise (find common ground).	1	2	3	4
13. encourage participation.	1	2	3	4
Self-oriented behaviors: In a group, I ...				
14. express hostility.	1	2	3	4
15. seek recognition.	1	2	3	4
16. avoid involvement.	1	2	3	4
17. dominate the group.	1	2	3	4
18. nitpick.	1	2	3	4

SOURCE: *Reprinted by permission from page 214 of* Organizational Behavior, *5th ed., by Don Hellriegel, John W. Slocum, Jr., and Richard W. Woodman. Copyright © 1989 by West Publishing Company. All rights reserved.*

click! http://www.3m.com/ about3M/index.html

generating ideas. Finally, and perhaps most importantly for creativity in groups, is the creation of an environment in which people can disagree without being disagreeable. In Skill Builder 10–1, you will have an opportunity to solve an unfamiliar problem first on your own and then in a small group. While working in the small group, make a conscious effort to carry out the concepts of listening, supporting, and differing.

TEAM BUILDING

Now that you have an insight into groups and group dynamics, we focus on teams and team building. Many supervisors are now shifting to the role of team leader, so we will use that term through the chapter. A **team** is a collection of people who must rely on group cooperation if the team is to experience the most success possible and thereby achieve its goals.[10] Experience has demonstrated that successful teams are "empowered to establish some or all of a team's goals, to make decisions about how to achieve those goals, to undertake the tasks required to meet them, and to be mutually accountable for their results.[11]

team
A collection of people who must rely on group cooperation.

Unfortunately, a number of teams do not achieve their optimum success and potential. This is often caused by the team leader's leadership style being too autocratic or too permissive in managing the group. Consequently, several of the characteristics of an effective team are lacking. These characteristics are shown in Exhibit 10–10. The following section gives an example of how many of these characteristics of an effective team are implemented through the use of a partnering change strategy. While the examples used come from the construction industry, the same concepts apply to internal organizational team building.

Partnering: Team Development Accelerated

Partnering, a variation of team building and strategic planning, initially was designed to improve efficiency and effectiveness in large construction projects, an ideal setting in which to analyze team development. Teams from the contractors and owners are brought together and have to form new teams, cooperating to solve problems. Moreover, complex construction projects take anywhere from two to five years to complete, so there is time to examine the progress or lack of progress in effective team development. Consider the following example:

> **It was a lack of progress that prompted engineer Dan Burns, chief of construction for the largest Corps of Engineers district—running from Panama to North Georgia—to initiate the first formal partnering effort in the public sector. In this case, a backlog of disputes between the Corps and its clients had too often resulted in costly litigation.**
>
> **As Burns explains the situation, "Frequently the time consumed between the initiation of a project and the final resolution of all administrative problems and financial responsibilities is two or three times the duration of the actual field work. Over 40 percent of my time as chief of construction has been involved in dispute resolution and conflict management; [we felt] there had to be a better way, [and so decided] to investigate the concept of partnering utilized in the private sector.**[12]

What Is Involved in Partnering?

The partnering process is closely related to total quality management and team development. Our definition of the partnering process includes a focus on developing trust, improving communications, and team building. The process identifies positive and resisting forces and then sets in motion the development of action plans to turn resisting forces into positive forces. It uses both value clarification and strategic planning to develop a common set of goals along with a partnering agreement that all parties sign.

As mentioned, we focus here on partnering in the construction industry, since the success rate on more than 200 projects exceeds 90 percent, whereas on most joint ventures the success rate has been only 30 percent. Furthermore, in 90 percent of the successfully partnered projects, the net result is development of one culture with a common set of values, beliefs, behavior patterns, action plans, and goals.

The process is typically initiated with a workshop lasting one and a half to two and a half days and involving key members from the participating organizations. For example, one of the authors facilitated a partnered project involving higher management of Magee Women's Hospital of Pittsburgh and

7 Explain what is involved in partnering and why it is successful.

partnering
A variation of team building and strategic planning, initially designed to improve efficiency and effectiveness in large construction projects.

 click! http://www.usace.army .mil/

Exhibit 10–10

Characteristics of an Effective Team

Clear Purpose		The vision, mission, goal, or task of the team has been defined and is now accepted by everyone. There is an action plan.
Informality		The climate tends to be informal, comfortable, and relaxed. There are no obvious tensions or signs of boredom.
Participation		There is much discussion, and everyone is encouraged to participate.
Listening		The members use effective listening techniques such as questioning, paraphrasing, and summarizing to get out ideas.
Civilized Disagreement		There is disagreement, but the team is comfortable with this and shows no signs of avoiding, smoothing over, or suppressing conflict.
Consensus Decisions		For important decisions, the goal is substantial but not necessarily unanimous agreement through open discussion of everyone's ideas, avoidance of formal voting, or easy compromises.
Open Communication		Team members feel free to express their feelings on the tasks as well as on the group's operation. There are few hidden agendas. Communication takes place outside of meetings.
Clear Roles and Work Assignments		There are clear expectations about the roles played by each team member. When action is taken, clear assignments are made, accepted, and carried out. Work is fairly distributed among team members.
Shared Leadership		While the team has a formal leader, leadership functions shift from time to time depending on the circumstances, the needs of the group, and the skills of the members. The formal leader models the appropriate behavior and helps establish positive norms.
External Relations		The team spends time developing key outside relationships, mobilizing resources, and building credibility with important players in other parts of the organization.
Style Diversity		The team has a broad spectrum of team-player types, including members who emphasize attention to task, goal setting, focus on process, and questions about how the team is functioning.
Self-Assessment		Periodically, the team stops to examine how well it is functioning and what may be interfering with its effectiveness.

SOURCE: *Jerry B. Harvey. "The Abilene Paradox and Other Meditations on Management." (Lexington, Mass: D.C. Heath 1988), and "The Abilene Paradox: The Management of Agreement,"* Organizational Dynamics, *Summer 1974. Copyright (c) 1974 with permission from Elsevier Science.*

Turner Construction Corporation. Exhibit 10–11 presents the agenda for the workshop for higher management along with a description of "What Is Partnering?" At a later date, a two-day workshop was held for the site team and subcontractors.

Partnering Successes

The Magee Women's Hospital project was successful and met all goals and expectations. The architectural firm involved in this project was so impressed with the partnering concept that it used the same facilitator to conduct internal team building and partnering sessions. The outcomes were a shift to a more participative team culture and continued growth and financial success. As a result of the success of the first few partnering programs, two major initiatives of the Corps of Engineers for the decade were partnering and the environment. One of these success stories was the Bonneville Navigation Lock partnering project on the Columbia River in Oregon. Exhibit 10–12 identifies the project's

Exhibit 10–11

*Magee Women's
Hospital Partnering
Workshop*

AGENDA
Partnering Workshop
Magee Woman's Hospital ACC Addition

General Objectives:

- To develop team-building skills
- To develop a common set of goals and a partnering commitment
- To develop specific project action plans
- To become a cooperative, effective project management team

Day 1—Friday, February 11, 1994

12:00–1:00	Lunch and introductions
1:00–2:15	Team-building exercise
2:15–2:45	Development of statement of goals and core values from viewpoint of respective partners
2:45–3:00	Break
3:00–3:30	Presentation, discussion, and synthesis of goals and core values
3:30–4:30	Identification and discussion of preferred individual conflict management styles
4:30–4:45	Break
4:45–5:45	Team-building exercise
5:45–7:15	Social time and dinner
7:15–8:00	Role play of a preferred conflict management style for the project; theory input on concept of principled negotiation and joint problem solving

Day 2—Saturday, February 12, 1994

8:00–9:15   Divide into three teams with the following assignments:

Team One. Develop a mission statement (partnering agreement) that all members sign.
Guidelines. Include reasonable achievable goals from Day 1 results. What are the corporate core values you want to drive this project?

Team Two. Develop a resolution process for dealing with issues and problems on the project.
Guidelines. What should our issue resolution process require? How should the issue resolution process work? What are the roles and responsibilities for all levels of the partnership in issue resolution? Who is involved at each level?

Team Three. Develop evaluation criteria and a process to periodically assess how the partnering team is doing.
Guidelines. How can we evaluate the progress of the partnership in achieving our goals? Who initiates the evaluation, who has input to the evaluation, and who sees it? How frequently is it administered, and what actions should the evaluation trigger?

9:15–10:00	Presentation and discussion of team plans
10:00–10:15	Break
10:15–11:30	Each partner develops and presents roles and responsibilities of key players. *Guidelines.* Include portrayal of relevant organization structure if deemed helpful.

What Is Partnering?

- Partnering is the process of bringing groups from different organizations together to create one team that collaborates to an unusually high degree to achieve a set of common and complementary objectives.
- Partnering is shared leadership and responsibility.
- Partnering is a recognition of interdependence and the development of a win-win attitude.
- Partnering is a proactive approach to project management and business relationships.
- Partnering is the essence of total quality.
- Partnering is fun!

Exhibit 10–12

*The Bonneville
Navigation Lock
Partnering Project*

Partnering at Bonneville was initiated in a three-day workshop attended by representatives of the contractor and the owners, the U.S. Army Corps of Engineers. The workshop focused on developing trust, improving communication, and team building. The Bonneville Partnering Mission Statement is a copy of the agreement, signed by all the participants at the end of the three-day workshop, detailing the partners' mission.

The participants' evaluation of the workshop highlighted that the norming stage had been successfully achieved by the workshop in developing teamwork, group cohesiveness, and openness of communication.

Although early results were quite favorable, "the proof of the pudding is in the eating." That is, how did the group function in Stage 4, performing? The Mission Statement Questionnaire details the mean response of participants as to how well they had accomplished their goals at the conclusion of the project, when the navigation lock was completed. All project goals had been met or surpassed, resulting in excellent evaluations on all items.

Mission Statement Questionnaire

1. We have constructed a quality project, on time, and under budget.

1	2	3	4	4.5	5
				mean	
Ineffective					Effective

2. We provided a safe work environment.

1	2	3	4	4.5	5
				mean	
Ineffective					Effective

3. We succeeded in developing a mutual, trusting, and cooperative relationship during the project.

1	2	3	4	4.5	5
				mean	
Ineffective					Effective

4. We were successful in minimizing the impact of visitor access to the Bonneville recreational facilities.

1	2	3	4	4.5	5
				mean	
Ineffective					Effective

5. We succeeded in the contractor and subcontractors receiving fair and reasonable profits.

1	2	3	4	4.5	5
				mean	
Ineffective					Effective

Bonneville Partnering Mission Statement

We, the partners involved in construction of the Bonneville Navigation Lock walls, adopt as our joint mission the following:

To construct a high-quality project, safely, in optimal time so that all stakeholders are proud to have contributed.

To develop a mutual trusting and cooperative relationship and execute the contract in such a manner that upon substantial completion, the project is administratively as well as physically complete and precludes the need for litigation.

To construct the project so that the contractor, its subcontractors, and suppliers, receive equitable compensation at a fair and reasonable price to the owner.

To minimize impact on visitor access and operation and maintenance of the Bonneville Powerhouse and recreational facilities.

mission statement, sometimes called a partnering agreement. The exhibit also identifies at the conclusion of the project how well the goals were achieved. Any item evaluated 4.5 or higher is in the "A" category.

The state of Arizona has had a most successful partnering program for a number of years. Since the implementation of partnering programs, the transportation department has reduced the size of its claims division from four people to one person. The money saved has been used to fund new construction.

Carl Henson, chief of construction of the Army Corps of Engineers for the Los Angeles District, has stated that, out of 22 projects that used partnering, only 21 have not met or exceeded expectations. The Synergistic Group has served as facilitator for over 300 projects and has a success rate of meeting or exceeding goals and expectations on over 90 percent of the projects. The Bonneville Lock construction on the Columbia River (Exhibit 10–14) is an example of one such project.

The partnering process is being tested by the management, coordination, and direction of the Central Artery/Tunnel (CA/T) project in Boston. The Massachusetts Highway Department states, "It is the largest construction project of its kind in America today. The project features units of cut-and-cover tunnels, immersed tube tunnels, highway viaducts, long-span bridges, and dozens of ancillary structures, such as vent buildings (each a multimillion dollar job by itself). It has some of the most complex urban utility rearrangement and construction staging challenges ever dealt with on a highway job. There has never been anything like it, and there may never be again."[13]

The management team of the Massachusetts Highway Department (MHD), the Federal Highway Administration (FHWA), and a joint venture of Bechtel/Parsons and Brinkeroff are committed and using both partnering and total quality management. Internal partnering champions are working with external facilitators, and the results are promising.

Most importantly, partnering has created well-organized teams with effective processes that allow TQM to be brought into play internally and throughout the CA/T project. The TQM initiative, stimulated by successful partnering, is called *Work Improvement Never Stops (WINS)*. Roger Daniels, a partnering coordinator, cites an example where an issue identified and resolved in a specific partnering workshop was the catalyst for a WINS effort at projectwide process improvement.[14]

Partnering Failures and Their Causes

In common with other types of change efforts, problems occur with partnering because of either a lack of support from top management or a Theory X philosophy of managing on the part of key leaders. A Theory X philosophy encompasses the belief that, since most people will try to get away with as much as they can, they must be constantly watched. Edgar Schein, an international expert on organization culture and process consultation, has stated, "You show me an organization that has a key leader with Theory X assumptions about people and I predict they will eventually screw things up."[15] In one major, complex partnering project involving three government agencies and three private construction firms, an on-site survey revealed that two of the government agencies had high-ranking off-site Theory X managers who were causing excessive and unnecessary difficulties in getting the project completed. Some of the consequences were high turnover and excessive on-site stress among employees, cost overruns, and the unnecessary firing of a primary contractor.

Other dangers include changes in key personnel at the site level without orienting them to a partnering approach, major unanticipated site conditions on which the original bid was not based, and inexperienced or incompetent facilitators. In one case with which we are familiar, an inexperienced facilitator encouraged partnering organizations to bring their respective lawyers to the initial partnering workshop. In this instance, a partnering agreement was never signed and the project has been involved in litigation.

⑧ Describe how to work with self-managing work groups.

self-managing work teams
Groups that tend to operate by member consensus rather than management direction.

 click! http://www.saturn.com/

SELF-MANAGING WORK TEAMS

Today, management in developed countries is undergoing a transformation, partly because of **self-managing work teams,** which tend to operate by member consensus rather than management direction. Europe has been in the forefront of experimenting with self-managing work teams, but managers in Canada and the United States are increasingly using teams as building blocks in a corporate renaissance.

The Saturn plant in Tennessee is based on the self-managing team concept, and the management at General Motors hopes it will be the model for the rest of the corporation. Estimates suggest that over 500 U.S. manufacturing plants use some form of self-managing work teams, illustrated by the experience of a small southern plant.

> **The small parts plant is owned by a large corporation and employs 320 workers. Most of the self-managed work teams consist of 8 to 12 members who select their own leader. At the next level are coordinators, who work with several teams. The coordinators report to an upper-management group called the support team. The coordinators operate primarily as developmental leaders. Their basic leadership practice is to encourage the teams to do things themselves—to be self-managing. Under this structure, there have been productivity gains of significantly more than 20 percent.[16]**

As more and more companies adopt a team approach to work, a number of them are discovering that their reward systems—pay, promotions, career paths, and so forth—do not support it. The following example shows what happens

The goal of today's supervisor is to enable work groups to manage themselves rather than depend upon a manager for constant direction.

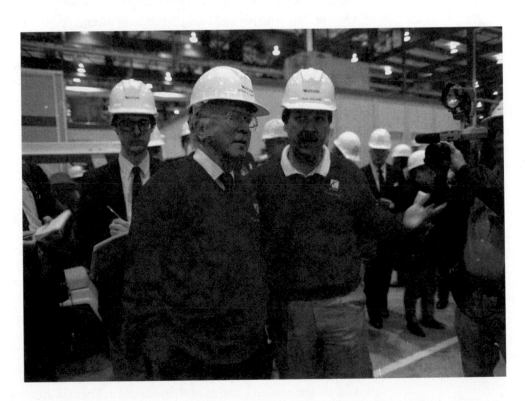

when the new team philosophy is sending one signal and the traditional reward system is sending another.

> **In 1988, the management of General Motors caused a near revolt among salaried workers when it revamped its performance appraisal system. Managers were required to rank employees according to individual performance, with at least 10 percent in the category of "inferior." Among other problems, this approach was so at odds with GM's new philosophy of teamwork that it was dropped after one year.[17]**

The important lesson from this and similar examples is that when companies move to a team approach, particularly with self-managed work teams, they need to ensure that their reward system reinforces the team approach. In the small southern plant studied by Manz and Sims, the reward system, which reflects the expertise level of employees, is based on the number of tasks the worker can competently perform. When workers feel they have mastered a task, they can be tested on it. The highest pay level is based on mastering the jobs of two work groups.

The trend in self-managed work teams is paying employees as they add to their knowledge and learn multiple skills. These "pay for knowledge" plans enjoy job rotation, continued individual growth, and increased expertise. Most importantly, they avoid the danger of increasing responsibilities and duties at lower levels without changing the reward system.

---

chapter review

① Appreciate the impact of change on individuals and organizations.

Organizational change is now occurring at an explosive rate. Internal and external forces cause change, and they must be considered in any change program.

② Compare and contrast the reactive approach to change to the proactive approach.

There are two ways of dealing with change: reacting to it or being proactive and planning for it. Obviously, being proactive and using a process of planned change is the preferred approach.

③ Understand planned change.

The use of team-building and participative management concepts can assist in the management of change and help overcome employee resistance to change. Insecurity, economic worries, prejudiced viewpoints and attitudes, and lack of advance notice are some of the reasons employees resist change. The organization and its team leaders can do a number of things to help employees develop a positive attitude toward change. Among these are timing changes carefully, giving employees plenty of advance notice and a chance to participate in the plans for change, taking employees' objections seriously, following up to make sure that changes are working out as planned, and letting employees share any economic benefits that result from the change.

④ Identify the stages of group development.

The focus then turns to the development of work groups; the types—formal and informal—and stages of development. Formal groups are those formed by management. Informal groups are those that are not part of the official organizational structure and evolve out of employees' affiliation needs. An examination of synergy tells us that two or more people working together in a cooperative way can accomplish more than the sum of their independent efforts, and in order to achieve synergy, it is important for a group to move through all four stages of group development: forming, storming, norming, and performing.

⑤ Compare the advantages and limitations of groups.

The primary advantages of groups are that they (1) give members an opportunity for needs satisfaction and (2) may function more effectively than individuals. Some limitations include the fact that they may (1) encourage social loafing, (2) diffuse responsibility, and (3) be less effective than individuals.

⑥ Describe the variables that determine a group's effectiveness.

Group effectiveness is determined by (1) group size, (2) member composition and roles, (3) norms, and (4) group cohesiveness. The Abilene paradox and groupthink can reduce group effectiveness.

⑦ Explain what is involved in partnering and why it is successful.

The chapter discussed a number of ways to encourage healthy team development, particularly in providing advice and making effective decisions. Partnering can accelerate group/team development, but it is essential that partnering have the support of top management. Empowering individuals and teams through decentralization of problem solving and decision making is also a key factor in effective implementation of partnering and team building.

⑧ Describe how to work with self-managing work groups.

Self-managing work teams have an impact on transforming organizations. Although some individuals and teams occasionally have difficulty coping with increased managerial responsibility, in general, employees in self-managing work teams are more satisfied, and production and quality show improvement. However, any company shifting to a participative team approach needs to ensure that the reward system is supportive or the move could backfire.

---

important terms

external change forces *277*
formal group *281*
group *281*
group cohesiveness *287*
informal group *281*
internal change forces *277*
norms *287*

organizational effectiveness *279*
partnering *290*
proactive (planned) process of change *279*
reactive process of change *278*
self-managing work teams *295*
synergy *281*
team *289*

---

questions for review and discussion

1. Is change as pervasive as the authors claim? Explain.
2. What are some of the primary reasons people resist change? What are some of the ways a team leader can ensure that change is accepted or at least not resisted?
3. What major changes in the last 10 years have had considerable impact on organizations? Do these changes provide support for or make a case against the use of team building in organizations? Defend your position.

4. Compare and contrast formal groups with informal groups. Explain the importance of leadership in both types of groups.
5. If groups have so many limitations, why are they so popular?
6. Of the factors affecting group effectiveness, do you think there is any order of importance? If so, rank the factors 1 through 4 and explain why you chose to rank them in that order.
7. Identify and discuss why partnering has been so successful. In your answer, include reasons why the process of partnering has been so successful in the construction industry.
8. Identify conditions and organizations where self-managing work teams would *not* be the way to organize. Then identify conditions and organizations where self-managing work teams *would* be the way to organize.
9. How would you deal with an informal leader in a task force who seemed to be totally opposed to the group's objectives?

skill builder 10–1

Team Building
group activity

Objective: To allow participants to "blue-sky" or fantasize their ideal training program.

Materials Required: Paper, flip chart.

Approximate Time Required: Thirty to 40 minutes.

Procedure: Divide the group into subgroups of four to five persons each. Tell them they have just received a call from their vice-president for human resource development (or similar authority) saying that the organization has just allocated $300,000 to be used strictly as they determine. Have each group member compose an individual "wish list," with an approximate budget figure for each item. (An example would be to visit personally five of the top human resource development authorities in the world. Costs would include airfare, food, lodging, consulting fees, and so forth.)

After 5 to 10 minutes for individual decision making, have each group discuss the individual priority listings and attempt to reach consensus on a group list. The group should record its results and report them to the entire audience.

SOURCE: *Adapted from Edward E. Scannell and John W. Newstrom,* More Games Trainers Play *(New York: McGraw-Hill, 1983), p. 289.*

Discussion Questions

1. After you had written your individual "wish list," how many of you altered your ideas or budgets after discussions with other members?
2. While group brainstorming ordinarily produces a better result, are there some cautions as well? If so, what are they?
3. If your top priority is really important, what are some ways you—as a group—could persuade the boss to budget the necessary dollars?

skill builder 10–2

Development of a Generic Project Partnering Approach
group activity

The Situation

In the past few years, a number of successful partnering projects have been initiated in the public sector of the construction industry. In the forefront of this innovative approach have been representatives from the U.S. Army Corps of Engineers, the U.S. Navy, and the U.S. Air

Force working with numerous contractors. This state-of-the-art process has dramatically improved the productivity and cost effectiveness of hundreds of millions of dollars worth of federal construction projects all over the United States.

As a result of these favorable outcomes, the U.S. Department of Commerce has decided to appoint a task force to develop a generic approach to effective partnering in the public sector. The task force will be composed of experienced personnel from both the public and the private sectors.

The Initial Assignment

You have been named to the newly formed task force. At the first meeting, the team will prioritize and sequence 12 activities, using the partnering approach. This approach is intended to lead to successful project completion.

Obviously, some of the activities are very important and others less important. Prior to the meeting, you decide to individually rank the activities from 1 through 12.

Step 1: Rank-order the activities individually without discussing the order with anyone.

Step 2: Assemble the task force and now, as a team, rank-order the importance and sequence of Activities 1 through 12.

You have until _____ o'clock to reach your decision.

Management Activities	Step 1 Individual Ranking	Step 2 Team Ranking	Step 3 Partnering Experts' Ranking	Step 4 Difference between Steps 1 and 3	Step 5 Difference between Steps 2 and 3
Develop a partnering logo and slogan					
Develop a common set of goals					
Time frame and schedule for common outings such as picnics, softball games					
Develop an evaluation instrument so you track partnering and project success					
Gain top management support for partnering concept					
Develop a strategy to bring subcontractors, lower levels, and new players into the partnering process					
Develop trust and open communication between the parties					
Develop a problem-solving process so problems are dealt with at lowest level					
Clarify site authority/responsibility versus home office					
Write a partnering agreement that all parties sign					
Develop a plan to maintain the partnership strengths to include follow-up workshops and continuing methods to keep the partnership motivated					
Conduct a partnership workshop before project gets under way or early into the project					
			Totals (the lower the score, the better)		
Developed by The Synergistic Group, 6 Schwaemmle Drive, Mobile, Alabama 36608.				Individual score Step 4	Team score Step 5

●skill builder 10–3

Creating an Organizational Culture

Assume you start your own business sometime after graduation. It can be any business of your choice that has a good opportunity for growth. After 10 years, the business has become quite successful and now employs 102 people.

1. Identify the business you have chosen.

2. Assume that initially you believed there is a positive correlation between having a strong culture and business success. Identify the specific actions you have consequently taken over a 10-year period to develop a strong organizational culture.

●skill builder 10–4

"Win as Much as You Can" Tally Sheet

The detailed instructions for completing this exercise will be provided by your instructor. Basically, for 10 successive rounds you and your partner choose either an X or a Y on the scorecard. The payoff for each round depends on the pattern of choices made in your group. The payoff schedule is given at the bottom of the scorecard provided.

You are to confer with your partner in each round and make a joint decision. In rounds 5, 8, and 10, you and your partner may first confer with the other partnerships in your group before making your joint decision.

	Round	Your Choice (Circle)		Cluster's Pattern of Choices	Payoff	Balance
	1	X	Y	__X __Y		
	2	X	Y	__X __Y		
	3	X	Y	__X __Y		
	4	X	Y	__X __Y		
Bonus Round Payoff × 3	5	X	Y	__X __Y		
	6	X	Y	__X __Y		
	7	X	Y	__X __Y		
Bonus Round Payoff × 5	8	X	Y	__X __Y		
	9	X	Y	__X __Y		
Bonus Round Payoff × 10	10	X	Y	__X __Y		

Payoff Schedule

4 Xs:	Lose $1.00 each
3 Xs:	Win $1.00 each
1 Y :	Lose $3.00 each
2 Xs:	Win $2.00 each
2 Ys:	Lose $2.00 each
1 X :	Win $3.00
3 Ys:	Lose $1.00 each
4 Ys:	Win $1.00 each

If there is no objection to a modest wager, each partnership may want to place a bet, ranging from 10 cents to a dollar, on the outcome of the game. The winner collects the money at the end of the exercise.

SOURCE: *Adapted from an exercise by William Gellermann, Ph.D., in J. Pfeiffer and J. Jones,* Structured Experiences for Human Relations Training, *Vol. II, published by University Associates, 1974.*

The Shift to Team Leadership
group activity

You work for a company interested in initiating a team leadership training program, and your plant manager has appointed you to an ad hoc task force to study the feasibility of implementing such a program in your plant. In one of the company's other plants, however, supervisors resisted team leadership, giving the following reasons:

1. Lack of time
2. Leader mind-set ("It's the leader's job to make the major decisions.")
3. Lack of trust in employees
4. Lack of confidence in employees' abilities or judgment
5. Potential for major negative consequences ("too risky," "too costly")
6. Leader's belief that the leader knows best
7. Leader's concern that developed employees will erode leader's base of power ("They're not dependent any more.")
8. Leader's perception that employees don't desire development ("They don't really care; they only want to do the minimum required.")

Instructions:

1. Divide the class into teams of three to six students.
2. Each team should brainstorm ways to overcome supervisors' predicted resistance to developmental leadership.
3. Each team is to outline an initial training agenda for the developmental leadership program to present to the plant manager.
4. The teams are to present their analysis and recommendations to the plant manager (represented by the instructor or a designated class member).
5. Vote with your class to determine which program appears to have the best chance of success. (*Note:* Students may not vote for their own team's program.)

case

Controlling

11   Exercising Control

12   Controlling Productivity, Quality, and Safety

5 part

Exercising Control

● outline

What Is Control?
Control's Close Links to Planning
Importance of Controls
Examples of Controls

Characteristics of Effective Control Systems

Types of Control Systems

Steps in the Control Process
Step 1: Establishing Performance Standards
Step 2: Measuring Performance
Step 3: Comparing Performance with Standards and Analyzing Deviations
Step 4: Taking Corrective Action If Necessary

Management by Exception

The Impact of Technology on Controls

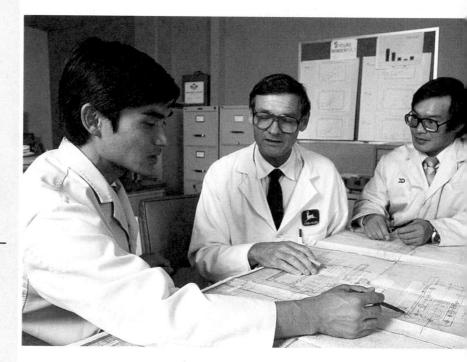

Management control seeks to compel events to conform to plans.

Billy Goetz

We tried to make some adjustments at halftime. They just didn't pan out.
Pro Football Coach After His Team Was Beaten in the Playoffs

Ron Johnston: Controlling Operations

Ronald L. Johnston is the facility engineering manager for the A.S.P.I. Division of Albertsons Inc. in Salt Lake City, Utah. Albertsons, one of the largest U.S. retail food and drug chains, began in Boise, Idaho, in 1939. The founder—Joe Albertson—changed the grocery business by introducing such unheard-of services as a "scratch" bakery, homemade ice cream, magazine racks, and an automatic donut machine. His stores were based on the concepts of high quality, good value, and excellent service.

These goals still prevail today in every aspect of the company. Johnston, who is the head of the engineering department, which is a vital part of Albertsons' store development team, plays a large part in accomplishing these goals.

The engineering department, under Johnston's direction, contributes directly to Albertsons' profitability by striving to achieve better operations through emphasizing personal communication, coordination, knowledge, and quality control. The people in the department do this by employing capable mechanical and electrical engineers and motivating them to achieve these goals through methods and procedures such as cross-discipline training sessions as well as sending employees to industry-related conventions and vendor seminars.

The engineering department consists of 40 people representing various trade and craft skills, as well as carefully selected front-line supervisors. In addition, Johnston is also responsible for the utilization of empowerment techniques to improve morale, increase efficiency, and develop personnel. Among these many and varied duties is the utilization of energy management techniques to sustain budget cost control and hold contractors and in-house personnel accountable. Johnston accomplishes these goals by using agreed-on schedules and performance reviews. He also sets budget objectives and develops contracts, which include high-dollar incentives for exceeding normal expectations. He tries to minimize bureaucracy by streamlining—or in some cases eliminating—procedure mandates and by using a common sense approach to control.

Johnston's primary responsibilities include new plant start-up, management of the engineering department, skill and diversity training, budget development, statutory authority for surveys and code compliance issues, cost improvement, utilization of manpower reduction, procurement of equipment and materials, project management, schedule development, plant and machinery surveys, contract negotiations, safety compliance, hazardous waste management, EPA compliance issues, and development and implementation of preventive and predictive maintenance programs.

The department's responsibilities also include the automation of the plant for central surveillance, along with an after-hours, dial-out paging system, which reduces the need for manpower. Johnston is also in charge of other control features that lead to reduced manpower needs, including use of

learning objectives

After reading and studying this chapter, you should be able to:

1. Define control and explain how it relates to planning.

2. Discuss the characteristics of effective control systems.

3. Discuss the three types of control systems.

4. Discuss the four steps in the control process.

5. Identify the different types of standards.

6. Explain the importance of strategic control points.

7. Discuss management by exception.

8. Discuss the impact of technology on control.

 http://www.albertsons.com

predictive maintenance techniques such as infrared scanning, vibration analysis, spectrum oil analysis, eddy-current testing, and so forth. These techniques lead to cost savings in both manpower and training. The department also uses competitive bidding and outsources software programming. Finally, Johnston is also involved with the planning and progress meetings on every new project and an evaluation meeting at the conclusion of each project.

In summary, Johnston helps maintain Albertsons' excellence by fine-tuning his department's operations so they are kept running smoothly at all times. In so doing, he is usually on call at all times, day and night—and weekends, too!

Many supervisors are taken by surprise when their activities do not "go according to plan." This failure is often the result of poor planning. But just as frequently, it is the result of poor control over the implementation of the plans!

In this chapter we give you a broad overview of what is involved in the control function. Chapter 12 will examine some specific areas of control that are crucial for supervisors.

WHAT IS CONTROL?

1 Define control and explain how it relates to planning.

Have you ever been driving a car on a trip and had one of the dashboard warning lights come on? Perhaps it was the oil pressure or temperature light. Basically, the light indicates that something is amiss. Without such a warning system, you would be caught by surprise when the car broke down, perhaps leaving you stranded far from home.

Managers and supervisors are often in a similar quandary! They go along not knowing whether things are as they should be or not. Unfortunately, many of them find that things are *not* as they should be only when it is too late to do anything about it. They do not have the advantage of periodic feedback or warning lights to tell them if they are on track. You might think of control as consisting of performance markers that tell you whether your unit's performance is moving in the right direction.

In Chapter 1, we defined *controlling* as the management function that involves comparing actual performance with planned performance and taking corrective action, if needed, to ensure that objectives are achieved. Basically, control has three phases: (1) anticipating the things that could go wrong and taking preventive measures to see that they don't, (2) monitoring or measuring performance in some way in order to compare what *is* happening with what *should be* happening, and (3) correcting performance problems that occur, which is the therapeutic aspect of control.

Control's Close Links to Planning

In Chapter 1, we also indicated that planning and controlling might be thought of as Siamese twins because they are so closely related. Planning "sets the ship's course," and controlling "keeps it on course." When a ship begins to veer off course, the navigator notices this and recommends a new heading designed to return the ship to its proper course. That's how supervisory control works. You set goals and seek information on whether they are being reached as planned. If not, you make the adjustments necessary to achieve your goals.

Thus, controlling may be thought of as the process that supervisors use to help accomplish their plans.

Importance of Controls

Perhaps you have heard the old adage: "Things never go as planned." That truth is a primary reason supervisors need to perform the controlling function effectively. Control is important in view of the many variables that can put things off track. Murphy's laws (some of which are listed in Exhibit 11–1) seem to operate everywhere. Because anything involving humans is imperfect, supervisors must use control to monitor progress and to make intelligent adjustments as required.

Examples of Controls

 click! http://www.jci.com

We live in a world of controls. Circuit breakers in our homes and offices are examples of controls. When an electrical overload occurs, the system adjusts by shutting itself down. Security alarm systems send out signals when a protected area is violated. As mentioned earlier, the dashboard in your car contains numerous control signals to warn you when something is not the way it is supposed to be—low oil pressure, overheated engine, alternator malfunction, keys left in car, seat belt not on, and so on. Exhibit 11–2 illustrates a number of other common examples of control.

2 Discuss the characteristics of effective control systems.

CHARACTERISTICS OF EFFECTIVE CONTROL SYSTEMS

To be effective, a control system must have certain characteristics. Among them, the following are the most important.

1. *Controls need to focus on appropriate activities.* Effective controls must focus on critical factors that affect both the individual's and the organization's abilities to achieve objectives. These critical objectives should include the essential areas of production and personnel activities, as well as related costs.

2. *Controls should be timely.* Information needed for comparisons and control purposes needs to be in a supervisor's hands in order for him or her to take

---

Exhibit 11–1

Murphy's Laws

- Left to themselves, things always go from bad to worse.
- There's never time to do it right, but always time to do it over.
- If anything can go wrong, it will.
- Of the things that can go wrong, the one that will is that which is capable of the most possible damage.
- If you think nothing can go wrong, you have obviously overlooked something.
- Of those things that "cannot" go wrong, the most unlikely one is that which will.
- Inside every large problem are many small problems struggling to get out.
- Any object will fall so that it lands in the one spot where it is capable of doing the most damage.

Exhibit 11–2

*Some Common
Examples of
Supervisory Control*

- At the end of the workday, a production supervisor spends 30 minutes examining a printout showing each employee's output, quality, and scrap. The supervisor notes those employees whose performance is below par and makes plans to discuss their performance with them the next day.
- A nursing supervisor studies a survey completed by all patients who were housed in her ward in the past six months. The survey lists items such as nurses' friendliness, professionalism, appearance, and a number of other factors related to job performance.
- A maintenance supervisor tours the building, examining the progress of each worker or work team.
- After a college football game, the head defensive coach views the game films several times, assigning performance grades to each defensive player. Grades below 60 reflect areas to which the coach must devote special attention during upcoming practices.

effective corrective action. Therefore, delays in generating, gathering, or disseminating information can prolong the occurrence—and extent—of deviations.

3. *Controls must be cost effective.* The benefits controls provide should be worth their costs of installation and operation. Too much control can be worse than too little. The key is that controls should be appropriate to the need and provide savings greater than the costs involved. An example of this need was pointed out by Senator William Cohen of Maine in the following statement:

> **The U.S. Department of Defense could save millions of dollars annually if it revamped regulations covering employee travel vouchers. . . . The system the Pentagon has created to protect itself against travel waste and fraud is the equivalent of assigning an armored division to guard an ATM machine. . . . The precautions cost more than the potential loss.**[1]

4. *Controls should be accurate and concise.* Controls must provide information about operations and people in sufficient quality and quantity to enable managers to make meaningful comparisons to operations standards. As with control, too much information can be worse than too little.

5. *Controls should be accepted by people they affect.* Controls and their applicability to specific situations should be communicated clearly to those responsible for implementing them and to those who will be controlled by them.

Although all of these characteristics are important, a given control system need not have all of them in order to do the job for which it is designed.

TYPES OF CONTROL SYSTEMS

3 Discuss the three types of control systems.

There are essentially three types of control systems. They are (1) feedforward controls, (2) concurrent controls, and (3) feedback controls.

Feedforward controls are preventive controls that try to anticipate problems and take corrective action before they occur. This type of control allows corrective action to be taken before a real problem develops. For example, Hart Schaffner & Marx, a leading producer of quality clothing, inspects every bolt of

feedforward controls
Preventive controls that try to anticipate problems and take corrective action before they occur.

concurrent controls
Sometimes called *screening controls* these controls are used while an activity is taking place.

feedback controls
Controls that measure completed activities and then take corrective action if needed.

cloth it plans to use in its tailored men's clothing before starting to cut pieces. See Exhibit 11–3 for some tips on establishing preventive controls. Notice that the first step is to focus on your goals or plans. Again, you can see how closely linked the planning and controlling processes are.

Concurrent controls (sometimes called *screening controls*) occur while an activity is taking place. Thus, an inspector can check items on the assembly line to see if they are up to standards. For example, in some of the more progressive Japanese plants, a worker who thinks there is something wrong with the product being produced can stop the assembly line.

Feedback controls measure activities that are already completed. Thus, corrections can take place after performance is over. Examples of these types of controls are financial and budgetary adjustments.

self-check

What type(s) of control is (are) used by Ronald Johnston in the chapter preview?

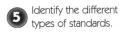
4 Discuss the four steps in the control process.

STEPS IN THE CONTROL PROCESS

The steps in the control process are illustrated in Exhibit 11-4. Note that step 4 may require going back to any of the previous three steps. It may consist of modifying the original standard, changing the frequency and manner of measuring performance, or achieving more insight into the possible cause of the problem. Let us examine the details of each of these steps.

5 Identify the different types of standards.

Step 1: Establishing Performance Standards

standard
A unit of measurement that can serve as a reference point for evaluating results.

The first step of the controlling process is really a planning step. You set your sights on something you want to accomplish. As a supervisor, you exercise control by comparing performance to some standard or goal. A **standard** is a unit of measurement that can serve as a reference point for evaluating results. Properly communicated and accepted by employees, standards become the bases for the supervisor's control activities.

click! http://www.nist.gov

Types of Standards. Standards can be either *tangible* or *intangible*. **Tangible standards** are standards that are quite clear, concrete, specific, and generally

---

Exhibit 11–3

Tips for Establishing Preventive Controls

1. Identify your department's major goals.
2. Identify those factors most crucial to accomplishing your department's major goals. These may be items such as properly running machinery and equipment, availability of raw materials, availability of key personnel, or a balanced demand for your department's services.
3. Determine the *most likely problems or circumstances* that could prevent the items in (2) from occurring. These could be factors such as machine breakdown or absence of key personnel.
4. Develop a plan for preventing the problems listed in (3). You might consider input from employees, staff personnel, your immediate supervisor, peers, and others in arriving at your preventive control plans.

Exhibit 11–4

The Process of Control

(1) Establish performance standards.

(2) Measure performance.

(3) Compare performance with standards and analyze deviations.

(4) **Take corrective action, if necessary.**

tangible standards
Clear, concrete, specific, and generally measurable.

numerical standards
Expressed in numbers.

monetary standards
Expressed in dollars and cents.

physical standards
Refer to quality, durability, size, weight.

time standards
Expressed in terms of time.

intangible standards
Are not expressed in terms of numbers, money, physical qualities, or time.

measurable. For instance, when you say, " I want the machine on line by 3 p.m.," the goal is very specific and concrete. Either the machine is on line at 3 p.m. or it is not.

Tangible standards can be further categorized as numerical, monetary, physical, or time related. **Numerical standards** are expressed in numbers, such as number of items produced, number of absences, percentage of successful sales calls, or number of personnel who successfully complete training. **Monetary standards** are expressed in dollars and cents. Examples of monetary standards are predetermined profit margins, payroll costs, scrap costs, and maintenance costs. **Physical standards** refer to quality, durability, size, weight, and other factors related to physical composition. **Time standards** refer to the speed with which the job should be done. Examples of time standards include printing deadlines, scheduled project completion dates, and rates of production.

Note that there may be some overlap among the types of tangible standards. For instance, when you say, "I want the machine on line by 3 p.m.," you have obviously communicated a time standard, but the standard is expressed numerically. Monetary standards are also expressed numerically, as are some physical standards.

In contrast to tangible standards, **intangible standards** are not expressed in terms of numbers, money, physical qualities, or time, because they relate to human characteristics that are difficult to measure. Examples of intangible standards are a desirable attitude, high morale, ethics, and cooperation (see Exhibit 11—5). Intangible standards pose special challenges to the supervisor, as the following example illustrates.

Supervisor Maude Leyden of the State Employment Office overheard one of her newer employment counselors, David Hoffman, berating a job applicant. The tone of his voice was domineering, as though he were scolding a child, although the applicant was perhaps 30 years his senior. She heard David conclude the interview with the words, "Now don't come back here and bother us again until you've had someone fill this form out properly. That's not what I'm paid to do!"

After the applicant left, Maude listened to David's explanation of what had just happened. He said he'd been under a lot of pressure that day and had grown very impatient, and he acknowledged his rudeness toward the applicant. Maude told him that he had not handled himself in a professional manner and discussed what he should have done differently. Later in the day, David was to call the applicant, apologize, and offer to be of further help.

He did call and apologize.

It is much more difficult to clearly explain an intangible standard, such as "interviewers must observe standards of professional conduct with clients," than to tell someone that the standard is "to service six malfunctioning computer systems each day." Just what *is* professional conduct? Is it patience, friendliness, courtesy, keeping a level head? Certainly it is less specific than "servicing six computers daily." As difficult as it may be, every supervisor has to establish, communicate, and control some types of intangible job standards.

self-check

Employee cooperation, desirable employee attitude, appropriate employee personal hygiene, and mature employee behavior are some intangible standards that organizations and individual supervisors typically must control. Can you think of others?

How Standards Are Set.   Standards can be set in many ways. The supervisor frequently sets standards on the basis of familiarity with the jobs being performed by his or her employees. The supervisor is generally knowledgeable

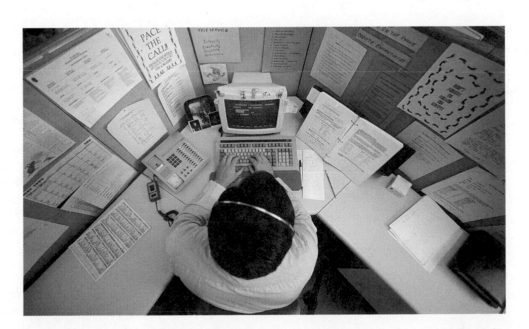

Customer service representatives are monitored against time standards, how quickly they answer the telephone, and how long they stay on the line with customers.

Exhibit 11–5

Controlling Intangible
Standards

about the time required to perform tasks, the quality necessary, and the expected employee behavior. This is especially true of supervisors who have been promoted through the ranks. If you are not technically knowledgeable about the work performed in your department, there are a number of ways to become familiar with standards. You can gain insights from past records of performance, if available, and from fellow supervisors, employees, and your own boss. Exhibit 11–6 presents some types of standards for a variety of positions.

For many jobs, various staff departments will strongly influence the standards set. The industrial engineering department, for example, may utilize systematic studies of movements and speed of workers to set quantity and time standards. The quality control department may establish standards for finish, luster, or precision. Cost accounting may develop standards for material costs or scrap. Thus, many standards may already be established for the people you will supervise.

Staff departments will also have a hand in setting standards for supervisors. For example, the budget department may help determine standards regarding material and payroll costs. Personnel may establish standards regarding the quantity and quality of grievances and turnover in a department. The ability to meet your departmental standards, in turn, will determine the amount of control that your own boss will exercise over your activities.

Step 2: Measuring Performance

Setting standards is an essential first step in control, but by itself it doesn't go far enough. A supervisor must monitor performance to ensure that it complies

Exhibit 11–6

Types of Standards for Various Positions

Position	Type of Standard
Bank teller	Monetary (balance), time (speed of teller line), physical (orderliness of work area)
Postal letter carrier	Time (hours taken to complete run)
Server in a large restaurant	Physical (appearance), time (speed), intangible (courtesy and friendliness)
Real estate salesperson	Monetary (volume), numerical (number of listings and closings)
Offensive-line football coach	Numerical (yards per game rushing), intangible (leadership of players)
Upholsterer in a manufacturing plant	Numerical (number of units completed), physical (quality of units)
Third-grade teacher	Intangible (appearance, classroom behavior), physical (quality of lesson plans)

with the established standards. Two issues the supervisor must deal with are (1) how often to measure performance and (2) how to measure performance.

How Often to Measure.   Determining how often to measure performance is an important control decision a supervisor must make. Sometimes this decision has already been made by the system, as shown in the following examples:

click! http://www .cargillfoods.com

> **Kay Davis, sales manager of City Motors, need only look at the sales chart prominently displayed on the sales floor outside her office to see how her sales personnel are doing. The chart lists the number of new and used cars sold by each salesperson for the week and the month, as well as sales volume.**

> **The production control room at DAVO Company provides a constant reading of activity on each of the production floor's operating machines. At any time, a production supervisor can visit the area and receive a printout of the work performed by any of the operators up to that time.**

6 Explain the importance of strategic control points.

strategic control point
A performance-measurement point located early in an activity to allow any corrective action to be taken.

Notice that in each of the preceding examples, performance is being constantly monitored. But this does not mean that a supervisor should spend the entire day monitoring performance. Instead, the supervisor should establish strategic control points. As shown in Exhibit 11–7, a **strategic control point** is a performance measurement point located sufficiently early in an activity to allow any necessary corrective actions to be taken to accomplish the objective. For each job, ask yourself: Considering the importance of this job, at what point do I need to know the progress being made so that I can make the required adjustments and still complete the job as planned?

Certain types of jobs, such as maintenance, personnel, and sales, don't lend themselves to frequent measurement of progress. Measurement takes time, unless an automated system is in place. Moreover, some jobs are more crucial to monitor effectively. For example, the work of an emergency room nurse requires more careful monitoring than does the work of a sales representative or a clerical worker.

Exhibit 11–7

*Setting Strategic
Control Points in the
Control Process*

How to Measure.   There are several basic ways for a supervisor to measure performance. These are:

1. Personal observation.
2. Written or oral reports by or about employees.
3. Automatic methods.
4. Inspections, tests, or samples.

   Exhibit 11–8 is an example of the second method, which could be used frequently, at very little cost. Notice how specifically the information requested is stated.

self-check

Can you suggest some instances or situations when each of these ways of measuring performance might be used?

In some jobs, supervisors and their employees work in the same area. The supervisor can easily move among the workers, observing their performance. In other departments, however, the supervisor may have workers spread out in various locations, which makes direct observation impractical. Consider a sanitation supervisor whose eight work crews collect garbage on various routes throughout the city. Such a supervisor must depend on written or oral reports or occasional inspections as the primary means of measurement. Here is what one sanitation supervisor said:

How do I know if my crews are doing the job properly? Mainly by the complaints I get from customers. Complaints range from garbage that isn't picked up on schedule to overturned trash cans, surrounded with litter. That's how I know what's going on directly in the field. Sometimes I will drive around and make an occasional inspection. We also annually survey residents to see if our people are considered timely, friendly, and efficient.

Exhibit 11–8

Example of a Written Report About an Employee

Management Encourages Your Comments

Date _5/19/2-_

Waiter or waitress _Phyllis_

Please circle meal   Breakfast   (Lunch)   Dinner

	Yes	No
1. Were you greeted by host or hostess promptly and courteously?	✓	__
2. Was your server prompt, courteous, and helpful?	✓	__
3. Was the quality of food to your expectations?	__	✓
4. Was the table setting and condition of overall restaurant appearance pleasing and in good taste?	✓	__
5. Will you return to our restaurant?	__	✓
6. Will you recommend our restaurant to your friends and associates?	__	✓

Comments

Food was overcooked. Potatoes were leftovers. Meat was tough. This was my second visit and I brought a friend with me. We were both very disappointed.

Name and address
(if you desire)

Please drop this in our quality improvement box located near the exit.

Thank you and have a good day.

SOURCE: *Adapted from Leon C. Megginson, Donald C. Mosley, and Paul N. Pietri, Jr.,* Management: Concepts and Applications, *3rd ed. (New York: Harper & Row, 1989), p. 417.*

Sales supervisors may seldom see their employees if the sales work takes them outside the office. As a result, salespersons are required to complete reports about number of calls made, sales results, travel expenses, customer comments, and numerous other matters. These reports are received by supervisors or the home office staff. Many salespersons, in fact, complain that they are required to do too much paperwork!

Supervisors who are not in frequent contact with their employees must come up with some meaningful, valid way to measure results. They need to find some means of making sure the measurements are reliable. Because of pressures to conform to standards, employees may attempt to falsify reports to make themselves appear better.

> **Several years ago, a nationally respected youth organization set very high membership goals for its local offices. The results appeared spectacular until it was discovered that a number of local chapters had considerably inflated the number of new members enrolled to avoid looking bad.**

In other words, you have to be careful about attempts to beat the control system. People may extort money, falsify documents, and distort oral reports. For example, if you ask an employee to give you an oral report on a job's progress, he or she may tell you, "Everything's just fine, boss," when, in fact, it is not.

Step 3: Comparing Performance with Standards and Analyzing Deviations

Unfortunately, many supervisors receive information that demonstrates a serious departure from standards but make little effort to understand what caused the difference between planned and actual performance. Failure to meet standards may result from a variety of causes. A supervisor needs to understand the reasons for below-average performance. Many supervisors jump to conclusions about the causes of problems; as a result, the corrective action they take is ineffective.

> **Suppose that the quality control standard for producing a certain part is 99/100. This means that there should be no more than one defective product per hundred units produced by a worker. You just received notice from the quality department that of the last 200 units produced by employee Kevin Rae, almost 13 percent were defective.**
>
> **What could have caused this problem? Could it have been poor materials? Might Rae's equipment be the cause? Is this like Rae? What will you do about it? These are some questions you have to ask yourself. Simply giving Rae an oral or written warning may be highly inappropriate and may not correct the problem!**

It is also important to compare results that are substantially above standard in order to determine why they varied from standard. The supervisor should check to see if all operating procedures are being followed, or if there is an improvement in operations that should be included in new standards.

It is important to find out the opinions of those close to a particular problem in order to determine why standards are not being met. For example, an employee's explanation or those of other employees or fellow supervisors might be obtained. Frequently, people in other departments can add insight. Here is what one supervisor said:

I was all set to really chew Emily out. She had an important job to complete for me this morning and didn't show up as scheduled. Fortunately, before I made a fool of myself, I learned from one of her friends that she'd gotten here early and the plant manager had asked her to do an even more important job. I checked this out with the plant manager, and, sure enough, that was the case. She was supposed to notify me but had just forgotten.

Step 4: Taking Corrective Action If Necessary

The final step in the control process is to take corrective action if necessary. You have undoubtedly seen many athletic contests turn completely around after halftime. This change is often due to corrective action taken by the coach—the modifications, adjustments, and fine-tuning done in response to problems encountered earlier.

The supervisor's job is much like that of a coach. Adjustments, fine-tuning, and perhaps even drastic actions may be necessary to pull off important tasks or to maintain standards. Examples of corrective actions a supervisor might take include:

1. Making a decision to retrain a new operator whose performance has not progressed as expected.
2. Shifting several employees from their normal jobs to help meet a deadline on another job.
3. Counseling an employee whose performance has recently been below standard.
4. Reprimanding an employee for failure to adhere to safety rules.
5. Shutting down a piece of equipment for maintenance after defective output is traced to it (see Exhibit 11–9).

Exhibit 11–9

Discuss management by exception.

MANAGEMENT BY EXCEPTION

Even under the best of circumstances, deviations from performance standards are bound to occur. Given the broad range of areas over which supervisors exert control, it is essential to distinguish between critical and less critical deviations. The fact that many performance deviations are due to normal operating variances means that supervisors must exercise some discretion in distinguishing between variations that are relevant and those that are less so.

management by exception
A supervisor focuses on critical control needs and allows employees to handle most routine deviations from the standard.

Under **management by exception,** a supervisor focuses on critical control needs and allows employees to handle most routine deviations from the standards. Exhibit 11–10 shows that the key issue is *whether or not a deviation is exceptional.* The key idea is to set priorities for activities, depending on their importance, and to focus your efforts on top-priority items. Management by exception works essentially the same way. Your attention should be focused on exceptional, rather than routine, problems.

Exhibit 11–10

Management by Exception

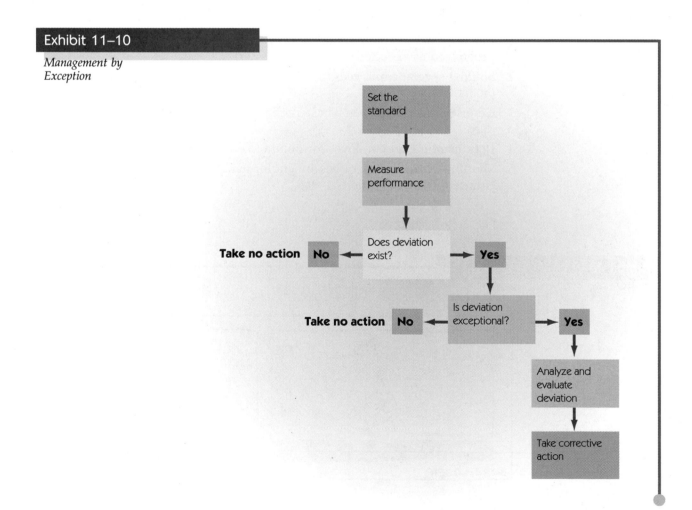

Preventative controls are key to limiting workers' compensation claims. Heightening awareness of safety issues can be accomplished in a variety of ways.

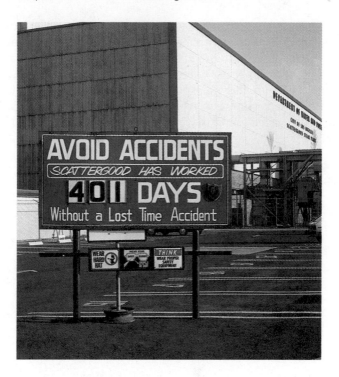

self-check

Suppose you are a sales supervisor and your departmental sales goal is 800 units weekly (or 3,200 units monthly). Each of your eight sales representatives, then, has a goal of 100 units weekly (or 400 units monthly). At the end of the first week, your sales results are as follows:

Salesperson	Weekly Goal	Units Sold
A	100	105
B	100	95
C	100	90
D	100	102
E	100	102
F	100	88
G	100	98
H	100	115
Total =	800	795

What corrective action will you take?

Managers who practice management by exception might do absolutely nothing about the previous situation. "But wait!" you say. "Look at Salesperson C, who performed 10 percent below standard, and Salesperson F, who was 12 percent below standard. Shouldn't a supervisor do something about these two employees?"

Of course, a supervisor should be aware of these deviations. However, re-call that only the first week has gone by. It is probably fairly normal to find such variances in a single week; the more pertinent information is how performance compares to the monthly benchmark of 3,200 units. With three weeks to go, the supervisor who gets too upset after Week 1 may be overreacting. Naturally, the supervisor should keep an eye on sales data in the upcoming weeks to see whether Salespersons C and F improve their performances. In this situation, the assumption of management by exception is that Salespersons B, C, F, and G realize that they are below standard and will be working to improve.

self-check

Suppose that at the end of the second week, sales results are as shown:

Salesperson	Weekly Goal	Week 1	Week 2
A	100	105	107
B	100	95	101
C	100	90	97
D	100	102	101
E	100	102	101
F	100	88	84
G	100	98	99
H	100	115	126
Total =	800	795	816

What will you do now?

Sales have perked up, and, with the exception of Salesperson F, everyone is in reasonable shape. As supervisor, you'd be justified in entering the control process with Salesperson F, as the red flag is still up on this one. You may want to discuss this person's results, try to identify actions that produce below-standard results, and develop a plan of corrective action.

Note that Salesperson H has been setting the standards on fire, averaging more than 20 percent *above* standard the first two weeks. This performance is also an exceptional departure from standard. What is behind these results? Is Salesperson H using some techniques that will work for others? Is this person's territory so choice that it becomes easy to make the standard? Should you modify the standard for Salesperson H? Management by exception can be applied to both favorable and unfavorable deviations from standard.

8 Discuss the impact of technology on control.

THE IMPACT OF TECHNOLOGY ON CONTROLS

As the world's economies—and their environments—continue to become more dynamic and complex, managers—including supervisors—must obtain, organize, and utilize huge amounts of information in order to make decisions and exercise control over them. Progressive managers are realizing that a high-speed information infrastructure is needed to cope with the rapid pace of operations in all types of economic activities.

One result of this "information revolution" is the redistribution of power in today's more advanced organizations. For example, decision making and control have now been shifted downward to lower levels of management, including the supervisory level. With practically unlimited types and sources of information at their fingertips, even operative employees no longer have to rely on others for facts and figures to make decisions. Thanks in part to networks and multimedia fusions, organizations are becoming more integrated.

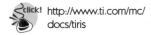

click! http://www.ti.com/mc/docs/tiris

> **For example, Tiris—a unit of Texas Instruments—is managed out of Bedford, England; its line of low-frequency transponders is designed in Freising, Germany; and the units are produced in Kuala Lumpur, Malaysia, whence they are shipped to customers around the world.[2]**

Organizations now have information and monitoring systems that permit supervisors to give instructions and control operations from a distance away from those activities.

click! http://www.ups.com

> **For example, at the start of his workday at 8:30 each morning, Washington R., a delivery person for United Parcel Service (UPS), picks up a bulky brown box resembling an oversize computer game. He carries the box with him all day as he makes his deliveries and returns to home base at night. His personal box has a window in which he can view all the day's tasks, each one timed to the minute.**
>
> **As he makes his deliveries, Washington keys the details into the box, which electronically transmits the data to his home depot. His supervisors can therefore determine at any time where he is and whether or not he is on schedule. At the end of the day, Washington hooks up his box to the UPS computer, and all the information he has accumulated during the day is automatically transferred to it.**
>
> **During the night, the computer downloads Washington's next day's itinerary and individual tasks into his box.[3]**

Today's information technology makes possible—for better or for worse—this form of digital monitoring and control.

---

chapter review

(1) Define control and explain how it relates to planning.

Controlling is the supervisory process of making plans and following through on them. Because of the many variables involved in executing and carrying out plans, supervisory control is an essential part of the management process.

(2) Discuss the characteristics of effective control systems.

For control systems to be effective, they should (1) focus on appropriate activities, (2) be timely, (3) be cost effective, (4) be accurate and concise, and (5) be accepted by people who will be controlled by them.

(3) Discuss the three types of control systems.

The three types of control systems are (1) feedforward controls, which try to anticipate problems and take corrective action before they occur; (2) concurrent controls, which are used while an activity is taking place; and (3) feedback controls, which measure activities that are completed and then take corrective action if needed.

(4) Discuss the four steps in the control process.

There are four steps in the control process: (1) Establish performance standards,

(2) measure performance, (3) compare performance with standards and analyze deviations, and (4) take corrective action if needed.

⑤ Identify the different types of standards.

There are several types of standards. They can be tangible (numerical, monetary, physical, and time) or intangible (attitudes, ethics, morals). They can be set by supervisors or staff departments.

⑥ Explain the importance of strategic control points.

It is important that the supervisor establish strategic control points. These points measure performance early enough in the process to permit sufficient adjustments or corrective actions to be made in order to achieve the goal. Supervisors measure performance through direct observation, by written or oral reports by or about employees, through automatic methods, and by inspections, samples, or tests.

⑦ Discuss management by exception.

Management by exception focuses supervisory attention on exceptional departures from standard rather than on routine variances.

⑧ Discuss the impact of technology on control.

The growth of information technology has redistributed power in organizations, thus enhancing the position of supervisors.

---

important terms

concurrent controls *309*	numerical standards *310*
feedback controls *309*	physical standards *310*
feedforward controls *308*	standard *309*
intangible standards *310*	strategic control point *313*
management by exception *318*	tangible standards *309*
monetary standards *310*	time standards *310*

---

questions for review and discussion

1. In what ways are planning and controlling related?
2. Discuss the following statement made by a supervisor: "I don't have to worry much about controlling. My view is that, if you plan a job properly, things will go right; so you don't have to worry about control."
3. Name the primary characteristics of effective control systems.
4. Identify and explain each of the four steps in controlling.
5. Give an example of each type of standard:
   a. Numerical standard
   b. Monetary standard
   c. Physical standard
   d. Time standard
   e. Intangible standard
6. Name and explain the three types of control systems.

7. In management by exception, the supervisor focuses on exceptional deviations from the standard rather than on every deviation. Will employees grow lax when they realize that they can perform below standard as long as they are not *too far* below? Discuss.
8. Explain the impact technology has had on control.

• skill builder 11–1

The Overcontrolling Supervisor

As a new operations supervisor, Clarise Rogers was very conscientious about wanting to do a good job and pleasing her boss. She spent a large part of the day watching her employees perform their jobs, moving from one work station to another. She inquired how things were going and tried to engage in friendly small talk.

One day a senior operator asked to see Clarise in her office. The operator said, "We know you mean well, but there's no need for you to be constantly checking up on everybody. We had one of the best departments in this company under Morgan [the previous supervisor], and she stayed off our backs. We're professionals, and we don't need somebody constantly looking over our shoulders. We're going to do a good job for you. Just give us some breathing space."

Answer the following questions:

1. What should Clarise do?
2. Suppose Clarise had just taken over one of the poorest performing departments in the company. Would this make a difference in the control techniques she should use? How?

• skill builder 11–2

Setting Standards and Measuring Performance
group activity

Instructions: Form into small groups to discuss each of the jobs listed below. Assume that each group member directly supervises that position. In each case, indicate the major type(s) of standard(s) that would be used (physical, monetary, time, or intangible) and the frequency and manner of measuring performance for each job.

Discuss with group members your ideas about how to handle each situation.

1. Bank teller
2. Postal letter carrier
3. Server in a large restaurant
4. Real estate salesperson
5. Offensive-line football coach
6. Upholsterer in a furniture manufacturing plant
7. Third-grade teacher in an elementary school

•skill builder 11–3

Setting Course Standards
group activity

Assume that you are the instructor in a supervisory management course at the college of your choice. In the class are 25 students completing the course for college credit. You are required to assign grades based on students' performances in the class.

Instructions:

1. Identify at least one standard that you can establish for the course in each of the following areas:

   a. Physical standards
   b. Numerical standards
   c. Time standards
   d. Intangible standards

2. In small groups, compare and discuss your lists of standards. Were your standards in any of the areas similar? Which standards were most common? In which areas was there the most variety among standards?

3. Present your overall findings to the class.

Controlling Absenteeism

Anna McIntyre had been named head nurse of the University Hospital pediatrics department the previous day. She would officially begin her new job in one week, when Carla Smith, the present head nurse, would be reassigned to a new department. Anna reflected on the conversation she'd had with Gail Sutherland, director of nursing, when Gail offered her the position. "Anna," Gail had said, "you'll be taking over a department that has 8 percent absenteeism compared to only 2 percent for other nursing units in the hospital. This has always been a problem, and Carla never could handle it— that's a major reason she was transferred. I want you to make it your number one priority."

Anna reflected on Carla's performance as head nurse. Carla had always been a skilled, competent nurse, but since being promoted to head nurse in pediatrics, she had just been too soft. Many nurses had taken advantage of her good nature—Carla had found it impossible to discipline—and the situation in pediatrics had begun to deteriorate. Anna knew from her own experience that absenteeism had been high in the department. This was especially true of weekend work. Carla never took action, even when it was obvious that personnel were making petty excuses.

Answer the following questions:

1. What additional information should Anna attempt to obtain regarding the absenteeism problem?
2. Advise Anna on the steps she should take to control absenteeism.
3. What types of standards should she use?
4. What strategic control points should she establish?

chapter 12

Controlling Productivity, Quality, and Safety

● outline

Improving Productivity and Cost Control
High U.S. Productivity Fuels the 1990s
Defining Productivity
Why Productivity Is Important
Groups Influencing Productivity
The Supervisor's Role in Improving Productivity
The Supervisor's Role in Cost Control
Some Recent Productivity Improvement Methods

Controlling Quality
TQM and Quality Control
Understanding Variance in Controlling Quality
Some Tools for Controlling Quality
The Supervisor's Role in Achieving Quality

Promoting Employee Safety
What OSHA Does
Factors Influencing Safety
Causes of Accidents
The Supervisor's Role in Promoting Safety

"*You can never inspect quality into products. You can only build it into them.*"

Akio Morita, Chairman, Sony Corporation

Productivity Increase or Else

As the financial community saw it, GFF had acquired Triaz, Inc., mainly to get its hands on Triaz's breadwinner division that served the aerospace industry. For years, Triaz had been a leading manufacturer of control devices, pumps, and gauges for the automotive and marine industries. In the last seven years, though, Triaz had shifted gears, emphasizing the aerospace and government industries.

About two months after the acquisition, Al Jackson, general manager of the division, was expected to eliminate marginally performing divisions, one of which was the Boaz facility. Boaz produced a variety of pumps for the automotive and marine industries. In the previous year, Boaz had lost $8 million on a volume of $320 million in sales. The plant was one of the oldest in the Triaz group, having been built in the 1920s. Two months after the GFF acquisition, Bert Mayfield, the newly named vice-president and general manager of Boaz and a former financial manager with Triaz, addressed the 200-plus managers of the division:

What I've just heard from New York is not very good news. It boils down to this: We have 12 months to turn things around at Boaz or we're all gonna go. We'll be sold, or if nobody wants us, we'll be shut down for good. These GFF folks know their stuff. Among the main things they're aware of are some that I already knew, namely,

1. *Our average costs are the highest in the industry—this includes our cost of goods sold as well as administra-*

tive costs. It costs us 12 percent more to make a pump than it does our competitors. These costs have severely affected our bottom line.

2. *Our cost of reworked parts—products that had to be reworked or scrapped because of poor quality—has increased steadily over the past five years and is significantly higher than our competitors'.*

3. *The quality of our finished products has deteriorated. Once, we had among the most reliable products on the market. But a recent GFF survey showed that customers now rank us fourth in quality out of six firms. Last year, we lost two long-time major contracts because of quality problems with the products we shipped to them.*

4. *Our safety performance at Boaz is at the bottom of the industry.*

After a brief pause, Mayfield continued:

Each department is going to have to make a significant contribution to productivity if we are to meet this challenge. In other words, we all have to become efficient at our jobs. I'll be meeting with all department heads, asking them to develop plans for increasing their department's productivity by 15 percent or more—that's the idea. We've got to get our costs back in line, our quality up, and those lost-time accidents down. Our line supervisors will play a big part in this, but everybody has to improve—production, purchasing, maintenance, engineering—you name it. We're all in this together, and if everyone shares the responsibility, we'll make it. If we don't, . . .

learning objectives

After reading and studying this chapter, you should be able to:

1. Explain the concept of productivity.

2. Identify and explain the ways in which management, government, unions, and employees affect productivity.

3. Describe some steps supervisors can take to increase productivity.

4. Differentiate between TQM and quality control.

5. Describe the role of variance in controlling quality.

6. Identify some important tools for controlling quality.

7. Explain what the Occupational Safety and Health Administration (OSHA) does.

8. Describe the supervisor's role in promoting safety.

 http://www.merck.com

It sounds as if this plant faces a challenge. The plant's unit cost did not rise to 12 percent over that of its competitors overnight. But only now has new management decided to exercise control, and it may be too late.

Notice the important role that department heads and line supervisors are expected to play in raising departmental productivity through their controlling function. This chapter focuses on several key areas of control that concern supervisors: (1) productivity and costs, (2) quality, and (3) safety.

IMPROVING PRODUCTIVITY AND COST CONTROL

1 Explain the concept of productivity.

Productivity has been an "in" word in American business for the past two decades. Another name for it is efficiency. We hear about productivity at work, read about it in magazines and newspapers, and see it discussed on television. It has become the subject of business- and government-sponsored seminars. "Productivity centers" have sprung up around the country to research the subject.

High U.S. Productivity Fuels the 1990s

On a global level, a country's productivity indicates how efficiently its human resources are utilized in producing goods and services. And the productivity of U.S. workers is higher than that of any other country's workers. Canadian workers, in fact, rank next to U.S. workers, producing about 95 percent of U.S. workers' output. Although the productivity of Japanese workers is much touted, actually the Japanese worker produces only about two-thirds of the output of the U.S. worker.

What troubled many people, though, was that in the 1980s we began losing our edge in productivity. The rate of growth of productivity in Japan, as well as in a number of other countries, exceeded that of the United States, cutting into our productivity lead. Plenty of blame was tossed around at management, government, unions, and employees. Recall how the U.S. lost its market dominance during this period, especially to the high-quality products from Japanese manufacturers. The 1990s saw a dramatic turnaround as U.S. companies took back the initiative. As shown in Exhibit 12–1, U.S. productivity boomed during the 1990s as a result of many factors: improved facilities, physical and information technology advancements, improved processes and work methods, investments in employee training, and other factors. Even despite the Asian financial crisis of the late 1990s, which reduced demand for U.S. goods and services abroad, the exceptionally high productivity rate of U.S. firms kept costs low, and enabled them to weather the storm.[1]

Defining Productivity

productivity
Measure of efficiency (inputs to outputs).

Basically, **productivity** is a measure that compares outputs to inputs. It tells you how efficiently a system is performing. For example, your car's gas mileage is a productivity measure of energy performance. For a certain input, say one gallon of gas, your car achieves a certain output, say 22 miles of travel. The figure of 22 miles per gallon (MPG) is the productivity measure of your car's energy performance. How is this figure useful? You now have a basis for comparing (1) your car's performance to that of other cars and (2) your car's present performance to its previous performance. For example, if your MPG were to fall to 15, you would know that your car's performance had fallen, and you would try

Exhibit 12-1

U.S. Productivity Growth in Manufacturing Output per Hour: 1960s–1999

Year	Annual Rate
1960s	2.2
1970s	2.7
1980s	1.4
1990	2.5
1991	2.3
1992	5.1
1993	2.2
1994	3.1
1995	3.9
1996	4.1
1997	5.0
1998	4.8
1999	5.5 (est.)

SOURCE: *U.S. Bureau of Labor Statistics.*

to determine the reasons—assuming, of course, that such an energy loss was important to you!

Productivity is expressed as a ratio; that is, output is divided by input. In our example of the car's gas mileage, the ratio might look like this:

$$\frac{\text{Total miles (220)}}{\text{Number of gallons (10)}} = 22 \text{ MPG}$$

self-check

What would be some meaningful input–output relationships for the following service organizations: restaurants, community colleges, beauty salons, insurance companies, department stores?

The official productivity measure of the United States as shown in Exhibit 12–1 is based on labor output and input per hour. This is the productivity that is announced each month by the government and discussed in the media. Basically, it is the ratio of the total output of the nation's goods and services to the total hours of labor that went into producing those goods and services.

Business organizations use numerous input–output performance measures, some of which are shown in Exhibit 12–2. Generally, when people in business discuss improved productivity, they are talking about total costs and total goods or services produced. That is what the plant manager had in mind in the chapter preview when he said that the plant needed to increase productivity by 15 percent. What he hoped was that, at the end of the next 12-month period, the productivity ratio would look like this:

$$\frac{\text{Total output of goods/services}}{\text{Total costs}} = \begin{array}{l} 15\% \text{ more} \\ \text{than previously} \\ \text{accomplished} \end{array}$$

Exhibit 12–2

*Examples of
Productivity
Measurements*

Input	Output
Salesperson labor hours	Sales volume per salesperson
Energy used, in BTUs	Number of pounds fabricated
Training hours for customer service personnel	Percent of error-free written orders
Number of hours of plantwide safety meetings	Number of accident-free days
Labor hours spent in preventive maintenance	Number of hours without a machine breakdown
Cost of raw materials	Quantity of finished goods produced
Total labor hours of service personnel	Total quantity of services produced
Total labor hours of production workforce	Total quantity of goods produced
Total costs	Total number (or value) of goods or services produced

Basically, there are three ways to accomplish the 15 percent productivity increase desired at Boaz:

1. *Increase* the total output without changing the total costs.
2. *Decrease* the total input costs without changing the total output.
3. *Increase* the output and *decrease* the input costs.

Assume that a department of Boaz produced 48,000 units (output) at a cost of $24,000 for raw materials, energy, and labor. The productivity ratio is:

$$\frac{48,000 \text{ units (output)}}{\$24,000 \text{ (input)}} = 2.0 \text{ units/dollar}$$

To achieve a 15 percent increase in productivity, the department would need to raise the final ratio by 0.3 (that is, 2.0 × 15%). In other words, the department would need a final productivity rate of 2.0 + 0.3 = 2.3 to achieve a 15 percent productivity increase. There are three basic ways to achieve this, as discussed next.

Example 1: Increasing Output. One approach to attaining the productivity increase is to hold the line on costs while increasing output. How much additional output would be needed to reach the new productivity rate of 2.3? This can be calculated by the following steps:

(a) $\dfrac{\text{Total units}}{\$24,000} = 2.3$ units per dollar

(b) Total units = 2.3 units per dollar × $24,000

(c) Total units = 55,200

Since the department is presently producing 48,000 units, it would have to produce 7,200 additional units without increasing costs to attain the 15 percent productivity increase.

Example 2: Decreasing Input. Another approach is to maintain present output while reducing costs. By how much would the department need to reduce costs to attain the 15 percent increase? This can be calculated by the following steps:

(a) $\dfrac{48{,}000 \text{ units}}{\text{Costs}} = 2.3$ units per dollar

(b) $\quad\text{Costs} = \dfrac{48{,}000 \text{ units}}{2.3 \text{ units per dollar}}$

(c) $\quad\text{Costs} = \$20{,}870$

Producing the 48,000 units at a cost of $20,870 would provide the 15 percent productivity ratio improvement. The department would have to maintain production of 48,000 units while reducing costs by $3,130 (that is, $24,000 − $20,870).

Example 3: Increasing Output and Decreasing Input. Suppose that the department could reduce costs by only $1,000. By how much would the department have to increase output to achieve the 15 percent productivity increase?

(a) $\dfrac{\text{Total units}}{\$24{,}000 - \$1{,}000} = 2.3$ units per dollar

(b) $\quad\dfrac{\text{Total units}}{\$23{,}000} = 2.3$ units per dollar

(c) $\quad\text{Total units} = 2.3$ units per dollar $\times \$23{,}000$

(d) $\quad\text{Total units} = 52{,}900$

Thus, reducing costs by $1,000 and increasing output by 4,900 units (52,900 − 48,000) would also provide the 15 percent productivity increase.

Why Productivity Is Important

Productivity is important for several reasons. From an individual company's standpoint, increased productivity translates into lower prices, larger market share, and greater profits. The firm's stronger financial position enables it to invest in research and development, to utilize new advanced technology, to increase wages and benefits, to improve working conditions, and so on.

Increasing productivity is exactly what Ford Motor Company had in mind when it made heavy investments in upgrading its assembly plants and technology, improving its processes, and training its workforce. These investments, coupled with its strong "Quality Is Job 1" theme, have paid off by making Ford the most productive and profitable North American car manufacturer. In 1999 the *Harbour Report,* the most widely recognized and quoted analysis of manufacturing productivity in the industry, ranked Ford the number one manufacturer in 10 of the 12 vehicle categories that it measures. Ford's Atlanta and Chicago plants, which build the Ford Taurus and Mercury Sable, ranked one and two in the midsize product. It also had the most productive plants for its Mustang, for three different pickup models and for its Econoline van.[2]

Productivity is also important for smaller and service-oriented businesses as well. Let us examine the following example:

Assume that you manage a steakhouse restaurant that utilizes seven waiters/waitresses. Their pay (including benefits but excluding tips) averages $10.00 hourly. The maximum number of tables that they can serve effectively is five per hour. Thus, the labor cost for serving each table is $10/5, or $2 per table. Assume that business has picked up re-

Ford motor assembly line workers have played a major part in making Ford plants the most productive in the United States.

cently. The kitchen can handle the extra business, and by rearranging tables, five new tables could be added. Since the current waiter/waitress maximum of five tables served per hour has already been reached, a new waiter/waitress must be hired to handle the extra workload. Before hiring another waitress, though, you pose the problem to your waiters and they come up with a plan.

"We could each handle an extra table an hour if we didn't have to set each table," they say. "Couldn't the hostess who seats the party distribute the silverware and menus? Also, might we arrange each waiter's tables in a more compact area? This would reduce walking time among tables. The time saved with these two changes might allow us to effectively serve another table hourly (which, by the way, would mean an additional tip)."

So you try it out, and behold, it works. Your workers handle the extra table per hour effectively. Let's calculate the effect on productivity—it has increased by one-fifth, or 20 percent. Moreover, your labor costs have decreased from $2.00 per table to $1.67 per table ($10.00 ÷ 6 tables = $1.67 per table). Since labor costs typically account for 30 to 60 percent of a company's expenses, increasing the efficiency of labor is very important to an organization's success.

On a larger scale, increased productivity enhances the economic growth and health of the United States. In the international market, companies from the United States compete with firms from other nations. Increased productivity in the United States keeps prices down, reduces inflation, and improves our standard of living.

2 Identify and explain the ways in which management, government, unions, and employees affect productivity.

Groups Influencing Productivity

As noted in Exhibit 12–1, the productivity growth rate of the United States picked up significant steam in the 1990s. But what caused the slowdown of U.S. companies' productivity in the 1980s? What is responsible for the impressive growth of the 1990s? Basically, four groups play important roles, as shown in Exhibit 12–3.

self-check

Who do you think is chiefly to blame for the lowered rate of productivity of U.S. companies during the 1980s? Is it management? Government? Workers? Unions?

Management. A major force in determining productivity is management. Many experts placed major blame on complacent, conservative management for the United States' deteriorating performance of the 1980s. The result was that we lost ground to many more efficient and highly productive foreign producers, especially the Japanese, in such industries as steel, autos, large earth-moving equipment, and so on. Fortunately, a turnaround in the 1990s was fueled by management decisions to build more modern plants, upgrade equipment, and improve processes, although some industries such as steel have never regained their dominant world market position.

Government. Another important productivity player is government. For example, tax incentives can encourage business investment in new facilities and technology; government regulations also play an important role. During the 1980s businesses spent huge amounts on the costs of compliance to satisfy, for instance, pollution and environmental controls, consumer protection requirements, and employee safety and health, to mention some of the more costly ar-

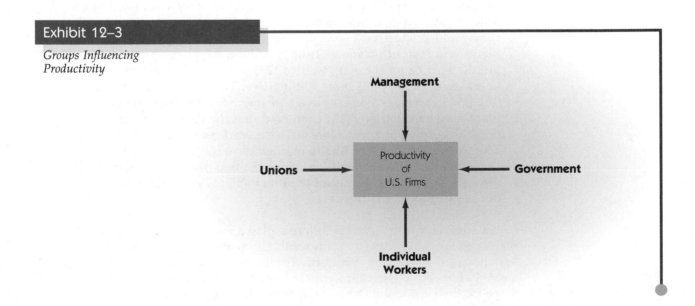

Exhibit 12–3

Groups Influencing Productivity

eas. This not only diverted expenditures from more efficient labor-saving technology, equipment, and plants, but it also required many new positions—such as equal employment opportunity (EEO) specialists, record keepers, and clerks—to be created to meet government requirements. These personnel do not contribute directly to output. While government regulation of business is necessary, the amount of regulation is a constant source of debate in this country as well as in others.

Individual Workers.   Another important productivity player is the individual worker. We saw in Chapter 8 that employees' ability, motivation, and commitment strongly affect individual and team performance. The age and education of employees impact their skill; during the 1980s the average age of workforce employees was much lower than in earlier years, which resulted in less experienced, less productive employees during that period. This situation has reversed itself in the 1990s and has fostered the United States' higher productivity during this period.

Unions.   Unions also play a role in productivity by their posture toward technology enhancements, new work methods, and displacement of inefficient jobs. We read about cases in which unions resist labor-saving devices and efficiencies and protect jobs that are considered nonproductive. Many people tried to make unions the scapegoat of the 1980s' productivity crisis; however, during this period, union membership was decreasing, as is the case today. Moreover, in the retail and wholesale industry, which had practically no union strength, the decline in productivity was similar to that which occurred in the more traditionally unionized industries.

> **General Motors in 1998 suffered a costly 54-day strike which shut down 26 of its 29 assembly plants and cost the company more than $2.5 billion. The strike was limited to two Flint, Michigan, parts plants which supply GM assembly plants. The issue: productivity. GM, lagging behind number one ranked Ford and Daimler-Chrysler in terms of efficiency and productivity, sought to upgrade, close, or sell noncompetitive plants and instead outsource from nonunion suppliers. The UAW, seeing the writing on the wall, wanted GM to spend the necessary money to make its parts plants more competitive. The union struck because it felt GM had reneged on its pledge to spend $300 million to make the plant more competitive; GM countered that the union resisted efforts to reduce payroll and adopt more efficient work methods at the two sites. The agreement that was finally reached gave the union a no sale, no close two-year commitment for one of the two plants. But experts said the agreement only postponed the inevitable: GM's need to boost productivity and competitiveness.[3]**

In summary then, all of these forces play a role in productivity. However, management, which directly controls decisions about facilities, technology, research, and the company "productivity climate," is most responsible in that it strongly impacts relationships with its union and sets the stage in numerous ways for the productivity of individual employees.

Describe some steps supervisors can take to increase productivity.

The Supervisor's Role in Improving Productivity

Supervisors often have little control over spending for technology and equipment, but as the persons in direct contact with operating employees, they are very important players in the productivity issue. But how do you go about it? Suppose that you work for Triad and head a department of 20 employees who produced a total of 10,000 units last year. Under your plant manager's new mandate, you must increase production to 11,500 units. How would you go about this? You could do some of the things listed in Exhibit 12–4, many of which have already been discussed elsewhere in the text or will be discussed in coming chapters.

The Supervisor's Role in Cost Control

As we pointed out earlier, the productivity of a department is based on its total outputs and total inputs. Upper management is cost conscious because costs represent major inputs. Supervisors direct the operating work of an organization; thus, they have a key role in controlling a firm's cost in labor hours and efficiency, maintenance of machinery and equipment, supplies, energy, and other matters.

Budgets are one aid that can help supervisors to control costs. Different budgets are normally prepared for sales, production, scrap, equipment, grievances, lost-work-time accidents, and the like. Moreover, they may be set for different time periods such as a week, a month, a quarter, or a year. Since a budget reflects expected performance, it becomes a basis for evaluating a department's actual performance (see Exhibit 12–5).

Exhibit 12–4

How Supervisors Can Improve Employee Productivity

- Train employees. Can their abilities be upgraded?
- Clearly communicate the need for high standards so that workers understand what is expected of them.
- Use motivation techniques to inspire workers to increase output. Pride, ego, and security are several important motivators available.
- Eliminate idleness, extended breaks, and early quitting time.
- Build in quality the first time work is done. Productivity is lost when items are scrapped or need to be reworked to be salvaged.
- Work on improving attendance and turnover in your work group.
- Reduce accidents. Accidents normally result in time lost to investigations, meetings, and reports—even if the employee does not suffer a lost-work-time injury.
- Seek to improve production measures. Will process or work-flow improvements help?
- Try to eliminate or reduce equipment or machinery breakdowns. Preventive maintenance is important.
- Exercise good control techniques. Follow up on performance and take corrective action promptly.
- Involve your employees in the process of improvement. Select their ideas and suggestions for improvement. Form special productivity improvement teams.

Exhibit 12–5

Performance Report

Name of department	Fabrication	Performance period	November 2006
Budgeted output	15,700 lbs.	Budgeted scrap	152 lbs.
Actual output	15,227 lbs.	Actual scrap	120 lbs.
Variance	−473 lbs.		+32 lbs.

Item	Actual	Budgeted	Variance
Direct labor	$32,000	$32,000	$ 0
Overtime	1,500	1,000	−500
Supplies	500	385	−115
Maintenance and repairs	4,250	3,000	−1,250
Utilities	1,300	1,200	−100
Scrapped material	1,200	1,520	+320
Total	$40,750	$39,105	−$1,645

self-check

Assume that you are supervisor of the fabrication department in Exhibit 12–5. If you were really trying to tighten up costs, which activities in your department would you focus on? Why?

Note in Exhibit 12–5 that the supervisor's department has performed well in some cost areas and not so well in others. Output is off by 473 pounds, overtime is 50 percent higher than budgeted, and maintenance and repairs are also over budget. On the plus side, the department has been efficient in using raw materials.

Budgets are not carved in stone; there will always be unusual occurrences that affect performance. An investigation of the unfavorable variances in Exhibit 12–5 may reveal that the supervisor or team member could have done little to avoid them. For example, perhaps a crucial piece of equipment had faulty parts, causing the high repair costs; or perhaps the high overtime resulted from an unexpected weekend job thrust upon the supervisor. A budget does, however, serve as an important supervisory tool by signaling areas that may need attention. Such attention might take the form of combining certain jobs, reducing scrap, achieving better quality production, or focusing on large-cost items rather than numerous smaller ones.

Recently, an important development has proved especially helpful to supervisors in achieving effective cost control. This was the advent of management information systems (MIS). It is now possible for supervisors in some circumstances to have up-to-the-minute cost data on payroll, raw materials, utilities, and other costs as nearby as a computer monitor or printer.

click! http://www.
inventorymanagement
.com

Some Recent Productivity Improvement Methods

In an effort to improve productivity, three relatively recent productivity improvement measures have been introduced in manufacturing firms. These improvements, which have been due to advances in computer and machinery technology, are (1) robotics, (2) just-in-time inventory control (JIT), and (3) computer-assisted manufacturing (CAM).

robot
A machine that is controlled by a computer.

Robotics.   A **robot** is a machine, controlled by a computer, that can be programmed to perform a number of repetitive manipulations of tools or materials. Japan makes the greatest use of robots in the world, with about 40 percent of the one million in use, or 1 for every 36 people employed in manufacturing. The United States employs about 100,000 robots, with over half in the automotive industry where they perform welding, painting, and other operations. However, they are also finding increased acceptance in electronics, food and beverage, pharmaceutical, consumer goods, and appliance industries, and other industries where materials handling and packing are required. It is estimated that these machines—often called "steel-collar workers"—operate for about $5 an hour, considerably less than the $15 to $20 per hour (including benefits) or higher wages paid to many employees.[4]

self-check

In addition to the $15 hourly payroll cost savings, can you think of any other advantages robots offer over human employees? Disadvantages?

just-in-time (JIT) inventory control
Materials arrive when they are needed in the production process.

Just-in-Time Inventory Control.   Under the **just-in-time (JIT) inventory control** system, needed materials arrive on the scene as close as is feasible to the time they are needed in the production process. Often, computers link the company with suppliers to keep them informed about the company's up-to-the-minute needs. With JIT, the proper components arrive in the right place at the right time. JIT allows an organization to minimize inventory holding and storage costs and to utilize the space previously occupied by inventory waiting to be used.

click! http://www.quality.nist .gov

The JIT approach has been used by many of the largest U.S. companies, such as Motorola, Chrysler, and other manufacturers. Retailers have also gotten into the act in a big way. Many large retail chains such as Home Depot and Wal-Mart practice just-in-time inventory control. Rather than stocking large amounts of inventory at each store, they depend on a just-in-time inventory control approach. A good example can be found at Dillards, a leading department store chain throughout the southeast and midwest. A computer-driven "direct response" program allows items such as Gant dress shirts and Christian Dior lingerie to be ordered directly from the vendor each week—by computer—based on the previous week's sales. And Dillards' goal is to reduce its average turnaround time from 12 days to 8 in the future.[5]

computer-assisted manufacturing (CAM)
Special computers assist equipment in performing processes.

Computer-Assisted Manufacturing.   In **computer-assisted manufacturing (CAM),** special computers assist automated equipment in performing the processes necessary for production. These computers can be reprogrammed to permit machinery to easily produce a product or part to different specifications. Whereas proper planning and coordination would normally take hours, CAM equipment can be programmed to make adjustments within seconds. CAM is especially useful when small orders of customized products must be filled. Once the computer has been programmed, the electronic signals control the machine processor, resulting in the correct sequence of steps to properly complete the task.

For example, at carpet manufacturers, computer software programs control patterns, weaves, and the size of carpets being produced. At apparel manufacturers such as Hart, Shafner, and Marx, computer software programs determine optimum cutting of patterns and sizes to minimize waste and ensure perfect cuts.

CONTROLLING QUALITY

In recent years, perhaps no other aspect of management has received the attention of organizations as the effort to improve quality. As you may recall, it was Deming who first publicized the link between increased quality and increased productivity and profitability. While quality is a concern at all management levels, it is most focused on at the operative level, since it is here that the basic work of functional departments is performed. As mentioned in Chapter 2, while the quality movement in service organizations, such as banks, hospitals, and hotels, has lagged behind that of manufacturers in the past, this is becoming less true today.

TQM and Quality Control

4 Differentiate between TQM and quality control.

Sometimes the terms *total quality management* and *quality control* are used interchangeably. However, as you learned in Chapter 2, they are not the same. Total quality management (TQM) refers to an organization's overall quality effort. This encompasses such factors as upper management's commitment, product and process design, employee training, relationships with customers and suppliers, continuous quality improvement, measurement of quality and management, and employee attitudes toward quality. **Quality control,** on the other hand, is a narrower process, consisting of the measurement and analysis of quality performance and actions taken to correct quality problems. It occurs during or after performance and may include inspection, testing, sampling, and statistical analysis.

quality control
Defined measurements designed to check whether the desired quality standards are being met.

Understanding Variance in Controlling Quality

5 Describe the role of variance in controlling quality.

Every product and service is the output or result of a process. You might consider a process to be a set of related activities designed to accomplish a goal. The nature of processes is to exhibit variation; for example, items produced in a machining or manufacturing process are not all exactly alike. Some measurable dimensions, such as length, diameter, or weight will vary. These variations may be quite small and imperceivable by the naked eye, but sophisticated gauges or test equipment will reveal these differences. Similarly, service processes are also subject to variation. Fast-food customers wait different periods of time before being served. Some luggage checked in on a commercial airline will not arrive with its owner. At a steakhouse, there is considerable variation among steaks prepared as "rare."

Two types of variation exist: common cause and special cause. Let's use a classic example to illustrate process variation: writing. Note the variations of handwritten letters below, though each one was carefully written by the same author.

You needn't use a magnifying glass to note that differences exist. The differences in each "P" are normal and to be expected. This we call *common cause variation*. Now look at the "a's." Note that the middle one is clearly different from the others. Perhaps the writer was bumped, or the paper quality in that one spot was different, or a different pen was used. (Actually, it was made by the same writer but using the other hand.) The variation is not routine or expected; clearly, there was excessive variation, or *special cause variation*. Common cause variation is a general, routine variation that is built into the system. Special cause variation occurs intermittently and is associated with a specific event.

Effective control of quality can have two focuses: (1) reducing common cause variation and (2) reducing special cause variation. As Deming and other quality experts note, special causes can sometimes be addressed by individual workers, but common causes can ordinarily only be corrected through management action to improve the process. This might include such things as upgrading raw materials, using more sophisticated equipment, additional training, and so on. Importantly, much of the effort by organizations to seek continuous quality improvement is aimed at reducing common cause variation by improving processes.

Reducing special cause variation entails identifying the problem, isolating it, examining the cause, and remedying it. This might mean, for instance, replacing an erratic piece of equipment, reassigning an employee who cannot keep pace with job demands, or reassigning personnel to handle peak customer demand periods. As a supervisor, it is important to understand variation and the extent to which different levels of quality performance can be attributed to normal or special cause variables. Statistical sampling is one useful tool for doing so, but is beyond our scope here. However, we will examine some other important tools.

Some Tools For Controlling Quality

(6) Identify some important tools for controlling quality.

A number of tools are available to assist in effective control of quality. Often, these are used by individuals who are part of special problem-solving or quality-improvement teams. Among the tools discussed here are flowcharts, histograms, run charts, Pareto charts, control charts, and fishbone diagrams. Some, such as histograms, run charts, and control charts, represent displays of the actual performance data which must be addressed. Keep in mind that these tools apply not just to the quality of manufacturing processes (although this is perhaps the most common application), but to service processes as well.

flowchart
Visual representation of the sequence of steps needed to complete a process.

Flowchart.   A **flowchart** is a visual representation of the sequence of steps needed to complete a process. Its purpose is to help individuals understand the *process* they are attempting to control. Flowcharts are frequently used by problem-solving teams to address quality issues involving processes with a number of sequential steps to complete (see Exhibit 12–6). Often such processes cut across departmental lines. The visual representation of the process enables team members to examine the relevant steps and note where improvements can be made, as reflected in the following example:

> **In one organization, its repair/remodeling group sought to improve the time it took to complete projects. It found that the average job was completed in 195 days, roughly six months of working time. Individually, each team member (e.g., a plumber, electrician, and carpenter) could not understand why the jobs took so long, since their own work lasted only**

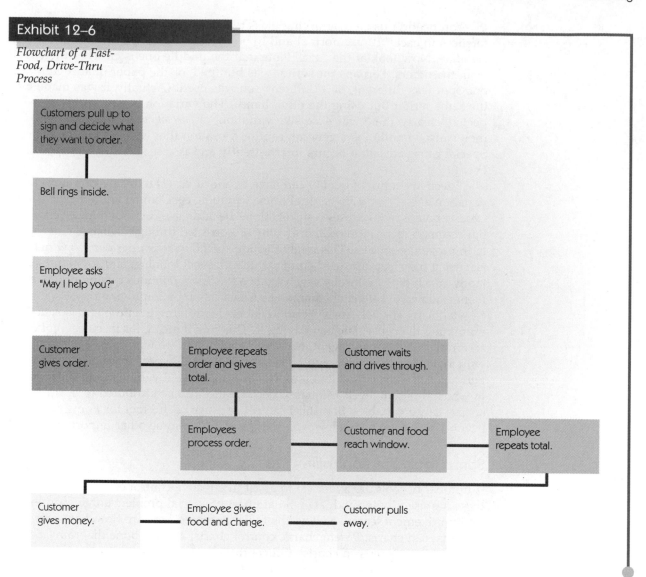

Exhibit 12–6

Flowchart of a Fast-Food, Drive-Thru Process

Customers pull up to sign and decide what they want to order.

Bell rings inside.

Employee asks "May I help you?"

Customer gives order.

Employee repeats order and gives total.

Customer waits and drives through.

Employees process order.

Customer and food reach window.

Employee repeats total.

Customer gives money.

Employee gives food and change.

Customer pulls away.

a few days or weeks. The group tackled the problem and began by developing a flowchart of the process. They discovered that another functional department received the work orders first and that it took ten days for the paperwork to make its way to the repair/remodeling group. "Why so long?" they asked. The person responsible said she did exactly as instructed—wait ten days before handing the job over. The explanation was that several years earlier the repair/remodeling department had trouble getting the material needed for their jobs. This being the case, the paperwork processor was told to slow down the paperwork, so that when it arrived, the material needed would be on hand. Eventually the problems with material inventory and delivery had been reconciled, but no one had eliminated the ten-day waiting period. Since another functional group controlled the paperwork, no one in repair/remodeling had a broad enough view of the process to see what was going on. In this

case, the flowchart showed the team how to immediately knock ten days off their time.[6]

histogram
Graphical representation of the variation found in a set of data.

Histogram.   A **histogram** is a graphical representation of the variation found in a set of performance data. It can provide clues about the population's characteristics. The visual presentation reflects how the process's output varies and what proportion of output falls outside of the performance targets. The histogram in Exhibit 12–7 represents data on the length of time that it took a bank to process loan requests. Note how easy it is to see how the output of the process varies and what proportion falls outside of any specification limits.

Run Chart.   A process sometimes performs differently over a period of time. A **run chart** is a data presentation that shows the results of a process plotted over a period of time. It might be used to show the number of hotel checkouts per hour, the number of employee absentees per day, or the percentage of customers waiting in excess of one minute to be seated. Note in Exhibit 12–8 how the run chart points out specific patterns of behavior in the process. The percentage of patrons who have to wait falls into a definite pattern. A much larger percentage waits early in the week, with the percentage decreasing throughout the week.

run chart
Data presentation showing results of a process plotted over time.

Pareto charts
Problem-analysis charts that use a histogram to illustrate sources of problems.

Pareto Chart.   **Pareto charts** are problem-analysis charts that use a histogram to graphically illustrate the sources of problems. They typically list problem

Exhibit 12–7

Histogram Showing Frequency and Length of Time Taken by Home Office to Process Loan Request

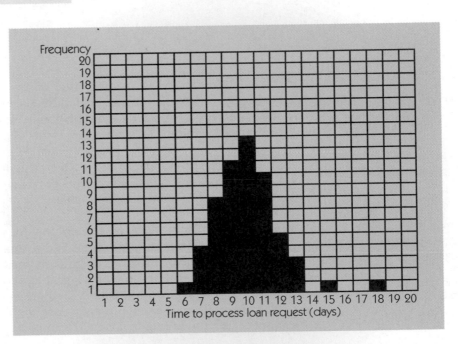

Exhibit 12–8

Run Chart of Percentage of Restaurant Customers Waiting in Excess of One Minute to Be Seated

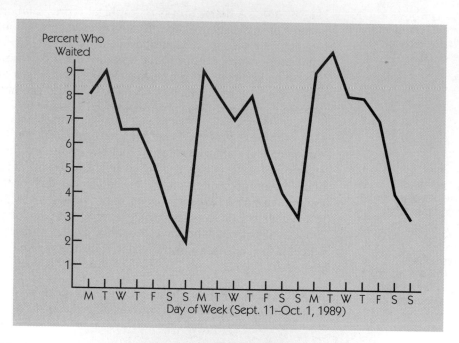

SOURCE: *From* Foundations of Total Quality Management: A Readings Book, 1st edition, *by J. G. Van Matre. Copyright © 1995. Reprinted with permission of South-Western College Publishing, a division of Thomson Learning. Fax 800-730-2215.*

causes from left to right in descending order of seriousness. Named after Vilfredo Pareto, the economist who originated the use of such analyses, the Pareto chart helps problem solvers zero in on the dominant rather than trivial problem. For example, Exhibit 12–9 shows the results of an extensive survey of customer complaints in a restaurant over an extended period of time. The chart serves as a consistent reminder to the problem-solving team that its time would be best used by focusing on the complaints of customers waiting for seats and dealing with a poorly organized buffet table.

Cause-and-Effect Diagram.   A very useful tool for understanding and identifying the causes of performance problems is the **cause-and-effect diagram.** This is also called a fishbone or Ishikawa diagram, named for the Japanese quality expert who popularized it. It represents a graphical display of a chain of causes and effects. The result, shown in Exhibit 12–10, resembles the skeletal system of a fish, with the horizontal line representing the problem being addressed and subsequent lines representing major causes and subcauses.

cause-and-effect diagram
A graphical display of a chain of causes and effects.

Control Chart.   The **control chart** is the "backbone" of statistical process control (SPC) and displays the "state of control" of a process. If a process is free from special cause variation, the process is said to be under control. An exam-

control chart
Displays the "state of control" of a process.

Exhibit 12–9

*Pareto Chart of
Customers'
Complaints About
Restaurants*

Code	Reason
A	Had to wait for seats
B	Buffet table not well organized
C	Table not clean
D	Room too drafty
E	Had to wait long time for coffee
F	Missing utensil at place setting
G	No dietetic sweetener provided
H	No ashtray on table

(June–September 1989)

SOURCE: *From* Foundations of Total Quality Management: A Readings Book, 1st *edition, by J. G. Van Matre. Copyright © 1995. Reprinted with permission of South-Western College Publishing, a division of Thomson Learning. Fax 800-730-2215.*

ple of a control chart is shown in Exhibit 12–11. In Exhibit 12–11, time is measured in terms of days on the horizontal axis; the value of a variable is on the vertical axis. The central horizontal line corresponds to the average value of the characteristic measured. In this case, as long as the values fall within 97 percent and 89 percent and no unusual pattern exists (such as succession of decreasing values), it is likely that no special cause variation is present and that the process is "under control."

The Supervisor's Role in Achieving Quality

Motivating workers to perform high-quality work consistently is one of the most difficult jobs a supervisor faces. Two ways to do this are to (1) let employees know you expect quality performance and (2) involve workers in achieving quality.

Let Employees Know You Expect Quality Performance. Many firms could be said to try to *inspect* quality into their products or services rather than *make it right* the first time. Fortunately, some companies and supervisors emphasize the right way from the start. They do this by stating their quality expectations for a job and including these expectations in their training of new personnel.

A large bank trains its new tellers not only in the technical aspects of the job, but also in how to interact with customers. In a number of trial runs, a "customer" walks up to the teller to complete a hypothetical transaction. The teller's actions are observed by a number of trainees and the trainer, and a critique is given of the way the customer was handled. Frequently, an experienced teller will demonstrate how the situation should have been handled. Included are such actions as smiling,

click! http://www.toyota
.com/times/manu/index
.html

Exhibit 12–10

Cause-and-Effect Diagram for "Why Tables Are Not Cleared Quickly"

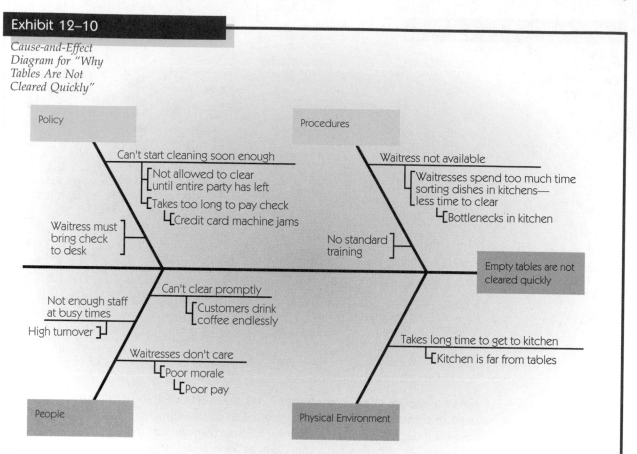

SOURCE: *From* Foundations of Total Quality Management: A Readings Book, 1st edition, *by J. G. Van Matre. Copyright © 1995. Reprinted with permission of South-Western College Publishing, a division of Thomson Learning. Fax 800-730-2215.*

looking directly at the customer, calling the customer by name, and efficiently handling the transaction. As a result, the bank's quality expectations are instilled in new tellers.

The best place to make an impact regarding your quality expectations is with the new employee. Yet many current employees may have spotty quality records. What can you do about this? We can tell you one thing not to do! Ignoring poor-quality performance results in the following:

1. The employee concerned gets the message that you do not expect any better or that mediocre quality is acceptable to you.

2. Other employees will also assume that mediocre performance is acceptable.

Assuming that workers know the quality standards, you must exercise supervisory control over quality. Sometimes a quality control specialist will help a line supervisor determine the quality of workers' performance by presenting run charts, histograms, or other statistical units. In many departments, however, the supervisor must play the only role.

Exhibit 12–11

Example of a Control Chart

Involve Workers in Achieving and Controlling Quality. As you learned in Chapters 2 and 10, many organizations have enlisted the efforts of operative-level employees to help improve quality. Let's look at an example:

Trident Precision Manufacturing, the Webster, New York, winner of the Malcolm Baldrige award for small businesses, is a good example of how employee involvement helps control quality and costs. Faced with a product defect rate of 3% in 1987, almost 10% of employee time was devoted to reworking nonconforming products. One manager stated the company's motto as "We make it nice because we make it twice." The company embarked on a quality approach that committed to employee involvement in the quality process. Employees in 1987 received a 25-hour training course in such skill areas as trigonometry, quality processes, interpersonal communication, and tools, such as run charts and Pareto diagrams. Employees were empowered to make quality decisions on their own, which included halting production for even the smallest flaws, or authority to spend up to $100 to fix each quality incident. The efforts have paid off handsomely—product defects have fallen since 1987 from 3% to 0.007%; employee time devoted to correcting quality problems has dropped from 10% to 1%. In 1997 the company's 179 employees, either as a part of problem-solving teams or as individuals, made over 2,200 process improvement suggestions, 98 percent of which were implemented. Recognition plays an important part in supporting quality; in 1997 over 1,700 items ranging from hockey tickets to dinners for two recognized employees' quality contribution. Today the company allots 5% of its payroll to employee training, compared to only 1% for

the typical firm. Employees obviously enjoy the new climate, as turnover dropped from 41% in 1987 to less than 4% in 1997.[7]

Quality teams have become an important part of the quality scene, as we pointed out earlier in Chapter 2. These may include special cross-functional teams, self-directed teams, or teams from within individual work groups. Problems (and opportunities) can be brought up by team members, team leaders, or higher management. Many companies allow these teams to call in staff experts for information or expertise as needed.

Ford Motor Company and the UAW have set up over 1,000 employee involvement groups (EIGs) in 68 plants across the country to carry out the theme "Quality Is Job 1."

Exhibit 12–12 presents the overall characteristics of effective employee involvement teams. The kinds of teams we have been discussing are implemented formally and require top management's approval and commitment. *Individual supervisors may, however, capture the spirit of employee involvement on their own.* The following comments, from the manager of a hotel convention center, show what can be achieved by encouraging employees to become involved:

The best quality ideas come from the people who are directly involved in the work. Frequently, poor quality is not caused by something they directly control. We noted that many clients would show up for a meeting and say the room arrangement was not what they had requested. This often required hurriedly rearranging a stage, tables, and chairs for as many as 700 people. The clients would get flustered, as did our people.

The problem was that our meeting coordinator would talk with the client, usually by phone, and take instructions as to how the meeting room needed to be set up. There was much room for interpretation as to just what the client wanted and last-minute changes would drive everyone nuts.

We presented this problem to a team of four of our workers who met, studied the process used by our meeting coordinator, and learned that she usually took instructions by phone. This left much room for interpreting what the client wanted. They also learned that often the person who called in to make the booking wasn't the one who had respon-

---

Exhibit 12–12

Characteristics of Effective Employee Involvement Teams

- Managers at all levels, especially at the top, should be committed to the concept and give it their unqualified support.
- Projects undertaken should relate directly—or at least indirectly—to participants' work.
- Projects should be team efforts, not individual activities.
- Participants should be trained in quality-control, decision making, and problem-solving techniques.
- Team leaders also should be trained in group dynamics and leadership of a group.
- Teams should be given feedback—in the form of results—regarding their recommendations and solutions.

sibility for the event, but was perhaps a secretary or assistant. This person's choice of room arrangement would then get overriden when the group arrived. Our team developed a form that graphically illustrates alternatives for arranging our rooms and audiovisual equipment we can provide. The client now selects the desired alternative, signs the form, and returns it to our coordinator. We now have something specific to go by, and our client is more committed to it. We'll still meet their last minute needs or make adjustments if needed. But we've only had two such major cases all year.

The lesson here is to seek out workers' advice on how to improve the quality of their work. Since they are so directly involved in the work, they frequently have excellent suggestions.

PROMOTING EMPLOYEE SAFETY

The final aspect of supervisory control that we will discuss in this chapter is employee safety. This subject has been in the business limelight since 1970, primarily as a result of the government's passage of the Occupational Safety and Health Act. But management has had an interest in employee safety for over a century because safety, efficiency, and productivity are closely related.

The results of poor safety are documented by the Bureau of Labor Statistics and the National Safety Council. Despite the fact that safety performance improved in the 1990s, in 1998 over 6,000 work fatalities occurred and 75 million workdays were lost.[8]

self-check

Do such organizations as banks, supermarkets, and department stores really need to be concerned about occupational safety and health?

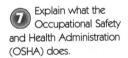

7 Explain what the Occupational Safety and Health Administration (OSHA) does.

OSHA
Created by the Occupational Safety and Health Act in 1970.

click! http://www.osha.gov

What OSHA Does

The **Occupational Safety and Health Administration (OSHA)** is a federal agency that was created by the Occupational Safety and Health Act in 1970 and went into operation in April 1971. Previously, different states had had different emphases on occupational health and safety. So the federal government stepped into the picture to ensure uniformity and enforcement. Basically, OSHA ensures that state governments, labor, and management provide consistently safer and healthier working conditions for employees.

OSHA requires organizations to keep safety logs and records of illnesses and injuries incurred on the job (see Exhibit 12–13). OSHA also has the right to develop standards, to conduct inspections to see that standards are met, and to enforce compliance by issuing citations and penalties against organizations that fail to comply. In addition, OSHA provides help by performing pre-investigations upon invitation from the organization.

Factors Influencing Safety

Several factors affect job safety. Among these are (1) the size of the organization, (2) the type of industry, and (3) the people.

Exhibit 12–13

*Record Keeping
Required by OSHA*

OSHA No. 101
Case or File No. _____

Form approved
OMB No. 44R 1453

Supplementary Record of Occupational Injuries and Illnesses

EMPLOYER

1. Name __Bradley Pulp & Paper Company__

2. Mail address __P.O. Box 1420__ __Sherman__ __Texas 75090__
   (No. and street) (City or town) (State)

3. Location, if different from mail address _____

INJURED OR ILL EMPLOYEE

4. Name __Herman__ __L.__ __Jackson__ Social Security No. __414-26-1000__
   (First name) (Middle name) (Last name)

5. Home address __707 Eighth Street__ __Sherman__ __Texas 75090__
   (No. and street) (City or town) (State)

6. Age __38__ 7. Sex: Male __✓__ Female _____ (Check one)

8. Occupation __Painter__
   (Enter regular job title, *not* the specific activity he was performing at time of injury.)

9. Department __Bleach Plant__
   (Enter name of department or division in which the injured person is regularly employed, even though he may have been temporarily working in another department at the time of injury.)

THE ACCIDENT OR EXPOSURE TO OCCUPATIONAL ILLNESS

10. Place of accident or exposure _____ __Sherman__ __Texas__
    (No. and street) (City or town) (State)
    If accident or exposure occurred on employer's premises, give address of plant or establishment in which it occurred. Do not indicate department or division within the plant or establishment. If accident occurred outside employer's premises at an identifiable address, give that address. If it occurred on a public highway or at any other place which cannot be identified by number and street, please provide place references locating the place of injury as accurately as possible.

11. Was place of accident or exposure on employer's premises? __Yes__ (Yes or No)

12. What was the employee doing when injured? __Employee had been cleaning pipes in preparation for__
    (Be specific. If he was using tools or equipment or handling material,
    painting. As he put his stepladder down, sodium hypochlorate dripped inside his face shield and went into his
    name them and tell what he was doing with them.)
    right eye.

13. How did the accident occur? __above__
    (Describe fully the events which resulted in the injury or occupational illness. Tell what
    happened and how it happened. Name any objects or substances involved and tell how they were involved. Give
    full details on all factors which led or contributed to the accident. Use separate sheet for additional space.)

OCCUPATIONAL INJURY OR OCCUPATIONAL ILLNESS

14. Describe the injury or illness in detail and indicate the part of body affected. _____
    chemical burn in right eye
    (e.g.: amputation of right index finger
    at second joint; fracture of ribs; lead poisoning; dermatitis of left hand, etc.)

15. Name the object or substance which directly injured the employee. (For example, the machine or thing he struck against or which struck him; the vapor or poison he inhaled or swallowed; the chemical or radiation which irritated his skin; or in cases of strains, hernias, etc., the thing he was lifting, pulling, etc.)
    sodium hypochlorate

16. Date of injury or initial diagnosis of occupational illness __July 16, 2000__
    (Date)

17. Did employee die? __No__ (Yes or No)

OTHER

18. Name and address of physician __Dr. Harry W. Myers__ __Sherman, Texas 75090__

19. If hospitalized, name and address of hospital _____

Date of report __July 16, 2000__ Prepared by __Joseph Dixon__
Official position __Supervisor__

Size of Organization. The safest places to work are the smallest and largest organizations. Companies with under 20 employees or over 1,000 employees have had better safety statistics than medium-sized organizations.

self-check

> What do you think accounts for the fact that large companies of, say, 10,000 employees have better safety performance than those with 100 employees?

In a small firm, the owner or manager is more personally involved with employees and tends to take on the role of safety officer. Very large firms have more resources available, such as safety departments, whose sole mission is to improve employee safety. Medium-sized firms have neither the direct personal involvement of the top manager nor the resources to create full-fledged safety departments. Often, the person assigned to oversee the safety function has additional job responsibilities. The safety focus may therefore be diluted by other important assignments.

Type of Industry. Some types of industry are safer than others. Exhibit 12–14 shows rates of occupational injury and illness for various industries. Note that the rates were highest for lumber and wood products, fabricated metal products, food processing, and air transportation. The more serious cases, involving numerous lost workdays, occurred in the air transportation industry.

People. The attitudes of managers and supervisors strongly influence the safety of work performance. Moreover, as shown in Chapter 13, employees themselves are important factors, as certain types of workers tend to have more accidents.

Despite increased safety emphasis, the fabricated metal products industry suffers from a high incidence of employee lost workdays due to job related injuries/illnesses.

Exhibit 12–14

Occupational Injury and Illness Rates per 100 Employees: Selected Industries, 1998

Industry	Total Cases	Lost Workdays
Mining	4.9	2.2
Food processing	13.6	2.9
Lumber and wood products	13.2	3.8
General building contractors	8.4	3.1
Fabricated metal products	13.9	3.4
Air transportation	14.5	7.4
Textile mill products	6.7	1.3
Chemicals and related products	4.9	1.0
Printing and publishing	5.4	1.7
Eating and drinking places	6.3	1.5
Hotels, lodging	7.3	2.0
General merchandise stores	9.0	2.6
Movie houses	3.5	0.6

SOURCE: *Bureau of Labor Statistics.*

Causes of Accidents

What causes on-the-job accidents? Basically, job-related accidents are caused by three types of factors: human, technical, and environmental. *Human factors* include carelessness, horseplay, fighting, use of drugs, poor understanding of equipment or processes, the thrill of taking risks, poor attitudes, and fatigue. Human factors account for most work-related injuries. *Technical factors* include unsafe mechanical, chemical, and physical conditions, such as those caused by defective tools and equipment, poor mechanical construction or design, or improper personal protective equipment (safety shoes, glasses, or mechanical guards or shields). *Environmental factors* are factors that surround the job, such as poor housekeeping, inadequate lighting and ventilation, or management pressure to increase output.

8 Describe the supervisor's role in promoting safety.

The Supervisor's Role in Promoting Safety

Good safety practices among employees help the supervisor in many ways. For one thing, on-the-job injuries can take up much of a supervisor's time as he or she may have to fill out accident reports, attend meetings to investigate the injury, and make recommendations (see Exhibit 12–15). Furthermore, safety is linked to productivity. The work group's productivity suffers when an injured employee is being treated or is recovering from an accident. Temporary or full-time replacements must be recruited, selected, and trained, and an inexperienced worker is unlikely to be as productive as the more experienced employee being replaced.

Because human factors are the major cause of work-related injuries, the supervisor, as top management's link with operating employees, plays a crucial role in employee safety. He or she is accountable for safety, just as for output or quality. Good safety control by the supervisor begins with a positive attitude.

"Safety is very important at the company and especially in my work unit," said Vera Edwards, a machine tender for Supreme Manufacturing.

Exhibit 12–15

Personal Injury Investigation

Injured:	Fred Hanna
Position:	Lab Assistant
Presiding:	L. C. Smithson, Technical Supt.
Date of meeting:	4/15/2000
Time of meeting:	2:34 p.m.
Place of meeting:	Plant Conference Room
Present:	L. C. Smithson (Technical Supt.), Fred Hanna (injured), Jim Berry (Housekeeping), Tom Ahens (Safety Director), Kim Jernigan (Supervisor)
Nature of injury:	Fractured distal end of radius, right arm
Lost time:	42 days (estimated)
Accident time and date:	4/13/2000 at 7:15 a.m.
Cause of injury:	Floor was wet—appeared to be water. Investigation revealed that bags of Seperan (a synthetic polymer) had been rearranged during the 11 p.m.–7 a.m. shift. One bag was torn, and its contents had trickled onto the floor, causing it to be exceptionally slippery when washed at the end of the shift. Janitor noticed but did not flag it or attempt to remove hazard, as he noted at the end of his shift.

Corrective steps/recommendations:

1. Apply grit to slippery areas; mark with appropriate warning signs.
2. Remind incoming shift personnel of hazardous conditions.
3. Communicate to incoming shift personnel any job priorities.
4. Store Seperan in a more remote area of the plant.

"When you drive into the parking lot, a large sign shows our company's safety record for the week and the year. Our supervisor is always talking safety, we have safety meetings monthly, and there are posters and signs throughout the work area. Our supervisor also makes us toe the line in following safety rules. He can really be tough on you when he catches you bending a rule such as not using your goggles or failing to put on your machine guard."

Exhibit 12–16 shows a number of steps that supervisors can take to improve safety performance in their departments. Even though supervisors play a critical role in controlling safety, they cannot do it alone. Top management must be committed to factors such as proper plant layout and design, safe machinery and equipment, and good physical working conditions. Note how recognition by management pays a major role in reinforcing safety for UPS:

At UPS drivers travel a million miles yearly with less than one avoidable accident! This performance is no coincidence; UPS strongly emphasizes driver safety. At five-year intervals, drivers with no avoidable accidents are feted with ceremonies at the local level. Drivers with a 25-year unblemished record are inducted into the company's Circle of Honor at a national celebration dinner where they receive a camel hair blazer and special plaque. Each year UPS publishes the names of its 2,700 plus Circle of Honor members in the *Wall Street Journal* and in *USA Today*.[9]

Exhibit 12–16

*What Supervisors Can
Do to Improve Safety*

- Push for upgraded safety equipment and safer work methods.
- Establish and communicate safety goals for the department.
- Clearly communicate safety requirements to all employees.
- Listen to employee job complaints about safety-related matters, including noise, fatigue, and working conditions.
- Make sure new employees thoroughly understand equipment and safety rules.
- Prohibit use of unsafe or damaged equipment.
- Encourage safety suggestions from your workers.
- Post safety bulletins, slogans, and posters to reinforce the need for safety.
- Refuse to let rush jobs cause relaxed safety standards.
- Set a proper example. Don't bend safety rules yourself.
- Conduct periodic safety meetings, with demonstrations by employee safety specialists or insurance representatives.
- Refuse to tolerate horseplay.
- Compete with other departments in safety contests.
- Report to employees any accidents that occur elsewhere in the company.
- Review past accident records for trends and insights.
- Encourage reporting of unsafe conditions.
- Make regular safety inspections of all major equipment.
- Enforce the rules when they are broken—take appropriate disciplinary action to demonstrate your safety commitment.
- Look for signs of fatigue in employees, such as massaging shoulders, rubbing eyes, and stretching or shifting position to relieve pain or fatigue. In such a case, relief for the employee may be warranted.
- Thoroughly investigate all accidents and attempt to remedy the causes.
- Develop a system for rewarding or acknowledging excellent safety conduct.

chapter review

1 **Explain the concept of productivity.**

This chapter examined three aspects of control that are important to supervisors. These are productivity, quality, and safety. Productivity is a measure of outputs compared to inputs. Company-wide, it refers to the total value of the units or services a company produced as compared to the total cost of producing them. Productivity can be increased by increasing output with the same input, decreasing input and maintaining the same output, or increasing output while decreasing input.

2 **Identify and explain the ways in which management, government, unions, and employees affect productivity.**

Four groups influence the productivity of U.S. firms. Management is considered by most experts to be the most influential group, since it controls spending for new or upgraded facilities and technology. Government also plays a role through its policies that require financial outlays by companies to meet federal laws for air and water pollution, energy, safety, and other regulatory requirements. Unions play a role in that, while management's job is to increase efficiency through new labor-saving technology and work methods, the role of unions is to protect the jobs of their members. Finally, employees play a role through their skill levels, motivation, and job commitment.

③ Describe some steps supervisors can take to increase productivity.

Actions that supervisors can take to increase productivity include upgrading workers' skills through training, improving worker motivation, using machinery and equipment better, improving quality, and preventing accidents.

Cost control is an important measure of a supervisor's productivity. One helpful device is a budget, which shows expected outcome for a given period expressed in numbers. Robotics, just-in-time inventory systems (JIT), and computer-assisted manufacturing (CAM) are three recent productivity enhancement measures.

④ Differentiate between TQM and quality control.

A second major area discussed in this chapter was quality. Total quality management or TQM is the entire system of policies, procedures, and guidelines an organization institutes so as to attain and maintain quality. Quality control, on the other hand, consists of after-the-fact measurements to see if quality standards are actually being met.

Quality control consists of actions taken during or after the fact to measure, analyze, and if necessary, correct quality problems. It is a much narrower concept than TQM, which is an organization-wide commitment to quality and includes such factors as top management commitment, employee training, relationships with customers and suppliers, continuous quality improvement, and employee involvement in the quality process.

⑤ Describe the role of variance in controlling quality.

An understanding of variance is important in controlling quality. Common cause variance is built into organizational processes and is considered normal. Common causes can normally only be corrected through management action to improve a process through such things as upgrading raw materials, using more sophisticated equipment, or additional training. On the other hand, special cause variance is nonroutine and entails identifying the problem, isolating it, examining the cause, and remedying it. It might involve an erratic piece of equipment, damaged raw materials, or an employee who is not performing properly.

⑥ Identify some important tools for controlling quality.

A number of tools are available to help in controlling quality. Often these tools are used by individuals who are part of special problem-solving or quality-improvement teams. These include such tools as flowcharts, histograms, run charts, Pareto charts, cause-and-effect diagrams, and control charts. These tools are applicable to a broad range of manufacturing and service-related situations.

⑦ Explain what the Occupational Safety and Health Administration (OSHA) does.

Employee safety has become important to organizations in recent years, especially since the passage of the Occupational Safety and Health Act in 1970. The

Occupational Safety and Health Administration, charged with enforcing compliance with the law, sets standards and regulations, requires organizations to maintain safety logs and records, conducts inspections, and has the authority to issue citations and penalties for violations found. Generally, the smallest and the largest organizations are the safest places to work. The nature of some industries makes them much more likely than others to have high injury incidence rates.

⑧ Describe the supervisor's role in promoting safety.

Supervisors play an important role in promoting safety. Because supervisors are the primary management link with operating employees, supervisory behavior greatly impacts employee safety performance. They do this in many ways, such as in setting departmental safety goals, assuring that employees understand safety requirements and procedures, conducting safety meetings, encouraging safety suggestions from employees, thoroughly investigating accidents, and enforcing rules when they are broken.

important terms

cause-and-effect diagram *342*
computer-assisted manufacturing (CAM) *337*
control chart *342*
flowchart *339*
histogram *341*
just-in-time (JIT) inventory control *337*

Occupational Safety and Health Administration (OSHA) *347*
Pareto charts *341*
productivity *328*
quality control *338*
robot *337*
run chart *341*

questions for review and discussion

1. Explain what has happened to productivity of U.S. firms in the 1990s.
2. Do you believe that management and unions must always be on opposite sides of the productivity issue? Why or why not?
3. Identify some of the steps that supervisors can take to improve their department's productivity.
4. How does quality control differ from total quality management? Explain.
5. Describe the role of variance in controlling quality.
6. Identify each of the following tools in controlling quality: Pareto chart, run chart, flowchart.
7. What does OSHA do?
8. Describe some ways in which supervisors impact safety performance.

skill builder 12–1

Quality Survey

Visit a local fast-food restaurant, such as McDonald's, Burger King, or Wendy's, and order a meal.

Instructions:

1. During your visit, perform a quality

analysis of the store, including but not limited to:

a. external store appearance, including shrubbery, cleanliness, and upkeep of outer building and parking lot

b. drive-thru, including ease, speed, and accuracy
c. cleanliness of inner store, including tables, floors, and restrooms
d. employee factors, including appearance, friendliness, and efficiency
e. service factors, including speed and accuracy
f. food quality, including taste, fresh-

ness, temperature, and portion size.

2. Assume that you were store manager and wanted to improve the areas that you found to be weak. Outline the corrective actions that you would take.

3. Meet with other student groups of five to six students to discuss your findings.

● skill builder 12–2

Increasing Safety Performance

Assume the role of a newly appointed store manager of a regional food chain superstore. All stores in the chain have been pressured to turn a profit in this highly competitive industry. And, while the former store manager achieved his profit goal, he fell far short in another: the store's safety performance. You are expected to do much better.

Last year the store accident rate was twice that of other stores in the chain: 16 reportable incidents per 100 employees, 9 of which involved lost workdays. These involved cuts, burns, slips, and falls. Many cuts occurred in the meat and deli areas; two burns occurred in the bakery area. One bagger sustained a fall in the parking lot while riding his empty grocery cart, a clear violation of policy. But the most serious fall resulted when a janitor left puddles of wax in an aisle and failed to put up warning cones when his work was interrupted to clean up a spill in another area. Another employee slipped on the wax and fell, injuring his left leg and

head. This injury resulted in nine months (and counting) of disability costs, nearly $200,000 of medical costs, and a reserve of about $150,000 for future rehabilitation payments. Analysis of the injuries showed that all of the accidents were caused by human error.

As new store manager, you are expected to immediately address the safety issue with your employees.

Instructions:

1. Outline a plan for bringing your employees' safety performance next year up to the average of other stores in the chain. You may assume your boss has approved a one-time $1,000 safety budget allocation to spend as needed to help you achieve this goal.

2. Meet with a group of other students to share your ideas. Your instructor may ask you to select a spokesperson to summarize the ideas of your team members.

Using Quality Tools

Welz Business Machines sells and services a variety of copiers, computers, and other office equipment. The company receives many calls daily for service, sales, accounting, and other departments. All calls are handled centrally by customer service representatives and routed to other individuals as appropriate. A number of customers had complained about long waits when calling for service. A market research study found that customers became irritated if the call was not answered within five rings. Scott Welz, the company president, authorized the customer service department manager, Tim Nagy, to study the problem and find a method to shorten the call-waiting time. Tim met with his service representatives, Robin Coder, Raul Venegas, LaMarr Jones, Mark Staley, and Nancy Shipe, who answered the calls, to attempt to determine the reasons for long waiting times. The following conversation ensued:

Nagy: This is a serious problem. How a customer phone inquiry is answered is the first impression the customer receives from us. As you know, this company was founded on efficient and friendly service to all our customers. It's obvious why customers have to wait: You're on the phone with another customer. Can you think of any reasons that might keep you on the phone for an unnecessarily long time?

Coder: I've noticed quite often that the person to whom I need to route the call is not present. It takes time to transfer the call and to see if it is answered. If the person is not there, I end up apologizing and transferring the call to another extension.

Nagy: You're right, Robin. Sales personnel often are out of the office on sales calls, away on trips to preview new products, or away from their desks for a variety of reasons. What else might cause this problem?

Venegas: I get irritated at customers who spend a great deal of time complaining about a problem that I cannot do anything about except refer to someone else. Of course, I listen and sympathize with them, but this eats up a lot of time.

Jones: Some customers call so often, they think we're long lost friends and strike up a personal conversation.

Nagy: That's not always a bad thing, you realize.

Jones: Sure, but it delays my answering other calls.

Shipe: It's not always the customer's fault. During lunch, we're not all available to answer the phone.

Venegas: Right after we open at 9 a.m., we get a rush of calls. I think that many of the delays are caused by these peak periods.

Coder: I've noticed the same thing between 4 and 5 p.m.

Nagy: I've had a few comments from department managers who received calls that didn't fall in their areas of responsibility and had to be transferred again.

Staley: But that doesn't cause delays at our end.

Shipe: That's right, Mark, but I just realized that sometimes I simply don't understand what the customer's problem really is. I spend a lot of time trying to get him or her to explain it better. Often, I have to route it to someone because other calls are waiting.

Venegas: Perhaps we need to have more knowledge of our products.

Nagy: Well, I think we've covered most of the major reasons why many customers have to wait. It seems to me that we have four major reasons: the phones are short-staffed, the receiving party is not present, the customer dominates the conversation, and you may not understand the customer's problem. Next, we need to collect some information about these possible causes. Raul, can you and Mark set up a data collection sheet that we can use to track some of these things?

The next day, Venegas and Staley produced a sheet that enabled the staff to record the data.

Over the next two weeks the staff collected data on the frequency of reasons why some callers had to wait. The results are summarized as follows:

Reason	Total Number
A Operators short-staffed	172
B Receiving party not present	73
C Customer dominates conversation	19
D Lack of operator understanding	61
E Other reasons	10

Instructions: Form a group of three to five students and based on the conversation between Nagy and his staff,

1. Draw a cause-and-effect diagram.
2. Perform a Pareto analysis of the data collected.
3. Develop some possible actions that the company might take to improve the situation.

SOURCE: *Adapted from "The Quest for Higher Quality: The Deming Prize and Quality Control," by RICOH of America, Inc., and presented in James W. Dean and James R. Evans* Total Quality *(Minneapolis/St. Paul: West Publishing Company, 1994), pp. 96–98.*

Skill Development

13   Coaching for Higher Performance

14   Meetings and Facilitation Skills

15   Facilitation Skills, Managing Conflict
and Stress

6 part

Coaching for Higher Performance

● **outline**

Introduction to Coaching
Coaching Is Performance Linked
Current Emphasis on Coaching
Why Supervisors Reject Coaching

The Coaching Functions
Tutoring
Mentoring
Confronting/Challenging
Counseling

Coaching and Understanding Diversity

The Skills of Coaching
Coaching: The Core Skills

**Coaching for Improved Performance:
Confronting and Challenging**

Coaching: The Counseling Function
Areas of Employee Counseling
Role of EAPs in Counseling

"My ultimate goal for every player is performance at the highest possible level."

Don Shula, Coauthor
Everyone's a Coach

Coaching in Action

Manager: Jeff, thanks for coming. I know you're getting ready for our one-week Supervisory Skills course at the Training Center next week. I see that you've read over the pretraining outline and materials. I always like to meet with participants before and after each course to discuss how I can help you put the skills into operation. Having looked over the outline and read the precourse materials, what would you most like to get from the course that would help you?

Jeff: Well, one thing I'd like to do better is to delegate tasks. Sometimes I'm too eager to do things myself. I guess it's just hard to let go.

Manager: Being pretty new to supervision, that's not unusual. It's especially a challenge to someone who is a strong technician, as you are.

Jeff: I must admit I could sometimes spend my whole day still interfacing with the departments working out their management information system problems. I'm afraid if you were to ask my technicians, they'd probably say I spend *too* much time still doing that, rather than delegating the challenging jobs to them. I guess it's my insecurity in supervision. . . .

Manager: So, you'd like the delegation session to help overcome some of this insecurity about your technicians. . . .

Jeff: Well, no, I wouldn't say it's so much insecurity about them, as it is about me. I guess I'm insecure about some of them; I mean they're younger and not as experienced. However, my key people are really talented professionals. Some of them know a lot more than I do about phases of our system. I've been supervising for only six months, and sometimes I feel as if I'm getting behind in my own technical expertise, which is to install and debug our systems. It's hard reconciling that. That's why I may assign a job, then follow up on it too closely. They probably see it as a lack of trust, when in fact, it's just my personal need to learn as much as I can to keep my own skills up.

Manager: Oh, I see what you're saying now. You feel as if you're losing some of your technical edge and miss doing the troubleshooting yourself. . . .

Jeff: Yeah, that's pretty much it. . . .

Manager: It seems as if that comes with your first management job. Technical expertise is a big plus, but it can also get in the way of your own employees' development.

Jeff: Yeah, so that's why in looking over the pre-course materials, being able to delegate better was one of the skill areas that jumped at me.

Manager: I think that's an excellent insight, Jeff. Our new culture is shifting to managers and supervisors becoming facilitators and developers and away from being the technical hub of expertise in their own departments. Our job now is to allow our people to run with the ball and help them do it. There's going to be a premium for supervisors and managers who can do this successfully. From what I know of the course, there's a strong emphasis on empowerment and delegation that will help you. Did any other areas particularly interest you? (The discussion continued for another 10–15 minutes.)

1 Explain what coaching is.

Introduction to Coaching

Did you ever play an organized sport, such as football, basketball, soccer, or volleyball? Or take individual lessons in piano, karate, or math? In each case you had a coach whose goal was to improve your performance. The essence of supervisory coaching—just as in those situations—is helping individuals become more effective performers. In the case that began this chapter, Jeff's manager is performing coaching—helping Jeff grow and learn new skills as a supervisor. The manager will also perform coaching during the follow-up meeting with Jeff after he returns from the course. That is the objective of this chapter: to help you learn more about coaching and the skills required to perform it effectively.

coaching
Supervisors helping individuals to reach their highest levels of performance.

You might think of **coaching** as the interpersonal process that supervisors and managers use to help individuals continually reach their highest levels of performance. It is a personal activity, a one-to-one relationship that starts when a new employee joins the team and continues throughout his or her tenure in the work unit. It may seem that new employees would be the primary focus of supervisory coaching. However, this is no longer true, given today's goals of *continuous* performance improvement. It is the job of supervisors to continually coach individuals to help them achieve increasingly higher levels of performance throughout their careers. As one well-known coaching expert puts it:

> **Coaching is the process by which managers stay in touch with subordinates. All the walking around in the world will not help managers to get the best from their employees unless they are walking around as coaches. Coaching is "eyeball to eyeball" management. Every conversation between managers and employees is potentially a coaching conversation. It is a chance to clarify goals, priorities, and standards of performance. It is a chance to reaffirm and reinforce the group's core values. It is a chance to hear ideas and involve employees in the processes of planning and problem solving.[1]**

Coaching Is Performance Linked

The focus of coaching conversations is employee performance. The underlying assumption is that through effective coaching, the supervisor can help an employee become an increasingly effective performer, as shown in Exhibit 13–1. If a topic has a present or future impact on an employee's performance, then it should be considered suitable for a coaching situation. Some situations are more obviously performance linked, such as helping an employee learn a new skill or addressing a problem of substandard work. Others are less directly performance related, such as helping an employee to prepare for advancement or to better understand and overcome insecurities. Notice the wide-reaching range

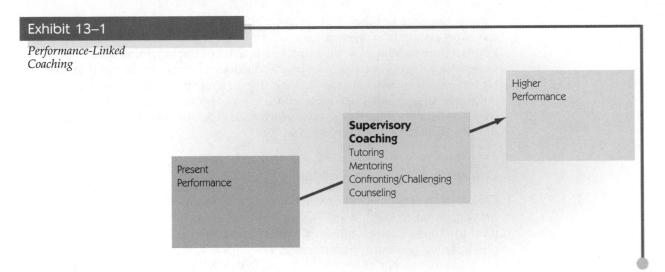

Exhibit 13–1

Performance-Linked Coaching

Present Performance → **Supervisory Coaching** Tutoring, Mentoring, Confronting/Challenging, Counseling → Higher Performance

of coaching situations shown in Exhibit 13–2 and how each is in some way performance linked. Quite a broad list, isn't it?

In the 1940s, a number of large organizations experimented by employing professionals to serve as organization-wide counselors. Their job was not to give advice, but essentially to become the organization's primary vehicle to listen to employees' job-related, personal, and emotional problems. Granted, it helped employees to vent their feelings about job frustrations and conflicts as well as personal problems, but the success of these programs was limited. Today, while a number of large organizations employ full-time counselors, it is the individual supervisor who is considered the "first line" of counseling. They are seen by employees as best able to help someone adjust to working conditions, work load and assignments, and employee–supervisor relationships. A team member's problems often affect his or her work performance (as well as

Exhibit 13–2

Examples of Coaching Situations

- Assigning a new challenging task; reviewing results.
- Determining with an employee his/her training needs.
- Showing an employee how to perform a task.
- Discussing a plan for employee career advancement.
- Listening to an employee's fears of job cutbacks.
- Providing an employee insight into company politics.
- Helping an employee adapt psychologically to job changes.
- Discussing poor employee performance.
- Helping an employee manage stress.
- Discussing how a long-term, excellent employee can reach an even higher performance level.
- Conducting a disciplinary interview.
- Discussing a problem of poor work or failure to follow organization rules/policy.
- Conducting a performance appraisal.
- Allowing an employee to "blow off" some emotional "steam."

the performance of others), attendance, and relationships on the job. Therefore, the supervisor has an immediate concern in these matters and assumes the legitimate role to address such employee problems. Supervisors cannot resolve personal problems such as poor health, substance abuse, or financial matters. However, the supervisor must at least understand the problem and urge the employee to seek adequate help if such a problem has the potential to negatively impact an employee's job performance. The supervisor's role in these situations is discussed later in the chapter.

Current Emphasis on Coaching

Coaching has only recently received recognition as a key supervisory activity. It first appeared in the mid-1970s, gained momentum in the 1980s, and is widely used in organizations today. In Chapter 2 you learned how the supervisor's role has changed from the autocratic, no-nonsense, technically proficient supervisor to a developer of people and a facilitator whose job is to help team members maximize their potential.

Because organizations and work units have become more culturally diverse, managers and supervisors must understand their people as individuals, taking into consideration their needs, competencies, goals, attitudes, insecurities, and concerns. Understanding individuals allows a supervisor to target his or her coaching efforts. In turn, coaching becomes an important vehicle for the supervisor to further his own understanding of his employees. Organizations also recognize that coaching efforts should be tailored to the individual being coached. Coaching directed toward the younger, more insecure employee, who must learn many job essentials, differs dramatically from coaching directed toward the senior employee, who values advancement to the next level.

Why Supervisors Reject Coaching

Coaching appears to be a natural activity; however, in actual practice there is a tendency for supervisors to neglect their coaching role. First, many lack confidence. They may feel uncomfortable counseling employees and embarrassed to discuss problems of substandard performance. There is always the risk that confronting a performance problem with an employee will create more problems than it resolves. The supervisor may have to deal with an employee's excuses, anger, or hurt feelings; the quality of a good relationship may be jeopardized. Ignoring a performance problem in the hope that it will resolve itself is often seen as a more desirable alternative.

Second, many supervisors see coaching as a passive process. They are more inclined through experience, and perhaps the expectation of their own managers, to have ready answers for everyone's problems and to deal with performance matters expeditiously. As one supervisor related in one of our coaching seminars:

> **All this listening makes coaching seem like a weak, "touchy-feely" approach that's too soft on people. When somebody's not doing his job, you get on his case and he'd better shape up. There's no way I can see myself sitting around saying "Oh, really." My own boss would think I've lost it. I've always been direct with people—you tell them exactly what they're to do, see that they do it, and get on them when they don't.**

We are all products of our past. Our parents told us what to do when we were young, as did our teachers. For those of us with military service experience, platoon leaders took over the telling. Then, when we went to work, our bosses told us what to do. When we become supervisors, it is only natural that we tend to become "tellers," which is an active, expeditious way to handle things.

However, as pointed out throughout this text, today's supervisory environment has changed considerably. The supportive relationship required for effective coaching does indeed involve more open, two-way communication and greater emphasis on the supervisor's listening skills. However, as you will see throughout this chapter, coaching behavior always distinctly addresses continually improving performance.

Third, coaching takes considerable time. Faced by many pressures, supervisors are not prepared to abandon their heroic firefighting pace. Many are so immersed into managing "details" that they cannot effectively employ coaching on the personal, one-to-one level that is required.

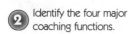 Identify the four major coaching functions.

THE COACHING FUNCTIONS

There are different ways to understand effective coaching. One is to examine *why* someone conducts a coaching session, that is, the *function* that coaching intends to serve. Another is to examine what *skills* a coach uses during a coaching session. We will examine the functions first, then the skills. Coaching serves four fundamental functions: (1) tutoring, (2) mentoring, (3) confronting/challenging, and (4) counseling.[2]

Tutoring

tutoring
Helps a team member gain knowledge, skill, and competency.

Tutoring involves a large range of coaching situations that help a team member gain knowledge, skill, and competency. Tutoring encourages team members to learn, grow, and develop. The goal is to avoid complacency with present skill levels and to develop a commitment to continuous learning. It also encourages members to put into practice those skills that are learned.

self-check

Note in the chapter preview that tutoring was the primary function being performed. The manager supported Jeff's attendance at the training course and drew out the major needs that Jeff hoped the course would address. The coach also established a follow-up meeting to review the course and discuss Jeff's plans for implementing the skills learned.

Mentoring

mentoring
Helps develop careers in others.

Mentoring is the coaching activity that helps develop careers in others. Mentoring may teach political savvy, understanding of the organization's culture, and the ways to advance one's career. It may also mean:

1. Helping an employee see the potentially negative impact of behavior he or she is considering.

 click! http://www.mentoring.org/

An important coaching function, "tutoring" refers to the guidance offered by a supervisor in helping employees master the skills necessary to perform their jobs.

2. Understanding how to approach and gain influence with powerful organization members.

3. Learning who key players are in given circumstances.

4. Understanding how relevant past or current events should impact the team member's actions and behavior.

Successful supervisory coaches help their team members to make key organizational contacts and to develop their own networks. They aid in giving good career guidance, and they keep a watchful eye out for effective development of their team members' careers.

It is estimated that supervisors perform formal mentoring in about 75 percent of the companies listed as *Computerworld's* "Top 100 Best Places to Work." At companies such as Harrah's Entertainment, Lincoln Electric, and Avon Cosmetics, employees receive heavy doses of training to keep them challenged, satisfied, and employed. Mentoring comes into play by being more personal, practical, and job specific than is training. It shows people shortcuts to using the skills learned in formal training. Or, as one manager puts it, mentoring shows people where the rocks and land mines are—how to avoid the mines and step on the rocks in moving toward career goals.[3]

confronting/ challenging
Establishes clear performance standards, compares actual performance against them, and addresses performance that doesn't meet those standards.

self-check

In what way was mentoring involved in the chapter preview?

Confronting/Challenging

The **confronting/challenging** coaching function is most directly performance related. Supervisory coaches establish clear performance standards, compare actual team member performance against those standards, and address performance that does not meet those standards. Through confronting/challenging, successful coaches help less-than-successful performers become successful and challenge successful ones to reach even higher levels.

Often supervisors, though they may be good, sensitive listeners and effective tutors and mentors, experience difficulty in confronting and challenging team members in the area of performance. They may find it uncomfortable to establish clear, concrete performance standards and to talk about performance directly. They may not be willing to address performance problems when a team member's behavior falls below standard. Confronting/challenging sessions, when finally held, may be superficial, apologetic, and may skirt the poor performance problem. We will discuss confronting/challenging in greater detail later in the chapter.

click! http://www.omnimgmt
.com/

Counseling

counseling
Supervisors helping an individual recognize, talk about, and solve either real or perceived problems that affect performance.

Counseling is the coaching function whereby the supervisor helps an individual recognize, talk about, gain insight into, and solve either real or perceived problems that affect performance. The manager's role is essentially to help the individual determine his or her own course of action. Many supervisors feel inept and poorly trained to deal with employees' personal problems. Perhaps the most common mistake is the tendency to give advice rather than to help the employee think through, understand, and develop alternatives to solving problems.

In conducting counseling, it is especially important to show sensitivity and to help a team member understand how personal problems impact, or potentially impact, job performance. It is also important to help a team member gain confidence in his/her ability to handle problems. In serious cases—such as drug abuse, financial problems, or health issues—this would mean recommending that the individual seek help through the company's employee assistance program or an outside professional.

You can gain more insight into the four coaching functions by examining the different outcomes associated with each function, as shown in Exhibit 13–3.

self-check

Re-examine Exhibit 13–1. Which functions—tutoring, mentoring, confronting/challenging, and counseling—are reflected by some of the coaching situations described?

All four functions have much in common and are often combined in a single coaching session. For example, when a new employee is struggling to perform, a single coaching session may involve confronting/challenging, counseling, and tutoring. Many of the skills and processes involved in all four functions are similar—the need for sensitivity, listening, and movement toward some form of closure.

COACHING AND UNDERSTANDING DIVERSITY

Throughout this book we have emphasized that today's organizations reflect considerably more employee diversity than in past years. And perhaps in no

Exhibit 13–3

*Outcomes of the Four
Coaching Functions*

click! http://www
.workteamcoaching
.com/books.htm

Tutoring

1. Increased technical know-how
2. Increased understanding of processes and systems
3. Increased pace of learning
4. Movement to expert status
5. Commitment to continual learning

Mentoring

1. Developing political understanding/savvy
2. Sensitivity to the organization's culture
3. Expanded personal networks
4. Increased sensitivity to key players' likes/dislikes
5. Greater proaction in managing own career

Confronting/Challenging

1. Clarification of performance expectations
2. Identification of performance shortcomings
3. Acceptance of more-difficult tasks
4. Strategies to improve future performance
5. Commitment to continual performance improvement

Counseling

1. Accurate descriptions of problems and their causes
2. Technical and organizational insight
3. Ventilation of strong feelings
4. Commitment to self-sufficiency
5. Deeper personal insight about own feelings and behavior
6. Changes in point of view

SOURCE: *Adapted from Dennis C. Kinlaw,* Coaching for Commitment *(San Diego, CA: Pfeiffer & Company, 1993), pp. 22–23.*

other supervisory activity is recognition of individual differences as important to success as is coaching. Because coaching requires a highly personal, one-to-one relationship, the supervisor's ability to relate to and understand an employee's needs, sensitivities, and uniqueness and to reflect these concerns in his or her interactions is crucial to successful coaching.

Sharon Olds, who we met in the Chapter 1 and 8 preview cases, marketing supervisor at AutoFin, supervises sixteen associates. Her department reflects a wide diversity of employees found in organizations today. There are eleven males, five females; ten Caucasians, four African Americans, one Asian, and one Hispanic. Their ages range from 23 to 59; three are single, never married; four are single and divorced or widowed. Half are college graduates, four never attended college, and four have completed some college or are presently attending college part time. Ten different religions are represented, not to mention the differences in individual values, needs, interpersonal styles, and cultures. "I always thought that a correct saying was that you treat people the same way that you would like to be treated, or you treat people the same. I've learned that that's not true. Some people are so different. I have to be consistent and fair, but a key to being a good supervisor is being able to relate differently to the individual needs of your people."

③ Describe some of the important skills used in coaching.

THE SKILLS OF COACHING

When a supervisor initiates a formal coaching session, he or she should have an objective to achieve and establish a basic framework for the session, adapted to the coaching function and the circumstances. However, the coaching process largely involves a number of spontaneous interactions that occur in a relaxed, personal setting. Many coaching interactions are initiated by the team member rather than the supervisor, and these may include requests for help, advice, or informal discussion of a work-related matter. In some cases, such as those of a personal nature, work may not be directly involved.

The supervisor must create a supportive atmosphere that encourages contact. He or she must maintain a climate that makes people feel welcome, respects their views and feelings, and shows patience when communicating with them. A supportive climate exists when a supervisor understands what team members want to accomplish and when members are encouraged to try new approaches without fear of reprisal. Effective listening is a critical coaching skill. It is difficult for many individuals to approach their supervisor for advice or to acknowledge job-related or personal problems that affect their job. Supervisors must establish an open, receptive communication climate.

Coaching: The Core Skills

The core coaching skills are discussed in the following sections. No single coaching session will necessarily involve all, or even most, of these. As you read through these skills, note the importance of an atmosphere of respect and understanding and a clear need for an outcome of the coaching effort.

acknowledging
Showing by nonevaluative verbal responses that you have listened to what the employee has stated.

Acknowledging. **Acknowledging** is showing through a range of nonevaluative verbal responses that you have listened to what the employee has stated. These comments may range from brief "uh huhs," "ohs," "hmmmms," or "I sees," to longer phrases like "I can understand that" or "So that's how it happened." The acknowledging skill is designed to bounce the communication ball back to the employee and allow him or her to further develop the information.

attending
Showing through nonverbal behavior that you are listening in an open, nonjudgmental manner.

Attending. **Attending** is showing through nonverbal behavior that you are listening in an open, nonjudgmental manner. In attending, your body language, such as alert posture, head nods, eye contact, and facial expressions, conveys full interest and attention. Nonattending behavior would include blank stares, nodding off, being distracted, glancing at your watch, or exhibiting other body language that displays uneasiness or disagreement with the topic being discussed. Effective attending behavior clearly communicates "I am interested and I am listening."

affirming
Communicating to an employee his or her value, strengths, and contributions.

Affirming. **Affirming** is communicating to an employee his or her value, strengths, and contributions or other positive factors. An example might be "You have made excellent progress learning the new system." Or "It always amazes me how quickly you catch on." Or "I've always valued your willingness to share your feelings with me about things. It's good knowing you'll level with me about the proposed changes."

confirming
Making sure an employee understands what has been said or agreed upon.

Confirming. **Confirming** is making sure that an employee understands what has been said or agreed upon. The coach can do this by summarizing and repeating the key points or by requesting the person being coached to do so. The coach might ask, "How about going over these steps in your own words and telling me how you would proceed?" Confirming may also occur with an eye to the future: "How about modifying your estimates as we've discussed, using the highest quality materials available, and let's take a look at this at 3 p.m. tomorrow."

pinpointing
Providing specific, tangible information about performance to an employee.

probing
Asking questions to obtain additional information.

reflecting
Stating your interpretation of what the employee has said.

resourcing
Providing information, assistance, and advice to employees.

reviewing
Reinforcing key points at the end of a coaching session to ensure common understanding.

summarizing
Pausing in the coaching conversation to summarize key points.

Pinpointing. **Pinpointing** is providing specific, tangible information. For instance, "You did a poor job on the write-up," is a vague general statement that covers wide territory. It is not as helpful as "The write-up used figures that were three years old, contained over 20 spelling and typographical errors, and lacked a specific recommendation."

Probing. **Probing** is asking questions to obtain additional information or exploring a topic at greater length, such as the following: "So you feel your group is ready to take on more responsibility. In what ways have they signaled this?" Or "So you would do it differently next time, given what you now know. Just what would you do differently?"

Reflecting. **Reflecting** is stating in your own words your interpretation of what the employee has said or feels, such as "So you feel that you should have received more help from your teammates on this?" or "It seems like you're really upset with them for not helping out."

Resourcing. Coaches should act as resources for their team members. **Resourcing** can be done by providing information, assistance, and advice: "I really wouldn't recommend by-passing Mason on this. It cost someone his job about five years ago when he did it." or "Talk to the human resources people. They should be able to answer your question." or "Let me show you how to do that."

Reviewing. At the end of a coaching session, reinforcing key points to ensure common understanding is the skill of **reviewing.** This can be done by the coach or coachee. "Let's pull this together. It seems we've identified three things you'll do with the survey data. First, you'll send your supervisors their individual results and the overall company results. Then you'll conduct one-on-one meetings with them to discuss their results. Following this, they'll develop a written plan, accepted by you as to what they'll do to improve." or "Let's make sure we're together on this. How about summarizing what you'll do with the survey results?"

Summarizing. **Summarizing** is pausing in the coaching conversation to summarize key points. "Let's see if I understand you. You believe three factors have hurt your sales performance: (1) our promotion strategy was changed, (2) extra committee work has taken a lot of time away from your sales group, and (3) your top sales rep has been out two weeks because of surgery."

Note that some skills, such as acknowledging and attending, relate to the atmosphere or environment of the coaching session—its openness and the fact that the coach is interested and is listening. Other skills such as pinpointing, probing, and resourcing are more directly tied to the *content* of the session, the issue(s) involved.

COACHING FOR IMPROVED PERFORMANCE: CONFRONTING AND CHALLENGING

One of the things supervisors must do, but often do poorly, is address problems in performance. Many managers do it in a blunt, threatening way that may cause resentment. Too often, they blame, lecture, put down, warn or coerce a

Exhibit 13–4

Suggestions for Confronting Poor Performance

1. Describe the performance situation in specific detail.
2. Seek and listen to the team member's point of view.
3. Get agreement on the problem.
4. Try to get the employee's involvement in determining a solution.
5. Agree on a plan of action to improve performance.
6. Summarize the agreement and reinforce the changed behavior.
7. Plan for follow-up, if needed.

person in attempting to make that person improve. Often, the result is no change, a half-hearted change, or resentment at having been called "on the carpet." Other supervisors avoid confronting a poor performer only to find that the poor performance escalates, making the inevitable coaching meeting involve more serious stakes than if it had occurred earlier. As indicated, this is a confronting/challenging function of coaching. The poor performance can relate not only to actual on-the-job work performance, but to other types of behavior as well, such as attendance, safety, attitude, and adherence to various company rules and policies.

While individual situations may differ, the suggestions for dealing with substandard performance contained in Exhibit 13–4 are often effective.

 Differentiate between general vs. pinpointed coaching statements.

It is essential that the issue of poor performance be addressed by the supervisor early in the meeting. The supervisor's comments should pinpoint the issues specifically. Instead of telling an employee, "Your job performance is poor," it'd be more informative to say "You reached only 75 percent of your work goal" or "You have been absent three times in the past two weeks." In this way, the employee is given something concrete. Exhibit 13–5 shows how general comments can be turned into more pinpointed ones.

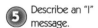 Describe an "I" message.

Tom Gordon, a well-known writer on leadership and interpersonal issues, advocates the use of what he calls "I" messages when we want to effectively alter someone's behavior.[4] He says there are three major parts of an **"I" message:**

Exhibit 13–5

General vs. Pinpointed Statement in Confronting/ Challenging Performance-Related Behavior

General	**Pinpointed**
1. Your attendance is poor.	1. You have missed a day in each of the past four pay periods.
2. You need to cooperate better with department heads.	2. Company policy is to give department heads the cost information when they request it.
3. You need to follow our safety rules.	3. This morning I saw you performing the job without wearing your safety goggles.
4. You haven't made the progress that you'd agreed on.	4. You and I agreed that you would complete the first draft by today, but you tell me you need two more days.

"I" message
An appeal, rather than a demand, that the other person change.

- *Feelings:* Indicate how you feel about the effects of the behavior (angry, embarrassed, frustrated, concerned, etc.).
- *Behavior:* Identify the specific behavior (absenteeism, not keeping appointments, not meeting quota, etc.).
- *Effect:* Spell out the end result of the behavior (poor example for others, making the work unit look unproductive, inconvenience to others in the unit, etc.).

When you send an "I" message, you make an appeal rather than a demand that the other person change. Note in the following examples that the focus is the *behavior,* its *effect,* and how it makes *you feel.* While no one likes being told their behavior is causing a problem, framing your displeasure in an "I" message addresses the problem more openly and tactfully and is more likely to pave the way toward a resolution in an objective, supportive manner.

"You" Message	**"I" Message**
You neglected to proofread that report. You should know better than to let a report go out like that.	When I noticed the many typos in the report, I was really upset. It makes our unit look careless and unprofessional.
You know I expect you to attend our regular meetings. You need to attend them from now on.	When you don't attend our regular meetings, I'm concerned that we miss your expertise and insight.

In using the "I" message, it is important to keep in mind the coaching skills from the previous section. The supervisor's goal is to correct the inadequate performance in a way that shields the employee's ego *and* maintains a positive relationship between supervisor and employee. Thus, the session should focus on the employee's *performance* rather than personality—in other words, the problem and not the person. Use of "I" messages can be an important tool in focusing on the employee's behavior rather than on the employee's ego.

COACHING: THE COUNSELING FUNCTION

6 Explain the extent to which a supervisor should counsel an employee about personal problems.

Counseling, one of the four coaching functions, involves a broad range of emotional areas, ranging from an employee's frustrations, insecurities, anger, and resentment to lack of commitment. The problem can be attributed to real or perceived factors and can be work related or personal. Basically, the objective of counseling is to help an employee better understand himself or herself and, when needed, to develop a plan of action to resolve the issue. The coach's job is to help the individual more fully discuss and understand the problem being experienced. Feelings, emotions, and attitudes may be exchanged. As shown in Exhibit 13–6, counseling attempts to identify and help both supervisor and team member better understand those "below-the-surface" factors that are influencing or may potentially influence the team member's performance. In counseling, the listening-related skills of attending, acknowledging, reflecting, and probing are especially essential.

A coach often has no advance notice as to when counseling is needed; these coaching opportunities are usually initiated by the team member. On other occasions, a team leader will plan to perform one of the other coaching functions, for instance, tutoring or confronting/challenging, when the need for counseling

Exhibit 13–6

Iceberg Model of Counseling

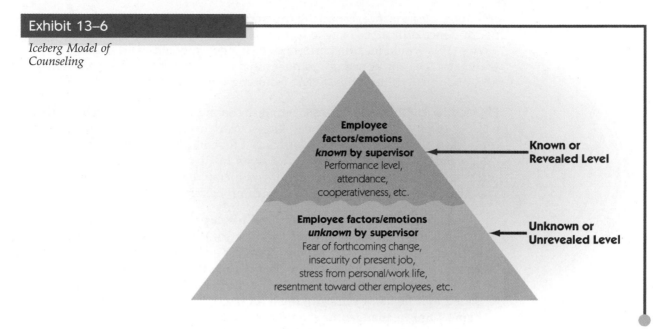

Employee factors/emotions *known* by supervisor
Performance level, attendance, cooperativeness, etc.

→ **Known or Revealed Level**

Employee factors/emotions *unknown* by supervisor
Fear of forthcoming change, insecurity of present job, stress from personal/work life, resentment toward other employees, etc.

→ **Unknown or Unrevealed Level**

arises. The leader must be sufficiently flexible to shift gears and address counseling, as pointed out below.

> **What started as a routine tutoring session for supervisor Rosa Bender turned out quite differently when she learned that Rudy Colquitt, a new technician, felt ignored by senior people in the department. Bender temporarily dropped her tutoring agenda and devoted about ten minutes to reflecting and probing why Colquitt, the youngest and newest member of the team, felt this way. Learning that he felt slighted because senior employees offered him little help, Bender helped him understand that senior employees, while likely supportive, were independent performers who thoroughly immersed themselves in their own work. Although perhaps they hadn't offered help, they would gladly help if asked. Colquitt agreed to ask senior employees for help when he needed it and to communicate to Bender his degree of success. Satisfied that this addressed the immediate counseling issue, Bender then shifted back to the tutoring session she had originally planned.**

Areas of Employee Counseling

Counseling is involved in virtually all aspects of the supervisor–employee relationship. It begins with the hiring phase and does not end until the employee leaves the company. Certain areas, though, are more likely to necessitate counseling than others.

Job Performance. We have already indicated that counseling is often used in combination with the other four coaching functions. It is especially important in the area of job performance. Numerous factors, many of which the supervisor is unaware, influence employees' job performance. A good rule of thumb is to always be prepared to engage in counseling when addressing below-standard employee performance, especially for employees who have in the past had no performance difficulties or who have only recently engaged in negative job behavior. This would include performance changes in quality and quantity of work, absenteeism, adherence to policy and rules, and changes in cooperativeness and relationships with others, including the supervisor.

Physical and Emotional Illness. Another common need for counseling arises because of physical and emotional illness. In some cases these are initially addressed by the supervisor as performance problems, but in many cases they may be initiated by the employee. Although the team leader must play a supportive, listening role in counseling, it is imperative that the employee clearly see the impact or potential impact of such problems upon performance.

> **When Avery Williard showed up late, his supervisor coincidentally happened to be present at Williard's work area. While Williard appeared quite uncomfortable and embarrassed, his supervisor expressed surprise because Williard was never late. It was then that the supervisor smelled alcohol. He asked Williard to join him in his office. Williard acknowledged that he had been drinking a lot lately because of "problems at home," but he pledged he would not do it again. His supervisor listened patiently, noting that Williard didn't volunteer particulars. He praised Williard for his excellent work and dependability over the years but reminded him that should it happen again, he would have no choice but to formally discipline him. Seeing that Williard was in no condition to work, he sent him home after setting a meeting for the next day. This meeting was to reinforce (1) his support for Williard and (2) the fact that Williard's behavior could not be tolerated again on the job. He also planned to strongly suggest that Williard consider referral to the company EAP (Employee Assistance Program) as a source of help.**

As in the situation above, supervisors are increasingly called on to counsel employees with many forms of physical and emotional problems. These problems range from substance abuse (see Exhibit 13–7) and job stress to debilitating physical illnesses such as cancer, heart disease, and AIDS. Moreover, the rash of corporate downsizings and mergers has created unparalleled emotional anxiety, as reflected by present and former employees who commit acts of physical violence against employers.

Personal Problems. To what extent should a supervisor counsel an employee with personal problems such as financial difficulties, health, or marital problems? The answer depends largely on the extent to which the problem impacts present or future job performance. If it affects job performance, it is essential that the supervisor use counseling to understand the nature of the problem, if for nothing more than to help the employee appreciate the need for professional assistance. However, a supervisor should tread carefully before becoming entwined in personal problems for several reasons:

1. Employees may feel resentful or embarrassed after "opening up" and disclosing highly personal matters. This may jeopardize their future job relationship with their supervisor.
2. If the supervisor makes too concerted an effort to probe into more than an employee cares to divulge, it will be resented.

Exhibit 13–7

Profile of the Typical Controlled-Substance Abuser

- Age 18 to 25, although cocaine use in particular is spreading to older age groups.
- Late to work three times more often than other employees.
- Requests early dismissal or time off during work 2.2 times more often.
- Has 2.5 times as many absences of eight days or more.
- Uses three times the normal level of sick benefits.
- Is five times more likely to file a workers' compensation claim.
- Is involved in accidents 3.6 times more often than other employees.
- Inconsistent work quality and lowered productivity.
- Increased mistakes, carelessness, errors in judgment.
- Mood swings, overreaction to criticism.
- Deliberate avoidance of coworkers and supervisors.
- Deteriorating personal appearance and ability to get along with others.
- Signs of poor morale and reduced productivity among coworkers, often because of time spent covering for the abuser.
- Needless risks taken in order to raise production following periods of low achievement.
- Careless handling and maintenance of machinery and equipment.
- Disregard for coworkers' safety.
- Increasing complaints about problems in the home and with family.
- Frequently recurring financial problems.

SOURCE: *Jerry Shriver, "Employers Are Helping Addicted Workers," USA TODAY, January 12, 1984, p. 5D. Copyright 1984, USA TODAY. Reprinted with permission.*

3. If the supervisor gives advice on personal problems—such as divorce, problems with children, or buying and selling property—and the results turn out unsatisfactorily, the supervisor will be blamed. Also, the supervisor and/or the company may be open to legal damages.

In general, counseling should be restricted to factors that affect job performance. Supervisors work hard to develop trusting, supportive relationships and are often placed in a position of counseling team members in problem areas only peripherally related to job performance. To reject the counseling opportunity outright may be perceived as lack of interest. The supervisor can always listen sufficiently to determine the nature of the employee's problem and then steer the individual toward a professional or other source of help.

Role of EAPs in Counseling

Employee Assistance Programs (EAP) Professional counseling and medical services for employees with unresolved personal or work-related problems.

From a handful of programs begun in the 1940s to address alcoholism, **Employee Assistance Programs (EAP)** have emerged to extend professional counseling and medical services to employees confronted by unresolved personal or work-related problems.[5] One survey of large- and medium-sized companies shows that over 70 percent have EAPs in place. Exhibit 13–8 gives you a good idea of what an EAP offers.

Where present, the EAP can be a big help to supervisors by handling referred cases at a professional level. EAPs can also help employees address their problems, many of which may have the potential to spill into the context of their work.

click! http://www.centerpoint .org/EAP.html

Exhibit 13–8

Example of an
Employee Assistance
Program (EAP)

Most of the time we like to think we are in control of our lives. All of us, however, occasionally experience personal crises that may cause us to feel out of control. These crises may be due to health problems, financial or legal difficulties, or emotional problems. Because we care about our employees, an Employee Assistance Program (EAP) has been implemented. The EAP will provide confidential, professional counseling and referral to employees who seek assistance with personal problems. Realizing that an employee may be affected by a family member's personal problem, the EAP is also available to the families of our employees.

What the EAP is:

- *Voluntary:* Employees or family members can contact the program directly. Participation in the program is always voluntary.

- *Independent:* The EAP is administered by Human Affairs Inc., a national company that provides assistance programs to many companies across the country.

- *Confidential:* Because of the two components mentioned above, EAP participants are assured that any information revealed to EAP staff will be held in the strictest professional confidence.

- *Professional:* All EAP staff are licensed Masters level therapists and counselors.

- *Free:* All counseling and referral services provided by the EAP are free to employees and their families. If an EAP counselor does recommend that employees consult a special outside resource, the counselor can let employees know what part of that service may be covered by their other medical benefits.

- *Accessible:* EAP counselors are available for emergency situations 24 hours a day, 7 days a week. Appointments are made for non-emergency situations during day or evening hours.

- *A Valuable Resource:* The EAP can serve as a resource concerning counseling, information, and management consultation to employees, supervisors, and family members.

What the EAP is NOT:

- *A Branch of Human Resources:* The EAP is not designed to replace any personnel or management procedures.

- *A Refuge for Poor Job Performance:* Participation in the EAP will not protect employees from disciplinary action.

Procedures

- *Self-Referral:* An employee or an immediate family member may use the service by contacting Human Affairs Inc. directly in complete privacy whenever they would like to consult with the counselor. Self-referrals are both anonymous and completely confidential. Self-referrals will not affect job security or promotional opportunity.

- *Supervisor/Management Referral:* A supervisor may recommend that an employee contact Human Affairs Inc. when there is a job performance or conduct problem which has not responded to ordinary supervisorial techniques. Whether or not the employee decides to contact Human Affairs Inc., it is the employee's responsibility to perform satisfactorily on the job; and if problems go unresolved and performance continues to deteriorate, disciplinary action up to and including discharge may result. Participation in the EAP is not a guarantee that these actions will not continue to occur, but improved performance often results from problem resolution.

The Company sincerely hopes that all staff and their dependents who might benefit from this service will take advantage of it.

SOURCE: *"Purpose of Company E.A.P.,"* Personnel Policy Briefs, *Sample Issue, n.d., p. 2., as found in Leon C. Megginson, Geralyn McLure Franklin, and M. Jane Byrd,* Human Resource Management *(Houston, TX: Dame Publications, Inc.), 1995, p. 296.*

chapter review

① Explain what coaching is.

Coaching is the interpersonal process used by supervisors and managers to help individuals continually reach their highest levels of performance. Coaching is performance oriented, whether it helps a new employee gain new skills or accept challenges or a seasoned employee to reach even higher levels of performance. Coaching is a relatively new management function, gaining momentum in the 1980s, and it reflects the changing role of supervisors as facilitators and developers of people.

Despite its importance, supervisors tend to experience difficulty in practicing effective coaching. Many lack the confidence in their communication skills, especially listening, to be an effective coach. Others see it as too passive and prefer to provide answers to employees rather than to work jointly with them to develop their own answers to problems. Still others are uncomfortable in spending the large amount of time that effective coaching takes.

② Identify the four major coaching functions.

There are four coaching functions. Tutoring helps a team member gain knowledge, skill, and competency. Mentoring develops political savvy, an understanding of key players, and the way to advance one's career. Confronting/challenging focuses directly upon performance itself—from setting clear objectives to follow-up meetings that discuss results. It can address performance problems and inspire top performers to continue to grow and improve. Counseling helps an individual recognize, talk about, and thereby gain insight into his or her real or perceived problems that may affect performance.

③ Describe some of the important skills used in coaching.

Coaching is a one-to-one relationship that utilizes such skills as acknowledging, attending, affirming, confirming, pinpointing, probing, reflecting, resourcing, reviewing, and summarizing.

④ Differentiate between general vs. pinpointed coaching statements.

In coaching designed to confront/challenge an employee with a performance problem, supervisors should pinpoint, in specific, concrete language, statements to describe the employee's performance level, rather than using general terms.

⑤ Describe an "I" message.

"I" messages, which indicate the problem behavior, its effect, and the supervisor's feelings, can be an effective way to focus on the performance problem. For example: "Your lunch break was in excess of an hour and a half. I was embarrassed when the plant manager came by looking for you on two occasions and found other people covering your work area."

⑥ Explain the extent to which a supervisor should counsel an employee about personal problems.

In general, supervisors should restrict their counseling to factors that affect an employee's job performance. Many personal problems, such as physical and emotional health, substance abuse, and financial and family problems, however, actually impact or may impact future performance. The supervisor should focus counseling on the performance-related aspects of the problem. Many firms today have an Employee Assistance Program (EAP) to which supervisors can refer troubled employees.

important terms

acknowledging *369*
affirming *369*
attending *369*
coaching *362*
confirming *369*
confronting/challenging *366*
counseling *367*
Employee Assistance Programs (EAP) *375*

"I" message *371*
mentoring *365*
pinpointing *370*
probing *370*
reflecting *370*
resourcing *370*
reviewing *370*
summarizing *370*
tutoring *365*

questions for review and discussion

1. What is meant by coaching?
2. Of the four major coaching functions—tutoring, mentoring, confronting/challenging, and counseling—which do you feel is most difficult? Why?
3. Describe the following coaching skills and give an example of each:
   a. attending
   b. affirming
   c. resourcing
   d. reviewing
4. Give an example of a "general" coaching statement as contrasted to a "pinpointed" coaching statement. Which is more effective and why?
5. What is an "I" message? Why is it an effective way to confront someone's behavior? Give an example.
6. To what extent should a supervisor counsel an employee about the employee's personal problems?
7. What is an EAP?

skill builder 13–1

Practicing "I" Messages
group activity

In reading this chapter, you learned that an "I" message consists of (1) how someone's behavior makes you *feel,* (2) what the *specific behavior* is, and (3) the *effect* of the behavior. The following three situations show a need for an "I" message.

a. Four of your employees share a single telephone line. You are aware that

one of them, Harry R., is especially long winded on the phone and talks for as long as 15 minutes. This prevents others from placing outgoing calls, and also ties up the line, preventing customers from getting through.

b. It is a requirement that waiters at the upscale restaurant you manage wear white shirts and ties. One waiter has been unloosening his tie, dropping the knot about two inches, and unbuttoning his shirt collar.

c. Coffee breaks for your office staff are normally 15 minutes. When someone occasionally takes a few minutes longer, it's not a big deal. But lately, one staff member has had three consecutive days when the break exceeded 20 minutes.

Instructions:

1. Write a hypothetical "I" message for each of the three situations.
2. Gather in groups of three to five students and share answers.
3. From your answers, select some good examples and present to the rest of the class.

●skill building 13–2

Practicing Coaching Responses

Assume the role of shipping supervisor at Apex Company. One of your employees, Jason, has been an excellent performer for the past five years. However, during the past two weeks, Jason has not seemed himself. He was operating a forklift when a careless accident caused about $2,000 in damages. Moreover, Jason has punched in late twice. When you discussed these incidents, he apologized, attributing his tardiness to car trouble. Normally outgoing and energetic, he has appeared tired and edgy. Usually one of the liveliest contributors at meetings of your group, he said nothing at yesterday's safety meeting. During afternoon break on the loading dock today, Spud, another employee, made a joking comment about Jason's favorite college football team, which had been beaten handily by its cross-state rival this past weekend. Jason responded angrily with an expletive, then got up and left the area. Another employee commented, "What's been eating Jason, anyway?" Everyone shrugged their shoulders. You decide to have a coaching meeting with Jason.

It is about two hours later. Jason has just walked into your office. You stand, acknowledge him, and close the door behind him. Jason takes a seat and as you move to sit down, he says, "So you wanted to see me about something."

A. Instruction: In the space below, write the opening statement you will make to Jason that pinpoints the reason for the meeting.

Assume that following your statement, a several minute discussion with Jason ensues. He seems very soft spoken and avoids eye contact. Then he looks you in the eye and says, "I'm glad I have this chance to talk with you. I feel like so much is going on with me lately. I guess I've just taken on more than I should . . . and I don't know what to do about it."

B. Instruction: In the space below, write the statement you will make to Jason that demonstrates reflecting.

Assume that the discussion continues. Jason is quite talkative now, volunteering information about financial problems brought on by a house addition, his son's college expenses, and a recent auto accident that cost him $750 to cover the deductible on his policy. To meet his financial needs, Jason tells you he has been moonlighting for 30 hours weekly as a security guard at a local hotel. He has gotten little sleep the past two weeks. He now worries that he can't sustain the pace, because his job performance at Apex is being affected. He says, "I know I haven't been much of a contributor around here lately."

C. Instruction: In the space below, write the statement you will make to Jason that demonstrates affirming but also reinforces the need for him to improve performance.

During the remaining discussion, Jason commits to making his present job performance his number one priority, despite his short-term financial needs. You discuss several alternatives that would allow him to do both, two of which he proposed: (1) Reduce his hotel hours with most of them being worked on weekends and (2) getting a loan from the company credit union or a bank. A third idea—taking his two-week vacation now, which would allow him to work his full

hotel hours for two weeks—was one you suggested he consider. You tell him you would look into waiving the normal two-week vacation notice. You also suggest he consider making an appointment with the company's EAP office, which can arrange for financial counseling for employees. Jason expresses interest in this. You agree to let Jason know tomorrow about the vacation matter, and to be available as needed to discuss things further should Jason need to talk. You note that Jason picks up his hard hat, which was placed on the floor, and says: "Well, I feel much better having talked with you about this. It's taken a lot off my mind, and it's helped me think some things through. Thanks for being so patient."

D. Instruction: In the space below, write the statement you will make to Jason that demonstrates confirming/summarizing and closes the meeting.

E. Meet with other students and compare your responses.

The Coaching Meeting

The following exchange took place between Charlene Rowe, Human Resources Manager, and one of her senior team members, Leonard Busche.

Rowe: Come in, Leonard, have a seat. (Leonard sits down.) I suppose you're wondering why I wanted us to get together.

Busche: Yes, I guess I am, Charlene.

Rowe: Leonard, recently something happened that I want to know your feelings about. It's about the report I asked you to put together for my Quality Steering Committee meeting yesterday afternoon.

Busche: (Somewhat defensively) What about it?

Rowe: To be quite frank, Leonard, I was too embarrassed to distribute it at the meeting. It just wasn't up to your usual standards. For one thing, it seemed superficial in that it described only a few of the programs we'd benchmarked, rather than all seven. Since this will be the major document the committee will be using as a reference, we needed coverage of *all* the visits we've made. Also, some of the most important processes were not included—like J&J's 360-degree feedback system and Motorola's team incentives.

Busche: (Only half joking) Gee, it seems as if I may need a union steward in here with me. (Leonard is a salaried, nonunion employee.)

Rowe: No, Leonard, I don't mean to give that impression. It's just that this job isn't like you at all, and that concerned me. You've always done exceptional work in putting together material like this for me. For all I know, it might have been my own fault, a misunderstanding between us. I wanted to meet and get your perspective on the situation.

Busche: Well, there isn't much to say. I guess I should have figured it wouldn't be of much help. (Getting a little emotional) I wasn't tickled about it either.

Rowe: You weren't pleased with it yourself?

Busche: No, I wasn't. Charlene, that report would have taken about 8–10 hours for me to do it up right. Do you know how long I had? About four hours, that's all. I couldn't do much in four hours.

Rowe: So you didn't get to put in the time on the report. . . .

Busche: No, I didn't. In fact, you weren't the only one embarrassed by it. But I can't promise it'll be the last lousy job. . . . I just can't handle everything that comes my way. I know we're a service department [human resources], but we're not the little outfit we were five years ago. I just can't keep up.

Rowe: It sounds as if the quality report is only part of the problem.

Busche: That's exactly what I'm saying. I'm expected to do everybody's odds and ends besides my regular job in training and safety. I've got the two accidents we're investigating from two weeks ago and all that paperwork. We're approaching our deadlines on the new training manuals. I'm heading up the newsletter committee that puts out our first edition next month. Then, you gave me the quality report with one week's notice. I would have gotten it done, but last week Bushman (VP and General Manager) asked me to be his facilitator. I had to put in some eight hours observing his meetings with the budget committee. So the quality report was lousy, I know. But if things continue as they are, it won't be the last. I hate it more than you do.

Rowe: Leonard, you know how we've all come to expect so much from you. Granted, we are a service department, but in retrospect, I wish you'd confided in me about this. I could have simply pushed back my quality committee meeting, which is what I essentially did, anyway. What can we do to help you?

Busche: How can we help? (Flippant) Oh, give me an assistant.

Rowe: Is additional help the answer?

Busche: I don't know the answer to that. I think what's really got me upset is Bushman. He didn't *ask* me to facilitate, he *told* me to. I should have turned him down, but I guess I haven't got the guts to say "no" to a vice-president. But then, I didn't want to let you down, either.

Rowe: I think it's terrific that Bushman values your abilities. Politically, it's in both of our interests for you to act as Bushman's facilitator. That is, if you want to do it.

Busche: Oh, I don't mind facilitating for Bushman. He needs a lot of help and he knows it. It would normally be a real compliment for me; it was just the timing that was bad.

Rowe: Leonard, you have a lot of things going on that I didn't know about. Maybe I'm the one who has to do some changing. I can see why, given your schedule the past two weeks, taking on that quality project was too much. It wasn't fair to you. Leonard, I need to feel confident that your work for me from now on will be what I can count on. What can we do to prevent this from happening again?

Busche: I could probably do a better job of letting you know what I've got going on. I could also be more honest with you. I just hate saying I can't do something, especially to my boss. You probably didn't know the newsletter was eating up my time last week, as were the safety problems. I guess I could keep you more up to date. I could also be more direct and tell you if I honestly don't have the time to take something on and do a good job. But it's hard for me to say no.

Rowe: O.K., let's give this a try. You'll give me a brief typed report on projects other than your normal training and safety activi-ties. If you're skeptical about a commitment request from outside the department, you'll discuss it with me before taking it on. You're also agreeing to level with me about whether you have time to commit to special projects that I throw your way. We'll try this process for a month and see what happens. Is that acceptable?

Busche: Yep, that sounds acceptable. Hopefully, I'll not get caught up in a bind like this again.

Instructions:

1. What type of coaching function was reflected in Rowe's meeting with Busche?

2. In terms of effectiveness on a 1–10 scale, with 1 being "poor" and 10 being "excellent," what score would you assign to Rowe's handling of the session? Why?

3. Identify comments by Rowe that reflect the following coaching skills: (a) reflecting, (b) pinpointing, (c) probing, (d) affirming, (e) confirming.

4. What other coaching skills can you identify?

5. Meet with a group of three to five other students, discuss your answers, and be prepared to report these to the rest of the class.

Meetings and Facilitation Skills

● outline

Purposes of Meetings
Information Giving
Information Exchange
Fact Finding
Problem Solving
Achieving Consensus

Approaches Used at Meetings
Leader-Controlled Approach
Group-Centered Approach
Which Approach Should You Use?

Advantages and Disadvantages of Meetings
Advantages of Meetings
Disadvantages of Meetings

Making Meetings Effective
Factors to Consider Before the Meeting
Factors to Consider During the Meeting
Factors to Consider After the Meeting

What Is Group Facilitation?
Role of the Facilitator
Process Consultation
Facilitating Teleconferencing

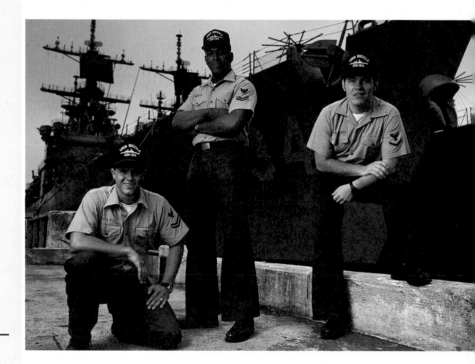

A meeting still performs functions that will never be taken over by telephones, teleprinters, Xerox copiers, tape recorders, television monitors, or any other technological instruments of the information revolution.

Antony Jay

Those who are unable to learn from past meetings are condemned to repeat them.

McKernan's Maxim

Chuck Dansby, Facilitator "Extraordinaire"

Facilitators are being called on increasingly to help groups and organizations become more effective. One of the best facilitators around is Chuck Dansby, total quality management supervisor with the Navy's Public Works Center in the San Francisco Bay area. Some public works representatives have suggested that a number of awards received by the center could not have been achieved without expert facilitation. The most prestigious of these awards was the Meritorious Unit Commendation Award issued by the Secretary of Defense.

After graduating from Chattanooga State Technical Institute, Chuck spent 12 years in the Navy, ending his tour as a First Class E6 Petty Officer. In 1988 he joined the Public Works Center, and in 1991 he was named the first quality improvement coordinator. During this time, the center was going through a period of expansion, and Chuck soon found himself operating a quality improvement department with a staff of seven people. Chuck and his team made helping units and groups to permanently improve processes their primary task. Even though Chuck and his group were in a staff capacity with no command authority, the following comments reveal why various managers called on him for assistance and what they said about him as a facilitator.

- Lt. Commander Bryan Johnson asked for Chuck's assistance when he needed to get the environmental group and construction group to work more effec-

tively together. He states, "Chuck was very helpful in teaming with me to get key people to talk through issues and concerns and in getting the groups to cooperate in achieving objectives." He especially appreciated Chuck's ability to ask questions, getting people to brainstorm and rethink alternatives. Program Manager Steve Worthington echoes these observations and states, "Chuck is an excellent listener and is very good at getting people to 'see the big picture.'"

- Security Officer Mike Shanlas states, "He gets people to rethink their ways of operating and does it by asking questions. In this manner, people stay focused on the process, and they come out with improved ways of operating. People become indebted to him because he helps them to succeed; he does not set people up for failure."

- Contract Manager John Teetsov gives insight as to the ideal quality of a facilitator when he states that Chuck can come into an unfamiliar area and "not knowing the business, can extract the right ideas and answers. Very importantly, he does things in a manner so that the group feels that they are being helped rather than manipulated."

Chuck has attended a number of schools while with the Navy, but the one that had the greatest impact on him as a future effective facilitator was W. Edward Deming's four-

learning objectives

After reading and studying this chapter, you should be able to:

1. Explain the four basic purposes of meetings.

2. Explain the process of consensus decision making in meetings.

3. Differentiate between the leader-controlled approach and the group-centered approach used in meetings.

4. Identify the advantages and disadvantages of meetings.

5. Describe the actions that a supervisor can take before, during, and after a meeting to make it effective.

6. Define group facilitation.

7. Explain the role of group facilitator.

8. Differentiate between process consultation and other models of consultation.

9. Specifically identify what can be done to make teleconferencing more effective.

day workshop on continual quality improvement. Deming and the course taught Chuck the value of asking the right questions. Today, the Navy's Public Works Center is going through a process of downsizing. In carrying out this process in a fair and human-

istic manner, Chuck is being called on for his expert facilitation skills in meeting the Public Works Center's greatest challenge.

SOURCE: *Conversations and correspondence with Chuck Dansby and others with the Navy's Public Works Center, San Francisco Bay area.*

To be effective when conducting meetings, a supervisor must be knowledgeable about small group behavior, discussed in Chapter 10. In addition, particularly with problem-solving meetings, a team leader must have certain facilitation skills. First let us examine the purposes of meetings.

 Explain the four basic purposes of meetings.

PURPOSES OF MEETINGS

Supervisors normally spend a great deal of time in meetings. In some meetings a supervisor functions as the meeting leader, or perhaps as a project or committee leader. In others, the supervisor functions as a participant rather than as a leader. But the fact of the matter is that meetings are a part of every supervisor's life. The more effectively a supervisor functions as a meeting leader, the more effectively he or she will do the total job.

Exhibit 14–1 shows that meetings generally are called to achieve one or more of the following purposes: (1) to give information, (2) to exchange information, (3) to obtain facts about a particular situation, and (4) to solve a problem.

Exhibit 14–1

Purposes of Meetings

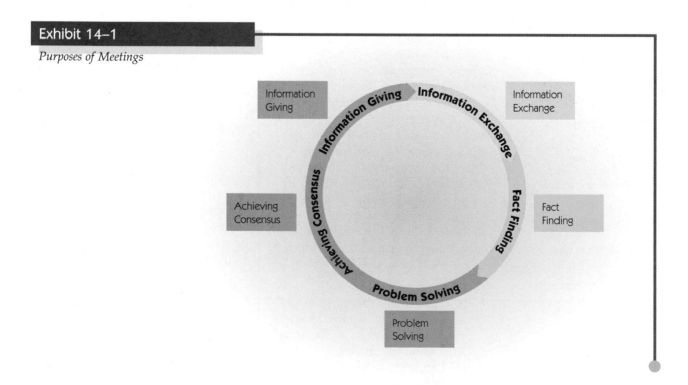

Information Giving

information-giving meeting
Held to announce new programs and policies or to update present ones.

The **information-giving meeting** is held to make announcements of new programs and policies or to update information on the present ones. Generally, it is closely controlled by the leader or those who are called on to provide information to the group, frequently by means of committee reports. There tends to be little feedback from group members unless they have questions to ask or points to clarify about the information presented. Normally this is the easiest type of meeting to conduct, since its format is highly structured and lends itself well to large groups.

Information Exchange

information exchange meeting
Held to obtain information from group members.

The **information exchange meeting** is called to obtain information from group members and to allow them to provide information to one another.

At Southeast Paper Manufacturing Company of Dublin, Georgia, a meeting of the plant manager and seven or eight of his key department heads is conducted each morning. Each of these department heads presents a status report on the previous day's activities and on any carryover information from the previous day. This daily exchange of information ensures that key department heads are "in the know" about the major activities in the plant.

Fact Finding

fact-finding meeting
Held to seek out relevant facts about a problem or situation.

Only relevant facts about a problem or situation should be sought in a **fact-finding meeting.** The meeting leader focuses not on finding solutions but

Information exchange meetings between domestic and overseas representatives of international companies can greatly enhance the success of their products and services.

rather on understanding the problem or situation. A supervisor might begin such a meeting as follows: "The reason I called this meeting is to discuss the high cost overruns we've been experiencing during the past month. I want to find out as much as I can about your perspective on the causes of this situation. Later we can consider some steps we can take to reduce these costs." Once the facts have been uncovered, the supervisor will have a better understanding of the situation.

Problem Solving

problem-solving meeting
Held to identify the problem, to discuss alternative solutions, and to decide on the proper action to take.

 click! http://www.tvo.org/ pdonline/forprincipals/ problemsolving.html

Typically, the **problem-solving meeting** combines the other purposes of information giving, information exchange, and fact finding. This type of meeting is held to identify the major elements of a problem, to discuss and evaluate alternative solutions, and ultimately to make a decision as to the proper action to take. Topics of problem-solving meetings might include any of the following:

1. Improving plant safety
2. Reducing machine downtime
3. Determining production schedules or job assignments
4. Implementing a new company policy in the best way

② Explain the process of consensus decision making in meetings.

Achieving Consensus

consensus
The acceptance by all members of the decision reached.

A particularly important concept, given the increasing popularity of problem-solving meetings, is the process of **consensus** decision making. When a group reaches consensus, all members agree to accept the decision reached, even though they may not personally favor it.

> **Try as he might, Charles Evans couldn't win support from other team members regarding his position on the team's planned recommendation to top management about a company parking lot policy. Evans favored a process that allocated preferred parking places for key personnel in the company—some by seniority, some by position. Other members favored a process that had no preferred parking.**
>
> **The team leader stressed the need for a consensus decision that all members could accept. Evans spoke openly about why he felt his approach was best, responded to questions raised by other team members about his position, and raised many questions about their position. The team leader had given him extra time to survey how other companies in the community handled the situation. Finally, after all issues seemed to have been fully discussed, she said: "I sense that after our full examination of the issue, the group favors a system that will operate as an open, first-come, first-serve system. Is this correct?" No one dissented. She continued: "That, then, is what we will send to the president. Charles, thank you for helping us to more fully explore all aspects of the system that we're recommending. Can you accept the team decision?"**
>
> **"Wow, she's really put me on the spot," thought Evans. "She's not asked whether I agree with it, but whether I accept it. How can I *not* accept it? It was a fair process. I presented my views; they just think differently on this one."**
>
> **Evans responded, "Yes, I can support it, even though I disagree with it." "Good," said the team leader. "We have a consensus."**

Consensus is more difficult when members have personal stakes in decision outcomes and when there is much diversity among the members themselves. Such is often the case with cross-functional teams. Consensus is not always achievable; some members openly state their intent not to support the group's decision. Perhaps they feel that others do not listen to dissenting views or that attacks are made on personality rather than position. At times, the team decision is hurried, the dissenter feels too strongly pressured, or takes the position "If it's not my way, I won't support it, period." Sometimes members will agree to accept the group's decision, but work to sabotage it or divorce themselves from it once the group leaves the meeting room.

Consensus is more likely when a group's members:

1. Openly state their true feelings, ideas, and disagreements.

2. Examine their different views fully.

3. Try to understand underlying reasons behind their differences on an issue.

4. Actively listen to and seek to understand other members' positions.

5. Focus on issues rather than on personalities.

6. Avoid actions that polarize members or lock them into positions. This may be the case with voting or taking sides, especially in early stages of discussion.

Seeking consensus is tough work; it typically takes longer than simply voting on decisions and requires a high degree of team-facilitation skills by the leader.

---

self-check

> In which of the four types of meetings do you feel group dynamics plays the strongest role? Why?

APPROACHES USED AT MEETINGS

 Differentiate between the leader-controlled approach and the group-centered approach used in meetings.

The interactions that take place at meetings vary greatly. Much depends on the purpose of the meeting and the meeting leader's personal style. One of two approaches is generally used in conducting meetings: (1) a leader-controlled approach or (2) a group-centered approach.

Leader-Controlled Approach

leader-controlled approach
Used at meetings of large groups in which the leader clearly runs the show and the open flow of information is impeded.

The **leader-controlled approach,** in which the leader clearly runs the show, is often used at information-giving meetings or when the large size of the group prohibits an open flow of information among members. The leader opens the meeting, makes announcements, or calls on those who have information to present. If anyone in the group has questions to ask or comments to make, he or she addresses them to the leader. The leader may answer the questions or bounce them to someone else. Exhibit 14–2 illustrates this approach. Should a stranger walk in after the meeting had begun, she or he would have no difficulty identifying who was in charge.

One advantage of this approach is that it is generally easier on the leader, because the fairly rigid structure means that there are few surprises. Another advantage is that this approach allows a large amount of material to be covered in a short period of time. It also lends itself to larger size groups.

Exhibit 14–2

Interaction in the Leader-Controlled Approach

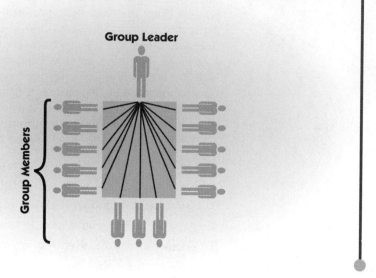

An obvious disadvantage of the leader-controlled approach is that it discourages a free flow of information. The fact that comments from the group must go through the leader means that spontaneous, direct remarks may go unmade. The creativity that results from the "piggybacking" of ideas is stifled. Another disadvantage is that members have no real opportunity to get sensitive and emotional issues out in the open and blow off steam.

Group-Centered Approach

group-centered approach
Used at meetings in which group members interact freely and address and question one another.

In a **group-centered approach,** group members interact more freely with one another, as shown in Exhibit 14–3. The meeting leader does not dominate the discussions; but neither does he or she simply sit back and allow the group to formulate its own direction. Quite the contrary; the leader keeps the meeting moving by directing/redirecting focus, asking for clarification, making sure that everyone speaks, summarizing the group's position, testing for consensus, moving the group to the next issue, and so on.

The advantages of the group-centered approach stem from the greater interaction that occurs at the meeting. First, it results in a better understanding of members' viewpoints. Second, if the purpose of the meeting is to solve a problem, the free flow of information may contribute to a better decision. Third, when people can express their emotions or disagreements, they feel better.

One disadvantage of the group-centered approach is that the meeting takes up a great deal more time than with the leader-controlled approach. Another disadvantage is that the increased interaction among members means that the leader's skills are tested more severely (see Exhibit 14–4). The leader must determine when to move the discussion of a topic along. He or she must make sure that everyone gets a chance to speak up and that discussions stay close to the subject. Also, since the leader must deal with diverse personalities, he or she must know how to handle emotions that may arise. A third disadvantage is that this approach is not well suited to large groups because of its interpersonal nature.

click! http://www.tvo.org/ pdonline/forprincipals/ meeting.html

Exhibit 14–3

*Interaction in the
Group-Centered
Approach*

Exhibit 14–4

SOURCE: *Copyright 1984, USA TODAY. Reprinted with permission.*

Which Approach Should You Use?

Which approach is better for you, as a supervisor, to use? The answer to this question depends on a number of factors, such as the size of the group, the ability of the group members, the amount of time allowed for the meeting, your skills, and the subjects to be discussed. Remember that you can shift from one approach to the other at a single meeting, depending on the nature of the items on your agenda.

> **Yoshi Tanabe's approach at meetings suits his purposes. Take Wednesday's meeting, for instance. The first item on his agenda was the new vacation-scheduling procedure. At this point Tanabe was the expert in the room. He made a three- to four-minute presentation on the new procedure and then fielded questions from the group.**
>
> **The next topic on the agenda was the need to develop and submit to higher management a plan for the department's participation in the company's 10-year anniversary open house for members of the community. Tanabe used a more open approach for the discussion of this topic. It took up about 20 minutes, with much interaction among the group. Within this time Tanabe and the group came up with a plan for the department's role during the open house.**

4 Identify the advantages and disadvantages of meetings.

ADVANTAGES AND DISADVANTAGES OF MEETINGS

Some supervisors despise attending and conducting meetings. They prefer to communicate on a one-to-one basis. But because meetings are a fact of life for supervisors, it is appropriate at this point to consider the advantages and disadvantages of meetings. Then, in the remainder of the chapter, we will provide pointers on how to make meetings more effective.

Advantages of Meetings

Meetings save time, ensure that the supervisor's communications are consistent, and permit a formal exchange of important information and ideas. Let's explore how these advantages work.

Save Time. Suppose you, as a supervisor, have a group of employees whose jobs are *not* performed in the same work area (as is the case with outside sales, delivery services, maintenance, or patient care). In order to communicate on a one-on-one basis, you would have to move from one location to another during the work period. By having a meeting, you can save a great deal of your personal time that would otherwise be spent tracking down each of your employees.

Moreover, when minutes of the meeting are distributed to members, they serve as a permanent record of what has occurred or been agreed on. In this way, they save time that might otherwise be needed to clarify or repeat what was said.

Ensure Consistency of Information. Meetings provide an opportunity for all present to hear the same message. If you communicate separately with each of your team members, you may present the information more effectively to some than to others. Also, some of your team members may ask questions or make comments that help clarify the communication or add a slightly different flavor to it. With one-on-one contacts, the grapevine goes to work, especially if there is a long lapse of time between when you talk with the first team member and when you talk with the last team member.

self-check

All members present at a meeting hear and see the same thing. Will they all interpret and remember it the same way? Explain.

Permit Formal Exchange of Information. Sometimes individual members of a work group have information that *must* be shared with all the other group members. This is particularly true when a problem confronts the work group. In a meeting, a comment made by one member frequently triggers an important idea in another member. This exchange can lead to solutions that might not have been thought of by any one member.

The degree of formality inherent in a meeting can be used to advantage by a supervisor. For example, suppose that you, a supervisor, have been told by the plant manager that production must be increased by 15 percent over the next year—otherwise the plant will be closed. Presenting this information to your work group in a meeting conveys the seriousness of the situation and dramatizes the impact of the message.

Disadvantages of Meetings

Meetings may result in watered-down decisions, may not be cost effective, and may be too impersonal. Let's see how these disadvantages arise.

May Water Down Decisions. Unless a meeting is properly conducted and its members are committed to effectiveness, the decisions made at the meeting may simply reflect the *average* input of members, rather than the ideas of the best members. Sometimes opinions voiced by the group's brightest or best informed members may not be accepted by the majority. At other times, knowledgeable members may suppress their own disagreements simply for the sake of harmony.

May Not Be Cost Effective. Meetings are more expensive than most people realize. When employees are attending meetings, they are not doing their normal jobs. Suppose 10 people, with an average annual salary of $50,000, attend a one-hour meeting. The cost of the meeting includes not only their salaries for that hour, but also costs for vacations, holidays, sick leave, medical insurance, Social Security, travel time, and so on. As shown in Exhibit 14–5, the cost of the meeting is $481. The meeting must therefore provide information important enough to justify the cost associated with it. And Exhibit 14–5 does not include the costs associated with time spent planning for the meeting. As we will point out shortly, the meeting leader may need to spend a considerable amount of time on the planning process.

May Become Too Impersonal. Meetings may not allow the personal interaction required for many sensitive issues. On a one-on-one basis, employees may communicate readily to their supervisor. But because a meeting involves a

Meetings Cost!

Have you ever thought about the cost of a meeting? The following table gives a rough approximation of hourly costs for managers at four salary levels. The hourly rates are illustrative and include loading for benefits, overhead, travel time, and the like.

Salary	Number of Participants in Meeting					
	10	9	8	7	6	5
$80,000	$766	$693	$613	$536	$460	$383
$60,000	$576	$520	$462	$403	$346	$288
$50,000	$481	$433	$384	$337	$289	$241
$30,000	$288	$260	$231	$201	$173	$144

SOURCE: *Updated and adapted from Edward F. Konczai, "Making the Most of Meetings,"* Supervisory Management 7 *(March 1982): 4. Reprinted by permission of publisher, from* SUPERVISORY MANAGEMENT, *March/1982 © 1982. American Management Association, New York. All rights reserved.*

click! http://www.tvo.org/
pdonline/forprincipals/
brainstorm.html

5 Describe the actions that a supervisor can take before, during, and after a meeting to make it effective.

more formal setting with many people present, some employees will be reluctant to speak up.

MAKING MEETINGS EFFECTIVE

This section presents some ideas that should help you conduct more effective meetings. Some of the actions discussed should be performed *before* the meeting, some *during* the meeting, and some *after* the meeting.

Factors to Consider Before the Meeting

The first step is to determine whether a meeting is really necessary. If so, you should clarify its purpose and then plan so that it will achieve its purpose.

Decide Whether a Meeting Is Needed. Before calling a meeting, you should determine whether the meeting is necessary. For example, could you convey the information you intend to give by other means, such as in a memo or over the telephone? Do all members of your group need the information or just a few? Will the format of the meeting help accomplish your purpose?

Many supervisors claim that they waste too much time in meetings called by their bosses, yet they themselves hold too many meetings with their own employees. So, when thinking about the next meeting you plan to hold, ask yourself, "Do I really need this meeting?"

Have a Clear Purpose. Assuming that a meeting is necessary, you should have a clear purpose for it. Otherwise you will waste everyone's time, including your own.

"Why are we having the meeting this afternoon, Rhoda?" asked Margaret Parker, one of the insurance clerks in the department. "I'm a little behind in some of my paperwork."

Rhoda, her supervisor, responded, "Well, Margaret, we always have a meeting the first Friday of the month, and today is the first Friday. But there's nothing important on my agenda, so don't worry about making it. Go ahead and catch up on your work."

self-check

What are the pros and cons of having regular weekly meetings at an established time?

Preplan the Meeting. Many meetings are doomed from the start because of poor initial planning. Perhaps another group has reserved the conference room, for example. Or the bulbs in the overhead projector are burned out. Or the people present at the meeting weren't notified that they should bring certain needed information. Or the leader simply hasn't done his or her homework! Proper planning requires you to do some work before the meeting begins. Such work might include the following:

1. Make sure that the people who are to attend the meeting have adequate advance notice (unless it's an emergency meeting).
2. Make sure that key people will be able to attend.
3. Let people know in advance if they will be expected to provide information or make a report.
4. Distribute copies of the meeting agenda in advance. This will enable people to bring essential documents with them or to gather information that may prove helpful.
5. Check to see that the meeting room is arranged as you desire and that the visual aids you intend to use are functioning properly.
6. Form a general idea of how long the meeting should last. You may want to indicate this to those who will attend. It is easier to predict the length of information-giving and information exchange meetings, however, than that of meetings held for fact finding or problem solving.

Factors to Consider During the Meeting

When the meeting time arrives, you can take a number of steps to help ensure the meeting's success. Among these are (1) starting the meeting on time, (2) designating someone to take minutes, (3) clarifying your objectives and expectations, (4) keeping the meeting on the desired topic, (5) encouraging participation, and (6) making sure there is closure.

Start on Time. There may be occasions when one or two employees do not arrive on time for a meeting. To avoid unnecessary delays, the supervisor should begin the meeting as scheduled. If a supervisor consistently waits for late arrivals, attendees may get the message that it's okay to be late, and successive meetings will start later and later. Such delays waste the time of those who arrive promptly.

Designate Someone to Take Minutes. Especially for information exchange, fact-finding, and problem-solving meetings, it is helpful to have someone

record the important points discussed and agreed on at the meeting. These
points are then outlined in a document called the **minutes** of the meeting,
copies of which are distributed after the meeting. If no one takes minutes, those
attending the meeting would be well advised to take notes on their own.

Clarify Your Expectations. Earlier in this chapter we stated that a meeting was
generally called to serve one or more of the following purposes: to give information, to exchange information, to obtain facts, or to solve a problem and
make a decision. As the leader of the meeting, make sure that you introduce
each item on the agenda by stating your purpose for including it. For example:

1. "I'd like to *give you some information* about . . . ." [information giving]
2. "Attached to the agenda that I sent each of you was the memo from the Human Resources Department regarding the new benefits. I'd like to *get your
   reactions* to these new benefits." [information exchange]
3. "The purpose of this meeting is to review the recent changes in our billing
   policy and their impact on collections. Your input will give me an idea of
   the success or failure of our new billing policy. In your experience, what has
   been *the effect of* the billing policy?" [fact finding]
4. "I'd like to get your ideas on what we can do to show our department in its
   best light during our open house. After hearing your ideas, *I'll put together
   our plan.*" [problem solving and decision making]
5. "The plant manager wants to know what our department's position is on
   switching to a week of four ten-hour days, as we discussed in our meeting
   last week. I can go any way you want to on this. *What do we want to do?*"
   [decision making]

In each example, the supervisor spelled out and clarified his or her expectations
regarding an item on the agenda. Take special notice of examples 4 and 5, in
which the supervisor carefully outlined the role of the group in the decision-
making process.

Provide Leadership. Ineffective leadership ruins many well-prepared meetings. The supervisor must be prepared to demonstrate leadership in the following ways:

1. *Keep the meeting moving.* Don't allow a meeting to drag on and on, and don't
   stray too far from the topic being discussed. If people wander from the
   topic, you might say, "We seem to have drifted from our major issue. Let's
   go back . . . "
2. *See to it that most or all members contribute to the discussion.* Don't allow one or
   two people to dominate the meeting. If this happens, call on others first for
   their comments or reactions.
3. *Summarize the apparent position of the group from time to time.* You might say,
   "Do I read the group properly? You seem to be saying that . . . "
4. *Address various problems related to participant behavior.* Exhibit 14–6 shows how
   to deal with some inappropriate behaviors.

Encourage Two-Way Communication. In most meetings the leader's job is to
facilitate openness and interaction among group members. This is particularly
important when the leader uses the group-centered approach. The leader must

Exhibit 14–6

Suggestions for Handling Disruptive and Inappropriate Behaviors at Meetings

Type	Behavior	Suggested Response
Hostile	"It'll never work." "That's a typical engineering viewpoint."	"How do others feel about this?" "You may be right, but let's review the facts and evidence." "It seems we have a different perspective on the details, but we agree on the principles."
Know-It-All	"I have worked on this project more than anyone else in this room. . . ." "I have a Ph.D. in economics, and . . ."	"Let's review the facts." (Avoid theory and speculation.) "Another noted authority on this subject has said . . ."
Loudmouth	Constantly blurts out ideas and questions. Tries to dominate the meeting.	Interrupt: "Can you summarize your main point/question for us?" "I appreciate your comments, but we should also hear from others." "Interesting point. Help us understand how it relates to our subject."
Interrupter	Starts talking before others are finished.	"Wait a minute, Jim. Let's let Jane finish what she was saying."
Interpreter	"What John is really trying to say is . . ." "John would respond to that question by saying . . ."	"Let's let John speak for himself. Go ahead, John, finish what you were saying." "John, how would you respond?" "John, do you think Jim correctly understood what you said?"
Gossiper	"Isn't there a regulation that you can't . . . ?" "I thought I heard the V.P. of Finance say . . ."	"Can anyone here verify this?" "Let's not take the time of the group until we can verify the accuracy of this information."
Whisperer	Carries on irritating side conversation.	Walk up close to the guilty parties and make eye contact. Stop talking and establish dead silence. Politely ask the whisperers to wait until the meeting is over to finish their conversation.
Silent Distractor	Reads newspapers, rolls eyes, shakes head, fidgets.	Ask questions to determine the distractor's level of interest, support, and expertise. Try to build an alliance by drawing him or her into the discussion. If that doesn't work, discuss your concerns with the individual during a break.
Busy-Busy	Ducks in and out of the meeting repeatedly, taking messages, dealing with crises.	Schedule the presentation away from the office. Check with common offenders before the meeting to make sure interruptions during the planned time will be minimal.
Latecomer	Comes late and interrupts the meeting.	Announce an odd time (8:46) for the meeting to emphasize the necessity for promptness. Make it inconvenient for latecomers to find a seat, and stop talking until they do. Establish a "latecomers' kitty" for refreshments.

Continued

Exhibit 14–6

concluded

Type	Behavior	Suggested Response
Early Leaver	Announces, with regret, the need to leave for another important activity.	Before starting, announce the ending time and ask if anyone has a scheduling conflict.

SOURCE: *Ten Deadly Sins of Poor Presentation from "Presentation Plus" by David Peoples, pp. 52–54. Copyright © 1988. John Wiley and Sons Inc., New York. Reprinted by permission of publisher.*

be an alert listener and be skilled in helping individuals in the group to express themselves. A key skill is the ability to use questions to involve individual members or the entire group in the communication process. Exhibit 14–7 shows some questioning techniques that can be used by the meeting leader.

Get Closure on Items Discussed. At many meetings that the authors have observed, an item will be discussed, but then the leader will go on to the next item on the agenda, leaving everyone to wonder what has been concluded. Achieving **closure** means reaching a conclusion with respect to a given agenda item that has been discussed. In the following example, notice how a department head achieves closure for a particular agenda item.

closure
Successfully accomplishing the objective for a given item on the agenda.

Martha Briem, a department head, presented comparative information showing that her department had a quality-rejection rate that was 10 percent higher than that of other departments in the company. She

Exhibit 14–7

Questioning Techniques for Leaders of Meetings

- *Clarifying or elaborating on a point made by someone.*
  Example: "Are you saying that . . . ?" or "Alice, would you mind giving us a little more detail about the situation? When did it happen?"
- *Calling on someone who is reluctant to talk.*
  Example: "Pete, you've been through more maintenance shutdowns than most of us. What do you think about all of this?"
- *Getting specific facts.*
  Example: "Exactly what were our production figures last month? Can someone give us those figures?"
- *Examining possible alternatives.*
  Example: "What are the pros and cons of converting to the new system?" or "Would we be able to keep up our quality under the new system?" or "What would happen if . . . ?"
- *Initiating group discussion.*
  Example: "What is your reaction to this new vacation policy?" or "Does this new policy affect anyone here?"
- *Obtaining more participation from the group.*
  Example: "We've heard two alternatives. Are there any more?"
- *Guiding the meeting tactfully in certain directions.*
  Example: "We seem to have already discussed this issue pretty thoroughly and agreed on a course of action. Is everyone ready to move on?"
- *"Testing the water" as to the group's feeling.*
  Example: "What would be your reaction if we went to the system we've been discussing? Would you support it?"

asked for her supervisors' input about possible actions. The discussion lasted about 25 minutes. Then she asked each supervisor to come up with a plan for improving product quality in his or her area and to make a 5-minute presentation at a meeting to be scheduled in two weeks.

Factors to Consider After the Meeting

Even though the meeting is over, your work isn't finished. Follow up by making sure that the minutes (if any) are distributed and that any important decisions or responsibilities assigned to specific individuals are carried out.

Distribute Copies of the Minutes. Distributing copies of the minutes of the meeting is important for the following reasons:

1. The minutes serve as a permanent record of what has been agreed on and committed to at the meeting.
2. The minutes identify topics on the agenda that have not been dealt with completely or that have been suggested for a future meeting.
3. The minutes permit a smooth transition, allowing you to take up where you left off at the next meeting.

Follow Up on Decisions Made. It is crucial that the supervisor follow up on any actions that were agreed on and any decisions that were made during the meeting. The follow-up may consist of personal observations or visits. It may also involve reports that keep the supervisor informed of progress regarding the agreed-on commitments.

> **"Oh, I make it a point to follow up on my meetings," stated Luis Santos. "We have a pretty active crowd who say what they think. If I feel that someone has really gotten ticked off or hurt by what was brought up at the meeting, I'll make it a point to try to smooth things out on a one-on-one basis. I also go one-on-one with somebody who said something I wanted to follow up on if I didn't feel the meeting was the place to do it."**

More and more organizations are using facilitators to help make their meetings more effective, and they are training team leaders in group facilitations. We examine this important area next.

WHAT IS GROUP FACILITATION?

6 Define group facilitation.

group facilitation
The process of intervening to help a group improve in goal setting, action planning, problem solving, conflict management, and decision making in order to increase the group's effectiveness.

Group facilitation is a process of intervening to help a group improve in goal setting, action planning, problem solving, conflict management, and decision making in order to increase the group's effectiveness. Although an outside facilitator can be helpful, as we saw in the opening case, the ideal is for managers and supervisors to gain facilitation skills and utilize shared leadership in carrying out the process.

As organizations cope with the world of increasingly rapid change, the need for facilitation to improve their effectiveness increases. Examples run the gamut from empowering employees, developing shared visions, and creating self-managing work teams to changing to a more participative organizational culture. It is hard to imagine successful change efforts in the areas of total quality management, reengineering, partnering, mergers, or downsizing without some form of facilitation.

Explain the role of group facilitator.

Role of the Facilitator

In our discussion of group dynamics and conducting meetings, you were introduced to facilitation challenges and suggestions for handling inappropriate behavior at meetings. A good foundation for being an effective facilitator requires experience and knowledge, not only of dynamics of the group but also of decision making, problem solving, communications, motivation, and leadership. In addition, the core skills shown in Exhibit 14–8 are essential.

8 Differentiate between process consultation and other models of consultation.

Process Consultation

Among the many roles facilitators must play is that of process consultant. In fact, process consultation skills are identified as being among the core skills of an effective facilitator. This role involves sitting in on team or task force meetings, observing the group's process, and intervening, if needed, to help the group function more effectively. Skill Builder 14–4 is designed to help you better understand when and how to intervene. Increasingly, facilitators are being used in major change efforts of total quality management, reengineering, and partnering. In essence, a facilitator becomes a consultant. The following sections describe three consultation models, and we draw extensively from author/consultant Edgar Schein in comparing them.

It is important to keep in mind that the effective facilitator is primarily a helper and wants the group to achieve long-term development and continuous process improvement. Exhibit 14–9 highlights this emphasis by showing the distinction between basic facilitation and developmental facilitation.

Purchase-of-Expertise Model. The most widely used form of consultation is the purchase of expert information. The organization, or someone within the organization, decides there is a need to call on an expert to help solve a problem or add a service. For example, someone to initiate an organizational attitude survey or introduce a performance evaluation system may be called. An individual who specializes in conducting marketing surveys or initiating total quality improvement programs may also be needed. Schein points out that this

Exhibit 14–8

Core Skills for the Effective Facilitator

- Communication skills—listening and asking the right questions.
- Leadership skills—participative management and developmental leadership.
- Problem-solving skills.
- Group dynamics skills.
- Conceptual and analytical skills.
- Conflict management skills—principled negotiation.
- Process consultation skills—intervention and diagnostic insights.

*Basic and
Developmental
Facilitation*

Characteristic	Basic Facilitation	Developmental Facilitation
Group objective	Solve a substantive problem or problems.	Achieve group goals along with solving substantive problems while learning to improve processes.
Facilitator role	Help group temporarily improve its processes.	Help group permanently improve its processes.
	Take primary responsibility for managing the group's processes.	Help group assume primary responsibility for achieving goals and managing processes.
Outcome for group	Emphasize dependence on facilitator for solving future problems.	Reduce dependence on facilitator for solving future problems.

SOURCE: *Roger M. Schwartz,* The Skilled Facilitator: Practical Wisdom for Developing Effective Groups, *Table 1.1, page 7, adapted as submitted. Copyright © 1994 Jossey-Bass Inc., Publishers.*

model has problems in that there is frequently a low rate of implementation of the consultant's recommendations. Further, this model is based on many assumptions that have to be met for it to succeed, and therein lies its weakness. The assumptions are:

1. The manager has correctly diagnosed the organization's needs.
2. The manager has correctly communicated those needs to the consultant.
3. The manager has accurately assessed the capabilities of the consultant to provide the information or the service.
4. The manager has considered the consequences of having the consultant gather such information and is willing to implement changes that may be recommended by the consultant.[1]

Another weakness is the fact that the model is based on a "tell and sell" method by the expert and there is no "ownership" or commitment by the client.

Doctor–Patient Model. A relationship between a consultant and an organization can be likened to that of a doctor and a patient. When an organization suffers symptoms such as declining sales or profits, low morale, or high turnover, a consultant may be brought in to check these problems. After the "checkup," the consultant prescribes what needs to be done to "get well" again. As Schein points out, this model places a great deal of power in the hands of the consultant in that he or she makes a diagnosis and also prescribes a treatment. The success of the model then depends on the following:

1. The initial client has accurately identified which person, group, or department is "sick."
2. The "patient" has revealed accurate information.
3. The "patient" accepts the prescription, that is, does what the "doctor" recommends.[2]

process consultation
A consultation model that involves others in making a joint diagnosis of the problem and eventually providing others with the skills and tools to make their own diagnoses.

Process Consultation Model. In contrast to the other models, **process consultation** involves others in making a joint diagnosis and eventually provides others with the skills and tools to make their own diagnoses. Also, even though the consultant may be an expert in the area of consultation, he or she refrains from solving the problem for the client. The emphasis is on facilitating the process so the client learns problem-solving skills. Although the facilitator may make suggestions or raise questions that broaden the diagnosis or develop more alternatives, the client makes the ultimate decision and develops the action plan or remedy. A summary of the underlying assumptions of the process consultation model follows:

1. Clients/managers often do not know what is wrong and need special help in diagnosing what their problems actually are.

2. Clients/managers often do not know what kinds of help consultants can give to them; they need to be informed of what kinds of help to seek.

3. Most clients/managers have a constructive intent to improve things, but they need help in identifying what to improve and how to improve it.

4. Most organizations can be more effective if they learn to diagnose and manage their own strengths and weaknesses.

5. A consultant probably cannot, without exhaustive and time-consuming study or actual participation in the client organization, learn enough about the culture of the organization to suggest reliable new courses of action. Therefore, unless remedies are worked out jointly with members of the organization, who do know what will and will not work in their culture, such remedies are likely either to be wrong or to be resisted because they come from an outsider.

6. Unless the client/manager learns to see the problem for himself and thinks through the remedy, he or she will not be willing or able to implement the solution. More importantly, he or she will not learn how to fix such problems should they recur. The process consultant can provide alternatives, but decision making about such alternatives must remain in the hands of the client.

7. The essential function of process consultation, or PC, is to teach the skills of how to diagnose and fix organizational problems. In this way, the client is able to continue on his or her own to improve the organization.[3]

How do facilitators determine whether or not they are being effective? One group that facilitates partnering workshops always asks the participants to evaluate both the effectiveness of the workshop and the facilitator(s). The following comments demonstrate that the facilitator provided good process consultation skills.

> **"The facilitators did an excellent job in serving as catalysts for dialogue."**
>
> **"The facilitator took the time to help each person or group with problem solving and with staying focused."**
>
> **"The techniques of the workshop leader improved communications and helped us to solve our problems in a collaborative manner."**
>
> **"The facilitator provided good, constructive, visionary thinking and identified personal and group blind spots."**

"The facilitator was collaborative, but firm enough to keep things focused and keep things moving."

"The facilitator's people skills were exceptional. He was genuinely interested in the individual and group needs, which made the workshop most effective."

"The facilitator achieved the goal of allowing *us* to solve our problems."

"The facilitator kept us focused without inhibiting the interaction of the participants."[4]

In two of the skill builders at the end of the chapter, you will have an opportunity to develop your process consultation and facilitation skills. Again more and more team leaders (supervisors) are asked to play facilitator roles that previously were the domain of outside consultants.

Facilitating Teleconferencing

(9) Specifically identify what can be done to make teleconferencing more effective.

Sometimes because of the expense of bringing people from distant locations to a meeting, a facilitator needs to set up or make arrangements for a teleconference. Susan Fox, executive director of the Society of American Archivists, has developed some excellent tips for facilitators in both profit and nonprofit organizations. They are presented in Exhibit 14–10.

Exhibit 14–10

Tips for Facilitating Teleconferencing

Preparation

1. *Decide who will be in on the call.* The first thing you need to consider is who should participate in the call. Usually conference calls address a specific issue that requires discussion leading to consensus. Think about including members who hold information relevant to the topic at hand. This may or may not include the obvious participants. You will also want to include key representatives from constituencies potentially affected by the outcomes resulting from the call.

2. *Establish a clear set of desired outcomes.* Ask yourself these kinds of questions:
   - Is this call necessary?
   - Can the issue wait?
   - If not, what needs to occur as a result of our discussion?
   - How quickly?
   - Who should be involved?
   - What will be the chief result?

3. *Create and distribute an agenda.* Once you have the rationale and desired outcome firmly established, develop an agenda and either fax or mail it to participants well in advance of the call, if at all possible. Remember to include clear instructions about how to dial into the call.

   All meetings, regardless of how they are convened, require an agenda. Don't try to cover too much ground. Keep the topic tightly focused, communicate your desired outcomes, and give each major agenda item a time limit. Cover minor items up front so that you can quickly move to items of substance. Conclude the agenda with next steps, which can be agreed on at the conclusion of the call.

Continued

Exhibit 14–10

concluded

Facilitation

Remember that a conference call is a cross between a face-to-face meeting and a telephone conversation. You will therefore need to draw on a number of skills. For example, similar to a face-to-face meeting, greet participants as they "check in," and engage those who are waiting for the quorum in small talk. Hold logistical and substantive topics until everyone is on line.

1. *Designate a timekeeper and note taker.* Once you have a quorum, ask one participant to be the timekeeper and another to take notes. You will, of course, take notes yourself, but having additional help will keep you focused on facilitation rather than dictation.

2. *Ask members to identify themselves each time they speak.* Because participants can't actually see one another, self-identification ultimately makes the discussion flow more easily. If a member forgets to identify himself or herself, take it upon yourself to make the identification as quickly and as unobtrusively as possible.

3. *Call on the silent.* Lack of visual clues can easily result in people stepping in on each other's conversation or, more likely, in one or two members dominating the discussion. It's up to you to provide balance and to call on those who remain quiet. You will need to ascertain whether their silence is the result of agreement, disagreement, or shyness.

4. *Poll each member.* It's up to you to solicit full participation. If you take a vote, register each participant. In fact, poll each member each time you reach a decision point. Bottom line, never assume.

5. *Watch the clock.* As in any meeting, work with your timekeeper. Groups naturally gravitate toward less difficult issues, which can quickly waste valuable time. Keep the discussion moving toward substantive issues and outcomes.

6. *Consider alternatives for difficult issues.* You may discover that the more difficult issues cannot be resolved on the telephone. If the group cannot reach consensus or engages in a heated disagreement, it may well be that a conference call is not the best communication mechanism for that particular issue. Acknowledge that fact and either give members time to reflect and eventually convene a second call or, if necessary, find another way to meet and work things out.

7. *Review assignments and close positively.* End the call on a positive note, then reiterate the tasks and deadlines and the individuals assigned to carry them out. Congratulate your colleagues on their fine work, and thank them for their time.

Follow-Up

As soon as the call is complete, prepare the to-do list with the deadlines and designees and send it out immediately. Within the week, if not sooner, gather your notes from the call and summarize the proceedings for all participants. Most of us tend to quickly forget what we say and promise to do, so this point can't be emphasized strongly enough.

It also helps to solicit feedback about how participants viewed the usefullness of the call. Did it accomplish its aims? Are there areas in which you can improve your facilitation skills? Most of us are unaware of our own telephone habits, and this kind of feedback can be enormously helpful.

chapter review

 Explain the four basic purposes of meetings.

Meetings can serve four general purposes: (1) to give information, (2) to exchange information, (3) to find facts, and (4) to solve problems. Group consensus is an important process in many meetings, especially in problem-solving meetings where decisions are made by the group.

② Explain the process of consensus decision making in meetings.

Group consensus means that members agree to accept the decision made by the group, even though not all of them may agree with it.

③ Differentiate between the leader-controlled approach and the group-centered approach used in meetings.

With a leader-controlled approach to a meeting, the leader clearly runs the show and conducts a very structured meeting. The advantages of this approach are that it lends itself better to established time frames, has more predictable outcomes, and is more appropriate for large groups. With a group-centered approach, there is more interaction among members. This approach permits greater understanding, and the exchange of ideas is more apt to generate creative solutions.

④ Identify the advantages and disadvantages of meetings.

The typical supervisor frequently must conduct meetings with his or her work group. Meetings have the following advantages over one-on-one contacts: (1) they save time, (2) they allow all present to hear exactly the same message, and (3) they lend a degree of formality. The disadvantages of meetings are that (1) they may result in watered-down decisions, (2) they may not be cost effective, and (3) they may become too impersonal.

⑤ Describe the actions that a supervisor can take before, during, and after a meeting to make it effective.

A number of actions can help to make meetings more effective. *Before* the meeting, the supervisor should determine whether a meeting is necessary, establish a clear purpose for the meeting, and plan it. *During* the meeting, the supervisor should start promptly, designate someone to take minutes, clarify his or her expectations, provide leadership, encourage two-way communication, and see to it that closure is achieved on the items discussed. *After* the meeting, minutes of the meeting should be distributed, and agreed-on commitments should be followed up.

⑥ Define group facilitation.

Group facilitation is a process of intervening to help a group improve in goal setting, action planning, problem solving, conflict management, and decision making in order to increase the group's effectiveness.

⑦ Explain the role of group facilitator.

Among the many roles facilitators play is that of process consultant. In carrying out that process, the effective facilitator is primarily a helper and wants the group to achieve long-term development and continuous process improvement.

⑧ Differentiate between process consultation and other models of consultation.

In contrast to other approaches, process consultation involves others and eventually provides others with the skills to diagnose and solve their own problems.

⑨ **Specifically identify what can be done to make teleconferencing more effective.**

Teleconferencing can be made more effective by carrying out the following guidelines.

1. Participants in the call should include those with information concerning the topic of the call and those affected by the outcome.
2. Establish desired outcomes and keep the call short.
3. Since the participants cannot see each other, the facilitator will involve all members and ask each to identify himself when he speaks; poll each member to insure full participation.
4. Consider alternative solutions for difficult issues and the possibility of another call or another way to meet.
5. Review the tasks and deadlines and the individuals responsible for working on them.
6. Finally, close on a positive note.

---

important terms

closure *398*
consensus *388*
fact-finding meeting *387*
group-centered approach *390*
group facilitation *399*
information exchange meeting *387*

information-giving meeting *387*
leader-controlled approach *389*
minutes *396*
problem-solving meeting *388*
process consultation *402*

---

questions for review and discussion

1. Name the four basic purposes of meetings. Of these, which generally requires the most skill on the part of the leader?
2. Explain the process of consensus decision making in meetings.
3. Differentiate between the leader-controlled approach and the group-centered approach used in meetings.
4. What are the advantages and disadvantages of meetings?
5. Describe the actions that a supervisor can take before, during, and after a meeting to make it effective.
6. Discuss the purpose of group facilitation and the role of the facilitator.
7. How does process consultation differ from other models of consultation?

● skill builder 14–1

Achieving Group Consensus
group activity

The table below lists the qualities most valued in a leader. These qualities appear in no special order and do not represent an all-inclusive listing. You will be asked to rank these according to your personal view of what is most important to what is least important.

Quality	Rank
a. intelligent	___
b. caring	___
c. dependable	___
d. inspiring	___
e. mature	___
f. forward-looking	___
g. courageous	___
h. honest	___
i. fair-minded	___
j. competent	___

Instructions:

1. Complete your personal ranking of the ten qualities listed. Rate as "1" your most important, "2" your second most important, and so on, with "10" being the least important.
2. Break into groups of seven to nine persons. The group will select a leader and two observers, who will follow additional instructions outlined below.
3. As a group, reread the discussion on the consensus process.
4. *The allotted time for this instruction is 30 minutes.* As a group, your leader will conduct a team meeting in which the team uses a consensus approach that results in a team ranking of the items. Make sure you fully explore differences of opinion among your members about the way your team will proceed to develop its ranking, as well as selection of what the team feels is #1, #2, etc. Try to avoid voting, which tends to restrict discussion of an issue. Make sure that all members "buy into" decisions of the group. *It is not necessary that you complete the ranking in the time per-*

mitted for the task. It is more important that you reach consensus on that which you *do* achieve rather than totally complete the ranking of items. If you complete half or more of the items in the time allowed, the likelihood is that you have sacrificed consensus to do so.

Instructions to the leader:

Your team will have 30 minutes to work on the task. Remember, do not forge ahead without full discussion of all relevant issues. The consensus process takes time; make sure differences are fully explored and consensus achieved before moving along to the next issue. Your effectiveness as a leader and as a team is not based on how many items you rank, but rather the extent to which you effectively lead your group toward consensus.

Instructions to observers:

1. Your task is to observe the meeting, taking notes. Evaluate (a) the effectiveness of the leader's behavior in conducting the meeting and (b) the extent to which consensus was actually achieved by the group. Complete the leader assessment scale below.

		Good	**Fair**	**Weak**
a.	Clearly established the objective of the meeting.	____	____	____
b.	Kept discussion relevant.	____	____	____
c.	Made sure everyone participated.	____	____	____
d.	Used questioning techniques effectively.	____	____	____
e.	Kept the meeting moving along.	____	____	____
f.	Helped the group fully examine issues.	____	____	____
g.	Summarized key points thoroughly.	____	____	____
h.	Achieved closure for each item on the agenda.	____	____	____
i.	Maintained "consensus" approach within the group.	____	____	____

2. After the instructor calls time, or when the meeting is complete, whichever comes first, report your observations to the group. (Keep the report to 5 minutes.)

skill builder 14–2

The Required Weekly Meeting

Emily Simon, who supervises 12 office employees at Integer Electronics, looked at the following memo, which had been placed on her desk.

TO: All Supervisors
FROM: Ramon Garcia, General Manager
SUBJECT: Weekly Meeting

Beginning October 1, all supervisors will conduct a meeting with their employees each Friday afternoon at 4:40 p.m. The purposes of these meetings will be to make announcements of interest, to update your work group on departmental and company progress, and to address problems, issues, and concerns that your work group may have. This action is being taken to improve communication in the plant. I appreciate your effort in making these meetings effective.

Shutting down 20 minutes early didn't bother Simon at all. Neither did the fact that a weekly meeting would probably waste everyone's time. What did concern her was that she had little experience running meetings and addressing large groups. How would she kill the time if there was nothing to say? What if her employees asked questions that she couldn't answer? Would these meetings end up being gripe sessions? "This might be just what a few people need as a platform to mouth off and stir up trouble," thought Simon. "It seems as if we've done pretty well around here without meetings in the past," she said to herself. Then she went to talk to Virgil Robinson, a good friend and supervisor in the purchasing department. She wondered what Virgil would have to say about this required weekly meeting.

Answer the following questions:

1. What are the pros and cons of the required meetings on Fridays?
2. To what extent are Emily Simon's concerns justified?
3. Assume that Simon comes to you for advice on how to conduct such meetings effectively. What suggestions would you offer?

●skill builder 14–3

Developing Skills as a Facilitator/Consultant
group activity

In preparation for this class, go back and reread the section on process consultation. Keep in mind that the primary role of the facilitator/consultant is that of helper to an individual, group, or organization.

Instructions:

1. Each member of the class is to identify a problem or issue on which he or she needs help. It may be that you need help improving your study habits and grades. It may be that you are having a problem at work with your boss or with someone who works with you or for you. The guideline is that it must be a real problem or issue and that you "own" the problem.
2. The class is to be divided into groups of three. Each member of the trio will take turns being the client and receiving help from the other two members. The client will start the process by stating the issue or problem and will have 20 minutes to receive help.
3. The other two members will ask questions to clarify, expand on, and sharpen the diagnosis. In carrying out the questioning, the facilitators will play an active listening role and ask questions that not only help them in

understanding the problem, but also aid the individual being helped to better understand. Examples of such questions would be: "When did you first start having this problem? Can you expand on the history of your relationship with this coworker?"

4. Ask the client what steps, if any, have been initiated to solve the problem.

5. Move into a joint problem-solving framework where all three of you engage in brainstorming ideas on how to deal with the problem.

6. Put together an action plan using the best ideas on specific actions the client can take to solve the problem.

● skill builder 14–4

Facilitator Training
group activity

Assume you are in training to become an external facilitator/consultant and are faced with the following situations:

Your Task

First you are to choose the correct answer from the three alternatives and write the letter (a, b, c) that corresponds to the answer provided under the heading "Your Answer." You will have ten minutes to complete the task.

Team Task

You will be assigned to a small team of trainees to develop a team answer. Although the team will arrive at its answer through consensus, remember that consensus does not always mean unanimity. It means everyone has an opportunity to have their views considered before a choice is made. You will have 30 minutes to complete the team task.

How would you handle the following situations if you were the facilitator?

1. You are the facilitator at a workshop with 35 participants. The participants have agreed on a common set of goals, and they have also identified five issues they need to deal with to achieve their goals. Five ad hoc subgroups of seven participants have been assigned to develop a plan to solve one of the top issues. The first step in the problem-solving process is to clearly state the problem. The members of one of the subgroups approach you as facilitator and state that they are having difficulty defining the problem and need your help.
   a. Tell them to do the best they can. (Your logic is that people learn from experience—success as well as failures.)
   b. Ask a few questions, and then write your version of the problem on the flip chart.
   c. Suggest that each person write a statement of the problem and then record all of them on the flip chart to see if one stands out or if there is a central theme.

Your Answer   *Team's Answer*   *Expert's Answer*

_____   _____   _____

2. You are facilitating a two-day workshop between the Navy and a contractor regarding the environmental clean-up progress of a Pacific island. Several former Navy personnel now work for the contractor. Toward the end of the first day, dur-

ing a break, a public works civilian from the Navy approaches you and expresses a concern that a former Navy captain, who now works for the contractor, always begins a suggestion or recommendation with the following comment: "When I was Captain of XYZ installation and we were faced with this situation, we did so and so."

a. Do nothing.

b. As facilitator, talk with the former captain and level with him about the concern of a member of the Navy's group. Suggest he make recommendations without mentioning his former leadership positions in the Navy.

c. As facilitator, mention the problem to the former captain's boss with the contractor. Leave it to him to decide whether or not he wants to say anything to the former captain.

Your Answer	*Team's Answer*	*Expert's Answer*
_____	_____	_____

3. You are facilitator for a group of 25 participants of two organizations who must work together to complete a major task such as building a dam. The two groups are having difficulties. As facilitator, you have taken them through a process where the group has identified and prioritized five issues they need to work on to ensure they will achieve their goals. After this task is completed, the group takes a short break before they start work on the priority issues. During the break, a key manager of one of the organizations comes to you and says that unless the lack of trust issue is addressed, very little progress will be made in resolving the other issues.

a. Tell the key manager to trust the process and that by working on the five prioritized issues, team building will occur and trust will develop.

b. Prior to reconvening, have a short meeting between four of the leaders, two from each organization, to gain their opinion on adding the trust issue to the list. Have the key manager present his case to them, and you, as facilitator, point out that developing trust is an important factor in successful teamwork and task accomplishment.

c. When the group reconvenes, you as facilitator add the trust issue to the list to be worked on.

Your Answer	*Team's Answer*	*Expert's Answer*
_____	_____	_____

4. Assume you are facilitating a quarterly improvement meeting between representatives from the production and maintenance departments of a chemical plant. There are seven participants: four from production and three from maintenance. The meeting has become bogged down and is not making progress because of the strong views of two participants—one from production and one from maintenance. It appears to you that although both views have merit, neither one is hearing what the other is saying, and each is strictly focusing on his or her own viewpoint.

a. Intervene and remind the participants of the time constraints and suggest they move on to something else.

b. Intervene and request to hear the views of the other participants.

c. Intervene by asking the production representative to summarize the maintenance representative's viewpoint to be sure the viewpoint was understood correctly by the production representative; then reverse the process.

Your Answer   *Team's Answer*   *Expert's Answer*

_____   _____   _____

5. Assume you are the facilitator/consultant for two medical firms located in a U.S. city with a population of 300,000 people. The firms are considering a merger; there are a number of win–win outcomes from such a merger (lower costs, better offices and facilities, more complete medical coverage, etc.). You are facilitating an initial, exploratory meeting with eight doctors, four from each firm. After three hours, the meeting is running into difficulties, despite several interventions by you to get things on track. The problem is that one of the doctors in the first firm is, from a leadership standpoint, very Theory X oriented and is strongly against the merger. It is obvious he basically does not trust the other doctors, and by voice tone and verbal and nonverbal actions, he is behaving in a very autocratic manner.

   a. Take a long break and have each group meet for an hour to decide if they really want to pursue the merger.

   b. Intervene by giving a short theory input on Theory X and Theory Y management philosophies, and for this discussion, suggest that a participative shared leadership discussion should prevail.

   c. Intervene by having all eight members respond on a 3 × 5 card to the following instructions:

   • Evaluate on a five-point scale how well we've done in focusing on substantive issues and ways to achieve our joint goals of better patient care, service, and profits.

1	*2*	*3*	*4*	*5*
Very poor		*Average*		*Very well*

   • Evaluate on a five-point scale how well we have done in carrying out good group dynamics of listening, supporting good ideas, sharing leadership, and differing without being disagreeable.

1	*2*	*3*	*4*	*5*
Very poor		*Average*		*Very well*

   • Post the results and use as a basis for the group to discuss how to improve the group's functioning and progress.

   Your Answer   *Team's Answer*   *Expert's Answer*

   _____   _____   _____

6. Assume you are the facilitator for a national sales organization that is changing its culture to a team approach from that of an individual entrepreneurial approach. The theme of the two-day workshop is "working together to grow stronger."

   After the national sales director reviews the overall company objectives and history, each regional team prioritizes issues, problems, and opportunities that they need to address to achieve overall company objectives. Next, each regional team works on an action plan involving the top-ranked item.

   As facilitator, you visit the four regional breakout rooms and are quite pleased that three of the four regional teams are progressing quite well and demonstrating most of the characteristics of an effective team—shared leadership, good participation and listening, etc. Unfortunately, the last regional team is having difficulty. After observing for some time, it is apparent the problem lies with the regional manager. He is doing 80 percent of the talking, cutting people off in mid-sentence who offer suggestions, and forcing his own viewpoint.

   a. As facilitator, suggest that they brainstorm ideas and write them on the flip chart before evaluating them.

   b. As facilitator, take over the leadership of the group by "playing traffic cop" and directing the flow of who talks when.

   c. Privately provide some coaching to the regional manager on how the session could be more productive.

Your Answer	*Team's Answer*	*Expert's Answer*
_____	_____	_____

7. This situation is a bonus question and provides an opportunity to provide an answer comparable to, or even better than, the expert's answer. The instructor with class input will decide if a bonus is deserved.

You have been asked as an outside facilitator to assist the chairperson of an appointed task force involving a department of the federal government. This department is moving into a new federal building under design and construction. The task force has been charged to determine such interior design questions as size and type of offices, paint color, size and number of conference rooms, etc.

The task force consists of 10 government employees and has had two meetings. There was no progress made in the meetings, however, primarily because of two disruptive task force members. One of the disruptive individuals is very skeptical about any new, innovative ideas and is playing the role of devil's advocate (challenger), to the point of causing frustration and unproductive meeting progress. The other individual obviously has no interest in being on the committee and has done paper work during both meetings.

What advice would you give the meeting chairperson regarding how to handle this situation?

Your Answer	*Team's Answer*	*Expert's Answer*
_____	_____	_____

SOURCE: *This skill builder was developed by the Synergistic Group, 6 Schwaemmle Drive, Mobile, AL 36608.*

Meeting Facilitation Challenges

Assume that you are the supervisor leading your work team in addressing an important issue. Each situation below represents an incident that crops up during the meeting.

1. Two of your team members, Betty Morton and Frank Jacobs, are hard-nosed members who often compete for attention. They often argue with each other as a way to get the spotlight. This meeting you're conducting is no exception. After stating the problem and requesting alternatives from the group, you had a good idea who the first two to make comments would be. Morton gave the first alternative. Jacobs gave his alter-

native, which was, of course, quite different from Morton's. Morton mounted a counterattack by defending her own proposal. As she speaks, you can see by Jacobs's body language that he is preparing his own counteroffensive.

2. One of your team members, Ernie Statler, is especially long winded. He always stretches what could be said in 10 seconds to a minute or more. The meeting has now lasted about 10 minutes and Statler has already spoken four or five times. You can see the boredom on everyone's face as he interrupts another member and gets set to talk again. You must intervene.

3. As your meeting moves along, Ann Stiles and Harry Litten have become distracting. They have whispered a few comments to each other, and you have noted some other team members' raised eyebrows and glances cast in their direction. Harold Pollock, one of your quiet, softspoken members has the floor as Stiles and Litten continue their private conversation. It's time you intervened.

4. It's now about 35 minutes into the meeting, and someone in the group makes a comment about the upcoming, big football game tomorrow between the state's two large college archrivals. Several members chime in with comments. Your group has some strong fans pulling for each school; several members are going as a group to see the game. They would obviously rather talk football than the subject at hand. You need to have them refocus.

5. At the start of the meeting you had told the group that you could live with any decision which they made. It's now about 45 minutes into the meeting and your team has fully discussed four workable alternatives. You feel one alternative is the best, but you can truly live with any of the alternatives offered. You say, "Well, we seem to have done a good job discussing the alternatives; let's see if we can now make a decision." At that point, one of the members asks which of the alternatives you favor.

6. Based on the team's responses, considerable time has been spent discussing the pros and cons and the best choice of the four. It appears that seven of your nine members favor alternative 3. The other two members favor alternatives 2 and 4. You feel that everyone has had a chance to speak up and hear each other out. You say, "It appears that, having heard from everyone on this issue, this group strongly favors alternative 3. Is this alternative workable with everyone?" Sam Stennett, one of the dissenting members, states "No, it's not okay with me. I'm firmly convinced it's not workable. I refuse to vote for something I don't think is best."

Instructions:

Indicate how you would handle each situation by writing down the exact words you would say.

chapter 15

Managing Conflict and Stress

• outline

Causes of Conflict

Conflict Management Styles

Using Principled Negotiation to Resolve Conflict

Overcoming Interpersonal Conflicts

What Is Stress?
Definition of Stress
The Costs of Stress
The Positive Aspects of Stress

Major Causes of Stress
Life Events
Personal Psychological Makeup
Organizational and Work-Related Factors
Burnout

Ways to Cope with Personal Stress
Physical Exercise
Relaxation Techniques
A Sense of Control

Developing and Maintaining Good Interpersonal Relationships

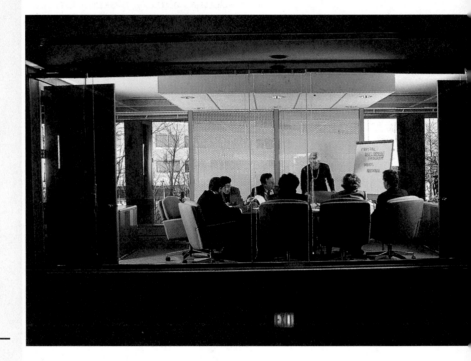

Nothing in life is to be feared. It is only to be understood.

Marie Curie

Everything that irritates us about others can lead us to an understanding of ourselves.

Carl Jung

Difficulties are meant to rouse, not discourage. The human spirit is to grow strong by conflict.

William Emery Channing

The Conflict-Laden, Stressful Plant Environment

The Davis Chemical Company recently acquired the chemical division of a smaller company in a friendly divestiture. In the acquisition they acquired three profitable chemical plants and one unprofitable plant that we will call Plant D.

After the acquisition, Davis Chemical Company sent a home office human relations manager, Beverly Rogers, to gather information, make a diagnosis, and provide recommendations to improve Plant D. In gathering data she utilized individual interviews and small-group discussion sessions. Beverly discovered considerable stress, insecurity, and low morale in the workforce of 500 people. In addition to a lack of teamwork, there was considerable conflict among departments, especially between production and maintenance.

Beverly was appalled at the heavy-handed manner used by the plant manager in his attempt to gain profitability for the plant. A year ago he decided to downsize in an effort to become profitable. After gaining the approval of his boss, he sent all employees a memo stating that within a year the company would rightsize and eliminate 150 more employees. That memo was sent six months ago, and since then 86 employees had been given pink slips. The backlash has taken the form of sabotage estimated at $2 million along with a record number of grievances. In addition, there was considerable finger-pointing and a culture of "blame the other group." The culture of blame was especially evident in the conflicts and divisiveness between production and maintenance. The unilateral autocratic leadership style of the plant manager seemed to be a major factor in the negative culture and lack of teamwork.

After completing her interviews, Beverly presented her report and recommendations to the Davis CEO and his top management team. Her primary recommendation was to remove the current plant manager and replace him with a manager from their company who had a reputation for team building and was skilled in developmental leadership. The manager she recommended had an undergraduate degree in chemical engineering, coupled with an M.B.A. degree. Additionally, she recommended that early in his tenure (within three months) the following action strategies take place:

1. Conduct a weekend retreat with the new plant manager's direct-report employees focusing on team building, action planning, and partnering within the lead team.
2. Conduct a joint session between the department heads and supervision from production and maintenance focusing on team building, conflict management, and joint problem solving.
3. After completing the first two strategies, conduct a communication/problem-solving session between the union leaders and plant leaders.

In conclusion Beverly recommended an outside facilitator/consultant be used to help in designing and implementing all three action strategies. The CEO and his team accepted all of the recommendations and immediately made the change in plant managers. As we go through this chapter we will refer back to this case.

We have seen in the preview case that excessive conflict is often very disruptive and damaging in organizations. A supervisor/team leader must possess a variety of skills and one of the most critical is conflict management. When conflict is excessive and dysfunctional, a significant amount of time must be spent on conflict management. However, we must keep in mind that a certain amount of conflict is healthy because it can lead to more effective decision making. For example, when conflict is present, the status quo is examined. Individuals grapple with various solutions through their analysis of the situation. In many cases, this evaluation leads to better decisions.

1 Identify the causes of conflict.

CAUSES OF CONFLICT

A supervisor/team leader must have a basic understanding of the causes of conflict before he or she can determine what is functional or dysfunctional. This section looks at some of the causes.

1. **Different goals or objectives.** If departments or individuals within an organization are working toward different goals, then conflict is almost always dysfunctional. In the partnering section we emphasized how important it is to develop a common set of goals that everyone supports.
2. **Communication.** Misunderstandings due to semantics, unfamiliar language, or ambiguous or incomplete information will surely lead to conflict.
3. **Structure.** Power struggles between departments with conflicting objectives or reward systems, competition for scarce resources, or interdependence of two or more groups to achieve their goals occur with organizational changes such as downsizing.
4. **Personal.** Incompatibility of personal goals or social values of employees with the role behavior required by their jobs will lead to conflict as will certain personality characteristics, such as authoritarianism or dogmatism.
5. **Change.** Fears associated with job security or the loss of personal power and prestige can cause abnormal behavior. Change can be threatening.

self-check

How many of the above causes of conflict were operative in the preview case?

2 Discuss conflict management styles and identify when each would be appropriate.

CONFLICT MANAGEMENT STYLES

Individuals must cope with all forms of interpersonal and intergroup conflict. It is important to properly diagnose the conflict situation so that it can be dealt with in a most effective manner. Exhibit 15–1 is a diagram of five conflict hanclick! http://www.cri.cc/

Exhibit 15–1

Interpersonal Conflict Management Styles

SOURCE: *Adapted from Thomas Ruble and Kenneth Thomas, "Support for a Two-Dimensional Model of Conflict Behavior,"* Organizational Behavior and Human Performance, *vol. 16 (1976), p. 145. Used with permission of Academic Press, Inc.*

dling styles which are based on the concern an individual has for oneself and for others. The five styles are as follows:

- **Avoiding.** Avoiding is an unassertive, uncooperative style in which the individual's concern for self and others is low. It is a useful style when dealing with trivial issues or when the negative consequences of confrontation outweigh the need for resolution.

- **Accommodating.** Accomodating is an unassertive, cooperative style in which the individual's concern for self is low while the concern for others is high. The accommodating approach downplays the parties' differences. It is an appropriate style to use when the issue is more important to the other party or the other party is right.

- **Forcing.** Forcing is an assertive, uncooperative style in which the individual's concern for self is high while the concern for others is low. This approach uses power to resolve conflict. A forcing style is useful in an emergency situation, where quick decisions are necessary. It is also useful for correcting unethical behavior.

- **Compromising.** Compromising is a somewhat assertive, cooperative style in which the individual has a moderate amount of concern for both self and others. The objective is to find a middle ground. The compromising style is appropriate when the parties have reached an impasse due to mutually exclusive goals.

- **Collaborating.** Collaborating is an assertive, cooperative approach in which the individual has a high concern for self and others. Collaboration is a problem-solving style. It is effective when dealing with conflict "head on," trying to surface all of the pertinent issues, and attempting to interpret differing points of view.

Conflict management styles must be adapted to fit the situation at hand.

Conflict management theory during most of the 1960s and 1970s supported collaboration as the appropriate approach to resolve conflict. Since collaboration in many cases leads to win–win outcomes, it is easy to discern why collaboration advocates supported this approach as "the model" for handling conflict. During the 1970s and 1980s, the contingency movement gained momentum. Proponents of this theory maintained that collaboration in all situations is unrealistic. For example, a management student, who is a member of a local emergency response team, made the following observation when conflict management styles were covered in class.

Her unit was activated shortly after a tragic train wreck occurred. The emergency response team prepares for these types of situations regularly. However, unanticipated problems arise that must be dealt with effectively as quickly as possible in order to save lives. Although the team members may utilize the collaborative approach during the planning stages, they do not have time to rely on this method while in the field. She indicated that the approach most often used by the team in the field was the forcing style, because it was the most effective.

The avoiding, accommodating, forcing, and compromising conflict management styles are usually best used when dealing with tactical, day-to-day, short-term problems. Whereas, collaboration (and compromising, to a limited extent) is a conflict management style more appropriate for ad hoc task forces and long-term strategic problems.

self-check

In the preview case what would be the preferred primary conflict management style to use in implementing the action strategies?

3 Describe principled negotiation.

USING PRINCIPLED NEGOTIATION TO RESOLVE CONFLICT

A real breakthrough in conflict management and resolution is found in the concepts proposed by Roger Fisher and William Ury of the Harvard negotiation project. They emphasize that, whether negotiation involves a peace settlement among nations or a business contract, people often engage in *positional bargaining*. This common form of negotiation involves proposing and then giving up a sequence of positions. The idea is to give up things that are not very important. Hence, proposals are "padded" initially. For this form of negotiation to succeed, it must meet three criteria of fair negotiation, which are: "It should produce a wise agreement if agreement is possible; it should be efficient; and it should improve, or at least not damage, the relationship between the parties."[1]

When people bargain over positions, they tend to back themselves into corners defending their positions, which results in a number of either *win–lose* or *lose–lose* outcomes. Moreover, arguing over positions often endangers an ongoing relationship by straining and sometimes shattering relationships. In a marriage this results in divorce, and in business the result can be the breakup of an otherwise successful operation. Many negotiations involve more than two parties, and in these cases positional bargaining compounds the problem of negotiating an agreement.

In their work with the Harvard negotiation project, Fisher and Ury developed an alternative to positional bargaining that they call **principled negotiation,** or negotiation on the merits. The four basic components of principled negotiation are:

principled negotiation Negotiation on the merits.

1. Separating the people from the problem.
2. Focusing on interests, not positions.
3. Generating a variety of possibilities before deciding what to do.
4. Insisting that the result be based on some objective standard.

Consultant facilitators for a number of joint ventures and partnerships involving multiple parties have noted that educating the joint venture parties in the concepts of principled negotiation has resulted in a high percentage of win–win resolutions in dispute settlements. Exhibit 15–2 illustrates the difference between positional bargaining and principled negotiation. Notice that in positional bargaining, one can either play "hardball" or "softball."

OVERCOMING INTERPERSONAL CONFLICTS

The authors are convinced that principled negotiation is an excellent approach for dealing with conflicts among departments within an organization or resolving conflicts in joint ventures or partnerships.

Perhaps a more pervasive challenge is managing interpersonal conflicts between individuals. This challenge has been accelerated because of fears of downsizing, mergers, and an unknown organizational future. Job insecurity fueled by these fears produces fertile ground for conflict as we saw in the preview case.

Industrial psychologist and trainer Dr. Jack Singer makes a strong case that human resource professionals and supervisors must learn conflict resolution strategies and teach them to other employees. He recommends a three-step pro-

Exhibit 15–2

Contrast of Positional Bargaining and Principled Negotiations

Problem **Positional Bargaining:** **Which Game Should You Play?**		**Solution** **Change the Game—** **Negotiate on the Merits**
Soft	**Hard**	**Principled**
Participants are friends.	Participants are adversaries.	Participants are problem solvers.
The goal is agreement.	The goal is victory.	The goal is a wise outcome reached efficiently and amicably.
Make concessions to cultivate the relationship.	Demand concessions as a condition of the relationship.	**Separate the people from the problem.**
Be soft on the people and the problem.	Be hard on the problem and the people.	Be soft on the people, hard on the problem.
Trust others.	Distrust others.	Proceed independent of trust.
Change your position easily.	Dig in to your position.	**Focus on interests, not positions.**
Make offers.	Make threats.	Explore interests.
Disclose your bottom line.	Mislead as to your bottom line.	Avoid having a bottom line.
Accept one-sided losses to reach agreement.	Demand one-sided gains as the price of agreement.	**Invent options for mutual gain.**
Search for the single answer: the one *they* will accept.	Search for the single answer: the one *you* will accept.	Develop multiple options to choose from; decide later.
Insist on agreement.	Insist on your position.	**Insist on using objective criteria.**
Try to avoid a contest of will.	Try to win a contest of will.	Try to reach a result based on standards independent of will.
Yield to pressure.	Apply pressure.	Reason and be open to reason; yield to principle, not pressure.

SOURCE: *"Positional Bargaining: Which Game Should You Play?" chart from* Getting to Yes, *2e by Roger Fisher, William Ury and Bruce Patton. Copyright © 1981, 1991 by Roger Fisher and William Ury. Reprinted by permission of Houghton Mifflin Co. All rights reserved.*

gram for assessing and implementing a conflict resolution strategy, as shown in Exhibit 15–3.

Many interpersonal conflicts occur when one person finds another person's behavior uncomfortable, bullying, or irritating. Robert Bramson has identified basic types of difficult behavior, three of which are particularly troublesome when trying to resolve conflicts. Exhibit 15–4 identifies these three types and gives suggestions for coping with them.

Exhibit 15–3

*Three-Step Program
for Conflict Resolution*

STEP 1. EVALUATING CONFLICT STYLE

Several self-assessment questionnaires have been developed over the years that are geared toward offering participants insight into how they react in typical conflict situations. Consider using them. The insight they provide allows you to understand what "buttons" get pushed when a person is provoked, and becomes useful as a tool to reevaluate and enhance one's behavior.

STEP 2. IDENTIFYING CONFLICT BEHAVIORS

Nonproductive Behaviors. Confronting, dominating, defending, using sarcasm and hostile humor, repressing emotions, insisting on being right, stonewalling, blaming.

Neutral Behaviors. Avoiding, cooling off, apologizing, giving in, backing off to avoid confrontation.

Positive Behaviors. Active listening, empathizing, disarming, inquiring, using "I feel" statements, recognizing how internal dialogue impacts emotional reactions. The goal is to eliminate negative and neutral behaviors and practice positive confrontation reduction skills until they become new habits.

STEP 3. LEARNING POWERFUL CONFRONTATION REDUCTION SKILLS

Active Listening. The key to all interpersonal communications is genuine listening, as opposed to defensive listening, where you plan your retort *while* the other person is talking to you. To begin to really listen, set up a role-playing environment.

First, paraphrase what the other person says in your own words, without judging, agreeing or disagreeing. Listen to and reflect upon the content, needs, and feelings of the other person.

Second, ask for feedback to determine whether you interpreted correctly. If you have not, ask for clarification.

Third, once you are sure you grasp the message and feelings of the other person, respond.

Fourth, the other person then should listen and paraphrase for you. This process continues until you have both clarified your positions.

Empathizing. This involves putting yourself in the other person's shoes and trying to see the world through his or her eyes, taking into account cultural, racial, gender and experiential differences.

Disarming. The fastest way to defuse an argument is to find some truth in what the other person is saying, even if you do not agree with the basic criticism or complaint. For example, saying "*I can understand* how you'd feel angry with me since you believed that I started the rumor" acknowledges and validates the angry person's feelings without actually agreeing with what was said. This opens the door to clarification.

Inquiring. By asking for clarification of ideas, needs and feelings *you* signal a feeling of working toward mutual understanding and compromise.

"I Feel" Statements. Expressing yourself with such statements as "I feel angry because you seem to be avoiding me" is much more productive than the accusatory, "*You* made me angry and it's *your* fault that I've had a bad day at work today." In the first scenario, *you* take responsibility for your own feelings and share them; in the second, you escalate the confrontation by blaming and putting the person on the defensive.

SOURCE: *Resources, Aberdeen Woods Conference Center, 201 Aberdeen Parkway, Peachtree City, GA 30269-1422. (Vol. 3, Issue 3, November 1997). Jack N. Singer,* Personality Collisions, *pp. 5–6.*

WHAT IS STRESS?

 http://www.stress.org/

A number of concepts presented earlier in this chapter and in previous chapters lend insight into how to manage stress. Organizations and supervisors can suffer serious consequences if stress is not understood and managed. We now examine the topic in more depth.

Exhibit 15–4

Coping with Difficult Behavior

Hostile-Aggressives: Hostile-aggressive behavior occurs when individuals bully other people by bombarding them with cutting remarks, or by throwing a tantrum when things do not go their way. Their focus is on attacking the other party in a conflict. Openly emotional, they use these displays to create discomfort or surprise in their adversaries. Underlying their behavior is a strong sense of "shoulds," internal rules about the way things ought to be. A key to dealing with hostile-aggressive behavior is to recognize the behavior and not to be drawn into it yourself.

HOSTILE-AGGRESSIVES:

- Stand up for yourself.
- Give them time to run down.
- Use self-assertive language.
- Avoid a direct confrontation.

Complainers: Complainers gripe constantly but never take action about what they complain about, usually because they feel powerless or they do not want to take responsibility. You may want to hear complainers out and let them know you understand their feelings, but do not get drawn into pitying them. Use a problem-solving stance. For instance, a manager might say, "Joan, what do you want the outcome of our meeting to be? What action needs to be taken?" This focuses the complainer on solutions, not complaints.

COMPLAINERS:

- Listen attentively.
- Acknowledge their feelings.
- Avoid complaining with them.
- State the facts without apology.
- Use a problem-solving mode.

Clams: Clams are silent and unresponsive when asked for opinions. They react to conflict by closing up (like their namesakes) and refusing to discuss problems. The challenge in coping with clams is getting them to open up and talk. Open-ended questions are invaluable, as is patience in allowing them their silence for a reasonable time.

CLAMS:

- Ask open-ended questions.
- Be patient in waiting for a response.
- Ask more open-ended questions.
- If no response occurs, tell clams what you plan to do, because no discussion has taken place.

SOURCE: *Adapted from* Coping with Difficult People, *Robert M. Bramson. Copyright © 1981 by Robert M. Bramson. Used by permission of Doubleday, a division of Random House and Carol Mann Literacy Agency, on behalf of the author.*

---

4 Explain why modern life makes us particularly vulnerable to stress.

stress
Any external stimulus that causes wear and tear on one's psychological or physical well-being.

Definition of Stress

For many years the medical community failed to take stress seriously. One of the reasons for this failure was the lack of an adequate definition of stress and of research into its effects. **Stress** can be defined as any external stimulus that causes wear and tear on one's psychological or physical well-being.[2]

Stress researchers point out that modern men and women sometimes react to the strains of work and everyday life the same way our primitive ancestors did. In the days of the caveman, when there was danger, a chemical reaction in the body geared our ancestors for either fight or flight. The problem for some modern men and women is that their bodies still react the same way to external stimuli, causing them to maintain a constant fight-or-flight readiness. The anxiety is similar to that of soldiers in combat, and it causes wear and tear on our bodies.

> **Jane Coleman was driving to work during the morning rush hour. An irresponsible driver nearly caused an accident by cutting into her lane. By the time Jane arrived at work, she was already tense; the problem was compounded when she discovered that one of her key employees was out with the flu. Two emergencies during the day caused her to end the day anxious and exhausted.**

Many of us face situations similar to Jane's. Note that stress can be caused by an external stimulus such as driving on the freeway or by conditions on the job. An excellent definition of job stress is "a condition arising from the interaction of people and their jobs and characterized by changes within people that force them to deviate from their normal functioning."[3] Under normal conditions, our bodies and minds are in a state of equilibrium (see Exhibit 15–5). As a result of occurrences on or off the job, however, our equilibrium may be disrupted. In attempting to recover from this imbalance, we function differently and sometimes generate a fight-or-flight chemical reaction. Obviously, Jane, as a supervisor, cannot leave her job or pick a fight with someone, but the chemical reaction in her body occurs anyway.

Exhibit 15–5

Equilibrium and Disequilibrium

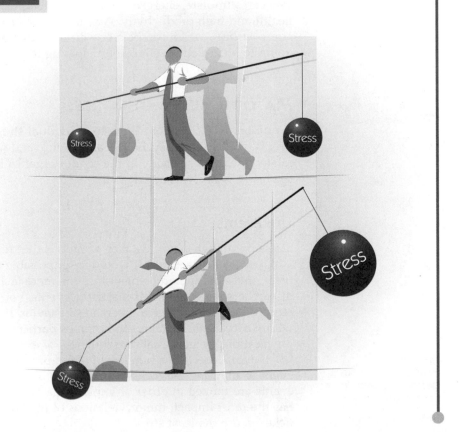

5 Describe both the costs and the benefits of stress.

The Costs of Stress

It has been estimated that two-thirds of all visits to doctors can be traced to stress-related symptoms. Stress, for example, is a major contributor to heart disease, cancer, lung problems, accidents, cirrhosis of the liver, and suicide.

Even the common cold and skin rashes are sometimes related to a person's experiencing prolonged and severe stress. Industry leaders are aware that such symptoms play a major role in absenteeism, accidents, and lost productivity.

Certainly a person under severe and/or prolonged stress cannot function as effectively as a person leading a more balanced life. We are not implying that stress is all negative, however, because a certain amount of stress adds zest to life.

The Positive Aspects of Stress

Some amount of stress is necessary to accomplish anything meaningful. The teams that play in the Super Bowl are certainly in a stressful situation. Anyone who has played a sport or spoken in front of a large group has been in a stressful situation. Without question, moderate amounts of stress improve performance. For example, difficult but attainable objectives motivate better than easy objectives.

People who seek types of work and leisure that engage their skills find life zestful and interesting. The secret is to involve oneself in challenging work and active leisure accompanied by sufficient rest and retreat. Life is full of stressors that can stimulate, energize, and aid in such positive outcomes as individual health and high productivity. We call the constructive dimensions of positive stress *eustress*, which can be a powerful motivator. Examples of eustress include going to an athletic event or participating in sports events.

6 Explain the major causes of stress.

MAJOR CAUSES OF STRESS

A number of factors contribute to individual stress. Among these are (1) life events, (2) personal psychological makeup, and (3) organizational and work-related factors. Especially in the case of organizational and work-related factors, the result is likely to be burnout.

Life Events

Stress occurs whenever we face situations that require changes in behavior and a higher level of activity. It would be impossible to list all of the situations that place stress on human beings, since the mere fact of living does so. However, researchers have identified major life events, both positive and negative, that require drastic changes in a person's behavior. If many of these events occur within a year's time, a person becomes particularly susceptible to unpleasant physical or psychological consequences of excessive stress.

Exhibit 15–6 lists a number of stress-provoking life events. A major **life event** is anything that causes a person to deviate from normal functioning. The events are ranked in order of impact on a person's life. The death of a spouse has the most impact; minor violations of the law, such as receiving a traffic ticket, cause the least stress.

life event
Anything that causes a person to deviate from normal functioning.

Exhibit 15–6

*Life Events from the
Social Readjustment
Rating Scale (SRRS)*

Event	Scale of Impact
Death of spouse	100
Divorce	73
Marital separation	65
Jail term	63
Death of close family member	63
Personal injury or illness	53
Marriage	50
Fired at work	47
Marital reconciliation	45
Retirement	45
Change in health of family member	44
Pregnancy	40
Sex difficulties	39
Gain of new family member	39
Business readjustment	39
Change in financial state	38
Death of close friend	37
Change to different line of work	36
Change in number of arguments with spouse	35
Foreclosure of mortgage or loan	30
Change in responsibilities at work	29
Son or daughter leaving home	29
Trouble with in-laws	29
Outstanding personal achievement	28
Wife begins or stops work	26
Begin or end school	26
Change in living conditions	25
Revision of personal habits	24
Trouble with boss	23
Change in work hours or conditions	20
Change in residence	20
Change in schools	20
Change in recreation	19
Change in church activities	19
Change in social activities	18
Change in sleeping habits	16
Change in number of family get-togethers	15
Change in eating habits	15
Vacation	13
Christmas	12
Minor violations of the law	11

SOURCE: *"The Stress of Adjusting to Change," from* The Relaxation Response, *by Herbert Benson, M.D., with Miriam Z. Klipper. Copyright 1975 by William Morrow Company, Inc. By permission of the publisher.*

Researchers have discovered a statistical correlation between scores on the SRRS and illness among managers and the general population. Individuals scoring 150 points or below have less than a 33 percent chance that a serious illness will occur in the next two years. With scores of 150–300, the probability increases to about 50 percent, and those who score over 300 have an 80 percent chance of serious illness.[4] Steps and action plans can be initiated to offset the probability of a high score, and thus a serious illness. We discuss this later in the chapter.

> **Patrick Hogan was a 34-year-old supervisor who seemed to have it all. He had a good job, was happily married, had two children, and was on top of the world. At work, he was highly productive and outgoing and was considered a leading candidate for advancement.**
>
> **In the course of a year, several events occurred in Patrick's life that completely disrupted his patterns of living. A long-time friend enticed him to invest in a steak house that the friend would operate. The restaurant lost money, and the friend left town, leaving Patrick responsible for the bank note. To save his investments, he started moonlighting at the restaurant, not getting home many nights until 1 a.m.**
>
> **While Patrick was struggling with the restaurant, his mother died after a lingering illness. Two weeks after the funeral, his wife had an accident and was confined to bed with a slipped disc. For the first time in his life, Patrick had to prepare meals, wash clothes, and care for the children while at the same time carrying on with his regular job and struggling with the restaurant.**
>
> **At work, Patrick's behavior changed drastically. He was impatient with his employees and lost his temper quickly. He became depressed and found it difficult to reach decisions about matters that he had previously handled decisively.**

self-check

Based on the above description of what happened in Patrick Hogan's life within the past year, calculate his score on the SRRS. Assume you are his supervisor and Patrick comes to you to talk about his situation. What advice would you give him?

⑦ Compare and contrast Type A behavior and Type B behavior.

Personal Psychological Makeup

Americans have long been noted for their emphasis on work. The United States has a justifiable reputation as a country where individuals, through hard work, can achieve considerable economic success. Some people, however, have become so caught up in the work ethic that work becomes the end itself rather than the means to an end. New Zealanders say that "Americans live to work and New Zealanders work to live." Our point is that some Americans have become workaholics, and this excessiveness has behavioral consequences that take a toll over a period of time.

Researchers have identified two basic types of behavior characterizing people in our society: Type A and Type B.

Type A Behavior. Cardiologists Meyer Friedman and Roy Rosenman first defined the term **Type A behavior.** Individuals who exhibit Type A behavior tend

Type A behavior
A behavior pattern characterized by (a) trying to accomplish too much in a short time and (b) lacking patience and struggling against time and other people to accomplish one's ends.

click! http://workhealth.org/
risk/rfotypea.htm

to try to accomplish too many things in a short time. Lacking patience, they struggle against time and other people to accomplish their ends. As a consequence, they become irritated by trivial things. Type A people also tend to be workaholics. Because of their psychological makeup they may be subject to stress over prolonged periods. For this reason, Type A people have a much higher risk of heart disease than Type B people.[5]

Type B behavior
A behavior pattern characterized by (a) tending to be calmer than someone with Type A behavior, (b) devoting more time to exercise, and (c) being more realistic in estimating the time it takes to complete an assignment.

Type B Behavior. People exhibiting **Type B behavior** tend to be calmer, to take more time to exercise, and to be more realistic than Type A in estimating the amount of time needed to complete an assignment. Type Bs also worry less and, in general, desire more satisfaction from their work.

Studies of Type A and B behaviors indicate that 60 percent of managers and supervisors fall into the category of Type A people. Many supervisors respond to all events as if they were emergencies or life-threatening situations. Managers and supervisors who exhibit extreme Type A behavior patterns tend to practice close supervision and find it difficult to delegate. They are concerned that errors might reflect on past achievements, and so they become excessively task oriented.[6]

self-check

Do you think of yourself as a Type A or a Type B personality? Exhibit 15–7 provides a quiz that will give you a rough idea of your behavioral pattern.

Organizational and Work-Related Factors

Throughout this book we have discussed many organizational and work-related factors that may cause excessive stress. As shown in Exhibit 15–8, these range from having poorly defined job descriptions to having autocratic or permissive leadership. If these factors exist in an organization over a period of time, they will cause extensive damage in the form of dissatisfaction, high turnover, low productivity, incomplete goal accomplishment, and job burnout.

As the following example shows, stress can even create an opportunity for union activity.

> **A union organizer approached several employees from the home office of XYZ Life & Casualty Insurance Company. He was quickly told that they were not interested in joining a union, since they had excellent pay, good working conditions, and a high regard for their supervisors.**
>
> **Six months later, a supervisor retired in the claims department. The new supervisor, after being on the job a month, called two long-time employees into the office and gave them dismissal notices without a reason for doing so. That night, five employees drove 90 miles to a meeting in another city with the union organizer. Upon their return, they obtained enough employee signatures to force an election to determine whether the union would represent employees in the XYZ home office.**

burnout
A malady caused by excessive stress in the setting where people invest most of their time and energy.

Burnout

One of the most common results of excessive stress is burnout. **Burnout** is a stress-related malady that generally originates in the setting where people in-

Exhibit 15–7

Behavior Type Quiz

To find out which behavior type you are, circle the number on the scale below for each trait that best characterizes your behavior.

Casual about appointments	1	2	3	4	5	6	7	8	Never late
Not competitive	1	2	3	4	5	6	7	8	Very competitive
Never feel rushed even under pressure	1	2	3	4	5	6	7	8	Always rushed
Take things one at a time	1	2	3	4	5	6	7	8	Try to do many things at once, think about what I'm going to do next.
Slow doing things	1	2	3	4	5	6	7	8	Fast (eating, walking, etc.)
Express feelings	1	2	3	4	5	6	7	8	"Sit on" feelings
Many interests	1	2	3	4	5	6	7	8	Few interests outside work

Total score: _____ Total score multiplied by 3: _____

The interpretation is as follows:

Number of Points	Type of Personality
Less than 90	B
90 to 99	B+
100 to 105	A−
106 to 119	A
120 or more	A+

SOURCE: *A. P. Brief, R. S. Schuler, and M. V. Sell,* **Managing Job Stress** *(Boston: Little, Brown & Co., 1981), p. 87.*

Exhibit 15–8

Organizational and Work-Related Factors that Cause Excessive Stress

- A highly centralized organization with decision making concentrated at the top.
- Many levels and narrow spans of control.
- Excessive and continuous pressure from higher levels.
- Conflicting demands on lower levels.
- Lack of clarity with respect to organizational and work objectives.
- Widespread autocratic leadership and close supervision.
- Little or no participation in decision making by supervisor and workers.
- Inconsistent application of company policies.
- Favoritism in decisions regarding layoffs, salary increases, promotions, and the like.
- Poor working conditions.
- Poor communication.
- Lack of structure and job descriptions.
- Widespread permissive leadership.
- Technical glitches with computer interfaces.

vest most of their time and energy. This setting is usually the work environment but could just as well be the home or the golf course.

The seriousness of the burnout problem has been highlighted by researchers Robert Golembiewski and Robert Munzenrider. Utilizing an adapted version of the *Maslach Burnout Inventory* (MBI), they discovered that 40 percent of more than 12,000 respondents in 33 organizations suffered from advanced phases of burnout.[7] Exhibit 15–9 explains the subscales used in the MBI and charts the eight phases of burnout.

A person scoring in Phase I would be highly energized and motivated by the positive aspects of stress. In Maslow's terms, such a person would be operating at the esteem and self-fulfillment level of the need hierarchy. To a lesser extent, the same would be true of a person in Phases II, III, IV, and V. Difficulties occur when a person reaches Phases VI, VII, and VIII, the advanced stages of burnout.

Candidates for job burnout have three distinguishing characteristics. First, they experience stress caused predominantly by job-related stressors. Second, they tend to be idealistic and/or self-motivated achievers. Third, they tend to seek unattainable goals.

Although over the long term the ideal way to deal with burnout is to address the factors that are causing it, in the short term burnout can be managed through use of any of a variety of strategies for coping with stress.

Some of the ways companies are preventing or attacking burnout are through providing an on-site fitness center or a subsidy program. "At Allied Signal, 74% of employees who use a fitness center or health club say working

Exhibit 15–9

MBI Subscales and Phases of Burnout

The adapted Maslach Burnout Inventory, or MBI, consists of 25 items, rated on a scale of 1 (very much *unlike* me) to 7 (very much *like* me). There are three subscales.

Depersonalization: Individuals with high scores on this subscale tend to view people as objects and to distance themselves from others. Example: "I worry that this job is hardening me emotionally."

Personal Accomplishment (reversed): Respondents with high scores on this subscale see themselves as not performing well on a task that they perceive as not being particularly worthwhile. Example: "I have accomplished few worthwhile things on this job."

Emotional Exhaustion: Individuals with high scores on this subscale see themselves as operating beyond comfortable coping limits and as approaching "the end of the rope" in psychological and emotional senses. Example: "I feel fatigued when I get up in the morning and have to face another day on the job."

Emotional exhaustion is considered most characteristic of advanced phases of burnout, and depersonalization is considered least virulent. Ratings of high or low on the three subscales determine the progressive phases of burnout, generating an eight-phase model of burnout:

	Progressive Phases of Burnout							
	I	II	III	IV	V	VI	VII	VIII
Depersonalization	Low	High	Low	High	Low	High	Low	High
Personal accomplishment	Low	Low	High	High	Low	Low	High	High
Emotional exhaustion	Low	Low	Low	Low	High	High	High	High

SOURCE: *Adapted from Robert T. Golembiewski and Robert F. Munzenrider,* Phases of Burnout *(Praeger Publishers, an imprint of Greenwood Publishing Group, Inc., Westport, CT, 1988), pp. 19–28. Reprinted with permission. All rights reserved.*

out raised their productivity and 62% say it improved stress coping abilities."[8]
"It is estimated that job stress and related problems cost companies an estimated $200 billion a year."[9]

Elaborate on personal ways to cope with stress.

WAYS TO COPE WITH PERSONAL STRESS

Four methods that have helped many supervisors to cope with stress are (1) engaging in physical exercise, (2) practicing relaxation techniques, (3) gaining a sense of control, and (4) developing and maintaining good interpersonal relationships.

Physical Exercise

People who exercise a minimum of two or three times a week are much less prone to the adverse symptoms of stress than those who do not. The exercise should be vigorous to the point of inducing perspiration. A person's muscles and circulatory system are not designed for a life of inactivity. People who revitalize their bodies are much less likely to worry and become upset over events and problems. The exercise can take many forms—tennis, handball, jogging, walking, swimming, gardening, or workouts at a health and exercise spa.

> **Earlier in the chapter, we highlighted the problems that Patrick Hogan was facing and saw how the stress of dealing with these problems had drastically changed his behavior. Patrick's manager noticed the change and counseled him regarding the situation. After Patrick had discussed his circumstances, the manager asked him if he engaged in regular exercise. Patrick answered that he simply did not have the time as a result of having to moonlight at the restaurant.**
>
> **Patrick's manager persuaded him to work out three times a week in the company exercise room. Within two week's time, Patrick's on-the-job behavior was back to normal, and he had begun developing a plan to cope with some of the problems outside of work.**

Relaxation Techniques

Exhibit 15–10 summarizes several of the relaxation techniques that are easy to use and are effective. These techniques are particularly useful to supervisors/team leaders because they are neither time consuming nor costly. Research shows that when practiced on a regular basis, these techniques enable one to deal more effectively with stress and may lower blood pressure and, in general, improve physical and emotional health.

A Sense of Control

Supervisors who have a sense of control over their own lives handle stress much better than those who feel they are manipulated by life's events or by other people. If they have other interests, supervisors are better able to look at work as only one aspect of life. Many of them also have a deep faith in religion, which allows them to cope with adversity. Some ways to gain control are as follows:

Exhibit 15–10

Relaxation Techniques

Relaxation Response. One of the best studied stress-relievers is the relaxation response, first described by Harvard's Herbert Benson, M.D., more than 20 years ago. Its great advantage is that it requires no special posture or place. Say you're stuck in traffic when you're expected at a meeting. Or you're having trouble falling asleep because your mind keeps replaying some awkward situation.

- Sit or recline comfortably. Close your eyes if you can, and relax your muscles.
- Breathe deeply. To make sure that you are breathing deeply, place one hand on your abdomen, the other on your chest. Breath in slowly through your nose, and as you do you should feel your abdomen (not your chest) rise.
- Slowly exhale. As you do, focus on your breathing. Some people do better if they silently repeat the word *one* as they exhale; it helps clear the mind.
- If thoughts intrude, do not dwell on them; allow them to pass on and return to focusing on your breathing.

Although you can turn to this exercise any time you feel stressed, doing it regularly for 10 to 20 minutes at least once a day can put you in a generally calm mode that can see you through otherwise stressful situations.

Cleansing Breath. Epstein, who has searched the world literature for techniques people have claimed valuable for coping, focuses on those that are simple and powerful. He calls them "gems," devices that work through differing means, can be learned in minutes, can be done anytime, anywhere, and have a pronounced physiologic effect. At the top of his list is the quickest of all—a cleansing breath.

Take a huge breathe in. Hold it for three to four seconds. Then let it out v-e-r-y s-l-o-w-l-y. As you blow out, blow out all the tension in your body.

Relaxing Postures. "The research literature demonstrates that sitting in certain positions, all by itself, has a pronounced effect," says Epstein. Sit anywhere. Relax your shoulders so that they are comfortably rounded. Allow your arms to drop by your sides. Rest your hands, palm side up, on top of your thighs. With your knees comfortably bent, extend your legs and allow your feet, supported on the heels, to fall gently outward. Let your jaw drop. Close your eyes and breathe deeply for a minute or two.

Passive Stretches. It's possible to relax muscles without effort; gravity can do it all. Start with your neck and let your head fall forward to the right. Breathe in and out normally. With every breath out, allow your head to fall more. Do the same for shoulders, arms, back.

Imagery. Find a comfortable posture and close your eyes. Imagine the most relaxed place you've ever been. We all have a place like this and can call it to mind anywhere, any time. For everyone it is different. It may be a lake. It may be a mountain. It may be a cottage at the beach. Are you there?

Five—Count 'Em, Five—Tricks. Since you can never have too many tricks in your little bag, here are some "proven stress-busters" from Paul Rosch, M.D., president of the American Institute of Stress:

- Curl your toes against the soles of your feet as hard as you can for 15 seconds, then relax them. Progressively tense and relax the muscles in your legs, stomach, back, shoulders, neck.
- Visualize lying on a beach, listening to waves coming in and feeling the warm sun and gentle breezes on your back. Or, if you prefer, imagine an erotic fantasy or picture yourself in whatever situation makes you happiest.
- Set aside 20 to 30 minutes a day to do anything you want—even nothing.
- Take a brisk walk.
- Keep a Walkman handy and loaded with relaxing, enjoyable music.

"Beating stress is a matter of removing yourself from the situation and taking a few breaths," says Rosch. "If I find myself getting stressed I ask myself 'is this going to matter to me in five years?' Usually the answer is no. If so, why get worked up over it?"

SOURCE: *Adapted from John Carpi, "A Smorgasbord of Stress-Stoppers,"* Psychology Today *29(1), January/ February 1996, p. 39.*

1. Plan. Look ahead, identifying both long- and short-term goals. Also, identify causes of stress and ways to alleviate them.

2. Get to know and like yourself. Identify your strengths and interests and pursue activities that capitalize on your strengths.

3. Perceive situations as challenges rather than as problems.

4. Take a long vacation rather than a series of short vacations.

5. Do things for others, either through a religious group or by becoming involved in some kind of volunteer work or youth activities such as Boy or Girl Scouts, Big Brother or Big Sister, or Junior Achievement.

6. Provide yourself with positive reinforcement when you do a task well. Treat yourself to a reward when you accomplish something worthwhile.

Developing and Maintaining Good Interpersonal Relationships

It is most important for one's mental health and happiness to give priority to close relationships—family and friends. These relationships provide a base of mutual support where one can discuss success, opportunities, issues, and problems. According to psychologist Alex Michalos, good interpersonal relationships are much more important to one's happiness and well-being than either income or looks.[10] When one is facing a major challenge or problem, it is helpful to be able to discuss it with a spouse or friend. It is also important to maintain relationships and confront problems between yourself and loved ones and friends through discussion rather than through avoidance. Exhibit 15–11 provides a summary of strategies that help make you feel great.

Exhibit 15–11

Strategies that Make You Feel Great

- Savor the moment. "Happiness," said Benjamin Franklin, "is produced not so much by great pieces of good fortune that seldom happen as by the little advantages that occur each day."

- Take control of your time. There is nevertheless a place for setting goals and managing time. Compared to those who've learned a sense of helplessness, those with an "internal locus of control" do better in school, cope better with stress, and live with greater well-being.

- Act happy. Study after study reveals three traits that mark happy people's lives: (1) They like themselves, (2) they are positive thinkers, and (3) they are outgoing. In experiments, people who feign high self-esteem begin feeling better about themselves.

- Seek work and leisure that engage your skills. Even if we make a lower but livable wage, it pays to seek work that we find interesting and challenging.

- Join the movement movement. A slew of recent studies reveal that aerobic exercise is an antidote for mild depression.

- Get rest. Happy people live active, vigorous lives, yet they reserve time for renewing sleep and solitude.

- Give priority to close relationships. People who can name several close, supportive friends—friends with whom they freely share their ups and downs—live with greater health and happiness.

- Take care of your soul. Actively religious people are much less likely than others to become delinquent, to abuse drugs and alcohol, to divorce, or to commit suicide. They're even physically healthier.

SOURCE: *Adapted from* The Pursuit of Happiness *by David G. Meyers. Copyright © by the David G. and Carol P. Meyers Charitable Foundation. Reprinted by permission of William Morrow & Company, Inc.*

chapter review

1 Identify the causes of conflict.

A key skill needed by supervisors is that of conflict management. Two of the causes of conflict are having unclear or different objectives and communication breakdowns.

2 Discuss conflict management styles and identify when each would be appropriate.

The five conflict management styles are avoiding, accommodating, forcing, compromising, and collaborating or joint problem solving. Two of the most widely used styles are forcing and collaborating. Collaborating seems to be most successful in dealing with conflicts caused by communication difficulties, whereas forcing is sometimes necessary when dealing with conflicts of personal values and personality.

3 Describe principled negotiation.

Principled negotiation holds promise in keeping personalities out of conflict by focusing on the problem rather than the person.

4 Explain why modern life makes us particularly vulnerable to stress.

Stress is any external stimulus that causes wear and tear on a person's psychological or physical well-being. Modern men and women react to stress as our primitive ancestors did, with a chemical reaction designed to ready the body for fight or flight. This chemical reaction is not helpful in normal situations today, so we need to develop ways to cope with and manage stress.

5 Describe both the costs and the benefits of stress.

When we are unsuccessful in coping with stress, the costs are enormous. Stress is a major cause of many illnesses, from the common cold to heart disease. It plays a role in absenteeism, accidents, and lost productivity. Not all stress is negative, however. Small and great achievements occur as a result of moderate amounts of stress.

6 Explain the major causes of stress.

Major causes of stress are life events, personal psychological makeup, and organizational and work-related factors. The death of a spouse or a divorce places tremendous stress on most individuals. Similarly, working in an extremely high-pressure environment under prolonged autocratic leadership can cause stress and job burnout.

7 Compare and contrast Type A behavior and Type B behavior.

A person's psychological makeup influences how that person handles stress. Type A people try to accomplish too many things in a short period of time and tend to lack patience when dealing with people. Type B people tend to be calmer and more realistic in their assessment of the length of time needed to complete an assignment.

8 Elaborate on personal ways to cope with stress.

Fortunately, many of us can do a better job of managing stress if we develop certain strategies and behaviors. On a personal level, we can (1) exercise, (2) practice relaxation techniques, (3) gain a sense of control over our lives, and (4) develop and maintain good interpersonal relationships. On the job, a supervisor can apply many of the concepts discussed throughout this book. Techniques particularly helpful in reducing stress in a work unit are to practice the concept of balance through participative management, when appropriate, and to delegate effectively without losing control.

important terms

burnout *427*	stress *422*
life event *424*	Type A behavior *426*
principled negotiation *419*	Type B behavior *427*

questions for review and discussion

1. Identify the five conflict management styles and describe when each one would be appropriate.
2. Discuss what is involved in principled negotiation. How does it differ from hard or soft negotiation?
3. Compare and contrast Type A behavior and Type B behavior.
4. What are the major causes of stress on the job? Off the job?
5. Explain why exercise and relaxation techniques are helpful for coping with stress.
6. What can a supervisor do to prevent stress in his or her unit?

● skill builder 15–1

The Conflict-Laden, Stressful Plant Environment

Divide the class into teams of five to seven people. Each group is to assume the role of a consulting team that has been asked to design a retreat for the new management group in the preview case of this chapter. Drawing from your own experience and from what you have learned in this class, develop objectives and an agenda for a two-day retreat for the top management group of the Davis Chemical Company.

Have two members from each team present their recommendations to the rest of the class. Each class member will then vote for the team (excluding his or her own team) that he or she thinks had the best retreat planned for the company.

● skill builder 15–2

Up in Smoke—Are You Burned Out?

Answer each question on a scale of 1 to 5 (1 = never; 2 = rarely; 3 = sometimes; 4 = often; 5 = always).

Do you

- Feel less competent or effective than you used to feel in your work? _____
- Consider yourself unappreciated or "used"? _____

- Dread going to work?   _____
- Feel overwhelmed in your work?   _____
- Feel your work is pointless or unimportant?   _____
- Watch the clock?   _____
- Avoid conversations with others (coworkers, customers, and supervisors
  in the work setting; family members in the home)?   _____
- Rigidly apply rules without considering creative solutions?   _____
- Get frustrated by your work?   _____
- Miss work often?   _____
- Feel unchallenged by your work?   _____

Does your work

- Overload you?   _____
- Deny you rest periods—breaks, lunch time, sick leave, or vacation?   _____
- Pay too little?   _____
- Depend on uncertain funding sources?   _____
- Provide inadequate support to accomplish the job (budget, equipment,
  tools, people, etc.)?   _____
- Lack clear guidelines?   _____
- Entail so many different tasks that you feel fragmented?   _____
- Require you to deal with major or rapid changes?   _____
- Lack access to a social or professional support group?   _____
- Demand coping with a negative job image or angry people?   _____
- Depress you?   _____

Add up your scores for the test and record your total: _____

Scores	Category
94–110	Burnout
76–93	Flame
58–75	Smoke
40–57	Sparks
22–39	No fire

The categories are interpreted as follows:

- *Burnout.* If your score is between 94 and 110, you are experiencing a very high level of stress in your work. Without some changes in yourself or your situation, your potential for stress-related illness is high. Consider seeking professional help for stress reduction and burnout prevention. Coping with stress at this level may also require help from others—supervisors, coworkers, and other associates at work, and spouse and other family members at home.
- *Flame.* If you have a score between 76 and 93, you have a high amount of work-related stress and may have begun to burn out. Mark each question that you scored 4 or above, and rank them in order of their effect on you, beginning with the ones that bother you the most. For at least your top three, evaluate what you can do to reduce the stresses involved, and act to improve your attitude or situation. If your body is reflecting the stress, get a medical checkup.
- *Smoke.* Scores between 58 and 75 represent a certain amount of stress in your work and are a sign that you have a fair chance of burning out unless you take corrective measures. For each question that you scored 4 or above, consider ways you can reduce the stresses involved. As soon as possible, take action to improve your atti-

tude or the situation surrounding those things that trouble you most.

- *Sparks.* If your score is between 40 and 57, you have a low amount of work-related stress and are unlikely to burn out. Look over those questions that you scored 3 or above, and think about what you can do to reduce the stresses involved.
- *No fire.* People with scores of 22 through 39 are mellow in their work, with almost no job-related stress. As long as they continue at this level, they are practically burnout-proof.

For many people, both the job and the home have the potential to produce high stress and burnout. For this reason, having at least one "port in a storm" is important. Ideally, if things are going badly on the job, rest and comfort can be found in the home. Similarly, if home conditions involve pressure, conflict, and frustration, having a satisfying work life helps. The person who faces problems on the job and problems in the home at the same time is fighting a war on two fronts and is a prime candidate for stress overload and burnout.

SOURCE: *Reprinted from George Manning and Kent Curtis, Stress Without Distress (Cincinnati, OH: South-Western Publishing 1988), pp. 143–145, with the permission of South-Western Publishing Co. Copyright © 1988 by South-Western Publishing Co. All rights reserved.*

● skill builder 15–3

A Planning Strategy to Cope with Success

List the things that are causing stress in your life at the present time. Determine which factors are causing positive stress and which are potentially negative and harmful.

Develop an action plan that will enable you to cope with the negative factors more effectively. A good action plan looks ahead and deals with what, when, where, and how to solve the problem.

CASE 15–1

The Missed Promotion

Susan Williamson was worried. For the past six months, her husband, Paul, had been a different person from the man she married. Up until that time, Paul had been a cheerful and caring husband and father. He took an interest in their children, was active in church, and had a zest for day-to-day living. In recent months he had been moody, abrupt, and withdrawn. He spent his time at home watching television and drinking beer. He never talked about his job as maintenance supervisor at the ABC Company as he once had. Recently Susan had asked if something at work was bothering him and, if so, whether he would discuss it with her. His reply was "No, there's nothing bothering me! You take care of the house and the children, and I'll take care of the job and making a living!"

Actually, the job had been bothering Paul for about a year. Before that, he was considered one of the outstanding maintenance supervisors. In those days, his two immediate supervisors, the maintenance superintendent and the maintenance manager, called on him frequently for advice and used him as a troubleshooter within the plant. Although Paul did not have a college degree in engineering, the maintenance manager had strongly hinted that when the maintenance superintendent retired, Paul would be promoted to his position. The maintenance manager had told Paul that, despite having three engineering graduates in the supervision group, he considered Paul the best in the department.

A year ago, the maintenance manager was transferred to another plant. A new maintenance manager came aboard who, from the start, favored college graduates. Gradually Paul was used less and less for troubleshooting assignments, and his advice was rarely sought. Then, six months later, the maintenance superintendent retired and a young engineering graduate named Bobbi, whom Paul had trained, was promoted to the superintendent's job. It was then that Paul's personality changed. He began sleeping longer each night, often falling asleep in front of the television set. He also developed a tightness in his stomach that was creating a burning sensation.

Bobbi, the engineer who had been promoted to maintenance superintendent, was worried. For the past several months she had been concerned about the performance and health of one of her maintenance supervisors, Paul Williamson. Paul had been Bobbi's boss at one time, and she had always admired his ability as a supervisor and his knowledge of the maintenance area.

Recently, while attending a regional meeting of maintenance managers from different plants of the ABC Company, Bobbi ran into the former maintenance manager at her plant, who was now at another plant. He asked how Paul was doing. Bobbi, glad to share her concern with someone, said that she was really worried about him. "His performance has slipped, for one thing. Also, he used to have perfect attendance, but lately he's been calling in sick a lot."

The maintenance manager replied, "I wonder if disappointment over not being promoted to maintenance superintendent has affected his performance. No reflection on you, of course, but before I left, the plant manager and I had agreed that Paul would be promoted to maintenance superintendent. Then the home office changed its corporate policy so that only college graduates could be promoted to superintendent. This made Paul ineligible, and you got the job instead."

Bobbi hadn't realized that Paul had been the first choice for the position she now held. Upon reflection, she decided to have a coaching and counseling session with him when she returned to the plant, as she certainly didn't want to lose him.

Answer the following questions:

1. How should Bobbi approach Paul about the situation?
2. What do you think Paul's reaction(s) will be?
3. Do you agree with the company's policy of promoting only college graduates to the maintenance superintendent position? Why or why not?

Managing Human Resources and Diversity

16   Selecting, Training, and
      Compensating Employees

17   Appraising and Disciplining
      Employees

18   The Supervisor and Labor Relations

7 part

Selecting, Training, and Compensating Employees

● outline

Responsibility for Selecting, Training, and Compensating Employees
A Shared Responsibility
The Supervisor's Role

Planning Human Resource Needs and Finding Employees to Fill the Jobs
Types and Number of Employees Needed
Filling Jobs from Within
Filling Jobs from the Outside

Complying with Equal Employment Opportunity Laws
Equal Employment Opportunity (EEO) Laws
Enforcement of EEO Laws

Selecting Employees for Specific Jobs
Requisition
Preliminary Screening
Application Form or Résumé
Preemployment Testing
Preemployment Interviewing
Checking References and Records
Preliminary Selection by the Supervisor
Final Selection
Physical Examination
Job Offer
Orientation

Training and Developing Employees
How to Determine Training Needs
How to Train Employees
Outside Assistance Available for Training

Compensating Employees
Importance of Compensation
Roles Played by Compensation
Types of Wages
Factors Affecting Wage Rates
The Comparable Worth Issue
Using Job Evaluation to Set Job Rates

Providing Employee Benefits
Legally Required Benefits
Voluntary Benefits
Flexible Benefits

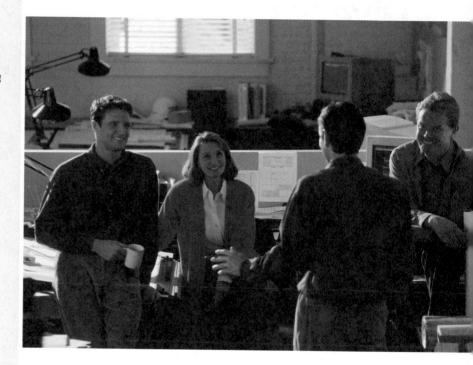

Here lies a man who knew how to enlist in his service better men than himself.

Andrew Carnegie's Epitaph

Happy employees, with good benefits, will make for good business.

Paul Strickland

It is not the employers who pay wages—they only handle the money. It is the product that pays wages.

Henry Ford

Bill Waldorf: Selecting and Supervising a Diverse High-Tech Work Team

William L. (Bill) Waldorf, marketing production manager, handles advertising for the 25 Gayfers/Maison Blanche Department Stores located throughout Alabama, Mississippi, Florida, and Louisiana. Gayfers/ Maison Blanche is a subsidiary of Mercantile Stores Company, Inc., which is based in Cincinnati, Ohio. Waldorf reports to the advertising director, who, in turn, reports to the president of Gayfers.

Waldorf is responsible for recruiting, interviewing, hiring, evaluating, rewarding, and disciplining his "associates," as employees are called. He selects his people from within the company, if feasible. His staff consists of 22 full-time employees who handle the creative and conceptual portion of the advertising and marketing activities for all the stores. There are an art director, four designers, a print production manager, a traffic manager, two copywriters, a photo studio manager, three photographers, three support personnel, three electronic pagination experts, a scanner operator, a darkroom technician, and a clerical/technical worker. The staff is composed of a diverse group of men and women, including minorities, who are highly skilled, conscientious, and largely self-motivated. While most of the employees are paid on an hourly basis, a few are paid a monthly or yearly salary.

Waldorf, who believes in empowering his associates, gives them freedom to make their own decisions and encourages them to come up with suggestions for work improvement throughout the company. He also uses the double incentives of (1) providing recognition for a job well done and (2) granting merit increases when deserved. Since most of his associates are creative people, he uses a *laissez-faire leadership style*. They mutually agree on what is to be done and what each person is to do; then he leaves them alone to do it—unless the job is not done effectively and on time.

As mentioned earlier, Waldorf is responsible for the creative portions of Gayfers' advertising operations. He frequently meets with the merchandise managers, their divisional managers, and the president of the company—if needed—to plan their marketing strategy. After they tell him what items they think will sell, Waldorf helps them identify who their customers are and what makes the items attractive to them. He then suggests themes, layout, color, artwork, and other factors that will make the items appealing.

Waldorf is also responsible for planning and supervising the photography activities and for the preparation and placement of ads in the electronic and print media used to advertise the merchandise. He checks daily sales figures on his e-mail terminal, by which internal letters are sent directly, quickly, and confidentially to him. He communicates via internet with headquarters in Ohio, which permits quicker and easier decision making.

Among his other activities, Waldorf supervises all TV, radio, and

learning objectives

After reading and studying this chapter, you should be able to:

1. Explain who is responsible for selecting, training, and compensating employees.

2. Describe how to plan human resource needs and how to find employees for specific jobs.

3. State the laws providing equal employment opportunity for protected groups of employees.

4. Describe the steps in the employee selection procedure, including the proper orientation of new employees.

5. Explain why training and development are necessary and describe how they are done.

6. Explain why employee compensation is so important and how it is determined.

7. Describe the most commonly provided employee benefits.

newspaper production, in addition to preparing and distributing direct mailing pieces. He also has access to the company's charge account list. Software programs can analyze many different types of information about these customers, which he can then use for various direct mail promotions.

Waldorf does extensive strategic and operational planning—part of which involves researching competitive marketing in other stores in order to evaluate their marketing strategy. In addition, he does weekly, monthly, quarterly, and annual planning, including evaluating which previous promotions were successful and which were not—and why. He then discusses with the merchandise managers which promotions to repeat.

Waldorf majored in commercial art at the University of Southern Alabama. He has also taken courses in illustration and design and computer courses in three-dimensional graphics and multimedia. As he has moved up in the company, he has attended leadership courses at Mercantile Stores University (MSU). At MSU, empowerment is highly stressed, as is decision making. Quality control is another subject he has studied.

One of the leadership techniques Waldorf learned at MSU was the use of management by objectives (MBO). He and each of his associates sit down at the beginning of the year to jointly set attainable goals. Then, they evaluate their own performance each quarter. At the end of the year, each associate fills out a self-evaluation form, giving specific examples of performance. That evaluation plays an important part in salary adjustments.

Waldorf was so successful in performing his diverse activities that he was immediately able to obtain a higher level—and higher paying—position when Mercantile was sold in 1998. He is now senior vice president of sales promotion for the McRae's Division of Saks Incorporated, Jackson, Mississippi.

click! http://www
.saksincorporated
.com/employment.html

We have discussed the functions of planning, organizing, and leading employees. Now we will look at the process of staffing the organization. When Art Linkletter, owner of over 75 companies, was asked the secret of his success, his answer was "I bet on people!" As the great industrialist Andrew Carnegie realized, an organization consists not merely of physical and financial resources but, most importantly, of people. Thus the supervisory challenge of the future will lie in properly selecting and developing people. Management must emphasize putting the right employees in the right jobs and then motivating them to perform.

Candidates for a given job can be obtained from inside or outside the organization, but there must be some method of selection to find capable people. Then, the organization must improve employees' performance through training and developing their abilities adequately and then compensating them. These and other aspects of human resource management are covered in this chapter.

We believe that supervisors need to "see the big picture" of the staffing process. Certainly not all supervisors are involved in the activities presented in this chapter, but, if they understand the total process of staffing, they will be in a better position to perform their part of this process.

① Explain who is responsible for selecting, training, and compensating employees.

RESPONSIBILITY FOR SELECTING, TRAINING, AND COMPENSATING EMPLOYEES

An organization can be successful only if it has the right number and types of people to do the required work. Therefore, a primary duty of all supervisors is the proper selection, placement, training and development, compensation, and utilization of competent employees. How well—or poorly—supervisors perform these functions is a major factor in their success or failure.

A Shared Responsibility

Like almost all aspects of supervision, selecting and training employees are shared tasks, though the primary responsibility should be left to supervisors. In general, the responsibilities are divided as follows:

1. *Top managers* set human resources objectives, establish policies, and do long-range planning and organizing.
2. *Middle managers* control the operating procedures needed to achieve these objectives and carry out personnel policies.
3. *Supervisors* interpret policies for employees and carry out higher management's wishes as to selecting and training employees. Also, they interpret and transmit workers' interests to higher management.

   With today's emphasis on *empowerment*, teams are often used at all three of these levels. It is especially important to have potential fellow-employees involved in an advisory role, at least.

The Supervisor's Role

Operative employees usually have little contact with high-level managers. Therefore, they tend to think of their supervisor as being "management" or "the organization." Because employees interpret their supervisor's actions, attitudes, and methods as representing those of all managers, supervisors are probably the most important people in achieving an organization's human resources objectives. Supervisors usually have the final word in selecting employees. Then they supervise and control the employees' daily activities. Finally, they appraise the employees' performance, often as the basis for giving employees further rewards and promotions.

self-check

In the Johnson Company, a large department store, sales positions are filled directly by the personnel office. When a selection decision is made, the sales department supervisor is notified, and the new employee reports to her or him for a job assignment. Typically, the new employee first meets his or her supervisor on the first day of work. What are the pros and cons of this system?

② Describe how to plan
human resource
needs and how to find
employees for specific
jobs.

PLANNING HUMAN RESOURCE NEEDS AND FINDING EMPLOYEES TO FILL THE JOBS

Most organizations cannot afford to have more workers than they need. Yet neither can they afford to do without the needed number of employees. Therefore, *the beginning of the staffing function is planning personnel needs.* There are two aspects to this step: (1) deciding what jobs need to be filled and what they involve and (2) determining the personal characteristics employees need to handle these jobs successfully. The first aspect involves the preparation of a *job description,* whereas the second aspect calls for a *job specification.* Both should be the responsibility of the supervisor, who best knows the job to be done and the knowledge and skills needed to do it.

One aspect of this staffing function is the effect of high labor turnover. Every time an employee leaves—voluntarily or otherwise—many visible and hidden costs arise when replacing her or him. Not only must a replacement be recruited and hired, but training costs are frequently quite high. In fact, a recent study done by one major employer indicated that the cost to replace *one* customer service representative earning $18,000 annually was nearly $58,000.[1] As you can see, the problem is particularly acute in the services industry.

If you know the reason(s) for high turnover, you may be able to reduce it. Exhibit 16–1 provides a partial answer to this problem.

click! http://www.alltel.com/
careers/careerpath/
careerpath.shtml

job description
Spell out the primary
duties and responsibilities of specific jobs.

Types and Number of Employees Needed

A **job description** is a written statement covering the duties, authority, responsibilities, and working conditions of a particular job. The supervisor can obtain

---

Exhibit 16–1

Why Good Workers Leave

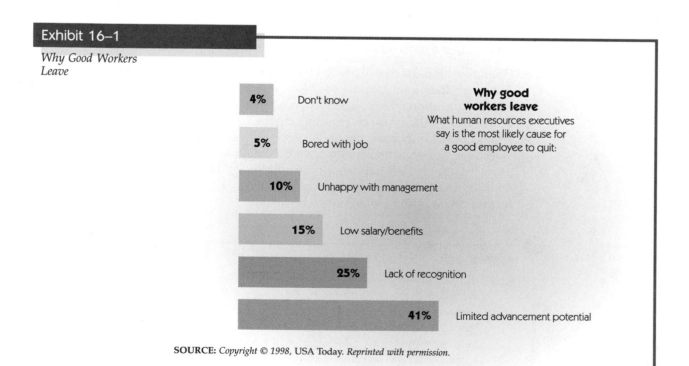

Why good workers leave
What human resources executives say is the most likely cause for a good employee to quit:

- 4% Don't know
- 5% Bored with job
- 10% Unhappy with management
- 15% Low salary/benefits
- 25% Lack of recognition
- 41% Limited advancement potential

SOURCE: *Copyright © 1998, USA Today. Reprinted with permission.*

job analysis
Gathering information and determining the elements of a job by observation and study.

job specification
Minimum standards a person should meet to perform the job satisfactorily.

click! http://www.eeoc.gov/

information about the job from experience in performing it, by observing other people performing it, or by doing a job analysis. **Job analysis** is the process of gathering information and determining the elements of a job through observation and study.

The job description also shows the relationship of the described job to others. Thus it becomes the basis not only for selecting someone for the job but also for further training workers and appraising their performance of the job. Exhibit 16–2 lists some typical components of a job description.

The personal characteristics required to perform a job are set forth in a **job specification,** which can be used to select the proper person for the job. Some of the categories of qualifications are education and training, aptitudes, temperament, interests, physical capabilities, experience, and attitudes. The job specification should state the minimum standards the person should meet in order to perform the job satisfactorily. One major reason for this is to be in compliance with the guidelines of the Equal Employment Opportunity Commission (EEOC), as discussed later in this chapter.

Finally, the number of people to be selected to fill each of the job and skill categories must be estimated. The supervisor first determines the total number of workers needed and then subtracts the number already employed; the difference is the number to be hired. (See Exhibit 16–3, "Job Specifications?")

Once the number and type(s) of employees needed for given jobs have been determined, the next step is to decide where to look for them. As Exhibit 16–4 shows, there are only two basic sources: within and outside the organization. A balanced program of acquiring people from both sources is better than relying on either source exclusively. A policy of promoting from within whenever possible and recruiting from outside when necessary provides for both continuity and new ideas.

self-check

In the chapter preview, where did Bill Waldorf obtain his employees? Do you think this is the best source for filling positions such as these? Explain.

Exhibit 16–2

Components of a Typical Job Description and Job Specification

- *Identification of job:* Job title, department, code, salary range, supervisor, etc.
- *Job description:*
  a. Physical demands of the job and the minimum physical requirements needed to fill it.
  b. Working conditions, including psychological conditions such as relationships with others and responsibilities for other people, money, and equipment.
  c. Summary of the duties and responsibilities of the job.
  d. Days and hours of work.
  e. Machines, tools, formulas, and equipment used.
- *Job specifications:*
  a. Educational background and knowledge, skills and techniques, and training and experience required to perform the job, as well as special training and development needed.
  b. Personal characteristics such as sociableness, articulateness, or aggressiveness.

Exhibit 16-3

Job Specifications?

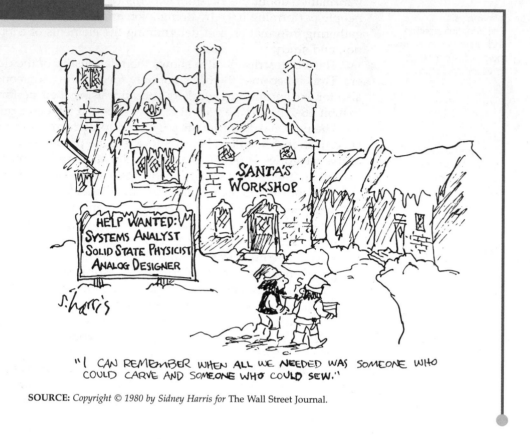

"I CAN REMEMBER WHEN ALL WE NEEDED WAS SOMEONE WHO COULD CARVE AND SOMEONE WHO COULD SEW."

SOURCE: *Copyright © 1980 by Sidney Harris for* The Wall Street Journal.

If personal qualifications have been established, then the sources most likely to produce people with such qualifications must be consulted. Some of these sources are more costly in both time and money than others. Although search costs should be taken into consideration, the source chosen should be the one that provides the best results from the standpoint of employee performance.

Filling Jobs from Within

There are many specific outside sources from which employees can be recruited, as you will soon see. However, most managers try to fill jobs from within, if possible.

Reasons For and Against Using Internal Sources. The reasons *for* using internal sources include (1) lower cost and (2) knowledge of the person's capabilities, strengths, and weaknesses. Promotion from within will probably provide continuity, enhance motivation, and also build the morale of other employees (except if an individual is bypassed and becomes jealous). The reasons for *not* using internal sources include (1) the lack of anyone capable of filling a job or willing to take it, (2) the conformity that may be produced by excessive reliance on internal sources, and (3) the possibility of developing complacency among current employees.

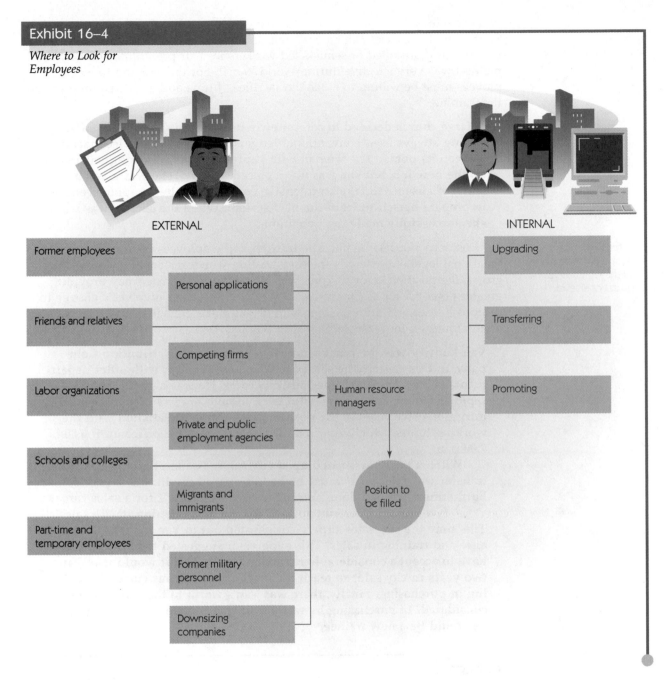

Exhibit 16–4

Where to Look for Employees

EXTERNAL

INTERNAL

Former employees

Personal applications

Friends and relatives

Competing firms

Labor organizations

Private and public
employment agencies

Schools and colleges

Migrants and
immigrants

Part-time and
temporary employees

Former military
personnel

Downsizing
companies

Human resource
managers

Position to
be filled

Upgrading

Transferring

Promoting

Methods of Obtaining Employees from Within. There are three methods of securing employees internally: (1) upgrading the employee currently holding the position, (2) transferring an employee from a similar position elsewhere in the organization, and (3) promoting an employee from a lower level job. A good training program throughout the organization is needed to provide the capable people needed for promotion.

Increasing skill requirements in various areas has led to technological unemployment, a situation in which employees can no longer perform their jobs

upgrading
Retraining unskilled or semiskilled workers to meet changing demands.

because educational or skill demands have increased beyond their capacity. Such virtual vacancies can be dealt with by **upgrading** present employees—that is, retraining unskilled or semiskilled workers in their present positions. This method was very effective during World War II. For this method to work, employees must be willing to make the sacrifice of time and effort required to take the training.

A large church decided to computerize its accounting processes after having always used conventional ledgers, journals, and office machines to keep its books. The woman who kept the books was not qualified to do the new job, but she was not replaced. Instead, she was given a leave of absence to take an intensive course from the computer vendor to prepare herself to learn the new system. When the change was made, she successfully made the transition.

transferring
Moving employees to a different job at the same organizational level.

Positions can also be filled by **transferring** employees from the same organizational level elsewhere in the organization. The transferee may have outgrown the position he or she previously held, or the transfer may provide greater potential for advancement. Essentially, a transfer involves a change in responsibilities and duties, either with or without a change in pay. Transfers are often requested for reasons other than pay increases.

Van Ludwig was the purchasing clerk at Tri-State Distribution Company. In this capacity he served and became familiar with other departments of the company, especially city sales. He was a good worker—rapid, efficient, and reliable. But even though his pay increased steadily during his five years in the position, he became dissatisfied with the working hours, which required him to remain at the office until 6:00 or 7:00 p.m.

When a position opened up at city sales, Van applied for it. But his transfer was rejected because he hadn't cleared it with his supervisor. Furthermore, he had done nothing to prepare himself for a sales career.

A few months later Van applied for the next opening in city sales. This time the city sales supervisor pointed out to Van his lack of experience and training in sales. This supervisor suggested that Van would have to accept a considerable reduction in pay, and it would take Van two years in city sales to reach the level of pay he was currently receiving in purchasing. Finally, there was Van's worth to the company to be considered. In purchasing he was a trained, efficient clerk; in city sales he would be a new trainee.

self-check

Would you have accepted Van as a transferee if you had been the city sales supervisor?

promoting
Moving a person from a lower to a higher level job.

Promoting is moving a person from a lower to a higher level job. Thus, a position is filled, but another one is vacated. The person who is promoted will need more skill and/or have more responsibility but may also gain more status, prestige, and income. One important reason for using promotion to fill higher positions is that the morale and motivation of employees are enhanced by this process.

Promoting from within an organization can be wonderful motivation for employees.

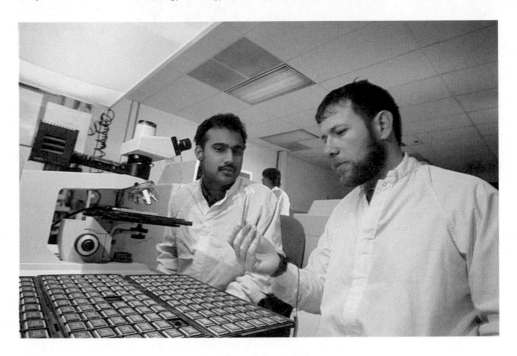

seniority
An employee's length of service in a company.

merit
An employee's ability to do the job better than others.

job posting
Announcing available job openings on a bulletin board.

click! http://monster.com/

dual promotion ladders
Enables skilled technical and scientific workers to get salary increases and higher job titles without becoming managers.

There are three bases for promotion: (1) **seniority,** or length of service, (2) **merit,** which refers to the employee's ability to do the job better than others, and (3) a combination of the two. In theory, promotions based on merit are more desirable from a motivational standpoint because they encourage employees to produce more in order to demonstrate their merit. For lower level jobs, however, particularly where unions are involved, seniority is the more common basis for promotion. There is considerable value in using a combination of length of service (seniority), which provides a good understanding of the job and the company, and merit, which guarantees that the employee has the mental and physical ability to do the job effectively.

If the employees are represented by a union, the firm will probably be required to post available job openings on a bulletin board to give present employees a chance to bid on them. This procedure, called **job posting,** has also been found to be a good method of complying with equal employment opportunity laws if there is no evidence of discrimination in the selection process later. Many nonunion firms are using it to foster employee growth and to prevent unionization.

Many companies are now using electronic job posting and computerized skills inventory systems to make filling jobs from within more efficient. For example, when Household International wanted to fill jobs from within during a growth spurt in the mid-1980s, the company used *Inside Tracks,* a job-posting software program, to help 1,300 displaced workers find another job somewhere in the company. All employees received a brochure with instructions for using the system.[2] The program was so successful that the employer made it available to all 14,500 employers at 450 offices around the country.[3]

Often, employees do not want to take a management job. So many companies are now using **dual promotion ladders,** whereby skilled technical and scientific workers can get salary increases and higher job titles without becoming managers. This practice is similar to the one used in professional sports, where outstanding players make far more than their coaches or management.

Filling Jobs from the Outside

Even if an employer has a policy of hiring from within, outside sources are often needed. As individual positions are filled by upgrading, transferring, or promoting employees, some vacated positions must be filled externally, as shown earlier in Exhibit 16–4. Some external sources of new employees are:

1. Former employees
2. Personal applications received in person or through the mail
3. Friends and relatives of employees
4. Competing firms
5. Labor organizations
6. Employment agencies, either public or private
7. Educational institutions, including high schools, business schools, vocational-technical schools, junior colleges, colleges, and manufacturers' training schools
8. Migrants and immigrants
9. Former military personnel
10. Companies in the area that are downsizing
11. Part-time or temporary employees

 click! http://www.manpower.com/

The use of part-time or temporary employees will become more important in the future. They provide a way to reduce hiring and benefits costs and also provide scheduling flexibility. No longer are these workers the after-school students seeking extra spending money. Instead, research by the National Association of Temporary and Staffing Services (NATSS) shows that older people—especially those available as a result of downsizing—are increasingly represented in the ranks of temporary workers.[4]

At about 2 percent of the U.S. daily workforce, these workers are becoming an integral part of our employment base. In 1998 alone, temporary help agencies filled about 2 percent of all jobs, up from 0.5 percent in the 1980s.[5] While these workers do provide temporary relief for the supervisor, they can pose discipline and accident problems, because they are often less skilled and less well trained.

Reasons for Using External Sources. A growing organization must go outside to obtain employees for at least its lowest level jobs. But there are also reasons for going outside for higher level personnel, and many of these reasons are associated with problems caused by computers and automation. When new skills are needed in a hurry, they must often be found in people from outside the organization who have the required education, training, and experience. Moreover, even when an internal promotion policy is followed, mistakes are inevitably made. It is almost impossible to anticipate all the skills that will be needed in the future. It is just as difficult to hire someone with those skills to join the organization at an entry-level position and progress through the organization at such a rate as to be available just when needed.

Methods of Recruiting from the Outside. Methods used to recruit new employees include:

1. Scouting at schools or colleges
2. Advertising through newspapers, trade journals, radio, billboards, and window displays
3. Using the services of private and public employment agencies
4. Acting on employee referrals
5. Electronic employment bulletin boards

The choice of the proper method to use is not an easy one, but it can be very important. The following example shows some problems with each of the more frequently used methods.

> **A store manager put a "Help Wanted" sign in the window. She found this practice time consuming because many unqualified applicants inquired about the job. Furthermore, when she rejected an applicant, she stood the risk of losing the applicant as a customer, and possibly that person's family and friends as well. The manager found that newspaper advertising also reached large groups of job seekers but still brought in many unqualified people. If the store's telephone number was given in the ad, calls tied up the line and customers couldn't reach the store.**

COMPLYING WITH EQUAL EMPLOYMENT OPPORTUNITY LAWS

③ State the laws providing equal employment opportunity for protected groups of employees.

All aspects of employment are affected by federal, state, and local laws, regulations, and court decisions. Some of the federal regulations and court decisions, and their effects on recruiting and selection, are now explained. It should be emphasized at this point, however, that EEO laws build on—and enhance— good human resource practices by most employers.

Equal Employment Opportunity (EEO) Laws

The Civil Rights Act of 1866, the Civil Rights Act of 1964, Executive Order 11246, the Civil Rights Act of 1991, and other legislation prohibit discrimination based on race, color, religion, sex, or national origin in all employment practices. Exhibit 16–5 shows additional laws that protect persons with disabilities, older workers, and Vietnam veterans. It also shows the laws' basic requirements and the agencies that enforce them.

Enforcement of EEO Laws

affirmative action programs (AAPs)
Programs to put the principle of equal employment opportunity into practice.

The Equal Employment Opportunity Commission (EEOC) is the primary agency enforcing EEO laws. It receives and investigates charges of discrimination, issues orders to stop violations, and may even go to a U.S. District Court to enforce its decrees. The Commission encourages **affirmative action programs (AAPs),** which are plans to put the principle of equal employment opportunity into practice. These programs are required by the Office of Federal Contract Compliance Programs (OFCCP) in the Labor Department, which enforces Executive Order 11246; by the Vocational Rehabilitation Act; and by the Vietnam Era Veterans' Assistance Act.

Exhibit 16–5

Legal Influences on Equal Employment Opportunity and Affirmative Action

Laws	Basic Requirements	Coverage	Enforcement Agencies
Section 1981 of Civil Rights Act of 1866	Prohibits racial discrimination in employment.	All private employers, labor unions, and employment agencies	Judicial system
Title VII of Civil Rights Act of 1964	Prohibits employment discrimination based on race, color, religion, sex, or national origin.	Private employers engaged in interstate commerce with 15 or more employees, labor unions, employment agencies, federal government workers, and state and local government workers	Equal Employment Opportunity Commission (EEOC)
Executive Order 11246 of 1965, as amended	Prohibits employment discrimination based on race, sex, color, religion, or national origin, and requires contractors employing 50 or more workers to develop affirmative action plans (AAPs) when contracts exceed $50,000 a year.	Federal contractors and subcontractors holding contracts of $10,000 or more	U.S. Department of Labor's Office of Federal Contract Compliance Programs (OFCCP)
Age Discrimination in Employment Act of 1967, as amended	Prohibits employment discrimination against persons over age 40.	Same as those under Title VII, except that private employers with 20 or more employees are covered	EEOC
Vocational Rehabilitation Act of 1973	Prohibits employment discrimination against otherwise qualified handicapped persons, requires reasonable accommodation, and requires development of AAPs.	Federal contractors and subcontractors holding contracts in excess of $2,500, organizations that receive federal assistance, and federal agencies	OFCCP
Vietnam Era Veterans' Assistance Act of 1974	Requires contractors to develop AAPs to recruit and employ qualified disabled veterans and veterans of the Vietnam War.	Federal contractors and subcontractors holding contracts in excess of $10,000	OFCCP
Immigration Reform and Control Act of 1986	Prohibits recruiting, hiring, or referring aliens who are not eligible to work in the United States; prohibits employment discrimination based on national origin or citizenship.	Private employers, labor unions, and employment agencies	U.S. Department of Justice's Special Counsel for Unfair Immigration-Related Employment
Americans with Disabilities Act of 1990	Prohibits employment discrimination against qualified individuals with a disability and requires reasonable accommodation.	Same as Title VII	EEOC

Exhibit 16–5

Concluded

Laws	Basic Requirements	Coverage	Enforcement Agencies
Civil Rights Act of 1991	Amends Title VII and the Americans with Disabilities Act to allow for punitive and compensatory damages in cases of intentional discrimination and more extensive use of jury trials.	Same as Title VII	EEOC

SOURCE: *From* Human Resource Management, 1st edition, *by Leon C. Megginson, Geralyn M. Franklin, and M. Jane Byrd, Copyright © 1995. Reprinted with permission of South-Western College Publishing, a division of Thomson Learning. Fax 800-730-2215.*

click! http://www.dol.gov/ dol/esa/public/ofcp_ org.htm

In essence, an organization, through an AAP, promises to do the following:

1. Make good-faith efforts to recruit from diverse groups (which include women, African-Americans, Hispanics, Vietnam-era veterans, native Americans, people with disabilities, and older workers) through state employment services.

2. Limit the questions that are asked of applicants on their application forms or during interviews (see Exhibit 16–6).

3. Set goals and timetables for hiring the protected groups.

4. Avoid testing applicants unless the tests meet established guidelines.

Exhibit 16–6

Topics to Avoid When Interviewing Applicants

Here is an up-to-date summary of 10 of the most dangerous questions or topics you might raise during an interview.

1. *Children.* Do not ask applicants whether they have children, or plan to have children, or have child care.
2. *Age.* Do not ask an applicant's age.
3. *Disabilities.* Do not ask whether the candidate has a physical or mental disability that would interfere with doing the job.
4. *Physical Characteristics.* Do not ask for such identifying characteristics as height or weight on an application.
5. *Name.* Do not ask a female candidate for her maiden name.
6. *Citizenship.* Do not ask applicants about their citizenship. However, the Immigration Reform and Control Act does require business operators to determine that their employees have a legal right to work in the United States.
7. *Lawsuits.* Do not ask a job candidate whether he or she has ever filed a suit or a claim against a former employer.
8. *Arrest Records.* Do not ask applicants about their arrest records.
9. *Smoking.* Do not ask whether a candidate smokes. While smokers are not protected under the Americans with Disabilities Act (ADA), asking applicants whether they smoke might lead to legal difficulties if an applicant is turned down because of fear that smoking would drive up the employer's health care costs.
10. *AIDS and HIV.* Never ask job candidates whether they have AIDS or are HIV-positive, because these questions violate the ADA and could violate state and federal civil rights laws.

SOURCE: *Adapted by permission,* Nation's Business, *July 1992. Copyright © 1992, U.S. Chamber of Commerce.*

A particularly perplexing area of concern for supervisors and their managers is how to handle the problem of fair and equal treatment of women. On June 22, 1999, the U.S. Supreme Court ruled that "victims of workplace sex discrimination can win punitive damages from employers even if the boss's behavior was not 'egregious.'"[6] Federal law now permits victims of such workplace bias to recover punitive damages of up to $300,000 from the employer, in addition to any actual losses—such as lost wages. In the 1999 discussion, the Court said that "... employers can defend themselves against such damages if they can show they made a sincere effort to prevent sex discrimination."

4 Describe the steps in the employee selection procedure, including the proper orientation of new employees.

SELECTING EMPLOYEES FOR SPECIFIC JOBS

A suggested procedure for selecting employees is shown in Exhibit 16–7. Individual employers may find it desirable to modify this procedure—or depart from it—under certain conditions. In this section, each of the steps listed in the exhibit is briefly explained.

Requisition

Selection really begins with a requisition from the supervisor to the human resource department. This requisition (see Exhibit 16–8), which is based on the previously prepared job description and specification, is the authorization the department needs to recruit applicants for the position(s) available. In many small and medium-sized firms, the supervisor makes an informal visit or phone call to the senior officer who is authorized to make the final job offer.

A reminder is needed at this point! If you, as a supervisor, are involved in selecting job applicants, all aspects of your procedure must conform to the EEOC's *Uniform Guidelines on Employee Selection Procedures.* Notice that the guidelines cover *all selection procedures,* not just testing. Your procedures should also comply with your affirmative action program for hiring people from various groups. The human resource officer, in particular, should be certain that the selection procedure conforms to national and local laws and customs.

Preliminary Screening

Whether formal or informal, some form of preliminary screening helps weed out those persons who do not seem to meet the employer's needs—thus saving their time and yours. This step deals with such obvious factors as educational background, training, experience, physical appearance, grooming, and speech—if these are relevant to job performance. Also, the applicant should know something about the organization and the job being sought.

An early study found that 9 percent of college applicants were eliminated at this point for "personal reasons." Some of the reasons cited for not hiring were bad breath, dirty fingernails, and uncombed hair.[7]

Mike, a bright young college student, applied at a local hotel for employment while home on summer break in 1994. He was rejected at the preliminary interview because his hair was below his collar—even though it was neatly pulled back. He was told that even the grounds

Exhibit 16–7

*Flowchart of a
Suggested Selection
Procedure**

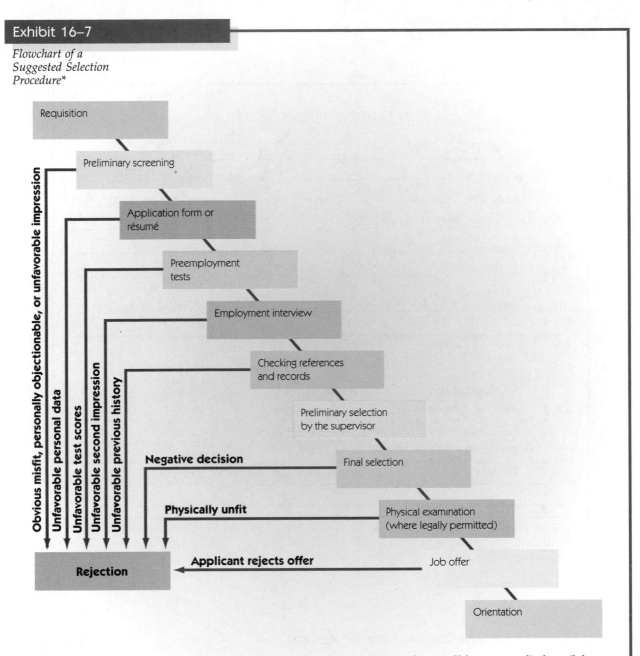

*This procedure is suggested for situations in which the applicant appears in person seeking employment. If the person applies by mail, fax, or e-mail, the preliminary screening would follow the receipt of the application or résumé.

SOURCE: *Donald C. Mosley, Paul H. Pietri, and Leon C. Megginson, "Management Leadership in Action." Copyright 1996 Addison Wesley Longman, Inc. Reprinted by permission of Addison Wesley Longman.*

keepers and dry cleaning plant workers had to have their hair above their collars.

In 1995, he was rejected by a grocery chain because he had a beard. He did find a lucrative job waiting tables at an English pub—with great tips and free meals.

Exhibit 16–8

*Sample Human
Resource Requisition*

HUMAN RESOURCE REQUISITION

Job Title: Warehouse worker   Job Code Number: 7-103

Number of employees needed   2   Date needed 2 March 2000

    Full-time ☐   Part-time ☐   Temporary ☑
                                               approx. 2 weeks

Whom to report to: ___ Norma Mills, Supervisor

Where to report: #1 warehouse, main office

Time to report: 8 AM

Requesting supervisor: Norma Mills   Date 20 Feb. 2000

(for use by Human Resource Department)

	Applicant's Name	Soc. Sec. No.	Date Available	Hire?
1.	Mike A. Johnson	344-62-9307	2 March	OK
2.	Carmen Carreon	433-54-3470	2 March	OK
3.	William S. Lloyd	460-65-0719	9 March	
4.	Laura Y. McGhee	478-60-3181	24 February	
5.				

Application Form or Résumé

After passing the preliminary screening, the job applicant usually completes an application form. (Some applications are submitted by mail or in person before preliminary screening.) The applicant lists employers for whom he or she has worked, titles of jobs held, and length of employment with each one. Background, education, military status, and other useful data are listed. The form should be carefully designed to provide the information needed about the applicant's potential performance; it should not be a hodgepodge of irrelevant data. The completion of the form in longhand will provide you with a simple test of the applicant's neatness, thoroughness, ability to answer questions—and literacy, as the following example illustrates:

> **The manager of a tire store once told one of the authors that he requires all applicants to fill out an application in person on the premises. "When they ask to take it home," he said, "I can be almost sure they're illiterate and need help in reading it and filling it out."**

The EEOC and many states have restrictions concerning the kinds of questions that may be included on an application form (refer back to Exhibit 16–6). Therefore, you should check any laws that your state may have on such practices.

Recruiters are now tending to react negatively to what showed signs of becoming a popular method of submitting résumés to potential employees—via e-mail. The very success of the method led to its troubles. Some companies are getting thousands of résumés dumped into e-mail boxes each day. In 1999, there were almost 5 million résumés on the Internet, and the number of job-related sites is expected to grow from around 200 in 1998 to 1,200 in 2002. Not only is the volume overwhelming employers, but many of the résumés contain attachments that are difficult to open or decipher.[8]

Preemployment Testing

Various tests can be used to assess an applicant's intelligence quotient (IQ), skills, aptitudes, vocational interests, personality, and performance. Preemployment testing, especially "personality" or psychological testing, is growing in use by industry. These test(s) can minimize turnover, because companies are now trying to hire for "fit" between the workers and employees, and testing can help them ensure that "fit." However, the tests must be EEOC approved and be valid and reliable. Only the most popular are discussed here.

Types of Tests. **IQ tests** are designed to measure the applicant's capacity to learn, to solve problems, and to understand relationships. They are particularly useful in selecting employees for supervisory and managerial positions. **Aptitude tests** are used to predict how a person might perform on a given job and are most applicable to operative jobs. **Vocational interest tests** are designed to determine the applicant's areas of major work interest. While interest does not guarantee competence, it can result in the employee's working and trying harder. **Personality tests** are supposed to measure the applicant's emotional adjustment and attitude. These tests are often used to evaluate interpersonal relationships and to see how the person might fit into an organization.

Probably the most effective tests the supervisor can use in selecting operative employees are **achievement, proficiency,** or **skill tests.** These tests measure fairly accurately the applicant's knowledge of and ability to do a given job. They can also spot *trade bluffers*—people who claim job knowledge, skills, and experience that they don't really have. One type of proficiency test is a **work sampling** or **work preview,** in which the prospective employee is asked to do a task that is representative of the work usually done on the job. In addition to showing whether the person can actually do the job, the test gives the applicant more realistic expectations about the job.

Perhaps the most frequently used test at present is for drug use. About 63 percent of companies now use some form of drug testing. Since January 1995,

---

IQ tests
Measure the applicant's capacity to learn, solve problems, and understand relationships.

aptitude tests
Predict how a person might perform on a given job.

vocational interest tests
Determine the applicant's areas of major work interest.

personality tests
Measure the applicant's emotional adjustment and attitude.

achievement, proficiency, *or* **skill tests**
Measure the applicant's knowledge of and ability to do a given job.

work sampling *or* **work preview**
A test in which the prospective employee must perform a task that is representative of the job.

 click! http://transit-safety .volpe.dot.gov/

around 7.5 million truck drivers, pilots, and other transportation workers have faced random alcohol breath tests as well as drug screens as a result of the Omnibus Transportation Employee Testing Act of 1991.[9] The U.S. Department of Transportation enforces the law.

Validity of Tests. If tests are used in making the selection decision, employers must be prepared to demonstrate their validity. **Validity** is demonstrated by a high positive correlation between the applicant's test scores and some identifiable measure of performance on the job. Furthermore, the tests must be designed, administered, and interpreted by a professional (usually a licensed psychologist); be culturally neutral so that they don't discriminate against any ethnic group; and be in complete conformity with EEOC guidelines.[10] Tests must also have **reliability;** that is, the results will be the same if the test is given to the same person by different testers or by the same tester at different times. Care should be exercised in interpreting test results, as some persons are adept at faking answers. Because of these and other problems, many firms are dropping testing in favor of other selection techniques.

It should be reemphasized at this point that *all selection techniques are subject to scrutiny by the EEOC.* It should also be mentioned that the most frequently used selection criteria are supervisory ratings and job performance.

Use of the Polygraph. The polygraph (lie detector) is a device used to evaluate a person's truthfulness by measuring physical changes in response to questioning. It is now being used sparingly to deal with the surge in employee thefts. It can be used for this purpose on three occasions: (1) during the preemployment security clearance exam, (2) when there is a specific loss, and (3) when a periodic spot check is made. *Because the polygraph hasn't been proven beyond a shadow of a doubt to be reliable, its use is severely restricted by federal and state laws. So use it cautiously!*

Preemployment Interviewing

In preparing for the employment interview, which is the only two-way part of the selection procedure, you should use the information on the application form and the test results to learn as much as you can about the applicant. A list of questions prepared before the interview can help you avoid missing information that might be significant in judging the applicant. Compare your list of questions with the job specification to ensure that you are matching the individual's personal qualifications with the job requirements. Some specific questions you might ask are:

1. What did you do on your last job?
2. How did you do it?
3. Why did you do it?
4. Of the jobs you have had, which did you like best? Which the least?
5. Why did you leave your last job?
6. What do you consider your strong and weak points?
7. Why do you want to work for us?

validity
A high positive correlation between the applicant's test scores and some objective measure of job performance.

reliability
The probability that test results won't change if given to the same person by different individuals.

If you are observant and perceptive during the interview, you can obtain some impressions about the candidate's abilities, personality, appearance, speech, and attitudes toward work. You should also provide the applicant with information about the company and the job. Remember, the applicant needs facts to decide whether to accept or reject the job, just as you need information to decide whether or not to offer it.

structured interviews
Standardized and controlled with regard to questions asked.

The interview may be carried out individually by the supervisor or in cooperation with someone else—the human resource officer or some other senior manager. It may be structured or unstructured. **Structured interviews** are standardized and controlled with regard to questions asked, sequence of questions, interpretation of replies, and weight given to factors considered in making the value judgment as to whether or not to hire the person. In unstructured interviews, the pattern of questions asked, the conditions under which they are asked, and the bases for evaluating results are determined by the interviewer.

Checking References and Records

The importance of carefully checking applicants' references cannot be overemphasized. Reference checks provide answers to questions concerning a candidate's performance on previous jobs. They are helpful in verifying information on the application form and other records, as well as statements made during the interviews. They are also useful in checking on possible omissions of information and in clarifying specific points. Yet, a Robert Half survey found that 68 percent of employers now find that former employers, fearing lawsuits, tend to say nothing—or only nice things—about past employees.[11] In fact, most former employers will only give dates of employment and position(s) held.

Reference checks made in person or by telephone are greatly preferable to written ones, as past employers are sometimes reluctant to commit to writing any uncomplimentary remarks about a former employee. Be sure to ask specific questions about the candidate's performance. The type of information you are allowed to seek is restricted by laws such as the Fair Credit Reporting Act and the Privacy Act. But you can check on dates and terms of employment, salary, whether termination was voluntary, and whether this employer would rehire the candidate.

Many organizations are now using credit checks to obtain information about prospective employees. If this source is used and is the basis for rejecting a candidate, he or she has the right to see the report.

Preliminary Selection by the Supervisor

By this point in the selection process, you—the supervisor—have narrowed the number of candidates to one or a very few. If there is only one, the applicant can be hired on a trial basis. If you have more than one qualified candidate, a review of the information collected should reveal the best choice. Although your preliminary selection may be subject to approval by the human resource department or some higher authority, usually the person will be offered the job.

Final Selection

Human resource officers are usually brought in on the final hiring decision because of their expertise. They ensure that all laws and regulations, as well as company policies, are followed. Also, they have a voice in such questions as salary and employee benefits to be offered to the applicant.

Physical Examination

Formerly, the final step in the selection procedure was a physical examination to see if the applicant could do the job. However, the Americans with Disabilities Act (ADA) has limited this part of the process. *Employers may not now require an exam before a preliminary job offer is made.*[12] *Then, when an exam is allowed, the exam may only determine whether the worker can do the job being sought, and no medical history may be taken.*[13]

Job Offer

Job offers to applicants for nonmanagerial and nonprofessional positions are usually made by the human resource office. They are often in writing and contain the terms and conditions of employment. At this point, the offer is either accepted or rejected. If it is rejected, an offer may be made to the next most qualified applicant. If there are no other qualified candidates, the selection procedure must start all over again.

After a candidate has accepted the job offer, those not hired should still be kept in mind for any possible future openings. It is common courtesy to notify them that someone else has been selected, and a diplomatic rejection will maintain their goodwill.

self-check

Have you ever applied for a job and been told, "We'll let you know within a week if we want you"? Even when the week was up, were you still hoping you might get a call, if only to say definitely that you had not been hired? How did this uncertainty make you feel toward the employer?

Orientation

orientation
Procedures of familiarizing a new employee with the company surroundings, policies, and job responsibilities.

The first day on a new job is confusing for anyone. Therefore, a new employee should be given a proper **orientation.** A job description should be given to him or her and explained in detail. Proper instructions, training, and observation will start the employee off on the right foot. A tour of the facilities and a look at the firm's product or service will help the new employee understand where he or she fits into the scheme of things.

The new employee needs to know the firm's objectives, policies, rules, and performance expectations. Frequent discussions should be held with him or her during the orientation program to answer questions and to ensure proper progress.

A formal interview with the new employee may be appropriate at some point during the first week. Other interviews can be held during the probationary period, which is usually from three to six months. The purpose of these interviews should be to correct any mistaken ideas the employee may have about the job and to determine whether he or she feels that you and your people are fulfilling your commitments.

After orientation is completed, a check list is usually gone over with the new employee. Then, the employee and a representative of the employer sign it, and it is placed in the employee's file as proof of knowledge of rules.

If done properly by the supervisor, orientation should accelerate the building of a positive working relationship with the new employee.

TRAINING AND DEVELOPING EMPLOYEES

5 Explain why training and development are necessary and describe how they are done.

One of the basic responsibilities of supervisors is training and developing employees. If they have the job skills and knowledge, supervisors can be the best trainers. Not only must new workers be trained in the details of the new job, but current employees must be retrained and their skills updated to meet rapidly changing environments and job requirements.

> **John Hancock Financial Services is one of the largest employers in the city of Boston. The company has found that "it used to be that managers expected people to come in the first day on the job ready for work; today's managers must accept the fact that they have no choice but to lengthen the learning curve for new employees. They can find workers if they are willing to spend the time necessary to train them."[14]**

click! http://www.petersons .com/

Why train employees? Training should result in (1) reduced employee turnover, (2) higher job satisfaction, (3) increased productivity, (4) increased earnings for the employee—and the employer, (5) less supervision as the employee becomes more self-reliant, and (6) decreased costs for materials, supplies, and equipment needed to correct errors.

> **According to Bill Saul, chairman of Remmele Engineering, Inc., an automation-equipment manufacturer, it can be profitable to train new employees. The Minneapolis, Minnesota, employer said: "Every time we bring in a new, well-trained employee, he can . . . bring in $90,000 in new sales. [At that rate] it doesn't take long to recoup training costs."[15]**

Another reason for training—especially of technical, professional, and managerial personnel—is to prepare promising employees for "fast track" promotions.

How to Determine Training Needs

A major problem with training is identifying *who* needs *how much* and *what type* of training. There are many ways to identify training needs. Some of the more practical ways are (1) supervisor's recommendations, (2) analysis of job requirements, (3) analysis of job performance, (4) test results, and (5) employee suggestions. A training needs survey may be conducted by asking supervisors to state their needs on a prepared form or by interviewing supervisors.

How to Train Employees

Once you know the employees' training needs, how do you train them? There are many ways a supervisor can train employees, including (1) on-the-job training, (2) apprenticeship training, (3) internship training, and (4) outside training. Another form of training is giving subordinates selected job assignments. This should help them prepare to accept responsibility.

on-the-job training (OJT)
Employees actually perform the work under the guidance of a supervisor.

On-the-Job Training. The most widely used method of training and developing employees is **on-the-job training (OJT)**, in which the employees actually perform work under the supervision and guidance of the supervisor or a trained worker or instructor. Thus, while learning to do the job, the person is also a regular employee producing the good or service that the business sells. This form of training always occurs, whether or not it is consciously planned. Although the techniques depend on the one doing the training, in general OJT involves:

1. Telling the worker what is to be done
2. Telling him or her how to do the job
3. Showing how it is to be done
4. Letting the worker do the job under the trainer's guidance
5. Telling—and showing—the learner what he or she did right, what he or she did wrong, and how to correct the wrong actions
6. Repeating the procedure until the learner has mastered the job

As with other aspects of supervision, there are many advantages and disadvantages of OJT. The main *advantages* are that production is carried on while the employee is being trained and that OJT results in low out-of-pocket costs. Also, no transition from classroom learning to actual production is required.

On the other hand, the *disadvantages* of OJT are the poor learning environment provided by the production area and the excessive waste caused by mistakes and/or lack of skill. Supervisors handle most OJT, but they are not necessarily the best ones to do it. Because their primary emphasis is on performing the operating tasks of the job, they are only secondarily concerned with training. If possible, another capable employee—or even an outside trainer—should be assigned this responsibility. Also, there should be a follow-up procedure to evaluate the results of the training and to serve as a basis for improving future development.

If the job of training is entrusted to fellow employees, they should be (1) *able* to do the training and (2) *willing* to do it. Also, arrangements should be made to ensure that they don't lose income by doing it. If a worker is paid at piecework rates or is required to fill a certain quota, time spent helping a new employee may cause the experienced worker to get less work done and hence earn less, which will certainly generate resentment and reluctance to help with future training.

Despite its disadvantages, OJT is still the best way to learn job skills. A structured OJT program not only trains and educates employees, it can also motivate them to produce more effectively.[16]

apprenticeship training
Blends the learning of theory in the classroom with practice on the job in the techniques of the job.

Apprenticeship Training. **Apprenticeship training** blends the learning of theory in the classroom with actual practice, on the job, in the techniques of the job. If job proficiency can be developed only over a long period of classroom instruction and actual learning experiences on the job, this method should be used. It usually encompasses two to seven years of both classroom learning and on-the-job training.

In 1992, Serigraphics Inc., a high-tech graphics and printing company in West Bend, Wisconsin, started cooperating with West Bend High School's new state-of-the-art apprenticeship program. The program is copied from the German program of "dual education," with two days a week at a high-tech center, namely Serigraphics Inc.[17]

Internship Training. Combining on-the-job training at a cooperating business with education at a school or college, **internship training** is generally used for students who are candidates for marketing or clerical positions or who are being prepared for management positions. This method can also be used for higher level positions. For example, the Georgia Institute of Technology's co-op program, which alternates quarters of academic work and internship with a cooperating employer, prepares students for engineering positions and also provides income to help them meet the cost of their education. Internship training gives students a chance to see if they would like to go to work for the company, and it gives management a chance to evaluate the student as a prospective full-time employee.

internship training
On-the-job training at a cooperating business is combined with class-work at a college.

Other Types of Training. Some job activities are so technical or specialized that they cannot be taught effectively on an informal basis by the supervisor. Instead, learners are sent to some outside source, such as a school, college, or equipment manufacturer, to learn the job. Drafting, computer programming, legal aid, and income tax accounting are some jobs of this nature. Some other types of development activities are extension courses, programmed (or video) instruction, closed-circuit television, job rotation, and college and university short courses and conferences.

Outside Assistance Available for Training

Where can you go for help in training employees? Many outside programs are available to help with training. For example, the National Apprenticeship Act of 1937, administered by the Bureau of Apprenticeship and Training in the Labor Department, sets policies and standards for apprenticeship programs. Also, all states have some form of **vocational-technical education programs,** in which vocational-technical schools, business schools, and junior colleges conduct regular or special training classes. Through such programs, potential employees can become qualified for skilled positions such as machinist, lathe operator, computer service technician, and legal assistant.

vocational-technical education programs
Regular or special training classes conducted by vocational-technical schools.

Other training activities for new employees are the **vocational rehabilitation programs** sponsored by the U.S. Department of Health and Human Services (HHS) in cooperation with state governments. These programs provide counseling, medical care, and vocational training for physically and mentally handicapped individuals.

vocational rehabilitation programs
Provide counseling, medical care, and vocational training for the physically and mentally handicapped.

The popular Job Training Partnership Act (JTPA) underwrites the most important public programs currently being used to help employers with training activities. These programs are developed and effectively controlled by private industry councils (PICs) and funded by block grants to the states. The PICs are headed by company executives and local business people, who probably know more than anyone else about what is needed to train people in the skills used in their areas. The funds provided must go for training, including on-the-job training; none of the funds can be used for stipends or wage supplements. In addition to getting cash reimbursement for hiring and training through PICs, firms can also get an investment tax credit to offset the cost of hiring eligible workers.

Finally, universities and professional management organizations offer seminars, conferences, and short courses that are effective methods of development.

6 Explain why employee compensation is so important and how it is determined.

COMPENSATING EMPLOYEES

An important aspect of human resource management is employee compensation. It is also an integral part of supervisory management.

Importance of Compensation

Of all supervisory problems, compensating employees is probably the most complex and difficult because it involves many emotional factors as well as economic and rational ones.

Compensation, in the form of wages and benefits, is very important to employees, because it is the primary—and often the only—source of income for them and their families. It is generally accepted that employees should receive "a fair day's wages for a fair day's work." Yet there are probably as many complaints from employees about the *relative* amount of their income as about the *absolute* amount, for everyone wants to be treated fairly when it comes to pay. Employees' *absolute level of income* determines their standard of living, but their *relative income* indicates status, prestige, and worth.

Wages and benefits are also becoming increasingly important to U.S. businesses because of foreign competition, deregulation of the transportation, finance, and energy industries, and the tightening of the economy. No longer can wages be increased without a corresponding increase in productivity unless the cost is passed along to consumers in the form of higher prices. In fact, employers paying a noncompetitive wage rate will soon find themselves in financial trouble because employee compensation and other types of costs interact with revenue to determine an employer's profit or loss, and the primary way to increase employee earnings is to increase productivity and the company's sales and profits.

In summary, the ideal situation is for employers to pay wages high enough to attract, motivate, and retain qualified employees, while at the same time keeping wages low enough to ensure adequate profits to expand productive facilities, attract new capital, and permit consumer satisfaction with the price.

Roles Played by Compensation

Appropriate compensation plays several roles: (1) It attracts capable employees, (2) it motivates employees to perform more effectively, and (3) it helps retain capable employees.

self-check

Before you read any further, complete Skill Builder 16–2, What Do You Want from Your Job?, at the end of this chapter. Then, return to this section and continue your reading.

Most employers try to remain competitive, both in their industry and in their community, by paying salaries and benefits that are similar to those paid by other employers. Thus, they try to find out what the average salaries are for different types of positions in their industry and local area. They do this by using wage surveys, which determine the going rate for jobs in the local labor market and in the industry. If it is not feasible to conduct a wage survey, an employer may use published wage survey information from sources such as trade associations and the U.S. Department of Labor.

It can be argued that most job applicants do not know the exact wages and benefits offered by different employers for similar jobs, and therefore the compensation rate isn't important to them, but we believe that prospective employees *do* compare job offers and pay scales before making decisions about where to work.

self-check

Which of the preceding arguments do you think is correct? Consider your own answers to Skill Builder 16–2. What did you put as the number one factor in choosing your first job? Was it "good salary"? You might want to compare notes with some of your fellow students to see how they answered the question. In our research with upper level business students since the 1957–1958 school year, we have found that "good salary" was number one in over 97 percent of the cases.

Compensation can also be used to motivate employees to improve performance. According to the *equity theory of motivation*, employees who believe that the employer's pay system, including wages and benefits, is fair and equitable to them will do a better job than those who do not. Moreover, the *expectancy theory of motivation* states that employee behavior that leads to reward tends to be repeated, whereas behavior that is not rewarded—or leads to punishment— tends not to be repeated. Thus, when an employee's income is what he or she expects, the employee will perform better.[18]

Our answer to the question "Does money motivate?" is yes it does, at least to the point that an employee's physical and safety needs have been satisfied. Above that level, money (especially day wages) tends to decline in importance.

Compensation can also act to retain employees, especially if it is in the form of favorable employee benefits. Although many factors cause employees to leave an organization, inadequate compensation is certainly an important one. Therefore, to retain good employees, employers must be sure that their compensation package is equitable not only in relation to that offered by other employers, but also in relation to that of other employees in the same organization.

Types of Wages

single rate
A compensation plan under which everyone who performs the same job is paid the same wage.

There are many types of wages used to compensate employees. Among the more commonly used types are (1) a single rate, (2) a rate range, (3) day work, or time wages, and (4) incentive wages.

When a **single rate** is used, everyone who performs the same job is paid the same wage, regardless of the level of performance. The single rate is used in many industries, especially those that are unionized, such as the automobile assembly, trucking, steel, trade, and service industries. It is also used for many occupations associated with crafts, production work, and maintenance.

A **rate range** offers a minimum and maximum wage rate for a given job, with employees paid at different rates depending on performance. The rate paid to an individual is usually determined by some form of performance appraisal, as will be discussed in the next chapter. Rate ranges are used for most technical, professional, and office workers, as well as for most government employees.

rate range
Minimum and maximum wage rates for a given job.

The two most common bases on which to compensate employees are (1) time worked and (2) output produced. The first of these methods, **time wages** or **day work,** pays the employee for the amount of time spent on the job, regardless of the output during that period. The second method, **incentive wages** or **performance pay,** pays the employee according to the amount of goods and services produced during a given period. The latter method links compensation to individual, team, or company performance. This form of payment is becoming more popular: the number of companies using it increased from under 50 percent to over 70 percent from 1990 to 1994.[19]

time wages or **day work**
Pay for the amount of time spent on the job, regardless of output.

incentive wages or **performance pay**
Wages determined by the amount of goods and services the employee produces.

In general, unions prefer single rates to rate ranges for the same type of job because rate ranges tend to cause competition among workers. Unions also tend to favor day work, or time wages, over incentive wages. Although unions will accept incentive wage plans that are based on group output rather than individual output, they insist that such plans be established according to the union's standards.

Factors Affecting Wage Rates

What most employers think they *should* pay is "competitive wages," but some specific factors affect what they actually pay. Most of these factors relate to what employers *have* to pay, but a final factor is what they are *able* to pay. These factors include (1) governmental factors, (2) collective bargaining, (3) cost-of-living adjustments (COLAs), (4) comparable wages, (5) market conditions, and (6) ability to pay.

Governmental Factors. Governmental laws, rules, and regulations largely determine what an employer *has to pay* workers. Some of these laws are the Fair Labor Standards Act, commonly called the Wage and Hour Law; the Walsh-Healey Act; the Davis-Bacon Act; the Equal Pay Act; and various EEO/AA laws, such as the Civil Rights Act, the Vocational Rehabilitation Act, the Americans with Disabilities Act, and the Vietnam Era Veterans' Assistance Act.

The Fair Labor Standards Act covers all employees working in interstate commerce, federal employees, and some state employees. Some employees, referred to as **exempt employees,** including executives, administrative and professional employees, outside sales personnel, and other selected groups, are not covered by the provisions of this law. All other employees, called **nonexempt employees,** are covered and must be paid at least the basic minimum wage ($5.15/hour at the time of this writing). If employees work over 40 hours in a given workweek, they must be paid one and a half times their regular rate of pay for each hour worked over 40 hours. However, there are provisions for employing full-time students at rates lower than the minimum wage. This law also prevents child labor. Age 14 is the minimum working age for most nonfarm jobs. On nonhazardous jobs, persons of age 14 and 15 can work no more than 3 hours on

exempt employees
Not covered by the provisions of the Fair Labor Standards Act.

nonexempt employees
Covered by the provisions of the Fair Labor Standards Act.

a school day, 8 hours on any other day, or 40 hours per week. Those who are 16 and 17 years old can work in nonhazardous jobs for unlimited hours.

The Davis-Bacon Act and the Walsh-Healey Act have different provisions. Construction firms with government contracts or subcontracts in excess of $2,000 are covered by the Davis-Bacon Act; other employers with government contracts exceeding $10,000 are covered by the Walsh-Healey Act. These acts differ from the Fair Labor Standards Act in two aspects. First, the actual rate of pay is set by the Secretary of Labor. This rate of pay is called the **prevailing wage rate** in the area and approximates the union wage scale for the area in the given type of work. A second difference is that overtime is paid at "time and a half" for all hours worked over 8 hours in a given day as well as over 40 hours in a given week.

prevailing wage rate Approximates the union wage scale for the area in the given type of work.

Public policy now prohibits discrimination in pay unless it is based on performance. For example, the Equal Pay Act prohibits different rates of pay for men and women doing the same type of work. Title VII of the Civil Rights Act prevents discrimination based on race, color, religion, sex, or national origin. The Age Discrimination in Employment Act prohibits discrimination against persons 40 years of age and older. Finally, the Vocational Rehabilitation Act and Americans with Disabilities Act prohibit discrimination against persons with handicaps.

Collective Bargaining. When unions are involved, basic wages, job differentials, individual rates of pay, and employee benefits tend to be determined through the collective bargaining process. The actual amount of compensation is determined by the relative strength of the union and the employer. However, even nonunionized employers are affected by the wage rates and the amounts of benefits paid by unionized firms.

cost-of-living adjustments (COLAs) Increases in wages in direct proportion to increases in the consumer price index.

Cost-of-Living Adjustments. Ever since 1948, **cost-of-living adjustments (COLAs)** have been included in many union contracts. Under a COLA arrangement, wages rise in direct proportion to increases in the consumer price index (CPI), which measures changes in the price of a group of goods and services that make up the typical consumer's budget. Such arrangements have been popular in the automobile, communications, electrical, mining, steel, transportation, and rubber industries. Many government employees have similar arrangements. COLAs are more popular when inflation increases rapidly, as it did in the late 1970s and early 1980s.

 click! http://stats.bls.gov/ cpihome.htm

Comparable Wage Rates. As indicated earlier, an employer must pay wage rates that are comparable to those paid in the area, the industry, and the occupation. If an employer in a given area pays less than the prevailing area rate, employees will move to higher paying jobs. The same is true for employers in given industries, such as steel, rubber, and automobile manufacturing, which are known as high-pay industries. Finally, there tends to be a relationship between wages for people in given occupations, such as professional and technical workers, managerial personnel, and sales personnel, regardless of who their employer is.

Market Conditions. The basic law of economics applies to wages. That is, as the supply of workers goes up relative to demand, wage rates tend to go down; and when the supply of workers goes down relative to demand, wage rates go up.

Employer's Ability to Pay. In spite of the above factors, individual wages are based ultimately on what the employer can afford to pay, or the amount of profit the private employer makes. This profit, in turn, is based on the productivity of the employees, prices charged, and the volume of goods sold or services provided. *Without profit, there cannot be higher wages, regardless of what happens outside the organization.*

The Comparable Worth Issue

In spite of the Equal Pay Act of 1963, which prohibits unequal pay for men and women doing the same job, women are still paid substantially less than men for *similar* jobs. There is much controversy as to the cause of this disparity. The problem, according to advocates of "pay equity," goes far beyond equal pay for the same job. The real issue is this: *Are women being systematically underpaid for work that requires the same skills, knowledge, and responsibility as similar jobs performed by men?*

comparable worth *or* pay equity
Jobs with equal points for the amount of education, effort, skill, and responsibility have equal pay.

Advocates say the solution lies in a system of **comparable worth,** or **pay equity,** in which a formula is used to assign points for the amount of education, effort, skill, and responsibility required for an individual job.[20] These points are then used, along with job evaluation, to set salary rates. Critics say such wage adjustments would destroy the market forces of supply and demand. The arguments of advocates and critics of comparable worth are shown in Exhibit 16–9.

Exhibit 16–9

Should Jobs of "Comparable Worth" Receive Comparable Pay?

Some women's groups believe that the principle of equal pay for work of equal value has been violated in that whole classes of jobs—such as those in the clerical area—are undervalued because they have traditionally been held by women. They want this practice changed so that pay for all jobs will be based on their value to the business or community, rather than on who holds the jobs.

The arguments *for* comparable pay for comparable work are:

1. If one employee contributes as much to the firm as another, the two should be paid the same.
2. It is needed to raise women's pay, which is now only about 65 percent of men's.
3. It will give women greater internal job mobility.
4. This is one way to further women's career ambitions.
5. It would serve to motivate women to be more productive.

The arguments *against* comparable pay are:

1. Federal law only requires equal pay for equal jobs.
2. It violates a firm's structured job evaluation system.
3. Employers must pay salaries competitive with those of other employers, which are based on what employees produce and on the economic value of the work performed.
4. Women receive less than men because two-thirds of new employees are women, and they always receive less than more senior employees.
5. It is practically impossible to determine accurately the real value of a job.

SOURCE: *Leon C. Megginson, Geralyn M. Franklin, and M. Jane Byrd,* Human Resource Management *(Houston: Dame Publications, 1995), p. 404.*

self-check

Do you think jobs of comparable worth should receive comparable pay? Which arguments in Exhibit 16–9 do you accept and why?

Using Job Evaluation to Set Job Rates

job evaluation
Determines the relative value of jobs to an employer so the appropriate earnings for employees doing given jobs can be determined objectively.

Job evaluation is a process used to determine the relative value of jobs to an employer to more objectively establish the earnings of employees doing different jobs. It is used to develop a fair and equitable scale of wages, especially for new employees. The relative value of each job to the organization is established as a basis for determining individual wage rates and satisfying EEO requirements. Job evaluation also provides information on the qualifications needed for a given job, thus helping supervisors to make more effective employee selections, promotions, demotions, and job changes.

While it is possible to obtain a reasonable degree of equity by using job evaluation, there are several problems with the process. First, the value of various occupations to an employer cannot be precisely measured by means of the same yardstick. Also, it is difficult to measure the relative value of work done by scientific, technical, professional, and managerial personnel. Finally, the worth of one job to the organization cannot be properly evaluated without considering its relationship to other jobs.

The usual procedure for using job evaluation to arrive at job rates or ranges is to do a job analysis, grade the jobs, price each job, and administer the resulting program. As shown in Exhibit 16–10, the process of *job analysis* results in *job descriptions,* which are then translated into *job specifications* that can be used as the basis for hiring new employees. These job specifications are then grouped into job *grades,* with jobs of the same relative value in the same grade. These job grades are then assigned a *price* based on the company's overall wage rate. These wage rates or ranges become the value of the job. By appraising the performance of each employee, management determines his or her individual wage rate within the wage range.

Exhibit 16–10

Steps in the Job Evaluation Procedure

Step	Procedures and Products Used	Resulting Product
Step 1: Analysis	Job analysis → job description →	Job specifications*
Step 2: Grading	Job specifications + job evaluation, or appraisal of the worth of the job →	Job grades
Step 3: Pricing	Job grades + overall wage rate →	Job wage rates or ranges
Step 4: Administering	Job wage rates or ranges + appraisal of performance or qualities of each employee →	Individual wage rate

These specifications can be used as the basis for performing the job evaluation procedure, or they can be used to prepare a statement of the personal qualifications needed to perform the job. This statement then becomes the basis for the recruitment and selection procedure.

7 Describe the most commonly provided employee benefits.

employee benefits
Financial rewards and services provided to employees in addition to their regular earnings.

PROVIDING EMPLOYEE BENEFITS

Employee benefits are financial rewards and services provided to employees in addition to their regular earnings. One way of classifying these benefits is according to whether they are legally required or are voluntary on the part of the employer.

Legally Required Benefits

Employers are required by law to provide all employees with Social Security and Medicare, workers' compensation, and unemployment insurance. Also, some employers must provide certain employees with family and medical leave. Each of these types of legally required benefits is explained below.

Social Security and Medicare. The Social Security system is in reality two separate systems. One provides retirement benefits for workers, and the other provides disability, survivors', and Medicare benefits. To be eligible for the program, a worker must have contributed taxes into the system for 10 years (or 40 quarters).

Benefits are financed by a payroll tax paid by both employer and employee. The tax rate, the earnings base on which it is paid, and the benefits are subject to frequent congressional changes. The Social Security tax rate for 2000 was 6.2 percent of the first $76,200 of an employee's earnings, with both the employer and the employee paying that amount. In addition, there is a Medicare tax of 1.45 percent on *all earnings*.

Workers' Compensation. All states have passed laws requiring workers' compensation. These laws protect employees and their families from permanent loss of income and high medical payments as a consequence of accidental injury, illness, or death resulting from the job. The amount to be paid for a given condition, such as loss of a hand or arm, is stipulated in the law.

Workers' compensation funds are provided primarily through employer contributions to a statewide fund. Employers may purchase insurance from private insurance companies to supplement these state funds. In general, employees are able to recover all medical expenses and up to two-thirds of the income loss due to disability or missed work.

experience rating
Determining, from the record of unemployed workers, the amount the employer must pay into the state's unemployment insurance fund.

Unemployment Insurance. In most states, unemployment insurance laws require that the government provide unemployed workers with benefits from a fund of payroll taxes imposed on employers. The amount paid into the fund by employers varies according to the unemployment rate within the state and the employer's record of unemployed or **experience rating.** To receive benefits under the law, the unemployed worker is required to register for employment at the state employment office and usually must have worked for a certain length of time before becoming unemployed.

Family and Medical Leave. The Family and Medical Leave Act of 1993 requires employers with 50 or more employees within a 75-mile radius of the home office, to offer employees—except *key employees*—up to 12 weeks of unpaid leave during a 12-month period for (1) birth of a child, (2) placement of a child for adoption or foster care, (3) caring for a spouse, child, or parent with a serious health condition, or (4) the employee's serious health condition. The employer must continue providing health care coverage during the absence and place the employee in the same or a comparable position upon return.

Voluntary Benefits

click! http://www.sun.com/ aboutsun/ehs/ ehs-workplace_health .html

In addition to the legally required benefits, many employers voluntarily provide other benefits. Some of these are in the general areas of (1) payment for time not worked, (2) health and insurance protection, and (3) retirement income.

Pay for Time Not Worked. Most employers today pay their employees for time not worked under certain circumstances. These benefits take such forms as paid vacations, paid holidays, paid sick leave, pay for jury duty, and paid compassionate leave for purposes such as to attend a funeral.

Health and Insurance Protection. Another group of benefits provides for medical and hospital care, along with pay, while an employee is sick. These benefits also include payments to an employee's beneficiary in case of the employee's death. Group medical, surgical, and dental plans are very popular with employees but are expensive for the employer. Most employers are now taking steps to limit these payments. Life insurance is another popular benefit received by many employees today. Group life insurance plans usually provide for death benefits to the employee's beneficiary and are generally based on the employee's income.

Retirement Income. A trend toward early retirement has developed in the United States. As this trend continues, employers are adopting various pension plans to help employees supplement their Social Security and other retirement benefits. The employee is usually provided with preretirement and postretirement counseling and a stipulated payment for the rest of the employee's life.

Employee benefits, such as medical coverage, are very important in today's world.

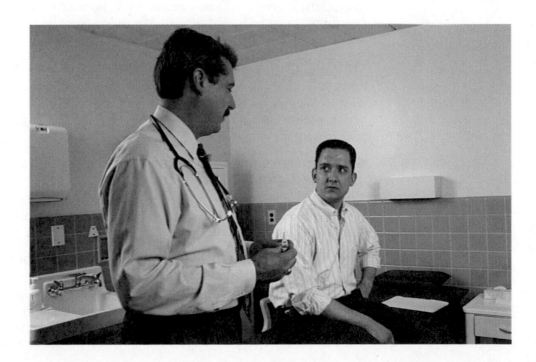

Flexible Benefits

flexcomp *or* **cafeteria benefit plans**
Providing employees with flexible benefit packages.

Many employers are now using some method of providing employees with flexible benefit packages. Called **flexcomp** or **cafeteria benefit plans**, these packages give each worker an individualized benefit package. Under these plans, all employees receive a statement of the total dollar amount of benefits they are entitled to, along with the amount earmarked for legally required benefits. Each employee then tells the employer how to allocate the balance among the programs available. Some advantages of this program are that (1) workers are more aware of the total value of their benefits, and (2) workers can choose which programs they want. As a result, workers are better satisfied and benefit packages are better tailored to individual needs.

chapter review

1 **Explain who is responsible for selecting, training, and compensating employees.**

This chapter has presented ways to select, train and develop, and compensate employees. In general, the human resource department is responsible for overall planning, recruiting, and handling the details of staffing. The role of supervisors is to requisition needed workers, interview applicants, orient new workers, and train new and current employees.

2 **Describe how to plan human resource needs and how to find employees for specific jobs.**

As part of planning human resource needs, the supervisor helps prepare job descriptions, which show the duties, authority, responsibilities, and working conditions of the job, as well as a set of job specifications, which lists the personal characteristics required, such as education, aptitudes, and experience.

Employees can be obtained from within an organization by upgrading present employees or by transferring or promoting people from other units, using job posting if feasible. Workers are recruited from outside by using such sources as former employees, personal applications, friends and relatives of present workers, competing firms, labor organizations, public or private employment agencies, schools and colleges, migrants and immigrants, former military personnel, surplus personnel from downsizing companies, and part-time and temporary employees.

3 **State the laws providing equal employment opportunity for protected groups of employees.**

Minorities, women, older workers, persons with disabilities, and Vietnam veterans are protected by various laws and regulations. The Equal Employment Opportunity Commission (EEOC) is the primary agency for enforcing these laws.

4 **Describe the steps in the employee selection procedure, including the proper orientation of new employees.**

The procedure for selecting employees for specific jobs includes (1) a requisition from the supervisor, (2) a preliminary screening-out of the obvious misfits, (3) the applicant's completion of an application form, (4) preemployment tests, (5) various interviews by the supervisor and human resource officer, (6) checking records and references, (7) a preliminary selection made by the supervisor, (8) physical exam, if legal, and (9) a job offer. If the offer is accepted, the new employee is given a job orientation by the supervisor.

(5) Explain why training and development are necessary and describe how they are done.

One of the basic supervisory responsibilities is training and developing employees—both new and currently employed—because such development has many benefits for both employees and employer. Training methods include (1) on-the-job training, (2) apprenticeship training, (3) internship training, (4) training given by outside institutions, and (5) giving promising employees selected job assignments. Assistance in training is available from many sources, especially state and federal government agencies. Apprenticeship programs are covered by the National Apprenticeship Act of 1937. The Job Training Partnership Act underwrites local training efforts developed by private industry councils. The federal government also works with states to provide vocational rehabilitation programs for people with disabilities, and most states offer some form of vocational-technical education programs to train workers for skilled occupations. Finally, universities and professional organizations provide seminars, conferences, and short courses.

(6) Explain why employee compensation is so important and how it is determined.

Another important management task is providing compensation for employees. Compensation is important to employees because it determines both their standard of living and their status, and it is important to employers because it represents a large proportion of costs. Appropriate compensation plays several roles: It attracts capable employees, it motivates employees to perform more effectively, and it helps retain employees.

Types of wages include a single rate for a given job and a rate range, with the actual pay based on seniority, performance, or some other criterion, including performance appraisal. Rates may be paid on a straight hourly basis—day work or time wages—or they may be based on output—incentive wages or performance pay.

Wage rates are affected by (1) governmental factors, (2) collective bargaining, (3) the cost of living in the area, (4) comparable wage rates, and (5) supply and demand. However, what employers can pay is ultimately limited by employee productivity and company profitability.

Despite laws requiring equal pay for the same job, women continue to be paid less than men overall, partly because compensation for jobs held primarily by women tends to be lower than that for jobs held primarily by men. Many proponents of pay equity insist that equal pay be offered for jobs of comparable worth. To establish the worth of a job, a complex process of job evaluation is needed; achieving accuracy and objectivity in this process is very difficult.

(7) Describe the most commonly provided employee benefits.

Employee benefits are noncash forms of compensation. Those that employers are legally required to provide are (1) Social Security and Medicare, (2) workers' compensation, (3) unemployment insurance, and (4) family and medical leave. Voluntary benefits usually include (1) pay for time not worked, (2) health and insurance protection, and (3) some form of retirement income. A modern trend is toward a flexible benefit policy, called *flexcomp* or *cafeteria benefit plans,* that allows employees to choose their own benefits up to a certain predetermined amount.

important terms

achievement, proficiency, *or* skill tests *457*
affirmative action programs (AAPs) *451*
apprenticeship training *462*
aptitude tests *457*
comparable worth *or* pay equity *468*
cost-of-living adjustments (COLAs) *467*
dual promotion ladders *449*
employee benefits *470*
exempt employees *466*
experience rating *470*
flexcomp *or* cafeteria benefit plans *472*
incentive wages *or* performance pay *466*
internship training *463*
IQ tests *457*
job analysis *445*
job description *444*
job evaluation *469*
job posting *449*
job specification *445*
merit *449*

nonexempt employees *466*
on-the-job training (OJT) *462*
orientation *460*
personality tests *457*
prevailing wage rate *467*
promoting *448*
rate range *466*
reliability *458*
seniority *449*
single rate *465*
structured interviews *459*
time wages *or* day work *466*
transferring *448*
upgrading *448*
validity *458*
vocational interest tests *457*
vocational rehabilitation programs *463*
vocational-technical education programs *463*
work sampling *or* work preview *457*

questions for review and discussion

1. What are some of the advantages and disadvantages of filling jobs from within?
2. Distinguish among upgrading, transferring, and promoting employees.
3. What outside sources can be used for finding new employees?
4. How do EEO laws affect recruiting and selecting of employees?
5. Name and explain the steps in the suggested procedure for selecting workers for specific jobs.
6. Describe several types of training and give examples of jobs each type of training is best suited for.
7. What is the responsibility of supervisors for training their employees?
8. Why is compensation so important to (a) employees and (b) employers?
9. Distinguish (a) between single rates and rate ranges and (b) between time wages and performance pay.
10. Discuss at least five factors affecting wage rates.
11. What is job evaluation, and what are some problems with its use?
12. Name and describe the four legally required employee benefits.
13. What are some of the more popular voluntary employee benefits?
14. What is flexcomp, and how does it work?

•skill builder 16–1

What Would You Do?

Three people have applied to you for an opening as a lathe operator. One is totally unqualified. One is experienced, but has a very poor attitude. The third lacks experience, but seems especially eager for the job; you think she would be a good worker if she had more experience, but you're not sure.

You have some rush work that you need to get out. Which of the following courses would you choose?

1. If the eager applicant has good references, hire her for a probationary period. But keep looking for a more qualified person in case she doesn't work out.
2. Pass up the three applicants. Keep looking.
3. Hire the experienced person, ignoring his attitude—you've got work to get out!

•skill builder 16–2

What Do You Want from Your Job?

Rank the employment factors in the following chart in order of their importance to you at three points in your career. In the first column, assume that you are about to graduate and are looking for your first full-time job. In the second column, assume that you have been gainfully employed for 5 to 10 years and are presently working for a reputable firm at the prevailing salary for the type of job and industry in which you work. In the third column, try to assume that 25 to 30 years from now you have found your niche in life and have been working for a reputable employer for several years. (Rank your first choice as "1," second as "2," and so forth, through "9.")

Employment Factor	Your Ranking		
	As You Seek Your First Full-Time Job	5–10 Years Later	15–20 Years Later
Employee benefits	____	____	____
Fair adjustment of grievances	____	____	____
Good job instruction and training	____	____	____
Effective job supervision by your supervisor	____	____	____
Promotion possibilities	____	____	____
Job safety	____	____	____
Job security (no threat of being dismissed or laid off)	____	____	____
Good salary	____	____	____
Good working conditions (nice office surroundings, good hours, and so on)	____	____	____

Answer the following questions:

1. What does your ranking tell you about your motivation now?
2. Is there any change in the second and third periods?
3. What changes are there, and why did you make them?

SOURCE: *Donald C. Mosley, Paul H. Pietri, and Leon C. Megginson,* Management: Leadership in Action. *Copyright 1996 Addison Wesley Longman, Inc. Reprinted by permission of Addison Wesley Longman.*

CASE 16–1

John Wolf: The Bypassed Employee

The Ames Manufacturing Company was a medium-sized company that produced various pumps and gauges for vehicles such as automobiles, buses, and trucks. The human resource needs of each department in the plant were usually filled by transfers from other departments within the company. John Wolf came to the production department of the firm from a human resources pool, with the oral recommendation of his former supervisor. After Wolf served the traditional three-month probationary period, his progress was reviewed. He was a borderline employee and a little slow in learning the work. This type of work and the absence of close supervision were completely new to him. Still, by mutual consent, he was retained past the probationary period. Wolf was cautioned, however, that he must improve his performance.

Each year for three years, Wolf's progress was reviewed. Although his work improved somewhat, he was not up to the caliber of the rest of the workforce. During this time, several new employees were added. They had been tested on general knowledge, mechanical aptitude, and personality traits and had been selected from among many applicants.

When a supervisor from another part of the department transferred out, Wolf called his department head. He informed the department head that he felt he was capable of assuming the vacated position, that he was the most knowledgeable person in his group, and that he expected to receive the promotion. After advising Wolf that he would be considered along with other eligible people, the department head held a meeting to review those employees available to fill the opening. The department head then explained to Wolf that, although he could get by in his own day-to-day work, there were other employees—hired more recently—who were more capable of being advanced.

Wolf was bypassed. Management explained to Wolf their thoughts that he was not ready to be promoted and might be better suited for work that was less mechanically complex and more closely supervised.

Answer the following questions:

1. Why was the internal source used in selecting John Wolf for the production department?
2. How did the recruitment of John Wolf from within work out?
3. Do you think he should have been promoted to supervisor? Why or why not?

chapter 7

Appraising and Disciplining Employees

outline

The Role of Performance Appraisals in Supervisory Management
What Is a Performance Appraisal?
How a Performance Appraisal Operates
Purposes of the Performance Appraisal
Legal Aspects of the Performance Appraisal

Who Should Do Performance Appraisals?
Employees Rating Themselves
Employees Rating Supervisors
Peers Rating One Another
Immediate Supervisor Rating Employees

Some Selected Methods of Appraising Performance
Traditional Methods of Performance Appraisal
New Ways of Appraising Performance
Barriers to Effective Appraisals

The Role of the Appraisal Interview

The Need for Discipline
What Is Discipline?
Positive and Negative Discipline
Discipline as Due Process

Types of Disciplinary Problems
Number and Frequency of Occurrences
Severity of Consequences
Sexual Harassment

How Disciplinary Due Process Operates
Establishing Rules of Conduct
Determining Penalties
Imposing the Penalty Only After a Fair Hearing

The Supervisor and Discipline
The Supervisor's Disciplinary Role
Principles of Effective Discipline: The Hot-Stove Rule
Applying Discipline
Supervisors' Personal Liability for Disciplining Employees

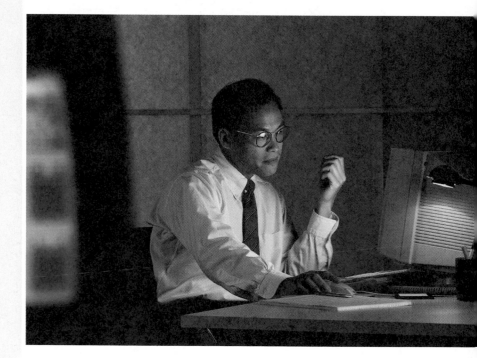

No one is free who cannot command himself.

Pythagoras

Good order is the foundation of all good things.

Edmund Burke

When the Transfer Backfires (A)

learning objectives

After reading and studying this chapter, you should be able to:

1 Explain what employee performance appraisal is and who performs it.

2 Describe some methods of appraising employee performance.

3 State why performance appraisal interviews are difficult for both the employee and the supervisor.

4 Define discipline and explain why it is necessary.

5 Discuss the differences between positive and negative discipline.

6 Describe how discipline is imposed under due process.

7 Explain the supervisor's disciplinary role.

Jane Smith abruptly rose and stormed out of the office of Robert Trent, the director of purchasing at a major eastern university. As she made her hasty exit, Trent began to wonder what had gone wrong with a seemingly perfect plan—one that would have rid his department of a "problem" employee. How could his well-constructed plan, using the university's formal transfer system, have failed so miserably, leaving him with an even more unmanageable situation?

It had all begun in January, when Trent decided that something must be done about Smith's performance and attitude. The process was made a little more awkward by the university's not having a formal employee performance-appraisal policy and program. Each department was left with the right to develop and conduct its own employee appraisals. This meant that each department could choose whether or not to appraise an employee, as well as choose the format and procedure to be used.

In January, Trent decided to conduct an appraisal of Smith. After writing down some weaknesses in her performance and attitude, he called her in to discuss them. He cited the various weaknesses to her, but, admittedly, most were highly subjective in nature. In only a few instances did he give specific and objective references, and he did not give Smith a copy of his findings. During the appraisal interview, he even hinted that possibly she didn't "fit in" and that she "probably would be much happier in some other place." In any event, he was satisfied that he had begun the process for eventually ridding the department of her. He reasoned that, if all else failed, this pressure would ultimately force her to quit. At the time, he hardly noticed that she was strangely quiet through the whole meeting.

As time went by, Smith's attitude and performance did not improve. In March, Trent was elated to learn that an opening existed in another department and that Smith was most interested in transferring. The university's formal transfer policy required that Trent complete the Employee Transfer Evaluation Form—which he gladly did. As a matter of fact, he rated Smith mostly "outstanding" on the performance and attitude factors. He was so pleased at having the opportunity to use the transfer system that he called the other department manager and spoke glowingly of Smith's abilities and performance. Although he had been the purchasing director for only eight months, having been recruited from another college, he even pointed with pride to Smith's five years' experience. In April, much to Trent's dismay, it was announced that Smith had lost the transfer opportunity to a better qualified candidate.

SOURCE: *Prepared by M. T. Bledsoe, Associate Professor of Business, Meredith College, Raleigh, North Carolina.*

The preview case illustrates an ongoing problem facing all supervisors—appraising employee performance, which is one of the least pleasant aspects of supervisory management. Yet an employee's performance is always being appraised, either formally or informally, poorly or well. Whenever a worker is praised or reprimanded, given a wage increase or passed over for one, promoted or not promoted, or transferred, laid off, or discharged, his or her job performance has been appraised and a value judgment made about it.

Another unpleasant—but necessary—aspect of the supervisor's job is discipline, which will be covered in detail here.

THE ROLE OF PERFORMANCE APPRAISALS IN SUPERVISORY MANAGEMENT

① Explain what employee performance appraisal is and who performs it.

Because performance appraisal is such an important part of the management process, enlightened managers are now trying to upgrade their appraisal programs. Most employers have already developed some kind of formal program for improving employee performance, growth, and development.

It should be strongly emphasized that performance appraisals—when properly designed, conducted, and discussed with the person being appraised—are beneficial to the employee as well as the organization. In other words, reviews can be positive and motivational if they are conducted with an attitude designed to improve performance and help each employee move toward maximizing his or her potential. Regardless of the appraisal method used, however, *the appraisal should be constructive* and future oriented.

What Is a Performance Appraisal?

performance appraisal Determines to what extent an employee is performing a job the way it was intended.

Performance appraisal is the process used to determine to what extent an employee is performing a job in the way it was intended to be done. Some other frequently used terms for this process are **merit rating, efficiency rating, service rating,** and **employee evaluation.** Regardless of the term used, the process always has the purpose of seeing how actual employee performance compares to the ideal or standard.[1]

How a Performance Appraisal Operates

If employees' output can be physically measured, then their rewards can be based on their actual output and there would be little need to formally appraise them. However, many jobs today do not lend themselves to physical measurement. Therefore, the supervisor tries to determine what personal characteristics an employee has that lead him or her to have satisfactory performance. As you can see from Exhibit 17–1, the process works as follows: An employee's personal qualities (1) lead to job behaviors (2) that result in work performance (3), which the manager appraises (4), and that appraisal results in some kind of personnel action (5).

An *employee's qualities* are abilities, attitudes, interests, skills, knowledge, and values. These qualities lead the employee to take certain actions that result in output or productivity. The manager appraises the employee's performance and then may reward the employee through a pay increase, transfer, promotion, training and development, or career progress.

Exhibit 17–1

How Performance Appraisals Operate

Aptitudes	Actions	Achievements	Evaluates	Rewards
Abilities	Conduct	Output	Measures	Pay increase
Attitudes	Functions	Productivity	Rates	Transfer
Interests	Motions			Promotion
Knowledge	Responses			Training
Motives				Career progress
Skills				Layoff
Values				Discharge
1. Employee's personal qualities	**2. Job behaviors**	**3. Work performance**	**4. Manager's appraisal**	**5. Personnel actions**

Most human resource departments now have computerized files on all employees. These *management staffing and development programs* should include appraisal criteria and ratings along with consistent definitions of skills, level of experience, and development activity.[2]

Purposes of the Performance Appraisal

Some specific reasons for appraising employee performance are (1) to recognize "good" performance, (2) to point out areas that need improvement, especially if the employee hopes to progress in the organization, (3) to validate selection techniques in order to meet Equal Employment Opportunity Commission (EEOC)/Affirmative Action Program (AAP) requirements (as discussed in Chapter 16), and (4) to provide a basis for administrative actions such as wage increases, promotions, transfers, layoffs, and/or discharges. Appraisal for these purposes is usually done by comparing the performance of one employee to that of others.

Administrative action sometimes takes the form of dealing with managers who are having problems, as well. A well-developed appraisal system can help detect "problem managers" in time to take appropriate action.[3]

click! http://www.eeoc.gov/

self-check

Notice in the chapter preview how Robert Trent manipulated the appraisal of Jane Smith to get her transferred. Although we do not condone the method he used, the case does show how a performance appraisal can be used as a basis for administrative action.

Performance appraisals can also be used for communications and motivational purposes, such as to provide a basis for giving advice, coaching, or counseling so that employees will have better expectations on the job, or as a basis for career planning and development. When used for these purposes, performance appraisal is usually done by comparing employees' actual performance to some previously determined work standard(s). In such cases, the role of the supervisor is that of a counselor, mentor, or instructor, and the appraisal should serve to motivate employees by giving them a better understanding of their job responsibilities, of what is expected of them, and of their training needs.

Legal Aspects of the Performance Appraisal

As discussed in Chapter 16, the EEOC has issued *Uniform Guidelines on Employee Selection Procedures,* which include guidelines for designing and conducting performance appraisals. These guidelines mandate that the characteristics, or job behaviors, measured by the appraisal be related to the successful performance of the employee's job. In other words, if the appraisal measures "skills," then those skills should be important to success in that job. This means that those responsible for designing the form and content of performance appraisals should be sure that what they purport to measure is relevant to the particular job being evaluated. Also, the employee should know in advance what the standards of performance are and how they are to be measured.

Second, the appraisal of a given employee should be based on the extent to which the person succeeds in carrying out the essential task(s) being measured. It also stands to reason that an appraisal should be nondiscriminatory and not reflect the appraiser's consideration of the employee's sex, race, age, disability, or any other protected category.

The person responsible for the appraising should be aware of the danger of letting personalities, personal biases, and personality conflicts get in the way of realistic evaluations. Appraisals should be an accurate assessment of performance and not tainted by extraneous attitudes and mind-sets.

WHO SHOULD DO PERFORMANCE APPRAISALS?

There are many individuals or groups who can do performance appraisals, but most appraisals are handled through (1) the employees rating themselves, (2) employees rating supervisors, (3) peers rating each other, or (4) the employees rating their immediate subordinates. In some service-oriented organizations, customers may also be called on to evaluate employees. Although we will discuss them all, performance appraisals done by the immediate supervisor are the most important for our purposes.

Employees Rating Themselves

A growing trend at progressive organizations is to let employees, especially managers, rate themselves. These ratings, which are not usually part of the regular performance appraisal, encourage employees to do personal career planning.

> **At some companies, such as Citibank, a senior manager simply hands employees an evaluation form and asks them to fill in their own ratings. Apparently this method works well. A manager at one such company said, "It's amazing how honest people are. They even put in things that are detrimental to their own progress and promotion." As a safeguard, however, the senior manager makes the final review of the ratings.**

Employees Rating Supervisors

 http://www.cognex .com/

If a main purpose of a performance appraisal is to improve employer–employee relationships, it may be useful to let employees rate their own supervisor. This method is also helpful to supervisors who sincerely want to improve their performance, especially their interpersonal relationships.

> For example, workers at Cognex Corporation, a Natick, Massachusetts, maker of machine-vision systems, started rating their supervisors in May 1995. The supervisors are rated on how well they promote teamwork, develop workers' skills, and evaluate employees' performance.[4]

Peers Rating One Another

peer rating
Each employee anonymously appraises the performance of peers.

Peer rating allows employees to rate one another. Under this method, each employee anonymously appraises the performance of the other members of the work group. The supervisor then tabulates the results for each employee. This method is often called the *mutual rating system*.

Immediate Supervisor Rating Employees

The most frequently used method of appraising performance is the rating of employees by their immediate supervisors, which is an unavoidable part of every supervisor's responsibility. Although it may be helpful to have input from the employees themselves or their peers, the immediate supervisor must be the ultimate appraiser of his or her own employees. Immediate supervisors are in the best position to know the job requirements and to know how well an employee is meeting them; thus, a supervisor can make the best judgment about the need for an employee to improve his or her performance.

A classic study found that 95 percent of the respondents were appraised by their immediate supervisor.[5] A more recent study showed that well over 80 percent of U.S. companies have appraisal systems for supervisory and middle managers as well as for office, professional, technical, and nonunion production workers.[6]

SOME SELECTED METHODS OF APPRAISING PERFORMANCE

2 Describe some methods of appraising employee performance.

We indicated earlier that employee performance is always being appraised, either formally or informally. For the purposes previously discussed, however, *formal* appraisals are preferred by most managers. This approach provides a record that can be used for any action resulting from the appraisal. Hence, formal performance appraisals are now conducted by most firms at regular intervals of every six months or a year. With new employees, the appraisal is often done after the first 90 days.

Traditional Methods of Performance Appraisal

There are many traditional approaches to performance appraisal. Most of them are aimed at attaining greater objectivity in the appraisal and reducing the influence of chance (see Exhibit 17–2). However, only the two most prevalent of

Exhibit 17-2

Suspicions Confirmed

Good ☐
Poor ☐
Very good ☐
Average ☐
Excellent ☐

these traditional methods are explained in detail. They are (1) the rating scale and (2) the employee comparison method.

Rating Scale. The oldest and most prevalent type of performance-rating procedure uses a **rating scale,** whereby an employee is rated on a number of characteristics on a point scale. An example of a rating scale is presented in Exhibit 17–3. Every 6 or 12 months, employees are rated on characteristics the organization considers important, such as quality of work, attitude toward work, ability to get along with others, and judgment. The point scale generally ranges from 5 for "exceptional" performance down to 1 for "very poor" performance. The points are totaled and the results are used to compare employees' performance and to point out where improvement is needed.

The major advantage of the rating scale system is its simplicity, but several disadvantages are also evident. The fact that an employee scores 35 does not necessarily mean that he or she is more effective on the job than another employee who receives a total score of 32. Moreover, different supervisors may have different standards in mind for "above average" or "average" work. In addition, supervisors may tend to rate their people high because it makes them look good, or because they honestly feel that their employees are "above average" or need a salary increase.

> After granting no general salary adjustments for a year and a half, one hospital's human resources committee decided to give a maximum raise of 6 percent. The managers and supervisors were told that each employee's increase would be based on appraisals by that employee's supervisor (which were done every six months).

rating scale
Rates an employee on a number of characteristics.

Exhibit 17–3

*A Typical Rating
Scale Appraisal Form*

Employee Evaluation Form

Employee Name *Fred Willis*   Position *Chief Engineer, Materials Research*
Period covered by evaluation: from *1/1/01*   to *6/30/01*

	Unsatis-factory (1)	Meets Minimum (2)	Average (3)	Above Average (4)	Out-standing (5)	Score
1. Quality and thoroughness of work		✓				2
2. Volume of work				✓		4
3. Knowledge of job, methods, and procedures				✓		4
4. Initiative and resourcefulness				✓		4
5. Cooperation, attitude, and teamwork			✓			3
6. Adaptability and ability to learn quickly					✓	5
7. Ability to express self clearly in speaking and writing			✓			3
8. Planning, organizing, and making work assignments		✓				2
9. Selection and development of employees		✓				2
10. Morale and loyalty of employees			✓			3

Total Score *32*

What steps can this employee take to improve his work? *Employee is an eager, innovative, resourceful person whose eagerness sometimes causes him to sacrifice quality of work. While highly talented, must learn to delegate more technical work to subordinates and assume more managerial tasks himself.*
Other comments: *Employee has been in position about 7 months. This is his first managerial job, and some problems in making the adjustment were expected.*

Total score:
10–15 Unsatisfactory
16–25 Meets Minimum
26–35 Average
36–45 Above Average
46–50 Outstanding

Supervisor's signature *Paul Batson*
Title *Head, Engineering Research*
Employee's signature *Frederick R. Willis*
Approved by *Horace Wilhelm*
Title *Director, Research & Development*

SOURCE: *Donald C. Mosley, Paul H. Pietri, and Leon C. Megginson,* Management: Leadership in Action. *Copyright 1996 Addison Wesley Longman, Inc. Reprinted by permission of Addison Wesley Longman.*

Of the appraisals received from the nursing department, 97 percent were "outstanding." These appraisals were returned to the director of nursing for an explanation. Her comment was, "Our supervisors thought their nurses deserved a good raise after going without one for 18 months."

employee comparison method
Supervisors rank the performance and value to the organization of their employees in comparison to others.

Employee Comparison Methods. To overcome the disadvantages of the rating scale, various employee comparison methods can be used. An **employee comparison method** differs from a rating scale system in that appraisers are required to rank each person in comparison to others in terms of performance and value to the organization. Thus, someone must end up being first, another second, and so on, down to the last employee. Some managers have modified this approach by selecting, for example, the top third, the middle third, and the bottom third of the work group and putting each employee in one of those groups.

One variant of the employee comparison method is the **paired-comparison technique.** Suppose a supervisor has five employees: Harrison, Jackson, Santos, Troy, and Willard. If the supervisor wants to appraise Harrison, the supervisor will compare Harrison with Jackson, Harrison with Santos, Harrison with Troy, and Harrison with Willard. The process is repeated until each employee has been compared with each of the others. The number of times one employee is ranked over another is recorded, and the result is an overall ranking based on who received the most votes, the second most votes, and so on. This technique probably provides a more realistic appraisal than the other methods mentioned, but it is more complex and is difficult to apply when the supervisor has a large number of employees.

paired-comparison technique
An employee is compared, in turn, to each of the other employees of the work group.

A word of caution is needed here! Employee comparison methods should be used judiciously. When all is said and done, *employees' performance should be appraised in relation to job duties and quality and quantity of output and not to other employees.*

New Ways of Appraising Performance

In recent years, the traditional approaches to appraising employees' work have been supplemented by management by objectives, or MBO, and behaviorally anchored rating scales. Because MBO was discussed in Chapter 3, it will only be reviewed here.

click! http://www.tvo.org/
pdonline/forprincipals/
performancereview
.html

Using Management by Objectives (MBO). MBO is also known as *joint target setting* or *appraisal by results.* As shown in Chapter 3, the supervisor's role in this approach is to help employees grow and fit their aims into the supervisor's broader objectives—and ultimately those of the organization. The tone of this approach is positive rather than negative, constructive rather than destructive.

With MBO, employees can see on a weekly or even daily basis the extent of their development toward the targets that have been set. They are thus actively involved in self-appraisal as they help establish their own goals, evaluate their strong and weak points, and periodically measure their own progress.

behaviorally anchored rating scales (BARS)
Specify more objectively the actual job behaviors being evaluated, because they are based on fuller descriptions of effective and ineffective job performance.

Using Behaviorally Anchored Rating Scales (BARS). **Behaviorally anchored rating scales (BARS)** were designed to specify more objectively the actual job behaviors being evaluated. Thus, they tend to be based on fuller descriptions of effective and ineffective job performance. There are several scale values on the forms. One scale value is used for each **job dimension,** which is a group of duties, activities, and responsibilities that are part of the job. **Anchors** are brief statements of actual worker behavior on the job. These indicate the specific degrees of job performance level, from the best, at the top, to the poorest, on the bottom.

job dimension
A group of duties, activities, and responsibilities that are part of the job.

anchors
Brief statements of actual worker behavior on the job.

Comparing employees with one another gives individuals a clear sense of their contribution to the success of the company.

In rating an employee using this system, the rater chooses the anchor that most nearly describes the employee's actual performance. Then the number to the left of the anchor scale that reflects the scale value is circled. After all the dimensions of the job have been evaluated, the circled scale values are totaled and averaged. The resulting figure is the employee's evaluation.[7]

BARS are most effective when used to develop plans for an MBO system, as they are based on job analysis, which makes them more job related. They provide statements of the desired employee behavior needed to reach objectives. Exhibit 17–4 is an example of this type of rating scale.

Barriers to Effective Appraisals

Like other human resource techniques, performance appraisals have validity and reliability problems. While appraisals are intended to evaluate employee performance and potential, they may not do so effectively because of various limitations on their use. The most common sources of error are (1) supervisors' reluctance to appraise employees, (2) appraiser bias(es), (3) halo and horn effects, and (4) the central tendency.

Supervisors' Reluctance to Appraise Employees. In general, supervisors are reluctant to appraise employees. In fact, it is one of their most unpleasant tasks. They tend to postpone it or find excuses not to do it. As you will soon see, the appraisal interview in particular is one of the most unpleasant of the supervisor's activities.

appraiser bias(es)
Conscious or unconscious educational, racial, or interpersonal conflict.

Appraiser Bias(es). An otherwise valid appraisal system may be invalidated by **appraiser bias(es)**, which may occur for reasons such as conscious or unconscious perceptions based on race, education, or interpersonal issues. Bias may also be a factor of time, as recent impressions are more likely to influence eval-

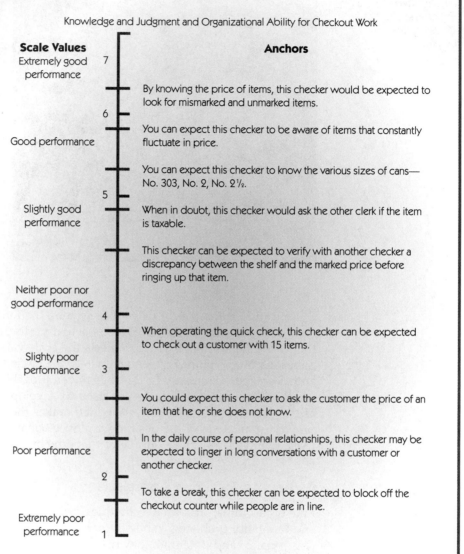

Exhibit 17–4

Example of a Behaviorally Anchored Rating Scale

Knowledge and Judgment and Organizational Ability for Checkout Work

Scale Values   **Anchors**

Extremely good performance   7

6   By knowing the price of items, this checker would be expected to look for mismarked and unmarked items.

Good performance   You can expect this checker to be aware of items that constantly fluctuate in price.

You can expect this checker to know the various sizes of cans— No. 303, No. 2, No. 2½.

5

Slightly good performance   When in doubt, this checker would ask the other clerk if the item is taxable.

This checker can be expected to verify with another checker a discrepancy between the shelf and the marked price before ringing up that item.

Neither poor nor good performance   4

When operating the quick check, this checker can be expected to check out a customer with 15 items.

Slighty poor performance   3

You could expect this checker to ask the customer the price of an item that he or she does not know.

Poor performance   In the daily course of personal relationships, this checker may be expected to linger in long conversations with a customer or another checker.

2

To take a break, this checker can be expected to block off the checkout counter while people are in line.

Extremely poor performance   1

SOURCE: *From "Development of First-Level Behavioral Job Criteria" by Lawrence Fogli, Charles L. Hulin, and Milton R. Blood ("Journal of Applied Psychology," 1971, 55 3–8), © by American Psychological Association. Reprinted by permission of the authors.*

uations. We tend to remember and give more weight to recent events than to distant occurrences.

The tendency to inflate ratings is another bias. Sometimes there is a general inflation of ratings by a supervisor over a period of time. Also, some individuals may consciously or unconsciously give ratings that are higher than those by other raters. In some cases, supervisors will intentionally inflate their employees' ratings because other managers are doing it, or because they think their workers need a raise in pay. One way to minimize this tendency is to separate—by, say, six months—the appraisals and salary adjustments.

It is difficult to prevent this tendency. However, employee comparison methods minimize it more than rating scale methods.

Halo and Horn Effects. The **halo effect** and its counterpart, the **horn effect,** reflect the rater's tendency to rate an employee high or low on *all factors being evaluated* as a result of the rater's impression of the employee's worth to the organization. If the appraiser likes the employee, he or she might rate the person high on all factors, failing to acknowledge that no employee is perfect in all areas. Conversely, if the rater does not like the person, low marks could be given on all factors.

Central Tendency. The **central tendency** results from the evaluator's reluctance to use the extremes of the rating scale. Instead, there is a tendency for the ratings to cluster around some intermediate point on the scale. This tendency reflects our inclination to not make hard choices at both ends of the scale.

halo effect
Tendency to rate an employee *high* on all factors being evaluated.

horn effect
Rater's tendency to rate an employee *low* on all factors being evaluated.

central tendency
Ratings clustering around some intermediate point on the scale.

THE ROLE OF THE APPRAISAL INTERVIEW

3 State why performance appraisal interviews are difficult for both the employee and the supervisor.

appraisal interview
Supervisor communicates the results of a performance appraisal to an employee.

Most organizations cannot afford poor performance, and workers cannot afford poor reviews. One way to satisfy both these requirements is for the supervisor to conduct an **appraisal interview** to communicate the results of a given performance appraisal to an employee. This method seems compatible with the objective of providing feedback on workers' progress and encouraging improvement on the job. However, conducting the appraisal interview is the job aspect that supervisors like least. This dislike, together with the poor way the appraisal interview is often handled, has caused this interview to be criticized heavily for damaging relationships between supervisors and employees. One of the main problems with such interviews is that too much is expected of them. The interview alone cannot improve performance, uncover training needs, and serve as the basis for pay increases, promotions, and so forth—but it can certainly help!

The appraisal interview is one of the most difficult duties required of a supervisor. Such an interview used to be along the lines of "Call Joe in and tell him what needs to be straightened out and what's expected of him." Today, however, interviewers are expected to aim at cooperation, constructiveness, and greater understanding.[8] Let us look at what tends to happen during the typical interview, even though it is conducted according to the rules of good performance appraisal interviewing.

Once a year Gloria Rogers calls her employees in one at a time for the appraisal interview. Both parties tend to "psych up" for this event. Rogers plans what she's going to say, and the employee tends to be apprehensive about what he or she is going to hear. At the beginning, Rogers tries to put the employee at ease by talking about the weather, the latest major league baseball game, or the employee's family. The employee knows that this is just the prelude to getting down to serious business—and tends to resent the delay.

Then Rogers explains her overall appraisal in broad terms. Initially, she'll mention some good aspects of the employee's performance and give the employee a chance to express his or her views. Next, she enumerates the employee's weaknesses and past failures. She allows the employee to explain these. Then, she explains what steps are needed to improve the employee's performance. At this point, she may ask for the employee's ideas on improvement.

One variation of the procedure allows the employee to give his or her own self-evaluation and compare it with Rogers's evaluation after it is given.

This conventional approach to the appraisal interview is emotionally upsetting for both the supervisor and the employee. There is no doubt in the employee's mind that he or she is in the hot seat and that there's little point in disagreeing with the supervisor about her judgments. It's best simply to remain submissive and accept the criticism, even if the employee disagrees with it.

Supervisors likewise tend to feel anxiety over performance appraisal, for, as management theorist Douglas McGregor points out,

Managers are uncomfortable when they are put in the position of "playing God. . . ." [We become] distressed when we must take responsibility for judging the personal worth of a fellow man. Yet the conventional approach to performance appraisal forces us not only to make such judgments and to see them acted upon, but also to communicate them to those we have judged. Small wonder we resist.[9]

It is fairly common practice for employers to require managers to discuss their appraisals with employees. The authors of this textbook have talked with numerous supervisors who suffer the double-barreled discomforts of performance appraisal. These supervisors dislike being appraised by their own bosses, and they dislike appraising their employees—or at least telling them the results. All this may lead to appraisal inflation. For example, in one company, when a policy was adopted requiring supervisors to give their appraisals to their employees, their appraisals of their employees suddenly jumped remarkably.[10]

Another important aspect of performance appraisals is that they should contain aspects of career planning for the employee. In other words, the appraisal should help the employee plan for the future.

In summary, the appraisal interview presents both an opportunity and a potential danger for the supervisor, as both praise and constructive criticism must be communicated. A major effort should be made to emphasize the positive aspects of the employee's performance while also discussing ways to make needed improvements. One classic study showed that one group of employees, who took some form of constructive action as a result of performance appraisals, did so because of the way their supervisor had conducted the appraisal interview and discussion.[11] Exhibit 17–5 provides some helpful hints for conducting a more effective interview.

THE NEED FOR DISCIPLINE

4 Define discipline and explain why it is necessary.

Effective job performance requires that both managerial and nonmanagerial employees maintain discipline. Most employees would rather work with a group that is well organized, well trained, and well disciplined than with one that is not. Employees benefit from discipline and suffer from disorder. An early study found that, although workers do not necessarily want to be personally punished, they do want to be supervised "not too much—but also not too little."[12] Successful supervisors know how to find the "middle road" that allows their

Exhibit 17–5

*Hints for the
Appraisal Interview*

Do

- Prepare in advance.
- Focus on performance and development.
- Be specific about reasons for ratings.
- Decide about specific steps to be taken for improvement.
- Consider your role in the employee's performance.
- Reinforce the behavior you want.
- Focus on future performance.

Don't

- Lecture the employee.
- Mix performance appraisal and salary or promotion issues.
- Concentrate only on the negative.
- Do all the talking.
- Be overcritical or "harp on" a failing.
- Feel it is necessary that both of you agree on all areas.
- Compare the employee with others.

SOURCE: *Robert L. Mathis and John H. Jackson,* Personnel/Human Resources Management *7th ed. (St. Paul, MN: West Publishing Co., 1994), p. 318.*

employees to know exactly what they may and may not do. These generalizations may lead to confusion unless the question "What is discipline?" is answered.

What Is Discipline?

To start out, let us emphasize that good discipline is based on good leadership. Based on that conclusion, the term *discipline* will be used in this chapter to refer to any of three concepts: (1) self-control, (2) conditions leading to orderly behavior in a work environment, or (3) punishment for improper behavior. Many companies say in their discipline policy that **discipline** is training that corrects, molds, or perfects knowledge, attitudes, behavior, or conduct. We agree with this overall definition.

discipline
Training that corrects and molds knowledge, attitudes, behavior.

Discipline as Self-Control. *Self-control* implies the orderly growth and development of a person, which enables the person to adjust to certain needs and demands. For example, athletes become disciplined when they've trained to the point of being ready for the big game. Astronauts train for years until they know exactly what is expected of them; then they are able to react as they should during an actual flight. You are disciplined if you do the intensive study that's necessary for you to pass your courses, as well as do the other things required of you. Self-discipline usually results from the actions—rather than the words—of the supervisor or higher level managers, as the following example shows.

> **The manager of a franchise selling and installing metal buildings had a problem with employees taking extra long lunch breaks. When he complained about it to his supervisors, one of them had the courage to say, "We could correct the problem more easily if you didn't take two-hour lunches yourself."**

Discipline as Orderly Behavior. The second meaning of discipline refers to the conditions necessary to obtain orderly behavior in an organization. Maintaining discipline implies keeping order among and controlling a group of

An organized work space helps promote the conditions necessary for orderly behavior in a work group.

workers by using methods that build morale and *esprit de corps.* You should be aware that, in order to create a workplace with better discipline, you should start by hiring workers that maintain a high level of self-discipline.

self-check

Have you had a class where order prevailed, seemingly without any effort on the part of the teacher or anyone else? Have you had one where conditions tended to be chaotic? Which did you prefer? Why?

punishment
Negative treatment for an undesirable act or omission.

Discipline as Punishment. The third meaning of discipline—**punishment**—refers to negative treatment that a person receives after an undesirable act or omission. The function of punishment is not to change past behavior but to prevent a recurrence of the undesirable act or omission in the future. Notice how this is shown in the following example, where a head nurse in a southern hospital recalls a difficult disciplinary problem.

> **One Saturday evening when staffing was short, a severe explosion and fire occurred at a petrochemical plant near us. As the injured were being admitted, we became very busy, especially in the burn unit, which needed another nurse.**
>
> **James Keiller,* the only male nurse on duty, was versatile and able to care for most patients. I asked him to work in the burn unit because of its heavy patient load. He became very angry and stated that if he wasn't needed in his assigned unit, he would go home. He said that I was unfair and that I always asked him to do extra work because he was the only male nurse in the house.**
>
> **I informed him that it would mean termination if he left a nursing unit understaffed. But he checked out and left. When I had time later that evening, I wrote out his termination slip.**

The punishment, discharge, was intended to prevent the nursing unit from being understaffed in the future.

---

*The name has been changed.

Positive and Negative Discipline

5 Discuss the differences between positive and negative discipline.

Discipline can be positive and constructive, or it can be negative and restraining. In either case, discipline is the force that prompts an individual or a group to comply with policies, rules, regulations, and procedures that are needed to attain the organization's objectives.

positive discipline
Promotes emotional satisfaction instead of emotional conflict by providing employees with greater freedom of expression.

Positive discipline promotes emotional satisfaction instead of emotional conflict by attempting to activate an inner force.[13] It provides workers with greater freedom of expression and results in coordination and cooperation with a minimum need for formal authority. Positive discipline can best be achieved when group objectives and procedures are well known and are a basis for individual behavior. It usually results from the supervisor's effective use of motivation, leadership, and communication, as the following example illustrates. This type of discipline also makes unconscious—or even conscious—use of peer pressure.

 click! http://www.teco.net/ TampaElectric.html

> **Tampa Electric Company uses positive discipline to turn around problem employees. First, they are given a day off, with pay, to think over their behavior and decide whether they really want to work for the company. Upon returning to work, the problem employee meets with his or her supervisor and tells what he or she is going to do. Then it is impressed upon the employee that what happens is his or her own fault. This process is enough to make most employees turn around. Those who do not are given the chance to resign, as they just do not fit into the company's program.**
>
> **For example, a lazy mechanic was given the day off to think about his behavior. At first he thought the "paid holiday" was wonderful. When he realized the company was in earnest, he made up his mind to "straighten up and fly right."[14]**

> **Another good example of the influence of positive discipline occurred recently at Prudential Insurance Company of America. When it offered its employees a free tape describing positive ways to discipline their children, 11,000 of its 90,000 workers requested a tape on the first day. This was four times the largest number of calls ever received in one day by Work Family Directions, the consultant hired by Prudential to handle the tape's distribution.[15]**

negative discipline
Designed to change a person's behavior.

malicious obedience
Following instructions exactly while knowing that the order is faulty and will cause problems.

Negative discipline involves an outside force or influence. This force will often cause a person to change outwardly, but not mentally and emotionally. Or it may lead a person to change *only* if punishment is repeated over a period of time. In fact, it sometimes results in **malicious obedience,** whereby an aggrieved employee does exactly what he or she is told to do, even knowing that the order given is faulty and will cause things to get fouled up (see Exhibit 17–6).

Negative discipline need not be extreme, and it is best used *only* when the positive type fails. Unfortunately, some organizations rely on negative discipline almost exclusively. Each supervisor must choose which type of discipline to use, and the effective supervisor will vary the type of discipline to suit the employee and the situation.

Whether you are engaged in positive discipline, negative discipline, or just a discussion with other members of your organization, any criticism you voice

Exhibit 17–6

*Negative Discipline
Can Lead to Malicious
Obedience*

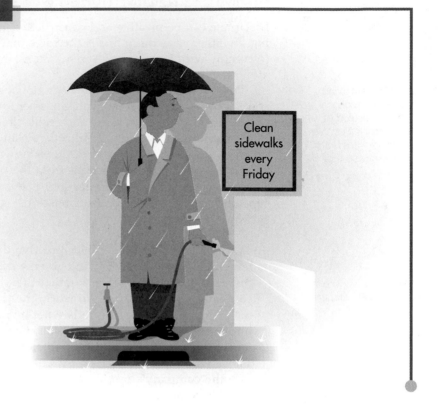

Clean
sidewalks
every
Friday

constructive criticism
Offered to help correct
a condition that can be
corrected.

should be constructive, not negative. You, as a supervisor, are perfectly right to engage in **constructive criticism** of any behavior or idea, as long as the environment is correct. When an argument is put forth in favor of a course of action and you see a disadvantage to it, you should voice that point if the advocate of the proposal fails to do so. When your boss or anyone else puts forth a proposal in your presence, he or she usually wants your honest reactions. Loyalty demands that you do your best to prevent a person from making a mistake or suffering some humiliation, when and where you can. Do not refuse an employee, a peer, or a supervisor such aid when you have it to give.

Discipline as Due Process

The Fourteenth Amendment to the U.S. Constitution guarantees every citizen due process under the law. Essentially, the following conditions ensure that an individual receives justice in the form of **due process:**

due process
Guarantees the individual accused of violating an established rule a hearing to determine the extent of guilt.

1. Rules or laws exist.
2. There are specific, fixed penalties for violating those rules, with progressive degrees in the severity of penalties.
3. Penalties are imposed only after a hearing has been conducted for the accused, at which time the extent of guilt is determined after considering the circumstances of the situation.

Unions have insisted that this same process be used within organizations in disciplining employees; even nonunion employers now use it. Today, most arbitrators will uphold a disciplinary action if it can be shown that (1) the rules are reasonable, (2) the penalty is related to the severity of the offense, and (3) the worker was given a fair hearing. Underlying the due-process concept is the assumption that the employer has the right to have a well-disciplined work environment and the right to administer discipline when rules are violated. Of course, where there's a union, its representative wants to be present when a member is disciplined. Disciplinary due process is explained in more detail later in this chapter. At this point, though, we would like to emphasize that employers can avoid employee grievance proceedings by developing equitable and objective disciplinary procedures.[16]

TYPES OF DISCIPLINARY PROBLEMS

Disciplinary problems can be classified in one of two basic ways: (1) according to the number and frequency of occurrences and (2) according to the severity of consequences. In both cases, we're dealing with the *degree* of the problem, not an absolute factor.[17] (See Exhibit 17–7 for examples.)

Number and Frequency of Occurrences

The Personnel Policies Forum of the Bureau of National Affairs, Inc., studied the most serious disciplinary problems in manufacturing, nonmanufacturing, and nonbusiness organizations. This classic study found that in 79 percent of the organizations surveyed, from the standpoint of frequency and number of occurrences, the worst disciplinary problems in all organizations were absenteeism and tardiness. Lack of productivity and poor work habits and/or attitudes were reported by 11 percent of the organizations, and 16 percent reported other problems.[18]

Severity of Consequences

In terms of the severity of their consequences, there are three categories of disciplinary problems: (1) minor infractions, (2) major violations, and (3) intolerable offenses.

minor infractions
Violations of rules that do little harm.

Minor Infractions. Minor infractions are disciplinary problems that do little harm or result in few serious consequences when they happen in isolation. But they may be serious when they happen frequently or in connection with other infractions.

Absenteeism and tardiness are the most frequently committed minor infractions. These problems involve workers' not being present when they are needed and having an apparent disregard for others. Other minor infractions are taking too long for breaks, leaving early, littering, slowing down production, distracting others with shouts or horseplay, and poor or careless performance. Operators, laborers, and service personnel have the highest rate of minor infractions; technical and professional employees and managerial personnel have the lowest rate.

major violations
Disciplinary problems that greatly interfere with orderly operations.

Major Violations. Disciplinary problems that substantially interfere with orderly operations are called **major violations.** Some of the most frequent major

Exhibit 17–7

*Example of
Disciplinary
Procedures Using
Graduated Penalties*

Offenses	Enforcement			
Minor Offenses	**First Action Step**	**Second Action Step**	**Third Action Step**	**Fourth Action Step**
Minor infractions that do not do great damage or have serious consequences when viewed individually, but may be considered serious when accumulated.	Education and informal warning(s) by first-line supervisor.	Warning in presence of union representative by first-line supervisor.	Warning or written reprimand by higher supervision in presence of union representative and/or suspension up to 2 days.	Becomes a major offense and is handled accordingly. (Does not necessarily involve immediate suspension.)
Major Offenses	**First Offense**	**Second Offense**	**Third Offense**	
Violations that substantially interfere with production or damage morale; or when seriousness of offense is apparent to a reasonable mind; or an accumulation of minor offenses.	Step 1: Immediately remove employee from job and have report to higher supervision. Step 2: Suspension up to 5 days, plus a written reprimand or written final warning, if necessary.	Step 1: Immediately remove employee from job and have report to higher supervision. Step 2: Written final warning. Suspension up to 10 days, or discharge if final warning was given for first offense.	Step 1: Immediately remove employee from job and have report to higher supervision. Step 2: Discharge.	
Intolerable Offenses	**First Offense**			
Offenses of a criminal or drastic nature which strain employment relationship or would be outrageous to most people.	Step 1: Immediately remove employee from job and have report to industrial relations department. Step 2: Discharge.			

Pointers

1. Economic penalties (such as suspensions, transfers, discharges) should be imposed only by higher supervision after consultation with industrial relationship department.

2. Written final warnings should always be accompanied by an economic penalty.

3. To be considered a second offense, violations should occur within a year of the first offense.

SOURCE: *Walter Collins and Herman Harrow, "Does the Penalty Match the Offense?" p. 20. Reprinted, by permission of the publisher, from* Supervisory Management *(September/1958) © 1958. American Management Association, New York. All rights reserved.*

violations involve lying, cheating, stealing, sleeping during working hours, willfully punching someone else's time card, violating safety rules, doing personal work on company time, and failing to carry out an order.

Intolerable Offenses. When the disciplinary problems are of such a drastic, dangerous, or illegal nature that they severely strain or endanger employment relationships, they are called **intolerable offenses.** These problems are so grave and their consequences so serious that they usually result in *immediate* discharge. The situation and the nature of the organization's operations tend to determine what is considered an intolerable offense. In other words, what is acceptable at one time or in one industry may not be acceptable at another time or in another industry.

intolerable offenses
Disciplinary problems of a drastic, dangerous, or illegal nature.

self-check

In a previous example, James Keiller was given a direct order by the head nurse. Notice that he was warned and given a chance to change his mind about checking out when he was needed in the burn unit. What category of disciplinary problem did he commit?

Do you think James Keiller's conduct in this example would have resulted in discharge during normal conditions at the hospital? Why or why not? Also, would it have resulted in discharge if he had been an employee in a research organization? Why or why not?

Some examples of intolerable offenses are fighting that results in serious harm to others; serious theft, including using company property to make something for personal use on company time; willful destruction of property; smoking in an area of inflammables where a "No Smoking" sign is posted; and any form of violence.[19] Look at the following example in which a head nurse in a large nursing home recalls a dreadful problem with Babs,* a loyal but drug-addicted registered nurse.

Bab's recent pattern of behavior was characterized by a state of being "high" and happy for a day or two, followed by extreme depression, slightly slurred speech, and muttering to herself. One afternoon, she went to the medicine room and picked up a bottle of capsules. She clutched them eagerly, saying, "Ah, what would I do without you?" Then she dropped a bottle of syrupy liquid on the floor. Finally, she shakily asked if she could go home. I told her to get a good night's sleep and see me in the morning at 10.

She was calm and back to normal the next morning. She said, "I realize you have no choice but to let me go, but please, please help me." Apparently her problems began when she had difficulty getting to sleep and was given a prescription for sleeping pills by her doctor. Because she was still sleepy when she awoke, she took a pep pill. This made her nervous, so another doctor prescribed a tranquilizer. Now she needed them all and was taking so many that she rarely felt or acted normally.

Both my department head and the human resource officer suggested that I fire her immediately!

---

*The name has been changed.

Sexual Harassment

At one time, sexually oriented "kidding" between supervisors and their employees was of no concern to management. Needless to say, this is no longer true! Instead, such verbal activities would now probably be considered sexual harassment.

sexual harassment
Unwelcome sexual advances that create a hostile, offensive, or intimidating work environment.

The EEOC's *Guidelines on Discrimination Because of Sex* defines **sexual harassment** as unwelcome sexual advances, requests for sexual favors, and other physical *or* verbal conduct, by a member of either sex, when such actions result in one of several consequences. Those consequences are (1) submission to the conduct is made, either implicitly or explicitly, a condition of employment; (2) submission to, or rejection of, the request(s) is used in making employment decisions involving the employee; or (3) the purpose or effect of such conduct is to unreasonably interfere with the employee's work performance or create a hostile, offensive, or intimidating work environment.[20]

Supervisors and their managers should take strong, quick, and positive measures to discourage sexual harassment, because *employers are responsible for such harassment by, or of, their employees.* Such measures should include express declarations against sexual harassment that are regularly—and clearly—communicated to all employees, and those statements should be quickly and effectively implemented. Also, internal procedures for conducting immediate, thorough, and impartial investigations should be well established and publicized. One way to ensure that such investigations are impartial is to have someone—such as a lawyer or employment specialist—from outside the organization to conduct them.[21]

The EEOC is now rigorously exploring sexual harassment charges. When guilt is determined, the penalties are steep, as the following example illustrates.

> **On August 4, 1995, a federal judge in Uniondale, New York, upheld the EEOC's largest sexual harassment lawsuit ever against Del Laboratories Inc. Del will pay $1.2 million to 15 women who claimed they were harassed by the CEO of the Farmingdale, New York, cosmetics company. He was accused of engaging in lewd behavior and using vulgar language. The company, while claiming the charges were "false and baseless," settled the case in order to avoid further costs and negative publicity.[22]**

HOW DISCIPLINARY DUE PROCESS OPERATES

6 Describe how discipline is imposed under due process.

As indicated earlier, disciplinary due process involves three steps. First, rules are established. Second, fixed penalties are set for each infraction of a rule (the penalties usually vary according to the degree of severity of the offense and how many times the rule is broken, as shown in Exhibit 17–7). Third, the penalty is imposed only after the employee has been given a fair hearing.

Establishing Rules of Conduct

If employees are to maintain self-discipline, they must know what they can and cannot do, and they must know it in advance. Therefore, most progressive organizations publish rules, usually in their employees' handbook. The Bureau of National Affairs study mentioned earlier found that 85 percent of the organizations published rules.

Determining Penalties

progressive discipline
Discipline that uses a graduated scale of penalties.

The types of penalties, as well as the ways they are used, generally are determined in consultation with the union. What usually results is termed **progressive discipline,** because it involves a graduated scale of penalties. If there is no union, the penalties stem from management's philosophy of how to treat employees, as well as from its fear of the entry of a union or government action.

The normal steps in a progressive-discipline policy are as follows:

1. *Oral warning* that does not go into the employee's record.
2. *Oral warning* that goes into the employee's record.
3. *Written reprimand,* which usually comes from some level above the supervisor.
4. *Suspension,* which usually consists of a layoff lasting from a day to a number of months.
5. *Discharge,* the ultimate penalty, which constitutes a break in service and wipes out the employee's seniority. Most supervisors are reluctant to use it because it is the economic equivalent of the death penalty and it affects the worker's family as well as the worker. Justification must be strictly established because discharge is almost always subject to the grievance procedure and arbitration.

Some other infrequently used penalties are demotions, transfers, and the withholding of benefits such as promotions, raises, or bonuses.

graduated scale of penalties
Penalties become progressively more severe each time the violation is repeated.

Unions, personnel managers, and most supervisors favor using a **graduated scale of penalties,** under which punishment for a given violation becomes progressively more severe each time the violation is repeated. The penalty may be, first, an oral warning; second, a written warning; third, suspension; and fourth, discharge. There is no gradation for intolerable offenses, however; the first time one is committed, the employee is discharged.

self-check

Was James Keiller, in a previous example, disciplined on the basis of a graduated scale of penalties?

Imposing the Penalty Only After a Fair Hearing

Supervisors must follow the correct procedure in taking any action against an employee. In other words, discipline must be properly administered in accordance with previously established and announced rules and procedures. Penalties should be based on specific charges, with notice given to the employee and the union, if there is one, usually in advance of management's attempt to take corrective action. The charges and their underlying reasons should be definite and provable. There should be provisions for a prompt hearing, witnesses, protests, and appeals. Finally, adequate remedies should be available to employees whose punishment has failed to meet the requirement of "fair play."

In summary, the main requirements for a proper disciplinary procedure are (1) to make definite charges, (2) to notify the employee (and union), in writing, of the offense, and (3) to have some provision for the employee to answer the charges either by protest or by appeal.

self-check

To what extent was the proper disciplinary procedure used in the examples given in this chapter (James Keiller, the male nurse, and Babs, the drug-addicted nurse)?

 Explain the supervisor's disciplinary role.

THE SUPERVISOR AND DISCIPLINE

Regardless of whether supervisors work in unionized firms, they must exercise discretion when recommending or imposing penalties on employees. In dealing with mistakes, supervisors must consider what the mistakes were and under what circumstances they were made. Mistakes resulting from continued carelessness call for disciplinary action. Honest mistakes should be corrected by counseling and positive discipline, not by punishment. These should be corrected in a way that will help the employee learn from the mistakes and become a more proficient and valuable worker.

The Supervisor's Disciplinary Role

One of the primary duties of present-day supervisors is to maintain discipline. Top managers expect—and depend on—their supervisors not only to set disciplinary limits but also to enforce them. Only then does an organization operate effectively.

In order to achieve this goal, supervisors must instill a desire for self-discipline in employees. If employees are not required to face up to the realities of their jobs, their goals, their resources, and their potential, they are in a poor position to function properly and make their best contribution to the organization. It's surprising how quickly organizational problems melt away when interpersonal forthrightness is applied.

When applying discipline, a supervisor must consider these points:

1. Every job should carry with it a certain margin for error.
2. Overconcern with avoiding errors stifles initiative and encourages employees to postpone decisions or avoid making them altogether.
3. A different way of doing something should not be mistaken for the wrong way of doing it.

Supervisors are more likely than higher level managers to avoid administering severe disciplinary action, because of the likelihood of generating undesirable effects. Other managers, including some personnel managers, take a stronger—perhaps more punitive—position on matters of discipline. A possible explanation is that supervisory managers are inclined to give stronger consideration to individual circumstances and behavior than are top managers. Also, supervisors are somewhat reluctant to follow rules strictly for fear they'll lose the cooperation of their employees if they're too severe.

hot-stove rule
Compares a good disciplinary system to that of a hot stove.

Principles of Effective Discipline: The Hot-Stove Rule

Four important principles of effective discipline are discussed in this section. These principles are often referred to as the **hot-stove rule,** because they draw a comparison between touching a hot stove and experiencing discipline. Here are the four principles, as illustrated in Exhibit 17–8:

1. You know what will happen if you touch a hot stove (it carries a clear warning).
2. If you touch a hot stove, it burns you right away (it is immediate).
3. A hot stove always burns you if you touch it (it is consistent).
4. A hot stove doesn't care whom it burns (it is impersonal).

Discipline Carries a Clear Warning. Employees should know what is and what is not expected of them. This means that there must be clear warning that a given offense will lead to discipline, and there must be clear warning of the amount of discipline that will be imposed for an offense.

Supervisor C. D. Yates* had long ignored a safety rule that the employees wear short-sleeved shirts while operating their machines. In fact, for over a year, several employees had routinely worn long-sleeved shirts in the department. After learning of an injury in another department when an employee's long-sleeved shirt got caught in a conveyor belt, Yates immediately wrote up warnings to five employees in his department who were wearing long-sleeved shirts that day.

Exhibit 17–8

The Hot-Stove Rule

SOURCE: *Based on concepts in Theo Haimann and Raymond L. Hilgert,* Instructor's Manual—Supervision: Concepts and Practices of Management, *6th ed. (Cincinnati: South-Western Publishing Co., 1995). Reproduced with permission.*

*The name has been changed.

self-check

If you were one of the five employees, would you consider Yates's action fair? Probably not. Since the safety rule was so openly ignored, it was the equivalent of no rule at all. For adequate warning to take place, Yates needed to communicate to his employees that, although the rule had been ignored in the past, it would now be enforced in the department. If you were an outside arbitrator, how would you rule? Why?

Discipline Is Immediate. The supervisor should begin the disciplinary process as soon as possible after he or she notices a violation. This is important for the following reasons:

1. An employee may feel that he or she is "putting one over" on the supervisor and may try to violate other rules.

2. An employee may assume that the supervisor is too weak to enforce the rules.

3. An employee may believe that the supervisor doesn't consider the rule important enough to be enforced. Thus, all the other employees may be encouraged to break or stretch the rule as well. It is not surprising to find an employee responding, "Well, I've been doing this for several days (or weeks) and nobody said anything about it to me before."

Discipline Is Consistent. This principle means that for similar circumstances, similar discipline should be administered. If two people commit the same offense under the same circumstances, they should receive the same punishment.

> **Helen* had a very high absenteeism record. Recently she missed work for two days without a legitimate excuse. Considering her past record, this offense would justify an immediate one-week suspension. However, her skills were badly needed by the supervisor, since the department was snowed under by a tremendous backlog of work. Helen was given only an oral warning.**

What will Helen's supervisor do when another worker misses work for two days without a legitimate excuse? If the supervisor is inconsistent, he or she will develop a reputation for playing favorites and lose credibility with employees. Does this mean a supervisor always has to dish out identical penalties for similar offenses? Note that we said the supervisor must be consistent as long as circumstances are similar. An employee's past record is a major factor to consider.

> **Two employees were caught drinking an alcoholic beverage on the job. The rules clearly prohibited this. For one employee, it was the first such offense; for the second worker, it was his third in the past year. Would the supervisor be justified in giving the second employee a more serious penalty than the first? You better believe it!**

---

*The name has been changed.

self-check

What are the pros and cons of giving an employee a "break" regarding discipline?

Discipline Is Impersonal. As a supervisor, you shouldn't get into personalities when administering discipline. You need to be as objective as possible. Moreover, after administering discipline to an employee, try to retain a normal relationship with that person. Two common mistakes supervisors make in imposing discipline are apologizing to employees and bawling out employees. Discipline the act, not the person. Your focus should be on *getting the employee's work behavior consistent with the rules.*

Applying Discipline

Two of the more unpleasant aspects of the supervisor's job are (1) laying off a worker for disciplinary reasons and (2) discharging an unsatisfactory employee.

disciplinary layoff or **suspension**
Time off without pay.

Disciplinary Layoff. If an employee has repeatedly committed major offenses and previous warnings have been ineffective, a **disciplinary layoff,** or **suspension,** is probably inevitable. Such a layoff involves a loss of time—and pay—for several days. This form of discipline usually comes as a rude shock to workers. It gets their attention! And generally it impresses on them the need to comply with the organization's rules and regulations.

Because this form of discipline is quite serious and involves a substantial penalty—loss of pay—most organizations limit the power to use it to managers who have attained at least the second level of management; often the human resources manager is involved as well. Yet supervisors have the right to recommend such action.

Not all managers believe the layoff is effective, and some seldom apply it as a disciplinary measure. First, they may need the worker to continue production. Second, they may feel that the worker will return with an even more negative attitude. Still, when properly used, it is an effective disciplinary tool.

termination-at-will rule
An employer can dismiss an employee for any reason.

Discharge. In 1884, a Tennessee court established the **termination-at-will rule,** whereby an employer could dismiss an employee for any reason—or even for no reason at all—unless there was an explicit contractual provision preventing such action.[23] The reasoning behind this decision was that if an employee can quit work for any reason, then the employer should be able to discharge for any reason.

Subsequent legislative enactments and court decisions, as well as union rules and public policy, have swung the pendulum of protection away from the employer and toward the employee by limiting the termination-at-will rule.[24] Most union agreements have a clause requiring "just cause" for disciplinary discharge and detailing the order in which employees can be laid off. EEO/AA regulations do essentially the same.

In general, court decisions suggest that the safest (legal) grounds for discharge include incompetent performance that does not respond to training or accommodation, gross or repeated insubordination, excessive unexcused absences, repeated and unexcused tardiness, verbal abuse of others, physical violence, falsification of records, drunkenness or drug abuse on the job, and theft.

Since discharge is so severe, supervisors can only recommend it. The discharge must be carried out by top management—usually with the advice and consent of the human resources manager.

Unions are quite involved in discipline when they represent the employees. Even many nonunionized organizations now follow the union's disciplinary procedure.

Supervisors' Personal Liability for Disciplining Employees

Recent court decisions holding supervisors personally liable for discharging disabled employees is making some supervisors reluctant to exercise their judgment in hiring, promoting, and firing employees. They are unwilling to take the punitive action indicated for unsatisfactory actions of employees if their personal assets, such as their houses or cars, can become subject to steep jury awards.

Previously, supervisors have been held individually liable in some blatant and serious sex and race harassment cases. But this trend is now changing, as the following example indicates.

click! http://www.usdoj.gov/ crt/ada/adahom1.htm

> **In 1993, a Chicago jury ordered Ruth Vrdolyak, president of AIC Security Investigations Ltd. (AIC), to pay $250,000 in damages to a disabled employee she fired. Later, the federal magistrate who heard the case reduced her portion of the punitive damages to $75,000. However, he let stand the verdict that Mrs. Vrdolyak had violated the Americans with Disabilities Act (ADA) by firing AIC's executive director because his inoperable brain cancer had reduced his cognitive abilities. But this jury concluded from the employee's videotaped testimony that Charles Wessel (who has since died) appeared mentally alert.**

chapter review

① Explain what employee performance appraisal is and who performs it.

An employee's performance is always being appraised, either formally or informally. The purpose of formal performance appraisals, however, is to compare employee performance to a standard or ideal—a sort of personnel quality control. Appraisal is more critical for employees whose output cannot be easily measured. Specific reasons for appraising employee performance are to provide a basis for some administrative action (such as a pay increase, promotion, transfer, layoff, discharge, or recommendation for training or development), to justify these actions for EEO/AA purposes, and to improve supervisor–employee relationships. Performance appraisals can be done by employees rating themselves, by employees rating supervisors, or by employees' peers rating each other, but the immediate supervisors should be ultimately responsible, since they are most familiar with their employees' work.

② Describe some methods of appraising employee performance.

Traditional appraisal methods include (1) rating scales, which compare performance to a standard, and (2) employee comparison methods, which compare employees to one another. In either case, it is important that employees' performance be evaluated in relation to their own duties and output. Newer methods include management by objectives (MBO) and behaviorally anchored rating scales (BARS).

(3) State why performance appraisal interviews are difficult for both the employee and the supervisor.

One of the jobs supervisors like least is conducting the appraisal interview, which is used to communicate the results of the appraisal to the concerned employee. A supervisor's reluctance to criticize employees may lead to appraisal inflation. One solution to this problem is the use of MBO, in which employees are involved with supervisors in setting their own goals and appraising their own performance.

(4) Define discipline and explain why it is necessary.

Another important supervisory activity is applying discipline. Because discipline is necessary for supervisory success, higher level managers expect supervisors to set and enforce disciplinary limits. There are three types of discipline: (1) self-control, (2) conditions for orderly behavior, and (3) punishment. Employee discipline is a process of control, either internally or externally imposed. As such, it is a method of maintaining management's authority—authority that is necessary to keep an organization operating effectively.

(5) Discuss the differences between positive and negative discipline.

Discipline may be positive or negative. Positive discipline provides workers with greater freedom of expression and results in cooperation and coordination with a minimum need for formal authority. In all disciplinary situations, the criticism itself must be constructive.

(6) Describe how discipline is imposed under due process.

Although the right to discipline is still management's responsibility, today supervisors must be sure they follow due process, which requires (1) stated rules, (2) specific penalties, and (3) an orderly procedure for assessing guilt and punishment. The rules usually classify offenses as (1) minor infractions, (2) major violations, or (3) intolerable offenses. Penalties can include (1) oral warnings, (2) oral warnings with a written record, (3) written reprimands, (4) suspension, and (5) discharge. Usually a graduated scale of penalties is imposed, in which the penalty increases with the frequency and severity of violations.

(7) Explain the supervisor's disciplinary role.

To be effective, discipline must be enforced. The manner of enforcement, in turn, affects the morale of the organization. One of the most difficult supervisory tasks is to strike an acceptable balance between severity and leniency in administering discipline. Four principles of effective discipline, collectively referred to as the "hot-stove rule," are that discipline should (1) carry a clear warning, (2) be immediate, (3) be consistent, and (4) be impersonal.

When lesser forms of discipline imposed by the supervisor are ineffective, it may be necessary to resort to layoff or discharge of the employee. Usually such action is carried out only by higher levels of management. In any case, it is important to be sure that due process has been observed and that there is just cause for such action.

---

important terms

anchors *486*
appraisal interview *489*
appraiser bias(es) *487*
behaviorally anchored rating scales
  (BARS) *486*
central tendency *489*
constructive criticism *494*
disciplinary layoff *or* suspension *503*
discipline *491*
due process *494*
employee comparison method *486*
graduated scale of penalties *499*
halo effect *489*
horn effect *489*
hot-stove rule *500*
intolerable offenses *497*

job dimension *486*
major violations *495*
malicious obedience *493*
minor infractions *495*
negative discipline *493*
paired-comparison technique *486*
peer rating *483*
performance appraisal *or* merit rating *or*
  efficiency rating *or* service rating *or*
  employee evaluation *480*
positive discipline *493*
progressive discipline *499*
punishment *492*
rating scale *484*
sexual harassment *498*
termination-at-will rule *503*

---

questions for review and discussion

1. Explain why performance appraisal is such an important part of the management process.
2. What is performance appraisal, and what are some of the other names for it?
3. What are some of the purposes of performance appraisal? Explain.
4. Name at least four persons or groups that do performance appraisals, and give reasons why each of these would be used.
5. Distinguish between the "halo effect" and the "horn effect."
6. Why is discipline so very important in organizations?
7. What is discipline? Explain it in at least three ways.
8. What is the due process of discipline, and why is it so important?
9. What is the union's role in the disciplinary process?
10. What procedure should be followed in administering discipline?
11. Why should disciplinary layoff and discharge decisions be restricted to higher levels of management?

●skill builder 17–1

Gloria Rogers Appraises Her Employees

Review the example of how Gloria Rogers (page 489) conducts her performance appraisal interviews. Notice that it is "conducted according to the rules of good performance appraisal interviewing."

Instructions:

Assume that you are Gloria's supervisor (manager). How would you advise her to improve her performance appraisals?

CASE 17–1

When the Transfer Backfires (B)

After incorrectly appraising Jane Smith's performance as mostly "outstanding" in order to get her transferred to another department (see chapter preview), Robert Trent was shocked when her transfer was turned down. To further complicate matters, Trent realized that he would have to face Smith in May when it would be time to discuss annual pay raises, which would include both merit pay considerations and cost-of-living adjustments. This would be even more difficult in view of the fact that Jane's performance and attitude had not improved since the January appraisal. If anything, they were worse.

Trent had just finished the May meeting with Smith by telling her the bad news: On the basis of both performance and attitude, she should not be recommended for a cost-of-living or merit-pay increase for the new year beginning July 1. Smith, armed with the transfer evaluation forms (completed and given to her in March), threatened to use all internal and external systems for organizational justice due her.

As Trent pondered this dilemma, he fully recognized Smith's unique status within the university community. She was the wife of a distinguished, tenured professor of business, and this situation provided additional pressure. As if this were not enough, he had to contend with the office social process pivoting around a weekly coffee group that was greatly influenced by Smith. It was not unusual for the former director of purchasing (who had retired after 25 years of service) to attend these gatherings. Of course, Smith had kept this group fully apprised of her continuing troubles with "this new, young purchasing director who is hardly dry behind the ears."

Answer the following questions:

1. What are the facts Trent must consider now?
2. What avenues are now open to Trent?
3. What does this case say to you about the need for supervisors to act morally?
4. Do you believe that some supervisors are untruthful where recommendations are concerned? Explain.
5. What three functions are salaries meant to perform?
6. To what extent should employee appraisals be used in salary adjustments? Explain.

SOURCE: *Prepared by M. T. Bledsoe, Associate Professor of Business, Meredith College, Raleigh, North Carolina.*

CASE 17–2

Poor Interpersonal Relationships

The division superintendent of a large plant was faced with a disciplinary problem in a certain department of his division. Here is his account:

In one department there are two workers who are badly needed by my division of the plant. Because of the nature of our work, it is important that the members of that department work as a team. At the present time, that department is not producing as efficiently

as it could because of the relentless bickering between these two workers. They are constantly angry with each other, and hurt feelings are the rule. Each feels offended, resented, and irritated by the other. In short, these two have a personality clash and apparently are unable to function together.

The first employee is older (by five years), has greater seniority (by two years), and more education (two years at a junior college). The second worker has only a high-school education, but is more capable of doing the job and is better able to relate to other employees.

Alone, and at different times, each was asked about his feelings toward the other. Then each was asked to be more understanding of the other and to try to work in greater harmony. They were told that the job had to be done, that they had to try to work together for the good of all, and that their present conduct toward each other could not be tolerated.

My department supervisors and I concluded that if, after I had talked to both workers, they could not work out their differences and work in harmony, I would be left with three choices. One solution would be to have them work on different shifts. Another possibility is to transfer one of them to another department. A last resort would be to discharge one or both of them.

The real problem is to decide what to do and then to do it. It will be a difficult problem determining which one will be transferred or fired, since help for this department is not readily available. The factors to be considered in the solution are fault, seniority, capability, and individual personality. These factors will have to be considered carefully, and a suitable decision will have to be made, based on the facts.

Answer the following questions:

1. If you were the division superintendent, what would you recommend doing with the two bickering employees? Why?
2. How would you implement your decision? In what order would you implement it?
3. What does this case illustrate about the need for a disciplined work environment?

The Supervisor and Labor Relations

● outline

What Are Labor Relations?

How Unions Developed in the United States
Early Union Activities
Period of Rapid Union Growth
Recent Limited Union Growth
Some Reasons for Declining Union Membership

Laws Governing Labor Relations
Basic Labor Laws
Administration of Labor Laws

Union Principles, Objectives, and Methods of Attaining Objectives
Organizing Employees
Becoming Recognized as the Employees'
Exclusive Bargaining Agent
Engaging in Collective Bargaining
Conducting a Strike or Lockout
Reaching an Agreement

Living with the Agreement
Supervisors' Rights Under the Agreement
The Supervisor and the Union Steward
The Role of Seniority
Handling Employee Complaints
Caution Needed in Terminations

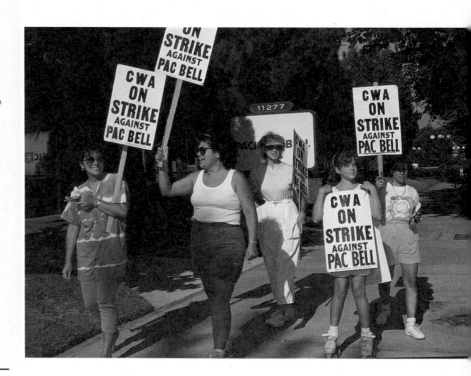

All your strength is in your union,
All your danger is in discord;
Therefore be at peace henceforward,
And as brothers live together.

Henry Wadsworth Longfellow

Long ago we stated the reason for labor organizations. We said that union was essential to give laborers opportunity to deal on an equality with their employer.

U.S. Supreme Court

The Union Organizer—Part I

Bobby Sutton managed Quality Service, a small hauling and delivery firm in California.* His father had just bought it from an aging proprietor who had let the business slide. The elder Sutton had retained the employees—a secretary, a clerk, two warehouse workers, and three drivers. A month had passed when Marvin Wiley, an organizer for the Teamsters Union, came in and demanded that Bobby recognize the union as the bargaining agent for the firm's warehouse workers and drivers. Marvin said that most of them had joined the union and wanted it to represent them. Also, the firm owed each of them $800 in back wages in order to bring them up to the union scale. Bobby indicated that he had no evidence that the workers either belonged to or wanted to belong to a union. When Marvin threatened to take the workers out on strike, Bobby said he'd consider them absent without permission and fire them if they walked off the job. Marvin said, "You'd better not do that," and left.

Bobby was quite upset and shaken by the incident. While he was trying to figure out what to do, Joe, a driver, came in to talk about the situation. Joe said he and the two warehouse workers did not want to join but that they were being pressured by Marvin and Bill, another driver. Bill was quite dissatisfied and was actively pushing the others to sign up. The third driver, Tony, was neutral and

*The names have been changed at the company's request.

would do what the majority wanted to do. Going back to his office, Bobby felt betrayed by Bill and Tony.

About a week after the incident at Quality Service took place, Marvin Wiley walked in, slapped a contract on Bobby Sutton's desk, and said, "Sign it!" After reading it, Bobby refused, explaining that he would go broke if he signed it. He said he was already paying near the union scale; he would pay the workers more when he could afford it and if they deserved it. Marvin said, "We'll see about that!" and angrily stalked out with the unsigned contract in his hand.

Although he could not do it legally, Bobby decided that if he was to keep the union out, he'd have to get rid of Bill. As business was slow during the winter months, Bobby laid Bill off, telling him he would rehire him when things picked up. Bobby would drive the third truck if this became necessary.

Things went well for Bobby during the next four years. Business grew and he had to add personnel. Each time he interviewed an applicant, he'd inquire as to the applicant's attitude toward various organizations, including unions. If the applicant showed a favorable attitude toward unions, Bobby would find a reason for not hiring him or her.

During its fifth year of operation, business was booming for Quality Service. Bobby Sutton had 22 employees, including 3 office employees, 7 warehouse workers, and 12 truck drivers. His father had

learning objectives

After reading and studying this chapter, you should be able to:

1. Explain what is meant by labor relations.

2. Trace the development of unions in the United States.

3. Explain why union membership is declining.

4. Name and explain the basic laws governing labor relations.

5. Describe union objectives and discuss the methods used to achieve those objectives.

6. Name three things that a supervisor must know in order to live with the union agreement.

bought another firm in a nearby city, and Bobby was running both businesses, with a supervisor at each location. Bobby had contracted to buy five new trucks and was trying to hire new drivers for them, but the number of capable drivers available for employment was quite limited.

After hearing nothing from the union for four years, Bobby was surprised when Marvin Wiley walked in and laid down authorization cards from five warehouse workers and two drivers. Marvin said, "Bobby, the last time I was here, you said you couldn't afford to unionize. But now you're the largest delivery firm in town. I think your people had better be working under a contract."

Again, Bobby refused to accept the union as the representative of his employees. The seven employees subsequently petitioned for an NLRB election, but lost it by a vote of 6 for the union and 13 against it. From then on, Bobby and his supervisors became more concerned about employee relations.

The opening quotations illustrate one of the most basic reasons why labor unions are needed. That is, individual employees cannot compete with the employer's resources by themselves. But when united, individual employees as a group can successfully contend with management.

labor union
An organization of workers banded together to achieve economic goals.

A **labor union** is an organization of workers banded together to achieve economic goals, especially increased wages and benefits, shorter working hours, improved working conditions, and both personal and job security. The individual employee has very little bargaining strength when negotiating with the employer. But when employees band together to form a labor union, they are better able to protect their interests and to obtain economic benefits.

It is impossible to cover everything about dealing with unions in one chapter, but we will include the most important ideas to help you understand the supervisor's role in labor relations. Even if you are—or expect to be—a supervisor in a nonunion firm, you need to understand how labor relations affect supervisory activities and relationships, for they affect nonunion employers as well as unionized ones.

self-check

Did you notice in Chapter 17 that, even in nonunion firms, supervisors use due process in applying discipline? This approach by enlightened supervisors improves labor–management relations.

 Explain what is meant by labor relations.

WHAT ARE LABOR RELATIONS?

labor relations
The relationship between an employer and unionized employees.

Terms such as **labor relations, union–management relations,** and **industrial relations** are often used to refer to the relationships between employers and their unionized employees. In this text, these terms will be used interchangeably.

The growth of unionism has forced managers—especially supervisors—to change many of their ways of dealing with employees, especially in matters concerning wages, hours, working conditions, and other terms and conditions of employment. Managers of unionized companies are constantly being challenged by union leaders in these areas. These challenges force supervisors to consider the rights of workers when developing and applying policies and procedures. Thus, management's freedom of choice has been greatly limited by the emergence of strong unions. For example, managers can no longer reward an employee on the basis of favoritism or punish one without just cause.

Labor relations are more than a power struggle between management and labor over economic matters that concern only themselves. Instead, hurt feelings, bruised egos, disappointments, and the hopes and ambitions of workers, managers, and labor leaders are involved. Also, these relationships affect and are affected by the total physical, economic, social, technological, legal, political, and cultural environment in which they occur.

self-check

Think about the last serious strike you can remember. Did it affect you in any way, either directly or indirectly? Even if it didn't affect you, what were the economic, social, political, and cultural effects on your community? On the nation? Did any workers in affected organizations lose jobs or wages? Did any companies lose output or go out of business? Were the sales at retail stores hurt? Were tax receipts reduced? Was there any violence? Did it affect any social or cultural events?

HOW UNIONS DEVELOPED IN THE UNITED STATES

In general, employees were treated well in the early colonies because of the severe shortage of workers. By the end of the 19th century, however, the situation had changed. The high birthrate, rapid and uncontrolled immigration, the concentration of wealth and industry in the hands of a few businessmen, political abuses by some employers, and the large numbers of workers in crowded industrial areas led to many abuses against workers. These included long hours, hard labor, unsafe and oppressive working conditions, crowded and unsanitary living conditions, low pay with no job security, and abuses of working women and children.

Early Union Activities

Trace the development of unions in the United States.

craft unions
Workers in a specific skill, craft, or trade.

http://www.aflcio.org/home.htm

There were labor unions in the United States as early as 1789, but they tended to be small, isolated, and ineffective **craft unions,** which are unions of skilled, experienced workers in specific skills, crafts, or trades.

More concerted action and stronger efforts were needed to improve the workers' plight. So several of the craft unions joined together in 1869 to form the Knights of Labor—the first nationwide union. Because its leadership was considered quite radical by most workers, it was only moderately successful. A more conservative national union was formed in 1881. It was named the American Federal of Labor (AFL) in 1886. Under the leadership of Samuel Gompers, the AFL grew and had great impact, especially during World War I and World War II. The basic concepts of a labor union were developed under his leadership. When asked what unions wanted for their members, Gompers invariably replied, "More!"

Period of Rapid Union Growth

During the 1920s and early 1930s, business became so powerful that workers again felt they were being exploited. They were hired, rewarded, punished, and fired at the whim of first-line supervisors, many of whom acted unfeelingly.

Therefore, several laws were passed in the 1930s that forced management to recognize unions and protected workers from exploitation (see the next section for details).

Until that time, the AFL and its affiliates had been organized on a craft basis. Union growth was thus limited, because there were few craft workers left to organize. But some workers had started organizing **industrial unions,** in which all the workers in a given industry—such as iron, coal, and autos—belonged to the same union, whether they were craftsmen, unskilled workers, or clerical employees. These unions broke away from the AFL in 1936 to form the Congress of Industrial Organizations (CIO).

Because of laws and government actions favorable to workers, the demand for workers resulting from World War II, and the prosperity that followed, union membership grew rapidly until 1945, when 35.5 percent of the workforce was unionized. Then, as Exhibit 18–1 shows, membership increased more slowly through the mid-1950s and afterward. Now only 13.9 percent of all nonagricultural wage and salary workers are members of unions. So, out of the

industrial unions
Unions composed of all the workers in an industry.

Exhibit 18–1

Membership of National Unions as a Percentage of the Total Labor Force

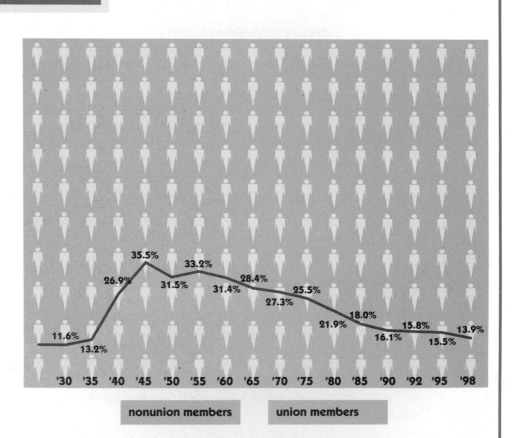

SOURCE: *U.S. Department of Labor, Bureau of Labor Statistics; and "Union Membership,"* Bulletin to Management *(a publication of the Bureau of National Affairs), March 4, 1993, pp. 68–70. Adapted from Leon C. Megginson, Geralyn M. Franklin, and M. Jane Byrd,* Human Resource Management *(Houston: Dame Publications, 1995), p. 480.*

total workforce, only 16.2 million are union members, and this number has held almost constant during the last decade.

Recent Limited Union Growth

After peaking at 35.5 percent of the total workforce in 1945, union membership declined until 1955, when it reached 33.2 percent of the workforce. That was the highest point reached in the post–World War II period. Because of this leveling off of union participation by American workers, and in hopes of reversing this trend, the AFL and CIO in 1955 merged into the AFL-CIO. But this move—and other concerted activities—did not stop the decline.

Total union membership did increase during the 1960s and 1970s when new types of unions, **employee associations,** emerged. For example, after President Kennedy issued Executive Order 10988 in 1962, the unionization of government workers escalated until 6.9 million, or 37.5 percent of all government employees, were unionized in 1998. At the same time, only 9.5 percent of all workers in private, nonagricultural industries were members of unions. As you can see from Exhibit 18–2, 42.6 percent of the 16.2 million unionized workers in 1998 were in government employment; 57.4 percent were in private employment. While only 28 percent of state employees are unionized, 34 percent of federal and 44 percent of local government employees were unionized in 1998.[1]

employee associations
Organizations that function as labor unions.

click! http://stats.bls.gov/
news.release/union2
.toc.htm

self-check

Nearly seven out of eight employed workers *do not* belong to a union. Why do you think this is so?

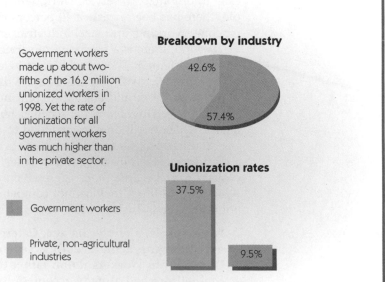

Government workers made up about two-fifths of the 16.2 million unionized workers in 1998. Yet the rate of unionization for all government workers was much higher than in the private sector.

Breakdown by industry

42.6%

57.4%

Government workers

Private, non-agricultural industries

Unionization rates

37.5%

9.5%

SOURCE: *Copyright 1999, USA Today. Reprinted with permission.*

*Women and minorities
are organized labor's
fastest growing
segment.*

③ Explain why union
membership is
declining.

Some Reasons for Declining Union Membership

There are many reasons for this declining union membership. First, a major reason is the shift in the economy from manufacturing jobs, which are relatively
easy to unionize, to service work, which is more difficult to organize. For example, there has been nearly a 40 percent drop in union membership in the auto,
machine-working, and steel industries in just the last 20 years.[2]

Second, there is a new kind of service worker—more educated and technologically oriented. These mobile employees are less interested in long-term
union contracts, with payments in the distant future, than in such things as
portable pensions and employer contributions to retirement plans. They also enjoy "employee involvement" schemes such as quality circles and self-managing
teams, which traditional unions tend to oppose.

Another problem for U.S. unions is the growing global economy. U.S. firms
are under pressure to cut costs in order to compete. Consequently, many employers have become more aggressive in opposing union organizing drives.[3]
Also, they feel that they cannot compete with foreign competitors if they are
bound by the industrywide bargaining required by U.S. unions.

 http://www.cat.com

**For example, a few years ago, Caterpillar, a leading producer of earth-
moving equipment, recently accepted a prolonged strike from the
United Auto Workers union rather than sign an agreement that its U.S.
competitors had already accepted. Its management believed that the
company would lose sales to "competitors with more flexible labor
deals abroad."[4]**

 http://www.uaw.org/

Fourth, the growing emphasis on part-time and temporary workers has also contributed to the decline in union membership. Currently there are over 20 million part-time employees in our workforce.[5] Also, the telecommuting "explosion" makes it difficult to organize workers. A 1997 study by Find/SVP, a New York research firm, estimated that 52 million Americans are self-employed, work as telecommuters, or otherwise work at home.[6]

Next, the growing "small is beautiful" world of business is working to discourage union membership. U.S. small businesses provide most of the new jobs in the United States. As an indication of the problem this trend poses for unions, there are now many more small business *owners* (around 23 million) than there are union members, and small firms are very difficult for unions to organize.[7]

Finally, the decline in union membership is partially due to the passage and enforcement of laws pushed by unions to protect employees. Also, some laws are designed to prevent union violence and corruption. For example, nearly every past president of the Teamster's Union has been convicted of a felony while serving as president of the union.

Laws Governing Labor Relations

4 Name and explain the basic laws governing labor relations.

The legal basis of union–management relations is provided by the National Labor Relations Act of 1935 (also called the *Wagner Act*), as amended by the Labor–Management Relations Act of 1947 (the Taft-Hartley Act), the Labor Management Reporting and Disclosure Act of 1959 (the Landrum-Griffin Act), and others. This complex of laws sets public policy and controls labor relations. Exhibit 18–3 shows the coverage, basic requirements, and agencies administering these laws. We'll provide only a few more details about them in the text.

Basic Labor Laws

In this section we examine why the basic labor laws were passed. We also point out the important features of these laws and explain how they are administered.

click! http://www.nlrb.gov/

Wagner Act. The National Labor Relations Act (Wagner Act) was passed to protect employees and unions by limiting management's rights. It gave workers the right to form and join unions of their own choosing and made collective bargaining mandatory. It also set up the National Labor Relations Board (NLRB) to enforce the law. The act defined specific **unfair labor practices** that management could not commit against the workers and the union, but it had no provision for unfair practices that unions might commit against workers and management. As a result, many union abuses arose. One major abuse was that unions could impose requirements as to how employees could get or keep a job. Many managers, as well as employees, assumed that the right to join a union carried with it the right *not* to do so. This assumption was changed during World War II, when agreements such as the union shop, the closed shop, and the agency shop became legal.

Under a **union shop** agreement, all employees must join the union within a specified period—usually 30 days—or be fired. Under a **closed shop** agreement, all prospective employees must be members of the recognized union before they can be employed, and all current employees must join within a speci-

unfair labor practices
Specific acts that management may not commit against the workers and the union.

union shop
All employees must join the union within a specified period.

closed shop
All prospective employees must be members of the recognized union before they can be employed.

Exhibit 18–3

*Basic Laws Governing
Labor Relations*

Laws	Coverage	Basic Provisions	Agencies Involved
National Labor Relations Act (NLRA) as amended (Wagner Act)	Nonmanagerial employees in nonagricultural private firms not covered by the Railway Labor Act; postal employees	Asserts the right of employees to form or join labor organizations (or to refuse to), to bargain collectively through their representatives, and to engage in other concerted activities such as strikes, picketing, and boycotts; establishes unfair labor practices that the employer cannot engage in.	National Labor Relations Board (NLRB)
Labor–Management Relations Act (LMRA) as amended (Taft-Hartley Act)	Same as above	Amended NLRA; permits states to pass laws prohibiting compulsory union membership; sets up methods to deal with strikes affecting national health and safety.	Federal Mediation and Conciliation Service
Labor–Management Reporting and Disclosure Act (Landrum-Griffin Act)	Same as above	Amended NLRA and LMRA; guarantees individual rights of union members in dealing with their union; requires financial disclosures by unions.	U.S. Department of Labor

SOURCE: *U.S. Department of Labor publications and the basic laws themselves, as amended.*

agency shop
All employees must pay union dues even if they choose not to join the union.

maintenance-of-membership clause
An employee who has joined the union must maintain that membership as a condition of employment.

fied time in order to retain their jobs. In an **agency shop,** all employees must pay the union dues even if they choose not to join the union. The **maintenance-of-membership clause** says that once an employee joins the union, he or she must maintain that membership as a condition of employment.

self-check

Do you have trouble seeing the difference between a union shop and a closed shop? In a union shop, management employs the people it chooses and then these people must become members of the union. In a closed shop, management must hire the workers sent by the union according to each worker's seniority as a member of the union.

right-to-work laws
The right of employees to join or refuse to join a union without being fired.

Taft-Hartley Act. Following World War II, with evidence of abuse of power by some union leaders, Congress passed the Labor–Management Relations Act (Taft-Hartley Act). Enacted in 1947, this act greatly changed the Wagner Act, making it more evenhanded, so that unions as well as management could be charged with unfair labor practices.

The Taft-Hartley Act prohibited the closed-shop agreement, except in the construction and shipping industries. Also, Section 14(b) of this act gave states the right to pass laws prohibiting the union shop. By 1996, 21 states had used Section 14(b) to pass **right-to-work laws,** which give workers the right to join or refuse to join a union without being fired. The states with right-to-work laws are highlighted in Exhibit 18–4.

Exhibit 18–4

States with Right-to-Work Laws

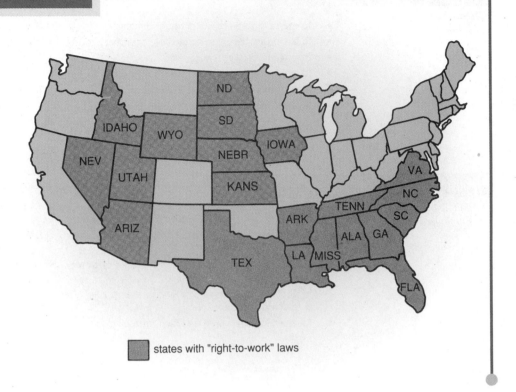

□ states with "right-to-work" laws

Landrum-Griffin Act. In 1959, Congress passed the Labor–Management Reporting and Disclosure Act (Landrum-Griffin Act) in an effort to prevent corruption and abuse of employees by some union leaders and managers. It provided an **employees' bill of rights,** which protects employees from possible abuse by unscrupulous managers and union leaders.

Employees, unions, and employers all have certain specified and implied rights and privileges under the basic labor laws. Exhibit 18–5 contains the rights of employees. Exhibit 18–6 shows what unions may not do, and Exhibit 18–7 lists what employers may not do under these laws.

employees' bill of rights
Protects employees from possible abuse by unscrupulous managers and union leaders.

Exhibit 18–5

Rights of Employees

- To organize.
- To bargain collectively.
- To expect no discrimination against them by management because they are union members.
- To expect no discrimination against them by management if they bring charges of unfair labor practices against the employer.
- To get a job without first being a member of a union.
- Not to have to join a union unless the union and the employer have signed a valid union-shop agreement in one of the states that do not have right-to-work laws.
- Not to be charged exorbitant initiation fees and dues by a union with a valid union-shop agreement.
- To receive financial reports from the union.

Exhibit 18-6

Unfair Labor Practices of Unions

- To coerce employees into or restrain them from engaging in union activities.
- To force management to discriminate against employees in violation of the law.
- To refuse to bargain in good faith.
- To require managers to pay money for work not done.
- To engage in a strike or boycott to force management to commit illegal acts.
- To charge excessive initiation fees and dues where there is a union shop.

Exhibit 18-7

Unfair Labor Practices of Employers

- To interfere with, restrain, or coerce employees who are exercising their rights under the law.
- To dominate or interfere with the forming or administering of unions, or to contribute support to them.
- To discriminate in hiring or in any other terms of employment in such a way as to encourage or discourage membership in a union.
- To discharge or otherwise discriminate against employees for filing charges against the employer or testifying under the law.
- To refuse to bargain with the union representative.

Administration of Labor Laws

The five-person National Labor Relations Board (NLRB) has the power to enforce the basic labor laws. The functions of the NLRB are (1) to certify unions as the exclusive bargaining agent for employees and (2) to see that unfair labor practices either are not committed or are punished. Its specific duties are:

- To hold an election to establish the bargaining agent for employees of a given firm.
- To investigate charges of unfair labor practices against the employer or the union.
- To issue complaints against either management or labor.
- To prosecute unfair labor practices and determine guilt.
- To assess fines and prison sentences.
- To ask federal courts to control activities of both management and labor by citing them for contempt.

5 Describe union objectives and discuss the methods used to achieve those objectives.

UNION PRINCIPLES, OBJECTIVES, AND METHODS OF ATTAINING OBJECTIVES

A wise man had seven sons who were intelligent, personable, and otherwise attractive, but they had one common fault—they were constantly fighting and squabbling with one another, even when being attacked by others outside the family. One day, the father decided to teach them a lesson. He called them together, gave each one of them a long wooden stick, and said to each one, in turn, "Break this stick over your knee." Each one of the sons broke his stick with very little effort.

Again, the wise man handed each son a stick, but this time said to them, "Bind the seven sticks together in a bundle." They did as he asked. "Now try to break the sticks," he said to each son as he handed him the bundle. None of them could break the bundle of sticks. "Remember," he said, "in union there is strength."*

This fable illustrates the truth that the main reason unions exist is to protect individual workers from the economic power of an employer or employer groups. Unions try to achieve certain objectives for their members and follow certain principles to achieve them.

Samuel Gompers, the AFL's first president, identified the following basic principles on which unionism is based: (1) strength through unity, (2) equal pay for the same job, and (3) employment practices based on seniority. If any one of these principles is threatened, the union and its members will fight back, as these are cardinal, non-negotiable beliefs. (A two-tiered wage system was introduced in airline bargaining during the 1980s, but it is now being revoked.)

These principles of unionism lead to the practical objectives unions have for their members. These goals are (1) higher pay, (2) shorter hours of work on a daily, weekly, or annual basis, (3) improved working conditions, both physical and psychological, and (4) improved security, both of the person and of the job.

How do unions achieve their objectives? The usual methods they employ are (1) to organize a firm's employees, (2) to become recognized as the employees' exclusive bargaining agent, (3) to engage in collective bargaining, (4) to go on strike or threaten to strike, and (5) to process grievances. Let us look at each of these methods.

Organizing Employees

union authorization card
Authorizes a particular union to be an employee's collective bargaining representative.

First, the union leader must persuade the employees of a firm to organize and join the union. The union organizer tries to get the employees to sign a **union authorization card,** which states that the employee wants the specified union to be his or her bargaining representative. An example of such a card is shown in Exhibit 18–8.

Understanding the Situation. Supervisors should first of all recognize that most union organizers are competent professionals who are committed to their work. By attending seminars and other programs, union organizers become expert in the provisions of the labor laws and in organizing techniques. Their international headquarters conducts continual research and supplies the organizers with current and effective information and carefully conceived and tested techniques. Carefully planned, methodically executed, and well-financed campaigns have replaced the heavy-muscled past attempts by amateurs to organize workers through intimidation or force.

The employer, and the conscientious supervisor in particular, may be shocked when first hit by the realization that a union is moving in to organize employees. Arriving at the plant gates one morning, the supervisor may be

---

*Aesop's Fables, "The Bundle of Sticks."

Exhibit 18–8

Example of a Representation Authorization Card

click! http://www.cwa-union.org/

COMMUNICATIONS WORKERS of AMERICA, A.F.L.-C.I.O.

Name _____

   (Please Print)   First   Middle   Last

Address _____

          Street

        City   State   Zip Code

Tel. No. _____ Job Title _____

I am an Employee of _____ ,

Department _____ , Section _____ , Shift _____
and I hereby designate the Communications Workers of America, as my
collective bargaining representative.

Date _____ Signature _____

FORM O-100   **REPRESENTATION AUTHORIZATION**   150
1-77

---

greeted by workers—including some of the oldest and most trusted employ-ees—carrying placards. The manager is often personally hurt, angered, and confused by this sudden defection. A natural reaction would be to strike back hard and fast against this threat. But precipitous action can cause management to lose the contest before the issues are drawn. Managers must know what to do—and, perhaps even more important, what not to do.

What Organizers Dislike to Find in an Organization. Union organizers have found that certain factors effectively reduce their chances of organizing employ-ees and gaining union recognition. They dislike finding the following in a tar-geted firm:

1. Employees who strongly believe that managers and supervisors are fair and are not taking advantage of them.

2. Employees who take pride in their work.

3. Good performance records kept by the management, for employees feel more secure when they know that their efforts are recognized and appreci-ated.

4. No claims of high-handed treatment, for employees respect firm but fair dis-cipline.

5. No claims of favoritism.

6. Supervisors who have established good relationships with employees, for union leaders know that good supervisor–employee relations stifle organiz-ing attempts.

As you can see, *supervisors are the key persons as far as employees are concerned, so they are an employer's first line of defense against the entry of a union.* The wise selection of supervisors is obviously very important; leadership abilities should be given more consideration than production abilities in the selection of supervisors.

Things to Do *Before* the Union Calls. There are many things supervisors and other managers can do to minimize the chances of employees' joining a union—if that's their wish. The most important ones are these:

1. The company and its higher level managers must pay close attention to supervisors, for they are the key to successful labor relations. Supervisors should receive substantially more pay than their employees. They should also get support from their boss for the orders they give and the decisions they make, because unhappy supervisors can do tremendous harm to an employer's labor relations. Treat supervisors right, keep them well informed, and make them an integral part of the management team.

2. Make sure that no item in the wage-benefit package lags far behind the norm for the area and industry.

3. Improve employee benefits as quickly and as extensively as is feasible.

4. Review jobs frequently to see if they need to be upgraded because responsibilities or working conditions have changed.

5. Make sure employee facilities are adequate, safe, well lighted, well ventilated, and reasonably clean.

6. Keep records of good—and bad—performance by employees, and have programs for boosting employee performance, loyalty, and morale.

7. Be firm but fair when imposing discipline.

8. Provide a practical release valve, such as a grievance committee, for employee frustrations and complaints.

9. Be alert for any complaints of abuse or favoritism by employees or supervisors.

10. Establish clear-cut lines for two-way communications with all employees.

11. Have clear, definite, and well-communicated work rules, making sure that their wording doesn't violate NLRB or EEO/AA rules.

12. Use discretion in hiring new employees.

Notice throughout the above list the importance of good supervisory practices. It cannot be said too strongly that first-line supervisors play an integral role in making unions unnecessary!

A classic research study found some marked differences in attitude between pro-union and pro-employer workers. In general, pro-employer workers showed a greater need for achievement, perfection, and success; a higher level of independence; and an identification with management. Pro-union workers showed a greater need for and dependence on attention, sympathy, and support from someone other than themselves. Their achievement level was low, as was their endurance.[8]

What the Supervisor Should Do—and Not Do—*When* the Union Enters. A tactic frequently used to gain recognition is for the union organizer to meet with the supervisor and hand over some signed authorization cards. Then, as illustrated in the chapter preview case of the Quality Service firm, the union representative says that he or she represents the workers and asks to be recognized as the workers' exclusive bargaining agent to sign or negotiate a contract.

Most labor-relations specialists suggest that supervisors not touch or examine the cards, for if they do, this action can be construed as acceptance of the union as the workers' agent. Nor should supervisors make any comments to the union representative. If the representative says, "Are you refusing to recognize the union?" the supervisor should reply, "Any comment concerning the company's position must await full consideration of the matter by higher levels of management." If the representative asks, the supervisor should give the name, address, and phone number of the company's labor relations manager. Of course, as soon as the representative leaves, the supervisor should inform his or her boss about the visit. Exhibit 18–9 contains some suggestions as to what you *may* legally do when a union tries to organize your employees. Some things you should *not* do are listed in Exhibit 18–10.

Becoming Recognized as the Employees' Exclusive Bargaining Agent

exclusive bargaining agent
Deals exclusively with management over questions of wages, hours, and other terms and conditions of employment.

Once the cards have been signed, the union tries to become recognized as the employees' exclusive bargaining agent. An **exclusive bargaining agent** is the employees' representative who has the exclusive right to deal with management over questions of wages, hours, and other terms and conditions of employment. A certified union has the sole right and legal responsibility to represent all of the employees—nonunion members as well as union members—in their dealings with management.

Management may voluntarily recognize the union or may be forced to accept it because of the union's superior bargaining strength. Ordinarily, a secret-ballot election is conducted by the NLRB when requested by the union or the company. If 30 percent or more of the eligible employees sign authorization cards or a petition requesting a representation election, the NLRB will conduct one. If a majority of the voting employees vote for the union, it is named the exclusive representative of the employees in their dealings with management.

Appeals Used by Union Organizers. The technique most commonly employed by union organizers to obtain union recognition is to compare the target company's practices to items in contracts that the union has with other companies, perhaps in an entirely different industry. If the terms of employment in the target company lag far behind, the union has a ready-made argument. Of course, the organizer will focus on those parts of the wage-benefit package that will make the employer look bad.

Union organizers appeal to five main desires of employees:

1. *Job protection.* Unions stress that they continually try to ensure that employees have a job—or at least an income—for a lifetime. With most employees already enjoying generous benefits, many seem more interested in job security than in higher pay rates. But there are exceptions to this generalization.

   Unionized employees at an Alcoa plant in Mobile, Alabama, voted to permit the plant to close rather than take cuts in income and benefits. They received quite high unemployment compensation, as well as supplemental payments from the company, for three years.

Exhibit 18–9

Things Supervisors May Do When a Union Tries to Organize Their Company

- Keep outside organizers off premises.
- Inform employees from time to time of the benefits they presently enjoy. (Avoid veiled promises or threats.)
- Inform employees that signing a union authorization card does not mean they must vote for the union if there is an election.
- Inform employees of the disadvantages of belonging to the union, such as the possibility of strikes, serving on a picket line, dues, fines, assessments, and rule by cliques or one individual.
- Inform employees that you prefer to deal with them rather than have the union or any other outsider settle grievances.
- Tell employees what you think about unions and about union policies.
- Inform employees about any prior experience you have had with unions and whatever you know about the union officials trying to organize them.
- Inform employees that the law permits you to hire a new employee to replace any employee who goes on strike for economic reasons.
- Inform employees that no union can obtain more than you as an employer are able to give.
- Inform employees how their wages and benefits compare with those in unionized or non-unionized concerns where wages are lower and benefits are less desirable.
- Inform employees that the local union probably will be dominated by the international union, and that they, the members, will have little say in its operations.
- Inform employees of any untrue or misleading statements made by the organizer. You may give employees corrections of these statements.
- Inform employees of any known racketeering or other undesirable elements that may be active in the union.
- Give opinions on the unions and union leaders, even in derogatory terms.
- Distribute information about unions such as disclosures of congressional committees.
- Reply to union attacks on company policies or practices.
- Give the legal position on labor-management matters.
- Advise employees of their legal rights, provided you do not engage in or finance an employee suit or proceeding.
- Declare a fixed policy in opposition to compulsory union membership contracts.
- Campaign against a union seeking to represent the employees.
- Insist that no solicitation of membership or discussion of union affairs be conducted during working time.
- Administer discipline, layoff, and grievance procedures without regard to union membership or nonmembership of the employees involved.
- Treat both union and nonunion employees alike in making assignments of preferred work or desired overtime.
- Enforce plant rules impartially, regardless of the employee's membership activity in a union.
- Tell employees, if they ask, that they are free to join or not to join any organization, so far as their status with the company is concerned.
- Tell employees that their personal and job security will be determined by the economic prosperity of the company.

SOURCE: *Leon C. Megginson et al.,* Successful Small Business Management, *6th ed. (Homewood, IL: Richard D. Irwin, 1991). pp. 821–822. Reprinted with permission of Richard D. Irwin.*

Exhibit 18–10

Things Supervisors May Not Do When a Union Tries to Organize Their Company

- Engage in surveillance of employees to determine who is and who is not participating in the union program; attend union meetings or engage in any undercover activities for this purpose.
- Threaten, intimidate, or punish employees who engage in union activity.
- Request information from employees about union matters, meetings, etc. Employees may, of their own volition, give such information without prompting. You may listen but not ask questions.
- Prevent employee union representatives from soliciting memberships during nonworking time.
- Grant wage increases, special concessions, or promises of any kind to keep the union out.
- Question a prospective employee about his or her affiliation with a labor organization.
- Threaten to close up or move the plant, curtail operations, or reduce employee benefits.
- Engage in any discriminatory practices, such as work assignments, overtime, layoffs, promotions, wage increases, or any other actions that could be regarded as preferential treatment for certain employees.
- Discriminate against union people when disciplining employees for a specific action, while permitting nonunion employees to go unpunished for the same action.
- Transfer workers on the basis of teaming up nonunion employees to separate them from union employees.
- Deviate in any way from company policies for the primary purpose of eliminating a union employee.
- Intimate, advise, or indicate in any way that unionization will force the company to lay off employees, take away company benefits or privileges enjoyed, or make any other changes that could be regarded as a curtailment of privileges.
- Make statements to the effect that you will not deal with a union.
- Give any financial support or other assistance to employees who support or oppose the union.
- Visit the homes of employees to urge them to oppose or reject the union in its campaign.
- Be a party to any petition or circular against the union or encourage employees to circulate such a petition.
- Make any promises of promotions, benefits, wage increases, or any other items that would induce employees to oppose the union.
- Engage in discussions or arguments that may lead to physical encounters with employees over the union question.
- Use a third party to threaten or coerce a union member, or attempt to influence any employee's vote through this medium.
- Question employees on whether or not they have been affiliated or signed with the union.
- Use the word *never* in any predictions or attitudes about unions or their promises or demands.
- Talk about tomorrow. When you give examples or reasons, you can talk about yesterday or today instead of tomorrow, to avoid making a prediction or conviction which may be interpreted as a threat or promise by the union or the NLRB.

SOURCE: *Leon C. Megginson et al.,* Successful Small Business Management, *6th ed. (Homewood, IL: Richard D. Irwin, 1991). pp. 823–824. Reprinted with permission of Richard D. Irwin.*

2. *Interference running.* Unions assure employees that they will act as their agents in grievances and disputes. They will go to bat for employees, and they claim to have the know-how to protect employees' interests.

3. *Participation in management.* Unions insist that they can and will give employees a greater voice in deciding the policies, procedures, and rules that affect them and the work they do.

4. *Economic gains.* Higher wages, reduced hours, and better benefits are still at the top of an organizer's checklist.

5. *Recognition and participation.* Knowing that pro-union workers need and are dependent on attention, sympathy, and support, union organizers promise employees that they'll have greater recognition and participation through union activities.

Additional Precautions for Supervisors. Besides observing the "dos" and "don'ts" given in Exhibits 18–9 and 18–10, management should make sure there is nothing in personnel policies and work rules that the NLRB can construe as being anti-union. For example, suppose a company has the following sign displayed: "No solicitation at this company." *This prohibition can actually be ruled an unfair labor practice unless it is enforced against all types of solicitation—even by charitable groups—not just union organizing.* A company is obliged to permit solicitation and distribution of literature by union organizers in nonwork areas such as locker rooms and parking lots. Of course, managers can prohibit nonemployees from being on company property at any time.

Next, supervisors and anyone else in a position to reward or punish voting employees should stay away from the voting area during a representation election.

Finally, neither threat of reprisal nor any promise of reward should be given before the election, although it is permissible to tell employees what has happened at other plants where workers unionized—if it is factual.

Engaging in Collective Bargaining

Once the union has been recognized as the employees' bargaining agent, it starts negotiating with management to try to reach an agreement (which in effect is a contract between the company and the union). Legally, **collective bargaining** is the process by which (1) representatives of the employer and the employees (2) meet at reasonable times and places (3) to confer in good faith (4) over wages, hours, and other terms and conditions of employment. Note that the representatives of the two parties are only required to meet in a "reasonable place," usually a conference room at a hotel or motel, and at a "reasonable time," usually the firm's normal daily working hours. They must negotiate "in good faith" by making valid offers and counteroffers about any question involving wages, hours, and other "terms and conditions of employment." Once an agreement has been reached, both parties must have the opportunity to sign it if they want to—which they usually do.

It's a "must" that supervisors be consulted at each step of this bargaining procedure. They should carefully examine every union proposal—and management counterproposal—to see how they would affect the supervisors' relationships with the employees. Also, supervisors should be consulted about concessions to be asked of the union negotiators.

If no agreement is reached, an impasse develops. At this point there are three alternatives: (1) to call in an outside **mediator,** provided by the Federal Mediation and Conciliation Service, who will bring the parties together and try to help them reach an agreement; (2) to agree to bring the issue to an outside **arbitrator,** who will make a decision that will be binding on both parties; or (3) for the union to go on strike or for management to stage a lockout.

collective bargaining
Conferring in good faith over wages, hours, and other terms and conditions of employment.

mediator
Tries to bring the parties together when collective bargaining has reached an impasse.

arbitrator
Will make a binding decision when collective bargaining reaches an impasse.

A strike is always viewed as a last resort to resolving disputes between labor and management.

Conducting a Strike or Lockout

strike
When employees withhold their services from an employer.

The ultimate strategy used by unions to achieve their objectives is the strike. A **strike** occurs when employees withhold their services from an employer in order to achieve a goal. The employees tell the public why they are striking by means of **picketing**—walking back and forth outside the place of employment, usually carrying signs (see Exhibit 18–11).

picketing
Walking back and forth outside the place of employment, usually carrying a sign.

It cannot be emphasized too strongly that most union leaders *do not like to use the strike.* It is costly, it carries a certain stigma for those walking the picket line, and it is potentially dangerous to the union because of the possible loss of membership and power if the strike fails. In fact, only a very small percentage of the thousands of contract negotiations conducted annually result in strikes. Although the strike itself is the ultimate device in collective bargaining and is the technique resorted to when all other methods of resolving differences fail, the *threat of a strike* is a continuing factor in almost all negotiations. Both the union and the employer frequently act as if one could occur.

lockout
A closing of a company's premises to the employees and refusing to let them work.

Just as the union can call a strike if it isn't satisfied with the progress of negotiations, so can management stage a lockout. A **lockout** is closing company premises to the employees and refusing to let them enter in order to resume work.

Reaching an Agreement

agreement or **contract**
Prepared when an accord has been reached to bind the company, union, and workers to specific clauses in it.

When an accord has been reached, a document is prepared that becomes the **agreement** or **contract** among the company, the union, and the workers. It usually contains clauses covering at least the following areas:

1. Union recognition
2. Wages

Exhibit 18–11

SOURCE: *Reprinted with permission of Tribune Media Service.*

3. Vacation and holidays

4. Working conditions

5. Layoffs and rehiring

6. Management prerogatives

7. Hours of work

8. Seniority

9. Arbitration

10. Renewal clause

Specifics are set forth in each of these areas, and rules are established that should be obeyed by management and the union. The management prerogatives clause defines the areas in which supervisors have the right to act, free from questioning or joint action by the union.

LIVING WITH THE AGREEMENT

6 Name three things that a supervisor must know in order to live with the union agreement.

Once the agreement has been signed, managers and supervisors have to live with the contract until it is time to negotiate a new one. Therefore, all management personnel—especially first-level supervisors—should be thoroughly briefed on its contents. The meaning and interpretation of each clause should be reviewed, and the wording of the contract should be clearly understood. Supervisors' questions should be answered to better prepare them to deal with labor-relations matters. Also, it should be impressed on supervisors that their counterpart—the union steward—will probably be better trained, know the contract provisions in greater detail, and be better equipped in the practice of contract administration.

Supervisors' Rights Under the Agreement

Supervisors should view the agreement as the rules of the game, for it spells out what they may and may not do. They should take a positive view of what they *may do* rather than a negative one of what they *may not do*. Although agreements differ in detail, most give supervisors the following rights:

1. To decide what work is to be done.
2. To decide how, when, and where it will be done.
3. To determine how many workers are needed to do the work safely.
4. To decide who will do each job, as long as the skill classifications and seniority provisions are observed.
5. To instruct, supervise, correct, and commend employees in the performance of their work.
6. To require that work performance and on-the-job personal behavior meet minimum standards.
7. To recommend promotions and pay increases, as long as they do not violate the union agreement.
8. To administer discipline according to the agreed-upon procedure.

See Exhibits 18–9 and 18–10 for a more definitive list of "do's" and "don'ts" for supervisors.

If uncertain as to their authority, supervisors should check with the firm's human resources or labor relations experts. Supervisors need to have a working knowledge of the agreement's details because the employees and their advocate, the union steward, will be aware of these details.

self-check

> Would you rather be a supervisor in a unionized or a nonunionized company? Why?

The Supervisor and the Union Steward

union steward
A union member elected by other members to represent their interests in relations with management.

The **union steward,** a union member who has been elected by other members to represent their interests in relations with management, is the supervisor's counterpart. He or she is the link between the workers and their union and between the union and the company, especially in case of controversy. The supervisor represents the company and its interests to workers, who play the dual roles of employees of the company and members of the union. The steward represents the union's position to the workers and to the company. The steward is at the same level in the union hierarchy as the supervisor is in the company hierarchy.

As equals, the steward and the supervisor must maintain production operations within the framework of the agreement. Frequently, the goals of the steward and the supervisor conflict, for the supervisor's job is to obtain maximum productivity, whereas the steward's aim is to protect the workers' interests—including not working too hard and not working themselves out of a job.

The Role of Seniority

seniority
An employee's length of service in a company; provides the basis for promotion and other benefits.

One of the most basic union principles is **seniority,** which means that workers who have been on the job the longest get preferred treatment and better benefits. One of the supervisor's greatest challenges is to maintain high productivity while assigning work, especially preferred jobs and overtime, to the most senior employee, who is not necessarily the most capable worker. Also, whom does the supervisor recommend for promotion—the most capable worker or the most senior employee? These issues, plus discipline, lead to most grievances against supervisors.

Handling Employee Complaints

grievance procedure
A formal way of handling employees' complaints.

In unionized companies, employees' complaints take the form of grievances. The **grievance procedure** is a formal way of handling these complaints. In nonunionized companies, employees may present their complaints to their supervisors for proper disposition.

Grievance Procedures. Exhibit 18–12 shows a typical grievance procedure, such as is usually found in unionized organizations. The form and substance of the grievance procedure depends on several factors:

1. The type of industry (the old-line, "smokestack" industries, such as steel, auto, and transportation, have the most formal and rigid procedures).

2. The size and structure of the organization (the larger, more highly structured organizations have the most formal and inflexible procedures).

Exhibit 18–12

Typical Grievance Procedure in a Unionized Organization

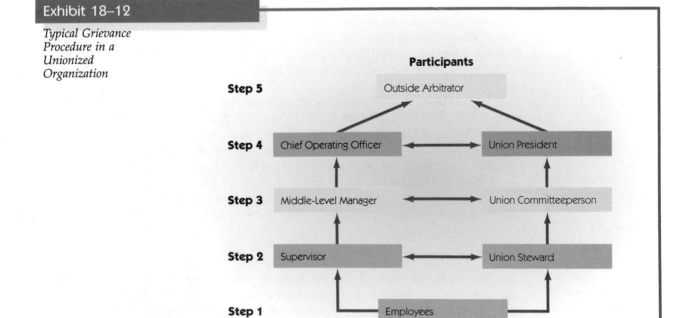

Participants

Step 5 — Outside Arbitrator

Step 4 — Chief Operating Officer ⟷ Union President

Step 3 — Middle-Level Manager ⟷ Union Committeeperson

Step 2 — Supervisor ⟷ Union Steward

Step 1 — Employees

3. The type of union (the older, craft-oriented unions tend to have a highly structured procedure).

There are usually five steps in a formal grievance procedure in a unionized organization. However, the *actual* number of steps taken will depend on the number of managerial levels in the organization and whether or not the grievance is submitted to arbitration.

1. Step 1 begins when an employee complains to the supervisor about a presumed wrong. From the employee's viewpoint, the supervisor may be violating the labor agreement or doing something that dissatisfies the employee. If the supervisor straightens out the matter satisfactorily, that's the end of the grievance.

2. Frequently, though, the issue is not resolved, so the employee goes to the union steward to present a grievance. The steward then tries to obtain satisfaction from the supervisor. This is Step 2. The vast majority of grievances are settled at this stage.

3. In Step 3, the union committeeperson or business agent tries to resolve the complaint with middle management, such as a department head.

4. In Step 4, the union president and the chief operating officer try to resolve the difference. If they succeed, that ends the grievance.

5. If the chief operating officer and the union president cannot resolve the grievance, it is submitted to outside arbitration. A mutually agreed upon arbitrator makes the decision. This is Step 5.

Complaint Procedures in Nonunionized Organizations. Many nonunion organizations have formal complaint procedures that are comparable in many ways to the formal union grievance procedures. These procedures permit complaints to go beyond the supervisor to committees composed of higher level executives, including the personnel officer and sometimes even top executives. However, they do not provide for arbitration, since the primary purpose of these procedures is to ensure fairness in employee relations and to improve employee attitudes, rather than to interpret human resources policies and practices. Such procedures are frequently found in public organizations such as government agencies.

Supervisors can improve employee–employer relationships if they understand the types of employees who are prone to file complaints or grievances. For example, an early study found that the more sensitive people are, the more apt they are to file. Young employees who are well educated but not well paid tend to file grievances, as do employees who have not been with the company long but are military veterans.[9] Supervisors have two alternatives for dealing with employees of these types. In some cases they may try to avoid hiring them; alternatively, they can try to find ways to accommodate them.

Caution Needed in Terminations

As discussed in Chapter 17, supervisors at one time had the right to terminate, or "fire," an employee in a nonunionized company "at will," that is, without having to show cause or even give a reason. However, subsequent legislation, union bargaining, and court decisions have largely eliminated that practice. Now an employer must offer a valid, documented reason for such action.

chapter review

(1) Explain what is meant by labor relations.

Labor relations, which are the relationships between employers and their unionized employees, are particularly important to supervisors, for they are the managers who must deal with operative employees on a day-to-day basis. An employer usually has good labor relations if the supervisors have good relationships with employees.

(2) Trace the development of unions in the United States.

Union activities grew slowly in the United States until the formation of the AFL. Then membership increased steadily until after World War I, when it leveled off. Membership mushroomed during the period from 1935 to 1950, when favorable laws were passed and industrial unions became popular. Since then, union membership has grown more slowly so that now only 13.9 percent of all employees, and only 9.5 percent of private employees, are members of a union.

(3) Explain why union membership is declining.

Some of the reasons for declining interest in unions among U.S. employees are (1) the economy has shifted from manufacturing jobs, which are relatively easy to unionize, to service work, which is more difficult to organize; (2) today's more educated and technologically oriented service workers are more interested in empowerment-type activities; (3) the global economy is forcing U.S. companies to cut costs by resisting organizing drives; (4) the influx of part-time workers resists unionization; and (5) the proliferation of small businesses makes organizing more difficult.

(4) Name and explain the basic laws governing labor relations.

The basic law governing labor relations is the Wagner Act, which gives workers the right to freely join unions of their choosing and to engage in concerted actions to achieve their goals. The Taft-Hartley Act prohibits the closed shop and provides for states to pass right-to-work laws prohibiting the union shop. The Landrum-Griffin Act provides employees with a bill of rights that protects them from exploitation by unscrupulous management and union leaders. These laws are administered by the National Labor Relations Board (NLRB), the Federal Mediation and Conciliation Service (FMCS), and the U.S. Department of Labor. The NLRB tries to prevent both unions and management from engaging in unfair labor practices.

(5) Describe union objectives and discuss the methods used to achieve those objectives.

Union objectives are higher pay, shorter hours of work, improved working conditions, and improved personal and job security. To achieve those objectives, unions organize (or recruit) an employer's workers into a union, then try to become recognized as their exclusive bargaining agent in dealing with management, usually through an NLRB-conducted, secret-ballot election. Unions have greater difficulty organizing employees in firms that have effective supervisors and good employee relations. Management can try to keep the union out as long as its policies and actions stay within the law.

When the union becomes the bargaining agent, it bargains collectively with representatives of management over wages, hours, and the other terms and conditions of employment. Supervisors are critical to success at this point, so they should help formulate demands to be made of the union, evaluate proposals made by the union bargaining team, and be kept informed of progress made in the negotiations.

If the two parties cannot agree and reach an impasse, there are several options: (1) they can call in an outside mediator, (2) they can agree to send the issue to an arbitrator, who will make a binding decision, or (3) the union can conduct a strike, or management can stage a lockout. Most negotiations end with an agreement, which becomes the contract between management and the employees.

(6) **Name three things that a supervisor must know in order to live with the union agreement.**

It is then up to the supervisor to live with the contract. Disagreements over interpretation of the agreement are settled through the grievance procedure. If agreement is not reached within the company, the issue goes to an arbitrator for resolution. Supervisors by and large can no longer terminate an employee without a valid, documented reason.

---

important terms

agency shop *518*
agreement *or* contract *528*
arbitrator *527*
closed shop *517*
collective bargaining *527*
craft unions *513*
employee associations *515*
employees' bill of rights *519*
exclusive bargaining agent *524*
grievance procedure *531*
industrial unions *514*
labor relations *or* union–management
   relations *or* industrial relations *512*

labor union *512*
lockout *528*
maintenance-of-membership clause *518*
mediator *527*
picketing *528*
right-to-work laws *518*
seniority *531*
strike *528*
unfair labor practices *517*
union authorization card *521*
union shop *517*
union steward *530*

---

questions for review and discussion

1. Define labor relations.
2. When did unions grow the fastest? Why?
3. Why has union growth slowed?
4. How do you interpret the union membership trends shown in Exhibits 18–1 and 18–2?
5. Do you believe that union power will increase or decrease in the future? Why?
6. Name the laws that form the legal basis for labor relations, and explain their general provisions.
7. What are the differences among the union shop, the closed shop, and the agency shop? Are these differences really significant? Explain.
8. What are "unfair labor practices," and what are some unfair labor practices that management sometimes commits?
9. What are some unfair labor practices that unions sometimes commit?
10. What are the primary objectives of unions?

11. What are the methods used by unions to achieve their objectives?
12. What provisions are usually included in a labor agreement?
13. Describe the typical grievance procedure.
14. Why has "termination at will" declined as a management tool?

●skill builder 18–1

The Union Organizer

Refer back to the chapter preview and assume that you are Marvin Wiley and are trying to get the employees of Quality Service to organize and vote for your union. What would you do? How would you go about getting the 13 employees who voted against the union (and any new ones) to sign authorization cards and vote for the union?

●skill builder 18–2

Would You Sign a Union Authorization Card?

Situation A: Assume that you encounter the following independent situations. You are 30 years old and have a job paying $8.50 per hour. Because of your personal situation, this is a fairly good job for you and will probably be the best job you can hold. Your spouse also does similar work at the company, so your combined income is about $34,000 per year (2,000 hours per person per year × $8.50/hour × 2 persons). Some of the workers are talking about joining a union.

Situation B: You hear that some lay-offs have recently been made to improve company profits. You also know that about once a month someone is injured.

Answer the following questions:

1. Would you sign a union authorization card in Situation A? Why or why not?
2. Would you sign a union authorization card in Situation B? Why or why not?

SOURCE: *H. Giles Schmid, Winona State University.*

CASE 18–1

Major League Baseball Umpires Foul Out

When future college textbooks are written on labor–management relations, the 1999 saga of baseball and its umpires may well be included as a case study in how not to do it—not only for unions but for employers as well.

On Thursday, September 2, 1999, 25 replacement umpires worked American and National League games, filling holes left by mass resignations of regular umpires, an ill-conceived strategy that backfired.

The leaders of the umpires union made a fatal mistake: They wrongly believed they had the power to shut down the business of baseball with a threat to withhold their services. As other unions have learned the hard way, a strike—by any name—is lost the moment the employer can keep going without them.

The tactic was almost certainly doomed from the start. An alternative, if not equally experienced, supply of qualified workers was readily available in the top minor leagues. And managers had not concealed their willingness to use that source.

While thinking they were cleverly getting around a no-strike agreement by resigning, the umpires foolishly placed themselves outside the coverage of the labor laws designed to protect the rights of bona fide strikers.

But management had no reason to rejoice, either, for the real roots of the confrontation lay in the fact that baseball's owners hadn't been "tending to business" in the matter of umpiring. Over time, the owners had delegated to the umpires their own prerogatives over everything from performance reviews to the location of the strike zone. The umpires had gradually gained veto power over who could supervise them, whether they could be required to stay in physical shape, and even whether they could be told to dust off home plate.

Thus, when the baseball commissioner's office, in the spring of 1999, tried to tell the umpires to call balls and strikes with some uniformity—and with at least a nod in the direction of the rule book—the umpires took it as an affront.

Such a posture would be laughable in most other workplaces, but it's hardly unique. Other employers have awoken too late to realize they have similarly given away control of their businesses. And restoring a proper balance is nearly always painful. But for both management stupidity and union arrogance, the umpires are hard to top.

Answer the following questions:

1. What does this case illustrate about the need for management to prepare for dealing with a union?
2. What should management have done differently?
3. What should the umpires have done differently?

SOURCE: *Adapted from "Umps Foul Out,"* USA Today, *September 3, 1999, p. 16A.*

Endnotes

Chapter 1

1. A. Janice Klein and Pamela Posey, "Good Supervisors Are Good Supervisors—Anywhere," *Harvard Business Review* 64, November–December 1986, pp. 125–128.

2. Rich Melchiomo, "The Changing Temporary Work Force: Managerial, Professional and Technical Workers in the Personnel Supply Services," *Occupational Outlook Quarterly*, Spring 1999, p. 24.

3. Howard Fullerton, "Table 6: Bureau of Labor Statistics Employment Projections, Civilian Labor Force, 1986 and 1996, and Projected 1996–2006," Bureau of Labor Statistics home page: http//stats.bls.gov/empstab3.htm; updated January 5, 1998; accessed July 3, 1999.

4. Jon Katzenbach, "The Right Kind of Teamwork," *The Wall Street Journal*, November 9, 1992, p. A10.

5. John Hillkirk, "Challenging Status Quo Now in Vogue," *USA Today*, November 9, 1993, pp. 1B and 2B.

6. Ibid., p. 2B.

7. John Hillkirk, "Reengineering Movement in Infancy," *USA Today*, November 9, 1993, p. 2B.

8. Daniel Eisenberg, "Rise of the Permatemp," *Time*, July 12, 1999, p. 48.

9. Rebecca Blumenstein and Solande Desantis, "AT&T and British Telecom to Buy Stake in Canada Wireless Firm Rogers Cantel," *The Wall Street Journal*, August 6, 1999, p. B4.

10. Patrick E. Conner, "Total Quality Management," *Public Administration Review*, November–December, 1997, p. 503.

11. Samuel K. M. Ho, "Change for the Better via ISO 9000 and TQM," *Management Decision*, March–April 1999, p. 5.

Chapter 2

1. Peter Drucker, "Twilight of the First Line Supervisor," *The Wall Street Journal*, June 7, 1983, p. B1.

2. Jennifer Laabs, "Job Cuts Reach Record Levels for 1998," *Workforce*, February 1999, p. 2.

3. David L. Corsun and Cathy Enz, "Predicting Psychological Empowerment Among Service Workers: The Effect of Support-Based Relationships," *Human Relations*, February 1999, p. 206.

4. Charles Garfield, *Second to None* (Homewood, Ill.: Business One Irwin, 1992), pp. 91–92.

5. James W. Dean and James R. Evans, *Total Quality* (St. Paul, Minn.: West Publishing Co., 1994), p. 7.

6. Les L. Landes, "Down with Duality Program-itis," *IABC Communication World*, February 1992, pp. 29–32.

7. James Lamprecht, *ISO 9000: Preparing for Registration* (New York: ASQC Quality Press, 1991) and Demo Stavros "The Standard for the 21st Century," *Industrial Distribution*, January 1997, pp. 44–47.

8. David A. Garvin, "Quality on the Line," *Harvard Business Review*, September–October 1993, pp. 41–54.

9. Dean and Evans, *Total Quality*.

10. Landes, "Down with Quality Program-itis."

11. George S. Easton and Sherry L. Farrell, "The Effects of Total Quality Management on Corporate Performance: An Empirical Investigation," *Journal of Business*, April 1998, pp. 253–308.

12. Edward Caldeira, "The Bottom Line on Quality," *Professional Builder*, November 1998, p. 26.

13. Thomas Peters and Robert Waterman, Jr., *In Search of Excellence* (New York: Harper and Row, 1982). See Chapter 6: "Close to the Customer."

14. Fred Luthans, *Organizational Behavior*, 7th ed. (New York: McGraw-Hill, 1995), p. 40.

15. "Tough at the Top," *The Economist*, January 6, 1996, p. 47.

16. Luthans, *Organizational Behavior*, p. 35.

17. Adapted from Dean and Evans, *Total Quality*, pp. 26–28.

Chapter 3

1. William L. Megginson, M. Jane Byrd, and Leon C. Megginson, *Small Business Management*, 3rd ed. (Burr Ridge, Ill.: Irwin McGraw-Hill, 2000), pp. 201–202.

2. Peter F. Drucker, *The Practice of Management* (New York: Harper & Row, 1954), p. 64.

Chapter 4

1. For further details, see *A Matter of Judgment and Ethics at Work,* videos produced by the Ethics Resource Center.
2. Patricia Haddock and Marilyn Manning, "Ethically Speaking," *Sky,* March 1990, p. 128.
3. William L. Megginson, Mary Jane Byrd, and Leon C. Megginson, *Small Business Management,* 3rd ed. (Burr Ridge, Ill.: Irwin McGraw-Hill, 2000), p. 255.
4. "Do Many Chief Executives Lose Their Drive as They Advance in Age?" *The Wall Street Journal,* November 18, 1997, p. 1A.
5. See Mortimer R. Feinberg and Aaron L. Wenstein, "How Do You Know When to Rely on Your Intuition?" *The Wall Street Journal,* June 21, 1982, p. 16.

Chapter 5

1. The material covering functional and product departmentalization first appeared in Donald C. Mosley, Paul H. Pietri, and Leon C. Megginson, *Management: Leadership in Action,* 5e (New York: HarperCollins, 1996), pp. 255–258.
2. James A. F. Stoner, *Management* (Englewood Cliffs, N.J.: Prentice-Hall, 1978), p. 284.
3. "Theme and Variation," *The Owen Manager* (Owen Graduate School of Management, Vanderbilt University) 4, Spring 1983, p. 2.
4. Thomas J. Peters and Robert Waterman, *In Search of Excellence: Lessons from America's Best-Run Companies* (New York: Harper & Row, 1982).
5. Peter Drucker, "The Coming of the New Organization, "*Harvard Business Review* 76, January–February 1988, pp. 45–53.
6. Richard L. Bunning, "The Dynamics of Downsizing," *Personnel Journal* 69, September 1990, p. 69.
7. Phillip R. Nienstedt, "Effective Downsizing Management Structures," *Human Resources Planning* 12, 1989, p. 156.
8. Bunning, "The Dynamics of Downsizing," p. 70.
9. Ronald Henkoff, "Getting Beyond Downsizing," *Fortune,* January 10, 1994, p. 58.
10. Wayne F. Cascio, "Downsizing: What Do We Know? What Have We Learned?" *Academy of Management Executive,* Vol. 2, No. 1, February 1993, p. 95.
11. This section is adapted from Michael Hammer and James Champy, *Reengineering the Corporation* (New York: Harper Business, 1993).
12. Ibid., p. 31.
13. Ibid., p. 32.
14. Adapted from Thomas A. Stewart, "Reengineering: The Hot New Managing Tool," *Fortune,* August 23, 1993, pp. 44–48.
15. Vincent K. Omachonu and Joel E. Ross, *Principles of Total Quality* (Delray Beach, Fla.: St. Lucie Press, 1994), pp. 138–139.
16. Ibid.
17. Frank Ostroff, *The Horizontal Organization* (New York: Oxford University Press, 1999), p. 130.
18. Ibid., pp. 23–24.
19. Nancy K. Austin, "Reorganizing the Organization Chart," *Working Woman,* September 1993, p. 24.
20. Ibid., pp. 24–25.

Chapter 6

1. Donald A. Laird and Eleanor C. Laird, *The Techniques of Delegating: How to Get Things Done Through Others* (New York: McGraw-Hill, 1957), pp. 107–108.
2. Claud S. George, *Supervision in Action: The Art of Managing Others,* 4th ed. (Upper Saddle River, N.J.: Prentice-Hall, 1985), p. 283. Reprinted by permission.
3. Dale D. McConkey, *No-Nonsense Delegation* (New York: AMACOM, 1974), pp. 90–100.
4. "Tom Peters' Formula for Supervisory Excellence," *Supervisory Management* 30, February 1985, pp. 2–3.
5. Suzanne Savory, "Ineffective Delegation—Symptom or Problem?" *Supervisory Management* 24, June 1979, p. 28.
6. Lawrence Peter and Raymond Hull, *The Peter Principle* (New York: William Morrow & Co., 1969).
7. Peter Reuters, "Study Finds Profit in Employee Empowerment," *USA Today,* June 6, 1995, p. 4B.

Chapter 7

1. Robert Kreitner and Angelo Kinicki, *Organizational Behavior,* 3rd ed. (Chicago, Ill.: Irwin, 1995), p. 368.
2. Albert Mehrabian, "Communication Without Words," *Psychology Today* 2, September 1968, pp. 53–55.
3. According to a Toyota advertisement in *Forbes,* June 19, 1995, p. 168.
4. Keith Davis, *Human Behavior at Work,* 8th ed. (New York: McGraw-Hill, 1989), p. 371.
5. John Thill and Courtland L. Bovee, *Excellence in Business Communication,* 4th ed. (Upper Saddle River, N.J.: Prentice-Hall, 1999), p. 40.
6. Deborah Tannen, "Language, Sex, and Power: Women and Men in the Workplace," *Training and Development,* September 1997, pp. 34–40.
7. "The Difference Japanese Management Makes," *Business Week,* July 14, 1986, p. 47.
8. J. Hart Seibert, "Listening in the Organizational Context," *Listening Behavior: Measurement and Application,* ed. Robert Bostrom (New York: The Guilford Press, 1990), pp. 119–127.

Chapter 8

1. Stephanie Armour, "Workplace Absenteeism Soars 25%, Costs Millions," *USA Today,* November 6, 1998, p. 1A.

2. Reported in Thomas J. Peters and Robert Waterman, *In Search of Excellence: Lessons from America's Best Run Companies* (New York: Harper & Row, 1982), p. xxi.
3. Alfred J. Marrow, *Behind the Executive Mask: Greater Managerial Competence through Deeper Self Understanding*, Report No. 79 (New York: AMACOM, 1964), p. 7.
4. Abraham H. Maslow, *Motivation and Personality* (New York: Harper & Row, 1954).
5. Robert Levering and Milton Moskowitz, "The 100 Best Companies to Work For," *Fortune*, January 12, 1998, p. 84.
6. Frederick Herzberg, Bernard Mausner, and Barbara Snyderman, *The Motivation to Work*, 2nd ed. (New York: John Wiley & Sons, 1959).
7. Stephanie Armour, "Cash or Critiques: Which Is Best?" *USA Today*, December 16, 1998, p. 6B.
8. Fred Luthans, *Organizational Behavior*, 7th ed. (New York: McGraw-Hill, 1995) p. 156.
9. See E. E. Locke and G. P. Latham, *Goal Setting: A Motivational Technique that Works* (Englewood Cliffs, N.J.: Prentice Hall, 1984).
10. Condensed from Peters and Waterman, *In Search of Excellence*, p. 68.

Chapter 9

1. Douglas McGregor, *The Human Side of Enterprise* (New York: McGraw-Hill Book Co., 1960), pp. 33–42.
2. Notes from Workshop on Process Consultation conducted by Edgar Schein, Albert Einstein Institute, Cape Cod, August 1991.
3. Interview with Dr. Paul Hersey, *Trainer's Bookshelf* (San Diego, Calif.: Learning Resources Corporation, 1982).
4. Robert R. Blake and Jane S. Mouton, *The Managerial Grid III: The Key to Leadership Excellence* (Houston: Gulf Publishing, 1985).
5. Paul Hersey and Kenneth H. Blanchard, *Management of Organizational Behavior: Utilizing Human Resources*, 3rd ed. (Englewood Cliffs, N.J.: Prentice-Hall, 1977), pp. 6161–6162.
6. Hersey and Blanchard acknowledge that they were strongly influenced by William J. Reddins, "3-D Management Style Theory," found in William J. Reddins, *Managerial Effectiveness* (New York: McGraw-Hill, 1970). We use Hersey and Blanchard's model because it is better known.
7. Robert Tannenbaum and Warren Schmidt, "How to Choose a Leadership Pattern," *Harvard Business Review* 51 (May–June 1973), pp. 162–180.
8. Leonard M. Apcar, "Middle Managers and Supervisors Resist Moves to More Participatory Management," *The Wall Street Journal*, September 16, 1985, p. 25.
9. David L. Bradford and Allen R. Cohen, *Managing for Excellence* (New York: John Wiley & Sons, 1984), pp. 71–98.
10. John MacGregor Burns, *Leadership* (New York: Harper & Row, 1978).
11. Bernard Bass, *Leadership and Performance Beyond Expectations* (New York: The Free Press, 1985).
12. B. M. Bass, B. J. Avolio, and L. Goodheim, "Biography and the Assessment of Transformational Leadership at the World Class Level," *Journal of Management* 13, Spring 1987, p. 7.
13. Ibid., p. 16.
14. George R. McAleer, "Leadership in the Military Environment," Association for Psychological Type, Special Topic Symposium, Type and Leadership, Crystal City, Va., March 5–7, 1993.
15. Bennett J. Sims, *Servanthood—Leadership for the Third Millennium* (Boston: Cowley Publications, 1997).
16. Operation Sagebrush, Fall 1955, experienced by Donald C. Mosley.
17. Robert K. Greenleaf, *Servant Leadership* (Mahwah, N.J.: Paulist Press, 1991), p. 3. Copyright by the Robert K. Greenleaf Center.
18. Ibid., p. 21.
19. William D. Hitt, "The Model Leader: A Fully Functioning Person," *Leadership and Organization Development Journal* 14, No. 7, December 1993, p. 10.

Chapter 10

1. Excerpts from handout from the Ritz-Carlton, Island of Maui, Hawaii; Edwin McDowell, "Ritz-Carlton's Keys to Good Service," *New York Times*, March 31, 1993, pp. C1–C3. *The Portrait*, the Ritz-Carlton Hotel Company; interviews and discussions with Lenny Litz, general manager, and staff of the Ritz-Carlton, Maui; discussion with Sue Musselman, assistant to the vice-president of quality; Ritz-Carlton Hotel Company, Atlanta, Georgia; and Mark Memmot, "The Quality Quest," *USA Today*, June 28, 1993, p. 2B.
2. Terrence R. Mitchell and William G. Scott, "America's Problems and Needed Reforms: Confronting the Ethic of Personal Advantage," *Academy of Management Executive* 4, August 1990, pp. 23–25.
3. B. W. Tuckman, "Developmental Sequence in Small Groups," *Psychological Bulletin*, May 1965, pp. 384–399.
4. See, for example, F. Steven Heinen and Eugene Jacobson, "A Model of Task Group Development in Complex Organizations and a Strategy of Implementation," *Academy of Management Review* 1, October 1976, pp. 98–111.
5. Don Hellriegel, John W. Slocum, Jr., and Richard Woodman, *Organizational Behavior*, 5th ed. (St. Paul: West Publishing, 1989), p. 210.

6. R. Mitchell, "How Ford Hit the Bull's Eye with Taurus," *Business Week,* June 30, 1986, pp. 69–70.

7. R. Bruce McAfee and Paul J. Champage, *Organizational Behavior: A Manager's View* (St. Paul: West Publishing, 1987), p. 250.

8. Don Hellriegel and John W. Slocum, Jr., *Management* (Reading, Mass.: Addison-Wesley, 1986), pp. 539–542.

9. W. Allen Randolph, *Understanding and Managing Organizational Behavior* (Homewood, Ill.: Richard D. Irwin, 1985), p. 399.

10. William G. Dyer, *Team Building: Issues and Alternatives* (Reading, Mass.: Addison-Wesley Publishing Co., 1977) p. 4.

11. Don Hellriegel and John W. Slocum, Jr., *Management,* 7th ed. (Cincinnati, Ohio: South-Western Publishing Co., 19XX), p. 52.

12. Donald C. Mosley, Carl Moore, Michelle Slagle, and Daniel Burns, "The Role of the O.D. Consultant in Partnering," *Organization Development Journal* 8(3), Fall 1990, pp. 43–49.

13. *Partnering: The Central Artery/Tunnel Manual* (Boston, Mass.: Massachusetts Highway Department, 1993), p. 2.

14. Roger Daniels, "WINS and Partnering Working Together to Improve the Way We Do Business on the CA/T," unpublished paper, December 1993.

15. Presentation by Edgar Schein at the Albert Einstein Summer Institute, Cape Cod, Mass., August 1992.

16. Charles C. Manz and Henry P. Sims, Jr. "Superleadership: Leading Others to Lead Themselves to Excellence," *The Manager's Bookshelf,* ed. Jan L. Pierce and John W. Newstrom (New York: Harper & Row, 1988), p. 328.

17. Carla O'Dell, "Team Play, Team Pay—New Ways of Keeping Score," *Across the Board* 26, Nov. 1989, pp. 38–45.

Chapter 11

1. "Pentagon Travel Costs," *USA Today,* March 28, 1995, p. 4A.

2. Myron Magnet, "Who's Winning the Information Revolution," *Fortune,* November 30, 1992, pp. 110–111.

3. Simon Head, "Big Brother in a Black Box," *Civilization,* August/September 1999, pp. 52–55.

Chapter 12

1. "U.S. Factories Are the Stars," *Business Week,* April 19, 1999, p. 30.

2. "Ford Continues Its Drive for Productivity Leadership: 1999 Harbour Report Tracks Success," Ford Motor Company Press Release, August 24, 1999.

3. Joe Miller, "Wait Until Next Year: Deal Dodges Tough Issues," *Automotive News,* August 3, 1998, p. 46.

4. "Robot Orders Rocket to Record in First Quarter," *Robotics World,* July–August, 1999, p. 12.

5. Lynda Radosevice, "EDI Spreads Across Different Business Lines," *Computerworld,* October 18, 1993, pp. 69–73; also, "Dillard Stores' Profit in April Quarter Was Flat, Disappointing Some Analysts," *The Wall Street Journal,* May 12, 1994, p. B4.

6. James W. Dean, Jr., and James R. Evans, *Total Quality* (St. Paul: West Publishing, 1994), p. 133.

7. Jennifer J. Laabs, "Quality Drives Trident's Success," *Workforce,* February 1998, pp. 44–49.

8. Bureau of Labor Statistics, National Census of Fatal Occupational Injuries, 1998, http://stats.bls.gov/oshome.html, released August 4, 1999.

9. Jennifer Laabs, "Cashing in on Safety," *Workforce,* August 1997, pp. 153–158.

Chapter 13

1. Dennis C. Kinlaw, *Coaching for Commitment* (San Diego, Calif.: Pfeiffer & Co., 1993), p. 19.

2. Dennis C. Kinlaw, *Coaching Skills for Inventory* (San Diego, Calif.: Pfeiffer & Co., 1993), pp. 1–13.

3. David Bicknell, "Keep It Personal and Keep Your Staff," *Computer Weekly,* July 8, 1999, p. 22.

4. Thomas Gordon, *Leader Effectiveness Training* (New York: Dryden Books, 1977), pp. 92–107.

5. Wayne C. Cascio, *Managing Human Resources,* 4th ed. (New York: McGraw-Hill, 1995), p. 550.

Chapter 14

1. Quoted in Alfred J. Marrow, *Behind the Executive Mask: Greater Managerial Competence Through Deeper Self-Understanding,* Report No. 79 (New York: AMA-COM, 1964), p. 7.

2. Edgar H. Schein, *Process Consultation,* Vol. 1, 2nd ed. (Reading, Mass.: Addison-Wesley Publishing Co., 1988), p. 6.

3. Ibid., p. 9.

4. Client evaluation feedback to the Synergistic Group, Mobile, AL.

Chapter 15

1. Roger Fisher and William Ury, *Getting to Yes* (New York: Penguin, 1993), pp. 3–4.

2. A. P. Brief, R. S. Schuler, and M. W. Sell, *Managing Job Stress* (Boston: Little, Brown, & Co., 1981) p. 2.

3. "The Road to Happiness," *Psychology Today* 27(4), July–August 1994, p. 34.

4. S. C. Kobasa, "Stressful Life Events, Personality, and Health: An Inquiry into Hardiness," *Journal of Personality and Social Psychology* 37, 1979, pp. 1–12.

5. Claudia Wallis, "Stress: Can We Cope?" *Time,* June 6, 1983, p. 52.

6. W. W. Suoganen and Donald R. Hudson, "Coping with Stress and Addictive Work Behavior," *Business*

(College of Business Administration, Georgia State University) 31, January–February 1980, p. 11.

7. Robert T. Golembiewski and Robert F. Munzenrider, *Phases of Burnout* (New York: Praeger, 1988), p. 220.

8. "Fitness Programs Are Working Out," *USA Today*, Wednesday, June 17, 1998, p. 5B.

9. Stephanie Armour, "Workplace Hazard Gets Attention," *USA Today*, May 5, 1998, p. 1B.

10. "The Road to Happiness," *Psychology Today* 27(4), July–August 1994, p. 37.

Chapter 16

1. Will Helmlinger, president of The Resource Development Group, Lake Oswego, Oregon, "The High Cost of Turnover," http://www.cratus.com/cratus/resources/willDec97.html; accessed November 19, 1999.

2. Sharon M. Tarrant, "Setting Up an Electronic Job-Posting System," *Training & Development* 48, January 1994, pp. 39–42.

3. Shari Caudron, "Online Job-Posting Facilitates Lateral Transfer at Household International," *Personnel Journal* 73, April 1994, p. 64J.

4. Robert Lewis, "Escaping from the Jobless Maze," *AARP Bulletin*, October 1994, p. 2.

5. Robert Samuelson, "A Quiet Revolution: Full Employment and Low Inflation," *Mobile* (Alabama) *Register*, June 25, 1999, p. 15A.

6. Tony Mauro, "Sex Bias Ruling Is 'Mixed,'" *USA Today*, June 23, 1999, p. 3A.

7. "Taking Advantage," WGN TV station (Chicago), February 19, 1984.

8. Stephanie Armour, "Employers: Enough Already with the e-Résumés," *USA Today*, July 15, 1999, p. 1B.

9. "Is the DOT Guilty of Overkill?" *Railway Age* 195, May 1994, pp. 65–67; and Lori Sharn, "Transport Workers Face Breath Tests," *USA Today*, February 4, 1994, p. 3A.

10. See "Adoption by Four Agencies of Uniform Guidelines on Employee Selection Procedures (1978)," *Federal Register* 43, August 1978, pp. 290–315.

11. "Labor Report," *The Wall Street Journal*, February 23, 1993, p. A1.

12. Julia Lawlor, "Disabilities No Longer a Job Barrier," *USA Today*, June 22, 1993, pp. 1A and 1B.

13. Michael A. Verespej, "How Will You Know Whom to Hire? No More Questions About Medical History," *Industry Week*, September 17, 1990, p. 70.

14. J. Fraser, "The Making of a Work Force," *Business Month*, September 1989, pp. 58, 60–61.

15. "In Search of Survival," *Inc.*, November 1985, p. 90.

16. Jerry McLain, "Practice Makes Perfect," *Office Systems* 9512, April 1995, pp. 74 and 76–77.

17. Hedrick Smith, "Future Jobs Less College-Oriented," *USA Today*, June 19, 1995, p. 11A.

18. William E. Reif, "Intrinsic versus Extrinsic Rewards: Resolving the Controversy," *Human Resources Management* 14, Summer 1975, p. 7.

19. Shawn Tully, "Are You Paid Enough?" *Fortune*, June 26, 1995, p. 72.

20. George Ming, "All the Parts of Comparable Worth," *Personnel Journal* 69, November 1990, p. 99.

Chapter 17

1. Robert Cyr, "Seven Steps to Better Performance Appraisals," *Training & Developing* 47, January 1993, pp. 18–19.

2. Ren Nardoni, "Corporatewide Management Staffing," *Personnel Journal* 69, April 1990, pp. 52–58.

3. Kenneth M. Golden, "Dealing with the Problem Manager," *Personnel* 66, August 1989, pp. 54–59.

4. "Evaluations Get a Makeover as Employers Seek to Make Them Useful," *The Wall Street Journal*, May 2, 1995, p. A1.

5. *Appraising Managerial Performance: Current Practice and Future Directions*, Conference Board Report No. 723 (New York: Conference Board, 1977), p. 26.

6. Robert L. Mathis and John H. Jackson, *Personnel/Human Resource Management* (St. Paul, Minn.: West Publishing Co., 1991), p. 299.

7. Leon C. Megginson, Geralyn M. Franklin, and M. Jane Byrd, *Human Resource Management* (Houston: Dame Publications, 1995), pp. 365–368.

8. Mary Mavis, "Painless Performance Evaluations," *Training & Development* 48, October 1994, pp. 40–44.

9. Douglas McGregor, "An Uneasy Look at Performance Appraisals," *Harvard Business Review* 35, May–June 1957, p. 90.

10. L. Stockford and W. H. Bissell, "Factors Involved in Establishing a Merit Rating Scale," *Personnel* 26, September 1949, p. 97.

11. H. H. Meyer and W. B. Walker, "A Study of Factors Relating to the Effectiveness of a Performance Appraisal Program," *Personnel Psychology* 14, August 1961, pp. 291–298.

12. For further details, see Irwin H. McMaster, "Universal Aspects of Discipline," *Supervision* 36, April 1974, p. 19.

13. Walter Kiechel, "How to Discipline in the Modern Age," *Fortune*, May 7, 1990, p. 179.

14. Laurie Baum, "Punishing Workers with a Day Off," *Business Week*, June 16, 1986, p. 80.

15. "Entry-Level Job Requirements Get Stiffer Every Year," *The Wall Street Journal*, May 16, 1995, p. A1.

16. M. Michael Markowich, "A Positive Approach to Discipline," *Personnel* 66, August 1989, pp. 60–65.

17. "Degree of Discipline," *Manager's Legal Bulletin*, April 15, 1991, pp. 1–2.

18. *Employee Conduct and Discipline,* Personnel Policies Forum Survey No. 102 (Washington, D.C.: The Bureau of National Affairs, Inc., August 1973), pp. 1–2.

19. Dennis Lindsey, "Of Sound Mind? Evaluating the Workforce," *Security Management* 38, September 1994, pp. 69–71.

20. Equal Employment Opportunity Commission, *Guidelines on Discrimination Because of Sex,* 29 C.F.R., Section 1064.11 (July 1, 1992).

21. Constance Johnson, "Court Cases Give Firms Guidance on Sexual Harassment," *The Wall Street Journal,* May 17, 1995, p. B2.

22. Margaret A. Jacobs, "Del Laboratories Agrees to Record Sum for Settling Sexual-Harassment Lawsuit," *The Wall Street Journal,* August 4, 1995, p. B2.

23. *Payne v. Western & A.R.P. Co.,* 81 Tenn. 507 (1884).

24. S. A. Youngblood and G. L. Tidwel, "Termination-at-Will: Some Changes in the Wind," *Personnel* 58, May–June 1981, p. 24.

Chapter 18

1. U.S. Department of Labor, Bureau of Labor Statistics, as reported in "Union Membership High in Government Jobs," *USA Today,* September 1, 1999, p. 1A.

2. "Unions on the Ropes," *USA Today,* June 14, 1995, p. 12A.

3. "Are Unions Striking Out?" *U.S. News & World Report,* June 12, 1995, p. 26.

4. "Unions on the Ropes."

5. "Union 'Downsizing' Fuels Struggle at Top," *Mobile* (Alabama) *Press Register,* July 5, 1995, p. 6–B.

6. Harriet Webster, "Would You Like to Work at Home?" *Reader's Digest,* March 1998, p. 130.

7. Mortimer B. Zuckerman, "The GOP's New Bedfellows," *U.S. News & World Report,* April 24, 1995, p. 72.

8. Joseph P. Cangemi et al., "Differences Between Pro-Union and Pro-Company Employees," *Personnel Journal* 55, September 1976, pp. 451–453.

9. Phillip Ash, "The Parties to the Grievance," *Personnel Psychology* 23, Spring 1970, pp. 13–37.

Glossary

A

accountability the obligation that is created when a person accepts duties and responsibilities from higher management. (p. 166)

achievement, proficiency, or skill tests a test that measures fairly accurately the applicant's knowledge of and ability to do a given job; used to spot trade bluffers. (p. 457)

acknowledging showing by nonevaluative verbal responses that you have listened to what the employee has stated. (p. 373)

active listening the listener makes a response so as to encourage feedback. (p. 209)

administrative skills establishing and following procedures to process paperwork in an orderly manner. (p. 15)

advisory authority authority of most staff departments to serve and advise line departments. (p. 143)

affirmative action programs (AAPs) programs encouraged by the Equal Employment Opportunity Commission to put the principle of equal employment opportunity into practice. (p. 451)

affirming communicating to an employee his or her value, strengths, and contributions. (p. 373)

agency shop an agreement under which all employees must pay union dues even if they choose not to join the union; compare to *closed shop, union shop.* (p. 518)

agreement or contract the document prepared when an accord has been reached to bind the company, union, and workers to specific clauses, which it spells out. (p. 528)

alternatives possible courses of action that can satisfy a need or solve a problem. (p. 107)

anchors brief statements of actual worker behavior on the job. (p. 486)

appraisal interview an interview in which the supervisor communicates the results of a performance appraisal to an employee. (p. 489)

appraiser bias(es) conscious or unconscious educational, racial, or interpersonal conflict. (p. 487)

apprenticeship training training that blends the learning of theory with practice in the techniques of the job; combines classroom instruction with hands-on experience. (p. 462)

aptitude tests employment tests used to predict how a person might perform on a given job; most useful for operative jobs. (p. 457)

arbitrator an outside agent, called in when collective bargaining reaches an impasse, who will make a binding decision. (p. 527)

attending showing through nonverbal behavior that you are listening in an open, nonjudgmental manner. (p. 373)

authority the right to tell others how to act to reach objectives. (p. 8)

authority compliance the leader's having a high concern for production results and using a directive approach. (p. 250)

B

behaviorally anchored rating scales (BARS) scales designed to specify more objectively the actual job behaviors being evaluated. (p. 486)

benchmarking comparing company practices against those of world-class performers. (p. 54)

body signals nonverbal signals communicated by body action. (p. 190)

budget a forecast of expected financial performance over time. (p. 85)

burnout a malady caused by excessive stress in the setting where people invest most of their time and energy. (p. 431)

C

cause-and-effect diagram a graphical display of a chain of causes and effects. (p. 346)

central tendency the tendency for the ratings to cluster around some intermediate point on the scale. (p. 489)

channel the means used to pass a message. (p. 188)

closed shop an agreement under which all prospective employees must be members of the recognized union before they can be employed and all current employees must join within a specified time in order to retain their jobs; compare to *agency shop, union shop.* (p. 517)

closure successfully accomplishing the objective for a given item on the agenda. (p. 402)

coaching supervisors helping individuals to reach their highest levels of performance. (p. 366)

coaching and selling style used with individuals or groups that have potential but haven't realized it fully. (p. 254)

collective bargaining the process in which the representatives of the employer and the employees meet at reasonable times and places to confer in good faith over wages, hours, and other terms and conditions of employment. (p. 527)

communication process model model of the five components of communication and their relationships. (p. 188)

comparable worth or pay equity the evaluation of work based on a formula whereby points are assigned for the amount of education, effort, skill, and responsibility required for an individual job; jobs with equal points have equal pay. (p. 468)

computer-assisted manufacturing (CAM) a manufacturing system in which special computers assist automated equipment in performing the processes necessary for production. (p. 341)

conceptual skills mental ability to become aware of and identifying relationships among different pieces of information. (p. 13)

concurrent controls used while an activity is taking place. (p. 313)

confirming making sure that an employee understands what has been said or agreed upon. (p. 373)

confronting/challenging establishes clear performance standards, compares actual performance against the standards, and addresses performance that doesn't meet those standards. (p. 370)

consensus the acceptance by all members of the decision reached. (p. 392)

constructive criticism criticism offered in a spirit of helpfulness toward correction of a condition that can be corrected. (p. 494)

contingency planning thinking in advance about possible problems or changes that might arise and having anticipated solutions available. (p. 72)

continuum of leadership behavior the full range of leadership behaviors in terms of the relationship between the use of authority by a supervisor and the employees' freedom. (p. 254)

control chart displays the "state of control" of a process. (p. 346)

controlling comparing actual performance with planned action and taking corrective action if needed. (p. 12)

cost/benefit analysis estimating and comparing the costs and benefits of alternatives. (p. 109)

cost-of-living adjustments (COLAs) increases in wages in direct proportion to increases in the *consumer price index (CPI).* (p. 467)

counseling the supervisor helps an individual recognize, talk about, and solve either real or perceived problems that affect performance. (p. 371)

country club management high concern for people. (p. 250)

craft unions a union of workers in a specific skill, craft, or trade. (p. 513)

critical path the series of activities in a PERT network that comprise the longest route, in terms of time, to complete the job. (p. 87)

D

decentralization the extent to which authority is delegated from one unit of the organization to another. (p. 146)

decision making considering and selecting a course of action from among alternatives. (p. 103)

delegating style used with exceptionally ready and capable individuals and groups. (p. 254)

delegation of authority managers grant authority to the people who report to them. (p. 164)

Deming's 85-15 rule assumes that when things go wrong, 85 percent of the time the cause is from elements controlled by management. (p. 45)

departmentalization the organizational process of determining how activities are to be grouped. (p. 134)

developmental leadership an approach that helps groups to evolve effectively and to achieve highly supportive, open, creative, committed, high-performing membership. (p. 256)

disciplinary layoff or suspension time off without pay given to serious disciplinary offenders to allow them to consider the possible consequences of their actions. (p. 503)

discipline training that corrects, molds, or perfects knowledge, attitudes, behavior, or conduct. (p. 491)

dissatifier factors factors that employees said most affected them negatively, or dissatisfied them about their job, including low pay, low benefits, and unfavorable working conditions. (p. 228)

diversity refers to the wide range of distinguishing employee characteristics such as sex, age, race, ethnic origin, and other factors. (p. 22)

downsizing striving to become leaner and more efficient by reducing the workforce and consolidating departments and work groups. (pp. 25, 148)

downward communication flows that originate with supervisors and passed down to employees. (p. 191)

dual promotion ladders   an advancement plan whereby skilled technical and scientific workers can get salary increases and higher job titles without becoming managers. (p. 449)

due process   a procedure which guarantees (a) that the individual accused of violating an established rule or law will get a hearing to determine the extent of guilt and (b) that the established penalties will be imposed only after the hearing is conducted. (p. 494)

E

ego need   the need for self-confidence, independence, appreciation, and status. (p. 226)

e-mail   documents created, transmitted, and read entirely on a computer. (p. 190)

Employee Assistance Program (EAP)   professional counseling and medical services for employees with unresolved personal or work-related problems. (p. 379)

employee associations   organizations composed of government, white-collar, agricultural, or service employees, as well as professionals, that function as labor unions. (p. 515)

employee benefits   financial rewards and services provided to employees in addition to their regular earnings. (p. 470)

employee comparison method   a traditional method of *performance appraisal* in which supervisors are required to rank the performance and value to the organization of each of their employees in comparison to the others. (p. 486)

employees' bill of rights   provisions of the Labor-Management Reporting and Disclosure Act (Landrum-Griffin Act) that protect employees from possible abuse by unscrupulous managers and union leaders. (p. 519)

empowerment   the granting of authority to employees to make key decisions within their areas of responsibility. (pp. 23, 37)

ethical dilemmas   situations in which the supervisor is not certain what the correct behavior is. (p. 26)

ethics   standards used to judge the "rightness" or "wrongness" of one person's behavior toward others. (p. 112)

exclusive bargaining agent   the employee's representative who deals exclusively with management over questions of wages, hours, and other terms and conditions of employment. (p. 524)

exempt employees   employees not covered by the provisions of the Fair Labor Standards Act; includes executives, administrative and professional employees, outside sales personnel, and other selected groups. (p. 466)

expectancy theory   views an individual's motivation as a conscious effort involving the expectancy that a reward will be given for a good result. (p. 230)

experience rating   an employer's record of unemployed workers, which is used, along with the state's unemployment rate, to determine the amount the employer must pay into the state's unemployment insurance fund. (p. 470)

experiential learning   one learns by doing and uses mistakes as an opportunity to figure out how to avoid them in the future. (p. 163)

external change forces   forces outside the organization that have a great impact on organizational change. (p. 277)

extrinsic motivation   behavior performed not for its own sake, but for the consequences associated with it. The consequences can include pay, benefits, job security, and working conditions. (p. 223)

F

fact-finding meeting   held to seek out relevant facts about a problem or situation. (p. 391)

feedback   the response that a communicator receives. (p. 189)

feedback controls   measure completed activities and then take corrective action if needed. (p. 313)

feedforward controls   preventive controls that try to anticipate problems and take corrective action before they occur. (p. 312)

feeling decision process   giving great weight to the "people" side of a decision. (p. 110)

financial resources   the money, capital, and credit an organization requires for operations. (p. 7)

financing   providing or using funds to produce and distribute the organization's product or service. (p. 6)

flexcomp or cafeteria benefit plans   a method of providing employees with flexible benefit packages. (p. 472)

flowchart   a visual representation of the sequence of steps needed to complete a process. (p. 343)

formal group   a group prescribed and/or established by the organization. (p. 281)

full empowerment   the total organization is involved. (p. 41)

functional authority   a staff person's limited line authority over a given *function*. (p. 145)

functional departmentalization   a form of departmentalization that groups together the common functions or similar activities to form an organizations unit. (p. 135)

G

Gantt chart a visual progress report that identifies work stages and scheduled completion dates. (p. 85)

glass ceiling invisible barriers that limit women from advancing in the organization. (p. 22)

goal-setting theory the theory that task goals, properly set and managed, can be an important employee motivator. (p. 233).

graduated scale of penalties a plan whereby punishment for a given violation becomes progressively more severe each time the violation is repeated. (p. 499)

grapevine the "rumor mill." (p. 197)

grievance procedure a formal way of handling employees' complaints; usually outlines the steps to be taken. (p. 531)

group two or more people who communicate and work together regularly in pursuit of one or more common objectives. (p. 281)

group cohesiveness the mutual liking and team feeling in a group. (p. 287)

group facilitation the process of intervening to help a group improve in goal setting, action planning, problem solving, conflict management, and decision making in order to increase the group's effectiveness. (p. 403)

group-centered approach used at meetings in which group members interact freely and address and question one another. (p. 394)

H

halo effect rater's tendency to rate an employee *high* on all factors being evaluated as a result of the rater's impression of the employee's worth to the organization. (p. 489)

heroic managers managers who have a great need for control and influence and who want to run things. (p. 257)

hierarchy of needs people's needs arrangement of in a hierarchy, or ranking of importance. (p. 225)

hierarchy of objectives a network with broad goals at the top level of the organization and narrower for individual divisions, departments, or employees. (p. 75)

histogram a graphical representation of the variation found in a set of data. (p. 345)

horizontal organization a flatter structure that uses a team to eliminate red tape and to meet the customer's needs. (p. 151)

horn effect rater's tendency to rate an employee low on all factors being evaluated as a result of the rater's impression of the employee's worth to the organization. (p. 489)

hot-stove rule a concept that compares a good disciplinary system to a hot stove in that discipline should (a) carry advance warning, (b) be immediate, (c) be consistent, and (d) be impersonal. (p. 500)

human relations skills understanding other people and interacting effectively. (p. 15)

human resources the people an organization requires for operations. (p. 7)

I

"I" message an appeal, rather than a demand, that the other person change. (p. 376)

impoverished management little concern for people or production. (p. 250)

incentive wages or performance pay a compensation method in which an employee's wages are determined by the amount of goods and services the employee produced (output). (p. 466)

industrial unions unions composed of all the workers in an industry, such as coal, whether they are craftsmen, unskilled workers, or clerical employees. (p. 514)

informal communication communication that occurs separately from the formal, established communication system. (p. 197)

informal group a group that evolves out of the formal organization but is not formed by management or shown in the organization's structure. (p. 281)

information exchange meeting held to obtain information from group members. (p. 391)

information-giving meeting held to announce new programs and policies or to update the present ones. (p. 391)

intangible standards are not expressed in terms of numbers, money, physical qualities, or time. (p. 314)

intermediaries go-betweens who act as mediators. (p. 18)

internal change forces pressures for change within the organization such as cultures and objectives. (p. 277)

internship training a method of learning in which on-the-job training at a cooperating business is combined with classwork at a school or college. (p. 463)

intolerable offenses disciplinary problems of such a drastic, dangerous, or illegal nature that they severely strain or endanger employment relationships. (p. 497)

intrinsic motivation behavior that an individual produces because of the pleasant experiences associated with the behavior itself. (p. 223)

intuition unconscious influence of a person's cultural background, education, and training, as well as knowledge of the situation. (p. 117)

inverted pyramid an organization form with a structure widest at the top and narrowing as it funnels down. (p. 153)

IQ tests tests designed to measure the applicant's capacity to learn, to solve problems, and to understand relationships. (p. 457)

ISO 9000 the global certification requirement of supplier firms that has been adopted by the United States and more than 90 other countries of the world. (p. 43)

J

job analysis the process of gathering information and determining the elements of a job by observation and study. (p. 445)

job descriptions written statements of the primary duties of specific jobs. (pp. 165, 444)

job dimensions a group of duties, activities, and responsibilities that are part of the job. (p. 486)

job evaluation a process used to determine the relative value of jobs to an employer in order to determine more objectively the appropriate earnings for employees doing given jobs. (p. 469)

job involvement employees use a broad variety of skills and control the work content of their jobs. (p. 40)

job posting the procedure of placing announcements of available job openings on a bulletin board to give current employees a chance to bid on them. (p. 449)

job specification a statement of the personal characteristics required of a person to perform a described job. (p. 445)

just-in-time (JIT) inventory control materials arrive when they are needed in the production process. (p. 341)

L

labor relations or union management relations or industrial relations the relationship between an employer and unionized employees. (p. 512)

labor union an organization of workers banded together to achieve economic goals, especially increased wages and benefits, shorter working hours, improved working conditions, and both personal and job security. (p. 512)

lateral-diagonal communication communication that takes place between individuals in the same department or in different departments. (p. 196)

leader-controlled approach used at meetings of large groups in which the leader clearly runs the show and the open flow of information is impeded. (p. 393)

leadership influencing individual and group activities toward goal achievement. (p. 246)

Leadership Grid® categorizes leadership styles according to concern for people and concern for production results. (p. 250)

leading conducting, guiding, influencing, and motivating employees in the performance of their duties and responsibilities. (p. 11)

life event anything that causes a person to deviate from normal functioning. (p. 248)

life-cycle theory of leadership leadership behaviors should be based on the readiness level of employees. (p. 252)

line authority power to directly command or exact performance from others. (p. 144)

line organization each person has clearly defined responsibilities and reports to an immediate supervisor. A line organization is concerned with the primary functions of the firm. (p. 130)

line personnel carry out the primary activities of a business. (p. 143)

line-and-staff organization an organization structure to which staff departments have been added to serve the basic line departments and help them accomplish the organization objectives more effectively. (p. 132)

lockout a company's closing its premises to the employee and refusing to let them work. (p. 528)

M

maintenance-of-membership clause a statement in a union agreement which says that an employee who has joined the union must maintain that membership as a condition of employment. (p. 518)

major violations disciplinary problems that substantially interfere with orderly operations. (p. 495)

Malcolm Baldrige National Quality Award a symbol of America's best in quality. (p. 47)

malicious obedience a reaction in which an aggrieved employee follows instructions exactly, knowing that the order is faulty and will cause problems. (p. 493)

management working with people to achieve objectives by effective decision making and coordination of available resources. (p. 7)

management by exception a supervisor focuses on critical control needs and allows employees to handle most routine deviations from the standard. (p. 322)

management by objectives (MBO) process whereby superior and subordinate managers jointly set overall organizational goals, define each individual's area(s) of responsibility in terms of the results expected, and use those measures as guides for operating the unit and assessing the contributions of each of its members. (p. 78)

managerial functions broad classification of activities that all managers perform. (p. 10)

marketing selling and distributing an organization's product or service. (p. 6)

matrix departmentalization a hybrid type of departmentalization in which personnel from several specialties are brought together to complete limited-life tasks. (p. 136)

mediator an outside agent, provided by the Federal Mediation and Conciliation Service, who tries to bring the parties together when collective bargaining has reached an impasse. (p. 527)

mentoring the coaching activity that helps develop careers in others. (p. 369)

merit an employee's ability to do the job better than others; a basis for promotion. (p. 449)

message words and/or nonverbal expressions that transmit meaning. (p. 188)

middle management responsible for a substantial part of the organization. (p. 9)

middle of the road management places equal emphasis on people and production. (p. 250)

minor infractions violations of rules that do little harm or result in few serious consequences. (p. 495)

minutes a written record of the important points discussed and agreed on at a meeting. (p. 400)

mission defines the purpose the organization serves and identifies its services, products, and customers. (p. 73)

monetary standards standards expressed in dollars and cents. (p. 314)

motivation willingness to work to achieve the organization's objectives. (p. 221)

N

negative discipline an outside force or influence designed to change a person's behavior. (p. 493)

nonexempt employees employees covered by the provisions of the Fair Labor Standards Act. (p. 466)

norms rules of behavior developed by group members to provide guidance for group activities. (p. 287)

numerical standards standards expressed in numbers. (p. 314)

O

object signals nonverbal messages sent by physical objects. (p. 191)

objectives the purposes, goals, and desired results for the organization and its parts. (p. 73)

Occupational Safety and Health Administration (OSHA) created by the Occupational Safety and Health Act in 1970. (p. 351)

on-the-job training (OJT) training in which employees actually perform the work under the supervision and guidance of the supervisor or a trained worker or instructor. (p. 462)

operational planning consists of intermediate and short-term planning. (p. 74)

operations producing an organization's product or service. (p. 6)

opportunity a chance for development or advancement. (p. 105)

organization a group of people working together in a structured situation for a common objective. (p. 6)

organizational effectiveness the result of activities that improve the organization's structure, technology, and people. (p. 279)

organizing deciding what activities are needed to reach goals and dividing human resources into work groups to achieve them. (p. 11)

orientation procedures of familiarizing a new employee with the company surroundings, policies, and job responsibilities. (p. 460)

P

paired-comparison technique a variant of the employee comparison method of *performance appraisal* in which an employee is compared, in turn, to each of the other employees in the work group. (p. 486)

Pareto chart problem-analysis charts that use a *histogram* to illustrate the sources of problems. (p. 345)

parity principle when duties are assigned, adequate authority is delegated to those who must carry out the assignments. (p. 168)

partnering a variation of team building and strategic planning, initially designed to improve efficiency and effectiveness in large construction projects. (p. 290)

peer rating a traditional method of *performance appraisal* wherein each employee anonymously appraises the performance of the other members of the work group. (p. 483)

perception the process by which one selects, organizes, and gives meaning to his or her world. (p. 199)

performance appraisal or merit rating or efficiency rating or service rating or employee evaluation the process used to determine to what extent an employee is performing a job in the way it was intended to be done. (p. 480)

personality tests employment tests that are supposed to measure the applicant's emotional adjustment and attitude; often used to evaluate interpersonal relationships and to see how a person might fit into an organization. (p. 457)

Peter principle states that in a hierarchy, every employee rises to his or her level of incompetence. (p. 178)

physical resources items an organization requires for operations. (p. 7)

physical standards refer to quality, durability, size, weight. (p. 314)

physiological need the need for food, water, air, and other physical necessities. (p. 225)

picketing demonstrating dissatisfaction with one's employer by walking back and forth outside the place of employment, usually carrying a sign explaining the reasons for one's dissatisfaction. (p. 528)

pinpointing providing specific, tangible information about performance to an employee. (p. 374)

planning selecting future courses of action and deciding how to achieve the desired results. (p. 10)

policy provides consistency among decision makers. (p. 82)

positive discipline an inner force that promotes emotional satisfaction instead of emotional conflict. (p. 493)

prevailing wage rate a rate of pay set by the Secretary of Labor that approximates the union wage scale for the area in the given type of work. (p. 467)

principled negotiation negotiation on the merits. (p. 423)

proactive (planned) process of change management tries to change things by setting a new course rather than by correcting the current one. (p. 279)

proactive quality approach building quality into the process in advance rather than "inspecting it into" the system. (p. 49)

probe directing attention to a particular aspect of the speaker's message. (p. 209)

probing asking questions to obtain additional information. (p. 374)

problem an existing unsatisfactory situation causing anxiety or distress. (p. 105)

problem-solving meeting held to identify the problem, to discuss alternative solutions, and to decide on the proper action to take. (p. 392)

problem-solving quality approach emphasizes identification of defects while seeking a remedy to these problems through quality teams. (p. 49)

procedure steps to be performed when a particular course of action is taken. (p. 84)

process consultation a consultation model that involves others in making a joint diagnosis of the problem and eventually providing others with the skills and tools to make their own diagnoses. (p. 406)

product departmentalization a form of departmentalization that groups together all the functions associated with a single product line. (p. 136)

productivity a measure of efficiency in terms of inputs as compared to outputs. (p. 332)

program a large-scale plan composed of a mix of objectives, policies, rules, and projects. (p. 85)

Program Evaluation and Review Technique (PERT) shows relationships among a network of activities to determine the completion time of a project. (p. 86)

programmed decisions decisions that are routine and repetitive. (p. 105)

progressive discipline discipline that uses a *graduated scale of penalties*. (p. 499)

project a distinct part of a *program*. (p. 85)

promoting moving a person from a lower- to a higher-level job; usually involves an increase in pay as well as responsibilities. (p. 448)

punishment a negative treatment that a person receives after an undesirable act or omission. (p. 492)

Q

quality control defined measurements designed to check whether the desired quality standards are being met. (p. 342)

R

rate range a range of minimum and maximum wage rates for a given job, with employees paid at different rates, depending on how well they perform. (p. 466)

rating scale a point scale used in a traditional method of *performance appraisal* to rate an employee on a number of characteristics. (p. 484)

reactive process of change management tries to keep the organization on a stead course by solving problems as they come up. (p. 278)

readiness level the state of a persons drive or need for achievement. (p. 248)

receiver the ultimate destination of the sender's message. (p. 189)

reengineering a rethinking and redesign process to dramatically improve cost, quality, service, and speed. (pp. 25, 54, 150)

reflecting stating your interpretation of what the employee has said. (p. 374)

reflective statement the listener repeats, in a summarizing way, what the speaker has just said. (p. 209)

reframing emphasizing management training and development programs. (p. 176)

reinforcement theory based on the law of effect, it holds that behaviors that meet with pleasant consequences tend to be repeated, whereas behaviors that meet with unpleasant consequences tend not to be repeated, and rewards and punishment are used as a way to shape the individual's behavior. (p. 234)

reinvention organizations dramatically changing themselves in such elements as size, organizational structure, and markets. (p. 25)

relationship behaviors leadership behaviors such as providing people with support, giving them positive feedback, and asking for their opinions and ideas. (p. 252)

reliability the probability that the results of a test will be the same if it is given to the same person by different individuals. (p. 458)

resourcing providing information, assistance, and advice to employees. (p. 374)

responsibility the obligation of an employee to accept a manager's delegated authority. (p. 8)

reviewing reinforcing key points at the end of a coaching session to ensure common understanding. (p. 374)

right-to-work laws state laws giving employees the right to join or refuse to join a union without being fired. (p. 518)

risk the possibility of defeat, disadvantage, injury, or loss. (p. 109)

robot a machine that is controlled by a computer. (p. 341)

roles parts played by managers in the performance of their functions. (p. 12)

run chart a data presentation that shows the results of a process plotted over time. (p. 345)

S

safety need the need for protection from danger, threat, or deprivation. (p. 225)

satisfier factors factors that employees said turned them on, such as recognition, advancement, achievement, challenging work, and being ones own boss. (p. 228)

self-fulfillment need needs concerned with the realization of one's potential, self-development, and creativity. (p. 226)

self-managed (autonomous) work teams teams that control many management aspects of their work, including scheduling, task assignments, and evaluation. (pp. 41, 295)

sender the person who originates and sends a message. (p. 188)

seniority an employee's length of service in a company; a basis for promotion. (pp. 449, 531)

servant leadership defines success as giving and measures achievement by devotion to serving and leading. (p. 262)

sexual harassment unwelcome sexual advances and requests for sexual favors or other physical or verbal conduct, by a member of either sex, when such actions interfere with an employee's work performance or create a hostile, offensive, or intimidating work environment. (p. 498)

"Siamese twins" of management planning and controlling, so called because planning is such an integral part of controlling. (p. 70)

single rate a compensation plan under which everyone who performs the same job is paid the same wage, regardless of level of performance. (p. 465)

single-use plans developed to accomplish a specific purpose and then discarded after use. (p. 85)

social need the need for belonging, acceptance by colleagues, friendship, and love. (p. 225)

space signals nonverbal messages sent based on physical distance from one another. (p. 191)

span of control principle states that there is a limit to the number of people a person can supervise effectively. (p. 140)

span of management the number of immediate employees a manager can supervise effectively. (p. 102)

staff personnel have the expertise to assist line people and aid top management. (p. 143)

staffing recruiting, training, promoting, rewarding people to do the organization's work. (p. 11)

standard a unit of measurement that can serve as a reference point for evaluating results. (p. 313)

standing plans or repeat-use plans plans that are used repeatedly over a period of time. (p. 80)

stereotyping the tendency to put similar things in the same categories to make them easier to deal with. (p. 200)

strategic control point a performance-measurement point located early in an activity to allow any corrective action to be taken. (p. 317)

strategic planning has longer time horizons, affects the entire organization, and deals with its interface to its external environment. (p. 72)

strategies the activities by which the organization adapts to its environment in order to achieve its objectives. (p. 74)

stress any external stimulus that causes wear and tear on one's psychological or physical well-being. (p. 426)

strike a situation that occurs when employees withhold their services from an employer in order to get something. (p. 528)

structured interviews employment interviews that are standardized and controlled with regard to questions asked, sequence of questions, interpretation of replies, and weight given to factors considered in making the value judgment as to whether or not to hire the applicant. (p. 459)

structuring and telling style   used with individuals or groups that are relatively less ready for a given task. (p. 254)

suggestion involvement   employees are actively encouraged to make suggestions to improve aspects of their work. (p. 39)

summarizing   pausing in the coaching conversation to summarize key points. (p. 374)

supervisory management   controls operations of smaller organizational units. (p. 9)

synergy   the concept that two or more people working together in a cooperative, coordinated way can accomplish more than the sum of their independent efforts. (p. 281)

T

tangible standards   clear, concrete, specific, and generally measurable. (p. 313)

task behaviors   clarifying a job, telling people what to do and how and when to do it, providing follow-up, and taking corrective action. (p. 252)

team advisors   share responsibility with the team for cost, quality, and prompt delivery of products. (p. 23)

team management   high concern for both people and production. (p. 252)

technical skills   understanding and being able to supervise effectively the specific processes required. (p. 16)

termination-at-will rule   the legal standard that states that an employer has a right to dismiss an employee for any reason, or without giving a reason, unless there is an explicit contractual provision preventing it. (p. 503)

Theory X   the average person has an inherent dislike of work and wishes to avoid responsibility. (p. 247)

Theory Y   work is as natural as play or rest. (p. 247)

thinking decision process   focuses predominantly on analysis, logic, and objectivity to solve problems. (p. 110)

time management   ability to use one's time to get things done when they should be done. (p. 87)

time signals   nonverbal messages sent by time actions. (p. 191)

time standards   expressed in terms of time. (p. 314)

time wages or day work   a compensation method in which an employee is paid for the amount of time spent on the job, regardless of output during that period of time. (p. 466)

top management   responsible for a major segment of the organization. (p. 8)

total quality approach (TQM)   reflects a major reorganization to achieve customer satisfaction through continuous improvement of products or services. (p. 49)

touching signals   nonverbal messages sent by body contact. (p. 191)

traditional quality approach   emphasizes quality assurance, quality control, or statistical quality control techniques based on random sampling. (p. 49)

transactional leadership   leaders identify desired performance standards and recognize what types of rewards employees want from their work. (p. 260)

transferring   moving employees to a different job at the same organizational level, involving a change in duties and responsibilities, with or without a change in pay. (p. 448)

transformational leadership   converts followers into leaders and may convert leaders into moral agents. (p. 260)

tutoring   the coaching situation that helps a team member gain knowledge, skill, and competency. (p. 369)

Type A behavior   a behavior pattern characterized by (a) trying to accomplish too much in a short time and (b) lacking patience and struggling against time and other people to accomplish one's ends. (p. 430)

Type B behavior   a behavior pattern characterized by (a) tending to be calmer than someone with Type A behavior, (b) devoting more time to exercise, and (c) being more realistic in estimating the time it takes to complete an assignment. (p. 431)

U

unfair labor practices   specific acts that management may not commit against the workers and the union, as defined by the National Labor Relations Act (Wagner Act). (p. 517)

unified planning   coordination of departments to ensure harmony rather than conflict or competition. (p. 77)

union authorization card   a card to be signed by an employee, authorizing a particular union to be his or her collective bargaining representative. (p. 521)

union shop   an agreement under which all employees must join the union within a specified period—usually 30 days—or be fired; compare to *agency shop, closed shop*. (p. 517)

union steward   a union member elected by other members to represent their interests to management. (pp. 21, 530)

unity of command principle   states that everyone should report to and be accountable to only one boss. (p. 138)

unprogrammed decisions   decisions that occur infrequently and require a separate response each time. (p. 105)

upgrading retraining unskilled or semiskilled workers to meet the changing demands of their present positions. (p. 448)

upward communication flows from lower to upper organizational levels. (p. 193)

V

validity a high positive correlation between the applicant's test scores and some identifiable, objective measure of performance on the job. (p. 458)

vocational interest tests employment tests designed to determine the applicant's areas of major work interest. (p. 457)

vocational rehabilitation programs programs that provide counseling, medical care, and vocational training for physically and mentally handicapped individuals. (p. 463)

vocational-technical education programs programs in which vocational-technical schools, business schools, and junior colleges conduct regular or special training classes. (p. 463)

voice signals signals sent by placing emphasis on certain words, pauses, or the tone of voice used. (p. 190)

W

wagon wheel an organization form in which figuratively there is a hub, a series of spokes radiating from the hub, and the outer rim. (p. 153)

work sampling or work preview a form of achievement or proficiency test in which the prospective employee must perform a task that is representative of the work usually done on the job. (p. 457)

Index of Web Addresses

http://academy.umd.edu, 265
http://monster.com/, 449
http://stats.bls.gov/cpihome.htm, 467
http://stats.bls.gov/news.release/union2.toc.htm, 515
http://transit-safety.volpe.dot.gov/, 457
http://workhealth.org/risk/rfotypea.htm, 427
http://www.3m.com/about3M/index.html, 289
http://www.aflcio.org/home.htm, 513
http://www.albertsons.com, 305
http://www.alltel.com/careers/careerpath/careerpath
    .shtml, 444
http://www.amazon.com, 74
http://www.americawest.com/, 37
http://www.benjerry.com/mission.html, 74
http://www.bmpcoe.org/bestpractices, 51
http://www.boeing.com/, 137
http://www.cargillfoods.com, 313
http://www.cat.com, 516
http://www.centerpoint.org/EAP.html, 375
http://www.cognex.com/, 483
http://www.cri.cc/, 417
http://www.cwa-union.org/, 522
http://www.daimlerchrysler.com/, 200
http://www.dell.com/corporate/vision/index.htm, 73
http://www.dol.gov/, 22
http://www.dol.gov/dol/esa/public/ofcp_org.htm, 453
http://www.eeoc.gov/, 445, 481
http://www.fambiz.com/, 90
http://www.frito-lay.com/, 222
http://www.ge.com, 165
http://www.generalmotors.com/company/
    community_involvement/diversity, 23
http://www.gpo.gov/usbudget/, 85
http://www.greenleaf.org, 264
http://www.honda2000.com/index.html, 204
http://www.hotmail.com, 190
http://www.hp.com, 235
http://www.ilr.cornell.edu/library/e_archive/
    glassceiling/, 22
http://www.internationalpaper.com, 259
http://www.inventorymanagement.com, 336
http://www.iso.ch/9000e/9k14ke.htm, 43
http://www.jci.com, 307
http://www.kraftfoods.com, 109
http://www.magnet.state.ma.us/mhd/, 162
http://www.manpower.com/, 450
http://www.mars.com/, 189

http://www.mentoring.org/, 365
http://www.merck.com, 327
http://www.nist.gov, 309
http://www.nlrb.gov/, 517
http://www.omnimgmt.com/, 367
http://www.osha.gov, 347
http://www.petersons.com/, 461
http://www.pfdf.org/, 36
http://www.pillsbury.com/, 109
http://www.quality.nist.gov/, 47, 337
http://www.reengineering.com/, 25
http://www.ritzcarlton.com/, 273
http://www.saksincorporated.com/employment.html, 442
http://www.saturn.com, 39, 167, 285
http://www.southwest.com/, 226
http://www.stanford.edu/group/decisions/, 106
http://www.stress.org/, 421
http://www.sun.com/aboutsun/ehs/ehs-workplace_health
    .html, 471
http://www.taci-hvac.com/frrbotto.htm, 249
http://www.teco.net/TampaElectric.html, 493
http://www.ti.com/mc/docs/tiris, 321
http://www.toyota.com/, 147
http://www.toyota.com/times/manu/index.html, 343
http://www.tvo.org/pdonline/forpincipals/brainstorm
    .html, 394
http://www.tvo.org/pdonline/forprincipals/delegate
    .html, 168
http://www.tvo.org/pdonline/forprincipals/meeting
    .html, 390
http://www.tvo.org/pdonline/forprincipals/norms.html, 283
http://www.tvo.org/pdonline/forprincipals/
    performancereview.html, 486
http://www.tvo.org/pdonline/forprincipals/
    problemsolving.html, 388
http://www.uaw.org/, 516
http://www.ups.com, 321
http://www.us.kpmg.com/ethics/dilema.html, 113
http://www.usace.army.mil/, 290
http://www.usdoj.gov/crt/ada/adahom1.htm, 504
http://www.wcom.com, 151
http://www.wendys.com, 261
http://www.whirlpoolcorp.com/whr/ics/story/value
    .html, 73
http://www.workteamcoaching.com/books.htm, 368
http://www.xerox.com, 150
http://www2.ford.com, 151

Subject Index

A

Accommodating, 417
Accountability
  def., 166
  requiring, 166
Achievement, proficiency, or
  skill tests, def., 457
Acknowledging, def., 369
Action plan, illus., 177
Active listening
  def., 209
  techniques, 209
Adjustments, cost-of-living
  (COLAs), 467
Administration of labor
  laws, 520
Administrative skills, def.,
  15
Advisors, team, 23
Advisory authority, def., 143
Affirmative action (AA), legal influences on, illus.,
  451–452
Affirmative action programs
  (AAPs), def., 451, 481
Affirming, def., 369
Age Discrimination in Em-
  ployment Act, 467
Agency shop, def., 518
Agent, exclusive bargaining,
  524
Agreement or contract
  def., 528
  living with, 529
  reaching an, 528
  supervisors' rights under,
  530
Alternative(s)
  collect, interpret, and
  evaluate information
  about each, 107
  def., 107
  develop, 107
  evaluating, illus., 108
  select the preferred, 107
American Federal of Labor
  (AFL), 513, 514

Americans with Disabilities
  Act, 466, 467
Analysis, cost/benefit, 109
Anchors, def., 486
Appeals used by union or-
  ganizers, 524
Applicants, topics to avoid
  when interviewing,
  illus., 453
Application form, 456
Appraisal
  barriers to effective, 487
  by results, 486
  performance, 480
Appraisal form, typical rating scale, illus., 485
Appraisal interview
  def., 489
  hints for, illus., 491
  role of, 489
Appraisers bias(es), def., 487
Apprenticeship training,
  def., 462
Approach
  group-centered, 390
  interaction in the group-
  centered, illus., 391
  leader-controlled, 389
  to managing quality, 49
  used at meetings, 389
  which should you use,
  392
Aptitude tests, def., 457
Arbitrator, def., 527
Assigning responsibility, 165
Assistants
  John Moody hires, illus.,
  129
  organization with assistants added (stage 2),
  128
Associations, employee, 515
Attending, def., 369
Attitude, "follow the
  leader," 118
Authority
  advisory, 143
  and status, 198

compliance, def., 250
def., 8
delegation of, 164–165
functional, 145
granting, 165
line, 144
of ideas, 143
of position, 116
Authorization card
  example of a representation, illus., 522
  union, 520

B

Bargaining, collective, 467
Barriers
  interpersonal and lan-
  guage, 199
  minimize status, 203
  organizational, 198
  to effective appraisals, 487
Barriers to effective supervisory communication,
  198
  interpersonal, illus., 200
Basic and developmental facilitation, illus., 401
Basic labor laws, 517
Basic laws governing labor
  relations, illus., 518
Behavior
  as a group member, evaluating, illus., 289
  at meetings, suggestions
  for handling disruptive
  and inappropriate,
  illus., 397–398
  continuum of leadership,
  254
  illus., 255
  coping with difficult,
  illus., 422
  discipline as orderly, 491
  improving ethical and
  social, 26
  relationship, 252
  task, 252
  Type A, 426

Type B, 427
  type quiz, illus., 428
Behaviorally anchored rating scales (BARS)
  def., 486
  example of, illus., 488
  using, 486
Belonging needs, 225
Benchmarking, def., 54
Benefit plans, flexcomp or
  cafeteria, 472
Benefits
  employee, 470
  flexible, 472
  legally required, 470
  of downsizing, 148
  providing employee, 470
  voluntary, 471
Bill of rights, employees',
  519
Biological needs, 225
Blanchard and Peale's
  "Ethics Check," illus.,
  113
Body signals, def., 190
Budget, def., 85
Burnout
  def., 427
  MBI subscales and phases
  of, illus., 429
Business Week, 42

C

Cafeteria benefit plans, flexcomp or, 472
Cause-and-effect diagram
  def., 342
  for "why tables are not
  cleared quickly," illus.,
  344
Causes of conflict, 416
Central tendency, def., 489
Centralization, decentralization versus, 146
Centralized versus a decentralized structure, layers of management re-
  flecting, illus., 147

Certification, ISO 9000: standards for, illus., 44
Change
 different responses to, illus., 280
 external and internal forces, illus., 277
 forces causing, 276
 managing organizational, 276
 proactive (planned), process of, 279
 reactive process of, 278
 results of ignoring, 278
 ways of dealing with, 278
Channel, def., 188
Charismatic leadership, 260
Charlotte Observer, 51
Civil Rights Act, 451, 466, 467
Climate, setting the proper, 202
Closed shop, def., 517
Closure
 def., 398
 on items discussed, 398
Coaching
 and selling style, def., 254
 and understanding diversity, 367
 current emphasis on, 364
 def., 362
 for improved performance: confronting and challenging, 370
 introduction to, 362
 is performance-linked, 362
 performance-linked, illus., 363
 situations, examples of, illus., 363
 skills of, 368
 the core skills, 369
 the counseling function, 372
 why supervisors reject, 364
Coaching functions, 365
 outcomes of the four, illus., 368
Codes of ethics, 112
Collaborating, 417
Collective bargaining, 467
 def., 527
 engaging in, 527
Command principle
 unity of, 138
 violating the unity of, illus., 140
Command, unity of, 138

Common vision, shaping, 258
Communication, 188
 barriers to effective supervisory, 198
 downward, 191
 electronic technology, 189
 encourage two-way, 396
 examples of planned, 204
 flows of, 191
 improving supervisory, 202
 in an organization, flow of formal, illus., 192
 informal, 197
 interpersonal barriers to effective supervisory, illus., 200
 lateral-diagonal, 196
 living with informal, 197
 plan for effective, 204
 purposes served by informal, 197
 upward, 193
 vertical flows: downward and upward, 191
 you like to receive from your supervisor, illus., 193
Communication matrix, managerial, 194
 illus., 195
Communication process model
 def., 188
 illus., 189
Comparable wage rates, 467
Comparable worth or pay equity, def., 468
Compensating employees, 464
Compensation
 importance of, 464
 roles played by, 464
 workers', 470
Complaint procedures in nonunionized organizations, 532
Complaints, handling employee, 531
Components of a typical job description and job specification, illus., 445
Compromising, 417
Computer-assisted manufacturing (CAM), def., 337
Conceptual skills, def., 13
Concurrent controls, def., 309
Conduct, establishing rules of, 498

Confirming, def., 369
Conflict management styles, 416
 interpersonal, illus., 417
Conflict resolution, three-step program for, illus., 421
Conflicts
 between line and staff, 143
 illus., 144
 causes of, 416
 overcoming interpersonal, 419
 using principled negotiation to resolve, 419
Confronting and challenging, 370
 def., 366
 performance-related behavior, general vs. pinpointed statement in, illus., 371
Congress of Industrial Organizations (CIO), 514
Consensus
 achieving, 388
 def., 388
Constructive criticism, def., 494
Consultation, process, 400, 402
Consumer price index (CPI), 467
Consumer Reports, 45
Contingency planning
 anticipates problems, 72
 def., 72
Continuous improvement, 51
 teams work in all sectors, illus., 53
Continuum of leadership behavior
 def., 254
 illus., 255
 Tannenbaum and Schmidt's, 254
Contract, agreement or, 528
Control(s), 306
 at the top, narrower span of, 140
 availability of, 147
 concurrent, 309
 delegating improves, 164
 different approaches to a supervisor's span of, 141
 examples of, 307
 factors contributing to a narrow or wide span of, illus., 142

feedback, 309
feedforward, 308
 impact of technology on, 320
 importance of, 307
 just-in-time inventory (JIT), 337
 must be cost effective, 308
 narrow, wide, and very wide, spans of, illus., 141
 need to focus on appropriate activities, 307
 process of, illus., 310
 quality, 338
 sense of, 430
 should be accepted by people they affect, 308
 should be accurate and concise, 308
 should be timely, 307
 some common examples of supervisory, illus., 308
 span of, 140
 tendency toward wider spans of, 142
 tips for establishing preventive, illus., 309
Control chart
 def., 342
 example of, illus., 345
Control point, strategic, 313
 illus., 314
Control principle, span of, 140
Control process
 setting strategic control points in, illus., 314
 steps in, 309
Control systems
 characteristics of effective, 307
 types of, 308
Control's close links to planning, 306
Controlled-substance abuser, profile of the typical, illus., 375
Controlling, 306
 def., 12
 intangible standards, illus., 312
 planning is most closely related to, 70
 process, 312, 316, 317
Controlling quality, 338
 involve workers in achieving and, 345
 some tools for, 339
 understanding variance

in, 338
Core leadership functions,
    264
Core skills
    coaching the, 369
    for the effective facilitator,
        illus., 400
Cost control
    improving productivity
        and, 328
    supervisor's role in, 335
Cost/benefit analysis, def.,
    109
Cost-of-living adjustments
    (COLAs), def., 467
Counseling
    def., 367
    iceberg model, illus., 373
    role of EAPs, 375
Counseling, areas of em-
        ployee, 373
    job performance, 373
    personal problems, 374
    physical and emotional
        illness, 374
Counseling function, coach-
        ing, 372
Country club management,
    def., 250
Craft unions, def., 513
Critical path, def., 87
Criticism, constructive, 494
Customer focus, 50
Cycle, nonplanner's, illus.,
    71

D

Daily time log, illus., 89
Davis-Bacon Act, 466, 467
Day work, time wages or,
    466
Decentralization
    def., 146
    factors affecting, 146
    on organizational struc-
        ture, effect of, 147
    versus centralization, 146
Decentralized structure, lay-
        ers of management re-
        flecting a centralized
        versus, illus., 147
Decision maker, thinking-or
        feeling-oriented, illus.,
        111
Decision making, 102
    advantages and disadvan-
        tages of each approach,
        114
    advantages and disadvan-
        tages of group, illus.,
        115

and problem solving re-
        late, how, 105
    approaches to, 114
    bases of, 116
    both feeling and thinking
        should be used, 110
    def., 103
    elements involved in, 103
    ethical considerations
        play a part, 112
    factors to keep in mind,
        109
    heart of supervisory man-
        agement, 100
    improves with practice, 111
    improving, 116
    in supervisory manage-
        ment, role of, 100
    individual and group, 114
    involves more than one
        alternative, 104
    is a conscious process, 103
    is the heart of supervisory
        management, illus., 101
    process, illus., 104
    role of supervisor and
        work group in, illus.,
        114
    seldom only one accept-
        able choice, 110
    steps in, illus., 106
    takes considerable time
        and effort, effective, 111
Decision process
    feeling, 110
    thinking, 110
Decisions, 106
    follow up on decisions
        made, 399
    implement (step 5), 109
    involve the future, 103
    may not be needed, 103
    may not please everyone,
        112
    may water down, 393
    programmed, 105
    right person should
        make, 109
    should contribute to ob-
        jectives, 110
    starts a chain reaction, 112
    step 1: define the idea or
        problem, 106
    step 2: develop alterna-
        tives, 107
    step 3: collect, interpret,
        and evaluate informa-
        tion about each alterna-
        tive, 107
    step 4: select the preferred
        alternative, 107

step 5: implement the de-
        cision, 109
    step 6: follow up, evalu-
        ate, and make
        changes—if needed,
        109
    types of decisions to be
        made104
    unprogrammed, 105
    why supervisors need to
        make so many, 100
Decreasing input, 330, 331
Defining productivity, 328
Delegate, 162
    knowing when to, 168
    why supervisors fail to,
        172
Delegating
    allows a supervisor to do
        other things, 163
    allows more work to be
        accomplished, 163
    develops people, 162
    improves control, 164
    style, def., 254
Delegation
    a solution for ineffective,
        176
    effective, 167
    parties involved in effec-
        tive, 171
    relating to success or fail-
        ure, 175
    steps in effective, illus., 170
    time required for effec-
        tive, 170
Delegation of authority, def.,
    164–165
Delegation process, 164
    effective, illus., 169
    how the process operates,
        168
    three aspects of, illus., 164
Delineating authority, how
        to avoid excessive line-
        staff conflict, 143
Deming's 85-15 rule, def., 45
Deming's fourteen points
    for quality, illus., 46
Departmentalization
    at the top-management
        level, functional, illus.,
        136
    def., 134
    functional, 135
    matrix, 136
        illus., 137
    product, 136
Desk-chair arrangements
    that affect formality,
        illus., 203

Developmental leadership,
        def., 256–257
Developmental managers,
    257
Diagram, cause-and-effect,
    342
    illus., 344
Different approaches to a
        supervisor's span of
        control, 141
Differing perceptions, 199
Difficult behavior, coping
        with, illus., 422
Dilemmas, ethical, 26
Discharge, 499, 503
Disciplinary due process op-
        erates, how, 498
Disciplinary layoff or sus-
        pension, def., 503
Disciplinary problems, types
        of, 494
Disciplinary procedures us-
        ing graduated penal-
        ties, example of, illus.,
        496
Disciplinary role, supervi-
        sor's, 500
Discipline, 491
    applying, 503
    as due process, 494
    as orderly behavior, 491
    as punishment, 492
    as self-control, 491
    carries a clear warning,
        501
    def., 491
    is consistent, 502
    is immediate, 502
    is impersonal, 503
    need for, 490
    negative, 493
    positive, 493
    progressive, 499
    supervisor and, 500
    the hot-stove rule, princi-
        ples of effective, 500
Disciplining employees, su-
        pervisor's personal lia-
        bility for, 504
Disequilibrium, equilibrium
        and, illus., 423
Dissatisfier or hygiene fac-
        tors, def., 228
    Herzberg's satisfier/moti-
        vator and, illus., 229
Distant drum, illus., 264
Diversity
    coaching and understand-
        ing, 367
    def., 22
Doctor-patient model, 401

Downsizing
 benefits of, 148
 costs of, 149
 def., 25, 148
 ways to get beyond, 149
Downward communication
 and upward communica-
  tion, vertical flows, 191
 def., 191
Dual promotion ladders,
 def., 449
Due process
 def., 494
 discipline as, 494
 how disciplinary due
  process operates, 498

E

Early union activities, 513
Economic gains, 527
EEO/AA laws, 466
Efficiency rating, 480
Ego or esteem needs, def., 226
Electronic communication
 technology, 189
E-mail, def., 190
Emphasizing team perform-
 ance, 23
Employee Assistance Pro-
 gram (EAP)
 def., 375
 example of, 376
 in counseling, role of, 375
Employee associations, def.,
 515
Employee benefits
 def., 470
 providing, 470
Employee comparison
 method, def., 486
Employee complaints, han-
 dling, 531
Employee counseling, areas
 of, 373
 job performance, 373
 personal problems, 374
 physical and emotional
  illness, 374
Employee evaluation, 480
Employee involvement, 55
 characteristics of effective
  teams, illus., 346
Employee safety, promoting,
 347
Employee with the primary
 responsibility, supervi-
 sor "placing the mon-
 key back" on, illus., 173
Employee, example of a
 written report about,
 illus., 315

Employee's qualities, 480
Employees
 compensating, 464
 dealing with ineffective,
  174
 exempt, 466
 five steps to motivating,
  235
 how to train, 461
 immediate supervisor rating, 483
 methods of obtaining
  from within, , 447
 nonexempt, 466
 organizing, 520
 rating supervisors, 483
 rating themselves, 482
 responsibility for selecting, training, and com-
  pensating, 443
 rights of, illus., 519
 selecting for specific jobs,
  454
 supervisor's personal liability for disciplining,
  504
 supervisors' reluctance to
  appraise, 487
 to whom authority is delegated, role of, 172
 training and developing,
  461
 types and number of
  needed, , 444
 where to look for, illus.,
  447
Employees' bill of rights,
 def., 519
Employees' exclusive bar-
 gaining agent, becom-
 ing recognized as, 524
Employees' jobs interesting,
 help to make, 236
Employees' performance efforts, support, 237
Employees' performance,
 reward, 237
Employers
 ability to pay, 468
 unfair labor practices of,
  illus., 520
Empowerment
 def., 23, 37
 full, 41
 levels of, 39
 illus., 40
 role of the supervisor in,
  56
 through job involvement,
  illus., 38
Environment, relaxed, 206

Environmental factors, 350
Equal employment opportu-
 nity (EEO) laws, 451
 complying with, 451
 enforcement of, 451
 legal influences on, illus.,
  451–452
Equal Employment Oppor-
 tunity Commission
 (EEOC), 451, 481
Equal Pay Act, 466, 467
Equilibrium and disequilibrium, illus., 423
Equity theory of motivation,
 465
Esteem needs, 226
Ethical behavior, improving,
 26
Ethical considerations play a
 part, 112
Ethical dilemmas, def., 26
Ethics
 check, Blanchard and
  Peale's, illus., 113
 codes of, 112
 def., 112
Exclusive bargaining agent
 becoming recognized as
  the employees', 524
 def., 524
Executive Order 11246, 451
Exempt employees, def., 466
Expectancy theory
 applying, illus., 232
 def., 230
 illus., 231
 of motivation, 465
Expectations, clarifying
 your, 396
Experience, 116
Experience rating, def., 470
Experiential learning, def.,
 163
External change forces, def.,
 illus., 277
External relationships, 22
External sources, reasons for
 using, 450
Extrinsic motivation
 def., 223
 link to intrinsic and, 229

F

Facilitation
 basic and developmental,
  illus., 401
 group, 399
Facilitators, 138
 core skills for the effective, illus., 400
 role of, 399

Fact-finding, 387
Fact-finding meeting, def.,
 387
Factors
 affecting choice of leadership style, illus., 247
 affecting decentralization,
  146
 affecting leadership style,
  246
 affecting wage rates, 466
 contributing to a narrow
  or wide span of con-
  trol, illus., 142
 dissatisfier or hygiene, 228
 environmental, 350
 governmental, 466
 human, 350
 influencing safety, 347
 language-related, 200
 organizational and work-
  related, 427
 satisfier or motivator, 228
 technical, 350
 to consider after the meeting, 399
 to consider before the
  meeting, 394
 to consider during the
  meeting, 395
 to keep in mind when
  making decisions, 109
Facts, 116
 intuition or, illus., 117
Failure
 eight ways to guarantee
  on the job, illus., 175
 relating delegation to, 175
Fair Labor Standards Act,
 466, 467
Family and medical leave,
 470
Feedback
 controls, def., 309
 def., 189
 encourage the use of, 206
 provide timely perform-
  ance, 237
 tips about, illus., 207
Feedforward controls, def.,
 308–309
Feeling decision process,
 def., 110
Filling jobs from within, 446
Financial resources, def., 7
Financing, def., 6
Flexcomp or cafeteria benefit plans, def., 472
Flexible benefits, 472
Flows of communication,
 191

"Follow the leader" attitude, 118
Forbes, 42
Forces causing change, 276
Forces, external and internal change, illus., 277
Formal appraisals, 483
Formal groups, def., 281
Formality, desk-chair arrangement that affect, illus., 203
Fortune, 42
Frame of reference, the receiver's, 205
Full empowerment, def., 41
Functional approach, advantages and disadvantages of, 135
Functional authority, def., 145
Functional departmentalization
    at the top-management level, illus., 136
    def., 135
Functions, 365
    coaching, 365
    how they are related, 12
    managerial, 10
    performed by managers, 10
Fundamentals, other listening, 210

G

Gantt chart
    def., 85
    example showing activities needed in production start-up, illus., 86
Geographic locations, 147
Glass ceiling, def., 22
Global challenges, meeting, 25
Goal, 74
Goal-setting theory, def., 233
Government, 333
Governmental factors, 466
Graduated scale of penalties, def., 499
Granting authority, 165
Grapevine, def., 197
Grievance procedure
    def., 531
    in a unionized organization, typical, illus., 531
Group(s)
    a manager's membership in different, illus., 282
    advantages of, 283
    cohesiveness, def., 287

def., 281
diffuse responsibility, 285
encourage social loafing, 285
evaluating your behavior as a member, illus., 289
evaluating, 283
facilitation, def., 399
formal, 281
how they develop, 282
importance of work, 281
influencing productivity, illus., 333
informal, 281
limitations of, 284
may be less effective than individuals, 285
may function more effectively than individuals, 284
member composition and roles, 287
possible effects of size on, illus., 286
provide opportunities for need satisfaction, 283
size, 286
stages of development, 283
task and maintenance roles in, illus., 288
types of, 281
Group decision making
    advantages and disadvantages of, illus., 115
    individual and, 114
Group effectiveness, 285
    model of, illus., 285
Group-centered approach
    def., 390
    interaction in, illus., 391
Guidelines on Discrimination Because of Sex, 498

H

Halo effect, def., 489
Harassment, sexual, 498
Health and insurance protection, 471
Heroic management approach, self-fulfilling consequences of using, illus., 258
Heroic managers, def., 257
Hersey and Blanchard's situational leadership, 252
Hersey-Blanchard Situational Leadership® Model, illus., 253
Herzberg's satisfier/motivator and dissatisfier/hy-

giene factors, illus., 229
Herzberg's theory, 228
    qualifying, 230
Hierarchy, levels of, 198
Hierarchy of needs
    def., 225
    Maslow's theory, 224
    illus., 225
Hierarchy of objectives
    def., 75–76
    for Computronix, illus., 76
Higher management, role of, 171
Hints for the appraisal interview, illus., 491
Histogram
    def., 341
    illus., 341
Horizontal organization, def., 151
Horn effect, def., 489
Hotels Magazine, 274
Hot-stove rule
    def., 500
    illus., 501
Human behavior, some fundamentals of understanding, 221
Human factors, 350
Human relations skills, def., 15
Human resources
    def., 7
    planning needs, 444
    sample requisition, illus., 456
Hybrid organization chart, illus., 152
Hygiene factors, 228

I

"I" message, def., 371–372
Ideas, authority of, 143
Illness, physical and emotional, 374
Impoverished management, def., 250
Improvement, continuous, 51
Improving productivity and cost control, 328
In Search of Excellence, 50, 148, 171
Incentive wages or performance pay, def., 466
Income, retirement, 471
Increasing output, 330, 331
Individual
    and group decision making, 114

may be less effective than groups, 285
may function more effectively than groups, 284
workers, 334
Individual skills, developing, 258
Individualized consideration, 261
Industrial relations, 512
Industrial unions, def., 514
Industry
    adjusting to shifts, 24
    occupational injury and illness rates, illus., 350
    type of, 349
Industry Week, 42
Ineffective employees, dealing with, 174
Informal communication
    def., 197
    living with, 197
    purposes served by, 197
Informal groups, def., 281
Information
    ensure consistency of, 392
    giving, 387
    permit formal exchange of, 393
Information exchange, 387
    meeting, def., 387
Information-giving meeting, def., 387
Infractions, minor, 495
Initiative, taking the, 206
Input, decreasing, 330, 331
Insurance protection, health and, 471
Insurance, unemployment, 470
Intangible standards
    controlling, illus., 312
    def., 310
Intellectual stimulation, 261
Interaction in the leader-controlled approach, illus., 390
Interference running, 526
Intermediaries, def., 18
Internal change forces, def., illus., 277
Internal sources, reasons for and against using, 446
International Paper's turn-around artist Bob Goins, illus., 259
Internship training, def., 463
Interpersonal barriers, 199
    to effective supervisory communication, illus., 200

Interpersonal conflict
management styles, illus., 417
overcoming, 419
Interpersonal relationships, developing and maintaining good, 432
Interview
appraisal, 489
hints for the appraisal, illus., 491
role of the appraisal, 489
structured, 459
Interviewing applicants, topics to avoid when, illus., 453
Interviewing, preemployment, 458
Intolerable offenses, def., 497
Intrinsic motivation
and extrinsic motivation, link to, 229
def., 223
Intuition or facts, def., illus., 117
Inventory control, just-in-time (JIT), 337
Inverted pyramid
def., 153
Nordstrom's, illus., 154
Investigation, personal injury, illus., 351
Involvement
employee, 55
empowerment through job, illus., 38
job, 40
suggestion, 39
IQ tests, def., 457
ISO 9000
def., 43
standards for certification, illus., 44

J

Job analysis, def., 445
Job description(s)
components of a typical, illus., 445
def., 444, 165
for a production supervisor, illus., 167
Job dimensions, def., 486
Job evaluation
def., 469
procedure, steps in, illus., 469
to set job rates, using, 469
Job involvement
def., 40

empowerment through, illus., 38
Job offer, 460
Job performance, 373
Job posting, def., 449
Job protection, 524
Job rates, using job evaluation to set, 469
Job specification
components of a typical, illus., 445
def., 445
illus., 446
Jobs
filling from the outside, 450
filling from within, 446
of "comparable worth" receive comparable pay, illus., 468
selecting employees for specific, 454
Joint target setting, 486
Just-in-time inventory control (JIT), def., 337

K

Kaizen, 51
Key ideas, using repetition to reinforce, 205

L

Labor force, membership of national unions as a percentage of the total, illus., 514
Labor laws
administration of, 520
basic, 517
Labor practices, unfair, 517
Labor relations
basic laws governing, illus., 518
laws governing, 517
or union-management relations or industrial relations, def., 512
Labor union, def., 512
Labor-Management Relations Act, 518
Landrum-Griffin Act, 519
Language barriers, interpersonal and, 199
Language-related factors, 200
Lateral-diagonal communication, def., 196
Lateral-diagonal flows, 196
Laws
governing labor relations, 517

Murphy's, illus., 307
right-to-work, 518
Layers of management reflecting a centralized versus a decentralized structure, illus., 147
Leader-controlled approach
def., 389
interaction in, illus., 390
Leadership, 246
approaches, contrasting, illus., 262
characteristics of servant, 263
charismatic, 260
comparison of transactional and transformations, 261
def., 246
developmental, 256
functions, core, 264
grid figure, illus., 251
Hersey and Blanchard's situational, 252
life-cycle theory of, 252
models, two, 250
provide, 396
servant, 262
ten characteristics of servant, illus., 265
the paradox of servant, 263
transactional, 260, 261
transformational, 260
Leadership behavior, continuum of, 254
illus., 255
Leadership continuum, Tannenbaum and Schmidt's, 254
Leadership Grid®, def., 250
Leadership style, 256
factors affecting, 246
illus., 247
Leadership® Model, Hersey-Blanchard Situational, illus., 253
Leadership® Model, Situational, 252
Leading, def., 11
Learning from successes and mistakes, illus., 163
Learning, experiential, 163
Leave, family and medical, 470
Legal aspects of the performance appraisal, 482
Legal influences on equal employment opportunity (EEO) and affirmative action (AA), illus., 451–452

Legally required benefits, 470
Levels of empowerment, 39
illus., 40
Levels of hierarchy, 198
Levels of management, 8
Life event, def., 424
Life events from the social readjustment rating scale (SRRS), illus., 425
Life-cycle theory of leadership, def., 252
Line and staff
conflicts between, 143
contacts, illus., 144
personnel, some reasons for conflict between, illus., 144
relationships between, 143
Line authority, def., 144
Line organization, 130
after ten years, John Moody's, illus., 132
def., 130
span of control in John Moody's, illus., 131
Line personnel, def., 143
Line-and-staff organization, 131
def., 132
John Moody's, illus., 134
Line-staff conflict: delineating authority, how to avoid excessive, 143
Linguistic styles, 201
Listener, becoming a better, 207
Listening
active, 209
fundamentals, other, 210
habits, rate your, illus., 208
techniques, active, 209
tips for better, illus., 210
Lockout
conducting a strike or, 528
def., 528

M

Maintenance-of-membership clause, def., 518
Major violations, def., 495
Malcolm Baldrige National Quality Award
def., 47
illus., 48
Malicious obedience
def., 493
negative discipline can lead to, illus., 494

Management, 6, 333
  authority and responsibility increase at higher levels, illus., 9
  by objectives. See MBO
  combines the organization's resources into a productive system, illus., 7
  country club, 250
  decision making: heart of supervisory, 100
    illus., 101
    def., 7
  impoverished, 250
  levels of, 8
  major impact at the supervisory level, 56
  middle, 9
  middle of the road, 250
  need for, 6
  participation in, 526
  planning at different levels, 72
    illus., 73
  reflecting a centralized versus a decentralized structure, layers of, illus., 147
  role of decision making in supervisory, 100
  role of higher, 171
  "Siamese twins" of, 70
  skills required for effective, 12
  span of, 102
  supervisory, 9
  task, 250
  team, 252
  three bases of total quality, illus., 51
  time, 87
  top, 8
  total quality, 338
  upward communication from workers to, illus., 194
Management by exception
  def., 318
  illus., 318
Management functions
  how they are related, illus., 13
  in action, illus., 11
Management philosophy, 150
  Theory X or Theory Y, 246
Management styles, conflict, 416
  interpersonal, illus., 417
Manager's list of potential rewards, illus., 233

Manager's membership in different groups, illus., 282
Managerial communication matrix, 194
  illus., 195
Managerial functions, def., 10
Managerial skills at different managerial levels, relative importance of, illus., 15
Managerial, special abilities required, 138
Managers, 9
  developmental, 257
  functions performed by, 10
  heroic, 257
  how they spend their time, illus., 10
  impact on remaining supervisors and, 149
  improving position of supervisory, 18
  middle, 443
  quality of, 147
  relationships with peers or other, 21
  roles played by, 12
    illus., 14
  tend to neglect planning, 70
  top, 443
Manager-to-employee relationships, 21
Managing your time, 87
Manufacturing
  computer-assisted (CAM), 337
  output per hour: 1960s–1999, U.S. productivity growth in, illus., 329
  quality issues in, illus., 43
Market conditions, 467
Marketing, def., 6
Maslow's hierarchy of needs theory, 224
  illus., 225
Matrix approach
  advantages of, 137
  disadvantages of, 138
Matrix departmentalization
  def., 136
  illus., 137
MBI subscales and phases of burnout, illus., 429
MBO
  def., 78–79
  how the process operates, illus., 79

  in action, illus., 81
  process, key aspects of, 79
  some problems with, 80
  supervisor and, 78
  underlying concepts, 79
  using, 486
Measure
  how often, 313
  how to, 314
Measurements, examples of productivity, illus., 330
Measuring performance (step 2), 312
Mediator, def., 527
Medical leave, family and, 470
Medicare, Social Security and, 470
Meetings
  approaches used at, 389
  cost, illus., 394
  decide whether it is needed, 394
  fact-finding, 387
  information exchange, 387
  information-giving, 387
  making effective, 394
  preplan, 395
  problem-solving, 388
  purposes of, illus., 386
  questioning techniques for leaders of, illus., 398
  suggestions for handling disruptive and inappropriate behaviors, illus., 397–398
Meetings, advantages of, 392
  ensure consistency of information, 392
  permit formal exchange of information, 393
  save time, 392
Meetings, disadvantages of, 392, 393
  may become too impersonal, 393
  may not be cost-effective, 393
  may water down decisions, 393
Meetings, factors to consider after, 399
  distribute copies of the minutes, 399
  follow up on decisions made, 399
Meetings, factors to consider before, 394
  decide whether is needed, 394

  have a clear purpose, 394
  preplan, 395
Meetings, factors to consider during, 395
  clarify your expectations, 396
  designate someone to take minutes, 386
  encourage two-way communication, 396
  get closure on items discussed, 398
  provide leadership, 396
  start on time, 395
Member composition and roles of groups, 287
Membership of national unions as a percentage of the total labor force, illus., 514
Mentoring, def., 365
Merit, def., 449
Merit rating, 480
Message, def., 188
Messages, importance of nonverbal, 190
Methods of appraising performance, some selected, 483
Methods of obtaining employees from within, 447
Methods of recruiting from the outside, 451
Middle management, def., 9
Middle managers, 443
Middle of the road management, def., 250
Minor infractions, def., 495
Minutes
  def., 396
  designate someone to take, 395
  distribute copies of, 399
Mission, def., 73–74
Mistakes, learning from, illus., 163
Model(s)
  communication process, 188
    illus., 189
  doctor-patient, 401
  of counseling, iceberg, illus., 373
  of group effectiveness, illus., 285
  process consultation, 402
  purchase-of-expertise, 400
  two leadership, 250
Monetary standards, def., 310

Motivation
  def., 221
  equity theory of, 465
  expectancy theory of, 465
  intrinsic and extrinsic, 223
  levels of, 221
  link to intrinsic and ex-
    trinsic, 229
  objectives as a stimulus
    for, 75
  other theories of, 230
  performance link, 223
  some fundamentals of
    understanding human
    behavior, 221
  three levels of, illus., 222
Motivator factors, 228
Multiple interpretations of
  words, illus., 201
Murphy's laws, illus., 307
Mutual rating system, 483

N

National Labor Relations
  Board (NLRB), 517, 527
National unions as a per-
  centage of the total labor force, membership
  of, illus., 514
Negative discipline
  can lead to malicious obe-
    dience, illus., 494
  def., 493
Negotiation, principled, 419
Nonexempt employees, def.,
  466
Nonplanner's cycle, illus.,
  71
Nonunionized organiza-
  tions, complaint proce-
  dures in, 532
Nonverbal messages, importance of, 190
Norms, def., 287
Number and frequency of
  occurrences, 494
Numerical standards, def.,
  310

O

Obedience, malicious, 493
Object signals, def., 191
Objectives, 74
  as a stimulus for motiva-
    tion and effort, 75
  decisions should con-
    tribute to, 110
  def., 73–74
  for Computronix, hierar-
    chy of, illus., 76
  guidelines for setting, 77

hierarchy of, 75–76
  importance of setting, 74
  provide clear perform-
    ance, 237
  unified planning through,
    77
  union principles, objec-
    tives, and methods of
    attaining, 520
Occupational injury and ill-
  ness rates per 100 em-
  ployees: selected indus-
  tries, 1998, illus., 350
Occupational safety and
  health administration.
  See OSHA
Occupational shifts, adjust-
  ing to, 24
Occurrences, number and
  frequency of, 494
Offenses, intolerable, 497
Office of Federal Contract
  Compliance Programs
  (OFCCP), 451
One-person organization,
  128
  John Moody's, illus., 129
On-the-job training (OJT),
  def., 462
Operational planning, def.,
  74
Operations, def., 6
Opportunity, def., 105
Oral warning, 499
Orderly behavior, discipline
  as, 491
Organization, 150
  after ten years, John
    Moody's line, illus., 132
  def., 6
  flow of formal communi-
    cation in, illus., 192
  four stages in growth of,
    128
  history of growth, 147
  horizontal, 151
  John Moody's after two
    years, illus., 130
  John Moody's line-and-
    staff, illus., 134
  John Moody's one-person,
    illus., 129
  line, 130
  line-and-staff, 131, 132
  one-person, 128
  size of, 349
  what organizers dislike to
    find in, 522
  with assistants added, 128
Organization chart
  hybrid, illus., 152

partial, illus., 4
Organizational and work-
  related factors, 427
  that cause excessive
    stress, illus., 428
Organizational barriers, 198
Organizational change,
  managing, 276
Organizational effectiveness
  def., 279
  result from changing
    structure, technology,
    and/or people, illus.,
    279
Organizational relationships,
  21
Organizational structure, effect of decentralization
  on, 147
Organizers, what they dislike to find in an or-
  ganization, 522
Organizing
  def., 11
  employees, 520
  principles, two important,
    138
Orientation, def., 460
OSHA
  def., 347
  record keeping required
    by, illus., 348
Output, increasing, 330, 331
Output per hour:
  1960s–1999, U.S. pro-
    ductivity growth in
    manufacturing, illus.,
    329
Outside assistance available
  for training, 463

P

Paired-comparison tech-
  nique, def., 486
Pareto chart
  def., 341
  of customers' complaints
    about restaurants,
    illus., 343
Parity of authority and responsibility, principle
  of, 168
Parity principle, def., 168
Partial organization chart,
  illus., 4
Participating and supporting style, def., 254
Participation, recognition
  and, 527
Parties involved in effective
  delegation, 171

Partnering
  def., 290
  failures and their causes,
    294
  successes, 291
  team development accel-
    erated, 290
  what is involved in, 290
  workshop, illus., 292, 293
Path critical, 87
Pay equity, comparable
  worth or, 468
Pay for time not worked,
  471
Peer rating, def., 483
Peers rating one another,
  483
Penalties
  determining, 499
  example of disciplinary
    procedures using grad-
    uated, illus., 496
  graduated scale of, 499
  imposing only after a fair
    hearing, 499
People, 349
Perception, def., 199
Perceptions, differing, 199
Performance
  coaching for improved,
    370
  emphasizing team, 23
  incentive wages or pay,
    466
  job, 373
  measuring (step 2), 312
  motivation link, 223
  new ways of appraising,
    486
  provide clear objectives,
    237
  provide timely feedback,
    237
  report, illus., 336
  reward employees', 237
  some selected methods of
    appraising, 483
  suggestions for con-
    fronting poor, illus.,
    371
  support employees' ef-
    forts, 237
  with standards and ana-
    lyzing deviations, com-
    paring (step 3), 316
Performance appraisal, 480
  how it operates, 480
    illus., 481
  in supervisory manage-
    ment, role of, 480
  legal aspects of, 482

or merit rating or efficiency rating or service rating or employee evaluation, def., 480
purposes of, 481
traditional methods of, 483
who should do, 482
Performance-linked coaching, 362
illus., 363
Period of rapid union growth, 513
Personal injury investigation, illus., 351
Personal problems, 374
Personal psychological makeup, 426
Personal relationships, 20
Personal stress, ways to cope with, 430
Personality tests, def., 457
Personnel
line, 143
some reasons for conflict between line and staff, illus., 144
staff, 143
Peter Principle, def., 178
Physical and emotional illness, 374
Physical examination, 460
Physical exercise, 430
Physical resources, def., 7
Physical standards, def., 310
Physiological or biological needs, def., 225
Picketing, def., 528
Pinpointing, def., 370
Planned change, 279
Planning
at different management levels, 72
illus., 73
basic steps in, 69
contingency, 72
control's close links to, 306
def., 10
human resource needs and finding employees to fill the jobs, 444
is most closely related to controlling, 70
lack of, illus., 70
managers tend to neglect, 70
operational, 74
some important points about, 68
three steps, illus., 69

unified, 77
Plans
single-use, 85
standing or repeat-use, 80
types of, 80
Policies, examples of, illus., 82
Policy, def., 82
Polygraph, use of, 458
Position, authority of, 116
Positional bargaining and principled negotiations, contrast of, illus., 420
Positive and negative discipline, 493
Positive aspects of stress, 424
Positive discipline, def., 493
Practice of Management, The, 78
Praise, how and when to, illus., 236
Preemployment interviewing, 458
Pre-employment testing, 457
Preliminary screening, 454
Preliminary selection by the supervisor, 459
Prevailing wage rate, def., 467
Preventive controls, tips for establishing, illus., 309
Principle(s)
of effective discipline: the hot-stove rule, 500
of parity of authority and responsibility, 168
of specialization, 199
parity, 168
Peter, 178
span of control, 140
two important organizing, 138
underlying the theory, 225
unity of command, 138
violating the unity of command, illus., 140
Principled negotiation
contrast of positional bargaining and, illus., 420
def., 419
to resolve conflict, using, 419
Priorities: a "must," setting, 90
Proactive (planned) process of change, def., 279
Proactive quality approach, def., 49
Probe, def., 209
Probing, def., 370

Problem
def., 105
define the idea or (step 1), 106
solving, 388
Problem-solving meeting, def., 388
Problem-solving quality approach, def., 49
Procedure
def., 84
grievance, 531
Process
decision-making, illus., 104
feeling decision, 110
of control, illus., 310
of delegation, 164
of effective delegation, illus., 169
thinking decision, 110
Process consultation, 400
def., 402
model, 402
Process of change,
proactive (planned), 279
reactive, 278
Product departmentalization, def., 136
Production start-up, example of Gantt chart showing activities needed in, illus., 86
Production supervisor, job description for, illus., 167
Productivity
and cost control, improving, 328
def., 328
defining, 328
fuels the 1990s, high U.S., 328
groups influencing, illus., 333
growth in manufacturing output per hour: 1960s–1999, U.S., illus., 329
how supervisors can improve employee, illus., 335
improvement methods, some recent, 336
improving, 26
measurements, examples of, illus., 330
supervisor's role in improving, 335
why it is important, 331

Profile of the typical controlled-substance abuser, illus., 375
Program
def., 85
vocational rehabilitation, 463
vocational-technical education, 463
Program evaluation and review technique (PERT)
def., 86
network for completing machine overhaul, illus., 87
Programmed decisions, def., 105
Progressive discipline, def., 499
Project, def., 85
Promoting
def., 448
employee safety, 347
Psychological makeup, personal, 426
Punishment
def., 492
discipline as, 492
Purchase-of-expertise model, 400
Purpose, clear, 394
Pyramid
inverted, 153
Nordstrom's inverted, illus., 154

Q

Qualifying Herzberg's theory, 230
Qualifying the theory, 227
Quality, 42
approaches to managing, 49
controlling, 338
Deming's fourteen points for, illus., 46
evolution of explosion in the United States, 45
improving, 26
involve workers in achieving and controlling, 345
is "Job 1," 42
issues in manufacturing and service, illus., 43
Motorola's fundamental objective and key beliefs, goals, and initiatives reflect commitment to, illus., 52
of managers, 147

reasons for the recent revolution, 42
some tools for controlling,
339
supervisor's role in
achieving, 343
understanding variance in
controlling, 338
Quality approach
proactive, 49
problem-solving, 49
total, 49
traditional, 49
Quality award, Malcolm
Baldrige National, 47
illus., 48
Quality chain, total, illus., 49
Quality control, def., 338
Quality management
(TQM), total, 50
Quality performance, let
employees know you
expect, 343

R

Rate range, def., 466
Rate, single, 465
Rating, merit or efficiency or
service, 480
Rating scales
behaviorally anchored
(BARS), 486
def., 484
example of a behaviorally
anchored, illus., 488
typical appraisal form,
illus., 485
using behaviorally an-
chored (BARS), 486
Rating system, mutual, 483
Reactive process of change,
def., 278
Readiness level
def., 248
the followers', 248
Receiver
consider frame of refer-
ence, 205
def., 189
supervisor as, illus., 189
Recognition and participation, 527
Record keeping required by
OSHA, illus., 348
Records, checking references
and, 459
Recruiting from the outside,
methods of, 451
Reengineering, def., 25, 54,
150

Reference, consider the receiver's frame of, 205
References and records,
checking, 459
Reflecting, def., 370
Reflective statement, def.,
209
Reframing, def., 176
Reinforcement theory, def.,
234
Reinvention, def., 25
Relations, labor, union-
management, and
industrial, 512
Relationship behaviors, def.,
252
Relationships
between line and staff,
143
developing and maintain-
ing good interpersonal,
432
external, 22
flow of supervisors' organizational, illus., 21
manager-to-employee, 21
organizational, 21
personal, 20
supervisor's, illus., 20
supervisor-to-manager, 21
supervisory, 20
with peers or other man-
agers, 21
Relaxation techniques, 430
illus., 431
Reliability, def., 458
Repeat-use plans, standing
or, 80
Report about an employee,
example of a written,
illus., 315
Report, performance, illus.,
336
Requisition, 454
sample human resource,
illus., 456
Resources
financial, 7
human, 7
into a productive system,
how management com-
bines the organiza-
tion's, illus., 7
physical, 7
Resourcing, def., 370
Responsibility
assigning, 165
def., 8
for selecting, training, and
compensating employ-
ees, 443

groups diffuse, 2895
shared, 443
Résumé, 456
Retirement income, 471
Reviewing, def., 370
Reward employees' per-
formance, 237
Rewards, manager's list of
potential, illus., 233
Rights of employees, illus.,
519
Right-to-work laws
def., 518
states with, illus., 519
Risk, def., 109
Ritz-Carlton credo, illus.,
275–276
Robot, def., 337
Robotics, 337
Roles
def., 12
of the supervisor in em-
powerment and total
quality, 56
played by managers, 12
illus., 14
Rule
def., 83
Deming's 85-15, 45
hot-stove, 500
illus., 501
termination-at-will, 503
Rules of conduct, establishing, 498
Rumor mill, 197
Run chart
def., 341
of percentage of restau-
rant customers waiting
in excess of one
minute to be seated, il-
lus., 342

S

Safety
factors influencing, 347
or security needs, def.,
225
promoting employee, 347
supervisor's role in pro-
moting, 350
what supervisors can do
to improve, illus., 352
Satisfier or motivator factors
and dissatisfier/hygiene
factors, Herzberg's,
illus., 229
def., 228
Schedule, def., 85
Security needs, 225

Selection procedure, flow
chart of a suggested,
illus., 455
Self-actualization needs, 226
Self-control, discipline as, 491
Self-fulfillment or self-
actualization needs,
def., 226
Self-managed (autonomous)
work teams, def., 41
Self-managing work teams,
def., 295
Sender
def., 188
supervisor as, illus., 189
Seniority
def., 449, 531
role of, 531
Sense of control, 430
Servant leadership
characteristics of, 263
def., 262–263
ten characteristics of,
illus., 265
the paradox of, 263
Service rating, 480
Service, quality issues in,
illus., 43
Setting priorities: a "must,"
90
Sexual harassment, def.,
498
Shared responsibility, 443
team, building, 257
"Siamese twins" of management, def., 70
Single rate, def., 465
Single-use plans, def., 85
Situational leadership,
Hersey and Blanchard,
252
Situational Leadership®
Model, def., 252
Situations, anticipating,
204
Size of organization, 349
Skill tests, 457
Skills, 365
administrative, 15
at different managerial
levels, relative impor-
tance of managerial,
illus., 15
conceptual, 13
developing individual,
258
human relations, 15
of coaching, 368
required for effective
management, 12
technical, 16

Social behavior, improving, 26
Social loafing, 285
Social or belonging needs, def., 225
Social readjustment rating scale (SRRS), life events from, illus., 425
Social Security and Medicare, 470
Solution, ineffective delegation, 176
Space signals, def., 191
Span of control, 140
  different approaches to a supervisor's, 141
  factors contributing to a narrow or wide, illus., 142
  in John Moody's line organization, illus., 131
  narrow, wide, and very wide, illus., 141
  narrower at the top, 140
  principle, def., 140
  tendency toward wider, 142
Span of management, def., 102
Special cause variation, 339
Specialization
  and its related jargon, 199
  principle of, 199
Staff personnel, def., 143
Staffing, def., 11
Stages of group development, 283
Standard(s)
  controlling intangible, illus., 312
  def., 309
  establishing performance (step 1), 309
  for certification, ISO 9000, illus., 44
  how they are set, 310
  intangible, 310
  monetary, 310
  numerical, 310
  physical, 310
  tangible, 309
  time, 310
  types of, 309
  types of for various positions, illus., 313
Standing plans or repeat-use plans, def., 80
Statement in confronting/ challenging performance-related behavior,

general vs. pinpointed, illus., 371
Statement, reflective, 209
States with right-to-work laws, illus., 519
Status barriers, minimize, 203
Status, authority and, 198
Stereotyping, def., 200
Strategic control point, def., 313
Strategic planning, def., 72–73
Strategies, 150
  def., 74
  that make you feel great, illus., 432
Strength, turning a weakness into, 176
Stress, 421
  costs of, 424
  def., 422
  major causes of, 424
  organizational and work-related factors that cause excessive, illus., 428
  positive aspects of, 424
  ways to cope with personal, 430
Strike
  def., 528
  or lockout, conducting, 528
Structure
  effect of decentralization on organizational, 147
  layers of management reflecting a centralized versus a decentralized, illus., 147
Structured interviews, def., 459
Structuring and telling style, def., 254
Success, relating delegation to, 175
Successes, learning from, illus., 163
Successful Meetings, 45
Suggestion involvement, def., 39
Summarizing, def., 370
Supervisors, 17, 443
  additional precautions for, 527
  and discipline, 500
  and managers, impact on remaining, 149
  and MBO, 78
  and the union steward, 530

and work group in decision making, role of, illus., 114
as a sender and a receiver, illus., 189
changing views of job, illus., 57
communications you like to receive from your, illus., 193
delegating allows them to do other things, 163
disciplinary role of, 500
emerging as teacher, leader, coach, 57
employees rating, 483
flow of organizational relationships, illus., 21
how they can improve employee productivity, illus., 335
in empowerment and total quality, role of, 56
in promoting safety, 350
job description for a production, illus., 167
personal liability for disciplining employees, 504
"placing the monkey back" on the employee with the primary responsibility, illus., 173
preliminary selection by, 459
rating employees, immediate, 483
reject coaching, why, 364
relationships, illus., 20
reluctance to appraise employees, 487
rights under the agreement, 530
role in achieving quality, 343
role in cost control, 335
role in improving productivity, 335
role of, 171, 443
situation faced by, 250
some current trends challenging, 22
things they may do when a union tries to organize their company, illus., 525
things they may not do when a union tries to organize their company, illus., 526
what they can do to improve safety, illus., 352

why they fail to delegate, 172
why they need to make so many decisions, 100
Supervisor-to-manager relationships, 21
Supervisory communication
  barriers to effective, 198
  interpersonal barriers to effective, illus., 200
  improving, 202
Supervisory control, some common examples of, illus., 308
Supervisory management
  decision making: heart of, 100
  illus., 101
  def., 9
  major impact at level, 56
  role of decision making in, 100
  role of performance appraisals in, 480
Supervisory managers, improving position of, 18
Supervisory relationships, 20
Suspension, 499, 503
Synergy, def., 281

T

Taft-Hartley Act, 518
Taking corrective action, 317
Tangible standards, def., 309–310
Tannenbaum and Schmidt's leadership continuum, 254
Task and maintenance roles in groups, illus., 288
Task behaviors, def., 252
Task management, 250
Team
  advisors, def., 23
  building, 289
  building a shared-responsibility, 257
  characteristics of an effective, illus., 291
  def., 289
  management, def., 252
  performance, emphasizing, 23
Technical factors, 350
Technical skills, def., 16
Technology, coping with exploding, 23
Teleconferencing, facilitating, 403
  illus., 403–404

Termination-at-will rule, def., 503
Terminations, caution needed in, 532
Testing, pre-employment, 457
Tests
achievement, proficiency or skill, 457
aptitude, 457
IQ, 457
personality, 457
types of, 457
validity of, 458
vocational interest, 457
Theories of motivation, other, 230
Theory
applying expectancy, illus., 232
expectancy, 230
illus., 231
goal-setting, 233
Herzberg's, 228, 230
Maslow's hierarchy of needs, 224
principles underlying, 225
qualifying, 227
reinforcement, 234
Theory X
def., 247
philosophy, 246
Theory Y
def., 247
management philosophy, 246
Thinking decision process, def., 110
Time
how to use more effectively, illus., 91
managing, 87
required for effective delegation, 170
start on, 395
Time log, daily, illus., 89
Time management, def., 87
Time management matrix, illus., 88
Time signals, def., 191
Time standards, def., 310
Time wages or day work, def., 466
Time wasters
eight common supervisory, illus., 90
handling the common, 90
Tools for controlling quality, some, 339
Top management, def., 8
Top managers, 443

Topics to avoid when interviewing applicants, illus., 453
Top-management level, functional departmentalization at, illus., 136
Top-management philosophy, 146
Total quality
approach (TQM), def., 49
chain, illus., 49
initiative (TQI), 35
role of the supervisor in, 56
Total quality management (TQM), 26, 50, 338
three bases of, illus., 51
Touching signals, def., 191
Trade bluffers, 457
Traditional methods of performance appraisal, 483
Traditional quality approach, def., 49
Training
and developing employees, 461
apprenticeship, 462
how to determine needs, 461
internship, 463
on-the-job (OJT), 462
other types, 463
outside assistance available for, 463
Transactional leadership, 261
and transformational leadership, comparison of, 261
def., 260
Transferring, def., 448
Transformational leadership
comparison of transactional and, 261
def., 260
Trust, establishing mutual, 202
Tutoring, def., 365
Two leadership models, 250
Type A behavior, def., 426
Type B behavior, def., 427
Type of industry, 349
Types and number of employees needed, 444
Typical rating scale appraisal form, illus., 485

U

U.S. productivity growth in manufacturing output

per hour: 1960s–1999, illus., 329
Unemployment insurance, 470
Unfair labor practices
def., 517
of employers, illus., 520
of unions, illus., 520
Unified planning through objectives, 77
Unified planning, def., 77
Uniform Guidelines on Employee Selection Procedures, 482
Union(s), 334
appeals used by organizers, 524
craft, 513
early activities, 513
how they developed in the United States, 513
industrial, 514
labor, 512
period of rapid growth, 513
principles, objectives, and methods of attaining objectives, 520
recent limited growth, 515
some reasons for declining membership, 516
things to do before they call, 523
what to do—and not do—when they enter, 523
Union authorization card, def., 520
Union shop, def., 517
Union steward
def., 21, 530
supervisor and, 530
Unionization rates high in government, illus., 515
Unionized organization, typical grievance procedure in, illus., 531
Union-management relations, 512
Unions, unfair labor practices of, illus., 520
Unity of command principle, def., 138
Unprogrammed decisions, def., 105
Upgrading, def., 448
Upward communication
def., 193
from workers to management, illus., 194

V

Validity
def., 458
of tests, 458
Variance in controlling quality, understanding, 338
Variation
common cause, 339
special cause, 339
Vertical flows: downward and upward communication, 191
Vietnam Era Veterans' Assistance Act, 451, 466
Violations, major, 495
Vision, shaping a common, 258
Vocational interest tests, def., 457
Vocational Rehabilitation Act, 451, 466, 467
Vocational rehabilitation programs, def., 463
Vocational-technical education programs, def., 463
Voice signals, def., 190
Voluntary benefits, 471

W

Wage and Hour Law, 466
Wage rate
comparable, 467
factors affecting, 466
prevailing, 467
Wages
incentive, 466
time, 466
types of, 465
Wagner Act, 517
Wagon wheel, def., 153
Wall Street Journal, The, 42
Walsh-Healey Act, 466, 467
Weakness, turning into a strength, 176
Wheel, wagon, 153
Words, multiple interpretations of, illus., 201
Work group in decision making, role of supervisor and, illus., 114
Work groups, importance of, 281
Work Improvement Never Stops (WINS), 294
Work sampling or work preview, def., 457
Work teams, self-managed (autonomous), 41, 295

Work to be accomplished, delegating allows more, 163

Workers, why the good leave, illus., 444

Workers' compensation, 470

Workforce, dealing with a more diverse, 22

Work-related factors, organizational and, 427
that cause excessive stress, illus., 428

Written report about an employee, example of, illus., 315

Written reprimand, 499

Photo Credits

p. 2 ©Spencer Grant/PhotoEdit
p. 6 ©David Young-Wolff/PhotoEdit
p. 16 ©Mark Richards/PhotoEdit
p. 23 ©Michael Newman/PhotoEdit
p. 34 ©Chip Henderson/Index Stock Imagery
p. 41 ©Mark Humphrey/AP/Wide World Photos
p. 47 ©Bettmann/Corbis
p. 55 ©Kevin Hare/AP/Wide World Photos
p. 66 ©Robert Maass/Corbis
p. 69 ©Bob Rowan/Corbis
p. 73 ©Michael S. Yamashita/Corbis
p. 84 ©A. Ramey/PhotoEdit
p. 98 ©Jeff Greenberg/PhotoEdit
p. 102 ©Mark Richards/PhotoEdit
p. 108 ©Mark Richards/PhotoEdit
p. 126 ©Layne Kennedy/Corbis
p. 135 ©Spencer Grant/PhotoEdit
p. 145 ©PhotoDisc, Inc.
p. 160 ©Michael Newman/PhotoEdit
p. 166 ©Dana White/PhotoEdit
p. 170 ©Michael Newman/PhotoEdit
p. 186 ©Bill Bachmann/PhotoEdit
p. 191 ©Scott Roper/Corbis
p. 196 ©Joe Polimeni/AP/Wide World Photos
p. 203 ©Dana White/PhotoEdit
p. 218 ©Michael Newman/PhotoEdit
p. 227 ©Bonnie Kamin/PhotoEdit

p. 244 ©Amy C. Etra/PhotoEdit
p. 249 ©Mark Richards/PhotoEdit
p. 260 ©Michael Newman/PhotoEdit
p. 272 ©Michael Newman/PhotoEdit
p. 284 ©PhotoDisc, Inc.
p. 295 ©Mark Humphrey/AP/Wide World Photos
p. 304 ©David Young-Wolff/PhotoEdit
p. 311 ©Mark Richards/PhotoEdit
p. 319 ©Elizabeth Zuckerman/PhotoEdit
p. 326 ©Kevin Wilton/Eye Ubiquitous/Corbis
p. 332 ©Paul A. Souders/Corbis
p. 349 ©Frank Sitemen/PhotoEdit
p. 360 ©Cindy Charles/PhotoEdit
p. 366 ©Michael Newman/PhotoEdit
p. 384 ©Jeff Zaruba/Tony Stone Images
p. 387 ©Cindy Charles
p. 414 ©John Neubauer/PhotoEdit
p. 418 ©Mark Richards/PhotoEdit
p. 440 ©R. W. Jones/Corbis
p. 449 ©Mark Richards/PhotoEdit
p. 471 ©Rhoda Sidney/PhotoEdit
p. 478 ©Royalty Free/Corbis
p. 487 ©Keith Brofsky/PhotoDisc
p. 497 ©Ryan McVay/PhotoDisc
p. 510 ©Robert Brenner/PhotoEdit
p. 516 ©Thomas Bowman/PhotoEdit
p. 528 ©Jonathan Nourol